Philosophy and Politics - Critical Explorations

Volume 15

The purpose of Philosophy and Politics - Critical Explorations is to publish high quality volumes that reflect original research pursued at the juncture of philosophy and politics. Over the past 20 years new important areas of inquiry at the crossroads of philosophy and politics have undergone impressive developments or have emerged anew. Among these, new approaches to human rights, transitional justice, religion and politics and especially the challenges of a post-secular society, global justice, public reason, global constitutionalism, multiple democracies, political liberalism and deliberative democracy can be included. Philosophy and Politics - Critical Explorations addresses each and any of these interrelated yet distinct fields as valuable manuscripts and proposal become available, with the aim of both being the forum where single breakthrough studies in one specific subject can be published and at the same time the areas of overlap and the intersecting themes across the various areas can be composed in the coherent image of a highly dynamic disciplinary continent. Some of the studies published are bold theoretical explorations of one specific theme, and thus primarily addressed to specialists, whereas others are suitable for a broader readership and possibly for wide adoption in graduate courses. The series includes monographs focusing on a specific topic, as well as collections of articles covering a theme or collections of articles by one author. Contributions to this series come from scholars on every continent and from a variety of scholarly orientations.

More information about this series at http://www.springer.com/series/13508

Hasan Aydin • Winston Langley
Editors

Human Rights in Turkey

Assaults on Human Dignity

Springer

Editors
Hasan Aydin
Department of Curriculum, Instruction, and Culture
Florida Gulf Coast University
Fort Myers, FL, USA

Winston Langley
University of Massachusetts
Boston, MA, USA

ISSN 2352-8370 ISSN 2352-8389 (electronic)
Philosophy and Politics - Critical Explorations
ISBN 978-3-030-57475-8 ISBN 978-3-030-57476-5 (eBook)
https://doi.org/10.1007/978-3-030-57476-5

This Springer imprint is published by the registered company Springer Nature Switzerland AG
The registered company address is: Gewerbestrasse 11, 6330 Cham, Switzerland

This book is dedicated to all the oppressed people of Turkey and other nations who, because of their religion, nationality, color, political beliefs, social class, language, ethnicity, gender identities, or other characteristics, have been the target of persecutions or faced all sorts of discrimination, oppression, and brutality by those in power. We also dedicate it to all children who drowned in the Maritsa River and the Aegean Sea while fleeing from such an oppressive regime. I (Hasan Aydin) dedicate this work to my three sons (Mustafa Ihsan, Ikram Agah, and Tarik Burhan) and all the children of their generation who have suffered extensively/immensely being separated indefinitely from their parents and families due to human rights violations. May justice and peace become a global reality in the future unfolding of the twenty-first century, accompanied by new hope, love, and faith.

Foreword

When we consider Turkey today in terms of human rights and, in particular, minority rights, that touchstone subset of human rights, we see a state that is in one sense the antithesis of the Ottoman Empire and in another sense its continuation.

Antithesis, because:

In the Ottoman Empire (1299–1922), fundamentally a Medieval empire,[1] there was naturally no such concept as human rights, seeing as how this term only entered into international documents following its first appearance in Article 1/3 of the 1945 UN Charter.[2]

The Republic of Turkey has been a part of the Council of Europe since the latter's foundation in 1949 — an international organization built on the ideal and principle of human rights, even if this does not mean that these rights were always implemented by Turkey. Turkey furthermore accepted the compulsory jurisdiction of the Council of Europe's judicial organ, the European Court of Human Rights, in January 1990 and is a signatory to a significant proportion of UN human rights agreements, even if by imposing interpretative declarations and reservations (Oran 2018, 69–83).

As for minority rights (which are granted so that the equality recognized for minorities will not remain a dead letter), notwithstanding the rights to religious autonomy granted to non-Muslim subjects in the Ottoman Empire, prior to the term *ekalliyet* (minority)—first used in 1913 by the Committee of Union and Progress,

[1]Historically, there have been two quite distinct types of empire: 1) the empires of Antiquity, between 3500 BCE and 476 CE (the Roman Empire in Europe, the Huns across Asia, and Han Dynasty in China, and so on), as well as the Medieval (800–1453) and Modern (1453–1789) empires (the Ottoman, Austro-Hungarian, and Russian Empires, and so on); 2) the colonialist and imperialist empires from 1789 to the present (Great Britain, France, Germany, and so on).

[2]Although the phrase previously appeared in France in the 1789 Declaration of the Rights of Man and of the Citizen, this document was national, and not international.

and first appearing in an official document in 1920 in Article 5 of the National Pact (*Misak-ı Milli*) (Bayir 2013, 68–69), there simply was no such concept or term.[3]

As for those rights and privileges accepted at the outset of the Ottoman Empire as a result of capitulations, these were given not to non-Muslim subjects, but to foreign Christian individuals and states.

As for the 1923 Turkish nation-state[4]—which aimed to rebuild the country from scratch on the basis of the secular concept of nation (*ulus*) —in the third section (Articles 37–44) of its foundational document, the Lausanne Peace Treaty, Turkey accepted, nominally and officially, non-Muslim Turkish citizens as minorities. Article 44 further granted such citizens minority rights that, in the language of the treaty, "shall not be modified," that "constitute obligations of international concern," that fall under the protection of the League of Nations, and that "shall not be modified without the assent of the majority of the Council of the League of Nations."

At the same time, the autonomy non-Muslims enjoyed in the Ottoman system was lifted. The religious leaders of every minority community had to answer to the assistant governor of Istanbul and were kept under tight control. They were treated *de facto* as second-class citizens, and, perceived from the onset as extensions of European power, were subjected to forms of ethno-religious cleansing described below.

Turkey has furthermore carried out, in a manner quite different than during the Ottoman Empire, very serious forms of oppression and discrimination against Kurds (who are Muslims, 75% of them Sunni) after the 1924 Constitution and, in particular, after the 1925 Sheik Said uprising. This is due to the fact that the nation-state in Turkey has yet to transform into a democratic state, and as such has been intolerant of all infra-identities.

---

[3]Long before the emergence, in sixteenth-century Europe, of the first type of minority in the world, religious minorities, the Ottoman Empire, from 1453 onwards, employed the *Millet* System (*millet* meaning here congregation), rooted in the Constitution of Medina dated to the first half of the seventh century in the Muslim Middle East. In this inegalitarian system whose social basis was the religious community, non-Muslim communities were referred to as *Millet-i Mahkume*, or those about whom rulings were made, whereas Muslims were collectively called *Millet-i Hakime*, those who made the rulings. Though the former were not counted as minorities and were most certainly second-class subjects, both nominally or formally, relative to the latter, they did have certain religious rights, including the right to collect taxes from their own religious communities. And in an Empire that had no such concept as ethnic minority, they were in fact autonomous in terms of religious manners, customs, and culture. What's more, the term *Millet-i Hakime* in practice meant Sunni Muslim. Alevis, who were heretics in the eyes of the Sunni state, as well as the "half community" (*buçuk millet*, from which the phrase "72.5 communities" comes) of Roma people were not counted by the Ottomans as part of the *Millet-i Hakime.* Without going into too much detail here, let us simply note that within the *Millet-i Hakime,* Alevis and Roma people constituted a sort of indeterminate grey zone.

[4]One must not conflate national state with nation-state. The former dates to 1789 (to the onset of nationalism), the latter to the final quarter of the nineteenth century (that is, to the era of imperialism). The national state declares that the source of sovereignty lies not in God or the king, but in the national people (*ulus*). The nation-state, meanwhile, names a type of state that rejects all infra-identities beyond the supra-identity of the dominant ethno-religious group in a society.

Continuation, because:

Turkey, just like the Ottoman Empire, has rejected the very existence of ethnic minorities within the country.

As in the Ottoman Empire, to be Muslim (indeed, Sunni Muslim) is fundamental in the Republic of Turkey. Despite all claims to secularism, in Turkey those who are not Muslim are simply not referred to as Turks. Rather, they are called "non-Muslim citizens," or "citizen" for short, as in the motto "Citizen! Speak Turkish" used in campaigns in the 1930s and 1960s banning the use of minority languages. The foundation of the laic nation (*ulus*) was, in other words, built atop the Ottoman *Millet* System. In a manner similar to the idea of WASP as a category of *de facto* acceptable citizenship in the USA, in Republican Turkey there operates a *de facto* supra-identity that I have called LAHASUMUT: **La**ic **Ha**nefi **Su**nni **Mu**slim **T**urk.

This book is made up of articles dealing exhaustively with the matter of human rights and minority rights in the Republic of Turkey and their violations, including those of sexual minorities. In this prologue, by way of an introduction to the subject, let us begin by making the following two opposing analytical distinctions:

First, with 1923 began a great wave of modernization, and in the newly established state, human rights were in fact more advanced relative to the Ottoman Empire. The reasons for this had to do with the fact that a Revolution from Above[5] brought an end to a situation in which the state was deemed to be the property of the Sultan. There was a jump from the religious concept of ummah or religious community to national community (which was declared, officially at least, to be secular), as well as from the concept of subject to that of citizen.

Second, in attempting to establish a new national community through the use of a new state itself established in the wake of three consecutive wars (the Balkan [1912–1913], First World [1914–1918], and Independence [1919–1922] wars), this Revolution from Above was naturally quite far from a democracy. And in this, non-Muslims and Kurds suffered the most, since at the very base of this new state were the monist and Turkish politicians of the Committee of Union and Progress of the Ottoman Empire.

External dynamics also negatively affected these internal dynamics, as the *zeitgeist* towards the end of the Second World War in what was then the center of the world, Europe, was, with few exceptions, enveloped by the oppressing waves of a fascist or at least fascistic atmosphere, from Portugal in the west to Turkey in the east. This atmosphere was not to come to an end immediately after the Second World War. On the contrary, anti-communism was to take over, and this situation in the Republic of Turkey, which lasted until at least the end of the 1950s, was to grow

[5]Because in pre-modern societies, the call for social progress does not come from the masses (that is, from below). In such conditions, Westernized elites "who emerge as representatives of the will of the people, and who wish when necessary to effect a leap forward in society despite the unenlightened convictions and positions of the masses" are able, by using the power of the state, to impose from above the advanced superstructure (namely, the law) of the West. This is termed a Revolution from Above.

more prominent and repeat itself during military coups: on May 27, 1960, and particularly on March 12, 1971, and September 12, 1980.

At the same time, in the early 2000s, Turkey was affected by the democratizing influences of external dynamics tied to Turkey's EU candidacy. Between 2001 and 2004, the country went through a second Revolution from Above, in the form of EU Harmonization Packages aiming to address the lack of democracy of the first Revolution.

These packages proved very important in addressing minority rights and human rights violations, particularly as they brought expanded freedom of expression. In this sense, important first steps were taken to move from a national security state to a human rights state, and important headway was made towards the protection of individuals from state oppression. Under the law, efforts began to distinguish thought from violence and criticism from insult. The military's political power, too, was delimited, and it became more difficult to carry out torture.

This second wave of modernization was at first supported by the then Prime Minister R. T. Erdoğan, though as he began gradually to set up an authoritarian regime, and in particular with the State of Emergency regime declared after the July 15, 2016, coup attempt in Turkey, this support was to disappear entirely. A new regime of oppression, the first signs of which came in 2005 with changes to the Criminal Code, was to steadily increase after 2013. And on July 15, 2016, following an unsuccessful coup attempt (the details of which remain unclear), the state of human rights gradually began to return to how things were before 1945, or even before 1923. As though he were waiting for precisely such an event to establish a One-Man Regime, Erdoğan set out not only to eradicate the followers of Fetullah Gülen but in fact to eradicate all opposition. This atmosphere further proved disastrous for Kurds, who in fact had nothing at all to do with the coup.

Why things were so for the Kurds is a question of central importance. After all, Erdoğan, in a first for Turkey, oversaw a significant "Solution Process" related to the Kurdish issue, beginning in 2009 and put into practice particularly in 2012 and 2013. When it became clear that he was losing votes across Turkey, Erdoğan put an end to this process in March 2015 and appealed to the Army to deal with the Kurdish issue by armed force alone. The Army, for its part, had already held firm to a principle, since the early days of the Republic, of disciplining the Kurds through the use of force.

This process coincided with a period in which competition between Erdoğan and the Gülen Movement had significantly escalated. Erdoğan, after all, had formed a remarkably close *de facto* coalition with the Gülen Movement early on due to the great need, in Erdoğan's party, for trained and experienced personnel, and in so doing had paved the way for the Gülen Movement to amass a great deal of power. Further, the period in question was also one in which Erdoğan's oppression, which gradually did away with democracy, met with the growing objections of the opposition.

Henceforth, having lost the support of the Gülen Movement, President Erdoğan began to rely on a coalition made up of four elements in order to stay in power, in an atmosphere of increased fear and anxiety by his claims of the existence of terror and an existential threat to the country: 1) Islamist AKP, 2) Turkist MHP, 3) Tamed putschist elements (Ergenekon), and 4) ex-Maoist Kemalists and Neo-Nationalists (followers of the politician Doğu Perinçek).

For this bizarre coalition (which I suggest we term the Four Horsemen of the Apocalypse), the only common ground is animosity towards Kurds. And to be able to receive the continued support of this coalition, the One-Man Regime started military interventions against the Kurds of Turkey, but also the ones in Syrian and Iraqi territory.

The State of Emergency regime is already sufficiently detailed in this book. Yet I would like here to mention a few additional points that I find important.

This regime of oppression, extended seven times at 3-month intervals, was finally lifted on July 18 2018, yet on that date a law was issued that transferred, for a 3-year term, the powers under the State of Emergency to governors who are appointed by the President. Also, the detention period in such collective activities as protests was extended to 12 days.

As noted below, Turkey has transitioned to a Presidential system that is lacking basic mechanisms of checks and balances. The Prime Ministry has been eliminated and the Parliament has clearly lost its importance as now everything is dealt with by Presidential decree.

All peaceful demonstrations, including those of environmental advocates, are immediately dispersed by the police and gendarme with tear gas and clubs. Police who kill during demonstrations end up nowhere to be found or else are cleared of charges in one way or another. The Saturday Mothers, who for decades have gathered in a public square in Istanbul, on the model of the mothers in Argentina's Plaza de Mayo, to keep alive the memory of their lost children without even a grave left behind to mark their absence, have been banned on the claim that they stand in the way of tourism. Pride Marches organized by LGBTI groups in cities and university campuses are also banned. And anyone who sets out on a hunger strike to protest such conditions is arrested.

A growing number of women in prison who are pregnant, have recently given birth, or who already have children face desperate conditions, unable even to find sanitary pads. Refugees who have escaped ISIS gangs to the south and sought passage to Europe find themselves used as bargaining chips in negotiations with EU countries as hundreds more in their situation drown in the Aegean Sea. Those who remain in Turkey have begun to experience growing forms of anti-Arab racism in response to their presence. Incidents like those of the 1990s, when many in Turkey were taken into custody never to return, are beginning to resurface. Throughout, the government and the Judiciary remain silent. Claims of torture that have begun to come in, one after the other from the prisons, are simply not investigated.

The number of civil servants and workers dismissed from duty by Emergency Degree (no questions asked) has surpassed 160,000. The number of academics dismissed from universities has surpassed 6,000. The severity of the situation can be understood from the fact that the number of academics dismissed from universities during the September 12, 1980, military coup totaled 77, all of whom were able to apply to the courts and return to work once the period of martial law was over, whereas now those dismissed by Emergency Decree cannot appeal to the courts. Currently, among those whose passports have not yet been seized, a serious brain drain to Europe is underway.

A summary of what, in addition to the right to work, is forbidden for those dismissed by Emergency Decree may shock the unfamiliar. Among their basic rights seized by means of a secret memorandum sent to various organizations (in a process likened to a form of "civil death") include: the right to hold a passport, to open bank accounts, to take a line of credit from the bank, to wire money from a bank, to obtain a business license, to sell one's home, to receive retirement salaries and social benefits, as well as to receive money from the insurance company for their damaged cars (Biskin, 2020).

It is impossible and unnecessary, in a short prologue, to summarize the book that follows. Yet I feel it is necessary to say a few words on the following two *sine qua non* matters of democracy:

Freedom of the press—democracy's first *sine qua non*—is now nonexistent. Nearly all newspapers and TV channels have been turned over, as a result of government pressure, to the holdings of businesspeople supporting those in power. 11,157 journalists are without work, and 91 are in prison. In 2019 alone, a total of 200 years of sentences were handed down to 59 journalists (11 bin 157 gazeteci işsiz 91 gazeteci cezaevinde, 2020).

The impartiality and independence of the judiciary—democracy's second *sine qua non*—is also nonexistent now. The reason lies in the fact that judges and prosecutors are overseen by the Board of Judges and Prosecutors, all of whose members are directly or indirectly selected by the ruling AKP. The Board immediately banishes to far-away locales any judges who exonerate newspaper writers or who release political prisoners and journalists—some, a number of times successively.

In particular, what set in motion this process—a process that has nullified the mechanisms of the separation of powers and checks and balances that are the *sine qua non* of presidency regimes—was a judicial organ itself at the highest of levels: The Constitutional Court.

According to the Constitution, the Constitutional Court cannot oversee State of Emergency decrees. Yet these decrees, according to the Constitution and to the internal bylaws of the Parliament, must be limited to events that necessitated the announcing of a State of Emergency and limited temporally to the duration of the State of Emergency. The Constitutional Court, by counting as State of Emergency decrees, from the beggining, decrees that in no way have such characteristics, and refusing to carry out due oversight, has paved the way for the AKP's constitutional violations. For instance, among these decrees are those issued on such matters as opening, closing, or changing the name of a university, banning television programs about marriage, and making it a requirement for drivers to use winter tires.

To summarize this final issue, it is instructive to relay *ad verbum* a January 19, 2020, statement from President and AKP Chairperson Erdoğan. Following the acquittal of once lieutenant general Metin İyidil, who had received a sentence of aggravated life imprisonment, he said:

> The judiciary has taken a truly very, very saddening step for our community. The interesting thing is this; *of course, we gave the necessary instructions for all of these* [italics mine], I mean, the fact that the person or people who gave this decision were *FETO'cü* shows just how far this has all reached...This is something incomprehensible. And, thankfully, our Ministry of Justice and our Office of the Attorney General has taken steps on this point. And these people were caught through operations carried out with the Interior Ministry (Erdoğan'dan Korgeneral İyidil'e beraat tepkisi 2020).

When talking about human rights, in every country minority rights ought to be considered first. The reason is that states, even when they do not oppress the dominant ethnic, religious, or sexual majority, may oppress their own minority citizens in some form and may violate their human rights and particularly their minority rights. Indeed, this is generally the case, and it is for these reasons that minority rights, as I stated at the outset, are *the* litmus test of human rights.

In order to be able to properly evaluate the national context of this matter of minority rights, let us conclude our prologue by having a look at the ways in which the Turkish state has approached the concept of minority. In this, we see two quite distinct categories.

The first such category is official minorities.

"Official" here refers to those minorities protected by Section III of the 1923 Lausanne Peace Treaty, chiefly (and as a continuation of the *Millet* System) Armenians, Jews, and Greeks of Turkey.

That said, what we might call the Big Three minorities (Greeks, Armenians, and Jews) have witnessed—as a result of a historical trauma known as Sèvres Paranoia, rooted in European intervention in the Ottoman Empire via non-Muslim minorities—how the rights granted to them by Lausanne have been implemented quite insufficiently (which is to say, have been violated).

In addition to the Big Three, are a number of other minorities who are also non-Muslims (that is, who possess rights according to Lausanne) but are overlooked by the nation-state: Antiochean/Arab Greek Orthodox Christians, Syrians (whose private foundations were only recognized very recently), and, further, those who are again non-Muslims citizens, yet for whom no minority rights at all are recognized: Bahaists, Yezidis, Protestants, Jehovah's Witnesses, and Levantines.

All of these non-Muslim groups have been subjected to ethno-religious cleansing. The reason is that in Turkey, the nation-state has carried out a policy of assimilation towards those infra-identities it was capable of assimilating (namely, to such Muslim yet non-Turkish groups as Bosnians and Circassians), whereas for those groups it believed to be incapable of assimilation (namely, non-Muslims), the policy has been ethno-religious cleansing. The decisive factor affecting the nation-state's choice on this matter is the simple reality that especially in the Middle East and the Balkans, it is religion and sect, and not race and language, that represent the foundations of identity.

In terms of ethno-religious cleansing, let us look at which types have been put into practice:

(1) Territorial purge from one's country and land (deportation, population exchange, exile)

(2) Physical attacks (being beaten, being killed, having one's possessions seized, the most well-known instance being the pogroms of September 6–7, 1955)
(3) Religious discrimination in laws, treaties, and policy implementation (the most well-known instances being the 1942 Wealth Tax (Wikipedia 2017) and the 1936 Declaration[6])

The second such category is that of groups recognized as minorities by international standards, yet whom the Turkish nation-state refuses to recognize.

International standards refer to certain fixed criteria in place since the Second World War: race, language, and religion. In the context of Turkey, because in the Lausanne Treaty only non-Muslims were accepted as minorities, Muslim non-Turkish groups (e.g., Laz, Georgians, Circassians, Albanians, Bosnians, Roma, Arabs, and, particularly, Kurds) are not accepted by the state as possessing minority rights.[7]

This situation is, because of Lausanne, legally neutral, yet many rights violations have come to the fore in terms not of minority rights but human rights. The reason for this is that although the title of Section III of Lausanne is "Protection of Minorities,"[8] it contains provisions related not just to minority rights but to human rights as well. Article 39/4 clearly accepts language rights as a human right, among this category. Looking more closely at the article, it is quite clear that outside of official spaces, citizens can use any language whenever and wherever they wish:

> No restrictions shall be imposed on the free use by any Turkish national of any language in private intercourse, in commerce, religion, in the press, or in publications of any kind or at public meetings.

In particular, Article 39/5 introduced a vital language right:

> Notwithstanding the existence of the official language, adequate facilities shall be given to Turkish nationals of non-Turkish speech for the oral use of their own language before the Courts.

Thus, came about the possibility of defending oneself in the courts (official space) by speaking in one's mother tongue.

Yet Turkey has never implemented these articles of its foundational treaty, and the courts have convicted those who speak and write in Kurdish and who wish to testify at hearings orally in Kurdish. The Constitutional Court has further closed a

[6]In 1936, the government, as a way of bringing an end to Islamist foundations, required all foundations to declare their real estate. In the 1970s, when the Cyprus imbroglio broke, this same policy was used to cripple minority foundations, ruling that the latter had no right to acquire properties beyond those listed in their 1936 Declarations. The state thus began to seize without compensation those properties acquired after 1936.

[7]It must be noted that because the term minority equates, for many in Turkey, to non-Muslims deemed to be part of a second-class, Kurds and Alevis, much like the state, strongly reject the term.

[8]The term human rights, as previously mentioned, only occurs in international documents in 1945, yet the term minority rights has been used in such documents since the sixteenth century.

total of 13 political parties on the grounds of the principle of "undermining the unity of the state with its territory and nation" and the ban on "creating a minority."

In addition to these language rights of Kurds, the religious rights of Alevis have also been violated. The Cemevis where the latter group performs its religious ceremonies have not been accepted as places of worship, and their children have been forced to take part in courses at school on Sunni Islam. The decisions of the European Court of Human Rights regarding both of these matters, meanwhile, have not been put into effect.

Finally, I wish to mention some of the consequences of these systematic violations of rights.

(1) The basic approach of the Turkish nation-state can be paraphrased as: Minorities upset the cohesion of the state and the people. This approach, which impedes democracy, divides the populace, and weakens Turkey internationally, has three basic consequences:

(a) Contemporary international law considers the protection of minorities through a four-sided approach: their existence will be protected, they will not be excluded, they will not be subjected to discrimination, and they will not be subject to assimilation (Bayir 2013, 8).

Yet the Turkish nation-state has implemented precisely the opposite of all these four principles: it has denied the existence of minorities and subjected them to exclusion, discrimination, and assimilation. In particular, discrimination and assimilation, those two great forms of divisiveness, have gone hand in hand.

(b) In terms of what is considered as an "acceptable citizen," the nation-state has stratified and divided citizens of the Republic of Turkey into a *de facto* four-part hierarchy to be ruled from high to low.

At the top is the category of LAHASÜMÜT that I mentioned earlier. Since the Islamist AKP passed to the One-Man Regime, increasingly this term has shed its first syllable, becoming simply HASÜMÜT—that is, Hanefi, Sunni, Muslim, Turk.

Below this group of citizens are the non-Turkish Muslims, groups subjected to assimilation.

Meanwhile, Kurds, as Muslims who openly rejected assimilation, occupy one place below the aforementioned group in terms of acceptability.

In last place are non-assimilable Muslims. As their assimilation was thought to be impossible, they occupy this lowest strata, and efforts have been made to have them leave the country entirely (as expressed by the widespread slogan "Love It or Leave It, *Ya Sev Ya Terk Et*") or, as is now the case, to have them remain only in symbolic numbers and recognized, if at all, only as a folkloric curiosity of sorts.

(c) While the monist mindset of the Revolution from Above of the 1920s and 1930s demonized, in the twentieth century, those who are different among the citizens of the Turkish Republic, the Islamist version of this same mindset has done the same in the twenty-first century, especially after

2013, by establishing an informal four-part coalition. By building its power on this nationalist coalition I have previously characterized as the Four Horsemen of the Apocalypse, it set in motion a true Counter-Revolution from Above on the basis of Islamist Turkism.

(2) As a result of this tangle of contradictions, the transition of Turkey from a "National Security State" to a "Human Rights State" has been significantly delayed, burgeoning into a serious problem. The happiness of individuals and communities and, consequently, the viability of the state have in turn been compromised.

The first wave of modernization brought about important advances, and its change indeed amounted to a very radical transformation. At the same time, though, in the first period of this Revolution from Above (the 1920s, the 30s, the 40s, then in a series of military coups), a significant proportion of citizens founded themselves in the position of "obligatory citizen," their infra-identities having been denied (in particular, for the Kurds).

This situation, as the result of the ongoing Counter-Revolution, is now on stage again: Those who are not Islamists find themselves in the position of "obligatory citizen."

A citizen whose identity has been rejected is an unhappy citizen and may represent a danger for the state. Since stationing a soldier with a bayonet beside each such citizen cannot be a solution, the only sensible path is to ensure that such citizens are not obligatory but voluntary citizens. To accomplish this end, it is imperative to address citizens not by the ethnic—indeed, ethno-religious—term *Türk*, but by the entirely territorial term *Türkiyeli* (of Turkey), and to wholly fulfill this obligation in law and in practice.

Emeritus Professor, Ankara University Baskın Oran
Turkey, Ankara, Turkey

References

11 bin 157 gazeteci işsiz 91 gazeteci cezaevinde. 2020. *Sözcü*, January 10. https://www.sozcu.com.tr/2020/gundem/11-bin-157-gazeteci-issiz-91-gazeteci-cezaevinde-5559717/

Bayir, Derya. 2013. *Minorities and Nationalism in Turkish Law*. United Kingdom: Ashgate Publishing Limited.

Biskin, Haci. 2020. KHK'lilere bir de 'gizemli genelge' darbesi. *Gazete Duvar*, January 9. https://www.gazeteduvar.com.tr/gundem/2020/01/09/khklilere-bir-de-gizemli-genelge-darbesi/

Erdoğan'dan Korgeneral İyidil'e beraat tepkisi: Yargı için çok üzücü bir adım, anlamak mümkün değil, bunların hepsinin talimatını verdik!. 2020. *T24*, January

19. https://t24.com.tr/haber/erdogan-berlin-ziyareti-oncesinde-aciklamalarda-bulunuyor,856639

Oran, Baskın. 2018. *Etnik ve Dinsel Azınlıklar: Tarih, Teori, Hukuk, Türkiye,* Literatür Yayınları, İstanbul [Updated English translation forthcoming: *Minorities and Minority Rights in Turkey: From the Ottoman Empire to the Present State*].

Wikipedia. 2017. *"Varlık Vergisi."* Last modified September 1, 2019. https://en.wikipedia.org/wiki/Varl%C4%B1k_Vergisi

Acknowledgments

As in any project of this magnitude, the completion of this collection involved the constructive intervention of more than just the editors and contributors. The idea of the book stemmed from our concern for a more inclusive and humanely grounded global understanding of the human rights violations in Turkey, and the relationship among those violations and the modern history and development of the country and its people.

We would like to thank those who have contributed to the fulfillment of this volume. First and foremost, we owe profound thanks to our colleague, the Dean of the College of Education, Florida Gulf Coast University, Dr. Eunsook Hyun, "Eunny," who selflessly advised us and provided us with suggestions to prepare this book. We would also like to thank all the contributors included in this volume for their enormous patience, hard work, and enthusiasm through the lengthy process, as well as for their willingness to persevere with this project. The chapter authors have been magnificent, scholarly, and patient. Without their keen interest and commitment and compliance with instructions, compiling this collection would have been impossible. We are inspired by each contributor's dedication, insights, and passion. Our involvement with them has been pleasurable and rewarding, and we consider them close colleagues and friends. We firmly believe that no author or editor could accomplish such as an enormous task as writing or editing a book without the help of innumerable people whose names are rarely mentioned or recognized.

We wish to offer an immense thanks to the many anonymous reviewers who, over the months, challenged and enriched the collection. They provided valuable critiques, positive feedback, coherence, content presentation, and critical insights to heighten the quality of each chapter. The entire process was an engaging and welcoming learning experience for us. As a result of these reviewers, the book is much more cohesive and fluent. We hope it will inspire others to research and critically examine the myriad of disjunctures and conjectures within the essential areas of human rights issues in Turkey.

We also thank our editorial assistant, Koksal Avincan, a scholar in exile and a scholar at risk, who has settled in a refugee camp in Germany. We have long admired him from afar for his work as an academic as well as his example as a fighter for human rights. He not only assisted us, but he undertook the laborious and often difficult task of tracking down sources, formatting footnotes, and preparing the tables. We are grateful beyond measure for his unwavering support of this project and for his friendship. His work has been exemplary and deserving of considerable credit. I also want to thank Tim Walters and Kristina Andrews for understanding the importance of such a project and for their excitement regarding the collection. We were very fortunate to have friends who are so passionate about editing and proofreading such relevant research on human rights violations in Turkey. This volume could never have been published in such a timely manner had it not been for Tim and Tina's strong support in this work.

We would also like to thank all the staff at Springer Publishing for their guidance and good humor, their understanding of the importance of such a collection, and their excitement regarding each manuscript. Special thanks go to Miranda Dijksman, Floor Oosting, and Alexander James for their admirable support in commissioning this book and for their exceptional dedication and hard work that brought forth this project to fruition. This collection could never have been published in such a timely manner had it not been for Miranda, Floor, and Alex's strong belief in the work.

Finally, we would like to thank numerous people in exile, whom, unfortunately, we cannot name, who believed in us and supported us in finishing this work to further spread the values, principles, and purposes of human rights across the world, the achievement of which we need more than ever before.

Contents

Part I An Overview of Human Rights in Turkey

1 **Introducing Human Rights in Turkey** 3
Hasan Aydin and Winston Langley

2 **Human Rights in Turkey: Past, Present and Future** 23
Ercan Balcioglu

Part II Freedom and Non-discrimination

3 **Freedom of the Media in Turkey Under the AKP Government** 51
Vedat Demir

4 **Discrimination Based on Religion: A Complex Story in Turkey** . . . 89
İştar Gözaydın

5 **Non-Discrimination, Minority Rights and Self-Determination: Turkey's Post-Coup State of Emergency and the Position of Turkey's Kurds** 109
Emre Turkut and Thomas Phillips

6 **Justice and Development (AKP) Attitudes Towards the LGBTI Community in Turkey** 131
Fait Muedini

7 **LGBTQ Rights in Turkey: Do Not Touch My Body!** 141
Barbaros Sansal

Part III The Rights of the Displaced

8 **Syrian Refugees in Turkey: (Un)Equal Opportunities in Education** 159
Alia Hadid and Rabia Hos

Part IV State of Emergency (OHAL)

9 **Authoritarianization and Human Rights in Turkey: How the AKP Legitimizes Human Rights Violations** 179
Mehmet Efe Caman

10 **Shunned and Purged: Turkey's Crackdown on the Hizmet (Gülen) Movement** 199
Sophia Pandya, Brenda Oliden, and Ibrahim Aytac Anli

11 **The Cases of Dismissal Under State of Emergency (OHAL): The Right to a Fair Trial as a Human Right** 227
Ufuk Yesil

12 **Intellectuals on Hunger Strike for Reinstatement to Their Job: The Case of the "Yuksel Resistance"** 261
Acun Karadag and Nazan Bozkurt

13 **Human Rights Violations and Medicolegal Approach** 293
Alper Keten

Part V Social and Economic Rights

14 **Right to Education: Challenges and Issues Under the Justice and Development Party Era** 319
Uzeyir Ogurlu and Koksal Avincan

15 **Academic Freedom and Living in Exile: Experiences of Academics in Turkey** 339
Hasan Aydin, Viktor Mak, and Kristina Andrews

16 **The Effects of Democratic Regression on Turkish Economy and the Brain Drain** 365
Zeliha Ozdogan

17 **Neoliberal De-Development in Turkey and the AKP's Socioeconomic War on the Counterhegemony** 383
Victoria Araj and Arin Y. Savran

Part VI Women and Children Rights

18 **Imprisoned Women and Children in Turkey: Human Rights Violations Under the State of Emergency** 411
Ömer Faruk Gergerlioğlu

19 **Trauma of Turkish Women and Children in an Era of Political Unrest** 435
Vonya Womack

Part VII Foreign Policy Initiative: A Case Review

20 Turkey's Accession to the European Union in Context of Its Human Rights Violations: Observations of a Journalist from Brussels 451
Gülsüm Alan

Contributors

Gülsüm Alan Euronews, Brussels, Belgium

Kristina Andrews Florida Gulf Coast University, Fort Myers, FL, USA

Ibrahim Aytac Anli Independent Researcher, Washington, DC, USA

Victoria Araj Women in International Affairs Network, London, UK

Koksal Avincan A Doctoral Student and Human Rights Activist at Florida International University, Miami, FL, USA

Hasan Aydin Department of Curriculum, Instruction, and Culture, Florida Gulf Coast University, Fort Myers, FL, USA

Ercan Balcioglu Faculty of Police and Security Management, Berlin School of Economics and Law, Berlin, Germany

Nazan Bozkurt Human Rights Activist, Düzce, Turkey

Mehmet Efe Caman Memorial University of Newfoundland, St. John's, Canada

Vedat Demir University of Potsdam, Potsdam, Germany

Ömer Faruk Gergerlioğlu Parliament Member for Peoples' of Democratic Party (HDP), Grand National Assembly of Turkey, Çankaya, Turkey

İştar Gözaydın Independent Researcher and Human Rights Activist, Istanbul, Turkey

Alia Hadid School of Education, University of Rhode Island, Kingston, RI, USA

Rabia Hos School of Education, University of Rhode Island, Kingston, RI, USA

Acun Karadag Human Rights Activist, Ankara, Turkey

Alper Keten Institute of Forensic and Traffic Medicine, Heidelberg University, Heidelberg, Germany

Winston Langley University of Massachusetts, Boston, MA, USA

Viktor Mak Human Rights Activist and Independent Researcher, Budapest, Hungary

Fait Muedini Department of International Studies, Butler University, Indianapolis, IN, USA

Uzeyir Ogurlu University of Wisconsin-Stevens Point, Stevens Point, WI, USA

Brenda Oliden California State University, Long Beach, CA, USA

Baskin Oran Emeritus Professor at Ankara University, Ankara, Turkey

Zeliha Ozdogan Penn State Harrisburg, Middletown, PA, USA

Sophia Pandya California State University, Long Beach, CA, USA

Thomas Phillips Liverpool John Moores University, Liverpool, UK

Barbaros Sansal Human Rights Activist, Ankara, Turkey

Arin Y. Savran University of Gothenburg, Gothenburg, Sweden

Emre Turkut Ghent Rolin-Jaequemyns International Law Institute (GRILI), Ghent University, Ghent, Belgium

Vonya Womack Cabrini University, Radnor, PA, USA

Ufuk Yesil Independent Researcher and Human Rights Activist, Istanbul, Turkey

About the Editors

Hasan Aydin earned his Ph.D. from the University of Nevada, Reno, in 2011. He has served many administrative positions, including Associate Chair of the Department of Curriculum and Instruction, Graduate Program Coordinator, Erasmus Exchange Student Coordinator, and Graduate Assistantship Coordinator at the College of Education at Yildiz Technical University, Istanbul, Turkey. He also has served as the chair of many masters and doctoral dissertation committees. Currently, Dr. Aydin is a human rights activist and a Professor of Multicultural Education in the Department of Curriculum, Instruction, and Culture at Florida Gulf Coast University. He also serves as a Director of Education and Youth Empowerment at the African Network of South-West Florida. His scholarship focuses on multicultural education, bilingual education, Kurdish language and cultural rights, human rights, social justice, diversity and equity in education, educating refugee students, citizenship education in a global context, and international education. Dr. Aydin's research cuts across local, national, and international contexts, and he has conducted research with and prepared educators in countries such as Germany, Turkey, Romania, Mongolia, and Nigeria. He is the author of several books, has published numerous articles, has had many conference presentations, and has translated several books from English into Turkish. These translations include James A. Banks' *An Introduction to Multicultural Education*, Geneva Gay's *Culturally Responsive Teaching: Theory, Research, and Practice*, and Bruce Berg and Howard Lune's *Qualitative Research Methods for the Social Sciences*. Dr. Aydin is a member of several professional organizations including the American Educational Research Association (AERA), the American Psychological Association (APA), the National Association for Multicultural Education (NAME), the Korean Association for Multicultural Education (KAME), the International Association for Intercultural Research (IAIE), and the Pi Beta Delta: International Honor Society for International Education.

Dr. Aydin is also a Founding Editor and Editor-in-Chief of the *Journal of Ethnic and Cultural Studies* and the *American Journal of Qualitative Research*, and an Associate Editor of *Intercultural Education*. He is on the editorial boards of several journals, including *Multicultural Education Review, International Journal of Education*, and *Journal of Cultural Analysis and Social Change.* In 2018 and 2019, he was awarded a college education professorship for his research, contributions, and publications. Dr. Aydin received the Human Rights Educator Award from the United Nations Human Rights Florida in 2019. In addition, in 2019, Dr. Aydin received an outstanding research award from The Marquis Who's Who Publication Board. Dr. Aydin served a Program Chair for the American Educational Research Association (AERA) 2020/SIG Multicultural/Multiethnic Education: Theory, Research, and Practice.

Winston Langley was a Provost and Vice Chancellor for Academic Affairs and the senior administrator in charge of advancing the University of Massachusetts Boston's academic mission and the quality of its intellectual life. A scholar with a rich, diverse academic background and a seasoned administrator, he has been instrumental in defining and developing UMass Boston's identity as a student-centered, urban public research university with a teaching soul. A professor of political science and international relations since 1982, Dr. Langley served as Director of the International Relations Program, Senior Associate Provost, Associate Chancellor, and Interim Provost and Vice Chancellor for Academic Affairs before he was appointed to his current position in 2009. Dr. Langley's scholarly interests include human rights, alternative models of world order, religion, and politics. His research has focused on the inadequacy of the nation-state system, the weakness of intergovernmental organizations (including the United Nations), non-governmental organizations expanding power and influence, and the paucity of alternative models for global ordering. Dr. Langley is the author of *Kazi Nazrul Islam: The Voice of Poetry and the Struggle for Human Wholeness* and the *Encyclopedia of Human Rights Issues Since 1945*, for which won the Choice Outstanding Academic Book Award. He is the Editor of *Human Rights: The Major Global Instruments* and (with Vivian Fox) *Women's Rights in the United States*, which won the Gustavus Myers Center for the Study of Bigotry and Human Rights Award for Outstanding Book on Human Rights in North America. He is a member of the American Society of International Law and a reviewer of nine publications, including *New Political Science*, *Transnational Perspectives* and the *International Journal of African Studies*. Dr. Langley earned a Bachelor of Arts in Biology from Atlantic Union College, a Master of Arts in European Diplomatic History, and a Doctor of Philosophy in Political Science and International Relations from Howard University, and a Doctor of Laws from Suffolk University.

List of Abbreviation

İdari Yargılama Usulü Kanunu, İYUK	Administrative Procedure
AI	Amnesty International
Uluslararası Af Örgütü Türkiye Şubesi, UAÖTŞ	Amnesty International Turkey
ATCS	Anti-Terrorism, Crime and Security Act
İnsan Hakları ve Mazlumlar için Dayanışma Derneği, MAZLUM-DER	Association for Human Rights and Solidarity for the Oppressed
CPT	Committee for the Prevention of Torture
CPJ	Committee to Protect Journalists
Telekomünikasyon İletişim Başkanlığı, TİB	Communications Directorate
CCTE	Conditional Cash Transfer for Education
Anayasa Uzlaşma Komisyonu, AUK	Constitutional Reconciliation Commission
CRC	Convention on the Rights of the Child
CoE	Council of Europe
Yükseköğretim Kurulu, YÖK	Council on Higher Education
DL	Decree Laws
Kanun Hükmünde Kararname, KHK	Decrees with Force of Law
Demokrat Parti, DP	Democrat Party
Demokratik Bölgeler Partisi, DBP	Democratic Regions Party
Güneydoğu Anadolu, ESA	East and Southeast Anatolia
ETÖ or Ergenekon	Ergenekon Terrorist Organization
EBRD	European Bank for Development and Reconstruction

ECHR	European Convention on Human Rights
ECtHR	European Court of Human Rights
EEC	European Economic Community
EHRC	European Human Rights Convention
EP	European Parliament
EU	European Union
Lezbiyen, Gey, Biseksüel, Trans, İnterseks + Aileleri ve Yakınları Derneği, LİSTAG	Families of LGBTs in Istanbul
Saadet Partisi, SP	Felicity Party
A name the Turkish government uses for the Gülen Movement, FETO	Fethullah Terror Organization
FDI	Foreign Direct Investment
Tevgera Jinen Azad, TJA	Free Women's Movement
GRECO	Group of States Against Corruption
GM	Gülen Movement
Helsinki Yurttaşlar Derneği, HYD	Helsinki Citizens' Assembly
Hâkimler ve Savcılar Yüksek Kurulu, HSYK	High Council of Judges and Prosecutors
HM	Hizmet Movement
İnsan Hakları Gündemi Derneği, İHGD	Human Rights Agenda Association
İnsan Hakları Derneği, İHD	Human Rights Association
Türkiye İnsan Hakları Vakfı, TİHV	Human Rights Foundation of Turkey
İnsan Hakları Ortak Platformu, İHOP	Human Rights Joint Platform
HRW	Human Rights Watch
Müstakil Sanayici ve İşadamları Derneği, MUSIAD	Independent Industrialists' and Businessmen's Association
IRB	Institutional Review Board
IPA	Instrument for Pre-Accession Assistance
IAMCR	International Association for Media and Communication Research
ICCPR	International Covenant on Civil and Political Rights
IDEA	International Institute for Democracy and Electoral Assistance
ILO	International Labor Organization
ILC	International Law Commission
ILGA	International Lesbian, Gay, Bisexual, Trans & Intersex Association
IMF	International Monetary Fund
IRFA	International Religious Freedom Act
ICNA	Islamic Circle of North America

ISIS	Islamic State of Iraq and Syria
Adalet ve Kalkınma Partisi, AKP	Justice and Development Party
KURDİ-DER	Kurdish Cultural Research and Development Association
KHRP	Kurdish Human Rights Project
PKK	Kurdistan Workers' Party
LGBTQ	Lesbian-Gay-Bisexual-Transgender-Questioning
LGBT	Lesbian, Gay, Bisexual, and Transgender
LGBTI	Lesbian, Gay, Bisexual, Transgender, and Intersex
MEDEL	Magistrats Européens pour la Démocratie et les Libertés
Milli Eğitim Bakanlığı, MEB	Ministry of National Education
MoNE	Ministry of National Education
MAS	Muslim American Society
NCTSN	National Child Traumatic Stress Network
Milli Selamet Partisi, MSP	National Salvation Party
Milli Güvenlik Kurulu, NSC	National Security Council
Milliyetçi Hareket Partisi, MHP	Nationalist Action Party
NGO	Non-Governmental Organization
NATO	North Atlantic Treaty Organization
OHCHR	Office of the United Nations High Commissioner for Human Rights
OECD	Organization for Economic Cooperation and Development
OSCE	Organization for Security and Cooperation in Europe
PACE	Parliamentary Assembly of the Council of Europe
Halkların Demokratik Partisi, HDP	People's Democratic Party
PTSD	Post-Traumatic Stress Disorder
Başbakanlık İletişim Merkezi, BIMER	Prime Ministry Communication Center
PISA	Program for International Student Assessment
PFDM	Public Finance and Debt Management Law
PFMCL	Public Financial Management and Control Law
Kamu Personeli Seçme Sınavı, KPSS	Public Service Personnel Selection Examination

RHTAC	Refugee Health Technical Assistance Center
RSF	Reporters Without Borders
Cumhuriyet Halk Partisi, CHP	Republican Peoples' Party
Tasarruf Mevduatı Sigorta Fonu, TMSF	Savings Deposit Insurance Fund
SAR	Scholars at Risk
SPoD	Social Policies, Gender Identity, and Sexual Orientation Studies Association
Güneydoğu Anadolu Projesi, GAP	South Eastern Anatolian Project
Toplu Konut İdaresi Başkanlığı, TOKİ	State Housing Development Administration
OHAL	State of Emergency
SCF	Stockholm Center for Freedom
Radyo ve Televizyon Üst Kurulu, RTÜK	Supreme Board of Radio and Television
Öğretim Üyesi Yetiştirme Programı, ÖYP	Teaching Staff Training Program
TECs	Temporary Education Centers
TEOG	Transition from Primary to Secondary Education
Doğru Yol Partisi, DYP	True Path Party
Türkiye Cumhuriyeti Anayasa Mahkemesi, TCC	Turkish Constitutional Court
Türkiye İstatistik Kurumu, TÜİK	Turkish Institute of Statistics
UNHRC	United Nations Human Rights Committee
UN	United Nations
UNESCO	United Nations Educational, Scientific and Cultural Organization
USCIRF	United States Commission on International Religious Freedom
UDHR	Universal Declaration of Human Rights
US DOS	US Department of State
Fazilet Partisi, FP	Virtue Party
WSJ	Wall Street Journal
Refah Partisi, RP	Welfare Party
Kadın ve Demokrasi Derneği, KADEM	Women and Democracy Association
WJP	World Justice Project
WMA	World Medical Association
WMAD	World Medical Association Declarations
WWII	World War Two

List of Figures

Fig. 3.1	Press Freedom Scores of Turkey, Reported by *Freedom House* (The data for the years 2018 and 2019 are based on "Freedom in the World" reports)	68
Fig. 3.2	Number of Imprisoned Journalists (CPJ)	72
Fig. 8.1	KidsRights report 2018 (Carlier 2018, Fig. 1)	161
Fig. 8.2	Data obtained from MoNE interview (Coşkun et al. 2017, Table 2)	166
Fig. 12.1	Acun Karadag's exposure to plastic bullets and pepper spray	272
Fig. 12.2	The harassing police chief (left) taking vengeance against Acun Karadag after she filed her complaint	273
Fig. 12.3	Yuksel protestor Merve Demirel being roughed up while being detained (Okatan 2019)	275
Fig. 12.4	Nazan Bozkurt's face after the police attack	277
Fig. 12.5	Gulnaz Bozkurt's hair after the police attack	277
Fig. 12.6	Perihan Pulat after the police attack	278
Fig. 12.7	Images of Mehmet Dersulu after police harassment	280
Fig. 12.8	Nuriye Gülmen before (left) and during (right) the hunger strike	283
Fig. 12.9	Semih Ozakca before the hunger strike (with his wife, Esra Ozakca)	284
Fig. 12.10	Semih Ozakca during the hunger strike	284
Fig. 17.1	Turkey leads in social media censorship: new Twitter transparency report (Turkey Blocks 2017)	400

List of Tables

Table 13.1 Common psychological reactions and symptoms; Holtan (1998) 302
Table 13.2 Diagnostic classifications (American Psychiatric Association 2013; WHO 2016) 303
Table 13.3 The points of psychological/psychiatric evaluation (Istanbul Protocol 2004; Rothbaum et al. 1992; Sutker et al. 1991) 304
Table 13.4 The reactions in children 305

Table 14.1 International agreements on the right to education 320
Table 14.2 The number of students who get into Kurdish literature programs in colleges 325
Table 14.3 Number of hired teachers of living languages in years 326

Table 15.1 Scholars at risk applications for assistance 346

Table 16.1 Some of the largest companies/assets seized by the Turkish Government (A Predatory Approach 2018) 377

Endorsers

Jay Albanese, PhD *Virginia Commonwealth University* *Wilder School of Government & Public Affairs*	A fascinating book detailing the rapid deterioration of human rights in Turkey, involving false imprisonment, job dismissals, media restrictions, and due process violations. A careful examination of the swift decline of democracy, transforming a prospering country into one where economic, educational, and social stability and the operation of the justice system were impacted by a government declaration of a State of Emergency. A comprehensive analysis of the ways in which a society changes when human rights are not enforced in accord with the principles of due process and the rule of law.
Haluk Savas, PhD *Professor of Psychiatry, Psychotherapist And Editor in Chief of KHK TV (Voice of Rights), Turkey*	As a human rights activist and a victim of severe human rights violations in Turkey, I recognize the value of the chapters, as they provide a thorough examination and analysis of subjects regarding human rights violations in Turkey. The book comprehensively chronicles the events pertaining to the steady rise of political authoritarianism. The relevancy of the issues addressed in each chapter makes the book important in regard to the emerging civil society movement in Turkey. Furthermore, the descriptions of the severe decline of human rights and the democratic backsliding towards authoritarianism and fascism during the last decade in Turkey highlight the significance of the book.
John M. Carey, Ph.D. *Wentworth Professor in the Social Sciences* *Dartmouth College, NH, USA*	Aydin and Langley's book addresses critical issues in a critical case. Turkey had been regarded as a rising democracy in a troubled region, but in recent years the country has experienced troubling signs of democratic erosion. Central to that decline is the precarious status of basic human

(continued)

	rights of expression, association, religion, and due process. This book explores what has happened and how it affects individuals and the Turkish polity more broadly.
Kati Piri *Member of the European Parliament and Delegation to the EU-Turkey Joint Parliamentary Committee*	*Human Rights in Turkey: Assaults on Human Dignity* fills a major gap in contemporary political scholarship. Its elucidation of Turkey's democratic backsliding into a one-man authoritarian regime is insightful and unique. Absolutely required reading for anyone who cares about this beautiful country, its wonderful people, and its uncertain future.
Jacob Torfing, PhD *Professor in Politics and Institutions, Roskilde University, Denmark*	Situated right at the border between East and West, Turkey and its volatile political development continues to attract attention from people interested in the prospect for democracy. This book offers an impressive and thorough account of the recent democratic backsliding and reveals that not only the hope for a consolidation of liberal democracy but also large sections of the population are victims of rising authoritarianism.
Eren Keskin *Lawyer and Human Rights Activist* *The Vice-president of the Human Rights Association, Turkey*	We are living in a "Geography of Genocide." Historically, Unionists (committtee of union and progress), who committed the 1915 Armenian Genocide, established the Republic of Turkey. As a result, a distorted history and official ideology for the state was established. Furthermore, "redlines" in the country, such as the Kurdish Question, the Armenian Genocide, and the Cyprus Issue, were fabricated. Until today, the Turkish Republic remains in denial of the problems that have caused major human rights violations. This book chronicles a very important reality that evaluates the "core state structure" in Turkey, which remains intact even though rulers have changed, through human rights violations.
Sevan Nisanyan, *Historian, Linguist, and Political Refugee, Greece*	Turkey was once a poster boy of the league of modernizing countries – a staunch ally of the West, an almost-democracy that would become better soon enough. It might even be the first Muslim country to join the European Union. That image now lies shattered under the erratic one-man-show of Tayyip Erdoğan. The police state reigns supreme, opposition is cowed, the courts are in shambles, and more journalists are jailed for their opinions than in any other country.
	How did it all come to this pass?
	This collection of essays examines the visible and obscure causes of the catclysmic events that have transformed Turkey. They question the long-established state of semi-freedom under secular

(continued)

	rule, as well as the "Islamic" challenges that have arisen since Erdoğan's rise to power.
David L. Carter, Ph.D. *Michigan State University*	As one who knows people who have been victimized by the authoritarian regime in Turkey, *Human Rights in Turkey* provides unique insights and perspectives on the changes that have befallen his wonderful country. It is truly insightful.
Hercules Millas, PhD *Political Scientist, Greece*	Human rights violations are a worldwide phenomenon, occurring in various capacities and to varying degrees in each country. However, unique to Turkey is the rapid increase in violations that are not the result of deeply rooted social practices, but rather are contingent upon political decisions. Therefore, the cases of these violations are worthy of study.

External Reviewers

- Ahmet Erdi Ozturk
- Alia Hadid
- Arda Kumbaracibasi
- Arin Savran
- Arzu Alvan Bozdereli
- Basak Ince
- Berk Esen
- Bettina Birmanns
- Brian Mello
- Caner Hazar
- Cengiz Aktar
- Edel Hughes
- Eleni Polymenopoulou
- Elvan Aktaş
- Emre Turkut
- Felisa Tibbitts
- Gulsum Alan
- Helen Avery
- İbrahim Ö. Kaboğlu
- İlhan Yildiz
- İsmail Hakki Yigit
- İstar Gozaydin
- Joshua Hendrick
- Louis Fishman
- Matthew Whiting
- Muehlenhoff Hanna
- Muhammed Emrah Tanyıldız
- Murat Akser
- Murat Issi
- Nikos Christofis

- Nikos Michailidis
- Ozlem Denli
- Özlem Kayhan Pusane
- Paul Kubicek
- Pierre Duterte
- Po-Han Lee
- Rabia Hos
- Seven Kaptan
- Sophia Pandya
- Stanley Thangaraj
- Stephen Lafer
- Tamer Balci
- Theresa Weitzhofer-Yurtisik
- Thomas Phillips
- Thomas Smith
- Tom Gerald Daly
- Tunde Szecsi
- Ugur Ozgoker
- Victoria Araj
- Viktor Mak
- Wim Lunsing
- Yusuf Incetas
- Zeliha Ozdogan

Part I
An Overview of Human Rights in Turkey

Chapter 1
Introducing Human Rights in Turkey

Hasan Aydin and Winston Langley

Abstract Since the foundation of the Republic of Turkey, the military and the media have been the leading traditional powers of oppressive, secularist, and nationalist regimes in the country. As a result, Turkey has been confronted with the anti-democratic practices of its governments. After a period of initial reforms, Recep Tayyip Erdoğan seized the levers of power and used them aggressively against his political enemies rather than eliminating the structures of the authoritarian state. He turned Turkey into a one-person regime after the failed coup attempt on July 15, 2016, and his actions have included the widespread violation of human rights. Among the repercussions of the actions taken were the imprisonment of hundreds of thousands of people, the shuttering of media, the dismissal of public employees, the dismissal of academics, and the misuse of the criminal justice system to victimize its citizens. Other adverse effects encompassed widespread violations of human rights, the abuse and mistreatment of prisoners, false imprisonment, torture, and the absence of the right to a fair trial. This introductory chapter addresses a brief historical background on human rights violations, specifically, under Erdogan's era. This chapter also gives a brief introduction to each essay, the full complement of which address all aspects of human rights in Turkey. This volume consists of twenty chapters that contain substantial new essays prepared by more than 30 leading Turkish and international researchers, human rights activists, scholars, and practitioners in the field. It also provides a complete overview of the issues that inform research, a "map" of the debates that animate the field, and provides readers with new perspectives on the most recent human rights issues from a multidisciplinary perspective.

H. Aydin (✉)
Department of Curriculum, Instruction, and Culture, Florida Gulf Coast University, Fort Myers, FL, USA
e-mail: haydin@fgcu.edu

W. Langley
University of Massachusetts, Boston, MA, USA
e-mail: winston.langley@umb.edu

H. Aydin, W. Langley (eds.), *Human Rights in Turkey*, Philosophy and Politics - Critical Explorations 15, https://doi.org/10.1007/978-3-030-57476-5_1

Keywords Human rights · Democracy · Torture · Persecution · Coup · State of Emergency (OHAL) · Turkey

Since the foundation of the Republic of Turkey, the military and the media have been the leading traditional powers of oppressive, secularist, and nationalist regimes in the country. After a period of initial reforms, Recep Tayyip Erdoğan seized the levers of power rather than eliminating the structures of the authoritarian state. He used them aggressively actual political enemies and turned Turkey into a one-person regime after the failed coup attempt on July 15, 2016. These actions include the widespread violation of human rights. This book tells the tale of the consequences of the measures taken after the failed coup attempt that has impacted the development of democracy and human rights in Turkey adversely, fundamentally altering the nation's course of history. Among the consequences of the actions taken have been the imprisonment of hundreds of thousands, the shuttering of media, the dismissal of public employees, the dismissal of academics, and the misuse of the criminal justice system to victimize the population. Adverse effects have included widespread violations of human rights including, torture, and abuse of prisoners, false imprisonment, and assault on the right to a fair trial (Aydin and Avincan 2020).

This volume examines some of the thorniest questions of Turkish democratization and human rights, including the underlying reasons for the decay of democracy and what has happened as a result of this decay. Among these are a deterioration of the educational system, a reduction in economic stability, the absence of the rule of law and due process, a radical transformation of the country, and violations of universal human rights.

Although Turkey is a signatory to the Universal Declaration of Human Rights that was adopted without dissent by the United Nations General Assembly on 10 December 1948, the State of Emergency declared in Turkey July of 2016 had drastic repercussions that altered the course of history in Turkey. In the immediate aftermath, more 125,000 public employees were dismissed from their jobs, more than 3000 foundations and institutions were shut down, newspapers and trade unions were shuttered, and an estimated 600,000 people were put under investigation. Numerous human rights were truncated. For example, the right to a fair trial, freedom of expression, and humane treatment in prisons. Indeed, many human rights organizations like the Human Rights Committee of the United Nations, Freedom House, and Amnesty International reported numerous gruesome reports of torture, false imprisonment, and the mal-treatment of men, women, and children (Aydin and Avincan 2020; Girdap 2020).

Over the last several decades, Turkey has been confronted with the anti-democratic practices of its government. The country has been unable to resolve critical issues affecting the rights of the nation's various ethnic minority groups, those who hold beliefs and ideologies different from the mainstream, and important matters related to gender (Kabasakal 2007). All these issues were among the primary concern of human rights defenders (Langley 2002). Even though in the early 2000s,

Turkey took several critical steps in the name of democratization, there were taken principally to help in its efforts to join the European, and these steps were not sustained. The country publicized its goals to increase democratic values, integrate laws with European standards, increase the prosperity of her citizens, and showing concern for the general welfare of Turkish society. During this period, Turkey achieved considerable progress and became recognized as one of the most successful countries in the world in decreasing human rights violations and promoting democratic values (Abramowitz 2018). Such progress ended as the politicians could not find their way to unite the country's differing interests into a politically cohesive whole. Under the current government, Turkish society has become more polarized than ever before under an autocratic regime that has brought a halt to the democratic transformation.

Beginning with the use of excessive force by law enforcement agencies which sought to disperse civilian activists fighting an urban development plan in Taksim Gezi Park in May 2013, human rights violations began to escalate in Turkey. The government response to the protests led to the killing of three people in the center of Istanbul, in Taksim Square, and the protest, a peaceful one at first, turned violent when police, at the behest of the political party in power, responded with undue force (Amnesty International 2015; Human Rights Watch 2014). Protests against the government followed nationwide, with approximately three and a half million people participating in almost 5000 demonstrations (de Bellaigue 2013). During these protests, 12 people lost their lives, one of whom was a child, Berkin Elvan, more than 4000 people were injured, and 5513 civilians were taken into custody. Hundreds of those arrested were charged with terrorism. More than a hundred organizations supporting what came to be called the Gezi Park Protests, formed a coalition called Taksim Solidarity which became the subject of criminal investigations. Prominent journalists and commentators opposed to the government's response to the Gezi Park protests were dismissed from their jobs due to the pressure of the government on their media outlets (Amnesty International 2015; Human Rights Watch 2014).

Even while the actions at Gezi Park were taking place, corruption related to the granting of government contracts came to the forefront in Turkey (Freedom House 2014, 2019). A corruption investigation that occurred between the 17th and 25th of December 2013 involved several high-level officials, including Ministers and their relatives, which many understood to be a serious threat to the possibility of a Turkish democracy (Freedom House 2014). Members of the government involved in the scandal denied the claims made against them and accused those conducting the investigation of staging a judicial coup. Prosecutors, judges, and police officers who took part in the investigation were eventually declared to be terrorists and were accused of working for a parallel state (Freedom House 2015). Instead of probing the corruption claims widely, the Turkish government accused the civil servants involved of participating, in a conspiracy (Freedom House 2019; Human Rights Watch 2016a). When the judiciary in-place attempted to bring the cases to trial, the government interceded and, with the help of pro-government members of the judiciary, brought the corruption hearings to an end (Amnesty International 2015; Human Rights Watch 2016b).

When trucks were seized and were found to be carrying weapons in Adana that were bound for Syria, a scandal broke out in January of 2014, and that scandal was made all the more troubling when the Turkish Gendarmerie who conducted the search were all fired from their positions and faced legal investigation. The first official statements about the incident were that the trucks were loaded with humanitarian aid for Turkmen groups located in northern Syria. Later, however, both Prime Minister Recep Tayyip Erdoğan and other government officials admitted the fact that those trucks were part of covert operations. Two prominent journalists, Erdem Gül and Can Dündar, who published stories revealing the actual content of the trucks in the daily newspaper *Cumhuriyet,* found themselves accused by the government of espionage. They were subsequently detained in prison for several months (Amnesty International 2016).

This singular event marked the beginning of a government campaign to control the media, and the pressure on the media escalated to the point at which the opposition media were silenced. The private cable channel, Digiturk, for example, stopped broadcasting TV channels belonging to the Gülen Movement. At the beginning of November of the very same year, daily newspapers and televisions channels belonging to Ipek Group were raided, and government trustees were assigned to take over the company. Further, the Turkish Satellite Communication Company, Turksat, dropped programming by the Samanyolu Group media outlet, and the chief executive of the group, Hidayet Karaca, was imprisoned. He was sentenced to life imprisonment in 2018 after 4 years of pretrial detention (Amnesty International 2015, 2016; Freedom House 2017, 2019a, b; Human Rights Watch 2014).

All the above-mentioned oppressive practices, as well as the decline of democracy, led to a reaction against the ruling AKP party in 2015. In a general election carried out on 7 June 2015, the AKP lost the majority it held in the parliament. To regain control, it decided to employ a war strategy to garner popular support. During this period, the process of finding peace with Kurdish elements in Turkish society was taking place. The government, however, escalated human rights violations against the Kurds to provoke a diversionary crisis, especially in southeastern Turkey. Attacks against the Kurdish media and the Kurdish political party (People's Democratic Party, HDP) increased significantly (Human Rights Watch 2016a). Such actions were consistent with previous actions by the Turkish government that reserved the right to close down political parties at will using the pretext that such entities posed a threat to the state (Lewis and Skutsch 1991). As a result, the ruling party launched operations against those who were clamoring for autonomy in southeastern Turkey. The excessive force used in those operations included torture, the destruction of houses belong to civilians, violence against women, disruption of medical care, and intentional creation of food and water shortages among the civilians (Human Rights Watch 2016a; Office of the United Nations High Commissioner for Human Rights 2017). According to some estimates, more than 350,000 people were compelled to evacuate their homes and to move to other cities (Human

Rights Watch 2016b). In subsequent security operations, civilians who wanted to return to their homes and repair the damage that the operations caused were not allowed to do so by Turkish authorities. Damaged houses and buildings were demolished by bulldozers to prevent the rebuilding of the settlements (Office of the United Nations High Commissioner for Human Rights 2017).

For some time, the anti-democratic actions of the repressive regime were prosecuted without a legal base. While seeking ways of how to create the legal environment in which such practices could be made legal and permanent, a coup was attempted on July 15, 2016. The government crack-down in response to the coup attempt caused serious damage to Turkish society. The response resulted in 237 civilian deaths, 2191 injures, and 34 arrests of coup plotters (Amnesty International 2017). After the coup attempt, the Turkish Government declared a three-month State of Emergency that was later extended to 2 years (Amnesty International 2017). The scope of the State of Emergency was not limited to prosecuting those involved in the coup attempt. Instead, it turned in to a "witch hunt" throughout Turkey (Abramowitz 2018). A considerable number of people who were not involved in the coup attempt, or any other crime, were persecuted without any legal grounds. Political opponents were accused of being terrorists and enemies of the state, and the ruling political party consistently used the term "enemy" in its campaign slogans during their elections in 2015 and 2018 (Abramowitz 2018).

Human rights violations reached unprecedented levels after the failed coup attempt. Beginning in July of 2016, the Turkish government dismissed thousands of people who never were involved in any violent acts from service (Girdap 2020; The New Humanitarian 2017). Included among the dismissed were high-ranking military officials, university professors, journalists, judges, human rights defenders, police officers, scientists, teachers, doctors, students, and others – many of whom were jailed. Turkey became a world leader in jailing intellectuals, opposition politicians, and journalists (Office of the United Nations High Commissioner for Human Rights 2018). During the declared a State of Emergency, in the aftermath of the coup attempt, the government reportedly suspended from employment, detained, or placed under investigation without any evidence of wrongdoing, a considerable number of people (Human Rights Watch 2017, 2018). The United States Department of State – Bureau of Democracy Human Rights and Labor (2018) reported that the number of people under investigation was 612,347; 2060 of whom were under the age of 18.

The Assembly of the Council of Europe (PACE) made calls for protection of between an estimated 16,000 and 20,000 women, some of whom were pregnant, as well as 700 children who were being held in pre-detention custody or prisons in Turkey (Stockholm Center for Freedom 2017). Exposing pregnant women to unhealthy conditions and increasing their numbers in prisons where the lack of medical equipment and staff makes them vulnerable to serious health risks ,such as birth complications and death (Amnesty International 2018), has become a common practice in Turkey (Stockholm Center for Freedom 2017).

In addition, Human Rights Watch (2019b) noted that Turkey has also seen mass arrests and trials on terrorism charges of hundreds of lawyers tried in proceedings that rights groups have documented as being politicized and unfair. While lawyers always have a critical role to play in protecting the rights of suspects in police custody and defendants in court, their role in protecting the rule of law and human rights is even more fundamental in the context of the current crackdown in Turkey. Yet, or more likely because of the latter role, as this report demonstrates, authorities have also targeted lawyers – criminal defense lawyers in particular (Amnesty International 2017; Office of the United Nations High Commissioner for Human Rights 2018). More than a thousand lawyers have been prosecuted for terrorism offenses in the past two and a half years, with several hundred held in prolonged pretrial detention. In April 2019, the Arrested Lawyers Initiative, a civic group, reported that 1546 lawyers had been prosecuted, with 274 of them being convicted in first-instance counts of membership of a terrorist organization and 598 having been held in pretrial detention for varying periods (The Arrested Lawyers Initiative 2019). Approximately 34 bar associations were shut down on the grounds of an alleged affiliation with a terrorist organization (Office of the United Nations High Commissioner for Human Rights 2018).

According to the State of Emergency Commission (The Inquiry Commission on the State of Emergency Measures 2018), more than 136,000 people have been purged from public service through emergency government decrees. Three hundred journalists have been arrested on the grounds (many of the arrested journalists are known to be liberal, leftist, pro-Kurdish, or nationalist) that their publications contained "apologist sentiments regarding terrorism" or other "verbal act offenses" or for "membership" in terrorist organizations. Hundreds more are currently on trial (Kingsley 2017). The individuals arrested have not been "provided with specific evidence against them and were unaware of investigations against them" (Office of the United Nations High Commissioner for Human Rights 2018). Because the stated purpose of the emergency regime was to restore the normal functioning of the democratic institutions, it is unclear how measures such as the eviction of families of civil servants from publicly-owned housing may contribute to this goal," an OHCHR report states. More than 200 media outlets and 1769 non-governmental organizations, such as associations, unions, and confederations, have been closed. In addition, more than 100,000 websites were reportedly blocked in 2016, including a high number of pro-Kurdish websites and satellite TV channels.

The Turkish Constitution was designed in 1982 in conformity with Turkey's strict adherence to the idea of a single Turkish nation (Kurdish Human Rights Project 2011). In the pursuit of this idea, Turkey has enacted laws that are either patently undemocratic or authoritarian, including those prohibiting minorities from getting primary education in their mother tongue (Ozfidan 2017). The country's largest minority, the Kurds, who comprise 23% of the population, have no right to self-determination even though Turkey has signed the International Covenant on Civil and Political Rights (ICCPR). This refusal is felt through Turkey's embargo of their language, cultural, and political freedoms (Kurdish Human Rights Project 2011). Cultural freedoms has resulted in violence and arbitrary detention for several decades. The country faces serious social, economic, and political challenges—particularly a deep division between the supporters and opponents of the current government and its more religious, nationalist, and populist agenda. For example, in the wake of the July 2016 coup attempt, the Turkish government shuttered 1500 civil society groups (CSOs) and many groups, such as Gülen Movement supporters, Kurdish groups, and liberal activist groups, as well as the rule of law organizations, are under tremendous pressure (Center of American Progress 2017). Scholars and human rights organizations are urging Turkey to recognize all the minorities in its territory and to provide them with the full opportunities to enjoy their economic, social, and cultural rights and to adopt the necessary plans of action for this purpose.

The quasi-legal practices of the administration during the State of Emergency have also seriously affected education rights in general. Looking at restrictions on the right to peaceful protests and assembly in Turkey, the World Report described attacks on academic freedom, and a failure to investigate allegations of torture in police custody (Human Rights Watch 2019a). More than 7257 academics were fired and 5705 academics were suspended and fired since July 2016 (United States Department of State – Bureau of Democracy Human Rights and Labor 2018). In addition to that, around 463 academics are estimated to have lost their jobs because they signed “the academic petition.” Apart from 26 academics who have been forced to retire, 437 academics have been dismissed without due process or legal recourse (Ozsoy 2018). The Petition for Peace Initiative called for an end to the war against Kurds in Turkey and protested the use of force against civilians and members of a trade union. Many of the hundreds who signed the petition have been subjected to suspensions from their jobs, disciplinary action, dismissals, criminal investigations, and even incarceration in solitary confinement. On September 8, 2016, the government also announced the suspension of 11,500 Kurdish teachers for alleged links to a terrorist organization (Butler and Toksabay 2016). An atmosphere of fear has been created to silence all democratic dissent. In the wake of the failed coup attempt of July, violations of fundamental rights and freedoms have further eroded democracy in Turkey.

Since the failed coup attempt more than 15 higher education institutions, 1069 private schools, 848 students’ dormitories, 301 university preparation schools (*dershane*), 19 unions and trade confederations, and many civil society organizations have been shut down (Stockholm Center for Freedom 2017, 2018; United States Department of State – Bureau of Democracy Human Rights and Labor 2019). More than twenty thousand academic faculties have been closed; their staffs fired. In addition, approximately 100,000 public and private school teachers across the country were abruptly dismissed from their jobs; most of them were detained or jailed and some of them are still under investigation. All 1576 deans serving at universities in Turkey were forced to resign, and a travel ban was imposed on all academics. All of those affected were dismissed on allegations of being members of terrorist organizations of undermining the national security of the state. None was afforded any procedural rights or confronted with any evidence to justify such allegations and dismissals, and no formal charges have been brought (Human Rights Watch 2017).

While the attempted coup represented a threat to democracy in Turkey, the dismantling of democracy was in the making before the coup attempt. The government’s measures constitute further attacks on all critical voices and the rule of law in the country. The targeting of individuals and institutions for their associations, real and alleged, without evidence of wrongdoing, is a violation of fundamental human rights. Where academic personnel and universities are involved, they constitute a severe assault on academic freedom that, in itself, is a threat to democracy. In addition, whether fired in the post-coup purge or for signing a petition decrying violence, scholars, academic, and other professionalisms are leaving the country in droves. It is unlikely, under the current conditions, that intellectuals will serve as civil servants in Turkey.

Because of the unlawful practices of the Turkish Government in recent years, Turkish people who have been severely affected by human rights violations, especially after a coup attempt on 15 July 2016, began to escape the political conflicts and the ill-treatment of the Turkish government. The UNHRC (2018) reported that Turkey ranked fifth among those nations whose citizens are seeking asylum in Europe. According to statistics, the number of asylum seekers from Turkey had gradually decreased from 2008 to 2016. However, a dramatic increase in the number of asylum applications occurred in 2016 in Europe; corresponding to the State of Emergency declared in Turkey. By 2018, the number of Turkish refugees in Europe seeking asylum had risen to 23,407, which was almost five times the number reported in 2016 (European Asylum Support Office 2019).

This book examines these events, their repercussions, and possible solutions to their associated problems, through analysis by way of history, survey, spatial analysis, and thematic analysis of interviews with those who have fled the continuing mayhem in Turkey. In addition, the book examines the historical setting of Turkey concerning the development of democracy, the treatment of cultural and ethnic minorities, and the short and long-term consequences of the crackdown, including its impacts on individuals, institutions like education and the media, the criminal justice system, the economy, and Turkey's standing in the international community.

The work, which is divided into seven parts, including an introductory section, addresses the violations of human rights in Turkey, with theoretical, empirical, and historical, descriptive analyses by experienced and well-known scholars, practitioners, or human rights activists. The editors are very fortunate to have received ninety-six proposals, from which the selections were made for the collection.

Unfortunately, two chapters initially intended for the volume are not included because the authors withdrew their chapters at the last moment because they did not want their names to appear. They believe that the Turkish government will arrest their family members who still live in Turkey. For this reason, this volume may not cover all aspects of current human rights violations for discussing challenges to the existence of human rights and state responsibility for human rights violations, and a general conclusion are not included in the text.

In Part I, the collection begins with chapters on the issues on human rights in the past, present, and future and investigates Turkey's long-run human rights violations and their social and political causes. In his chapter, Ercan Balcioglu argues that Turkey has had a history of human rights issues with minorities, including Kurds, Alevis, and Armenians, that spans nearly two centuries. A fully functioning democracy and legal system with competent institutions and established rules have not been as yet established. Furthermore, the occasional progress of Turkey in furthering fundamental rights has been characterized by waves of adverse interventions, as in the case in the post-coup conditions of July 15, 2016, and many others that preceded it.

In considering the history of human rights in Turkey, two contradictory images that reflect different realities in Turkey emerge. The first image is that of a modernizing, developing and democratizing Turkey that is evolving with an unwavering rule of law. Unfortunately, a second image reflects widespread and targeted anti-democratic political processes in which the rule of law and separation of powers have not been achieved, and the "law of the ruler" dominates the social order. Today, the judiciary is neither impartial nor independent. Control and balanced systems, the social division of labor, and the fair income distribution are missing in the frame. Systematic discrimination exists against specific social segments, such as Kurds and some religious groups. The social system is unjust and unequal. Finally, this section includes dual identity conflicts and paradoxical interventions.

In Part II of the collection, the contributors discuss theoretical foundations, historical traditions, and empirical evidence in the area of freedom, and antidiscrimination in religious, media, Kurdish, and LGBT communities. In his chapter, Vedat Demir addresses violations of freedom of media, including the press, and of speech that have been violated by the Justice and Development Party (AKP) government in several respects. Demir argues that since the foundation of the Republic of Turkey, the military and media had always been the traditional central powers of the oppressive, secularist, and the nationalist regime in the country. Initially, Recep Tayyip Erdoğan and his AKP challenged this structure, after coming to power in 2002 with two primary objectives: to break the stranglehold of Turkey's political establishments and to push forward Turkey's planned integration into the European Union. As a result of their progressive policies, AKP swiftly gained the support of liberals, democrats, Kurds and religious conservatives. However, these reforms helped Erdoğan establish the foundations of his own political agenda. Erdoğan overcame many challenges that would be problematic for his political agenda by weakening the military influence and reforming the secular foundation of the Turkish Republic. In time, however, Erdoğan adopted the traditional perspective of the Turkish state, even though he came to power as an anti-statist alternative. After a period of initial reforms, rather than eliminating the structures of the authoritarian state, he seized and used them aggressively against his political enemies and turned Turkey into a one-person regime.

The authoritarian policies of the Erdoğan government became apparent during the anti-government Gezi Park protests in May 2013 and the vast corruption scandal in of that year. Journalists were harassed and assaulted, while attempting to cover the Gezi Park protests, and dozens were fired or forced to resign, in response to their reporting on the demonstrations. The same year, more journalists were fired over their coverage of "sensitive issues" that could weaken Erdoğan and his party. Demir further argues that media freedom in Turkey deteriorated at an alarming rate in 2015. The Erdoğan government started to use the penal code, criminal defamation legislation, and the country's antiterrorism laws aggressively to punish critical reporting while journalists faced growing violence, harassment, and intimidation from both state and non-state actors throughout the year. The most aggressive form of state intervention against media enterprises was the direct seizure of assets. Several major media outlets were seized by the government and swiftly turned into government mouthpieces. The state-owned national broadcaster and news agency also became propaganda tools for Erdoğan, while he repeatedly interfered with the rest of the media outlets' editorial decisions and exerted pressure on them to fire critical journalists. The coup attempt in July 2016 became an unprecedented turning point for the Turkish media. During the 3-year State of Emergency, declared after the coup attempt, a massive purge was carried out against the critics of Erdoğan. The emergency decrees passed in this period resulted in the shutdown of hundreds of newspapers, news agencies, radio stations, television networks, and magazines, while thousands of journalists were left unemployed. Hundreds of critical journalists were arrested. Turkey has become the world's biggest jailer of journalists in a short period. In this chapter, the author answered the question of the freedom of the media in Turkey and its dramatic deterioration under the AKP government as well as how Erdoğan has used the media to realize his political agenda over the last two decades.

In the next chapter, Istar Gozaydin discusses religious discrimination, focusing explicitly on the non-Muslim population. Although Turkey has been constitutionally, a secular state that guarantees substitute rights to religious minorities, since its foundation, discriminatory laws and gaps in practice remain severe. Gozaydin emphasizes that discrimination is not only against non-Muslim religious individuals and groups. Most significantly, the Alevi faith has been a subject of discrimination in terms of non-acknowledgement with repercussions in denial of venues of prayer and rituals, educational services, and financial subsidies, to mention a few. She evaluates the freedom of religion has always been a thorny issue in Turkey. Even though in black letter law, a substantial number of regulations exist, discrimination in this regard has been very multi-layered in modern Turkey. In her chapter, she evaluates political and legal/judicial aspects of the issue in the context of human rights throughout republican Turkey, starting with its roots in the Ottoman past and differentiating policies regarding religion with their impacts on various groups in society. Moreover, she considers non-believers and share their discriminatory practices based on religion in her chapter as well.

Next, Emre Turkut and Thomas Phillips address non-discrimination, minority rights, and self-determination during and after Turkey's post-coup State of Emergency and the position of Turkey's Kurds. The authors underline the underlying problems of the accommodations to Kurds, and the extraordinary limitations of rights arising from them, as well as their striking effect on minorities in Turkey during the State of Emergency (OHAL). Also, Turgut and Phillips argue that the declaration of the State of Emergency that constituted a response to an attempted coup, which the Gülen Movement alleged orchestrated, also targeted "other individuals and organizations," mainly those allegedly connected to the PKK (Kurdistan Workers' Party), and thus extended to Turkey's Kurdish periphery. Their chapter maps the impact of the Turkish post-coup derogation measures on Turkey's Kurds and tests them against non-discrimination principles, minority rights, and the right of self-determination.

Fuat Muedini's chapter considers the theoretical foundation LGBTI community in Turkey. Muedini examines these levels of discrimination in Turkey, as well as explores how activists are working to improve human rights for LGBTI individuals living in this hostile environment. Muedini bases his analysis on interviews from several NGO leaders and activists of leading LGBTI organizations in the region, including Lambda Istanbul, Kaos GL, Pembe Hayat, Social Policies, Gender Identity and Sexual Orientation Studies Association (SPoD), and Families of LGBT's in Istanbul (LİSTAG).

The last chapter in this section is a discussion on LGBTQ Rights and, using empirical evidence, shows how historically the Turkish government violated human rights. In it, Barbaros Sansal presents several stories of LGBTQ individuals who have experienced discrimination, physical abuse, and even death in Turkey. This chapter addresses several stories including Ahmet Yıldız, who is thought to have been killed by his father because he was gay; Hande Buse Şeker who was shot by a police officer who was a client while he was a sex worker; and Hande Kader, a gay activist who was subjected to police violence during the march of honor in 2015 and was burned to death. Sansal argues that the stories of gay people suggest that all systems in Turkey are united in discriminatory policies against LGBTQ people, and civil society organizations have been unable to protect gay rights. Even though the Turkish Constitution and the Universal Declaration of Human Rights, to which Turkey is a signatory, guarantee equal rights, the rights of LGBTQ people continue to be abrogated.

Part III of the collection addresses the rights of the displaces Syrian refugees who resided in Turkey after Syrian civil was in 2011. In the initial chapter, Alia Hadid and Rabia Hos show that the number of Syrian refugees who are seeking shelter in Turkey continues to rise as Syria enters its ninth year of violence. The authors of this chapter argue that the ongoing crisis has resulted in more than 3.5 million registered Syrian refugees (United Nations High Commissioner for Refugees 2019). Although researchers in this field have studied the multiple social, economic, and security related debates, the scope of this chapter focuses on the education rights of the Syrian refugees in Turkey. Despite the importance of such challenges, a much more pressing issue exists, which is providing education to all children who constitute 1.6 million Syrian refugees, of which more than 430.000 are out of school (UNICEF 2018) in Turkey. Hos and Hadid provide a detailed review of the current situation of schooling Syrian refugee children in Turkey. The authors refer to UN documents, non-governmental organization (NGO) reports, and scholarly work to present an overview of the Syrian refugee education in Turkey. The authors investigates how Turkey responded to meet the Syrian refugees' educational needs and how the continuing efforts are still in violation of the fundamental human rights of refuges, in part, because around half a million of them are still out of school (Karasapan and Sajjad 2018). In the concluding section, the authors end with a discussion of how the responses thus far have not improved even though many years have passed and show how this violates fundamental human rights.

The process of human rights issues under the State of Emergency and some of the main concepts now widely discussed form the heart of Part IV. In his chapter,

Mehmet Efe Caman, a long-time major figure in the development of democratization and human rights law and its context in Turkey, examines the positive experience of democratization and transformation from the Edict of Gulhane in 1839 to the First Constitutional Era of 1876. During that period, Turkey had a history of constitutional democracy and human rights. This long history, however, has not ensured a continuing and durable standard on human rights in Turkey. Caman argues that Turkey's aspiration for membership in the European Union (EU) was a remarkable external factor that influenced the Turkish democratization process. AKP recognized this and deliberately integrated a reform policy into its party program. When the AKP came to power in 2002, it implemented an intensive reform program to fulfill the EU accession criteria. The level of human rights in Turkey as of 2004 (when the EU decided to start negotiations for Turkish membership) presents an example of how deep penetration of political modernization, and a sophisticated organization of the state architecture, promoted a specific basis for further democratization. Caman also highlights how after the Gezi Park protests of Spring 2013 and the corruption scandal in December 2013, Turkish democracy began to decline. In 2014, the government terminated the Peace Process and ended the moderate course with the Kurds, and the Turkish military launched a massive military offensive in Kurdish towns. As a result, tens of thousands of people left their homes, and entire neighborhoods in Kurdish cities were utterly destroyed. Caman discusses how AKP purged academics (peace petitioners) supporting a peaceful solution of the conflict after the crack-down following the coup attempt, which witnessed hundreds of thousands of public servants discharged and purged, tens of thousands of people imprisoned, and Turkish human rights standards considerably reduced. Thousands of Gülen Movement followers and hundreds of Kurdish politicians – about 10 MPs and numerous elected Kurdish mayors – were removed from their elected posts and jailed. Caman also deals with the thorniest issues of Turkish democratization and human rights practices which are at once the underlying issues in the progressive democratic decay and the explanation for the decision of the AKP to subvert the democratization process.

Next, Sophia Pandya, Brenda Oliden, and Ibrahim Anli examine the reasons why the Hizmet Gülen Movement has become a primary target of Erdoğan and offer an analysis of the characteristics and strategies of conservative, authoritarian populism, the processes used to destroy the Gülen Movement network in Turkey and the attempts to neutralize it abroad. The authors also shed light on the human consequences of the purge or crackdown against the movement. They argue that their work is informed, in part, by scholarship on populist state-sponsored violence and the effects of collective trauma. The mechanisms by which Erdoğan has carried out his crackdown have been effective and they have had far-reaching consequences. These include firing people at random, seizing property, kidnapping, arbitrary arrests (without due process), promoting a climate of fear, silencing, scapegoating, and social and religious shunning (or "takfirism"). The authors employed qualitative research shaped by participant/observation ethnographic methodology and semi-structured interviews collected via a mixture of purposive and snowball sampling that was carried out from June 2016 to July 2018. The goal of the authors was to interview those HGM participants who had recently fled Turkey due to political oppression and or fear of imminent arrest to seek asylum in the United States. The authors asked informants why they had left Turkey, what their experiences were, and how those experiences impacted them and their families.

In his chapter, Ufuk Yesil discusses the rights to a fair trial as a human right under OHAL. Yesil indicates that, after the failed coup attempt on July 15, 2016, in Turkey, more than 125,000 public servants were dismissed from their professions without any concrete justification, and their names were added to lists announced by the decree law, along with the decision that they would not be reinstated in the future. Yesil underlines that the individuals were accused of being members of a terrorist organization, and rights connected with the European Convention on Human Rights (ECHR) were not afforded to them. Furthermore, Yesil states that the presumption of innocence was violated, and even their fundamental right to defend themselves was not granted. Because they were officially classified as terrorists, they became isolated from social life and in practice, were sentenced to "*civil death*." This chapter concludes with the denial of fundamental rights, including that of a fair trial.

In their chapter, Acun Karadag and Nazan Bozkurt provide empirical data with several case studies on intellectuals on hunger strike for reinstatement to their job, including a case of "*Yuksel Resistance.*" Karadag and Bozkurt emphasize various human and constitutional rights violations in Turkey and demonstrate them systematically. They collected data through interviews, reports, and open-source media articles written after a protest in Ankara named "*We Want Our Jobs Back.*" The chapter also employs verbal histories of activists including Acun Karadag, Nazan Bozkurt and Mehmet Dersulu, and participant observation in activities in which the researchers have been involved since the beginning of the State of Emergency. Five human rights activists were interviewed for data collection. The chapter revealed two themes: *Violence and Unlawful Intervention*, and *Resistance and Determination*. The chapter presents evidence with the photographs under these two themes. The chapter concludes that the Turkish government has violated fundamental human rights including the right to a fair trial and right to peacefully assemble and demonstrate. In addition, Karadag and Bozkurt argue that the Turkish police disproportionately intervened using unnecessary and extreme violence in cases where Decree-Law victims were trying to exercise their Constitutional rights.

The final chapter in this part provides evidence and evaluation of the human rights violations within a Medicolegal Approach. Alper Keten argues that in Turkey, the number of people directly exposed to torture is estimated at several million during OHAL that lasted for 730 days from July 20, 2016, to 20 July 2018. In this process, through ministerial decrees, 150,348 public servants, including judges, prosecutors, state officials, teachers, bureaucrats, medical doctors, and academics, were dismissed without any investigation. Keten indicated that the right not to be tortured had been stated clearly and definitely in international law. The United Nations have been trying to put forward standards to provide adequate protection against torture and other cruel, inhumane and insulting treatments practiced upon people for years. The agreements, declarations, and decisions accepted by the member states of the United

Nations manifest clearly that no exceptions should exist in terms of torture prohibition and has imposed other obligations to protect against similar violations.

The tasks of care and inspections are handled in many declarations of the World Medical Association. Those declarations clearly state that doctors are responsible for taking proper care of their patients, including prisoners and persons who have been claimed to be guilty of wrong-doing. The International Medical Ethic Rules of the World Medical Association Declarations emphasize that doctors have the responsibility to provide medical care in a professionally, morally independent, and compassionate way that is compatible with human dignity. This declaration indicates that the doctors are not only responsible for providing treatment that benefits a patient, but also, they should show loyalty to their patients. Keten evaluated the Istanbul Protocol that was prepared by many scientists around the world and accepted by the United Nations in 1999. The Istanbul Protocol was intended to establish international guidelines for the assessment of persons who have been subjected to torture, inhumane, or degrading treatment for the investigation of cases of alleged torture and the reporting of findings to the judiciary and other investigative bodies. Medical evaluations with a forensic purpose were to be carried out objectively and unbiasedly. The chapter concludes with the discussions of the medicolegal issues related to human rights violations in Turkey.

Part V of this collection provides an evaluation of the human rights violations on social, economic, and educational rights. The first chapter in this section focuses on the right to education and challenges issues raised under the AKP. In it, Uzeyir Ogurlu and Koksal Avincan note that the right to education has been recognized as a human right by several international conventions. The Constitution of the Republic of Turkey also provides for the right to education. However, the government, ruled by AKP since 2002, has failed to protect and fulfill this right for all. Although education in one's mother tongue, compulsory religious education and a teaching recruitment system have been among the most debated education rights, July 15, 2016, which is the date of the failed coup attempt, represents a turning point in the history of violation of human rights in the Republic of Turkey. The controversies and violations of human rights were exacerbated after the failed coup attempt with a massive purge of dissidents. Thousands of teachers were dismissed, and thousands of public and private schools, dormitories, and unions were closed as part of the crackdown. This chapter concludes with a summary of the violations of education rights in Turkey under the AKP era, especially after the July 15 failed coup attempt, in the light of international agreements on rights to education.

The next chapter, Hasan Aydin, Viktor Mak and Kristina Andrews address on academic freedom in Turkey. The authors interviewed scholars who are in exile after the failed coup attempt in 2016 and the highlight how Turkish government began a massive crackdown against dissent, and thousands of academics were targeted, suspended and fired from their jobs. While there is a precedent for academic institutions being political targets in Turkey after coups and attempted coups (Weiker 1962), the scale of the purge was shocking, particularly given the positive recent trends in democracy in Turkey, as it hoped to join the European Union.

Aydin, Mak, and Andrews highlight that the violations of academic freedom are widespread and comprehensive as hundreds of signatories have lost their jobs at Turkish universities. The Turkish government has used the Peace Petition to send a strong message to academics to silence their dissent and to withdraw into an apolitical existence (Redden 2019). After that, many academics chose to flee Turkey to pursue their research in universities abroad. In this chapter, the authors report the findings of their empirical study, which explored the perspectives of academics on academic freedom that they experienced before and after the coup in 2016 in Turkey. The authors linked their evidence to The Lima Declaration on Academic Freedom and Autonomy of Institutions of Higher Education (1989), referring to the UN Agreements on Human Rights, which stressed that the members of the academic community are entitled to freedom of thought, expression, assembly, organization, individual rights, and travel (Gokbel and Seggie 2015). As Summak (1997) noted, insights into academics' perceptions of their academic freedom can be gained directly by asking them. This study focuses on individual academic freedom as a human right, which involves intellectual freedom, the absence of limitation on the exercise of intellectual capacities, and freedom of inquiry (Gokbel and Seggie 2015). The authors used a qualitative phenomenology approach because the researchers were interested in the lived experiences of ten faculty who left Turkey after they had been fired and removed from their university position. The findings of the chapter indicate that although most participants stated their apolitical behavior before the coup, a few noted that their research (e.g., Kurdish culture, religion, Syrian refugees, language) could be perceived as a particular political stand. Regardless, they found themselves to be victims of the political system in which their attempts to advance their fields brought brutal and unjustified repercussions. The academics who participated in the study were successful within their fields and respected in the international academic community for their quests to seek truth and knowledge. The chapter concludes with recommendations for policies for Turkish and international organizations.

Zeliha Ozdogan's chapter discusses the effects of democratic regression on the Turkish economy and the brain drain after the deep financial crisis in 2001 in a country that had previously experienced rapid economic growth. Ozdogan underlines that Turkey's economy had become stable and robust by the end of the 2000s. Alongside the economic progression, European Union accession talks generated optimism about democratic consolidation and the EU membership. She focused on 2013 when the government increased its authoritarian grasp in the aftermath of the Gezi Park protests, in which the government used excessive force to expel the protestors with minimal dialogue between the two parties involved and a corruption scandal that included the highest-level government officials. Ozdogan discusses the expansion of the government's authoritarian power after 2013 that grew in such a way as to thwart all opposition in the country and eradicate the checks over the government's executive power. The chapter highlights that Turkey has drastically dropped to the bottom of the lists in international indexes of democracy and human rights.

Meanwhile, Turkey's economic stability has stalled; all freedoms, including property rights, have been disrespected and violated, and many intellectuals and scientists have fled from the country. In addition, the author discusses the theoretical foundation of the nexus between political and economic development. The chapter presents the trajectory of the Turkish economy during the last decade. It explores the effect of democratic regression on the economy, particularly in the areas of property rights and brain drain.

The final chapter in this part concerns the neoliberal de-development in Turkey and the AKP's socioeconomic war on the counterhegemony. Victoria Araj and Arin Savran critically examine the politics of Turkey's AKP that have resulted its monopolization of power and rising authoritarianism, as well as the resulting impediments on fundamental rights and freedoms. The chapter enriches a theoretical foundation by reconnoitering the importance and centrality of the neoliberal[1] (Harvey 2005, 2) development and de-development of the country's socioeconomic structures, as part of the Islamic-rooted AKP's quest for domestic and regional hegemonic power. The chapter further analyzes the evolution of the de-development of subaltern (especially Kurdish) space in Turkey on both the national and regional levels. It also discusses the resistance against the AKP's attempts at hegemonic dominance.

Araj and Savran focus explicitly on two patterns of rights violations. In section one, they discuss the AKP's authoritarian neoliberal development policies and the emerging counter hegemonic resistance from the subaltern against the commodification of the commons, gentrification of homes, privatization of the Turkish economy, and human rights violations. Section two analyses the AKP power bloc's intensified de-development and authoritarian practices plus the use of extreme force to maintain public consent and repress subaltern resistance and agency, thus widening the democratic deficit. The chapter concludes with an examination of where this leaves the prospect of counterhegemonic resistance in Turkey today, particularly after the July 2016 attempted coup d'état, the 2017 presidential referendum, and the 2019 municipal elections.

Part VI of the volume provides empirical evidence of human rights violations in relationship to women and children. The chapters in this section investigate the human rights violations of imprisoned women and children after the coup attempt. In the first chapter of this section, Omer Faruk Gergerlioglu examines violations of rights committed against women and children during the State of Emergency declared after the coup attempt on July 15, 2016. Gergerlioglu uses the narrative analysis of 44 victimized women and children form data that were gathered through messages sent to social media accounts, letters received, social media communications, as well as face-to-face interviews. Three major themes emerged from the

[1]Borrowing from Harvey, we broadly conceptualize *neoliberalism* as a theory of political economy, which advances the idea that "human wellbeing can best be advanced by liberating individual entrepreneurial freedoms and skills within an institutional framework characterized by strong private property rights, free markets, and free trade"

including *ostracism, civil death, torture, and persecution*. The findings in this chapter indicate that the coup attempt of July 15 was used as a pretext to eliminate a group of people. The evidence shows that the women and children in question had nothing to do with the coup attempt but were victimized for their alleged ties with the Gülen Movement. Women were exposed to all types of abuse during the State of Emergency, including job dismissals to detentions and arrests (even and commonly during pregnancy or postpartum period), threats, harassments, intimidations, ostracization, inability to find accommodation, inability to find work, economic difficulties, illnesses, psychological problems, forced displacement, forced separation from loved ones, abortion, suicide and death. Women generally experienced those victimizations with their children.

In the following chapter, Vonya Womack examines the trauma of Turkish women and children in an era of political unrest and highlights, through a series of vignettes drawn from interviews, how recent developments in the Justice and Development Party (AKP)/Hizmet Gülen Movement (HGM) split has affected women and children's rights. The chapter explores human rights violations, displacement, and individual and communal trauma. Through family stories, the author explores political, ethical, psychological, and cultural factors impacting refugee Turkish women and children. Woman concludes that these traumas can potentially awaken the global community to action by understanding the plight and resilience of the human spirit of these Turkish women and children.

Part VII of the collection reflects on the recent debates about the attempts to provide some visual evidence of human rights violations in Turkey. In his chapter, Gulsum Alan focuses on Turkey's Accession to the European the Union in Context as a journalist observation. Alan argues that 1999 is considered a turning point in Turkey's effort to gain European Union membership, as this was when Turkey's European Union candidacy application was officially approved. Brussels, stating that Turkey sufficiently met the political criteria, decided to begin accession negotiations in 2005. Alan states that after the failed coup of 2016, the European Parliament seriously concerned the rule of law, media freedom and the fight against corruption in Turkey and recommended suspending EU accession negotiations with Turkey. Alan underlines that Brussels said Ankara was moving away from the norms of the European Union values and that no new chapter could be opened until the situation was resolved. One of the most critical indicators of Turkey's commitment to European values is its membership in the Council of Europe, of which the European Court of Human Rights is a part. Although the Court has no organic ties to the EU, it often takes a stance against human rights violations throughout the EU and in Turkey, whose violations escalated after the July 15, 2016, failed coup. For its part, the European Union has considered Turkey's stance against the Court's assessments and evaluations. The author concludes this chapter with an examination of Turkey's relations with the European Union during the 1990s, 2000s, and 2011.

References

Abramowitz, Michael J. 2018. *Freedom in The World 2018: Democracy in Crisis*. Freedom House. https://freedomhouse.org/sites/default/files/FH_FITW_Report_2018_Final_SinglePage.pdf.

Amnesty International. 2015. *Amnesty International Report 2014/2015-The State of the World's Human Rights*. https://www.amnesty.org/download/Documents/POL1000012015ENGLISH.PDF.

———. 2016. *Amnesty International Report 2015/16-The State of the World's Human Rights*. https://www.amnesty.org/download/Documents/POL1025522016ENGLISH.PDF.

———. 2017. *Amnesty International Report 2016/17- The State of the World's Human Rights*. https://www.amnesty.org/download/Documents/POL1048002017ENGLISH.PDF.

———. 2018. *Amnesty International Report 2017/18- The State of the World's Human Rights*. https://www.amnesty.org/download/Documents/POL1067002018ENGLISH.PDF.

Aydin, Hasan, and Koksal Avincan. 2020. Intellectual Crimes and Serious Violation of Human Rights in Turkey: A Narrative Inquiry. *The International Journal of Human Rights* 24 (8): 1127–1155. https://doi.org/10.1080/13642987.2020.1713108.

Butler, Daren, and Ece Toksabay. 2016. Turkey Suspends Thousands of Teachers, Wages' Biggest Campaign' Against Kurds. *Reuters,* September 8.

Center for American Progress. 2017. *Trends in Turkish civil society*. https://www.americanprogress.org/issues/security/reports/2017/07/10/435475/trends-turkish-civil-society/.

de Bellaigue, Christopher. 2013. Turkey: "Surreal, Menacing . . . Pompous". *The New York Review of Books,* December 19.

European Asylum Support Office. 2019. *EASO EU+ Asylum Trends 2018 Overview*. https://easo.europa.eu/sites/default/files/EASO-2018-EU-Asylum-Trends-Overview.pdf.

Fernando, Laksiri. 1989. The Lima Declaration on Academic Freedom and Autonomy of Institutions of Higher Education. *Higher Education Policy* 2 (1): 49–51.

Freedom House. 2014. *Freedom in the World 2014*. http://freedomhouse.org/sites/default/files/FIW2014Booklet.pdf.

———. 2015. *Freedom in the World 2015*. https://freedomhouse.org/sites/default/files/01152015_FIW_2015_final.pdf.

———. 2017. *Freedom in the World 2017*. https://freedomhouse.org/report/freedom-world/2017/turkey.

———. 2019. *Freedom in the World 2019*. https://freedomhouse.org/report/freedom-world/freedom-world-2019/democracy-in-retreat.

Girdap, Hafza. 2020. Human rights, conflicts, and dislocation: The case of Turkey in a global Spectrum. *American Journal of Qualitative Research 2020* 4 (1): 69–84. https://doi.org/10.29333/ajqr/8266.

Gökbel, Veysel, and Fatma Nevra Seggie. 2015. *Academic Freedom in Turkey*. SETA.

Harvey, David. 2005. *A Brief History of Neoliberalism*. Oxford: Oxford University Press.

Human Rights Watch. 2014. *Human Rights World Report 2014*. https://www.hrw.org/world-report/2014/country-chapters/.

———. 2016a. *Turkey: State Blocks Probes of Southeast Killings*. https://www.hrw.org/news/2016/07/11/turkey-state-blocks-probes-southeast-killings.

———. 2016b. *World Report 2016*. https://www.hrw.org/world-report/2016/country-chapters/turkey.

———. 2017. *World Report 2017*. https://www.hrw.org/sites/default/files/world_report_download/wr2017-web.pdf.

———. 2018. *World Report 2018*. https://www.hrw.org/world-report/2018.

———. 2019a. *World Report 2019*. https://www.hrw.org/world-report/2019.

———. 2019b. *Lawyers on Trial: Abusive Prosecutions and Erosion of Fair Trial Rights in Turkey*. https://www.hrw.org/report/2019/04/10/lawyers-trial/abusive-prosecutions-and-erosion-fair-trial-rights-turkey.

Kabasakal Arat, Zehra, ed. 2007. *Human Rights in Turkey*. Philadelphia: University of Pennsylvania Press.

Karasapan, Omer, and Shah Sajjad.(2018). Syrian Refugees and the Schooling Challenge. *The Brookings Institution,* October 23. https://www.brookings.edu/blog/future-development/2018/10/23/syrian-refugees-and-the-schooling-challenge/.

Kingsley, Patrick. 2017. Turkey Purges 4,000 More Officials, and Blocks Wikipedia. *New York Times,* April 30. https://www.nytimes.com/2017/04/30/world/europe/turkey-purge-wikipedia-tv-dating-shows.html.

Kurdish Human Rights Project. 2011. *Kurdish Economic, Social and Cultural Rights in Turkey.* https://kurdistancommentary.wordpress.com/2011/05/30/kurdish-economic-social-cultural-rights-in-turkey/.

Langley, Winston E. 2002. Encyclopedia of Human Rights Issues Since 1945. *Journal of Government Information.* https://doi.org/10.1016/s1352-0237(01)00332-x.

Lewis, James R, and Carl Skutsch. 1991. *The Human Rights Encyclopedia, Volume Two.*

Office of the United Nations High Commissioner for Human Rights. 2017. *Report on the Human Rights Situation In South-East Turkey from July 2015 to December 2016.* https://www.ohchr.org/Documents/Countries/TR/OHCHR_South-East_TurkeyReport_10March2017.pdf.

———. 2018. *Report on the Impact of the State of Emergency on Human Rights in Turkey, Including an Update on the South-East from January-December 2017.* https://www.ohchr.org/Documents/Countries/TR/2018-03-19_Second_OHCHR_Turkey_Report.pdf.

Ozfidan, Burhan. 2017. Academic Value of Bilingual Education: Factors in Learning on Culture and Language *Revista de. Cercetare Si Interventie Sociala* 59: 34–47.

Ozsoy, Elif Ceylan. 2018. Academics for Peace – Imprisonment , Censorship Continue. *University World News,* June 15. https://www.universityworldnews.com/post.php?story=2018061309132653.

Redden, Elizabeth. 2019. Peace Petition Signatories Face Continued Prosecutions. *Insider Higher Ed,* July 1. https://www.insidehighered.com/news/2019/07/01/about-700-academics-have-been-criminally-charged-turkey-their-signatures-petition.

Stockholm Center for Freedom. 2017. *Jailing Women in Turkey – Systematic Campaign of Persecution and Fear.* https://stockholmcf.org/wp-content/uploads/2017/04/Jailing-women-in-Turkey.pdf.

———. 2018. *Free Thought Under Siege in Turkey: The Crackdown on Education.* https://stockholmcf.org/wp-content/uploads/2018/07/The-Crackdown-On-Education-in-Turkey_june_2018.pdf.

Summak, Mehmet Semih. 1997. An Analysis of Academic Staff Members' Perceptions of the Problem-Solving Processes, General Administrative Problems andthe Academic Rights and Freedoms at Turkish Public Universities. *Yayinlanmamis Doktora Tezi,* Sosyal Bilimler Enstitüsü, Gaziantep Üniversitesi 294.

The Arrested Lawyers Initiative. 2019. *Incarceration of Turkish Lawyers: Unjust Arrests and Convictions (2016–2018).* https://arrestedlawyers.org/2019/04/01/new-report-incarceration-of-turkish-lawyers-unjust-arrests-and-convictions-2016-2019/.

The Inquiry Commission on the State of Emergency Measures. 2018. *Olağanüstü Hal İşlemleri İnceleme Komisyonu Faaliyet Raporu 2018* [Disaster Recovery Commission Annual Report 2018]. https://ohalkomisyonu.tccb.gov.tr/docs/OHAL_FaaliyetRaporu_2018.pdf.

The New Humanitarin. 2017. *Crackdown: Prison Conditions Worsen in Post-Coup Turkey.* https://www.thenewhumanitarian.org/investigations/2017/09/06/crackdown-prison-conditions-worsen-post-coup-turkey.

UNICEF. 2018. *UNICEF Turkey 2018 Humanitarian Situation Report, 24.* https://reliefweb.int/sites/reliefweb.int/files/resources/UNICEF%20Turkey%20Humanitarian%20Situation%20Report%20No.%2024%20-%20August%202018.pdf.

United Nations High Commissioner for Refugees. 2019. *Situation Syria Regional Refugee Response.* https://data2.unhcr.org/en/situations/syria/location/113.

United States Department of State – Bureau of Democracy Human Rights and Labor. 2018. *Turkey 2017 Human Rights Report*. https://www.state.gov/wp-content/uploads/2019/01/Turkey.pdf.
———. 2019. *Turkey 2018 Human Rights Report*. https://www.state.gov/reports/2018-country-reports-on-human-rights-practices/turkey/.
Weiker, Walter F. 1962. Academic Freedom and Problems of Higher Education in Turkey. *Middle East Journal* 16 (3): 279–294.

Hasan Aydin earned his Ph.D. from the University of Nevada, Reno in 2011. Dr. Aydin is a Professor of Multicultural Education in the Department of Curriculum, Instruction, and Culture at Florida Gulf Coast University. His scholarship focuses on multicultural education, bilingual education, Kurdish language and cultural rights, human rights, social justice, diversity and equity in education, educating refugee students, citizenship education in a global context, and international education. Dr. Aydin's research cuts across local, national, and international contexts, and he has conducted research with and prepared educators in countries such as Germany, Turkey, Romania, Mongolia, and Nigeria. He is the author of several books, has published numerous articles, and has had many conference presentations. Dr. is also a founding editor and editor-in-chief for the *Journal of Ethnic and Cultural Studies* and the *American Journal of Qualitative Research*, and an associate editor for the *Journal of Intercultural Education.* In 2018 and 2019, he was awarded a College of Education a professorship for his research, contributions, and publications. Dr. Aydin received the Human Right Educator Award from the United Nations Human Rights Florida in 2019. In addition, in 2019, Dr. Aydin received an outstanding research award from The Marquis Who's Who Publication Board. Dr. Aydin also served a program chair for American Educational Research Association (AERA)-2020/ SIG: Multicultural/Multiethnic Education: Theory, Research, and Practice.

Winston Langley is Provost and Vice Chancellor for Academic Affairs and the senior administrator in charge of advancing the University of Massachusetts Boston's academic mission and the quality of its intellectual life. A scholar with a rich, diverse academic background and a seasoned administrator, he has been instrumental in defining and developing UMass Boston's identity as a student-+, urban public research university with a teaching soul. A professor of political science and international relations since 1982, Dr. Langley served as director of the International Relations Program, senior associate provost, associate chancellor, and interim provost and vice chancellor for academic affairs before he was named to his current position in 2009. Dr. Langley's scholarly interests include human rights, alternative models of world order, religion, and politics. His research has focused on the inadequacy of the nation-state system, the weakness of intergovernmental organizations (including the United Nations), non-governmental organizations expanding power and influence, and the paucity of alternative models for global ordering. Dr. Langley is the author of *Kazi Nazrul Islam: The Voice of Poetry and the Struggle for Human Wholeness* and the *Encyclopedia of Human Rights Issues Since 1945*, for which won the Choice Outstanding Academic Book Award. He is the editor of *Human Rights: The Major Global Instruments* and (with Vivian Fox) *Women's Rights in the United States*, which won the Gustavus Myers Center for the Study of Bigotry and Human Rights Award for Outstanding Book on Human Rights in North America. He is a member of the American Society of International Law and a reviewer of nine publications, including *New Political Science*, *Transnational Perspectives*, and the *International Journal of African Studies*. Dr. Langley earned a Bachelor of Arts in biology from Atlantic Union College, a Master of Arts in European diplomatic history and a Doctor of Philosophy in political science and international relations from Howard University, and a Doctor of Laws from Suffolk University.

Chapter 2
Human Rights in Turkey: Past, Present and Future

Ercan Balcioglu

Abstract This article investigates Turkey's long-term human rights problems and their social and political causes. In the modern sense, Turkey has a human rights history that is nearly two centuries long. Despite this long sociological background, a fully functioning democracy and legal system with competent institutions and established rules have not been built till this day. Furthermore, the country's occasional progress in furthering fundamental rights has been characterized with tidal backslides of interventions and backsliding as in the case in the post-coup conditions of July 15, 2016, and many other periods that preceded. In this way, considering the history of human rights in Turkey, two contradictory images reflect different realities in Turkey. In the first image, a modernizing, developing and democratizing Turkey is evolving with an unwavering rule of law. The second picture, however, reflects widespread and targeted anti-democratic political processes, during which rule of law and separation of powers are still not achieved and social order is dominated by the law of the ruler. The judiciary is not impartial and independent. Control and balance systems, the social division of labor and fair income distribution are missing in the frame. There is systematic discrimination against certain social segments such as Kurds and some religious groups. The social system is run unjustly and unequally. The deep-rooted problems in the sociology of Turkey are reflected in the constant intervention of the ruling elites to the demands of the civil society for established democratic structures and progress in human rights and freedoms.

Keywords Human rights · Rule of law · Constitutional failure · Modernization · Turkey

---

E. Balcioglu (✉)
Faculty of Police and Security Management, Berlin School of Economics and Law, Berlin, Germany

H. Aydin, W. Langley (eds.), *Human Rights in Turkey*, Philosophy and Politics - Critical Explorations 15, https://doi.org/10.1007/978-3-030-57476-5_2

2.1 Introduction

The Turkish modernization process has been plagued with a Jacobin tradition that has persisted for well more than two centuries now. In general, human rights and constitutional developments in Turkey were instrumentalized as foreign policy tools, to signal accreditation and integration with the western world as well as to prevent foreign intervention in affairs with domestic ethnic communities and state unity. Yet, the modernization project was implemented through a series of top-down reforms rather than the conventional bottom-up, fed by the feedback of the development in society leading to demand structural changes. Especially during the late Ottoman era and early years of the republic (1923–1945), neither public opinion nor social maturity reflected the designed modernization path (Kongar 1998). Despite becoming a multi-party democratic system as a requirement for membership in the Western political system of the post-Second World War era, which prioritized fundamental rights and freedoms, this transition did not establish a strong civil order in Turkey. After the 1960s, the Jacobin tradition again emerged with its adverse stance towards Human Rights and Democracy that was fueled by many military interventions, ultimately leading to adverse anti-democratic conditions in the post-coup era after July 15th, 2016.

The Ottoman political legacy, which the new elites of the Turkish Republic inherited, made up the basis of its political culture. Prioritizing the building of a nation-state on a modern Turkish identity (Baran 2010; Güvenç 1997; Kösebalaban 2011), the top-down and antidemocratic approach of ruling elites for reformation transferred the social paradox of the late Ottoman Empire to the new republic. The social paradox was between the Kemalist principles of the militarist elites who held a strict national security perspective and, ironically, the increased Western integration and the inevitable modernization and civil consciousness that came with it. Nevertheless, the paradox is not exclusive to Kemalism, rather, the democratic rise and authoritative hold of the Islamist political leader Recep Tayyip Erdoğan and his Justice and Development Party (AKP) have demonstrated that it is, indeed, deeply embedded in the Turkish culture of governance. In the meantime, however, civil society has established itself to an even greater degree with increased consciousness of democracy, and rights and freedoms. This was due to the persistent violations throughout the history of the republic, which has touched the lives of people from all religious and ideological segments. This article presents an analysis of the stated paradox, the development of civil society and its struggle with the anti-democratic establishment, together with Turkey's long-run human rights problems and their social and political causes.

The article starts with a section on the historical account of key developments central to the development of Human Rights in Turkey. The second section introduces the sociological background of Ottoman modernization vis-à-vis an incompatible social structure. In the third section, the human rights legacy of the Empire and its reflection in the early years of the Turkish Republic are explained. The section following details the civilian-military relations that are characterized by the top-down approach to guard Kemalist principles embedded in the structure and ideology of the republic. Furthermore, this section also elaborates on the EU accession process, the rise of AKP and political Islam in the form of Erdoğanism, and the brief dawn and subsequent fade of fundamental rights and freedoms. The fifth section details the current persisting eclipse of human rights and its consequences as reported by scientific studies reports published by national and international NGOs. Finally, the article finishes with concluding remarks.

2.2 Historical Background

The nineteenth-century Ottoman modernization process brought about the search for a new social order. In this context, the imperial edicts of *Gulhane and Islahat*, the *Mecelle* as the civil code, and *Kanun-i Esasi* the first constitution were declared. Although not enough in terms of human rights, there were partial developments that consequently brought about the *Young Turks*, a generation of pro-Western elites, soldiers and bureaucrats (Ahmad 1964). The Republic of Turkey inherited a modernization and Westernization processes that existed in the political, social and cultural spheres of Ottoman society. It was this Ottoman military-bureaucratic elite that established The Republic of Turkey in the early 1920s (Akçam 2004) and the 1921 Constitution adopted during the War of Independence reflected this legacy. Between the years 1923 and 1939, during the Atatürk era, developments were made in the field of human rights with the 1924 constitution and various reforms that followed. However, issues especially concerning human rights and democracy inherited from the Ottoman society have haunted the republic in various contexts and levels.

Particularly, during the establishment of the new Turkish Republic as a modern nation-state, the Lausanne Treaty (1923) inherited a categorical crisis that defined a complex, multi-ethnic and multi-religious society as "Turkish". Due to this misconceptualization of the Ottoman *Millet* system, the republic effectively disregarded the existence of other ethnicities and beliefs within its people, causing continuous human rights violations in its relationships with its ethnic, such as Armenian, Kurdish, Greek, as well as religious minorities, as in Alevis, Christians, various Sunni groups (Miller et al. 2010).

The primary policy of the Turkish Modernization adopted from the late empire strategy was continued integration and participation in key Western institutions such as the United Nations (UN), North Atlantic Treaty Organization (NATO), Organization for Security and Cooperation in Europe (OSCE), Council of Europe Organization for Economic Cooperation and Development (OECD) and the European Economic Community (EEC). Turkey, as a UN founding member signed the UN Human Rights Charter in 1945 shortly after which the first, however controversial, multiparty elections were held in 1946 (Akşin 1996, 291). In 1959, Turkey made an application for membership in the European Coal and Steel Community. Despite active membership at the key Western institutions formed in the aftermath of World War II and the many reforms applied, the structural problems in the field of democracy and human rights in Turkey have lingered. Due to the misconceptualization in its very foundations and the subsequent paradoxical relationship with its citizens, the relations among the state, society and the individual have not achieved a healthy structure as in developed societies.

Coming after the authoritarian single-party rule which lasted until 1950, the 1960 military coup was the first in the history of the Republic; however, it was not the last. Following the military coup, the 1961 Constitution was proclaimed. Despite all the new rights and institutions that were brought with the 1961 Constitution, the 1971 military memorandum and the 1980 military coup that followed have clearly demonstrated that Turkey's democracy and human rights issues could not be solved systematically. Later, with the 1982 Constitution and the 1983 elections, the rules and institutions attempted to revert the country to a democratic state of law. Both the 1961 Constitution prepared after the 1960 military coup and the 1982 constitution written after the 1980 military coup were designed by the soldiers with military tutelage mechanisms and experiences in military crackdowns. Even though both constitutions were adopted with high acceptance rates due to popular referendum campaign and vote-counting system, Turkey's chronic anti-democratic governance and the rule of law problem were not solved by the 1982 constitution. Both constitutions were prepared by the Advisory Councils whose members were elected by the military junta and worked under military pressure and anti-democratic conditions.

Nevertheless the years between 1982 and 2011 saw further Westernization that came with further integration into global and regional human rights mechanisms. Yet, during the subsequent years, a gradual regression in human rights was seen under the Erdoğan Administration, and, following the failed coup of 15th July 2016, the transformation sped up radically. This current transition is a paradoxical reflection of the previous post-coup contexts in 1960, 1982 and 1997, with a never seen before authoritarian might concentrated in the hands of a civilian authority.

2.3 The Sociological Background of Turkey's Human Rights Paradox

According to Marxist theory, the economic structure determines the social superstructure and assimilates the institutions through which it operates, such as the law, state, politics, and family (Marx 1977). Consequently, as the infrastructure changes in a healthy society, the superstructure adapts. Accordingly, the nineteenth century social and political developments changed the social structures of Western societies, when the structural changes in the economic (feudalism-capitalism) and political (aristocracy-bourgeoisie) realms came hand in hand. With the progress in science and industry, Western societies changed the mode of production and economic relations. In this way, developments in technology and the consequent changes in the field of law and politics led to the birth of a social order based on Individual

Freedom and Human Rights. Based on this background, capitalism emerged and dominated in the Western society but the new individual-oriented social order brought with it a modern set of social problems, political demands and subsequent definitions in newly and yet-to-be formed industrialized societies.

These interactions between the economy and all other social institutions of the superstructure were not present in the nineteenth century Ottoman Empire, which still had a feudal economic structure. The Ottoman society had not undergone the same transformation from feudalist to capitalist society as in Western societies as no significant and generalizable change was present in the relations between the means of production, labor and capital in the Ottoman Empire (Durkheim 1966). When the history of Ottoman human rights is examined within this context and time of developments, this gap in social development between Western societies and the Ottoman society could not be closed with the reforms that lacked the foundation of established individualism. In fact, the reforms made in the field of human rights, freedoms, and democracy remained as a strategy pursued by the political elite and intellectuals that were primarily instrumentalized as to fulfill the requirements of the empire's desire to catch-up and integrate itself into the emerging international system (Ahmad 1964).

In its period of decline and disintegration, the empire lost its territories, and many national groups broke away (Gocek 2011; Hanioğlu 2008). It was during this period that the Ottoman Empire became overwhelmingly Sunni Muslim, from a largely heterogeneous society made up of a wide range of religions, ethnicities, and local cultures. The country was unable to secure justice and to establish a fair social order within. Land losses forced the Ottoman Empire to make military reforms. Further reforms in fundamental rights and democracy aimed to revive the empire's setbacks by integrating it into the Western modernization process, and, in this way, became a crucial element of the empire's foreign policy. These were reflected in the form of constitutional developments that highlighted individual and human rights during the most challenging century of the empire, which, however, did not deliver the expected transformation and relief in the public (Ortaylı 2005). Many structural arrangements were made in the field of democracy and law such as the imperial edict of Gulhane and Islahat and Kanun-i Esasi the first constitution and 1st Constitutional Monarchy. These advancements, controversially, transformed the previous Ottoman governing structure that gave significant local authority to the many ethnicities it ruled over into an increasingly centralized and authoritarian state type (Berkes 1964; Zurcher 2004). Despite attempts to clone a modernization process with political reforms, it was the security bureaucracy or the military class that still held an important privilege in what essentially continued to be the classical Ottoman social order.

2.3.1 The French Revolution and Ottoman Modernization

The French Revolution of 1789 lead to the removal of the French aristocracy and transformed the existing socio-political order in France and beyond in terms of history of human rights and freedoms (Bosher 1989, 131). All over Europe, the end of the eighteenth century was a time of a total and unprecedented breakdown of monarchies (McPhee 2002, 56). The people of France set the stage for the foundation of the first French Republic. Shortly after, in 1789, they also drafted the Declaration of the Rights of Man and of the Citizen, which became a key statement of the revolution's values and a pillar of human rights and individual dignity. The French revolution also accelerated the shift in the European states system from the dynastic land state to the nation-state (Bukovansky 2002, 165). As a consequence, the revolution fundamentally challenged monarchies throughout Europe and effected the Ottoman Empire with the emerging nationalism among many ethnic groups under its rule. As in the case of Greeks and Serbs in the Balkans, Ottoman minorities revolted against the Ottoman rule after gaining a strong consciousness of independence with the French Enlightenment (Inalcık 1994; Karpat 2002).

The Ottoman modernization process, which began in the late eighteenth century, aimed at the integration of the Ottoman Empire into the European system of states. Until the eighteenth century, after starting to lose wars and land, the Ottoman Empire could not admit to itself that it was in a period of decline and only started modernizing initially in the military field. This was primarily because land-based production was very important to its traditional army in the feudal social order (Karpat 2000). In its classical governance culture, the Ottoman Empire had a highly decentralized governance system allowing considerable autonomy to its *Eyalets,* or provinces. In this context, the conditions after the eighteenth century created a paradox – centralization was essential to implement reforms necessary for the survival of the Ottoman Empire; however, it was also centralization that exacerbated social problems and further stirred the anger of various ethnic groups it ruled. During the nineteenth century, the empire suffered the repeated loss of wars and land and became susceptible as it never was before to armed conflict and its immediate aftermath (Inalcık 1994). These were crucial factors that had primary effects in the politicization of communal identities and the breakdown of the Ottoman imperial rule. The regression and disintegration period of the Ottoman Empire started in early nineteenth century and continued until the first quarter of the twentieth century, leading to a painful process that eventually founded a nation-state: the Turkish Republic. Nevertheless, the fear of disintegration was inherited and, indeed, was yet to find ground in the *Weltanschauung* of the republic.

2.3.2 The Ottoman Social Structure

Another primary reason that frustrated the modernization efforts was largely was the stark difference of the social structures in the Ottoman Empire and European states (Berkes 2002). The Ottoman social system was based on agricultural production organized around the manorial "Millet System" (Eryılmaz 1992). In the Ottoman constitution of 1876, the term "Millet," which translates as "Nation," is not used as a reference to ethnicity (Lewis 2002; Strauss 2010). Instead, it is used to refer to a wider population of people who share the same belief or religion.

In this way, in the Ottoman Empire, each confessional community or "Millet" had an independent court of law pertaining to their personal law under which they were allowed to rule under their own rules and regulation. Muslims were subject to the Sharia, Christians to the Canon Law and the Jews to the Halakha. Therefore, an overarching structure was not enforced on the millets as a whole and non-Muslims were given a significant degree of autonomy within their own community.

This autonomy was crucial in deterring the nationalistic attitudes of Ottoman minorities, as well as instrumental in preventing the intervention of foreign powers on the backdrop of the rights, freedoms and separatist agenda. The primary aim of legal reforms in the Ottoman Empire was not to address the social problems and the demands of the people like in the West, nor was it to build an individual-oriented social order. Rather, it was to prevent the destruction of the Ottoman state (Oran 2007).

Human rights abuses in the twentieth century were a primary cause of the collapse of the Ottoman State. Republic of Turkey, the successor state of the Ottoman Empire, was also the heir to a problematic human rights legacy (Finkel 2006). Since its birth until today, human rights crises were not absent in the Turkish Republic and became more visible especially whenever its social structure took steps towards further democratization. It should not be forgotten that every authoritarian regime may have reserves of democratic policy and practice in its pocket. Similarly, every democratic regime may have potential autocratic policy reserves in its toolbox (Ahlers and Stitchweh 2019, 4). In other words, if basic principles such as transparency, accountability, governance and traceability cannot be implemented in a democratic country, then a constant risk of a backward transformation is present.

2.4 The Inherited Paradox of the New Republic: Military Dominated Nation Building in the Early Republican Era

The Turkish Republic is the heir to the sociological and political legacy of the late Ottoman Empire (Kongar 1998). Traces of the previously existent social structures and definitions were transferred to the essential codes of the new republic with the Treaty of Lausanne. Similar to the social conception of the Millet System that essentially makes a categorization based on a religious belief based on Muslim or non-Muslim identities, the treaty defined a Turkish supra-identity that subsumed all existent Muslim identities and all other identities as minorities. This condition set the ground for an identity crisis of non-Turkish Muslim minorities and a restraint in granting basic rights and freedoms to the republic's religious and ethnic minorities. The place of the Kurdish minority and their rights was effectively ignored after the creation of an identity crisis. Standing on this categorical crisis, Christians, Jewish, Alevits and some Sunni groups were effectively suppressed by the Turkish State (Miller et al. 2010; Oran 2007).

This categorical identity crisis put in motion by the Treaty of Lausanne was not the only issue that the new republic faced. Paralleling the approach taken to reformation and modernization during the late period of the Ottoman Empire, constitutional developments in human rights were regarded with a means-for-ends calculation and did not deliver the desired transformation in the new republic. Unfortunately, the very same foundational structural problems in human rights and freedoms have survived to the present day. During the Ottoman times, such policies and reforms, implemented by intellectuals and bureaucrats with a top-down approach, were aimed at preventing the decline and disintegration of the Ottoman social order (Kongar 1998; Yasa 1970).

In the Turkish Republic, reforms were not fruits of democratic processes and lacked the backing of social demands and movements. It is notable, nevertheless, that Turkey was governed with the functional 1921 Constitution during its War of Independence with the presence of a strong opposition group in the parliament until the first elections in 1923. However, the same top-down elitist approach to reformation was applied by the designers of the new republic, especially following the 1924 Constitution. Shortly after the establishment of the republic on October 29, 1923, the 1924 constitution was ratified on April 20, 1924, by the Turkish Parliament. As a first amendment, on April 10, 1928, Article 2 was changed and the "Religion of the Turkish state is Islam" statement was annulled. Women were given the right to vote and stand for election in 1931 and 1934 respectively. Further changes followed in 1937 when the constitution was amended with Law No. 3115 of February 5, 1937, that enshrined the six fundamental principles of *Kemalism* into the 1924 Constitution.

In the period between 1923 and 1946, Turkey was ruled by a single-party system during which the nation-state was built. The dominance of military tutelage and Jacobinism was a key characteristic of the period. A key figure and a perfect reflection of the time was İsmet İnönü – a prominent Turkish general turned politician. İnönü, who also signed the foundational Lausanne treaty, served as the first Chief of the Staff from 1922 to 1924. Then he succeeded Atatürk, becoming the second President of Turkey from 1938 to 1950. During his presidency, he officialized the title of "National Chief" for himself. Before and after his 12-year presidency he completed four terms as the first Prime Minister from 1923 to 1924, 1925 to 1937, and finally from 1961 to 1965. The 1924 constitution remained in force until the military coup of 1960, after which it was replaced by the Constitution of 1961. The military junta that Cemal Gürsel effectively defined this constitution and he became the fourth President of Turkey. In no small measure, today's Turkish society, in addition to the previously existing democracy and human rights issues, faces problems in adapting to the new social developments that have emerged with globalization and the post-1980s information era. The 1982 constitution was far from responding to demands of change and transformation and its legal order annulled the on-paper freedoms granted with the 1961 constitution (Barkey 2014).

2.4.1 History of Human Rights vis-à-vis Western Alignment in the Turkish Republic

When examining the legal background of Turkey's human rights history, starting with the 1877 constitution of the Ottoman Empire, the 1921, 1924, 1960, 1982 constitutions follow relatively the same line of with the international community regarding advancements in fundamental rights and freedoms (Türkmen 2007, 253–259). The Universal Declaration of Human Rights of UN and the European Convention on Human Rights (ECHR) which were also recognized by Turkey, applies for every segment of the society and covers every individual. However, it is not possible to say that these rights are equally applied to all citizens in Turkey. Despite a historical discussion of constitutional and human rights and freedoms debated in Turkey for more than two centuries now, no civil constitution has been designed and ratified based on the will of the people, in free conditions and enacted by social consensus. Today, Turkey does not have a democratic civil constitution, endorsed by the society by means of a free and fair referendum (Arkan et al. 2017; Barın 2014).

The 1982 constitution and its legal order were far from responding to the necessities of change and transformation. Since the Second World War, Turkey has been closely following international developments in the field of human rights and freedoms. Even though international human rights instruments had been signed and set, their participation in the international human rights system was long delayed until the early 2000s due to political reserves in both regional human rights mechanisms and global human rights mechanisms (Smith 2007, 262). Human rights protection mechanisms in Turkey were established formally; however, the legal order remains incompatible with international human rights mechanisms and, because of this, has not been an effective legal order in the absence of accreditation for international standards and safeguards (Bahçecik 2015). In this way, despite de jure confirmations of international human rights treaties and documents, many of the problems regarding implementation are de facto frozen (Kabasakal Arat 2007). In this context, it is very risky for judicial professionals to accept these norms and rules and to take them into consideration in decision-making processes (Açik 2011; Alemdar 2011; Altıparmak 2010; Güneş 2018).

In effect, there has been considerable integration of Turkey into the Western alliance. Despite not bringing true and sustained progress in rights and freedoms, this political-historical background has nevertheless led to a cultural accumulation in the field of relative democratization, modernization and legal order as well as human rights and freedoms. Atatürk, as the founding father of modern Turkey, implemented a series of reforms, including secularization and industrialization, which intended to "Europeanize" or Westernize the country (Keyman and Duzgit 2007). Turkey has ever since been part of the Western World. The new republic joined the League of Nations by invitation, and during World War II, remained neutral until February 1945, when it joined the Western Allies. Turkey then became a founding member of the United Nations, a member of the Council of Europe in 1949, and a member of

NATO in 1952. During the Cold War, with strategic concerns, Turkey allied itself at the side of the Western Alliance consisted of the United States and Western Europe, which mandated itself to defend freedom, democracy and human rights. Turkey has also played a vital role in the defense of the European continent as a member of the European Council, Organization on Security and Cooperation in Europe, the OECD, and an associate member of the European Economic Community and after joining the European Customs Union in 1995.

2.4.2 Turkey's Participation in the International Human Rights Mechanism

Turkey is a participant in two international human rights mechanisms and, therefore, subject to the monitoring of two agencies. Since the very early days of the UN-led global human rights regime, Turkey, as a founding member, participated actively in the drafting of the Universal Declaration of Human Rights. However, due to political reasons, Turkey did not ratify the covenants of the declaration until 2003 (Türkmen 2007, 252).

The UN system has tried to set up an effective sanctions mechanism following the post-Cold war, including adding additional protocols on human rights and freedoms to the existing conventions and the recent formation of the International Criminal Court. Still, a widely spoken criticism is that the United Nations system has not been efficacious, especially in the field of human rights due to the heterogeneous membership of the organization, which makes it a mixture of democracies and authoritarian regimes. The United Nations has a heavy bureaucratic machinery, characterized by a lack of coordination and enforcement power. One criticism is that the UN regime gives members "strong promotion" with "weak monitoring procedures" (Donnelly 1986, 634). This was especially valid throughout the Cold War in sustaining the ideological struggle between the blocs. The bipolar bloc politics in the UN determined the relations among the member states and allowed the UN to avoid explicit references to its members in human rights reports during the Cold War period.

Turkey, which has the second-largest army in NATO, is also a major arms buyer. For the general part of the Cold War period, the United States as a prominent member of NATO retained a policy of silence relative to Turkey. Similarly, European countries were also largely indifferent to human rights violations in Turkey until the 1980s, which was also rooted in their completion for the Turkish arms market. Thus, Turkey could find a chance to mute its highly selective treaty ratification record at the UN for a long time (Kabasakal Arat 2007, 287).

The European Convention for the Protection of Human Rights and Fundamental Freedoms, which is the first regional human rights instrument, was adopted in 1950. Designed by the Council of Europe, it operates than the UN mechanisms with legally binding human rights instruments (Davidson 1997, 101). The Human Rights

Convention has two enforcement mechanisms, which are the European Commission on Human Rights as an interstate complaint system, and the European Court of Human Rights for individual applications. In 1999 the two mechanisms were merged to form a permanent court of Human Rights at which member states are judged and ordered to pay indemnities to the victims when appropriate. Through these mechanisms, respective states were pushed into taking the necessary measures to prevent violations that were subsequently monitored by the Council's Committee of Ministers.

The human rights system of the Council of Europe has been gradually moving toward a further integration with the European Union. The Maastricht Treaty of 1992, formally known as Treaty on European Union, recognized the Human Rights Convention as a general legal principle. Following the end of the Cold War, young democracies of Central and Eastern Europe had to fulfill the Copenhagen criteria, which emphasized maintaining the rule of law, respect for human rights, protection of minorities, and the application of the market economy rules before joining the union. In 1997, these criteria were formally incorporated into the Amsterdam Treaty, and a further step taken in 2000 consolidated them when the EU Charter of Fundamental Rights was adopted.

Turkey had joined the European Human Rights Regime in 1954 and ratified the European Convention on Human Rights and Fundamental Freedoms and its binding jurisdiction in 1989 (Smith 2007, 262; Türkmen 2007, 254). As a more effective system than the UN mechanism, the European Human Rights Regime has ever since been a primary watchdog and enforcer of human rights in Turkey.

Human rights in Turkey have been shaped by its aspiration for Europeanization, the endogenous factors deriving from Turkey's two-century-old modernization experience and the exogenous factors of the two regimes it has been a member of since the Second World War (Bürgin 2019). These developments were important in both strengthening democratic institutions and the establishment of the rule of law in Turkey and, more importantly, its participation in regional and international accountability mechanisms.

2.5 The Civilian-Military Dilemma Post WWII: Political Establishment and Human Rights

The civilian-military relationship is the reflection of the long-standing sociological paradox that has long deterred progress in human rights and freedoms in Turkey. The *Weltanschauung* of the common people would desire a transition to a civil society, but this desire is at odds with the ruling elites, and, because of this, cannot shape the superstructure accordingly (Kongar 1998). The military was key in firstly establishing and then sustaining the structure set by the founding ideology of the Turkish Republic that has strict definitions regarding the recognition of the existence of a diverse social structure in terms of ethnicity and religion. After the rise of consciousness regarding individual rights and democracy, the militarist establishment again deterred any change that would alter the status quo. Consequently, steps taken towards further democratization have been met with crushing anti-democratic responses with the many military interventions in the history of the republic (Keyman and Düzgit 2007).

More recently, the ruling AKP has been utilizing the very same paradox by first, using ruling power to implement policies despite popular dissent and second, while establishing a political system in which rule of law and separation of powers do not function, sustaining it by crushing human rights and freedoms. This section will first start with an account of civil-military relations in the Republic of Turkey and then detail on the military responses to the Western alignment of Turkey. Finally, an account of the transition from the Jacobinism of the militarist establishment of Kemalism to that of the traditionalist establishment of Erdoğan's Political Islamism will be given. For this, it is crucial to understand the long-charged desire for democratization in the society and the EU accession process that Erdoğan utilized.

2.5.1 The History of Military Influence over Civil Politics

The establishment of a democratic constitutional order requires the armed forces to be controlled by civilian rulers. However, this has never been the case in Turkey, where the military has held a tight grip over fundamental rights and freedoms, the development of democracy, the design of a civilian constitution and the development of an impartial and competent judiciary. Since the Ottoman times and the foundation of the Turkish republic in 1923, the army has maintained an essential role in Turkish society (Toktaş and Kurt 2010). A central figure for the Turkish Republic was Mustafa Kemal Atatürk, who, as a former Ottoman general, emerged as the protagonist in the establishment of the new modern Turkish and headed the army in the 1923 Turkish war of independence. Becoming the first president of the republic, he is an endlessly adored historical figure as the founder and commander-in-chief of the Turkish Republic; however, he is also seen as a controversial figure for his autocratic rule.

The many radical and top-down reforms Atatürk introduced to modernize the country to promote secularism, and institutional reforms formed the foundation of Kemalism as a state ideology (Kongar 1998; Ozbudun 2000). As a parallel to this line of thought, the army is considered as a highly respected symbol that is also mandated to protect the internal stability of the state. The Turkish army has, therefore, considered itself as the founder of the Turkish Republic and the untouchable protector of Atatürk's principles like "national unity" and "secularism." This characteristic was to become crucial in justifying future actions when authority was to be yielded. After the Second World War, the ruling military elite yielded some of their power to the democratically elected political parties, as a necessity of Turkey's decision to join the Western alliance (Akçam 2004). Even though certain laws explicitly prohibited the involvement of active military personnel in politics, many political and state institutions were governed with people who had a military background until recent past. For example, all the presidents of the Republic of Turkey had a military background, until the 8th President Turgut Özal, with an exception for Celâl Bayar who was toppled by the military. Yet, when civil society increased its demands for further liberalization, each successive coup and intervention in 1960, 1971, 1980, 1997, 2007, the military elite exercises its power (CESRAN 2011; Cizre 2004).

The Armed Forces, in this way, used coups and post-coup contexts to suppress undesired elements of the society with brutal measures like torture, mass arrests, martial law or general limitation of democracy in the state (Keyman 2012). With a direct reference to the preservation of Kemalism, when taking power from the civilian governments, presidents General Cemal Gürsel of the 1960 coup and General Kenan Evren of the 1980 coup justified their actions via perceived threats against the nation's unity and the country's integrity. The military ensured its veto power and control over civil politics through institutional mechanisms such as the National Security Council, the State Security Courts, and various departments, groups, and centers established within the General Staff through the legal order established by the 1961 and 1982 constitutions (Jevčák 2015; Kuru 2012; Salah 2013).

2.5.2 *Human Rights in Turkey and EU Accession on the Background of Military*

Turkey has long been trying to improve its human rights record and its relations with the European Union during which civil society has also increased its demands for further liberalization and fundamental rights. An important indicator to understand Turkey's human rights policy is, therefore, Turkey's relation with the EU and the European Court of Human Rights. The military elite has acted to exert its power with each successive military coup of 1960, 1971, 1980 and 2016, and the post-modern coups of 1997 and 2007 (Akçam 2004). This back-and-forth struggle can be referred to as a kind of political interplay between civil society and state elites.

Turkey's relations with European institutions during the Cold War period, especially its relations with the European Union, is an important metric for understanding the development of human rights, freedoms, and democracy in Turkey (Yilmaz et al. 2007). The relationship between the European Union and Turkey is a difficult but an important process (Özcan 1999). Turkey's bid to integrate with Europe started with its application for full membership of the European Economic Community (EEC) on 31 July 1959. Since then, relations between the EU and Turkey have never been as Turkey had desired. After the 1963 Ankara Agreement signed between the EU and Turkey, some changes occurred in the expectations of both sides, but neither Turkey nor the Union wanted to end this process. The continuing development of the EU brought new barriers to Turkey's membership process. Since Turkey's bid, the union enlarged itself from six to twenty-eight member states. The obstacles to the full EU membership, are not rooted merely in the reservations of the EU. Rather, considerable responsibility also falls on Turkey due to many problems such as military interventions, and the lack of a democratic political system and legal order that is respectful of universal rights and freedoms. Today, every state that desires to take an active position in the modern world must measure their political, economic, legal systems and institutions against the principles of democracy and the rule of law. Yet today, the main obstacle to full membership is Turkey's will to comply with the Copenhagen Criteria, namely, "the institutionalized practices for democracy and legal order, and protection of human rights" (Kardas 2002).

Nevertheless, the regional integration of Turkey and its European Union membership process is an important enhancing factor for civil liberty and its implementations (Tekin et al. 2013). The 1982 constitution is in complete contrast to the requirements this course of action and is systematically problematic for fundamental human rights, democratic rule, the rule of law and judicial independence. Turkey has experienced many political and economic crises and has yet not achieved a civilian constitution. Therefore, for nearly a quarter-century, the discussion about designing a new civilian constitution has dominated the discourse and not left the centrality of politics ever since. This dire condition reflects the long-standing sociological paradox that deters progress. Because of the harsh contrast between the common people and ruling class, the common people cannot shape the superstructure according to its *Weltanschauung*. Consequently, steps towards further democratization have been met with crushing anti-democratic responses. Particularly, this cleavage between the public and the military and political elites has made itself evident in Turkey's history of human rights and democratization with the decennial political crisis (Keyman and Duzgit 2007).

2.5.3 Erdoğan, AKP & The Rise and Fade of Human Rights

In the process of achieving political, economic and social development, the essence of establishing sound civilian rule remains one of the key factors in consolidating democracy alongside reinforcing the rule of law and human rights. 1991 was the year of the collapse of the former Soviet Union and the end of bipolarity in the world of the cold war. Especially after Cold War, Turkey has experienced several rapid institutional and legal changes parallel to its harmonization processes with European institutions such as the Council of Europe, the European Court of Human Rights, and the European Union. These integrations intended to prevent the Turkish Armed Forces from intervening in politics and bring Turkish civil-military relations into European standards (Uluçakar and Çağlar 2017, 42). Certainly, these steps were important developments for harmonization with EU standards and for the civil-military relationship to normalize just as in the consolidated democracies (Demirel 2010). However, the impact areas of the military on civil life have not been eliminated at all (Aknur 2013). The Turkish modernization process has faced the necessity of making irreversible and inevitable reforms after the Cold War during a time, which was characterized by weak coalition governments and corrupt management. Aside from the numerous political crisis, Turkey had two major economic crises in 1994 and in 2001. During this period, a general demand appeared for democratic rule and civilian constitution as well as to secure law and democracy in Turkish society.

Against the background described above, Prime Minister Recep Tayyip Erdoğan's Justice and Development Party (AKP) came to power with a strong emphasis to human rights and democracy in the first general elections after the 2001 economic crisis. As a reflection of this demand and with the primary aim of European Union membership, Erdoğan's first cabinet made many reforms from late 2002 until 2007 and sent key signals that upheld human rights and rule of law, such as the annulation of the 15-year State of Emergency that had long paralyzed 13 provinces in the southeastern region. As a direct consequence of the EU reforms after 2002, the army started losing the institutional leverage mechanisms that it had previously set and enjoyed. Consequently, the military elite started exerting political preference through informal measures and non-institutional mechanisms that were especially influential between 2003 and 2007, such as the frequent speeches that senior members of the Armed Forces gave on domestic and foreign policy issues.

Erdoğan's first term was, therefore, characterized by a solid democratic attitude accompanied by successful economic and foreign policies. However, despite having a two-thirds majority in the parliament, Erdoğan did not eagerly follow the necessary agenda and policies to build a new civil constitution (Erdoğan and Yazıcı 2011). Many constitutional amendments were made between 2002 and which, however, instead of building a civil constitution, were characterized with a skewed impression of renewal. In the second period (2007–2011), Erdoğan seized the system with the opportunities of the anti-democratic system to create a one-man rule effectively, despite running on an ultimate agenda of a new constitution in his political rhetoric (Barın 2014, 11). It was at this time that the Turkish civil-military relations went through a dramatic transformation through which the traditionally powerful role of the military in domestic, foreign and security policies was effectively diminished. Especially, the military authority was dented between 2007 and 2011 with the *Ergenekon and Balyoz* and a series of spinoff *Sarıkız* (Blonde Girl), *Ayışığı* (Moonlight), *Yakamoz* (Sea Sparkle), *Eldiven* (Glove) investigations that followed. Some 300 junior and senior military officers were placed in pretrial detention under allegations of plotting coups to overthrow the democratically elected AKP government.

Between 2002 and 2011 Erdoğan stood close to the political views of democrats, liberals, the Gülen Movement and the Kurds that favored democratic development. By exploiting this popular opinion, his actual political Islamic ideology was obscured from domestic and international public opinion. In the crisis of the 2007 parliamentary election for the president and the referendum that followed the same year, he reached out to masses in the name of the so-called "democratic identity" and changed the election system. Until 2011, the post-coup constitution of 1980 was unable to be replaced with a civil one and was amended seventeen times with the aim of aligning it with international standards, and referendums were held in 1987, 2007 and 2010. The public support for the 2007 referendum led to another key political advantage, guaranteeing that Erdoğan would remain in power for an extended period. In 2010, AKP garnered almost 58% of the vote, which was accompanied with the mandate to bring the Turkish constitution into further compliance with European Union standards 2010 (Özer 2015). Overall, 113 of the 177 articles of the 1982 Constitution were amended; however, the constitution never reached the consistency and maturity that guarantees fundamental rights and freedoms.

The political developments and successes prompted AKP to pursuit desecuritization policies and aggressively consolidate its power in politics. During the third term of the Erdoğan administration, between 2011 and 2015, Erdoğan and AKP started to deliberately act for the establishment of a cultural, social and political reality based on political Islam. Especially, educational reforms of 2012 were tailored to strengthen the conservative electoral base. As a result of the 2012 reforms, many regular schools were converted to Imam-Hatips leaving hundreds of thousands of pupils from the age of ten with no options other than attending Islamic schooling. Despite serious critics regarding the violation of freedom of education and belief, Erdoğan used this policy to reinvigorate a politically charged pious generation aligned with the ideals of Erdoğan's justice and development party.

As a result of the serious regressions in fundamental rights and policies, a considerable section of the population was upset with the third term of AKP. The dismay was particularly highlighted with the May 2013 Gezi protests, which first started in opposition to Erdoğan's plan of demolishing the Gezi Park in Istanbul and was subsequently joined by hundreds of thousands against Erdoğan's rising authoritarianism. The protests were held for 134-days until they were brutally suppressed violating freedom of assembly. Later the same year, between 17 and 25 December, Erdoğan and AKP were embarrassed with the corruption scandals of cabinet ministers. These events marked the beginning of a downward spiral, accelerated by the 2-year post-coup state of emergency declared after July 15, 2016.

After the last coup that failed miserably, it remains unclear whether the military has yielded its power, and if Turkey is moving towards more democratic and normalized governance in its civil-military relations as in developed democracies. Nevertheless, the constitutional reforms that followed during the successive state of emergency and the referendum of April 16 have yet again undermined freedoms and provided legal justification to human rights violations that marked the transition to the presidential system. The policies of AKP in its third and fourth terms have killed the idea of a Turkey that has an open civil society based on a system that upholds democracy and fundamental rights & freedoms (Gözler 2017). Republican People's Party (CHP) Vice President Aykut Erdoğdu accurately illustrates the current condition and the absence of a constitution that upholds human rights, freedoms and the independence of judiciary: "After the referendum (the referendum of April 16, 2017), there is no constitution of the Republic of Turkey and the Turkish nation. It is not a 'constitution' in force today. The text that doesn't bring separation of powers and doesn't guarantee fundamental rights and freedoms cannot be called a constitution. Turkey currently has no constitution" (Erdoğdu 2019).

2.6 Current Human Rights Situation in Turkey After July 15, 2016

At the beginning of the 2000s, Turkey was a country that was regarded as having made significant progress in human rights and freedoms. The frequent military coups that toppled Turkish governments in 1960, 1971, 1980, and 1997 frequently led to the rewriting of the Turkish constitution, and the instalment of new governments (Öztürk 2006). This started to change in the early 2000s when Turkey's attempts to join the EU had left the military with little power. Indeed, the EU reform packages had reduced the power of the military in civilian affairs. In the aftermath of the unprecedented coup attempt came on the night of July 15, 2016, the *OHAL* (state of emergency) was declared and remained in force for the next 2 years. This paved the way for unlawful restrictions and systematic violations of human rights and allowed the government to pass laws beyond the effective scrutiny of Parliament and the courts (Freedom House 2019a).

Under the state of emergency, public officials were dismissed or suspended by decree without due process and fair trial. Even though the coup had failed, in the absence of any direct responsibility in the intervention, hundreds of media outlets, associations, foundations, private hospitals, and educational establishments were tied to the putsch and were consequently shut down by the government. With the many decrees issued, the assets of these institutions were confiscated without compensation, and almost all remain closed as of today. It is particularly interesting that following the failed attempt, at least 152,000 civil servants were dismissed, of whom tens of thousands were arrested for alleged connections with the coup, including 107,944 individuals named in lists of the emergency decrees.[1] Massive dismissals of teachers and academics with alleged links to the Gülen Movement, a former ally of the ruling Justice and Development Party (AKP), have significantly affected the education sector and thereby the right to education (OHCHR 2018).

More than 80,000 people were in pre-trial detention on charges linked to membership to the Gülen Movement, labeled as the "Fethullahist Terrorist Organization" ('FETÖ') for allegedly orchestrating the 2016 coup attempt (United States Department of State 2018). A similar number were released on bail and were subjected to reporting requirements. Only a tiny minority of them were accused of taking part in the actual events of the attempted coup. The judiciary, itself decimated by the dismissal or detention of up to a third of Turkey's judges and prosecutors, remained under extreme political pressure. Arbitrary, lengthy and punitive pre-trial detention

[1]Decree 667, available at http://www.resmigazete.gov.tr/eskiler/2016/07/20160723-8.htm; Decree 668, available at http://www.resmigazete.gov.tr/eskiler/2016/07/20160727M2-1.pdf; Decree 669, available at http://www.resmigazete.gov.tr/eskiler/2016/07/20160731-5.htm; Decree 670, available at http://www.resmigazete.gov.tr/eskiler/2016/08/20160817-17.htm; Decree 673, available at http://www.resmigazete.gov.tr/eskiler/2016/09/20160901M2-1.pdf; Decree 677, available at http://www.resmigazete.gov.tr/eskiler/2016/10/20161029-4.htm.

and violations of fair trial became a routine of the law enforcement and jurisprudence (Aydin and Avincan 2020; Girdap 2020).

More than 4200 judges and prosecutors were dismissed through executive orders of the High Council of Judges and Prosecutors while the Constitutional Court dismissed two judges. An additional 22,474 people lost their jobs due to closure of private institutions, such as foundations, trade unions and media outlets. Some 570 lawyers were arrested, 1480 faced prosecution, and 79 were sentenced to long-term imprisonment. Moreover, approximately 34 bar associations were shut down on the ground of alleged affiliation to a terrorist organization. OHCHR also identified a pattern of persecution of lawyers representing individuals accused of terrorism offences. According to the Ministry of Interior, 159,506 individuals had been arrested in relation to the emergency decrees by the end of December 2017. OHCHR also received reports on the arrest and detention of approximately 300 journalists for "membership" in terrorist organizations, on the grounds that their publications contained apologist sentiments regarding terrorism or other "verbal act offences." (Human Rights Watch 2019; OHCHR 2018).

The post-July 15th state of emergency created a basis for human rights violations like the previous post-coup contexts of the past. Dissent was ruthlessly suppressed, with journalists, academicians, politicians including members of parliament, mayors, lawyers, judges and prosecutors, teachers, political activists, and human rights defenders among those targeted. Opposition and protest were not tolerated and were met with torture under police custody and in prisons (Aydin and Avincan 2020). Under the conditions of the state of emergency, unfair and unequal election campaigns were conducted. At the same time, the use of social media and the Internet became difficult, thus, effectively blocking the opposition. Currently, Turkey scores 37 of 100 in Internet Freedom metrics according to the "Freedom on the Net 2019" report released by the Freedom House and is also the only country in Europe whose Internet is "not free" (Freedom House 2019c). Any effective investigation of human rights violations committed by state officials has been prevented by pervasive impunity in the orders of state of emergency. After more than three and a half years since the coup, the crackdown is still ongoing and affecting the lives of hundreds of thousands. Despite the end of "state of emergency" measures, no resolution has been found for individuals whose fundamental rights and freedoms have been violated in the persistent eclipse of law and democracy.

In this context, following the 10 April 2017 referendum with which the transition to the presidential system was approved, the presidential and the parliamentary elections were also held during the state of emergency on 24 June 2018. The anti-democratic conditions of "state of emergency" government were key to the design of the new political system. Interestingly, the state of emergency was abolished just a month after the setting of the new political order that consolidated Erdoğan's political ambitions (Freedom House 2019b).

Politicians and elected officials representing constituencies in the predominantly Kurdish east and southeast of Turkey were especially targeted during the post-coup period. Nine parliamentarians from the pro-Kurdish leftist Peoples' Democracy Party (HDP), including the party's two leaders, sixty elected mayors of the

Democratic Regions Party (DBP), the sister party of HDP were jailed on terrorism charges. The assignment of unelected trustees appointed by the governing AKP has continued until today. The authoritarian character of the regime has also included expanded influence over major cities. In October 2017, six elected mayors including those representing Ankara and Istanbul, were left with no option but to resign after being requested to do so by the President. As a result, a third of Turkey's population was not being represented by the people they had elected at the 2014 local elections.

The country's foreign affairs have also seen similar aggression. Armed clashes continue between the Kurdistan Workers' Party (PKK) and state security forces. Furthermore, Turkish armed forces also carried out military operations against armed groups within Syria and Iraq. Its alliances are shaken by arbitrary decisions ignoring common interests and established understandings.

Turkey ranks fourth among 47 countries in the number of applications to the European Court of Human Rights (ECtHR), according to the tally of submissions to the court. In cases filed against Republic of Turkey, Turks followed the citizens of Russia, Romania and Ukraine, making up the 12.6% (7100) of the total number of cases brought to ECtHR in 2018. Most of these cases involve lengthy periods of pre-trial detention. Since the failed coup in July 2016, Turkey has jailed tens of thousands of people on coup charges and has enforced long pre-detention periods even without the filing of an indictment.

Since 2016, EU accession negotiations have also been stalled. The EU has accused and criticized Turkey for human rights violations and deficits in the rule of law. In 2017, EU officials said that post-coup policies of Turkey violated the Copenhagen criteria of eligibility for an EU membership. On June 26th, 2018, the EU's General Affairs Council stated that Turkey's recent diversion from the European Union were grounds for effectively freezing the accession negotiations and opening of further chapters. Furthermore, the council added that it is "especially concerned about the continuing and deeply worrying backsliding on the rule of law and on fundamental rights including the freedom of expression" (Council of the European Union 2018; Reuters 2019).

Facts regarding the nosedive of the human rights and democracy in Turkey has been widely debated and have noted that the development of a democratic and civil society in the EU process had seriously regressed during the state of emergency and its aftermath. This erosion has also been reported by independent civil society organizations such as Freedom House, World Justice Project and Amnesty International, as well as international organizations and bodies such as the United Nations High Commissioner for Human Rights, the European Court of Human Rights (ECtHR), Council of Europe (CE) and EU.

The European Commission stated in its 2018 Report on Turkey that the capacity of Turkey to ensure effective domestic legal remedies in the sense of the ECtHR had been further undermined by several unfortunate precedents. The European Commission emphasized that Turkey has yet to address key recommendations of the Council of Europe and its bodies. Reforms in the field of the rule of law and fundamental rights remain strategic priorities for the EU cooperation with Turkey with a view to reverse the backsliding over the recent period. The full respect of the rule of law and of fundamental rights and freedoms remain as crucial prerequisites for EU assistance. The "Revised Indicative Strategy Paper for Turkey" recognized the need to prioritize the prevention of violations of the European Convention on Human Rights – like the condition in the 1990s. According to the European Commission, the availability and applicability of key fundamental rights, which have been curtailed by Turkey under the State of Emergency like pre-trial detention and the removal of crucial safeguards that protect detainees, have to be prioritized via making key legislative changes that align with the ECtHR, (European Commission 2018).

Freedom in the World 2018 report of Freedom House on political rights and freedoms stated that Turkey has declined from the "Partly Free" category to "Not Free" category – a first time for Turkey in 18 years since the report was first published. The report emphasized that Turkish President Erdoğan had intensified and broadened the crackdown on his perceived opponents whom he declared as terrorists and traitors (Freedom House 2018). According to the Freedom in the World 2019 report, Turkey was rated as "Not free" for the second consecutive year (Freedom House 2019b).

The International Institute for Democracy and Electoral Assistance (IDEA) reported in 2018 that Turkish and Haitian democracies had a very weak and fragile performance with low levels of fundamental rights. The Turkish democracy was cited as having the most widespread democratic erosion and backsliding in the past 5 years (IDEA 2019). The World Justice Project (WJP) has reported that the fundamental rights in Turkey were rated as 122nd of 126 countries with a score of 0.32/1 in its 2019 Rule of Law Index (WJP 2019).

An important recent report is "Social Costs Report of the State of Emergency in its Second Year," published by *Justice for Victims*, a Turkish civil society initiative that records and studies the victims of the OHAL (state of emergency). Based on the responses of 3776 participants in January 2019, the report demonstrated the great extent of the absence of "State of Law" during the OHAL, which created a context in which the Turkish legal order was incapable of assuring its citizens of their fundamental rights and freedoms. As a result, 133,351 people were dismissed from their profession in public service without a fair trial including academicians, judges, prosecutors, police, doctors, nurses, teachers, and bureaucrats with the 16 different Decree Laws of between July 2016 and July 2018 (Aydin and Avincan 2020; Mağdurlar için Adalet 2019). The number of citizens directly victimized by Decree Laws probably exceeded 250,000. However, the reach of the decrees also includes secondary victims; that is, the relatives of the citizens directly victimized by decree laws. When the relatives and dependents of the victims are added to this calculation, the overall total of the secondary victims easily reaches 1,500,000 (Mağdurlar için Adalet 2019).

On the night of July 15th, 2016, the Turkish government survived a coup plotted against president Erdoğan and his governance by the "Peace at Home Council", whose *nom de guerre* is a direct reference to a renowned Atatürk quotation (Haugom 2019). The July 15th coup was the first one to fail in the history of a republic that has been plagued with many direct and indirect military interventions. Interestingly, the

2016 failed coup has led to virtually identical consequences as to that of the classic military coups and interventions. In fact, the coup has been repeatedly framed as a gift and chance by Erdoğan and other AKP politicians to enable an unprecedented crackdown (Dündar 2019). The state of emergency declared immediately after the coup was not different in function than the ones issued following the successful coups of 1960 and 1980. During the 2-year-long state of emergency, an anti-democratic and fearful society was created, and the political and legal structures were re-designed to repress civil society and its proponents. Paradoxically, the result of this coup too curbed the vision for progress towards a complete civil society with a functional democracy upholding human rights. It is certain that Turkish civil society has been targeted by a sophisticated civil coup d'état in the aftermath of the July 15th. Currently, the aspirations for completing the modernity process, which had been especially highlighted with the EU membership process, are now stranded along forgotten shores after Erdoğan's authoritarian consolidation with the new presidential system set up in the aftermath of the post-2016 state of emergency (Human Rights Watch 2019).

2.7 Conclusion

The constitutional development in Turkey, unlike in Western societies, has not emerged as a reconciliation of popular movements demanding fundamental rights and freedoms from the state. In general, human rights and constitutional developments in Turkey were instrumentalized as foreign policy tools to signal accreditation and integration as well as to prevent foreign intervention in affairs with domestic ethnic communities and state unity. The condition of late modernization has come with a top-down approach to modernity rather than the conventional bottom-up, fed by the feedback of the development in societies (Kongar 1998). Instead of the natural causality between the base and superstructure where the latter is shaped by the developments in the former, the two-centuries-old Turkish modernization process has had a persistent and paradoxical Jacobinism as a central characteristic. In the absence of key developments in science, industry and culture, and most crucially, the subsequent political demands regarding fundamental rights and freedoms, the Turkish society could not transition from a feudal to a modern capitalist society in a timely and healthy manner (Giddens 1990; Keyder 1987). The late and abrupt introduction of the Ottoman Empire to modernization, in this sense, has created the fault lines of a paradox that still determines Turkish modernization experience.

In this sense, Turkey's democracy and legal history are filled with tidal periods reflecting the discrepancy between the aimed standards and on-the-ground experience. Turkey, at a certain level, has participated in the UN and European human rights mechanisms after the Second World War. However, it has yet not established a democratic state of law with all its institutions and rules delivering robust checks and balances in international standards. This has become a significant obstacle for the development of a modern society. Furthermore, the higher ruling class and political elites both military and civil, in the Turkish experience, apply and sustain repeated measures of direct and indirect control over democracy, further halting the development of an open civil society in Turkey. Military dominance until the end of WWII and the interventions in 1960, 1971, 1980, 1997 and 2016 with the successive political and legal order established have not allowed the progress of a functional human rights mechanism in line with international standards. This creates a paradoxical vicious cycle wherein the unmatched heightened demands of the society are reflected with social, economic and political crises.

For a long time, Turkey tried to replace the 1982 constitution with a civilian constitution to establish a democratic state respecting human rights and based on the rule of law. With the EU membership process starting in the early 2000s, the Turkish civil society seized the chance to complete its process of integration with modernity. This was especially thanks to the alignment of the civil society with political elites that held a pro-democracy stance that favored modernization and integration with European accession as the final echelon. It was during the Constitutional Reconciliation Commission (AUK) process that a significant constitutional accumulation was achieved. In the AUK experience, a cross-party resolution agreed on 60 articles that were primarily concerned the enhancement of fundamental rights and freedoms and created a roadmap for future civil, constitutional developments in Turkey (Barın 2014). In fact, these developments can be regarded as counterpoint to the post-2016 conditions that have created a serious backsliding in the invaluable gains of the previous years. Even though the commission was unable to write a new civil constitution after all, this experience of critical evaluation will be especially useful in shedding light on future civil, constitutional debates (Arkan et al. 2017; Barın 2014; Gönenç 2015).

Turkey has two crucial assets that may reverse the unfortunate backward trend. First, the long history of the modernization discourse has granted Turkish society considerable maturity, which had materialized in the accession process. Second, the EU accession process has created the necessary mechanisms for rapid and steadfast reintegration once civil consciousness is back. A first crucial step to take in starting to solve the current paradox lies in the founding of a sound legal basis that strengthens democracy upholds the rule of law and provides ultimate judicial independence. Then, the institutional structure of the criminal justice system can be brought in alignment with international standards and accreditation in which the roles and statuses of criminal justice professionals such as judges, prosecutors and lawyers are clearly defined and are not susceptible to political extortion. Finally, this approach can win over the military and civilian elites who do not reflect the popular demand for a democracy and human rights.

References

Açik, Coşkun. 2011. *Ulusal Insan Haklari Kurumları ve Türkiye Örneğine Eleştirel Yaklaşım* [The National Human Rights Institutions and Critical Approaches to Turkey]. Unpublished master's thesis. Ankara University, Institute of Social Sciences, Political Science and Public Administration Department.

Ahlers, Anna L., and Rudolf Stichweh. 2019. The Bipolarity of Democracy and Authoritarianism: Value Patterns, Inclusion Roles and Forms of Internal Differentiation of Political Systems. *Sociologia & Antropologia* 9 (3): 819–846.

Ahmad, Feroz. 1964. *The Young Turks*. Oxford: The Clarendon Press.

Akçam, Taner. 2004. *From Empire to Republic: Turkish Nationalism and the Armenian Genocide*. New York: Zed Books Ltd.

Aknur, Müge. 2013. Towards More Democratic Civil-Military Relations in Turkey. *L'Europe en Formation 1* (367): 31–50.

Akşin, Sina. 1996. *Ana Çizgileriyle Türkiye'nin Yakın Tarihi* (İkinci Baskı) [Outline of Recent History of Turkey] (2nd ed.). Ankara: İmaj Yayıncılık.

Alemdar, Zeynep. 2011. *Sarmal Modeli Yarı Sarmak: Türkiye'de İnsan Hakları Kurumları-Devlet-AB İlişkisi* [Are We There Yet? Spiral Model: Human Rights Institutions-State-EU Relations in Turkey]. Uluslararası İlişkiler, Cilt 7, Sayı 28 s. 111–128.

Altıparmak, Kerem. 2010. *Köprüden Önce Son Çıkış: Türkiye İnsan Hakları Kurumu Kanun Tasarısı'nın Eleştirel Değerlendirilmesi* [Last Exit Before the Bridge: Human Rights Institutions of Turkey a Critical Evaluation of the DRAFT LAw]. Ankara Üniversitesi Siyasal Bilgiler Fakültesi İnsan Hakları Merkezi İnsan Hakları Çalışma Metinleri XIII Ankara. http://ihm.politics.ankara.edu.tr/userfiles/file/Kopruden%20son%20cikis.pdf.

Arkan, Atilla, Cem Duran Uzun, Erdal Tanas Karagöl, İsmail Çağlar, Murat Yeşiltaş, Nebi Miş, Nurullah Gür, and Ufuk Ulutaş. 2017. *2017'de Hukuk ve İnsan Hakları* [Law and Human Rights in 2017]. Ankara: SETA Vakfı.

Aydin, Hasan, and Koksal Avincan. 2020. Intellectual Crimes and Serious Violation of Human Rights in Turkey: A Narrative Inquiry. *The International Journal of Human Rights* 24 (8): 1127–1155. https://doi.org/10.1080/13642987.2020.1713108.

Bahçecik, Şerif Onur. 2015. The Power Effects of Human Rights Reforms in Turkey: Enhanced Surveillance and Depoliticisation. *Third World Quarterly 36* (6): 1222–1236. https://doi.org/10.1080/01436597.2015.1047204.

Baran, Zeyno. 2010. *Torn Country: Turkey Between Secularism and Islamism*. Stanford: Hoover Institution Press Publication.

Barın, Taylan. 2014. *Türkiye'nin Yeni Arnayasa Arayışı: 2011–2013 TBMM Anayasa Uzlaşma Komisyonu Tecrübesi* [Turkey's Quest for a New Constitutional: 2011–2013 Constitutional Reconciliation Commission Experience]. İstanbul: On İki Levha Publishing.

Barkey, Henri. 2014. Turkish Democracy: Two Steps Forward, Two Steps Backwards. *Harvard International Review 35* (4): 75–78.

Berkes, Niyazi. 1964. *The Development of Secularism in Turkey*. Montreal: McGill University Press.

———. 2002. *Türkiye'de Çağdaşlaşma* [Modernization in Turkey]. İstanbul: YKY Yay.

Bosher, John Francis. 1989. *The French Revolution*. London: Weidenfeld and Nicolson.

Bukovansky, Mlada. 2002. *Legitimacy and Power Politics*. Princeton: Princeton University Press.

Bürgin, Alexander. 2019. Policy Learning: An Understudied Mechanism of EU Influence on Turkish Domestic Politics. *Turkish Studies 20* (4): 493–511. https://doi.org/10.1080/14683849.2019.1601562.

CESRAN. 2011. *The Paradox of Turkish Civil Military Relations*. http://cesran.org/cesran-papers-1.

Cizre, Umit. 2004. Problems of Democratic Governance of Civil-Military Relations in Turkey and the European Union Enlargement Zone. *European Journal of Political Research 43* (1): 110–125. https://doi.org/10.1111/j.1475-6765.2004.00147.x.

Council of the European Union. 2018. *Enlargement and Stabilization and Association Process Council Conclusions*. https://www.consilium.europa.eu/media/35863/st10555-en18.pdf.
Davidson, Scott. 1997. *Human Rights*. Buckingham: Open University Press.
Demirel, Tanel. 2010. 2000'li Yıllarda Asker ve Siyaset: Kontrollü Değişim ile Statüko Arasında Türk Ordusu [Military and politics in 2000s: Turkish army between controlled change and status quo]. *SETA Analiz,* Sayı: 18. SETA Siyaset Ekonomi ve Toplum Araştırmaları Vakfı, Ankara.
Donnelly, Jack. 1986. International Human Rights: A Regime Analysis. *International Organization 40* (3): 599–642.
Dündar, Can. 2019. Der 15. Juli: "Ein Geschenk Allahs" für Erdoğan [July 15: "A gift from Allah" for Erdoğan]. *Deutsche Welle*, July 15. https://www.dw.com/de/alarm-f%C3%BCr-Erdoğan-zum-jahrestag-des-t%C3%BCrkischen-putschversuchs/a-49567356.
Durkheim, Emile. 1966. *The Division of Labour in Society*. New York: The Free Press.
Erdoğan, Mustafa, and Serap Yazıcı. 2011. *Türkiye'nin Yeni Anayasasına Doğru* [Towards Turkey's New Constitution]. İstanbul: TESEV Anayasa Komisyonu Raporu.
Erdoğdu, Aykut. 2019, Korkutan Iki Yıllık Senaryo [Frightening Two-Year Scenario], *Odatv,* January 12. https://odatv.com/korkutan-iki-yillik-senaryo-01121901.html.
Eryılmaz, Bilal. 1992. *Ottoman Millet System*. Istanbul: Ağaç Yayıncılık.
European Commission. 2018. Commission implementing decision of 5.12.2018 adopting an Annual Action Programme for Turkey for the year 2018, Brussels. https://ec.europa.eu/neighbourhood-enlargement/sites/near/files/aap-and-annex-turkey-2018_0.pdf.
Finkel, Caroline. 2006. *Osman's Dream: The Story of the Ottoman Empire 1300–1923*. New York: Basic Books.
Freedom House. 2018. *Freedom in the World 2018*. https://freedomhouse.org/print/50067.
———. 2019a. *Freedom in the World 2019*. https://freedomhouse.org/report/countries-world-freedom-2019.
———. 2019b. *Turkey in Transit: Democratization in Turkey*. https://freedomhouse.org/sites/default/files/inline_images/Turkey%20in%20Transit.pdf.
———. 2019c. *Freedom on the Net 2019: The Crisis of Social Media*. https://www.freedomonthenet.org/countries-in-detail.
Giddens, Anthony. 1990. *The Consequences of Modernity*. Stanford: Stanford University Press.
Girdap, Hafza. 2020. Human Rights, Conflicts, and Dislocation: The Case of Turkey in a Global Spectrum. *American Journal of Qualitative Research 4* (1): 69–84. https://doi.org/10.29333/ajqr/8266.
Gocek, Fatma Müge. 2011. *Transformation of Turkey: Redefining State and Society from the Ottoman*. New York: Ibtauris.
Gönenç, Levent. 2015. *Türkiye'nin Anayasa Uzlaşma Komisyonu Deneyimi* [Turkey's Constitutional Reconciliation Commission Experience]. Ankara: Türkiye Ekonomi Politikaları Araştırma Vakfı. https://www.tepav.org.tr/tr/yayin/s/762.
Gözler, Kemal. 2017. *Elveda Anayasa: 16 Nisan 2017'de Oylayacağımız Anayasa Değişikliği Hakkında Eleştiriler* [Farewell Constitution: Criticism About the Constitutional Amendment We Will Vote on April 16, 2017]. Bursa: Ekin Yayınları.
Güneş, Ümran. 2018. National Human Rights Institutions for the Protection of Human Rights in Turkey: Ombudsman Institution and Human Rights and Equality Institution in Turkey. *Trakya University Journal of Social Science 20* (1): 165–186.
Güvenç, Bozkurt. 1997. Secular Trends and Turkish Identity Perceptions. *Journal of International Affairs 2* (4). https://dergipark.org.tr/en/pub/perception/issue/49038/625582.
Hanioğlu, M.Şükrü. 2008. *A Brief History of the Late Ottoman Empire*. Princeton: Princeton University Press.
Haugom, Lars. 2019. The Turkish Armed Forces and Civil-Military Relations in Turkey After the 15 July 2016 Coup Attempt. *Scandinavian Journal of Military Studies 2* (1): 1–8. https://doi.org/10.31374/sjms.14.
Human Rights Watch. 2019. *Events of Turkey*. https://www.hrw.org/world-report/2019/country-chapters/turkey.

IDEA. 2019. *The Global State of Democracy 2019 Addressing the Ills, Reviving the Promise*. Stockholm: International IDEA.
Inalcık, Halil. 1994. *An Economic and Social History of the Ottoman Empire*. Cambridge: CUP.
Jevčák, Matus. 2015. *Comparison of Civil-Military Relations in Turkey Before and After 2002*. Unpublished master's thesis. Masaryk University, Faculty of Social Studies Department of Political Science.
Kabasakal Arat, Zehra F. 2007. Turkey's Prospects and Broader Implications. In *Human Rights in Turkey*, ed. Z.F.K. Arat, 262–275. Philadelphia: University of Pennsylvania Press.
Kardas, Şaban. 2002. Human Rights and democracy Promotion: The Case of Turkey-EU Relations. *Alternatives: Turkish Journal of International Relations 1* (3): 136–150.
Karpat, Kemal H. 2000. *Ottoman Past and Today's Turkey*. Boston: Brill.
———. 2002. *Studies on Ottoman Social and Political History: Selected Articles and essAys*. Boston: Brill.
Keyder, Çağlar. 1987. *State and Class in Turkey: A Study in Capitalist Development*. London: Verso.
Keyman, Ariana. 2012. *Civil-Military Relations in Turkey*. http://www.e-ir.info/2012/05/21/civil-military-relations-in-turkey/.
Keyman, E. Fuat, and Senem Aydın Duzgit. 2007. Europeanization, Democratization and Human Rights in Turkey. In *Turkey and the European Union*, ed. E. LaGro and Knud Erik Jørgensen, 69–88. New York: Palgrave Macmillan.
Kongar, Emre. 1998. *21. Yüzyılda Türkiye: 2000'li Yıllarda, Türkiye'nin Toplumsal Yapısı* [Turkey in the 21st Century: Turkey's Social Structure]. Remzi Kitabevi.
Kösebalaban, Hasan. 2011. Ottoman Origins of Turkish Identity Discourses. In *Turkish Foreign Policy*, 25–46. New York: Palgrave Macmillan.
Kuru, Ahmet T. 2012. The Rise and Fall of Military Tutelage in Turkey: Fears of Islamism, Kurdism, and Communism. *Insight Turkey 14* (2): 37–57.
Lewis, Bernard. 2002. *The emergence of modern Turkey*. Oxford: OUP.
Mağdurlar için Adalet. 2019. *Social Costs Report of the State of Emergency in Its Second Year*. Ankara: Mağdurlar için Adalet Topluluğu.
Marx, Karl. 1977. *A Contribution to the Critique of Political Economy*. Moscow: Progress Publishers.
McPhee, Peter. 2002. *The French Revolution 1789–1799*. Oxford: Oxford University Press.
Miller, Frederic P., Agnes F. Vandome, and John McBrewster (eds). 2010. *Human Rights of Kurdish People in Turkey*. Alphascript Publishing.
OHCHR. 2018. *Report on the Impact of the State of Emergency on Human Rights in Turkey*, including an update on the South-East January–December 2017, United Nations High Commissioner for Human Rights.
Oran, Baskın. 2007. The Minority Concept and Rights in Turkey. In *Human Rights in Turkey*, ed. Z.F.K. Arat, 35–56. Philadelphia: University of Pennsylvania Press.
Ortaylı, İlber. 2005. *İmparatorluğun En Uzun Yüzyılı* [The Longest Century of the Empire]. İstanbul: İletişim Yayınları.
Ozbudun, Ergun. 2000. *Contemporary Turkish Politics: Challenges to Democratic Consolidation*. Boulder: Lynne Rienner Publishers, Inc.
Özcan, Mehmet. 1999. Avrupa Birliği-Türkiye İlişkilerinde Temel Belirleyici Unsur Olarak İnsan Hakları [Key Determinants of Human Rights as EU-Turkey Relations.]. *Polis Bilimleri Dergisi*, 2(5–6). Polis Teşkilatinin 155. Yili Özel Sayisi.
Özer, Yonca. 2015. AB'ye Üyelik Sürecinde Türkiye'de Demokratikleşme [Democratization in Turkey During the EU Accession Process]. *Marmara Üniversitesi Avrupa Topluluğu Enstitüsü Avrupa Araştırmaları Dergisi 23*(2), 143–168. https://dergipark.org.tr/tr/pub/maruaad/issue/42386/510475.
Öztürk, Osman Metin. 2006. *Ordu ve Politika* [Army and Policies] (2. Baskı). Ankara: Fark Yayınları.

Reuters. 2019. Turkey Condemns European Parliament Committee Call to Suspend Accession. *Reuters*, February 21. https://www.reuters.com/article/us-turkey-eu/turkey-condemns-european-parliament-committee-call-to-suspend-accession-idUSKCN1QA0MJ.
Salah, Mehmet. 2013. *The Turkish Working Class and Socialist Movement in Perspective*. https://libcom.org/library/turkish-working-class-socialist-movement-perspective.
Smith, Thomas W. 2007. Leveraging Norms: The ECHR and Turkey's Human Rights Reforms. In *Human Rights in Turkey*, ed. Z.F.K. Arat, 262–275. Philadelphia: University of Pennsylvania Press.
Strauss, Johann. 2010. A Constitution for a Multilingual Empire: Translations of the Kanun-ı Esasi and Other Official Texts into Minority Languages. In *The first Ottoman Experiment in Democracy*, ed. C. Herzog and M. Sharif, 21–51. Wurzburg: Orient-Institut.
Tekin, Ömer Faruk, Mehmet Göküş, and Ali Şahin. 2013. Civil-Military Relationship Between 2000 and 2012 in Turkey in the Context of Modern State. In *Proceedings of IISES, 6th International Academic Conference* (pp. 448–456). June 23–26, Bergen, Norway.
Toktaş, Şule, and Ümit Kurt. 2010. The Turkish Military's Autonomy, JDP Rule and the EU Reform Process in the 2000s: An Assessment of the Turkish Version of Democratic Control of Armed Forces (DECAF). *Turkish Studies 11* (3): 387–403.
Türkmen, Füsun. 2007. Turkey's Participation in Global and Regional Human Rights Regimes. In *Human Rights in Turkey*, ed. Z.F.K. Arat, 249–261. Philadelphia: University of Pennsylvania Press.
Uluçakar, Mustafa, and Ali Çağlar. 2017. An Analysis of Two Different Models of Civil-Military Relations: The Case of Turkey. *Uluslararası İlişkiler 14* (55): 41–57.
United States Department of State. 2018. *Turkey 2018 Human Rights Report*. Washington, DC: Bureau of Democracy, Human Rights and Labor. https://www.state.gov/wp-content/uploads/2019/03/TURKEY-2018-HUMAN-RIGHTS-REPORT.pdf.
WJP. 2019. *2019 WJP Rule of Law Index*. Washington, DC: World Justice Project. https://worldjusticeproject.org/sites/default/files/documents/ROLI-2019-Reduced.pdf.
Yasa, Ibrahim. 1970. *Türkiye'nin Toplumsal Yapısı ve Temel Sorunları* [Turkey's Social Structure and Key Issues]. Türkiye ve Orta Doğu Amme Idaresi Enstitüsü Yayinlari.
Yilmaz, Ömer, Bülent Çiçekli, and M. Bedri Eryılmaz. 2007. *The Analysis of European Court of Human Rights' Decisions Related to Turkey (2002 – 2005)*. Ankara: USAK.
Zurcher, Erik J. 2004. *Turkey: A Modern History*. London: Tauris.

Ercan Balcioglu graduated from Mersin University's department of Sociology in 2000. Between the years of 2000 and 2004, he obtained his MA from the Sociology Department of the Institute for Social Sciences at Mersin University, Turkey. He was then appointed as a research assistant at the Turkish National Police University (TNPU) in 2007. In 2010, he spent 5 months at Kean University, New Jersey, as a *visiting researcher* to study police deviancy and police crimes. He received his Ph. D. from the Institute for Security Sciences at TNPU in 2012. After receiving his Ph.D. from the Institute for Security Sciences at TNPU, he was a visiting professor at the Criminology Department of University of Leicester in UK between 2013 and 2014. Ercan Balcioglu currently works at the Department of Police and Security Management, Berlin School of Economics and Law (HWR). Dr. Balcioglu has participated and collaborated in many criminological research projects at both national and international levels funded by different institutions. In addition to his regular teaching activities at Berlin School of Economics and Law (HWR), he also taught courses about crime and delinquency at various universities. Dr. Balcioglu has been researching on criminology, victimology and criminal justice system for over 13 years.

Part II
Freedom and Non-discrimination

Chapter 3
Freedom of the Media in Turkey Under the AKP Government

Vedat Demir

Abstract Freedom of expression is an essential human right that forms the basis of an open government and a well-informed society through public debate as well as free and independent media. Therefore, ensuring freedom of expression and having free, independent, and diverse media are vital elements for any healthy and strong democracy. This chapter analyses the history of the press and media freedom in Turkey by focusing on the last two decades under Recep Tayyip Erdoğan and the Justice and Development Party (Adalet ve Kalkınma Partisi, AKP). The chapter closely examines the tools and methods the Erdogan government used to take the media under control and establish an authoritarian one-man regime in Turkey.

Keywords Freedom of expression · Authoritarianism · Turkish media · Erdoğan regime · Silencing media · Jailing journalists

3.1 Introduction

Communication is one of the most essential human rights, and it does not only consist of sharing and receiving information. Instead, it is a two-way process in which people are involved in a democratic and balanced dialogue individually and collectively. Freedom of communication started to take its place in international documents as a human right in the first half of the twentieth century. In the Universal Declaration of Human Right, adopted by the United Nations General Assembly on December 10, 1948, the right to freedom of communication is secured through the following articles:

> Article 18. Everyone has the right to freedom of thought, conscience and religion; this right includes freedom to change his religion or belief, and freedom, either alone or in community with others and in public or private, to manifest his religion or belief in teaching, practice, worship and observance.

V. Demir (✉)
University of Potsdam, Potsdam, Germany

H. Aydin, W. Langley (eds.), *Human Rights in Turkey*, Philosophy and Politics - Critical Explorations 15, https://doi.org/10.1007/978-3-030-57476-5_3

> Article 19. Everyone has the right to freedom of opinion and expression; this right includes freedom to hold opinions without interference and to seek, receive and impart information and ideas through any media and regardless of frontiers.

In 1950, the definition of freedom of expression is stated in Article 10 of the European Convention on Human Rights that established the European Court of Human Rights as follows:

> Everyone has the right to freedom of expression. This right shall include freedom to hold opinions and to receive and impart information and ideas without interference by public authority and regardless of frontiers. This Article shall not prevent States from requiring the licensing of broadcasting, television or cinema enterprises.

The state parties of the International Covenant on Civil and Political Rights (ICCPR) and the European Convention on Human Rights, such as the Republic of Turkey, are obligated to respect, protect and promote the rights set out in these binding treaties.

The MacBride Report, published in 1980 by UNESCO, defined the right of communication, its elements, and the vision of its intentions (MacBride 1980, 173):

> Everyone has the right to communicate: the components of this comprehensive Human Right include but are not limited to the following specific communication rights:
>
> (a) A right to assemble, a right to discuss, a right to participate and related association rights;
> (b) A right to inquire, a right to be informed, a right to inform, and related information rights; and
> (c) A right to culture, a right to choose, a right to privacy, and related human development rights.
>
> The achievement of a right to communicate would require that communication resources be available for the satisfaction of human communication needs.

Throughout history, people fought against political, economic, religious, and social powers curtailing their right of communication. Only those who were successful were able to gain freedom of speech, press, and information. The same struggle, of course, still exists today but people have new demands such as two-way flow, free exchange, access, and participation (MacBride 1980, 172). In today's world, freedom of expression and independent media form the basis of a democratic society that is well-informed through public discussions and communication. Therefore, a free, independent, and diverse media is a vital element for any healthy and strong democracy in which freedom of communication exists.

Turkey is one of the salient examples of the countries that have experienced democratic backsliding in the last decade. The deterioration in media freedom in Turkey played a key role in its transformation from being an exemplar democracy in the MENA region to an oppressive one-man rule. In order to understand this transformation, this chapter analyzes the history of media and media freedom in Turkey by focusing on the last two decades under Recep Tayyip Erdoğan and the Justice and Development Party (Adalet ve Kalkınma Partisi, AKP) as well as the tools and methods they used to take the media under their control and establish an authoritarian regime.

3.2 The Development of the Turkish Press

The fundamental goal of the Turkish modernization and westernization reforms was saving the state rather than creating a modern society. In one of his articles published in 1872, Namık Kemal, a distinguished Turkish intellectual, points out this reality and discusses the intentions of the "Tanzimat" a series of reform movements that started the period of westernization and modernization in the Ottoman Empire (Lewis 1968, 170):

> Indeed [he says if] one looks at its external aspect, one would think it to have been made as a surety for the life, property, and honor of every individual. But the truth of the matter is that it was proclaimed for the purpose of securing the life of the state.

The military defeats and territory losses stimulated the Ottomans to look for the factors underlying the Western military superiority which was the main problem of the Ottoman modernization process (Mardin 2000, 134–35). Initially, the Ottoman Sultans attempted to address the growing Western challenge by reforming the military and assembling a modern army. By the nineteenth century, however, the Ottoman elites came to the realization that military reforms would not be enough and a modern political, social and economic structure was necessary to keep up with the Western world (Ahmad 1993, 3). A developed press that could inform the public was a fundamental part of this modern structure.

3.2.1 Emergence of the Turkish Press

Other than the ones in the military field, the most important technical innovation adopted from the West was printing. In 1727, an Imperial decree was issued, giving permission for the establishment of a Turkish press and the printing of Turkish books in Istanbul. During the time between the appearance of the first book in 1729 and the closing of the printing house in 1742, seventeen books had been printed. The development of printing in Turkey proceeded rapidly after the printing house was reopened in 1784 (Lewis 1968, 50–51).

3.2.1.1 First Turkish Newspaper

Under Sultan Mahmud II (1808–1839), the Ottomans started to take a considerably different approach to the institutionalization of Westernization than their predecessors. During this time, Westernization became a formal policy as a part of bureaucratic reforms and was put into effect with brutal force. The new schools provided the necessary manpower while a government newspaper was used to support the reforms through propaganda for the first time (Hanioğlu 2008, 63). As Ahmet Emin Yalman, Turkish journalist and professor, stated, the Sultan had seen the necessity of securing the support and cooperation of his people in order to modernize Turkey (1914, 27).

Newspapers in French had already been published in Turkey before by French nationals. Towards the end of the first quarter of the nineteenth century, newspapers in other foreign languages started to be issued. In 1828, the first newspaper in the Islamic world, *Vakayi Mısrıya* (Events of Egypt), was established by Mehmet Ali, the semi-independent governor of the Ottoman-ruled Egypt, and published in Turkish and Arabic. This encouraged Sultan Mahmud II to establish the first official Turkish newspaper, called *Takvim-i Vekayi* (Calendar of Events) which was a required reading for public officials, in 1831. Historiographer Esad was assigned as the editor of *Takvim-i Vekayi* while Alexandre Blaque, who already had published a French newspaper in Smyrna (İzmir), edited the French edition, entitled *Moniteur Ottoman* (Berkes 1998, 126). *Takvim-i Vekayi* became a much more efficient way to inform the public about the purposes of the Sultan's policies with the inauguration of the postal system in 1834 (Lewis 1968, 95).

3.2.1.2 First Semi-Official and Private Newspapers

In 1840, an Englishman, William Churchill, established a Turkish weekly focusing on foreign politics called *Ceride-i Havadis* (Register of News), which was issued five times a week later on. It received a subvention of about fourteen hundred dollars annually (Yalman 1914, 32). *Ceride-i Havadis* was a virtual monopoly of journalism in Turkish language for 20 years and played a key role in accustoming the Turkish reader to news and features as well as training a new generation of journalists and developing the other necessary parts of the newspaper business such as printing and distribution (Lewis 1968, 147).

The first non-official and self-supporting newspaper, *Tercüman-i Ahval* (Interpreter of Conditions), was launched in 1860. This publication started a new era in Turkish literature and Turkish language as it was not only the first non-official newspaper, but also the first publication of the modernist school in Turkey (Yalman 1914, 34).

3.2.1.3 First Shut Down of a Paper

Ceride-i Havadis and *Tercüman-i Ahval* suddenly found themselves competing against each other. *Ceride-i Havadis* started to put out a supplementary daily news bulletin to address this challenge. *Tercüman-ı Ahval,* on the other hand, boasted of its independence stating that its competitors were owned by the imperial government and an Englishman while it represented the "people of Islam." A further argument on questions of education between the two newspapers resulted with the first official suspension of a Turkish journal when *Tercüman-ı Ahval* was shut down for 2 weeks (Davison 1963, 186).

In 1862 a new paper called *Tasvir-i Efkar* (Illustration of Opinion) started to be published. *Tasvir-i Efkar* had a slightly more advanced approach and its radicalism was more cultural than political. It attracted some attention to political issues in the

Ottoman Empire and called for financial and legal reforms. In March 1863, it was followed by a newspaper called *Mir'at* (Mirror) which had only three issues published (Lewis 1968, 148–49).

3.2.1.4 Regulations on the Press

In 1865, for the first time, the Ottoman government felt the need to put some kind of restraint upon the press to keep it under control. The Press Law of January 1865 was declared, and a press bureau was established to watch over the execution of these set of laws (Yalman 1914, 36). According to the new law, every paper and editor needed to obtain an official permit, and they were required to deliver a signed copy of each issue to the government for review and were responsible for penalties as a result of a violation of regulations (Davison 1963, 186).

A more radical newspaper called *Muhbir* (Informer) was established and started to be published on January 1, 1867. The vigorous and sensational articles appeared on *Muhbir* angered the Ottoman administration in a short span of time. The editors of *Muhbir* were exiled to Anatolia and the newspaper stopped being published on March 8, 1867. In the meantime, several other newspapers had started to be published in Istanbul. The rapid increase in the number of newspapers caused concern within the Ottoman administration which made the government more and more autocratic especially after the accession of the new sultan, Abdülaziz, in 1861 (Lewis 1968, 149).

3.2.1.5 Suppressions and the Exile of the Press

The Ottoman administration realized in a short span of time that the press laws failed in checking the revolutionary publications and the personal attacks against those in power. The next step taken by the government characterized a defining feature of the Turkish system of government that has been in effect since then. The government decided that "on account of considerations of public order, to act, as often as the interests of the country required, through administrative channels, and independently of the existing press law, against newspapers which should disregard the principles, the observation of which is the essential condition of a national press" (Yalman 1914, 36). The authoritarian measures taken by the government started an era of severe pressure on the press, suppressing more and more newspapers, and causing the press departure for Europe of their more prominent contributors. As a result of the oppressive policies, the most significant Turkish newspapers had to be published in exile in London, Paris, and Geneva in the following years (Lewis 1968, 150).

Despite the government and oppression, the Turkish press continued to grow and develop, both in number and in quality. In 1860, there was only one official and one semi-official newspaper established and run through the government support. In 1872, there were three dailies, two papers published three times a week, a satirical weekly, a semi-weekly, a weekly police gazette, a military weekly, and a commercial weekly (Yalman 1914, 40–41).

In the following years, the press proved to be a tool giving a voice to the opponents of the Ottoman administration while the numbers of papers were increasing remarkably. There was no considerable Turkish middle class to play the role taken by the bourgeoises in Western countries, and most of the Turkish intellectuals were attached to the administration through official posts. They, however, could oppose and criticize the administration and the newly developed Turkish press gave them an opportunity to raise their voices (Davison 1963, 187).

3.2.1.6 The Press Under Control of the State and Censorship

After his accession to the throne in 1876, Sultan Abdülhamid used all of his power to oppress the opposing voices in the society and control the press. As a result of his policies, the free intellectual life of Turkey transferred itself to France, Egypt and other places together with the press activity in Turkey (Yalman 1914, 16).

Censorship was already well established in the time of Sultan Abdülaziz, and it became more widespread and extended from newspapers to any kind of printed matter under the rule of Abdülhamid (Lewis 1968, 187). During this time, a censorship department in the Ministry of Education was established to enforce the press and publication laws and criticism against the government was strictly forbidden. The writings of some Turkish authors were banned as well as the writings of some European authors such as Racine, Rousseau, Voltaire, Hugo, and Zola (Shaw and Shaw 1977, 251).

The government censorship prohibited any political discussions, especially ones related to liberalism, nationalism and constitutionalism. The newspapers were also restrained from discussing current affairs in any meaningful ways, and therefore the press published papers filled with encyclopedic articles rather than news. They attempted to inform the Ottoman reading public, which was still only a fraction of the population, about the outside world this way (Zürcher 2017, 74). The press in Istanbul avoided any serious political comment or the reporting of news, but they unobtrusively continued to instill European social ideas and attitudes in their readers and keep them connected to the modern world of which Turkey was now a part (Lewis 1968, 194).

3.2.1.7 Constitutional Period

After the 1876 Constitution was put into action again with the Young Turk Revolution in 1908, the press started to enjoy a status incomparably better than the previous oppressive period (Yalman 1914, 16). Censorship was lifted and newspapers and magazines filled with diverse opinions started to be published to satisfy the long-lasting need of the public (Ahmad 1993, 31). The government oppression on the press returned again after 1909. However, even the increasing bullying of the administration and the conditions of war were not able to prevent the flow of progressive thoughts and arguments within the empire (Lewis 1968, 230–31). The Second Turkish Constitutional Regime was declared in 1908. Although it lasted longer than the first attempt, it also failed. The Constitution, however, remained in force and elections were still held while the regime turned into a military oligarchy of the Young Turk leaders. The regime eventually ended with the defeat of the Ottoman Empire in 1918 as a result of the First World War (Lewis 1968, 211).

3.2.2 Turkish Press in the Republic Period

After the Greek army landed in Izmir and invaded the rest of western Anatolia in May 1919, the Turkish nationalist forces, led by General Mustafa Kemal, organized a resistance movement against the invasion. The nationalists were able to restore the Turkish authority in Anatolia after 3 years of fighting on different fronts which was followed by diplomatic successes such as the Treaty of Lausanne, drawing the new borders of Turkey. On October 29, 1919, the Republic was established, setting in motion the process of creating a new and modern Turkey, by the nationalist leadership that was overwhelmingly military in its composition (Ahmad 1993, 2–3).

The new government, led by Mustafa Kemal Atatürk, gained its legitimacy through victory in the independence war and started to make crucial reforms to modernize Turkey. The state structure inherited from the Ottomans were replaced with "Kemalist" ideology, based on Westernization, secularism, Turkish nationalism and the cult of Atatürk. The Turkish army was assigned as the protector of this ideology that formed the foundations of the new state and it crushed the resistance against the new order when needed.

During the Cold War, Turkey was the frontline state, further strengthening the power of the Kemalist military over the state and judicial establishments. Turkey was eventually introduced to democracy when the single party regime, that had been in power since the foundation of the republic, ended in 1950. The Turkish military, however, stood above the politics and kept controlling the following cabinets until the end of the century through formal and informal methods. The military intervened and suspended the constitutional order many times through military coups in 1960 and 1980 as well as government dismissals in 1971 and 1997 (Matusiak 2015, 9–10).

After the Democrat Party (DP) ended the single party regime in 1950 by defeating the Republican People's Party (Cumhuriyet Halk Partisi, CHP), founded by Atatürk, the new administration made liberal reforms during its initial years in power and loosened the repressive press laws. After they were elected for the second time in 1954, however, the Democrat Party adopted authoritarian policies and harassed the opposition parties and press. In May 27, 1960, the Turkish military carried out a coup and took control of the government in order to end the polarization between the government and the opposition (Özbudun 2011, 41).

The Turkish military carried out another coup 20 years later on September 12, 1980 and declared the Constitution of 1982 that reversed the more liberal constitution declared in 1961. The new constitution concentrated the power in the hands of the executive and gave even more power to the president and the National Security Council while limiting the freedom of the press and trade unions as well as basic human rights and liberties. Although basic human rights, such as freedom of speech, were included in the constitution, it was stipulated that they could be annulled, suspended or limited due to purposes of national interest, public order, national security and protection of the republican order (Zürcher 2017, 286). This enabled future administrations to abuse any essential rights through arbitrary decisions and manufactured excuses.

3.2.3 The Formation of the Turkish Press' Character

Since the early days of the history of the Turkish press, journalists have been threatened, censored and fired from their jobs. They were also exiled, harassed, imprisoned or killed through formal and informal methods due to their opinions critical of the government or the Turkish state.

Development of newspapers in Turkey was the result of political factors rather than social and economic conditions. Due to the initial state impact, the Turkish press has always been very open to any influence from the state and political powers through its 200 years of history (Demir 2007, 233).

The press was established as a government institution like every other modernization reform in Turkey, and maintained this character until 1860. An independent class of reformers took the press under their control between 1860 and 1876, and the press acted as an unrestricted intermediary of opinions between Turkey and the West. There has been a tendency, however, altering in degree with the constant political changes, towards repressing adverse political criticism (Yalman 1914, 16).

The first journalists were amateurs, writers, officials and politicians who wrote part-time and failed to appreciate the full potentials of this new and powerful medium. To some extent, this was also true during the period of Abdülhamid in which many journalists had other professions. Professional journalism, however, was clearly and rapidly developing in Turkey and many skilled journalists started to earn their livelihood through the press. With a rise in the literacy rate, an increased demand for news and information made the press a profitable business, providing a new class of journalists a new status and influence over the society (Lewis 1968, 462).

The Turkish press, with its tradition of opposition and criticism, has always played a significant role in the social and political modernization of Turkey throughout its history. Journalists played key roles in introducing the liberal democratic values of the West both in the Ottoman Empire and in the Turkish Republic. The press has always been responsible for protecting democracy in the country but has also failed in this task many times. For instance, the mainstream media supported the military interventions in 1960, 1971 and 1980 (Şahin 2010, 377, 385).

The new conservative policies implemented in the United States and Europe and the collapse of socialism in the 1980s and 1990s started the period of commercialization in media in Turkey. In this period, media conglomerates had a significant influence on the government as well as the state of Turkish politics. One of the most controversial issues was the relationship between economy, politics and media (Demir 2007, 234; 2011).

In 1996, the Islamist Welfare Party (Refah Partisi, RP) came to power in Turkey by forming a coalition government with the center right the True Path Party (Doğru Yol Partisi, DYP). This put the army in alert as it felt responsible for protecting the values of the republic. In 1997, the National Security Council issued the government with a list of demands to prevent "creeping Islamization" in the country and to fortify the secular system. The pressure forced the coalition government to resign and led to the shutdown of the Islamist Welfare Party by the Constitutional Court of Turkey that also banned the key leaders of the party from active politics (Cizre 2008a, 310–11). During this time, the two biggest media conglomerates in Turkey were the main supporters of the military pressure and the forced resignation of the government (Şahin 2010, 377). The consequences of the military memorandum would shape at least the next 20 years of the Turkish people and drastically change the fundamentals of the Turkish Republic as it led to the rise of Recep Tayyip Erdoğan and his Justice and Development Party.

3.3 Freedom of the Media Under the Justice and Development Party (AKP) and Erdoğan Regime

The Milli Görüş (National Outlook) movement emerged in the early 1970s and became the core ideology of many successive political parties that mobilized and represented marginalized conservatives in the country through Islamic discourse. Due to their Islamic political discourse and their anti-secular activities, several of these parties, including the Welfare Party, were shut down by the Constitutional Court. The successor of the Welfare Party, the Virtue Party (Fazilet Partisi, FP) was also shut down on June 22, 2001 for its anti-secular activities and reconstituting a permanently dissolved party. As a result, the movement split into two in August 2001. The traditionalist wing founded the Felicity Party (Saadet Partisi, SP) while the reformist wing founded the Justice and Development Party (Adalet ve Kalkınma Partisi, AKP). The AKP came to power in the 2002 Elections and became the dominant party by establishing an electoral hegemony in the following elections (Cizre 2008a, 346; Gumuscu 2016, 6).

The personality of Erdoğan played an important role in the success of the AKP. He and his party gained the support of the mass of the population who identified themselves with him due to his background. He grew up in a poor neighborhood in Istanbul and was the son of migrants who moved to Istanbul from the eastern Black

Sea coast. After the electoral victory of the Welfare Party in 1994, he became the mayor of Istanbul with an emerging popularity (Zürcher 2017, 339).

The AKP rule since 2002 could be divided into more specific periods. The reform period was only limited to its first 3 years, ending in 2005. Between 2005 and 2007, the AKP government focused on strengthening its power and successfully demonstrated its power in the 2007 presidential election. From 2007 to 2010, the AKP, in alliance with the Gülen Movement, fought against the secular establishments in Turkish state. In 2011, Erdoğan started to work to realize his ambition of a one-man rule. After 2013, Erdoğan has started to take more authoritarian actions as a result of the Gezi Park protests, the tension between the AKP and the Gülen Movement, and the massive corruption cases against AKP ministers. Although Erdoğan aligned with the military against the Gülen Movement, his party lost the majority vote in the 2015 Elections (Bipartisan Policy Center 2015, 41). The coup attempt in 2016 gave Erdoğan the opportunity to become more powerful than ever and finally establish his one-man rule.

The best way to understand the rule of the AKP would be analyzing it in two terms. Its first term between 2003 to 2011 could be called "the Period of the Justice and Development Party (AKP)." In this time frame, the AKP appeared as a reformist party that made democratic reforms and increased freedoms, including the press freedom, as a result of the European Union process. During this time, the policies of the AKP government were also heavily influenced and supported by the liberals, democrats, secular reformists, Kurds and of course conservatives who were oppressed due to secular policies in the past (The Economist 2016, 4).

During the formation period of the AKP, the administration of the party could be grouped into two subgroups. One of these groups consisted of Erdoğan and his associates who worked with him when he served as the mayor of Istanbul, while the other group was the reformist wing of the Virtue Party led by Abdullah Gül, Bülent Arınç, and Abdullatif Şener (Aydin and Dalmış 2008, 202). Although Erdoğan was the least experienced in politics among them and had a weaker personnel base, he eventually took leadership of the party and the state (Matusiak 2015, 17).

The second term of the AKP after 2011 could be called "the Period of the Erdoğan regime." Until 2011, Erdoğan, as the prime minister and the leader of the AKP, constantly strengthened his power and started to neutralize both social and political groups opposing him as well as the ones he allied with in the first period of the AKP. After the Gezi Park protests and the corruption investigations in 2013, Erdoğan's attacks on government critics became much more visible as he accused every opposition movement of being a conspiracy to overthrow him. After the 2016 coup attempt, Erdoğan finally established his authoritarian regime and silenced every critical voice in the country.

3.3.1 The Period of the Justice and Development Party (AKP)

When it was established and came to power, the AKP rejected any continuity with its predecessors and Islamist parties, and identified itself as a "conservative democratic" party. The AKP's agenda and statements made by its leaders during the 2002 and 2007 elections strongly promoted universal values such as human rights, the rule of law, limited government, pluralism, diversity and tolerance for all (Hale and Özbudun 2010, 20). The AKP took lessons from previous failed coalitions and party shutdowns. As a result, they denied their Islamist pedigree and adopted a moderate and non-religious discourse. They also focused on Turkey's accession to the European Union not only as a reform strategy but also as a way of transforming the domestic power balance (Cizre 2008a, 320–21).

According to the Human Rights Watch (HRW) Report in 2016 (12), the AKP governments from 2003 to 2009, introduced many legal reforms that increased the legal protection of political, social, and cultural rights of Turkish citizens including freedom of expression regardless of their religious or ethnic backgrounds. Since 2011, however, Turkey has had a worrying rollback of human rights due to the AKP's increasing intolerance of opposition and critical media.

The general elections on November 3, 2002 resulted with the predicted but still impressive victory of the AKP. It became the first party to win the majority in the Turkish parliament since 1987 by gaining about a third of the valid votes and controlling two-thirds of the seats in the parliament (Çarkoğlu and Kalaycıoğlu 2007, 1).

The AKP summarized its political aspirations in five points (Gögüs and Mannitz 2016, 7):

- Enactment of a new constitution based on the rule of law which secures the principles and standards of the Universal Declaration of Human Rights and the European Convention on Human Rights.
- Protection of the fundamental rights and freedoms of each citizen regardless of ethnic, religious or ideological background.
- Full membership in the European Union and acceptance of the economic and political criteria of the EU.
- Development and economic stabilization.
- Participatory democracy rather than parliamentary representation.

3.3.1.1 Democratization Reforms and the European Union Process

After coming to power, the AKP first sought to start Turkey's EU membership process. The idea of becoming a part of Europe was endorsed widely by the public. The elite supported the idea for partly ideological reasons because Turkey's accession in Europe would ensure its Western alignment. It was supported by most of the population for a practical reason: simply improving their living standards. However, the EU membership requirements were adopted by the AKP so as to apply the

AKP's own political agenda and take control of the state (Zürcher 2017, 340). Although the core supporters of the AKP were not fond of the idea of being a part of the European Union, the newly elected government was eager to visit capitals in Europe and start the process for the membership. After all, in December 2004, Turkey was promised a starting date for the EU membership negotiations and the negotiations began in October 2005 (Çarkoğlu and Kalaycıoğlu 2007, 55).

The AKP was not overly afraid of the opposition, but they kept in memory the 1997 "post-modern coup" It was enough reason for them feel vulnerable at that point. Although the AKP had the government and majority in the parliament, "the state machinery," including the judiciary, police, and army were not in their control. The following years would observe the AKP's struggle to shatter the sovereignty of the state and establish political control over its organs, especially the army, by receiving a strong endorsement from the European Union (Zürcher 2017, 340).

The National Security Council (MGK), functioning as "the shadow government," had been the military's instrument to influence politics. The new reform packages which were put into effect on August 7, 2003 turned MGK into an advisory body and the majority of its members into civilians. Therefore, the military's impact on politics was reduced. Implementing these democratic reform packages was a historic legislative achievement. The AKP government consciously made this decision which could have potentially led to a confrontation with the military's leadership. This bold step indicated that the government was confident enough to establish a civilian rule. When the 8th Harmonization Package passed on May 21st, 2004, civilians extended their presence over the defense budget, and military representatives no longer held a position on the Council on Higher Education (YÖK) and the Supreme Board of Radio and Television (RTÜK). State security courts, remnants of the era after the military coup of 1980 where the state had been held to trial of crime, were also eliminated. The right of the military courts was diminished when it came to try citizens who criticized the military (Cizre 2008a, 321–22).

With an overwhelming speed, many legal changes took place between 2002–2006. The parliament passed 261 new laws from October 2003 to July 2004. Many of the new laws were related to the military's status in the political system, legal procedures, and human rights. The next year, additional 166 laws were passed. Although the pace of the reforms slowed down in the following years, these legal reforms which took place in the first years of the AKP government were great achievements (Zürcher 2017, 341).

The reform packages, started in November 2002, included the following:

- Increased freedom of expression;
- Abolished anti-terrorism arrangements that authorized punishment for verbal propaganda against the unity of state;
- Abolished the death penalty;
- Gave retrial rights to citizens whose court decisions were revoked by the European Court of Human Rights;
- Gave permission for Kurdish language education and broadcasting;

- Ended the intransigence of the Turkish foreign policy regarding the Cyprus issue (Cizre 2008b, 2).

Press freedom made significant progress in Turkey after the implementation of the EU reform packages. On June 9, 2004, a more liberal press law replaced the then-current law which had been in effect since 1950 (Demir 2007, 230).

According to the new regulations, only a court order and a decision of the public prosecutor in urgent cases made the seizure of printed material possible. For urgent cases, the public prosecutor had to submit his decision within 24 h to receive the approval of a competent judge. If not approved in 48 h, it would be automatically dismissed. With the new rules, the owners, general editors, and author journals, periodicals also could not be pressured to disclose the sources of their news reports (Hale and Özbudun 2010, 58–59).

A decade long rule of the AKP's initial phase granted Turkey a fast transformation and aspiring prosperity as a result of the reforms which aimed to fulfill the EU standards. In 2005, Turkey officially started the negotiations with the European Union. Around 2012, the AKP finally changed the game to its favor against the military in terms of dominance over politics, and civilians started to have influence over the military for the first time in Turkish history. This ended the supremacy of the Kemalist state-establishment and the secular-nationalist ideology, and the Turkish public no longer shared their values or regarded them as political choices. The Republic of Turkey was simply at its height in terms of prestige, position and influence about a decade after the AKP's coming to power (Matusiak 2015, 14).

3.3.2 The Period of Erdoğan's Authoritarian Regime

Compared to the first period of the AKP, the EU process and democratization reforms lost momentum after the AKP's second election victory in 2007. After the 2010 referendum on a number of changes to Turkish Constitution and 2011 General Elections victory, Erdoğan and the AKP started to follow their own agenda to establish an authoritarian one-man regime.

After 2007, three most prominent figures in the AKP were Abdullah Gül, Tayyip Erdoğan and Bülent Arınç. They were all among the founders of the party in 2001 and now holding the three highest position in Turkish government as president, prime minister and speaker of the parliament. The AKP won three consecutive elections and had a stable majority in the parliament. The political challenges from the opposition, Kemalist civil society and organizations as well as the army which was the biggest threat at the time, had all been met successfully. The AKP almost faced the same consequence as their predecessors but avoided the threat of a ban by the constitutional court in 2008. By holding the three key positions in the state, especially the presidency, it was now able to carry through all the appointments of top bureaucrats, provincial administrators, judges and public prosecutors. Negotiations with the European Union had stalled by this time, but the EU process had helped the AKP overcome its biggest challenge by functioning as a crowbar to destroy the Kemalist state (Zürcher 2017, 347–48).

As the AKP was gaining more and more power in the second period of the AKP, the system of the Turkish government had turned into the personal rule of Erdoğan. It was in this time that the first signs of monopolizing tendencies became more apparent and Erdoğan started to make religious references and morally patronizing comments in public. This created concern among Turkish seculars and liberals and led them to question Erdoğan's intentions (Gögüs and Mannitz 2016, 10).

The concerns about the AKP's tendency towards an authoritarian regime had been raised by many journalists and academics. In an interview, published in 2007, Şerif Mardin, a distinguished Turkish political scientist, pointed out the rising religiosity and conservatism in the country and created a new sociological term called "Neighborhood Pressure" referring to the communal pressure on individuals that force them to comply with the religious and conservative norms in their everyday lives (Çakır 2007). In late 2009, Nuray Mert, an academician and journalist, expressed her concerns on the rise of authoritarian politics under the label of civil government in her column at *Radikal* newspaper (2009). In 2011, Faruk Birtek who is a prominent sociology professor said, "I am afraid, I am worried, I do not trust" and then added, "I'm scared when I make this statement. Because I don't know what's going to happen. The police can come and raid the house, find something that suits him. I wasn't that kind of person" (Mengi 2011).

In the conclusion of their study on the AKP, published in 2010, William Hale and Ergun Özbudun analyze the possible paths that the AKP could take at the time and state, "It appeared that at the beginning of 2009 the AKP was at a crossroads. It might either return to its old policy of vigorously pursuing the reformist path with the ultimate aim of becoming an EU member, or to compromise with the state elites and accept the status quo perhaps with some minor improvements" (158). The AKP and Erdoğan, however, took none of these paths. Instead, they gradually turned Turkey into an authoritarian one-man regime in the following years.

Unlike their first two terms, the AKP was very confident in their third term in office. This was mainly because of controlling the executive and legislative offices and the result of the 2010 Referendum that reduced the political balancing power of the judiciary and the military. They finally had the ability to reshape the landscape of Turkish politics (Kirdiş 2016, 34). The AKP and Erdoğan, however, used this opportunity to gain even more power in the government for their own benefits. Erdoğan's rule has disregarded and undermined the state's legal and political order and has become increasingly authoritarian and especially repressive against critics. According to the HRW Report published in 2012, the government stopped prioritizing human rights reforms after 2005, and freedom of expression and association were both damaged by the ongoing prosecution of journalists, writers, and hundreds of Kurdish political activists (503). Another report, published by the Committee to Protect Journalists (CPJ) in 2012, states the following about the Erdoğan government's policies towards the media (6):

> The government of Prime Minister Recep Tayyip Erdoğan has waged one of the world's biggest crackdowns on press freedom in recent history. Authorities have imprisoned journalists on a mass scale on terror- ism or anti-state charges, launched thousands of other criminal prosecutions on charges such as denigrating Turkishness or influencing court proceedings, and used pressure tactics to sow self-censorship Erdoğan has publicly deprecated journalists, urged media outlets to discipline or fire critical staff members, and filed numerous high-profile defamation lawsuits.

These authoritarian actions, which were the opposite of what the AKP had done in its first period, led to the erosion of the state's constitutional order and changed the image of Turkey to an authoritarian, unpredictable, and unreliable country (Matusiak 2015, 5). In the following years, freedom of speech and press freedom in Turkey sharply deteriorated as Erdoğan's government became more and more authoritarian.

3.3.2.1 Gezi Park Protests and Corruption Investigations in 2013

As the AKP was becoming more powerful and having more control over the levers of power, they gradually stopped being interested in democracy, Europe, and liberal economics. In their first term, the AKP implemented some of the most thorough economic and political reforms in the history of modern Turkey. These reforms generated an enormous amount of goodwill in the West for Erdoğan and his party, which lasted until the Gezi Park protests in 2013 although the AKP had started to take authoritarian actions long before (Bipartisan Policy Center 2015, 40–41). In 2013, the Gezi Park protests in May, and the corruption investigations against the AKP in December, also known as "the 17–25 December Investigations", became breaking points for Turkish democracy. In response to these events, the AKP government quickly became more authoritarian than ever and Erdoğan became the one-man in control of the whole regime he had established.

Since the AKP's victory in the 2010 referendum, Erdoğan had been heavily using religious and nationalist references in his speeches. For example, in 2012, then Prime Minister Erdoğan declared in public how he and his party defined the role of Islam in current government politics by saying, "We have four main red [important] topics: one state, one nation, one flag and one religion" (Göğüş and Mannitz 2016, 13–14). As a result of the discourse used by Erdoğan, Turkish society was becoming more and more polarized each day. The tensions that had been building up in the society finally exploded in May 2013.

On May 28, a small group of environmentalists started to camp out at Gezi Park, located next to Taksim Square at the center of Istanbul. They were protesting against the government's plan to destroy one of the last public parks in the city to build a shopping mall. In response, the police attacked the protestors by using excessive force. The news and videos of police brutality spread rapidly through social media and sparked massive protests in many cities in Turkey. The police kept using excessive force and brutally attacked the protesters which resulted in the death of some demonstrators. Erdoğan called the demonstrators "vandals" and "unbelievers" who had no respect for the "national will." Erdoğan also accused the protesters of working together with, what he called, the "interest-rate lobby," which supposedly intended to weaken the Turkish economy through the protests while some of the officials of the AKP hinted at a global Jewish conspiracy. During this time, the foreign media and their reporters in Turkey were also heavily targeted by Erdoğan and his party (The Economist 2016, 6; Zürcher 2017, 355–56).

One of the results of the demonstrations is that it caused the AKP and Erdoğan to abandon their understanding of a liberal democracy based on enlarged participation rights as well as tolerance towards the critical voices. Majoritarian rule and freedom of speech were no longer criterions of democracy for Erdoğan (Gögüs and Mannitz 2016, 21–22).

Media During the Gezi Protests

The consequences of the AKP's influence on the Turkish media for the last 10 years had become apparent for the first time during the Gezi Park protests. Many television channels refused to report the demonstrations happening in the biggest cities of Turkey. *CNN Turk* franchise aired a documentary about penguins when the demonstrations first erupted; as a result, the penguin was adapted by the protestors as their visual mascot. Another big and respected television channel, *NTV*, asserted that the protests were a part of a well-organized conspiracy against Turkey. The protestors were already expecting this kind of coverage from the pro-government media, but the portrayal of the demonstrations by the more secular as well as trusted television stations and newspapers was disappointing. Erdoğan's control on the media eventually pushed people to social media where they were able to access news reported without the influence of the government (Finkel 2015, 18).

The deterioration of fundamental human rights in Turkey became more apparent and obvious with the way the government handled the Gezi Park protests and aftermath. The police used brutal methods to stop the demonstrations. Many journalists were imprisoned. Internet bans on social media platforms such as Twitter, Facebook and YouTube were imposed. These social media platforms were frequently used by the protestors for communication and to communicate information to each other as the Turkish media refused to report the events (Gögüs, Mannitz 2016, 26).

The Gezi Park protests also accelerated the dismissal of journalists who had dissenting opinions against the government. Some newspapers fired their senior columnists and other journalists with arbitrary excuses. For instance, *Sabah* newspaper dismissed its ombudsman, Yavuz Baydar, simply for doing his job and trying to deal with reader complaints. Some other examples include a health correspondent who was fired for criticizing a hospital care and a duty photographer for talking with his protester friend on his way to work (Finkel 2015, 9).

2013 Corruption Investigation

December 2013 is usually considered as the turning point of the AKP's and Erdoğan's stance towards democracy and rule of law. On December 17, the Turkish police arrested 47 people for being involved in a corruption circle. These people included businessmen, state officials, and sons of some of the AKP cabinet ministers. Soon after, recordings of the suspects' phone conversations, including the ones with Erdoğan, leaked and circulated on the internet. Erdoğan denied the authenticity of the tapes. The recordings revealed the AKP's system of nepotism and influence-peddling, mostly in being linked with profitable construction deals being given to the party loyalists (The Economist, 2016, 6). In retaliation, the AKP government sought to restrict police power and extend executive power over the establishment that administers the judiciary. In addition to reallocating judges and police officers, the government also arrested police officers who took part in the corruption probe (HRW 2014a).

Erdoğan called the corruption investigations a plot against his government conducted by a "parallel structure." He made it clear that a state within the state must be eliminated. During his hostile election campaign, Erdoğan accused both liberal opposition and the Gülen Movement as plotters and proxies who worked for "interest lobbies". As a result, the AKP won the March 2014 municipal elections (Zürcher 2017, 358).

The authoritarian policies of Erdoğan government became even more manifest during the anti-government Gezi Park protests in May 2013 and the huge corruption scandal in December 2013. The Turkish government already had a long tradition of limiting press freedom, social media, and rights for the unions and organizations. After the 2013 Gezi protests, the AKP government heightened the restrictions in these areas. The AKP also attempted to prevent discussions and information concerning the December 2014 corruption probe by blocking YouTube and Twitter in the country. Between 2013 and 2014, many media workers lost their jobs including well-respected mainstream journalists and writers who were outspoken against the government (HRW 2015, 549).

Erdoğan scaled up the purge of state institutions by getting rid of the suspected members of the Gülen Movement. Since early 2015, pro-government media has adopted a new term for the movement which was previously called "Parallel Structure;" It was now called the "Fethullahist Terrorist Organization (FETO)." In addition, the Gezi Protests were still in the memory of the Erdoğan government which increased the pressure on the remaining independent media. Critical websites and social media accounts were systematically shut down. The AKP and pro-government media has increasingly used anti-western rhetoric mostly hinting that the Gülen Movement, the PKK (Kurdistan Workers' Party), and the independent media serve the interests of foreign powers and receive protection from these powers (Zürcher 2017, xi).

In June 2015 Elections, the AKP lost the majority in the parliament. However, the opposition parties failed in forming a government, and Turkey went to the ballot box one more time on November 15, 2015. The AKP secured a precious victory and guaranteed a fourth term in the office. The AKP and the President, elected in 2014, continued policies that violated human rights, democracy, and the rule of law in Turkey. After the election in November 2015, the AKP government also halted the peace talks with the PKK and started an intense military offensive against them in southeastern regions in Turkey. Emma Sinclair-Webb, senior Turkey researcher at the HRW, said "Turkey's trajectory is toward authoritarianism and the dismantling of all checks on the power of its leaders. The combination of the breakdown of the

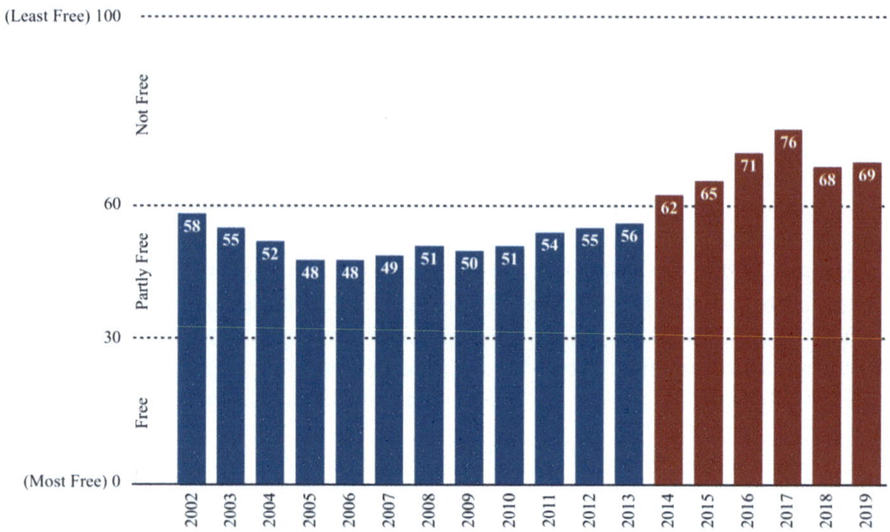

Fig. 3.1 Press Freedom Scores of Turkey, Reported by *Freedom House* (The data for the years 2018 and 2019 are based on "Freedom in the World" reports).

Kurdish peace process and crackdown on media and political opponents over the past year spell dark times ahead and take Turkey further away from the goal of being a rights-respecting country" (HRW 2016a).

Turkey, From "Partly Free" To "Not Free"

After the 2013 corruption investigations, the government tightened internet laws and blocked Twitter and YouTube for several weeks in the country as these social media platforms were mainly used to spread the leaked phone calls implicating ministers and family members in corruption. This prompted a joint statement from three United Nations special rapporteurs. The Constitutional Court ruled against the blocking orders in April and May, and as a result, both Twitter and YouTube reopened shortly after (HRW Report 2015, 549). Journalists were harassed and assaulted during and following the aftermath of the Gezi Park protests, and dozens were dismissed or forced to resign from their positions due to their reports on the demonstrations. The same year, other prominent journalists were fired over their coverage of "sensitive issues" that could weaken Erdoğan and the AKP. As a result of this sharp deterioration in press freedom, Turkey's status declined from "Partly Free" to "Not Free" with the worst score it had received since the AKP came to power in 2002 (Freedom House 2014, 11–12). In the following years, Turkey's press freedom score would continue to deteriorate and reach record low numbers, especially after the July 15th Coup Attempt in 2016 (Fig. 3.1).

According to the HRW Annual Report in 2016, human rights in Turkey deteriorated as the fragile Kurdish peace process ended in 2015 which was followed by the escalation of violence in southeastern Turkey. The government also continued its crackdown, much more aggressively, on the media as well as political opponents of the government and Erdoğan.

> In November 2015, *Cumhuriyet*'s editor Can Dündar and journalist Erdem Gül were arrested and jailed pending trial. In October, police raided the İpek Media group, including TV stations and newspapers, two days after the government had appointed trustees to run the parent company, Koza İpek Holding. The government similarly moved against the Samanyolu Broadcasting Group, by ending distribution of its TV channels on the state-owned TURKSAT satellite dish distribution platform. The publisher Cevheri Güven and editor Murat Çapan of weekly news magazine *Nokta* were arrested and jailed pending trial for "inciting an armed insurrection against the government" for a satirical picture of Erdoğan and report.
>
> Journalists continued to be fired from mainstream press outlets in 2015 for critical reporting, commentary, and tweets. Social media postings critical of the president and politicians by ordinary people also led to criminal defamation charges and convictions. A new trend in 2015 saw courts in several cases order pretrial detention of people for several months for allegedly insulting Erdoğan via social media or during demonstrations. In March 2015, parliament passed new legislation allowing ministers to request the Communications Directorate (TİB) to block online content or remove it within four hours to "protect life and property, national security, the public order, [or] to prevent crime and to protect general health." A court must approve the decision within 48 hours (580–82).

The annual report published by the Freedom House in 2016 also points out that media freedom in Turkey deteriorated at an alarming rate in 2015:

> Erdoğan government started to use the penal code, criminal defamation legislation, and the country's antiterrorism law aggressively to punish critical reporting while journalists faced growing violence, harassment, and intimidation from both state and nonstate actors throughout the year. The most aggressive form of state intervention against media enterprises was the direct seizure of assets. Several major media outlets were seized by the government and swiftly turned into government mouthpieces. The state-owned national broadcaster and news agency also became propaganda tools for Erdoğan while he repeatedly interfered with the rest of the media outlets' editorial decisions and exerted pressure on them to fire critical journalists. (26 April 2016)

From the time they came to power in 2002 to the 2015 General Elections in which the AKP lost the parliamentary majority, the AKP and its policies changed drastically. The AKP started as a government committed to civil libertarianism and decentralization but turned into a regime that is careless of the rule of law, intolerant, discriminatory, and committed to ideological uniformity (Finkel 2015, 9).

3.3.2.2 Freedom of the Media After the July 15 Coup Attempt

Turkey's political system has undergone a significant change under Erdoğan's leadership. Erdoğan and the AKP managed to break down a sclerotic semi-authoritarian form of government, a regime of military tutelage, and the identity of the informal rulers of the regime. They, however, failed to break down the structure of the regime itself. In fact, once Erdoğan overcame the former regime and its instruments, he immediately started to build a new form of semi-authoritarian government by promoting a presidential system in which he would be the sole ruler without checks and balances (Bipartisan Policy Center 2015, 57).

The reasons behind the July 15th Coup Attempt and the details about it still remain a mystery to this day. What is known is the fact that it was defined as a "gift from God" by Erdoğan and it gave him an excuse to carry out a widespread purge and crackdown on all opposition while expanding his hold over the state. Shortly after the coup attempt, the government declared a state of emergency for 3 months which was expanded multiple times and eventually ended long after in July 2018. With the State of Emergency, Erdoğan gained the power of presiding over the cabinet, issuing decrees that bypassed Parliament and preventing them from being appealed at the Constitutional Court (Lord 2018, 275).

Although it was not clear who exactly was behind the coup attempt, Erdoğan, his government and the pro-government media pointed the finger at the Gülen Movement, referred by the government as the "Fethullahist Terrorist Organization (FETO)," as the only power behind the plot. As a result, a huge purge began targeting anyone who was suspicious of having the remotest link with the Gulenists (Zürcher 2017, xi). The government issued decrees that undermined the foundations of the rule of law by claiming to fight threats to "national security and unity." This opened the way to arbitrary arrests and dismissals as well as direct interference to the judicial system by the government. The witch-hunt targeted the allegedly pro-Gulen media and journalists but also the representatives of the Kurdish, secularist and left-wing media outlets. The prosecutors and judges who expressed any sympathy for the Gülen Movement were directly accused of being a part of the failed coup (RSF 2016, 2–3). Expressing sympathy, of course, also meant giving the government critics a fair trial instead of giving them the sentence that Erdoğan and his government wanted.

In the English Pen report, published in 2018, the government's authoritarian actions against freedom of expression after the coup attempt is discussed as follows:

> Even prior to the failed coup, criminal investigations and prosecutions were a course of action used to silence dissent, alongside prior restraints on publications; legal action aimed at inflicting harm; abuse of the legal right of reply in print media; forced removal of internet content, news reports and social media posts, especially by the opposition; frequent blocking of websites and social media platforms; administrative sanctions and tax investigations against media outlets and their owners; and forced dismissal of journalists critical of the government and its policies. All of these are ongoing interventions carried out within the 'boundaries of the law'. These wide-ranging and systematic practices and their silencing and chilling effects were never confined to print and broadcast media and journalists. However, in the post-coup period following 15 July 2016, they have been extended to regularly target NGOs, human rights activists, businesspeople, writers, publishers, scholars and academic institutions (Akdeniz and Altıparmak 2018, 3).

Mass Arrests of Journalists

In the first 2 months of the State of Emergency, dozens of renowned journalists, including leading reporters and editors of newspaper and magazines, were placed in detention or arrested and a total of 620 press credentials were canceled. The scale of the roundups of jailed journalists was astonishing. For instance, 42 arrest warrants were issued on journalists on July 25, and another 47 were issued 2 days later. Reporters Without Borders (RSF) analyzed the attained interrogation records and stated that "many journalists are being targeted above all for working for media sympathetic to the Gülen Movement. Their work as journalists is equated to membership of the movement, and this in turn is equated to complicity in the coup attempt" (2016, 5).

Following the coup attempt, 160 media outlets, allegedly associated with the Gülen Movement or Kurdish media, were shut down by government decrees. In mid-November, the number of journalists in pretrial detention on the basis of their writing and journalistic activities raised to 144, making Turkey the worldwide leader in jailing journalists. Many of these reporters and columnists were detained with no evidence (HRW 2017, 603). Among those jailed were veteran journalists and commentators who have been prominent liberal intellectuals and government critics, such as Nazlı Ilıcak, Şahin Alpay, Ahmet Altan, and Mehmet Altan. Nazlı Ilıcak, a 73 years old veteran journalist, was a former supporter of Erdoğan's early reforms and the Virtue Party (FP) representative in the parliament. She had been dismissed from her position at the pro-government daily, *Sabah*, in 2013 for stating that the government ministers who were implicated in December 2013 corruption investigations should resign and face trial. She then started to write at the oppositional *Özgür Düşünce,* one of the 160 media outlets that were closed down after the coup attempt (RSF World Report 2016, 5).

The government also detained many journalists and writers by accusing them of having ties with the PKK, with no evidence. Among these were famous Turkish literary critic, Necmiye Alpay, and novelist, Aslı Erdoğan. In August 2016, a pro-Kurdish daily, *Özgür Gündem,* was shut down by authorities. Many journalists had participated in solidarity campaigns to support the newspaper, and as a result, dozens of them were put under investigation for "spreading terrorist propaganda." In November, Murat Sabuncu, who became the editor of *Cumhuriyet* after Dündar, and nine writers and board members of the oldest newspaper of Turkey were arrested (HRW World Report 2017, 603).

Although the state-owned media had always been a supporter of Erdoğan and taken direct orders from him, hundreds of employees of the state-owned news agency *Anadolu* and the state-owned broadcaster *TRT* were also dismissed from their positions and became victims of Erdoğan's purge (RSF 2016, 10).

According to Committee to Protect Journalists (CPJ), the number of imprisoned journalists in Turkey rose from 14 to 86 in 2016, which made Turkey the world's worst jailer of journalists. In 2016, Turkey was accountable for more than 30% of all imprisoned journalists worldwide and more than double the amount of its closest rival, China. The promising era that started with the AKP reforms and decrease in the number of jailed journalists completely ended. Since 2016, Turkey has remained the world's worst jailer of journalists (Fig. 3.2).

Purge of Academics and Journalists

According to Akdeniz and Altıparmak (2018, 13–14) the "general term to describe the new State of Emergency is 'lustration.'" Under the State of Emergency, the AKP government embarked on sweeping purges against the Gülen Movement, which the government claimed to have been behind the coup attempt, as well as the Kurds and other groups and organizations that the government saw as a danger to national security. Public institutions as well as the private sector took their part in the purge.

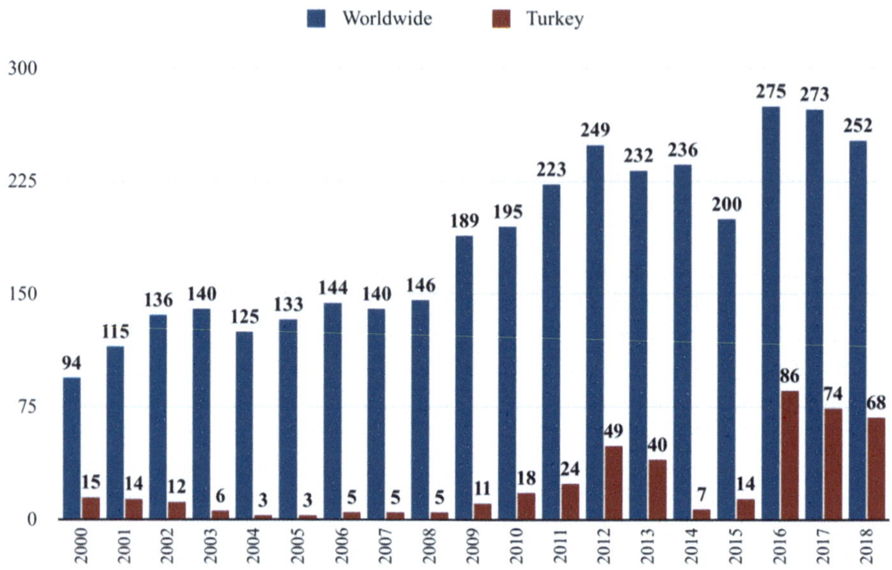

Fig. 3.2 Number of Imprisoned Journalists (CPJ)

Most of these private establishments were educational institutions and media outlets (Aydin and Avincan 2020). According to the State of Emergency Report of IHOP (2018, 45–51) "a total of 179 media agencies and publishing and distribution companies were shut down during the State of Emergency. These were 7 news agencies, 50 newspapers, 20 periodicals, 39 radio stations, 33 Television channels and 30 publishing houses and distribution companies."

As Akdeniz and Altıparmak said (2018, 14), the methods of the purge resembled the legacy of the Eastern European experience after the cold war. Contrary to these countries, there was no regime change in Turkey, and the purge process was not based on predetermined rules or consequences of investigations. The lustration process was executed through arbitrary Emergency Decrees.

According to the IHOP Report of 2018, 112,679 civil servants have been dismissed from their positions. 5705 of these were academics who were dismissed from 119 public universities. Of the dismissed academics 386 were the signatories of "Academics for Peace" who condemned the government-conducted military operations against the Kurdish regions in Turkey in January 2016. 3041 academics working at 15 foundation universities, which were closed down by government decrees, became unemployed in this period too (24,39,44).

In July 2018, the State of Emergency was finally lifted after 2 years of being in effect. However, the new counterterrorism legislation, passed in parliament in August 2018, gave authorities similar powers to which they had during the emergency rule. Turkey still ranked as the number one for jailing journalists in the world. According to the HRW report "an estimated 175 journalists and media workers are in pretrial detention or serving sentences for terrorism offenses at the time of writing.

Hundreds more are on trial but at liberty. Most media lack independence and promote the government's political line" (2019, 588–89).

In 2018, the courts came to their final decisions concerning politically motivated trials of journalists. These trials were based on journalistic activities that did not support violence but were accused of having links to terrorist organizations as well as the coup attempt. Prominent writers and critics like Ahmet Altan, Mehmet Altan, and Nazlı Ilıcak were given life sentences without parole on false charges of being involved in the coup attempt. The courts also issued a verdict for the trial of *Cumhuriyet* newspaper staff including journalists, executives, and editors. Fourteen of them were given sentences from two to eight years in prison on baseless terrorism charges. Some websites including Wikipedia remained blocked, and online content removal continued. Thousands of people went through investigations and prosecutions for their social media posts (HRW Report 2019, 588–89).

As the RSF reported, "persecution of critics had already been growing in before the state of emergency in Turkey in what was the clearest sign of President Erdoğan's authoritarian tendencies. Judicial harassment of journalists, systematic internet censorship, curbs on pluralism and the increasingly concentrated ownership of leading media outlets in the hands of the government's friends had become the norm. The state of emergency removed the few remaining safety nets and brought arbitrary governmental decision-making to new unprecedented heights: journalists have been jailed without any reason being given, media outlets have been closed with the stroke of pen, and punitive measures have been taken without any form of trial" (2016, 4).

The July 15 Coup Attempt turned into an unprecedented twist for the Turkish media. After the coup attempt, the State of Emergency was declared, and lasted for 2 years. During this period, the Turkish government implemented an immense purge against the critics of Erdoğan. Hundreds of critical journalists were arrested, making Turkey the world's biggest jailer of journalists in a short period of time (Freedom House 2017). With the emergency degrees issued during this time, over hundreds of newspapers, news agencies, radio stations, television networks, and magazines were shut down which caused over thousands of journalists to lose their jobs. About 889 press cards were cancelled by the government. (Hurriyet Daily News 2017). As Akdeniz and Altıparmak stated (2018, 43), "The grave picture observed prior to the attempted coup of 15 July 2016 has turned into one in which media freedom in particular has been completely undermined since the declaration of the State of Emergency."

Discourse of the Government and Media

Following the failed coup attempt in July 2016, Erdoğan embarked on a series of brutal and arbitrary purges in the military, police, judiciary, media and education, targeting the Gulenists, liberals, leftists, and Kurdish opposition. The use of conspiratorial and anti-Western rhetoric played a key role for Erdoğan in gaining popular support to carry out massive purges and to push through draconian laws. The rhetoric Erdoğan used set the stage for him to establish a one-man regime and cut Turkey off from the West.

Erdoğan used the coup attempt to control the polarized Turkish society as one through his discourse of defending Turkey against "internal traitors" and enemies of the state that were controlled by other countries. (Yılmaz et al. 2019, 8). The self-censorship in Turkish media helped Erdoğan easily control the public discourse. Erdoğan depicted himself as the main victim of the coup attempt which enabled him to unite the Turkish society, regardless of their political opinions, against the coup attempt and a common external enemy, the West. By uniting the polarized Turkish society against the Gülen Movement, the Kurdish opposition and their Western allies, Erdoğan consolidated all of the power in Turkey. Standing against Erdoğan or criticizing his policies became synonymous with supporting the coup plotters or being a Gulenist (Guiler 2016, 28–31).

3.3.3 The Methods and Instruments Used by Erdogan to Silence the Media

Turkey's media was a clear example of the AKP's domination in the public area. Pressuring private media bosses, using the laws against incitement, defamation, and the spread of terrorist propaganda were the methods of the AKP to eventually have a grip over the entirety of Turkish media excluding a few broadcasters and publishers (The Economist 2016, 5).

The long-time assaults on independent media and crackdown on press freedom intensified by the government after the coup attempt in 2016. Censorship of journalism had always been employed as a method for a long time, but President Erdoğan and the AKP government utilized more creative methods to silence critics (HRW 2016, 2).

In the 80s and 90s of Turkey, most of the freedom expression related prosecutions were about the defamation of Atatürk, Turkishness, and the national integrity of Turkey. According to Akdeniz and Altıparmak (2018 5), "under the rule of the AKP, these have been replaced by prosecutions involving denigration of religion, the government and defamation of the President. In terms of attacking freedoms, the AKP government developed a much more subtle and sophisticated mechanism involving different methods, in contrast with the 'rough' methods employed in the 80s and 90s. It not only employs prosecutions and criminal sanctions but also prior restraints, decisions of the newly established Criminal Judgeships for Peace blocking access to websites and social media platforms, harsh governmental control exercised by the Supreme Board of Radio and Television (RTUK), and onslaughts by pro-government media outlets against journalists and newspapers."

As the HRW specified (2017, 602) "the government-led efforts to silence media criticism and scrutiny of government policy in Turkey involves five main trends: the prosecution and jailing of journalists; takeover of media companies by appointing government-approved trustees and seizing assets and the closing down of media; removal of critical television stations from the main state-owned satellite distribution platform and their closure; physical attacks and threats against journalists; and government pressure on media to fire critical journalists and cancel their press accreditation. Blocking of news websites critical to the government also increased. Turkey made the highest number of requests to Twitter of any country to censor individual accounts."

The AKP government and President Erdoğan have used various methods, some of which were used by the state in the past, to control and silence the media. In this chapter, these methods will be classified under the following headings:

1. Transferring media ownership in favor of the government.
2. Economic and financial support or suppression.
3. Judicial suppression: the prosecution and jailing of journalists.
4. Confiscation of media groups.
5. Other Methods.

3.3.3.1 Transferring the Media Ownership

Many media conglomerates had already collapsed due to the 2001 Turkish Economic Crisis, and therefore the state was the largest media boss in Turkey when the AKP came to power in 2002. Erdoğan used this situation in favor of his government and supporters. He handed over the state-owned media outlets to businessmen who had ties with him. Those transferred media corporations were gradually turned into propaganda organs of the AKP government, followed by the dismissal of critical columnists and journalists.

Turkey's media played a significant role in maintaining public support for the AKP, and therefore it was crucial for Erdoğan to control the entire media. He and his party came to exercise control over all media by putting pressure on private owners who were not supporters of Erdoğan. They utilized state power to their advantage and made arbitrary laws against incitement, defamation and the spread of "terrorist propaganda." Eventually, only a small number of broadcasters and news publishers were able to criticize Erdoğan's actions in Turkey (The Economist 2016, 5).

In terms of media ownership, the biggest winner of the 2001 Turkish Economic Crisis was *Dogan Group*. As its rivals were wiped out during and after the crisis due to varying reasons, Dogan ended up controlling about 40% of the Turkish media as the biggest media conglomerate in the country in 2004 (Öncü 2012, 129).

The circumstances that helped the AKP come to power in 2002 also put many large media groups in public receivership. The government eventually transformed these media groups into business conglomerates controlled by supporters of the AKP. For instance, the government seized the assets of *Ciner Group*, owner of *Sabah* newspaper and *ATV*, and sold off many of its media properties to *Calık Group*, a conglomerate run by Erdoğan's son-in-law, Berat Albayrak, who would later serve as a minister in Erdoğan's cabinets in different positions. *Calık Group* was the sole bidder in the auction and purchased the properties with the help of loans from two state banks. *Cukurova Media Group*, which owned *Akşam* and *Güneş* newspapers as well as *Sky360 TV*, was seized in a similar way in 2013 and sold off to another businessman from Erdoğan's close circle (CPJ 2012, 12; Finkel 2015, 15).

3.3.3.2 Economic and Financial Support or Suppression

Many businessmen had gained prominence under the AKP government as a result of their support to Erdoğan. For instance, Hasan Kalyoncu, the owner of *Kalyon Group*, played a role in the establishment of the AKP and had been closely associated with the Islamist Movement in Turkey, and therefore was rewarded by Erdoğan many times. *Kalyon Group* has been a key beneficiary of public tenders since the AKP came to power. They were given many state projects by the government including major infrastructure projects worth an estimated 100 billion TRY. In return, *Kalyon Group* helped Erdoğan acquire media groups, such as *Sabah* and *ATV*, and turn them into government mouthpieces in a short span of time (Lord 2018, 265).

Erdoğan also used government instruments to punish and tame media groups and other business conglomerates that challenged his policies. In 2011, *Dogan Group* was forced to sell some of its media properties, such as *Milliyet*, due to their giant tax fine assessing $2.5 billion. The tax fine was clearly Erdoğan's politically motivated move to tame *Dogan Group* and its flagship, *Hürriyet*, due to their increasing criticism against the government and their influence on public opinion (CPJ 2012, 12–28).

3.3.3.3 Judicial Suppressions

The exploitation of the criminal justice system is another one of Erdoğan's methods to suppress free media. The core of all human rights problems in Turkey, including press freedom violations caused by the faulty rule of law, is a profound structural issue. Without addressing this problem, it is impossible to explain any issue regarding fundamental rights in Turkey. Constant abuse in the judiciary during the last decade turned the judiciary into a government instrument. After winning the 2010 constitutional referendum, the AKP took control of the High Council of Judges and Prosecutors.

New changes on the Criminal Procedure Law eliminated the Criminal Courts of Peace, whose judgments could be contested before Criminal Courts of First Instance and forming the Criminal Judgeships for Peace. Now, a decision made by a Criminal Judgeship for Peace could only be challenged before another Criminal Judgeship for Peace (Akdeniz and Altıparmak 2018, 8-9). With these new amendments, the Criminal Judgeships for Peace was established in June 2014, and it has become the most effective tool used by the Erdoğan regime to silence journalists, academics, writers and all opposition.

The AKP government and Erdoğan carried out a massive purge in the judiciary and tightened its grip on it after the July 15 coup attempt. According to Akdeniz and Altıparmak, "A total of 4,140 judges and prosecutors were dismissed from office including 333 judges and two prosecutors of the Court of Cassation, 276 members of the Council of State, two chief public prosecutors, 1,280 public prosecutors, 2,346 criminal and civil court judges and two members of the Constitutional Court. Of these, 2,200 were placed in detention" (2018, 10).

In the June 2018 parliamentary and presidential elections, Recep Tayyip Erdoğan was reelected to the office, and the AKP retained control of the parliament through a coalition with the nationalist party. The June 2018 elections took place under the State of Emergency which was declared after the coup attempt in July 2016. The election campaigns were carried out in a climate where media censorship and repression of perceived government enemies and critics continued throughout the year. During the elections, many journalists, parliamentarians from the opposition, and the pro-Kurdish party's presidential candidate were jailed. According to the HRW Report, "The election brought into force the presidential system of governance agreed in a 2017 referendum. The system lacked sufficient checks and balances against abuse of executive power, greatly diminished the powers of parliament and consolidates presidential control over most judicial appointments" (2019, 588).

The AKP government also increased the pressure on judges and prosecutors. If they issued verdicts which the AKP did not like, they would find themselves unemployed or languishing in prison. During the first hearing of journalists who were accused of having ties with terrorist organizations, the court decided to release 21 defendants who were held at lengthy pre-trial detention. However, the pro-government media was quick to fiercely criticize the court's decision of releasing the defendants. An appeal against the release of eight of the 21 and a new investigation against the other 13 were issued; therefore, none of the defendants were released. Afterwards, the High Council of Judges and Prosecutors suspended the three judges who made the decision to release the journalists and the prosecutor at the hearing (HRW World Report 2017, 561–62).

In their article published by English PEN, Akdeniz and Altıparmak states as follows:

> In Turkey under the rule of Erdoğan, not even high judges and courts have any safeguards against the government. Within a period of seven years, hundreds of judges in the highest courts of the country were replaced and thousands of judges and prosecutors were arrested and detained. Under these conditions, it is evident that no judge can pass an independent judgment in any case that is likely to have political implications. More importantly, writers, academics, journalists and individuals with oppositional views are announced as having links with multiple illegal organizations despite a lack of any concrete evidence. Again, the various illegal organizations, which have nothing in common with one another, are given joint reference in investigations with no evidence whatsoever and a vast number of people are placed in detention on grounds such as membership to such organizations. In reaching these conclusions, articles written by journalists, their remarks on television shows and social media posts are presented as the sole evidence of their crime (2018, 11).

On March 3, 2011, nine journalists and writers were arrested for allegedly having ties to the "Ergenekon Terrorist Organization" (ETÖ or Ergenekon). Two journalists, Ahmet Şık and Nedim Şener, who were outspoken critics of the Turkish criminal justice system and police, were arrested. On February 17, three other *Oda*

TV journalists—Soner Yalçın, Barış Pehlivan and Barış Terkoğlu were detained and held in pre-trial detention on various charges including being a member of Ergenekon. Two other journalists, Mustafa Balbay and Tuncay Özkan, had already been behind bars for 2 years and two and half years respectively on charges of being a member of the same organization (HRW 2011). While the Ergenekon trials were ongoing, Erdoğan had declared, "I am the prosecutor of Ergenekon" (Vatan 2008).

According to The Committee to Protect Journalists (CPJ) "about 30 percent of journalists jailed in August 2012 were accused of taking part in anti-government plots or being members of outlawed political groups. Several have been linked to the alleged Ergenekon conspiracy, which prosecutors have described as a vast plot aimed at overthrowing the government through a military coup. According to the government's theory, journalists were using news coverage to create the kind of societal chaos conducive to a coup" (2012, 6).

In its 2012 report, the CPJ stated the following about the Erdoğan government's policies towards the media:

> The government of Prime Minister Recep Tayyip Erdoğan has waged one of the world's biggest crackdowns on press freedom in recent history. Authorities have imprisoned journalists on a mass scale on terrorism or anti-state charges, launched thousands of other criminal prosecutions on charges such as denigrating Turkishness or influencing court proceedings, and used pressure tactics to sow self-censorship. Erdoğan has publicly deprecated journalists, urged media outlets to discipline or fire critical staff members, and filed numerous high-profile defamation lawsuits (2012, 6).

On December 14, 2014, Turkey's biggest circulation daily, *Zaman* newspaper's editor, Ekrem Dumanlı and a columnist from the daily were arrested. The head of national *Samanyolu Broadcasting Group*, Hidayet Karaca, three workers from the group, and a journalist from *Bugün* newspaper were also arrested. In a speech on December 12, Erdoğan hinted that the arrests of others would soon be carried out. "The timing of this operation had coincided almost exactly a year after the December 17, 2013, corruption allegations broke," said the HRW (2014b). *Zaman* and *Samanyolu*'s reporting had mainly focused on the corruption investigation related arrests and allegations.

The AKP government's influence on the judiciary had become increasingly apparent. If the government did not like the decision of the Constitutional Court, which is the last stop internally to reverse the human rights violations, the first courts were able to ignore the ruling. Disregarding the judgments of Constitutional courts by the local courts, the country's rule of law and constitution were dragged into a crisis, and therefore freedom of expression in Turkey was also in a crisis (Akdeniz and Altıparmak 2018, 11).

"I don't concur with the decision and I have no respect for it," Erdoğan said on February 28, 2016 regarding the Constitutional Court ruling that paved the way for the release of *Cumhuriyet* editor-in-chief Can Dündar and Ankara bureau chief Erdem Gül who were arrested on terror and espionage charges (Hurriyet Daily News 2016).

After the December 2013 Corruption Probe, the editors, journalists, and columnists linked to the Gülen Movement and some other critical journalists were arrested and held in pretrial detention, joining the Kurdish and leftist journalists who used to be the main victims of lengthy pretrial detention on terrorism charges. After the failed coup attempt, the prosecution of journalists who were associated with the Gülen Movement reached a zenith. Nearly 80 journalists were placed in pretrial detention for having ties to the Gülen Movement or the failed coup attempt. On October 2016, eleven senior staff members of *Cumhuriyet* newspaper along with its editor-in-chief were arrested on charges of being associated with both the PKK and the Gülen Movement (HRW 2016, 3–5).

Erdoğan's fierce criticism or the pro-government media's organized smear campaign, which recycled the same reports and articles, usually stimulated the judicial process to begin and prosecutors to take action against the people targeted by Erdogan. This would not only intimidate the people who were being investigated but also those who held similar opinions (Akdeniz and Altıparmak 2018, 43).

3.3.3.4 Confiscation of Media Groups

Among the Turkish constitutions, the 1961 Constitution is considered to hold the most liberal regulation for the freedom of the press. After 1923 when the Republic of Turkey was born as well as the single-party era and multi-party period after 1946, governments tended to keep the press under control and avoid diverse voices. Because of negative experiences in the past, articles protecting freedom of expression and the press had been included in the new constitution in 1961. Article 33, which was also kept in the following 1982 Constitution, is as follows:

> **Article 30.** A printing house and its annexes, duly established as a press enterprise under law, and press equipment shall not be seized, confiscated, or barred from operation on the grounds of having been used in a crime.

Despite the explicitly stated article in the constitution, the Erdoğan government seized the opposition media and quickly converted them into government mouthpieces. Before the July 15 failed coup attempt, in 2015 and 2016, the AKP government confiscated two major private media companies which owned several television and radio stations as well as newspapers. The government appointed trustees to those private media companies, and pro-government broadcasting and publishing by these media companies started the next day.

In October 2015, the Turkish police stormed the *Ipek Media Group* including its television stations and newspapers two days after the government appointed trustees to its parent company, *Koza Ipek Holding*. The trustees fired the staff and appointed new editors to turn them into pro-government media organs (HRW World Report 2016, 582). In March 2016, the government appointed trustees to *Feza Media Group*. This decision by an Istanbul prosecutor displayed the president's and government's efforts to silence the critical media. Consequently, *Feza Media Group* which owned *Zaman* newspaper, *Today's Zaman, Aksiyon* and *Cihan News Agency* were taken over by the government. (HRW 2016b). These two media companies were forced to shift their editorial policies and transform their television channels and newspapers to become pro-government. Feza Group's *Zaman* had lost a significant number of subscribers. After the failed coup attempt in 2016, over 100 media outlets were shut down by the government along with Ipek and Feza Media Groups for their alleged links to the Gülen Movement (HRW 2016, 6).

3.3.3.5 Other Methods of the AKP Government

Violence Against Journalists
Many oppositional journalists and their families were threatened and attacked by Erdoğan supporters as a result of being pointed as a target by the pro-Erdoğan media as well as Erdoğan himself. These attacks aimed to silence government critics and force them to self-exile.

For instance, on September 9, 2015, Cem Küçük, who worked at pro-government daily *Star* and was known for targeting government critics, wrote a column about Ahmet Hakan, a prominent columnist working at *Hürriyet* and a TV political talk-show host. In reference to Hakan, Küçük stated, “Like schizophrenia patients, you think you are still living in the days when *Hürriyet* was running the country. If we want, we can squash you like a fly. You are only still alive because we have showed mercy so far.” After the article was published, Hakan started to receive serious threats, and he was violently assaulted near his home in Istanbul a couple of weeks later. He sustained multiple injuries including a broken nose and ribs.

On May 6, 2016, Can Dündar, *Cumhuriyet's* editor-in-chief, faced an assassination attempt. A gunman attacked and shot at Dündar while he was standing with his wife outside a courthouse awaiting the verdict in a controversial case accusing him and Erdem Gül, *Cumhuriyet*'s Ankara bureau chief, of revealing state secrets. Erdoğan had threatened both journalists in public many times before the attack, saying they will “pay the price” (HRW 2016, 35–37; CNN 2016).

On July 5, 2019, Turkey's Foundation for Political, Economic, and Social Research (SETA), a pro-government organization that has close ties with the ruling AKP, released a report that targets various journalists working for foreign media outlets and described them as “anti-government” and “pro-terrorism” (SETA 2019). The report accused the journalists of being biased against Turkey and making false news to damage Turkey's reputation. It also included the photos of these journalists and columnists, including Gülsüm Alan, Ece Temelkuran, Barbaros Şansal, Fatih Polat and Banu Güven, as well as schemes demonstrating where they worked in the past and who they were in contact with.

Removal of Critical TV Channels
Another silencing method of the government was ordering the removal of oppositional television channels from satellite distribution and digital platforms which eventually led to the shutdown of those TV channels.

In October 2015, Turkey's most popular satellite network and TV operator, *Digiturk*, stopped streaming seven critical TV channels to its customers. Turkey's largest and state-controlled signal provider, *TÜRKSAT*, followed *Digiturk* by also dropping the seven channels from its service despite a warning issued by the Supreme Radio and Television Board (RTÜK). The warning from RTÜK stated that the channels' removal violated the requirements for broadcasting platform operators to be impartial and was inconsistent with standard legal procedure. A couple of months later on February 24, 2016, *TÜRKSAT* also removed the signal of independent opposition television channel *İMC TV* after receiving a letter from the government about an investigation accusing the channel of spreading terrorist propaganda (HRW 2016, 61–62).

3.3.4 Erdoğan's Direct Intervention in Media Content and His Hate Speech Against the Opposition

3.3.4.1 Interfering in Media Content

The content of Turkish newspapers and television channels was constantly intervened by Erdoğan. This could be clearly seen in one of the leaked recordings between Erdoğan and a *Habertürk* senior executive, which spread on YouTube and Twitter. The recording demonstrates how Erdoğan controls the way the private *Habertürk* television channel covers its news. He insults and yells at the senior executive on the phone for broadcasting the views of an opposition politician on the news ticker. As a result of the phone call, the part about the opposition politician was quickly removed from the news ticker (Hurriyet Daily News 2014a).

In another leaked phone conversation, Erdoğan addresses the elderly head of the *Demirören Group* and makes him cry due to a story about government's Kurdish policy published in his newspaper, *Milliyet*. "How did I get involved in this business?" the head asks between sobs. In addition to media, *Demirören*'s other interests include property development and liquefied natural gas enterprises dependent on Erdoğan's grace and favor (Finkel 2015, 10).

In 2016, emails belonging to Berat Albayrak, Erdoğan's son-in-law and then-energy minister, were leaked by a hacking group called *Redhack*. One of the emails revealed that the head of *Doğan Media Group* was regularly reporting to Albayrak on editorial decisions (HRW 2016, 56).

Seeing newspapers with the exact same pro-government headlines has become something usual in Erdoğan's Turkey. During the Gezi Park protests, "Democracy demands sacrifice," was the copycat headline of six separate pro-government newspapers on a single day, depicting Erdoğan as the real victim, instead of the protestors, and as though he was ready to lay down his life (Finkel 2015, 19).

3.3.4.2 Use of Hate Speech Against the Opposition

Erdoğan frequently targeted, vilified, threatened and insulted opposition groups, government critics, journalists, and academics. Over the years, hate speech became a political tool for Erdoğan to maintain his public support. Even in 2012, he was particularly harsh and confrontational against the oppositional media and publicly scolded individual journalist, filed legal complaints against them and put pressure on to the media outlets to silence oppositional voices. Many media outlets have demoted or fired prominent columnist and commentators who were against Erdoğan's policies (CPJ 2012, 11).

A TV program, run by Nuray Mert, who is a journalist and an academic, had been abruptly taken off the air after Erdoğan targeted her in one of his election campaign speeches in May 2011. In his speech, Erdoğan mocked Mert's last name, which means "brave, trustworthy, and honest," and called her "Namert," meaning "despicable and coward" (CPJ 2012, 13). Making derogatory adjectives out of government critics' names is a popular part of Erdoğan's hate speeches. Erdoğan also made remarks to encourage the judiciary to take action against journalists he disliked and to give them the highest possible sentence. After prominent journalist Ahmet Şık was arrested in March 2011, Erdoğan likened his book, which had not been even published, to "a bomb" (CPJ 2012, 15).

Erdoğan publicly and personally threatened Can Dündar, the editor-in-chief of *Cumhuriyet,* many times due to revealing and covering a story about a variety of weapons being sent to Syria by the Turkish intelligence agency in 2015. "This slander and this illegitimate operation against the National Intelligence Organization [MİT] are, in a way, an act of espionage. This newspaper got involved in this espionage activity, too," Erdoğan stated during an interview on *TRT* on May 31, 2015. He then added, "The person who wrote this news shall pay a heavy price for it, I won't just let it go" (Hurriyet Daily News 2015). On June 2, Erdoğan lodged a complaint with the Ankara prosecutor against Dündar, accusing him of publishing "fake images and information" as well as "attempting to overthrow the government, or partial or total prevention of government duties," a crime for which the penalty is life imprisonment (HRW 2015). Soon after, Dündar was detained on November 26 together with Erdem Gül, *Cumhuriyet*'s Ankara bureau chief, to pay the heavy price Erdoğan had indicated.

In response to the Academics for Peace, who condemned the Turkish government's security operations in southern eastern Turkey, Erdoğan started a harsh campaign attacking these academics in at least five speeches in which he called them "vile," "equal to terrorists," and "base and dark" while encouraging the Turkish judiciary to take action against them (HRW 2016c). In a speech given to a group of lawyers on April 5, 2015, Erdoğan implied that critical journalists, academics and lawyers are terrorists by stating the following:

> Terrorism supporters in the guise of academics, spies in the guise of journalists, activists in the guise of politicians and militants in the guise of government officials are no different from members of terrorist organizations holding guns and bombs. They serve the same purpose. We have to watch out as a nation. We do not have to carry those who betray the state and the nation on our backs (HRW 2016, 38–39).

Erdoğan has also publicly encouraged collective punishment against government critics many times especially against the members of the Gülen Movement. "If this is called a 'witch hunt,' then yes, we perform a 'witch hunt," stated Erdoğan in 2014, referring to the persecution of Gulenists. He then added, "In order to sterilize this dirty water that has contaminated the milk, we will either boil or molecularize it," and asked party members and his supporters to help him in this "witch-hunt" (Hurriyet Daily News 2014b).

While Erdoğan has constantly used hate speech against government critics as well as oppositional groups and parties, any criticism against him is considered a crime under the Article 299 of the Criminal Code on Defamation of the President. The cases filed under this article had a significant exponential increase after the election of Erdoğan as President in 2014. Even though the article is about the defamation of the President as an individual, the Turkish judiciary exploited it to criminalize any criticism against Erdoğan as an attack on the Turkish state and tried defendants with allegations of terrorism-related crimes (Akdeniz and Altıparmak 2018, 7).

3.4 Conclusion

Freedom of expression, an essential human right, forms the basis of an open government and a well-informed society through public debate and independent media. Ensuring freedom of expression and a free, independent, and diverse media is a vital element for any healthy and strong democracy. Therefore, freedom of communication has its place in international documents as a human right.

The establishment of the first Turkish newspaper was one of the consequences of the Ottoman modernization and westernization reforms that mainly aimed "to save the state." The first Turkish newspaper was published in 1831 by the state as a propaganda tool and for the necessity of maintaining the support and cooperation of the people. The first private newspapers were also dependent on government support and therefore under the control of the government. Due to the state influence on its development, the Turkish press has always been very open to any influence from the state and political powers throughout its history.

Generally, the Turkish press was a useful instrument of the forcibly imposed modernization process in the country. Often, the press voluntarily adopted this mission, and it became the voice of the state rather than the voice of the people.

There were rare times when the press supported democratic processes too. However, these time periods, in which the free and independent press was strong and effective, were generally very brief in Turkish history. During both the empire and the republic, the press was subjected to oppressions and restraints by the government. Since the beginning of the Turkish press history, journalists have been threatened, censored, sacked, exiled, harassed, imprisoned or killed.

The military and media had always been the main traditional powers of the oppressive, secularist, and nationalist regime in Repulic of Turkey since it was founded in 1923. In the history of Turkish democracy, the mainstream press backed mainly authoritarian single party regimes or military interventions in Turkey.

When the AKP came to power in 2002, it was a party which represented the common interest. Its supporters varied from hard-core Islamists, traditional religious groups, Islamist modernizers, socially conservative businessmen, to liberal intellectuals, secular reformists and the Kurds. There was relatively a few influential political actors among the party members.

In this chapter, the Justice and Development Party (AKP) was analyzed under two periods. The period from its first term of coming to power to the 2011 elections, was defined as "the Period of the Justice and Development Party (AKP)." In this period, the AKP appeared as a reformist party which stimulated democratization and expanded freedoms. During this period, crucial improvements in democracy and press freedom were made in the country with the impact of the EU accession process.

The AKP's second term, after 2011, was defined as "the Period of the Erdoğan regime." After winning his first and second elections, the AKP leader and prime minister, Recep Tayyip Erdoğan strengthened his power and started eliminating both the social and political groups he allied with as well as the different voices within the party. The government's authoritarian tendencies became more visible with the 2013 Gezi protests. After the corruption investigations targeting his close circles and the AKP's cabinet ministers, Erdoğan increased his strength and authoritarian rule by blaming the opposition groups for plotting to remove him from power. After the failed coup attempt in July 2016, Erdoğan finally managed to establish his authoritarian one-man regime.

From 2002 to 2009, the AKP government had launched positive legal reforms that aimed to increase the legal protection of political, social, and cultural rights of the Turkish citizens regardless of their ethnic and religious origins. Contrary to the first period of the AKP, the EU accession process and democratization reforms weakened after the AKP's second election victory in 2007. After the 2011 elections, the AKP government started to become less tolerant and more oppressive towards social and political dissidents as well as the free media. As a result of the deterioration in press freedom in 2014, Turkey's status declined from "Partly Free" to "Not Free" according to the Freedom House Report.

The mysterious July 15 Coup Attempt in 2016, called a "gift from God" by Erdoğan, gave the government an excuse and unlimited power to carry out widespread purges and establish a fully authoritarian regime. Through the state of emergency declared right after the coup attempt, Erdoğan held the power to preside over the cabinet, issuing decrees that bypassed the Parliament and the Constitutional Court.

During the state of emergency that lasted much longer than initially announced, the government implemented massive purges, generally defined as a "lustration" by academics from different fields. Hundreds of thousands of officials were dismissed from their positions. About 6000 of these were faculty members who were dismissed from 119 public universities. The government also shut down 15 foundation universities by government decrees, causing more than 3000 academics to be unemployed. Erdoğan's purge also targeted the media and private sectors. More than 175 journalists were arrested with terrorism charges. Many prominent oppositional newspapers, news agencies, radio stations, television networks, and magazines were closed down by decrees, leaving hundreds of journalists unemployed.

The government has also used other ways and instruments to silence the free press and create a party media under Erdoğan's control. Erdoğan has implemented many methods used by authoritarian regimes in the past as well as new and creative ways to control the media. Some of these methods are jailing, threatening and physically attacking journalists; pressuring the media to fire critical journalists and canceling their press accreditation; taking over media companies; seizing the assets of media companies or shutting them down by using judiciary power; personally intervening in newspaper and television content; removing critical television channels from satellite platforms and streaming services; and blocking news websites.

In addition, Erdoğan has used the state's financial and economical sources to control the rest of the media by handing over the state-owned or seized media outlets to the businessmen in his close circle. In a short span of time, every one of these media organizations has turned into a government mouthpiece just like the other media organizations in the country, excluding a handful of small newspapers and local television channels.

Under Erdoğan's regime, Turkey has transformed from being an exemplar country in its region with a stable democracy and liberties to an oppressive one-man rule. The era that started with the AKP's reforms and the EU accession process was followed by the authoritarian actions of Erdoğan and his crackdown on liberties and press freedom that gave Turkey the title of "the world's biggest jailer of journalists." Controlling the media and therefore the information flow in the country played a key role in establishing Erdoğan's new regime that is built upon conspiracy theories and hate speech against government critics and the West.

References

Ahmad, Feroz. 1993. *The Making of Modern Turkey*. London: Routledge.

Akdeniz, Yaman, and Kerem Altıparmak. 2018. Turkey: Freedom of Expression in Jeopardy: Violations of the Rights of Authors, Publishers and Academics Under the State of Emergency. *English Pen Report*. https://www.englishpen.org/wp-content/uploads/2018/03/Turkey_Freedom_of_Expression_in_Jeopardy_ENG.pdf. Accessed 15 Dec 2019.

Aydin, Ertan, and İbrahim Dalmış. 2008. The Social Bases of the Justice and Development Party. In *Secular and Islamic Politics in Turkey the Making of the Justice and Development Party*, ed. Ümit Cizre, 201–222. Oxon: Routledge.

Aydin, Hasan, and Koksal Avincan. 2020. Intellectual Crimes and Serious Violation of Human Rights in Turkey: A Narrative Inquiry. *The International Journal of Human Rights* 24 (8): 1127–1155. https://doi.org/10.1080/13642987.2020.1713108.

Berkes, Niyazi. 1998. *The Development of Secularism in Turkey*. London: Hurst & Company.

Bipartisan Policy Center. 2015. *Turkey Transformed: The Origins and Evolution of Authoritarianism and Islamization Under the AKP. October 2015*. https://bipartisanpolicy.org/wp-content/uploads/2019/03/BPC-Turkey-Transformed.pdf. Accessed 15 Dec 2019.

Çakır, Ruşen. 2007. Prof. Şerif Mardin: Mahalle Havası Diye Bir Şey Var ki AKP'yi Bile Döver. [There Is Such Thing as Neighborhood Pressure That Could Even Overcome the AKP]. *Vatan*,

May 15. http://rusencakir.com/Prof-Serif-Mardin-Mahalle-havasi-diye-bir-sey-var-ki-AKPyi-bile-dover/749. Accessed 15 Dec 2019.
Çarkoğlu, Ali, and Ersin Kalaycıoğlu. 2007. *Turkish Democracy Today: Elections, Protest and Stability in an Islamic Society*. London: I.B. Tauris.
Cizre, Ümit. 2008a. Ideology, Context and Interest: The Turkish Military. In *The Cambridge History of Turkey-Turkey in the Modern World*, ed. Reşat Kasaba, vol. 4, 301–332. New York: Cambridge University Press.
———. 2008b. Introduction: The Justice and Development Party: Making Choices, Revisions and Reversals Interactively. In *Secular and Islamic Politics in Turkey the Making of the Justice and Development Party*, ed. Ümit Cizre, 2–14. Oxon: Routledge.
CNN. 2016. *Turkish Journalist Can Dundar Shot At Outside Court*. May 7 https://edition.cnn.com/2016/05/06/europe/turkish-journalist-escapes-court-shooting/. Accessed 15 Dec 2019.
CPJ. 2012. Turkey's Press Freedom Crisis the Dark Days of Jailing Journalists and Criminalizing Dissent. *A Special Report by the Committee to Protect Journalists*. https://cpj.org/reports/Turkey2012.English.pdf. Accessed 15 Dec 2019.
Davison, Roderic H. 1963. *Reform in the Ottoman Empire 1856–1876*. Princeton: Princeton University Press.
Demir, Vedat. 2007. *Türkiye'de Medya Siyaset İlişkisi* [The Relationship Between Media and Politics in Turkey]. İstanbul: Beta.
———. 2011. Türkiye'de 2000'li Yıllarda Medya-Sermaye İlişkileri [The Relationships Between Media and Capital in Turkey in the 2000s]. In *2000'li Yıllar Türkiye'de Medya* [Media in Turkey in the 2000s], ed. Nabi Avcı, 77–100. İstanbul: Meydan.
Finkel, Andrew. 2015. Captured News Media: The Case of Turkey. *The Center for International Media Assistance (CIMA) Report*. October 2015. https://www.cima.ned.org/wp-content/uploads/2015/10/CIMA-Captured-News-Media_The-Case-of-Turkey2.pdf. Accessed 15 Dec 2019.
Freedom House. 2014. *Freedom of the Press 2014*. https://freedomhouse.org/sites/default/files/FOTP_2014.pdf. Accessed 15 Dec 2019.
———. 2016. *Freedom of the press 2016 – Turkey*, 26 April. https://freedomhouse.org/report/freedom-¬press/2016/turkey. Accessed 15 Dec 2019.
———. 2017. *Freedom of the Press 2017*. https://freedomhouse.org/sites/default/files/FH_FIW_2017_Report_Final.pdf. Accessed 15 Dec 2019.
Gögüs, Sezer Idil, and Sabina Mannitz. 2016. The World Culture Entered Turkey: New Conflict Lines and the Challenges for Democratic Consolidation in Turkey. *Peace Research Institute Frankfurt (PRIF) Report*. https://nbn-resolving.org/urn:nbn:de:0168-ssoar-46689-3. Accessed 15 Dec 2019.
Guiler, Kimberly. 2016. Towards Erdoğan and the East: Conspiracies and Public Perception in Post-Coup Turkey. In Contemporary Turkish Politics. December 7. *The Project on Middle East Political Science (POMEPS)*, 28–31. https://www.bakerinstitute.org/media/files/files/6240636c/POMEPS_Studies_22_Turkish_Politics_Web-2_95rZWni.pdf. Accessed 15 Dec 2019.
Gumuscu, Sebnem. 2016. The Clash of Islamists: The Crisis of the Turkish State and Democracy. In Contemporary Turkish Politics. December 7, 2016. *The Project on Middle East Political Science (POMEPS)*, 6–11. https://www.bakerinstitute.org/media/files/files/6240636c/POMEPS_Studies_22_Turkish_Politics_Web-2_95rZWni.pdf. Accessed 15 Dec 2019.
Hale, William, and Ergun Özbudun. 2010. *Islamism, Democracy and Liberalism in Turkey the Case of the AKP*. Oxon: Routledge.
Hanioğlu, M.Şükrü. 2008. *A Brief History of the Late Ottoman Empire*. Princeton: Princeton University Press.
HRW Report. 2015. *World Report of Events of 2014*. New York: Seven Stories Press.
———. 2016. *World Report of Events of 2015*. New York: Seven Stories Press.
———. 2017. *World Report of Events of 2016*. New York: Seven Stories Press.
———. 2019. *World Report of Events of 2018*. New York: Seven Stories Press.

HRW. 2011. *Turkey: Journalists' Arrests Chills Free Speech*. March 4. https://www.hrw.org/news/2011/03/04/turkey-journalists-arrests-chills-free-speech. Accessed 15 Dec 2019.

———. 2014a. *Turkey's Human Rights Rollback Recommendations for Reform*. September 29. https://www.hrw.org/report/2014/09/29/turkeys-human-rights-rollback/recommendations-reform. Accessed 15 Dec 2019.

———. 2014b. *Turkey: Crackdown on Opposition Media Arrests Damage Press Freedom*. December 19. https://www.hrw.org/news/2014/12/19/turkey-crackdown-opposition-media. Accessed 15 Dec 2019.

———. 2015. *Turkey: Newspaper Under Threat Over Syria Arms Story*. https://www.hrw.org/news/2015/06/03/turkey-newspaper-under-threat-over-syria-arms-story. Accessed 15 Dec 2019.

———. 2016. *Silencing Turkey's Media the Government's Deepening Assault on Critical Journalism*. https://www.hrw.org/sites/default/files/report_pdf/turkey1216_web.pdf. Accessed 15 Dec 2019.

———. 2016a. *Turkey: Deteriorating Climate for Rights*. https://www.hrw.org/news/2016/01/27/turkey-deteriorating-climate-rights. Accessed 15 Dec 2019.

———. 2016b. *Turkey: Court Orders Newspaper Takeover. Zaman Latest Critical Voice Government Seeks to Silence*. March 5. https://www.hrw.org/news/2016/03/05/turkey-court-orders-newspaper-takeover. Accessed 15 Dec 2019.

———. 2016c. *Turkey: Academics Jailed for Signing Petition*. https://www.hrw.org/news/2016/03/16/turkey-academics-jailed-signing-petition.

Hurriyet Daily News. 2014a. *Turkish PM Acknowledges Phone Call to Media Executive*. February 12. http://www.hurriyetdailynews.com/turkish-pm-acknowledges-phone-call-to-media-executive-62368. Accessed 15 Dec 2019.

———. 2014b. *Turkish PM Erdoğan Vows 'to Sterilize' Gulen Movement 'by Boiling or Molecularizing'*. May 11. http://www.hurriyetdailynews.com/turkish-pm-Erdoğan-vows-to-sterilize-gulen-movement-by-boiling-or-molecularizing-66327. Accessed 15 Dec 2019.

———. 2015. *Cumhuriyet's Editor-in-Chief to 'Pay Heavy Price,' Says Turkish President*. June 1. http://www.hurriyetdailynews.com/cumhuriyets-editor-in-chief-to-pay-heavy-price-says-turkish-president%2D%2D83269. Accessed 15 Dec 2019.

———. 2016. *Erdoğan Says He 'Does Not Respect, Will Not Obey' Top Court Ruling on Arrested Journalists*. February 28. http://www.hurriyetdailynews.com/Erdoğan-says-he-does-not-respect-will-not-obey-top-court-ruling-on-arrested-journalists-95784. Accessed 15 Dec 2019.

———. 2017. *Press Cards of 889 Journalists Canceled in Turkey in 2016: Justice Minister*. October 15. http://www.hurriyetdailynews.com/press-cards-of-889-journalists-canceled-in-turkey-in-2016-justice-minister-120858. Accessed 15 Dec 2019.

İHOP. 2018. Updated Situation Report-State of Emergency in Turkey 21 July 2016–20 March 2018. *Human Rights Joint Platform (İHOP) Report*, April 17. https://www.ihoorg.tr/wp-content/uploads/2018/04/SoE_17042018.pdf. Accessed 15 Dec 2019.

Kirdis, Esen. 2016. *AKP's Foreign Policy and Its Party Identity Contemporary Turkish Politics*. December 7. The Project on Middle East Political Science (POMEPS), p 32–36. https://www.bakerinstitute.org/media/files/files/6240636c/POMEPS_Studies_22_Turkish_Politics_Web-2_95rZWni.pdf. Accessed 15 Dec 2019.

Lewis, Bernard. 1968. *The Emergence of Modern Turkey*. 2nd edn. London: Oxford University Press.

Lord, Ceren. 2018. *Religious Politics in Turkey from the Birth of the Republic to the AKP*. Cambridge: Cambridge University Press.

MacBride Report. 1980. *Many Voices, One World*. Report by the International Commission for the Study of Communication Problems, UNESCO. The Anchor Press Ltd, Essex.

Mardin, Şerif. 2000. *The Genesis of Young Ottoman Thought a Study in the Modernization of Turkish Political Ideas*. Syracuse: Syracuse University Press.

Matusiak, Marek. 2015. *The Great Leap Turkey Under Erdoğan*. Warsaw: Centre for Eastern Studies. Ośrodek Studiów Wschodnich im Marka Karpia. https://www.osw.waw.pl/sites/default/files/pw_51_ang_great_leap_net.pdf. Accessed 15 Dec 2019.

Mengi, Ruhat. 2011. Profesörler de korkar! [Professors Are Afraid Too]. *Vatan*, January 24. http://www.gazetevatan.com/ruhat-mengi-354983-yazar-yazisi-profesorler-de-korkar/. Accessed 15 Dec 2019.

Öncü, Ayşe. 2012. Television and Media. In *The Routledge Handbook of Modern Turkey*, ed. Metin Heper and Sabri Sayan, 125–138. Oxon: Routledge.

Özbudun, Ergun. 2011. *The Constitutional System of Turkey 1876 to the Present*. New York: Palgrave Macmillan.

Reporters Without Borders (RSF). 2016. *Turkey: State of Emergency, State of Arbitrary*. September 2016. https://rsf.org/sites/default/files/turquie.etatdurgence.eng_.def_.pdf. Accessed 15 Dec 2019.

Şahin, Alpay. 2010. Two Faces of the Press in Turkey: The Role of the Media. In *Turkey's Engagement with Modernity Conflict and Change in the Twentieth Century*, ed. Celia Kerslake, Kerem Öktem, and Philip Robins, 370–387. Hampshire: Palgrave Macmillan.

SETA. 2019. Uluslararası Medya Kuruluşlarının Türkiye Uzantıları [International Media Outlets' Extensions in Turkey]. In *Foundation for Political, Economic, and Social Research (SETA) Report*. İstanbul: SETA.

Shaw, Stanford J., and Ezel Kural Shaw. 1977. *History of the Ottoman Empire and Modern Turkey vol. II: Reform, Revolution, and Republic: The Rise of Modern Turkey, 1808–1975*. Cambridge: Cambridge University Press.

The Economist Special Reports Turkey. 2016. Erdoğan's New Sultanate. *The Economist*, February 4. https://www.economist.com/special-report/2016/02/04/erdogans-new-sultanate.

Vatan. 2008. Evet, Ergenekon'un Savcısıyım [Yes, I Am the Prosecutor of Ergenekon]. July 16. http://www.gazetevatan.com/-evet-ergenekon-un-savcisiyim%2D%2D189246-siyaset/. Accessed 15 Dec 2019.

Yalman, Ahmet Emin. 1914. *The Development of Modern Turkey as Measured by Its Press*. New York: Columbia University Press.

Yılmaz, Ihsan, Mehmet Efe Caman, and Galip Bashirov. 2019. How an Islamist Party Managed to Legitimate Its Authoritarianization in the Eyes of the Secularist Opposition: The Case of Turkey. *Democratization*. https://doi.org/10.1080/13510347.2019.1679772.

Zürcher, Eric J. 2017. *Turkey a Modern History*. 4th ed. London: I. B. Tauris & Company.

Vedat Demir is an exiled academic who is currently a visiting professor at the University of Potsdam in Germany as a Philipp Schwartz fellow. He was a professor at Istanbul University where he taught political communication, media ethics, and mass media and politics. Dr. Demir received his bachelor and master's degrees from Marmara University and his Ph.D. from Istanbul University. His research expertise focuses on political communication and public diplomacy. He served as the General Secretary of the Turkish Press Council from 2000 to 2003 and was a visiting scholar at Ithaca College and Cornell University between 2012 and 2014. Dr. Demir is the author of Medya Etiği [The Ethics of Media] (2006), Türkiye'de Medya Siyaset İlişkileri [The Relationship Between Media and Politics in Turkey] (2007), and Kamu Diplomasisi ve Yumuşak Güç [Public Diplomacy and Soft Power] (2012).

Chapter 4
Discrimination Based on Religion: A Complex Story in Turkey

İştar Gözaydın

Abstract Discrimination is the unjust or prejudicial treatment of different categories of people. Historically, when the term "discrimination based on religion" is used in the context of Turkey, mostly it covers the non-Muslim population. Turkey is a majority Muslim country, but also constitutionally a secular state of almost 100 years that guarantees substantial rights to religious minorities. However, discriminatory laws and gaps in practice remain severely. Moreover, discrimination is not only against non-Muslim religious individuals and groups. Having a *de facto* understanding of official Islam since the Ottoman past, all other approaches of Islam in Turkey have always been getting their share of discrimination. Most significantly the Alevi faith has been a subject of discrimination in terms of non-acknowledgement with repercussions in denial of venues of prayer and rituals, educational services, financial subsidies, to mention the least. Actually, freedom of religion has always been a thorny issue in Turkey. Even though in black letter law there exist a substantial number of regulations, discrimination in this regard has been very multi-layered in modern Turkey. In this chapter I would like to evaluate political and legal/judicial aspects of the issue in the context of human rights throughout the republican Turkey with glancing at its roots in the Ottoman past and by differentiating policies regarding religion with their impacts on various groups in society. It should certainly be noted that a freedom of a category also involves freedom from that category. In other words, I will be including non-believers, and their share in discrimination (s) based on religion in the chapter as well.

Keywords Religious discrimination · Religion rights · Turkey's non-Muslims · Turkey's Alevis

İ. Gözaydın (✉)
Independent Researcher and Human Rights Activist, Istanbul, Turkey

H. Aydin, W. Langley (eds.), *Human Rights in Turkey*, Philosophy and Politics - Critical Explorations 15, https://doi.org/10.1007/978-3-030-57476-5_4

4.1 Historical Background of Religion Discrimination

Republican Turkey established politically and legally in 1923 has been a project of modernity. Especially during the single party period from 1923 to 1945, the state occupied a central role in the social and cultural engineering. Initial consideration for laicist[1] policies and legislation of the republican decision making elite of Turkey were to alter not only the supra-structure of the country towards a modern/Western body like their predecessors in the late Ottoman times, but also to transform the whole Turkish society into a modern one. Traditional belief systems appeared there as a threat. In other words, religion was perceived as a rival to modernity as in almost all other states in similar processes.[2] Therefore, the Republic of Turkey's founding elite implemented policies to remove religion from the public realm and reduce it to a matter of faith and practice of the individual, so that the principle of freedom of religion was to protect privatized religion[3] only. Thus Islam, the predominant faith system of the land since the thirteenth century,[4] has been relegated to the private sphere.

The Ottoman state was based on divine legitimacy[5] as almost all pre-modern political bodies, however the Ottoman rulers applied a corpus of secular laws in addition to sharia n (Islamic law) since the fifteenth century.[6] As Karen Barkey puts it, "The Ottoman Empire ... developed a supranational ideology based on the Ottoman dynasty representing the realm of Islam against the infidels. Yet, although the dynastic element was always there, the Islamic segment of the supranational

---

[1]I use the term laicists for those who that prefer the state's control of religion as opposed to secularism which implies the separation of state and religion. As Rex Ahdar and Ian Leigh point out, "The longstanding French policy of *laicité* exemplifies ... desire to restrict, if not eliminate, clerical and religious influence, over the state. ... The modern Islamic society of Turkey is similarly an example of a state founded on strongly secular principles where restrictions on individual religious liberty have been introduced to prevent pressure being exerted by the predominant religious group" (Ahdar and Leigh 2005, 73). For a comprehensive argumentation on the terms laic and secular, and their derivatives, see Davidson 2003. I totally agree with Davison in his arguments, thus I prefer to use the term 'laicist' for republican state practice in Turkey. Furthermore, *laiklik* (laicité) is the concept that is preferred by the Republican decision-making elite of Turkey in all legislations and other legal regulations.

[2]For a profound scrutiny of religion in modern times and secularisms, one of the pillars of modernity, see Cady and Hurd 2010.

[3]For "religion is a private affair" understanding and its consequences in modernization processes, see Casanova 1994, 40–66.

[4]It should also be noted that the religious picture of Anatolia in the thirteenth and fourteenth centuries appears to be complex. See for a conceptualization as 'metadoxy' for this period, see Kafadar 1995, 74–77.

[5]"In retrospect one sees that the contribution of Ottoman Hanafi Islam was stronger in terms of religo-administrative innovations than in terms of theological speculation." (Mardin 1997, 125).

[6]See, for productions of *kanun-name* (lawbooks) to take care of increasing complexity of the administrative apparatus Babinger 1978, 433; İnalcık 1973.

idiom was not always articulated or used."[7] This was a means of perfected administrative skills legitimating a normative order. Heinrich von Treitschke states that in the one hand, under the Crescent everyone was permitted to live in his/her own faith; on the other hand, this was a subtle means of enslavement for non-Muslims. However as long as the *dhimmi*, the non-Muslim population, paid their taxes punctually and avoided conflicts with the Muslims, they could survive peacefully (Treitschke 1916).[8] Non-Muslim religious minorities had potential autonomy, especially in the major cities, Jews, Greeks and Armenians had been established as communities (*millet*), with internal jurisdiction of their affairs (Barkey 1994, 43). This was an expression of limited tolerance for maintaining the empire. Daniel Goofman compares late medieval European Christian and Ottoman political rulers: "... European Christians often managed relations with the 'other', particularly the Jew and the Muslim, by vigorous persecution and expulsion. The Ottomans handled their 'others' less violently by asserting a theoretical Muslim supremacy –signified by a head-tax upon non-Muslims and certain often symbolic sumptuary restrictions- and simultaneously practicing a nearly absolute but effective disregard in which the various religions ... within the empire co-existed and comingled virtually at will."(Goffman 2002, 9). "In contrast, the Ottoman state was not so tolerant of its Muslim populations and victimized all kinds of heterodox Islamic movements ..."[9] This was a ruthless means of social organization of dissent over all religious groups that fought against the Ottoman State's centralizing efforts after the fifteenth century.

"(T)he liberal individualist notion of civil and political equality that makes the modern conception of freedom of belief possible was not the paradigm in (the) premodern world" (Mahmood 2015, 143), however by the shift of the paradigms facilitating the modernization processes, yet other forms of persecutions got unleashed. *Tanzimat* rescript of 1839 and the Reform rescript (*Islahat Fermanı*) of 1856 guaranteed a set of religious liberties to all Ottoman subjects, Muslim and non-Muslim alike, including to choose whatever religion they wanted to belong to.[10] One effect of the reform movement was to undermine the traditional Ottoman legal categories of Muslim, dhimmi, and non-Muslim foreigner; but the state continued to recognize the religious foundation of the millets, drafting organic laws governing the self-administration of the three major non-Muslim communities: the Greek Orthodox (1862), the Armenians of the Apostolic Church (1863), and the Jews (1865) (Hanioğlu 2008, 74–76). In the context of *Tanzimat* reforms "... it was possible to envisage a rapidly modernizing state with legal guarantees for individual citizens (and) religious freedom" (Keyder 1997, 34). Moreover, although in the Constitution of 1876, Islam remained the official state religion, for the first time in history, all

[7]Barkey 2008, 99; for the role of Islam see 104–108, "... although Islam was understood as the religion of the state, it was subordinated to the *raison d'etat*". 105.

[8]See Treitschke's remarks in his *Politics II*, 40.

[9]Barkey 2008, 160; for persecutions over several groups see 160–191.

[10]The Ottomans interpreted "freedom of religion" (*serbesti-i idyan*) as the "freedom to defend their religion" (Deringil 1998, 115–117).

subjects were declared to be Ottomans with equal rights regardless of their religion. All Ottoman bureaucratic positions became accessible to non-Muslims on paper, however the implementation had issues.[11] A legal system providing rights with sanctions and political Islam (Türköne 1991) were both products of the modernization process. As Selim Deringil makes clear, the Islamic elements of Abdülhamit's regime were not simply a return to past practice. Rather, Islamic symbols of legitimacy were re-employed to defend the modernization program of the Ottoman state (Deringil 1998, 44–46). Later, accumulations of nationalist milieu loaded by poor economic conditions by World War One led to atrocities of 1915 committed primarily against the Armenians, but the Syriac and Chaldean Christians as well.

"With the founding of the Republic, (Ottoman) religious cosmology was exchanged for a nationalist ontology and a positivist epistemology. Social order was no longer thought to issue from a religious order but from a configuration of national values (…). The state was … the discoverer of nationalist morality, its guardian, and its disseminator as well" (Sunar 1987, 85–86. Thus in 1924, *Diyanet İşleri Başkanlığı* (Presidency of Religious Affairs; hereinafter *Diyanet*), a laic administrative unit to execute services regarding Islamic faith and practices; to enlighten society about religion; and to carry out the management of places of prayer got established (Gözaydın 2008, 2020, 216–227). This agency was instituted to regulate Islamic services, but it actually was a means of controlling 'religion' and 'securing' secularity by disseminating an official understanding of Islam.[12] In the mentality of the founding elite of Republican Turkey, religion was to remain in the personal domain; the public aspect was to be managed by *Diyanet* only. Thus, on 30 November 1925 Sufi/dervish brotherhoods/orders were legally banned.[13]

On 24 July 1923, Lausanne Treaty was signed. It provided a number of negative as well as positive rights for non-Muslim minorities of Turkey, with non-Muslim being interpreted as only including three major communities of the Greek Orthodox, Armenian Orthodox and Jewish.[14] Therefore, the rights of other, then existing non-Muslim groups, such as the Syriac Orthodox and Syriac Chaldean, Latin Catholic, and those of Bahai faith, have not been viewed by Turkey as subject to

[11]To study the extent of which *Tanzimat* declarations were really implemented, see Findley 1982, 339–368.

[12]"Kurdish Nakşibendis rebelled in 1925; with time, other Nakşibendis sought jobs in the Directorate of Religious Affairs, colonizing it from within." For a claim of "colonizing" *Diyanet* within see, Findley 2010, 382–383.

[13]*Tekke ve Zaviyelerle Türbelerin Seddine ve Türbedarlıklar ile Bir Takım Unvanların Men ve İlgasına Dair Kanun* [Law on the Closure of Dervish Lodges, Hospices and Shrines and on Abolition and Prohibition of the Use of Certain Titles] No. 677, December 13, 1925. For a brief commentary on the *tarikats* see, Lewis 1961/1979, 404–412. For a detailed analysis of different religious orders in the nineteenth century see, Abu-Manneh 2001. For an account of religious communities in the Republican times see, Özdalga 2010, 69–91.

[14]For rights covered by the Lausanne Treaty see, Yıldırım 2015, 167–173.

the Lausanne protection scheme.[15] Moreover, implementation even with regard to the three major communities has been deficient;[16] especially regarding property issues and religious/educational institutions.[17] To identify Turkish citizenship and Turkish nationality were the priorities of modern Turkey of the 1920's. Heavy debates in the Parliament on article 88 of 1924 Constitution which defined the inhabitants of Turkey reveal a lot of discriminatory statements that some to the extent which may be qualified as hate speech.[18] Campaigning for Turkification and marginalization of non-Muslim population were heated in the 1920's.[19] Nevertheless, "... negative legacy of the past would resurface later in the atmosphere of World War Two and recreate the trauma of the years of the Armistice and War of Independence. As a result, the Capital Tax levy promulgated in 1942, which rightfully intended to tax profits earned from speculations and black market operations, would be implemented in a totally discriminatory manner against citizens of the Jewish and Christian faiths and those of Dönme origin." (Bali 2006, 49)

Late 1940's was a time for the ruling party *Cumhuriyet Halk Partisi* (Republican Peoples' Party: CHP) to make a number of concessions to a part of the population with Islamic sensitivities. For example, *İmam-Hatip* schools were introduced in 1948 to provide basic vocational training to imams and preachers, sacred tombs were re-opened, optional Islamic lessons were allowed in primary schools for 10 to 12-year old, and a faculty of theology was permitted (1949). However after decades of single-party rule an alternative party, *Demokrat Parti* (Democrat Party: DP) was allowed to participate in elections of 1946 as a transition to multi-party regime. "The DP was able to utilize religious feelings that many people still possessed who had generally not been immersed within secular establishments and disliked the dismissal of traditional institutions." (Vertigans 2003, 48) In 1950 election DP won 55% of the vote. On 16 June 1950, barely a month after they came to power, they passed a law restoring the call to prayer (*ezan*) in Arabic again.[20] In the preceding years DP had worked hard to build up an electorate by acquiring support among local Islamic leaders and networks, particularly among followers of the Kurdish

[15]Currently, newer non-Muslim groups like the Jehova's Witnesses or Protestants with Turkish citizenship are not recognized as non-Muslim minorities as protected under the Lausanne Treaty.

[16]Governmental policies and politics influence perceptions and attitudes in the society as well: "... at the level of popular culture, there is a strong tendency to consider non-Muslim Turkish citizens not as equal citizens but as aliens whose loyalty to the Turkish state is dubious." (Özbudun 2012, 68).

[17]For shortcomings in the implementation of rights provided by the Lausanne Treaty, see Aydın Düzgit 2014, 319.

[18]*TBMM Zabıt Ceridesi*, term II, vol 8/1: 908–911.

[19]For "speak Turkish" campaigns and other activities of nuisance against non-Muslim population in the 1920's and 1930's see, Cagaptay 2006.

[20]The *ezan* had been called in Turkish since June 1941. For repercussions of this act, see Azak 2012, 59–78.

Islamic scholar and preacher Bediüzzaman Said Nursi.[21] DP was a source of hope in the late 1940's and through the 1950's, unfortunately produced little more than bitter disappointment.

"... (I)n 1955 came the worst mistake of modern Turkish history, when shady interests ... caused riots against the Greeks in Istanbul." (Stone 2010, 160)[22] Looters not only attacked properties affiliated to non-Muslims (predominantly Greek, but other religious minorities as well), but also churches and cemeteries: holy pictures, crucifixes, icons and other sacred objects were destroyed. All 73 orthodox churches in Istanbul were set on fire (Korkut 2019). The Turkish state's policy to remove all minorities from Anatolia had been substantially achieved by the 1950's. In this light, the pogrom of 6/7 September was to prove to be a particularly successful continuation of the removal of the Christian communities in Istanbul.

Following the initial military intervention of 1960 that was to be succeeded by many others, regretfully in terms of democracy and human rights, a new constitution got produced. The 1961 Constitution provided the people of Turkey with a greater degree of rights and freedom than they had ever enjoyed since the establishment of the Republic. New political parties formed and from 1965 on wards the conservative-liberal policies of the DP were continued by the *Adalet Partisi* (Justice Party), led by Süleyman Demirel. In January 1970 *Milli Nizam Partisi* (National Order Party), the first pro-Islamic political party in Republican Turkey, was established to be shut down judicially in May 1971. Soon after on 11 October 1972 *Milli Selamet Partisi* (National Salvation Party/hereinafter MSP) was founded, thus in Turkish democratic politics, a predominantly pro-Islamic vein affiliated by Necmettin Erbakan,[23] no matter under what political party name, started to run.[24] On 31 March 1975, Demirel formed a rightist coalition with MSP and ultranationalist *Milliyetçi Hareket Partisi* (Nationalist Action Party; MHP), known as the 'Nationalist Front'. Thus, "The militants of the Right considered themselves as part of the state now that their leaders were in governing coalition which gave them protection and the ability to terrorize their political opponents. They ... attacked ... the Alevis ... because they supported the Republicans who were secular and ultranationalist." (Ahmad 2003, 142) In 1978 in Kahramanmaraş, assaults primarily against Alevis that lasted seven days ended with more than a hundred dead, and hundreds of wounded. 210 homes and 70 offices were destroyed.[25]

[21]Nursi initially supported the Kemalist revolution, but became an important opponent in the 1930's. See, Mardin 1989. It should be noted that Mardin's reading of Nursi have been much criticized in Islamic circles. See also, Vahide 2005; Akbulut Kuru and Ahmet T. Kuru 2008, 99–111.

[22]For a detailed analysis on events of 6–7 September 1955, the organization of the riots, the interaction between the 6–7 September events and the Cyprus issue see Güven 2011.

[23]See Shankland 1999, 87–131.

[24]For an account of this line of Islamic political parties and their *Milli Görüş* (The National View) ideology see 2015, 109–117; Sunier and Landman 2015, 24 and 68–80. For a field study in Ümraniye focusing on supporters of this line of parties see White 2002.

[25]In the media, see http://bianet.org/english/english/103813-remembering-the-maras-massacre-in-1978; http://bianet.org/english/politics/170324-37-years-after-maras-massacre

Despite the fact that 1961 Constitution was a legislation that rights were regulated democratically, the military intervention of 12 March 1971 and restrictive amendments that were made consequently, altered the milieu of freedom. In 1970's the State targeted primarily and violently the 'left'; however it was also a fact that many were convicted in accordance with article 163 of the Penal Code for 'illegal conduct' due to activities such as reading collectively the corpus of Bediüzzaman.[26]

In September 1980, Turkey experienced yet another *coup d'etat* and later had a much less libertarian constitution than the previous one. Throughout the 1980's, the National Security Council and General Evren ensured that politics were confined to the straitjacket of military oversight, yet civil society and new political movements emerged nevertheless. Indeed, 1980's is the first decade in Turkey that civil society organizations got overwhelmingly established. *İnsan Hakları Derneği* (İHD), the longest lasting human rights organization in Turkey was founded on 17 July 1986 and *Türkiye İnsan Hakları Vakfı* (TİHV) followed it. Later came *İnsan Hakları ve Mazlumlar için Dayanışma Derneği* (MAZLUM-DER), *Helsinki Yurttaşlar Derneği* (HYD), *Uluslararası Af Örgütü Türkiye Şubesi* (UAÖTŞ), *İnsan Hakları Gündemi Derneği* (İHGD) and *Barış Derneği* (Anar 1996, 163–174).

1990's was a decade of violence not only against Kurds but also for the Alevi groups. Alevi spiritual leaders, intellectuals, artists, and lay people from all over Turkey gathered for a festival in Sivas were massacred by an Islamist fundamentalist mob on 2 July 1993; 35 were dead, more than 50 were heavily wounded. Another assault on Alevis took place in Istanbul's Gazi quarter in March 1995. In four days that riots continued, 22 persons died, 155 persons were wounded severely. Official statements defended perpetrators and perpetrators weren't persecuted, is still another main issue too.

On 28 February 1997, the members of the General Staff 'requested' government leaders Necmettin Erbakan and Tansu Çiller, tighter control of Islamic brotherhoods, curtailment of religious vocational high schools (*İmam Hatip Liseleri*) and Qur'an courses, the marginalization of 'green capital' and the clousure of radio and TV stations deemed anti-secular. In the course of these demands, *Yüksek Öğretim Kurulu*/YÖK (Higher Education Council) proscribed the wearing of headscarf at all universities. Women who refused to take off their head covering were not allowed to matriculate or attend examinations. The Constitutional Court duly banned Refah Partisi (Welfare Party) headed by Necmettin Erbakan in January 1998; and thereby closed down the largest party in the Parliament.

The impressive electoral victory of *Adalet ve Kalkınma Partisi* (Justice and Development Party/AKP) in the parliamentary elections of 2002 was a profound change in Turkish politics. However, from 2007 signs of yet another fundamental transition emerged; this was a change of policies from emphasis on democracy to attempts of constructing a hegemonic authoritarian regime through a narrative of conservative Islamic discourse. This shift may be read as a reaction of AKP to a series of efforts of the "ancient regime". 27 April 2007 "memorandum" may be

[26]For a judicial account of these cases see Berk 1975.

considered as a breaking point in this process. On 27 April 2007 at 11.20 pm., a statement on alleged threats to the secular regime appeared at the official website of *Türk Silahlı Kuvvetleri* (Turkish Armed Forces) referring to the approaching presidential elections.[27] 2008 attempted closure trial to close AKP and ban its 71 leading members from politics for five years, based on the charge that the party violated the principle of separation of religion and state in Turkey was also crucial as a turning point especially in Erdoğan's conduct. With 6 members voting for a closure (7 would have been needed), the Constitutional Court rejected the demands of the prosecutor and did not ban the party. The court gave its verdict on 9 July 2009 rejecting the demand, and the case against AKP was terminated.[28] Nevertheless, Gezi protests[29]; the so-called "17–25 December process"[30] and finally the failed coup attempt of 15 July 2016 was the penultimate stage of Turkey's clear path in the direction of authoritarianism. In July 2018, having triumphed in the presidential elections the previous month, Erdoğan began to formally transform Turkey's long-standing parliamentary system into a heavily centralized presidential one. Amendments in the Constitution of Turkey provided the President various powers sufficient to form a one-man government.

Legally and politically *Diyanet* has been transformed into a useful instrument by 2010's to disseminate new state policies domestically and internationally. Social engineering attempts were once again active. I disagree with Çınar and Duran's claim that "(Diyanet) has a minor role in the representation of the Islamist movement or in the production of Islamic discourses" (Çınar and Duran 2008, 21). Which was probably valid before the AKP governments. However, "(a)s the mystic communities lost power and the AKP came to power, the (government controlled) Directorate of Religious Affairs became more legitimate, the people turned to it more, they started to hang its calendars on the walls as a sign of respect and acceptance (also concomitant with the Islamic turn of the directorate)" (Tuğal 2009, 200). Empowerment of an institution for religious affairs that has clearly been favoring Sunni Islam was an indication for further discriminatory action against "others".

Various monitoring reports on religious freedom and its implementation in Turkey reveal some ongoing violations, and several discriminatory acts. I would like to focus on two of these monitoring processes due to their specific commitment in freedom of religion. United States Commission on International Religious Freedom (USCIRF) is an independent, bipartisan U.S. federal government commission

---

[27]For an account of this so called e-memorandum see Gözaydın, 2017, 257–258; Yavuz 2009, 240–245.

[28]For the closure case against the AKP see Hale and Özbudun 2010, 74–75; for a journalistic evaluation of the Court decision see Tavernise and Arsu 2008. http://www.nytimes.com/2008/07/31/world/europe/31turkey.html?fta=y.&_r=0

[29]For a thorough account of the Gezi events see Özkırımlı 2014.

[30]Initiation of judicial processes against some ministers due to corruption allegations in December 2013, made an ongoing dispute between Fethullah Gülen and Recep Tayyip Erdoğan public. See *Kuru* 2017, http://www.themontrealreview.com/2009/Islam-And-Democracy-In-Turkey.php; Yavuz, 2018; Watmough and Öztürk 2018.

created by the 1998 International Religious Freedom Act (IRFA) that monitors the universal right to freedom of religion or belief abroad. This Commission issues annual reports and makes policy recommendations to the President, the Secretary of State, and Congress. In the monitoring process there exists three categories as, Tier 1: Countries of Particular Concern; Tier 2; Other countries and regions monitored. Turkey was taken in monitoring list in 2009, and remained there in 2010 and in 2011. In 2012, Turkey was placed in Tier 1 list of 'countries of particular concern'. Turkey's Ministry of Foreign Affairs as well as the Diyanet officially made public statements to protest such categorization. In 2013, Turkey was among countries to be monitored; however in the following years it was categorized as a Tier 2 country. 2019 report gave way in Turkey to negative reactions due to the statements on Gülen and his supporters.

The Freedom of Belief Initiative, which I would like to take as a second reference body, was launched in September 2011 with the aim of monitoring issues related to freedom of thought, religion, of belief in Turkey, and to make legal standards and monitoring reports related to such topics accessible to all stakeholders. Four reports that have been issued[31] since 2013 reveal their observations under two main headings, one to be freedom of thought, religion or belief; the other to be freedom to manifest religion or belief.

Two issues that take prominent place in the reports of The Freedom of Belief Initiative but not in United States Commission on International Religious Freedom reports are the right to conscientious, or religious or belief- based objection to mandatory military service; and right to legal personality as a belief-group. Although these rights are in the very scope of freedom of religion regimes; in the context of discrimination, I would like to focus on the following ongoing violations and discriminatory conduct:

[31]The Right to Freedom of Religion or Belief in Turkey – Monitoring Report January–June 2013: https://inancozgurlugugirisimi.org/en/nhciog-report-the-right-to-freedom-of-religion-or-belief-in-turkey-monitoring-report-january-june-2013-now-available-in-english/

In Need of a Principled Approach Monitoring Report on The Right to Freedom of Religion or Belief In Turkey, July 2013–June 2014: https://inancozgurlugugirisimi.org/en/new-report-in-need-of-a-principled-approach-monitoring-report-on-the-right-to-freedom-of-religion-or-belief-in-turkey-july-2013-june-2014/

Monitoring Report On The Right To Freedom Of Religion Or Belief In Turkey 2015: https://inancozgurlugugirisimi.org/en/monitoring-report-on-the-right-to-freedom-of-religion-or-belief-in-turkey-2015-is-published/

2019 Report Pursuing Rights And Equality: Monitoring Report On The Right To Freedom Of Religion Or Belief In Turkey: https://inancozgurlugugirisimi.org/en/2019-report-pursuing-rights-and-equality-monitoring-report-on-the-right-to-freedom-of-religion-or-belief-in-turkey/

4.2 Freedom from Religion

Freedom from religion encompasses several categories: "That a person not believing in a religion does not automatically mean that one does not believe in god. In principle, atheists do not believe in any religion, also in a god or gods. But a person who, while not belonging to any religion, may believe in a god (deism), or can look askance at the idea of god (skepticism) or may think that presence or absence of a god is not able to be determined (agnosticism), or may be unconcerned with religious matters."[32] On current national ID cards there exists no field for religious affiliation; however it is in cards' micro- chips which is still a coercion to declare one's religion or belief. Moreover, the majority of people have been nevertheless reluctant as regards the matter of leaving the religion section blanc, as this may create the potential for discrimination in Turkey where Muslims constitute the majority. Any critical approach to issues related to religion may be made subject of punishment, as in the case of Aydın Tatlav when the applicant wrote that Islam legitimizes social injustice by portraying it 'God's will'.[33] There is no crematorium in Turkey, and authorities have not assigned any places for non-religious funerals. Association of Atheism has been a target of hate speech and assaults since it was established in 2014.[34]

4.2.1 The Right to Change One's Religion or Belief

Converting to another religion from Islam has been one of the most severely attacked rights in Turkey. Claims of missionary activities, which actually are perfectly legitimate in the context of the right to change one's religion may end up in violence. In 2006 the Italian catholic priest Father Santoro was killed in Trabzon by a nationalist teenager. In 2007 a young man stabbed a Catholic priest in Izmir, claiming he was inspired by a movie depicted missionaries as trying to take over Turkey. In April 2007 one German and two Turkish Protestant converts in Malatya were murdered by five young Turks upon hours of torture.[35]

[32] See Şirin (2014), 59–88. Research on these categories are very scarce in Turkey.

[33] Aydın Tatlav v. Turkey, 2 May 2006, European Court of Human Rights, no. 50692/99.

[34] See https://www.ateizmdernegi.org.tr

[35] For detailed account of these violations see White 2013, 82–83, 90.

4.2.2 Slanderous Discourse Targeting Minority Belief Groups

Despite the fact of various positive developments initiated by AKP in the context of rights of non-Muslim communities,[36] discourse emphasizing the superiority of Islam over other religions pronounced by Erdoğan himself[37] facilitates pavement to frequent use of hate-speech against non-Muslim groups.[38] Within this context, pejorative labeling of non-Muslims as 'traitors' and 'exploiters' became more evident.[39]

4.2.3 Halki Seminary

The Heybeliada Theological School was found on a supranational base to educate clergymen in 1844. In 1971 the school was closed legally due to an act to reorganize higher education and prohibiting operation of privately owned schools. 1970's was a decade that frictions over Cyprus have started between Turkey and Greece. Since then Halki Seminary has been a subject of political bargaining between the two states. Preventing the re-opening of the seminary is a intersecting violation of religious and educational rights (Kırlıdökme 2010, 41).

4.2.4 Compulsory "Religious Culture and Knowledge of Ethics" Courses

Children of Jewish and Christian families are exempt from the "Religious Culture and Knowledge of Ethics" lessons during their education. However, in order to be able to use the right to exemption, students and parents have to present a copy of their identity cards with the respective religion stated in the religion section. Initially this results in an obligation to declare one's religion which is not compatible with the

---

[36]See Beylunioğlu 2017.

[37]"*Erdoğan: Bizim tek derdimiz var, İslam İslam İslam*" (Erdoğan: We have only one concern, Islam Islam Islam). http://bianet.org/bianet/siyaset/166454-erdogan-bizim-tek-derdimiz-var-islam-islam-islam

[38]The Hrant Dink Foundation monitors hate speech in media and publishes periodical reports: the most recent one for 2019 mentions not only Jewish, Armenians and Syrians as most often subject to hate speech in media, but also against Christians, Buddhists, atheists, deists, etc. https://hrantdink.org/attachments/article/2003/Medyada-Nefret-Soylemi-ve-Ayrimci-Soylem-2018.pdf

[39]In Turkey's current society it is quite a wide perception that non-Muslim are "foreigners". Surveys on xenophobia reveal sources of slandering discourses against religious minorities. See Çarkoğlu 2006, 170.

rulings of European Court of Human Rights. Moreover, the standardized "Transition from Primary to Secondary Education" (*TEOG*) test, which began being administered during the 2013–2014 school year has been a source of discrimination for these students. In calculating the *TEOG* test results announced in June 2015, it was determined that minority students exempt from religious education were automatically listed as having taken compulsory religious classes, though this was corrected by the authorities later.[40]

4.2.5 Discrimination Against the Alevi Communities

State Islam has always had a Sunni orientation in Turkey, and has thus kept the Alevi communities mostly outside the Republican administrative circles of influence. The historical animosities between the Alevi and Sunni communities have kept their sectarian identities[41] concealed in the public realm under threat of severe discrimination. While most Alevis regard Alevism as a non-Sunni variation of Islam, some claim that Alevism is not part of Islamic tradition, and others insist that it is not a religion at all (Hurd 2015, 87–108). Elizabeth Özdalga in an article in 2008 claims that, "(w)hen Alevis are asked to spell out their frustration, the issues most frequently referred to are obligatory religious education in school; difficulties in getting permission and/or funding for the building of *cemevis*; and lack of representation at state level." (Özdalga 2008). After more than a decade that the abovementioned article was published, demands appear to be almost constant due to the ongoing fact that "whereas debates on identity and diversity have indisputably become more widespread in Turkey since 1980's, difference, and even more particularism, are still illegitimate and stigmatized." (Massicard 2006, 82).

In recent years there have been significant legal developments on behalf of the Alevi communities in Turkey through several judgements of the European Court of Human Rights (hereinafter the ECtHR). Following is an account of three prominent cases and Turkey's conduct in the expected process of application of the decisions thereof. Three groups of judgements regarding to education, benefitting from financial exemptions for places of worship, and status of *cemevis* rendered by the ECtHR reveal discriminations that the Alevis have been subjected to in Turkey.

[40]http://www.agos.com.tr/tr/yazi/10305/el-yordamiyla-teog

[41]For a query on religious beliefs and practices Sunnis versus Alevis see Çarkoğlu and Kalaycıoğlu 2009, 28–30.

4.2.5.1 Cases of Hasan and Eylem Zengin v. Turkey Application No. 1448/04 and Mansur Yalçın and Others v. Turkey Application No. 21163/11

In the aftermath of the 1980 military *coup d'etat* in Turkey, the state began to re-emphasize the role of religion and the significance of religious education, hence the new government introduced compulsory courses on 'religion and morals' by a clause in the new Constitution of 1982. The content of the curriculum and the textbooks included information only about the Sunni interpretations of Islam with little references to other world religions.

The pioneering case on the issue of religious education was *Hasan and Eylem Zengin v. Turkey*, which set the case law. In the lawsuit, Hasan Zengin accused Turkey of violating his parental rights on his daughter's education. The state representatives in their defence highlighted the "unbiased" nature of Turkish education and claimed that the syllabus "did not take into consideration the vision of members of *mezhep* (a branch of Islam) or *tarikat* (a religious order) represented in the country." After the assessment of the case, the ECtHR acknowledged that 9th grade textbook included some information on Alevi religious figures, however the overall content of the textbooks and the curriculum was insufficient to address the demands of Zengin. Additionally, the compulsory nature of religious education was a further violation point. The ECHR ruled in 2007, "The exemption procedure is not an appropriate method and does not provide sufficient protection" since it required citizens to declare their religious affiliation. The judgment was finalized on 9 January 2008.

Meanwhile, on June 22, 2005, fourteen parents of school-aged children including a Mansur Yalçın submitted a petition to the Ministry of National Education, demanding a revision in the content of religious education. The applicants asked Alevi culture and philosophy to be incorporated into the program, and demanded that the revisions in the curriculum to be consulted with officials of the Alevi faith. The applicants also called for revisions in the training of teachers of religious education. In its response, the Ministry emphasized the "supra-confessional approach" of the curriculum preparation process and declined the request. In due law, in sequence of the response of the Ministry, a class-action suit was filed in the same year. After exhausting all domestic judicial processes, the case was introduced to ECtHR on February 2, 2011 by the applicants Mansur Yalçın, Yüksel Polat and Hasan Kılıç whom submitted that the way in which the compulsory classes in religious culture and ethics were delivered in primary and secondary schools infringed their rights under the second sentence of Article 2 of Protocol No. 1 to the European Convention on Human Rights.

In response to the criticism on the content of religious education textbooks, the Ministry of Education prepared new textbooks to be used in the 2011–2012 school year. Although new material introduced the concept and issues related to Alevi faith, the revised text continued to put strong emphasis on the Sunni interpretations of Islam. Hence, it may be said that the revisions were actually a cosmetic change; the content of the textbooks and curriculum continued to be an "education of a religion" rather "education *about* religions."

Eventually, assessing the *Mansur Yalçın and Others v. Turkey* case, the ECtHR held in the judgment rendered on 16 September 2014 that the Turkish education system was inadequate because it has not been able to develop a method that would meet the conditions of objectivity and pluralism and respect for the religious beliefs of parents. However, the latest curriculum which started to be applied in 2018 is also not impartial to all religions and belief systems, it does not adopt a moral code that is independent from religious beliefs, and it does not provide a general education on religious beliefs based on the principles of neutrality, objectivity and pluralism. A study on "Religious Culture and Ethics" books reveal that number of pages referring to Alevi belief are 20 in 1782 pages of the nine books of the secondary level education.

4.2.5.2 Cumhuriyetçi Eğitim ve Kültür Vakfı v. Turkey. Application No.32093/10

Cemevi, the place of worship for the Alevi communities, has not been acknowledged legally as a temple in Turkey. In order to challenge this discriminatory conduct against the *cemevis*, a case got filed by *Cumhuriyetçi Eğitim Ve Kültür Merkezi Vakfı* (Foundation for Republican Education and Culture). The applicant association is a foundation established under Turkish law, which was set up in 1995 and has public utility status. This religious foundation runs, throughout Turkey, many *cemevis*, which are premises dedicated to the practice of Alevism. In particular, it runs the Yenibosna Cultural Centre, a complex which houses, among other things, the applicant foundation's headquarters, a mass hall, library, conference hall, classroom, a room for funerals and a *cemevi*. Exhausting all judicial processes, the case was brought to the ECtHR in 2010. The ECtHR concluded that the difference in treatment sustained by the applicant foundation had no objective or reasonable justification. It observed that the system for granting exemptions from payment of electricity bills for places of worship under Turkish law thus entailed discrimination on the ground of religion. The ECtHR held, unanimously, that there had been a violation of Article 14 (prohibition of discrimination) taken together with Article 9 (freedom of thought, conscience and religion) of the European Convention on Human Rights.

Consequently some *cemevis* refused to pay their electricity bills and in the due process their energy supplies were cut off. Some of those *cemevis* filed cases against those administrative actions in local courts and each of them had judgments on their favors, thus they are now exempt from paying for electricity bills for their worship halls *per se*. In brief, when a *cemevi* files a case, judicial process ends in its favor. However as there are thousands of *cemevis* in Turkey, and there exists no umbrella legislation prepared and/or declared, in order to be exempt from paying electricity bills each individual *cemevi* is forced to file an individual case before a local court.

So far no legislative arrangements have been done to allow all *cemevis* in general to benefit from this exemption.

The Turkish Government, in its Action Plan dated 5 January 2016 and presented to the Committee of Ministers, in reference to the 64th Government's programme, announced its intention to grant legal status both to traditional centers of culture and *cemevis*. To this date no changes has not been reported in that direction.

4.2.5.3 Case of İzzettin Doğan and Others v. Turkey Application No. 62649/10

On 22 June 2005, applicants individually submitted a petition to the Prime Minister requesting that:

- services connected with the practice of the Alevi faith constitute a public service,
- Alevi places of worship (*cemevis*) be granted the status of places of worship,
- Alevi clergy providing religious services be recruited as civil servants,
- special provision be made in the budget for the practice of the Alevi faith,.

After exhausting all judicial processes, on 31 August 2010, 203 applicants filed an application with the ECtHR claiming that by refusing to provide to members of their community religious public services, as it is provided for the Sunni individuals was a violation. On 26 April 2016, the Grand Chamber held that there had been a violation articles 9 and 14 under the European Convention of Human Rights in the case of *Izzettin Doğan and Others v. Turkey*.

4.3 In Lieu of a Conclusion

Despite abovementioned decisions, still belief groups in Turkey do not have any legal identity, nor there is neither any progress nor preparations in that aspect. Worship places of Alevi, Protestant Christian and some others are not recognized, interventions to election procedure of Armenian Patriarch has been publicized recently,[42] a portion of the properties of minority foundations have been returned to communities but a great number of minority foundations are still non-recognized.

As a final note I should underline that primary consideration for regimes of protection of rights and freedoms relies on fairness. The U.N. Declaration on the Elimination of All Forms of Intolerance and of Discrimination Based on Religion or Belief of 1981 is clearly a very important international instrument regarding

[42]On 22 May 2019 the Constitutional Court of Turkey decided that it is a violation of Article 24 of the Constitution to intervene in the election process for the Armenian Patriarch. (*Levon Berç Kuzukoğlu ve Ohannes Garbis Balmumciyan* (application No: 2014/17354). https://www.anayasa.gov.tr/media/6037/2014-17354.pdf

religious rights and as it is required by Article 7, the rights and freedoms set forth in the Declaration should be accorded in national legislation in such a manner that everyone shall be able to avail themselves of such rights and freedoms in practice. However, no one's religion should be used to harm others, as well. Religion may often be used as an excuse to discriminate against LGBTQ people, women, religious minorities, non-believers and others (Millhiser 2020).[43] Thus, struggle against discrimination based on religion should always cover discrimination in the name of religion as well.

References

Abu-Manneh, Butrus. 2001. *Studies on Islam and the Ottoman Empire in the 19th Century (1826–1876)*. Istanbul: The ISIS Press.

Ahdar, Rex, and Ian Leigh. 2005. *Religious Freedom in the Liberal State*. Oxford/New York: Oxford University Press.

Ahmad, Fero. 2003. *Turkey: The Quest for Identity*. Oxford: Oneworld.

Akbulut Kuru, Zeynep, and Ahmet T. Kuru. 2008. A Political Interpretation of Islam: Said Nursi's Faith Based Activism in Comparison with Political Islamism and Sufism. *Islam and Christian-Muslim Relations* 19/1: 99–111. https://doi.org/10.1080/13510340701770311.

Anar, Erol. 1996. *İnsan Hakları Tarihi*. İstanbul: Çiviyazıları.

Aydın-Düzgit, Senem. 2014. Human Rights in Turkey. In *Turkey's Democratization Process*, ed. Carmen Rodriguez, Antonio Avalos, Hakan Yılmaz, and Ana I. Planet. London/New York: Routledge.

Azak, Umut. 2012. Secularists as the Saviors of Islam: Rearticulation of Secularism and Freedom of Conciense in Turkey (1950). In *Secular State and Religious Society: Two Forces in Play in Turkey*, ed. Berna Turam. New York: Palgrave Macmillan.

Babinger, Franz. 1978. *Mehmed the Conquerer and His Time*. Trans. Ralph Manheim. Princeton: Princeton University Press.

Bali, Rifat N. 2006. The Politics of Turkification During the Single Party Period. In *Turkey Beyond Nationalism Towards Post-Nationalist Identities*, ed. Hans-Lukas Kieser. London/New York: I. B.Tauris.

Barkey, Karen. 1994. *Bandits and Bureaucrats: The Ottoman Route to State Centralization*. Ithaca/London: Cornell University Press.

———. 2008. *Empire of Difference: The Ottomans in Comparative Perspective*. New York: Cambridge University Press.

Berk, Bekir. 1975. *Nurculuk Davası*. Istanbul: Yeni Asya Yayınları.

Beylunioğlu, Anna Maria. 2017. Recasting the Parameters of Freedom of Religion in Turkey: Non-Muslims and the AKP. In *Authoritarian Politics in Turkey: Elections, Resistance and the AKP*, ed. Bahar Başer and Ahmet Erdi Öztürk. London/New York: I.B.Tauris.

Cady, Linell E., and Elizabeth Shakman Hurd. 2010. *Comparative Secularisms in a Global Age*. New York: Palgrave Macmillan.

Cagaptay, Soner. 2006. *Islam, Secularism, and Nationalism in Modern Turkey: Who is a Turk?* London/New York: Routledge.

[43]For Fulton v. City of Philadelphia which is likely to deal a severe blow to LGBTQ rights see, Ian Milhiser, "The fight over whether religion is a license to discriminate is back before the Supreme Court", February 25, 2020; https://www.vox.com/2020/2/25/21150692/supreme-court-religion-discrimination-lgbtq-foster-fulton-philadelphia-first-amendment

Çarkoğlu, Ali, and Ersin Kalaycıoğlu. 2009. *The Rising Tide of Conservatism in Turkey*. New York: Palgrave Macmillan.

Çarkoğlu, Ali. 2006. The New Generation Pro-Islamists in Turkey: Bases of Justice and Development Party in Changing Electoral Space. In *The Emergence of a New Turkey: Democracy and the AK Parti*, ed. M. Hakan Yavuz. Salt Lake City: The University of Utah Press.

Casanova, Jose. 1994. *Public Religions in the Modern World*. Chicago/London: The University of Chicago Press.

Çınar, Menderes, and Burhanettin Duran. 2008. Evolution of Contemporary Political Islam. In *Secular and Islamic Politics in Turkey: The Making of the Justice and Development Party*, ed. Ümit Cizre. London/New York: Routledge.

Davison, Andrew. 2003. Turkey, a 'Secular' State? The Challenge of Description. *The South Atlantic Quarterly* 102 (2): 333–350.

Deringil, Selim. 1998. *The Well-Protected Domains: Ideology and the Legitimation of Power in the Ottoman Empire 1876–1909*. London/New York: I.B. Tauris.

Findley, Carter V. 1982. The Acid Test of Ottomanism: The Acceptance of Non-Muslims in the Late Ottoman Bureaucracy. In *Christians and Jews in the Ottoman Empire: The Functioning of a Plural Society*, ed. Benjamin Braude and Bernard Lewis. New York: Holmes and Meier Publishers.

Findley, Carter Vaughn. 2010. *Turkey, Islam, Nationalism, and Modernity: A History, 1789–2007*. New Haven and London: Yale University Press.

Goffman, Daniel. 2002. *The Ottoman Empire and Early Modern Europe*. New York: Cambridge University Press.

Gözaydın, İştar B. 2008. Diyanet and Politics. *The Muslim World* 98-2 (3): 216–227.

Gözaydın, İştar. 2017. Epilogue: The Desire is There. In *Authoritarian Politics in Turkey: Elections, Resistance and the AKP*, ed. Bahar Başer and Ahmet Erdi Öztürk. London/New York: I.B. Tauris.

———. 2020. *Diyanet: Türkiye'de Din Siyaseti*. rev ed. Istanbul: İletişim.

Güven, Dilek. 2011. Riots Against the non-Muslims of Turkey: 6/ September 1955 in the context of demographic engineering. *European journal of Turkish studies – Social Sciences on Contemporary Turkey* 12. https://journals.openedition.org/ejts/4538.

Hale, William, and Ergun Özbudun. 2010. *Islamism, Democracy and Liberalism in Turkey: The case of the AKP*. London/New York: Routledge.

Hanioğlu, M.Şükrü. 2008. *A Brief History of the Late Ottoman Empire*. Princeton/Oxford: Princeton University Press.

İnalcık, Halil. 1973. *The Ottoman Empire: The Classical Age 1300–1600*. New York: Weidenfeld and Nicolson.

Kafadar, Cemal. 1995. *Between Two Worls: The Construction of the Ottoman State*. Berkley/Los Angeles/London: University of California Press.

Keyder, Çağlar. 1997. The Ottoman Empire. In *After Empire: Multiethnic Societies and Nation Building – The Soviet Union and the Russian, Ottoman and Habsburg Empires*, ed. Karen Barkey and Mark von Hagen. Colorado/Oxford: Westview.

Kırlıdökme, Utku. 2010. The Greek Orthodox Patriarchate of Istanbul and the Heybeli Theology School (Halki Seminary): History, Discussions and JDP Government's Policy. *The Turkish Yearbook of International Relations* 41: 31–58.

Korkut, Tolga. 2019. What happened on 6–7 September? *Bianet*. https://m.bianet.org/english/minorities/116914-what-happened-on-6-7-september.

Kuru, Ahmet T. 2017. Islam and Democracy in Turkey: Analyzing the Failure. *The Montréal Review*. http://www.themontrealreview.com/2009/Islam-And-Democracy-In-Turkey.php.

Lewis, Bernard. 1961/1979. *The Emergence of Modern Turkey*. London/Oxford/New York: Oxford University Press.

Mahmood, Saba. 2015. Religious Freedom, Minority Rights, and Geopolitics. In *Politics of Religious Freedom*, ed. Winnnifred Fallers Sullivan, Elizabeth Shakman Hurd, Saba Mahmood, and Peter G. Danchin. Chicago/London: The University of Chicago Press.

Mardin, Şerif. 1989. *Religion and Social Change in Modern Turkey: The Case of Bediüzzaman Said Nursi*. Albany: State University of New York Press.
———. 1997. The Ottoman Empire. In *After Empire: Multiethnic Societies and Nation Building – The Soviet Union and the Russian, Ottoman and Habsburg Empires*, ed. Karen Barkey and Mark von Hagen. Colorado/Oxford: Westview.
Massicard, Elise. 2006. Claiming Difference in an Unitarist Frame: The Case of Alevism. In *Turkey Beyond Nationalism: Towards Post-Nationalist Identities*, ed. Hans-Lukas Kieser. London/New York: I.B.Tauris.
Millhiser, Ian. 2020. *The Fight Over Whether Religion Is a License to Discriminate Is Back Before the Supreme Court*. February 25, 2020. https://www.vox.com/2020/2/25/21150692/supreme-court-religion-discrimination-lgbtq-foster-fulton-philadelphia-first-amendment.
Özbudun, Ergun. 2012. Turkey – Plural Society and Monolithic State. In *Democracy, Islam & Secularism in Turkey*, ed. Ahmet Kuru and Alfred Stephan. New York: Columbia University Press.
Özdalga, Elizabeth. 2008. The Alevis – A "New" Religious Minority? Identity Politics in Turkey and Its Relation to the EU Integration Process. In *Religion, Politics, and Turkey's EU Accession*, ed. Dietrich Jung and Catharina Raudvere. New York: Palgrave Macmillan.
———. 2010. Transformation of Sufi-Based Communities in Modern Turkey: The Nakşibendis, the Nurcus, and the Gülen Community. In *Turkey's Engagement with Modernity: Conflict and Change in the Twentieth Century*, ed. Celia Kerslake, Kerem Öktem, and Philip Robins. Oxford: Palgrave Macmillan.
Özkırımlı, Umut. 2014. *The Making of a Protest Movement in Turkey*. London: Palgrave Macmillan.
Shakman Hurd, Elizabeth. 2015. *Beyond Religious Freedom: The New Global Politics of Religion*. Princeton/Oxford: Princeton University Press.
Shankland, David. 1999. *Islam and Society in Turkey*. Cambridgeshire: The Eothen Press.
Şirin, Tolga. 2014. Freedom From Religion in Turkey. In *Freedom of Religion and Belief in Turkey*, ed. Özgür Heval Çınar and Mine Yıldırım. Newcastle upon Tyne: Cambridge Scholars Publishing.
Stone, Norman. 2010. *Turkey: A Short History*. London: Thames & Hudson.
Sunar, İlkay. 1987. State and Economy in the Ottoman Empire. In *The Ottoman Empire and the World-Economy*, ed. Huri İslamoğlu-İnan. New York: Cambridge University Press.
Sunier, Thijl, and Nico Landman. 2015. *Transnational Turkish Islam: Shifting Geographies of Religious Activism and Community Building in Turkey and Europe*. London: Palgrave Macmillan.
Tavernise, Sabrina, and Şebnem Arsu. Turkish Court Calls Turkish Party Constitutional. *The New York Times*, 31 July 2008.
Treitschke, Heinrich von. 1916. *Politics II*. Trans. Blanche Dugdale & Torben de Bille. New York: The Macmillan Company.
Tuğal, Cihan. 2009. *Passive Revolution: Absorbing the Islamic Challenge to Capitalism*. Stanford: Stanford University Press.
Türköne, Mümtazer. 1991. *Siyasal İdeoloji Olarak İslamcılığın Doğuşu*. İstanbul: İletişim.
Vahide, Şükran. 2005. *Islam in Modern Turkey: An Intellectual Biography of Bediuzzaman Said Nursi*. Albany: State University of New York Press.
Vertigans, Stephen. 2003. *Islamic Roots and Resurgence in Turkey: Understanding and Explaining the Muslim Resurgence*. Westport/Connecticut/London: Praeger.
Watmough, Simon, and Ahmet Erdi Öztürk. 2018. From 'Diaspora by Design' to Transnational Political Exile: The Gülen Movement in Transition. *Politics, Religion & Ideology* 19: 1–10. https://doi.org/10.1080/21567689.2018.1453244.
White, Jenny B. 2002. *Islamist Mobilization in Turkey: A Study in Vernacular Politics*. Seattle and London: University of Washington Press.
White, Jenny. 2013. *Muslim Nationalism and the New Turks*. Princeton/Oxford: Princeton University Press.

Yavuz, M.Hakan. 2009. *Secularism and Muslim Democracy in Turkey*. New York: Cambridge University Press.

———. 2018. A Framework for Understanding the Intra-Islamist Conflict Between the AK Party and the Gülen Movement. *Politics, Religion & Ideology* 19: 11–32. https://doi.org/10.1080/21567689.2018.1453247.

Yıldırım, Mine. 2015. *The Collective Dimension of Freedom of Religion or Belief in International Law: The Application of Findings to the Case of Turkey*. Abo: Abo Akademi University Press.

İştar Gözaydın studied law at Istanbul University (1981) and New York University (1987). Starting her academic career in 1983, she became a tenured full professor in 2006 focusing on state-religion relations, the role of religion in Turkey's foreign policy, religious discrimination, and law-politics relations. Gözaydın was deprived of her freedom by being jailed in Turkey upon alleged charges in the context of "Anti-Terror Law" between December 2016 and March 2017. She was fully acquitted in 2018, however since Gözaydın had an international travel ban for three years, she has not been able to physically attend the Leibniz Professorship position that she was granted in 2018 at Leibniz University. Being a founding member of Helsinki Citizens Assembly, a prominent human rights NGO, and having published extensive work domestically and internationally, Gözaydın was granted Lisl and Leo Eitinger Human Rights Award by Oslo University in 2017. She has been producing and presenting radio programs on law, politics and music (currently on J.S. Bach) at *Açık Radyo* since 1995 where she was one of the founding members. She has been attending *Femfikir* debate programs where national and international politics are discussed by a group of female experts since it was launched in December 2017 at *Medyascope*, an independent internet medium based in Istanbul. Gözaydın lost her beloved husband İskender Savaşır in June 2018 after a short episode of 4.5 months after a diagnosis of two primary cancers.

Chapter 5
Non-Discrimination, Minority Rights and Self-Determination: Turkey's Post-Coup State of Emergency and the Position of Turkey's Kurds

Emre Turkut and Thomas Phillips

Abstract States of emergency are often declared due to underlying problems of minority group accommodation, and the extraordinary limitation of rights arising from them tends to have a particularly striking effect on such groups. This was true, for instance, with the emergency measures adopted by the British authorities in the context of the 'Troubles' in Northern Ireland. The same appears true in respect of the Turkish state of emergency in the aftermath of the failed military coup of 15 July 2016 *vis-à-vis* the position of Turkey's Kurds. In spite of the fact that the declaration of the state of emergency constituted a response to an attempted coup which was, allegedly, orchestrated by the Gülen Movement, it is clear that the resulting derogating measures have also targeted 'other individuals and organizations', mainly those allegedly connected to the PKK (Kurdistan Workers' Party), and thus extended to Turkey's Kurdish periphery. This chapter seeks to map the impact of the Turkish post-coup derogation measures on Turkey's Kurds and to test them against the non-discrimination principle, minority rights, and the right of self-determination.

Keywords Emergency · Kurds · Non-discrimination · Minority rights · Self-determination · Turkey

---

E. Turkut (✉)
Ghent Rolin-Jaequemyns International Law Institute (GRILI), Ghent University, Ghent, Belgium
e-mail: Emre.Turkut@UGent.be

T. Phillips
Liverpool John Moores University, Liverpool, UK
e-mail: T.J.Phillips@ljmu.ac.uk

H. Aydin, W. Langley (eds.), *Human Rights in Turkey*, Philosophy and Politics - Critical Explorations 15, https://doi.org/10.1007/978-3-030-57476-5_5

5.1 Introduction

The application of human rights during public emergencies is one of the main legal challenges of our times. Based on ample evidence of actual practice (i.e. France and the United Kingdom), emergency regimes—particularly when coupled with broad-reaching and vague anti-terrorism laws—tend to be accompanied by gross and systematic human rights abuses as when states arrogate extraordinary powers to address threats to public order (OSCE 2018). This trend is recently exemplified by the far-reaching derogation measures adopted by Turkish authorities after the failed military coup of 15 July 2016.

In the aftermath of the attempted coup, on 21 July 2016, Turkey declared a nationwide state of emergency and lodged a derogation notice with the Council of Europe (CoE) to derogate from the European Convention on Human Rights (ECHR) pursuant to Article 15 thereof, referring to *the 15 July coup attempt and its aftermath together with the 'other' terrorist attacks*.[1] A similar notification was lodged with the UN Secretary-General on 2 August 2016 pursuant to Article 4 of the International Covenant on Civil and Political Rights (ICCPR).[2] Since the initial declaration, the state of emergency was prolonged seven times for a total period of 24 months until it was eventually lifted on 17 July 2018.[3]

A closer examination of the derogation measures undertaken by Turkey during the period of emergency rule suggests that the post-coup measures reached their apotheosis through mass detentions and institutional closures, and through the collective dismissals of public servants (Ruys and Turkut 2018). Turkey adopted a *scattergun* approach to human rights curtailment, which involved severe repression based, in many cases, on a very tenuous connection with the *raison d'être* of the state of emergency (Turkut 2019). As a result, the emergency decrees targeted a wide range of human rights. Although the state of emergency was lifted in July 2018, many of the exceptional emergency powers have concretized into new, permanent anti-terrorism legislation, which has been described as 'normalizing the state of emergency' (EU Progress Report 2019), and have found institutional form in Turkey's new presidential system of government, which is incompatible with elementary constitutional principles such as the separation of powers (Human Rights Watch 2018).

States of emergency are often linked to the inadequate or non-existent protection of minority rights, and the extraordinary limitation of rights during these crises tends to have a striking impact on minorities both collectively and individually. This was true, for instance, with the emergency measures adopted by Britain, particularly the

[1]See, Turkey, Derogation to the Convention on the Protection of Human Rights and Fundamental Freedoms Notification (ETS No.5), JJ8187C Tr./005–191, 22 July 2016.

[2]See, Turkey, Notification under Article 4(3) of International Covenant on Civil and Political Rights, C.N.580.2016.Treaties-iv.4, 2 August 2016.

[3]See, Turkey, Derogation to the Convention on the Protection of Human Rights and Fundamental Freedoms Notification (ETS No.5), JJ8719C Tr./005–223, 8 August 2018.

unequal use of detention and internment against the Catholic minority, in the context of the 'Troubles' in Northern Ireland (Bakircioglu and Dickson 2017). More recently, warrantless house raids and arrests of Muslims during France's state of emergency in the aftermath of the 2015 Paris attacks have raised similar 'community profiling' and 'discrimination' concerns (Human Rights Watch 2016; Codaccioni 2018). The same also appears true in respect of the Turkish state of emergency and the parlous situation of its Kurdish population. Although the declaration of the state of emergency was an immediate response to the attempted coup, the derogating measures have not been targeted exclusively at the Gülen Movement (GM), a group designated by government as the 'Fetullahist Terrorist Organization/the Parallel State Structure' ('FETÖ/PDY') (which, it is claimed, was responsible for the failed coup), but have also extended to the Kurdish periphery where the PKK has been engaged in a fierce fight with the Turkish state since the mid-1980s.[4] The decimation of many prominent pro-Kurdish associations, TV channels, news agencies and radio stations; the dismissal of over 11,000 schoolteachers deemed to be linked with the Kurdistan Workers' Party (PKK); the removal of over 90 mayors of the pro-Kurdish Peoples' Democratic Party (HDP) and its regional sister-party, the DBP (Democratic Regions Party); and the detention of over 10 HDP deputies on an array of charges related to alleged involvement in, and support for, terrorism are salient examples.

International human rights law seeks to protect the rights of minorities during states of emergency. Most notably, the ICCPR explicitly incorporates 'as one of the conditions for the justifiability of any derogation' in Article 4 that the derogation measures should not 'involve discrimination *solely* on the ground of race, color, sex, language, religion or social origin'. The ECHR, on the other hand, does not explicitly pronounce on the prohibition of discrimination in its derogation clause of Article 15, but it does contain two legal norms on non-discrimination.[5] Article 14 ECHR provides that Convention rights shall be secured without discrimination on a number of grounds, including 'association with a national minority' (ECtHR, *Thlimmenos v Greece* [2000] para. 33). Protocol 12 to the ECHR provides a more general prohibition of discrimination.

Moreover, Article 27 ICCPR more directly protects the rights of minorities. As explained below, derogation from *some* elements of Article 27 is legally impermissible. The ECHR, on the other hand, contains no minority rights provision. Therefore, there is no direct way for members of minority groups to claim minority rights in the ECHR regime though the European Court of Human Rights (ECtHR) has held that member states are under an obligation to uphold "international standards in the field of the protection of human and minority rights" (ECtHR *Denizci v Cyprus*

[4]The PKK and Da'esh are the only 'other terrorist organizations' mentioned by name in the Turkish Government's Memorandum to the Venice Commission. See, Turkey, '*Memorandum prepared by the Ministry of Justice of Turkey for the visit of the delegation of the Venice Commission to Ankara on 3 and 4 November 2016 in connection with the emergency decree laws*', CDL-REF (2016)067, 23 November 2016.

[5]Despite its lack of a minority rights provision, the ECHR is not completely blind to questions of minority group protection and does, to a limited extent, engage with them indirectly.

[2001] para. 410). Furthermore, reference must also be made to the overlapping yet normatively independent group right of self-determination of peoples, a norm of *jus cogens* (ILC, Fourth Report on Peremptory Norms of General International Law 2019) and *erga omnes* character (ICJ, *Portugal v Australia* [1995] and *Advisory Opinion* [2004]), which is enshrined, in international treaties (Article 1 of the ICCPR & ICESCR) and forms part of modern customary international law (UNGA, Resolution 1514 (XV) [1960] and Resolution 2625 (XXV) [1970]).

Against that background, this chapter seeks to shed light on an unexplored aspect of the Turkish post-coup emergency regime.[6] In particular, it seeks to map the impact of the Turkish derogation measures on Turkey's Kurds, and to test the derogation measures against the non-discrimination principle, minority rights, and the right of self-determination. Section I examines the scope of the Turkish post-coup emergency and the consequences thereof. It then zooms-in on the operation of the derogation measures vis-à-vis the Kurdish people by arguing that they cannot be understood merely as extraordinary actions taken against the specific threat arising from the failed coup (or so called, 'other terrorist attacks'); rather, they must be understood *in a much wider sense* encompassing the historical and ongoing persecution of the Kurdish minority.

The following two sections analyze the state of emergency through the lens of certain human rights. Section II focuses on the individual right of non-discrimination and minority rights. The section scrutinizes the principles of necessity, proportionality and non-discrimination within the derogations regime. The section argues that notwithstanding the negative impact on the Kurds it seems unlikely that the human rights bodies will resort to a broad and encompassing use of the non-discrimination principle. It then considers the linked question of whether the minority rights contained in Article 27 of the ICCPR tell us anything about the legality of particular state of emergency measures. It will be argued that one can build a plausible case that certain measures taken during the state of emergency, and which Turkey might plausibly claim to be covered by its derogations, were in violation of Article 27.

Section III takes the argument further by engaging with the crux of the Kurdish Question in Turkey, namely the group right of self-determination. In concrete terms, insofar as the derogation measures have arguably disproportionately targeted Turkey's Kurds and shrunk the political space for articulating Kurdish demands, it is important to establish whether they can be reconciled with the right of

[6]There is an emerging literature on the Turkish state of emergency in the aftermath of the 15 July coup attempt and the post-coup emergency measures. The existing scholarship has so far focused on the legality of the collective dismissals of thousands of public servants from the perspective of ECHR law (see, Ruys and Turkut 2018); on the use of exceptional national security and emergency powers in the fight against terrorism in Turkey (see, Turkut 2019); on the question whether the Turkish failed coup could be regarded as an 'emergency that threatens the life of a nation' under Article 4 ICCPR and Article 15 ECHR (see, Nugraha 2018); on the legitimacy and proportionality of Turkey's post-coup derogation (See, Altiparmak and Gürol 2019); and on the perceptions of the victims of human rights violation during the post-coup crackdown (see, Aydin and Avincan 2020). Finally, for a comparative analysis in the context the recent declarations of state of emergencies by Ukraine, France, and Turkey, see Mariniello 2019.

self-determination of Turkey's Kurds by analyzing the normative guiding principles that might be derived from international law. The section argues that certain state of emergency measures run counter to the procedural and substantive aspects of that *jus cogens* right.

5.2 The Post-Coup Emergency and the Kurdish People in Turkey

5.2.1 The Scope of the Post-Coup Emergency

Before fully embarking on mapping the Turkish derogation measures with a particular focus on Turkey's Kurds, one must consider the scope of the state of emergency. As noted above, Turkey's derogation notices are broad in scope, and cover a wider range of threats than those posed by the groups, which were directly involved in the planning and implementation of the failed coup. By making a very general reference to the series of events that unfolded in Turkey on the night of 15 July 2016, and by mentioning *'other terrorist acts'* with no further elaboration, the notices indicated Turkey's intention to "take required measures in the most speedy and effective manner" in its *fight against all terrorist organizations*.

The Turkish Government purported to justify this position in a notification letter of 25 July 2016 to the CoE, in which it asserted that 'FETÖ's "widespread infiltration" combined with "grave and violent attacks against national security" made it necessary (where it was not previously thought necessary) to derogate from certain human rights obligations.[7] Later, in its Memorandum of 23 November 2016 to the Venice Commission, the Turkish authorities asserted that there are close links between GM and the PKK, with the latter taking advantage of the state's perceived vulnerability.

Leaving aside the question of what sort of *close* relationship can be drawn between GM and the PKK (and leaving aside the questionable assumption that any entity that might benefit from the actions of another is therefore closely linked with it) the most relevant question is whether the Turkish Government was "reasonably entitled to consider that normal legislation offered insufficient resources for the campaign against terrorism and that recourse to measures outside the scope of the ordinary law...was called for" (ECtHR, *Ireland v UK* [1978] para.117). Put differently, could the public emergency in post-coup Turkey justify a lawful derogation from Turkey's international human rights obligations given that a derogation regime is normally intended to be a response to the circumstances of a *specific* emergency? And if so, could the emergency measures be justified if the focus shifts primarily towards 'other terrorist attacks' (Venice Commission 2016)? As aptly observed, "[a] lthough the notion of a public emergency might be defined in the abstract with

[7]See, Turkey, Derogation to the Convention on the Protection of Human Rights and Fundamental Freedoms Notification (ETS No.5), JJ8190C Tr./005–192, 25 July 2016.

relative ease, the application *in concreto* of such definition gives rise to numerous legal problems to which, so far, either only partial solutions have been found, or none at all" (Svensson-McCarthy 1998, 195).

The ECtHR, when it ruled on the validity and legitimacy of the Turkish derogation for the first time in the *Mehmet Altan and Sahin Alpay* cases of 20 March 2018 did not question this factual basis for the scope of the Turkish post-coup state of emergency. It relied on the finding by the Turkish Constitutional Court (TCC) in the *Aydın Yavuz and Others* (TCC, [2017]) case that "the fact that the attempted coup had taken place at a time when Turkey had been under violent attack from numerous terrorist organizations had made the country even more vulnerable". By simply highlighting that "...the attempted military coup disclosed the existence of a 'public emergency threatening the life of the nation' within the meaning of the Convention", thus justifying Turkey's recourse to the derogation clause under Article 15 ECHR (seemingly) in connection with the 15 July attempted coup, the ECtHR failed to take into account the dangers allegedly posed by these 'other terrorist organizations' and refrained from making a determination on the Turkish recourse to measures outside the scope of the its ordinary law in its broader fight against terrorism (ECtHR, *Altan v Turkey* [2018] para.92 and *Alpay v Turkey* [2018] para.76). In other words, the ECtHR too uncritically rode on the coat tails of the TCC.

This amplified the deference effect seen in the context of national security at a domestic level by giving it an international dimension. To date, the human rights bodies have conceded the government's assertion of a state of emergency although in principle there must be a close *nexus* between the circumstances of the public emergency and the proportionality of measures taken in response thereto (UNHRC, General Comment No. 29 (2001) para.4) On the ECHR level, with only one exception, the European organs have consistently deferred to national authorities' assessment of whether or not a 'public emergency threatening the life of the nation' exists.[8] The ECtHR has even acquiesced to the UK Government's assertion that the threat of terrorism prior to any actual attack was a public emergency threatening the life of the nation (ECtHR, *A & Others v United Kingdom* [2009]). As regards the ICCPR regime, the United Nations Human Rights Committee (UN HRC or Committee) has traditionally been reluctant to determine the existence of a state of emergency and, in one instance, based its finding on "the *assumption* that there exists a situation of emergency" while generally acknowledging "the sovereign right of a State to declare a state of emergency is not questioned" (UNHRC, *Landinelli Silva v Uruguay* [1981]). As early as 1978, reacting to this clear disconnect between principles under international human rights treaties and the deferential practice of treaty bodies, one commentator observed how "a critical on-looker would be justified in concluding that the chances of a state being found guilty of wrongly declaring an emergency are somewhat remote" (Green 1979, 548).

---

[8]The exception concerns the European Commission on Human Rights' rejection of the claim by the Greek "Colonel's regime" that a state of emergency existed that justified its having taken certain measures following the 1967 military coup that had brought it to power.

5.2.2 *Mapping the Impact of the Turkish State of Emergency on the Kurdish People*

After the failed coup, Turkey adopted a wide range of emergency decrees, which granted "very far-reaching, almost unlimited discretionary powers for administrative authorities" (CoE Commissioner for Human Rights 2016) and targeted anyone deemed a terrorist to counter the severe dangers to public security and order from terrorist activities, whether or not the latter are related to the coup attempt. Unsurprisingly, the Kurdish movement has borne the brunt of the emergency, suffering a crackdown marked by higher levels of political imprisonment and greater restrictions on freedom of assembly and association and on electoral aspects of self-determination (UN OHCHR 2017, 22).

The re-securitization of the Kurdish question, whereby Turkey seeks to turn every move towards Kurdish rights into an existential threat, makes the situation even more threatening from a Kurdish perspective (Bezwan 2018, 62). This situation is not unique in Turkish history: from the beginning of the Republic in 1923, Turkey adopted repressive measures towards Kurdish culture and language, and established a military presence in the Kurdish region, leading to the announcement of martial law and state of emergency in the Turkish southeast (McDowall 2004) This is particularly due to the fact that Turkey has clung to the idea of a Turkish identity as the origin of national unity with one language and one nation (See Article 3 of the Turkish Constitution) and sought to impose a common set of traditions and historical-cultural narratives on all segments of society and, in case of resistance, eliminate other identities and ethnic minorities through a policy of denial and suppression (Yeğen 1999; Oeter 2018, 212). Due to this mind-set, the 'Kurdish problem' has been reduced to a security issue and the important cultural and socio-political elements of the Kurdish Question have been sidelined (Barkey and Fuller 1998). Rather than addressing the *cause* of the security issue by engaging with the Kurds' very real and legitimate grievances (a strategy that was, eventually, adopted by the UK in regards to Northern Ireland with much success), Turkey has opted to focus intently on the violent *effects* of those unaddressed grievances.

The collapse of the peace process in 2015 led to this re-securitization narrative. It is argued that a resolution of the Kurdish issue proved beyond reach of a peace process marked with "divergent understandings and irreconcilable expectations and the lack of a concrete roadmap" (International Crisis Group 2015). Since July 2015, the Turkish Government has adopted a policy reminiscent of the violence of the 1990s, which is marked by a campaign of counter-insurgency, the declaration of open-ended curfews and 'temporary security zones',[9] and anti-terrorism operations

---

[9]In June 2007, the Turkish Armed Forces announced via their website that 'temporary security zones' would be formed in three Kurdish provinces: Şırnak, Siirt and Hakkari. Since then, many additional areas have been declared as provisional security zones. The Law on Prohibited Military Zones and Security Zones No. 2565 provided the legal basis of 'temporary security zones'. The Law No. 2565 was adopted on 18 December 1981 by the 12 September military regime and it still

that killed and displaced a large number of civilians[10] and caused destruction in the Kurdish majority region. Echoing these human rights concerns, in early 2016, the United Nations Committee on the Elimination of Racial Discrimination stressed that in the context of the fight against terrorism, the enforcement of anti-terrorism legislation and security-oriented policies have resulted in racial profiling of members of the Kurdish community (UNCERD Report 2016). Such legislation has been applied to curtail the right to freedom of expression and association and led to the unwarranted arrest, detention and prosecution of thousands of Kurds.

This trend against the Kurdish minority reached a new peak via far-reaching powers under the state of emergency. Amid a growing onslaught against Kurdish opposition voices during the state of emergency period, on 1 September 2016, the Turkish Ministry of Education suspended 11,500 schoolteachers deemed to be linked with the PKK and revoked their licenses to teach, over 90 percent of whom were serving in Kurdish-speaking municipalities.[11] Turkey, however, provided little evidence, thus giving rise to concerns that they were dismissed as a precautionary measure based on mere suspicion (UN OHCHR 2017).

On the same day, Turkey adopted Decree No. 674 that allowed for the removal and replacement of locally elected officials with trustees appointed by the Turkish Ministry of Interior where a mayor, deputy mayor or member of municipal council has been dismissed or arrested due to the offences of aiding and abetting terrorism and terrorist organizations. An overwhelming number of those replaced had links with the Kurdish movement (DBP Local Authorities Commission Report 2017). Despite the official termination of the Turkish post-coup state of emergency, this practice has continued in the Kurdish regions. The majority of replaced co-mayors have been jailed on politically motivated terrorism charges after their removal from elected office (HDP Report 2019).

Throughout the emergency period, Turkey permanently closed at least 20 Kurdish media outlets for 'spreading terrorist propaganda' (Amnesty International 2017). It

---

remains in effect. When the PKK announced to end the cease-fire in July 2015, a total of 37 areas had become 'temporary security zones' in Turkey's east and southeast. The declaration of such zones enables the military to effectively occupy the area and exercise powers similar to those, which existed under the state of emergency regimes. It has been argued, however, that since then a de facto state of emergency has continued to exist in a legally dubious form and substance in the context of 'temporary security zones'. Thus, despite a de jure revocation in 2002, a de facto exceptional regime has continued to raise the spectre of past emergency rule in Turkey's southeast. See also Yıldız and Breau 2010, 22 and KHRP 2008, 14.

[10]"According to official figures related to Sur, for example, 22,000 persons were displaced for 50 terrorists rendered ineffective; a ratio of 440." See, Memorandum on the Human Rights Implications of Anti-Terrorism Operations in South-Eastern Turkey, Council of Europe Commissioner for Human Rights, Comm.DH (2016) 39, 2 December 2016, para.28.

[11]Many lower level public servants, such as schoolteachers, not mentioned in the appended lists of Decrees, have been dismissed by decisions of the relevant administrative entities and judicial bodies. As envisaged in Article 4(1) of Decree no.667, these dismissals take place "upon the proposal of the commission to be established by the minister in the relevant ministries and with the approval of the Minister."

also took steps to erode the institutional base of the Kurdish movement and severely restricted their right to organize via political parties. Thousands of HDP and DBP party officials, including its two-chairs, have been detained on anti-terror grounds (Human Rights Watch 2017). More than 10 HDP deputies have been stripped of their seats in parliament on the same grounds (EU Progress Report 2019).

5.3 Testing Turkey's Post-Coup Measures Against the Non-Discrimination Principle and Minority Rights

5.3.1 Non-Discrimination

The post-coup derogation measures significantly targeting the Kurdish minority *prima facie* raise an issue of non-discrimination. For example, in relation to the mass dismissals of the Kurdish school teachers, the OHCHR noted its concerns that this practice poses the question of the political or racial profiling of members of an ethnic group and thus of Turkey's compliance with the prohibition of discrimination (UN OHCHR 2017). Relatedly, the Kurdish representatives alleged that this measure was introduced as a form of collective punishment based on their ethnic origin and language (UN OHCHR 2017).

However, these measures do not necessarily violate the principle of non-discrimination. According to the consistent case law of international human rights bodies, a difference in treatment on the basis of criteria such as race, ethnicity or national origin may be considered lawful if it pursues a *legitimate aim* (in the ECtHR jargon) or in other words, has *reasonable and objective justification* (in the UN HRC jargon) and if there is reasonable *relationship of proportionality* between the means employed and the aim sought to be realized.

The argument here is that it is unlikely that the human rights bodies will resort to an imaginative use of the non-discrimination principle with regard to the Turkish derogation measures affecting the Kurdish minority. There are at least three reasons for this - one contextual, the others technical. The contextual argument is that, as is clear from Turkey's derogation notice, at least on paper the post-coup state of emergency was declared to counter the threats arising from the failed coup and other terrorist attacks, rather than being targeted against a particular minority group (Kurdish minority) or a religious group (Gülen Movement). More specifically, various reasons or justifications were given by the Turkish government for the use of policies of detention/dismissals towards Kurdish people in light of their alleged affiliation with the out-lawed PKK. It is also worth noting that after the declaration of the state of emergency in July 2016, several other terrorist attacks were committed in Turkey, attributed to the PKK, which may justify certain measures with exceptional character taken as part of the Turkey's effort to protect itself against such attacks (Venice Commission 2016).

The Turkish state may therefore be able to meet the *legitimate aim* requirement by referring to its national security interests. This test has however been criticized as being a mere rhetorical assertion and redundant (Arnardóttir 2003; Partsch 1993). Perhaps more can be made of the second leg of the justification test: proportionality between means and ends. As such, the assessment will mainly hinge upon the proportionality test, which "requires that the distinction on which a given measure is based is assessed for its suitability and effectiveness in relation to the aim pursued and for its effects on individuals and groups" (Moeckli 2008, 94).

This takes us to our technical arguments. These interrelated arguments stem from the fact that emergency situations put the non-discrimination principles in a reverse spotlight – minimizing their potential role in such situations. The first argument is that the proportionality tests contained in all derogation clauses are almost identical to the proportionality test under the non-discrimination principle (Oraá 1992). This is to say that any derogating measure would have to be strictly required by the exigencies of the situation—a test unlikely to be met by a derogating measure that involves discrimination. To put it the other way round, the impermissible restrictions on the right to non-discrimination (either because not supported by objective or reasonable justification or not proportionate to the threat) are also not lawful for the operation of the derogation clause. Following this line of thought, it is clear that derogation measures that are carried out discriminatorily are very unlikely to be 'strictly required'. Based on this, human rights bodies tend to examine such discrimination claims in times of emergency primarily from the perspective of the proportionality test under the derogation clause. For example, in the context of the ECHR, this is patently evidenced in the *A & Others v. UK* case when the ECtHR was required to consider the application of the British *Anti-Terrorism, Crime and Security Act* (ATCS Act 2001), which permitted an extended power for the UK Government to arrest and detain the non-British –foreign national- terrorist suspects in the context of public emergency said to flow from the terrorist attacks of 11 September 2001 (ECtHR, *A & Others v United Kingdom* [2009]). Notwithstanding its considerable deference and the low threshold as regards what is encompassed by the notion of 'public emergency threatening the life of the nation', the European Court found that 'the derogating measures were disproportionate in that they discriminated unjustifiably between nationals and non-nationals' (ECtHR, *A & Others v United Kingdom* [2009] para.191). Here, the Strasbourg Court simply saw no need to consider the complaints concerning Article 14 ECHR separately because the measures were found to be disproportionate to the threat and to be discriminatory in their effect.

The second technical argument is closely related to the first: the question of proportionality is closely linked to the doctrine of margin of appreciation. The *tendency* of human rights bodies towards a wide margin of appreciation during emergency situations complicates the issue further. Although the ECHR, for example, in its general holdings on Article 14 ECHR, stated that where a differential treatment that goes beyond the reasonable permissible limitations is based on race or ethnic origin, 'the notion of objective and reasonable justification must be interpreted as strictly as possible',[12] it has frequently conceded a certain margin of appreciation for the states 'in assessing whether and to what extent differences in otherwise similar situations justify a different treatment' (Arai-Takahashi 2002, 23). Although the UN HRC does not expressly refer to the margin of appreciation, its supervisory practice reveals a similar approach to the ECtHR (Henrard 2011). In any case, derogation from human rights treaties produces an unclear *aporia* in international jurisprudence where it contains the most extreme statements of the margin of appreciation.

Cases arising from the fifteen years of emergency governance in the Kurdish dominated southeast of Turkey between 1987 and 2002 are particularly illustrative. In its judgment in *Aksoy v. Turkey*, the ECtHR acknowledged that "...the particular extent and impact of PKK terrorist activity in South-East Turkey has undoubtedly created, in the region concerned, a public emergency threatening the life of the nation" ([1996] para.70), yet the most grave human rights violations were recorded as the Turkish state pursued oppressive policies against the Kurdish people (Reidy et al. 1997). This approach escalated to a point where Turkish officials engaged in torture, disappearances, extra-judicial killings, and forced displacement of civilians (Kurban and Gülalp 2013). Most cases concerned alleged discrimination in relation to Kurdish identity; the contentions of the applicants, however, were found to be unsubstantiated (*Akdivar and Others v Turkey* [1998] and *Menteş and Others v Turkey* [1998]) or manifestly ill-founded (*Doğan v Turkey* [2004]) and thus, not proved to be based on race or ethnic origin.[13] In a number of cases, moreover, the Court simply declined to review altogether (*Sadak and Others v Turkey* [2001]). In this respect, it is argued that the wide margin of appreciation is hardly conducive to a proper 'objective and reasonable justification' scrutiny' (Arnardóttir 2003, 171). This leads to the conclusion that, as for the protection of minorities, there seems to be little role for the non-discrimination principle (David et al. 2009).

5.3.2 Minority Rights

In its notification under Article 4(3), Turkey derogated from its obligations under Article 27 of the ICCPR, which provides for the rights of ethnic, religious and linguistic minorities "to enjoy their culture, to profess or practice their own religion, or to use their own language" in community with others. The right applies to individuals differentiated by their membership of a minority community. The most widely accepted definition of a minority community for the purpose of Article

[12]See i.a. *Orsus and others v Coratia* ([2010] para. 149) in which the European Court held that "very weighty reasons would have to be put forward before the Court could regard a difference of treatment based exclusively on the ground of ethnic origin as compatible with the Convention".

[13]It is of great significance to note that in many cases before the ECtHR where the Kurds alleged discrimination, they mostly based those claims on grounds of ethnic origin, rather than of being member of a national minority. See, Kurban and Gülalp 2013, 170.

27 refers to the group's non-dominance, numerical inferiority, nationality of the state concerned, differing ethnic, religious, or linguistic characteristics, and to their sense of solidarity directed towards preserving their identities (Capotorti 1979). The existence *vel non* of a minority falls to be determined objectively, whether or not a state party decides to recognize a particular group as such (UNHRC, General Comment No. 23 (2001) para.4). Whatever the indeterminacies inherent in the definition of a minority, there is no reasonable doubt that Turkey's Kurds fall within its ambit.

The substantive protections derived from or integral to Article 27 are multifaceted. At its most basic level, the right requires protection of the physical existence of the minority community (Thornberry 1980). This is reflected in Article 1 of the *UN Declaration on the Rights of Persons Belonging to National or Ethnic, Religious and Linguistic Minorities*, which obligates states to protect the "existence" of their minorities (UNGA Res. 47/135). It also requires the application of generally applicable non-discrimination and equality rights to members of minority communities (UNGA Res. 47/135 Article 4/1). Together, these basic elements of minority rights protection may be described as "essential starting points" to facilitate Article 27 (Pentassuglia 2002). But the right in Article 27 is much more substantial than a commitment to formal, legal equality and physical existence because it is concerned with the *maintenance and development of minority identities*. In short, minority rights are about ensuring that members of minority groups are not assimilated against their will (UN Economic and Social Council 2005, para.27). One might describe it as "a legal prohibition on acts of cultural genocide" (Wheatley 2005, 35), but one should also be cognizant of the fact that unwanted assimilation can be achieved without the necessary *intent* (so crucial a part of the definition of genocide) to do so. Indeed, the canon of legal instruments pertaining to minority rights seeks, to some extent, to tackle 'hidden' or structural causes of assimilation.

In order to fulfill the rights under Article 27, states are under an obligation to take positive measures aimed at creating favorable conditions to enable members of minority communities to maintain and develop their cultures, languages, religions, traditions and customs (UNGA Res. 47/135 Article 4/2). This includes, for example, an obligation to provide opportunities for minorities to learn their mother tongue or (more importantly) to learn *via the medium of* their mother tongue (UN Economic and Social Council 2005, para.27). Article 27 is therefore concerned with enabling members of minority groups to do something that members of the majority take for granted—namely, to maintain and develop their identities. In that sense, the right is concerned with equality in a substantive rather than a merely formal sense insofar as it ensures that members of minority groups are not legally viewed as abstract human beings, completely divorced from their cultural backgrounds.

Despite the importance of Article 27, Article 4(2) of the ICCPR does not include it among the list of non-derogable rights, and its normative status is open to doubt. The Badinter Arbitration Committee (Opinion Nos. 1–2, 1992) opined that minority rights have *jus cogens* status, but scholars have cast doubt on that opinion (Craven 1996) and the most recent report of the International Law Commission's Special Rapporteur on Peremptory Norms of International Law in 2019 makes no mention of it. To make matters even more complicated, Turkey's reservation to Article 27 purports to limit its scope to particular non-Muslim communities, excluding the Kurdish minority (Bayir 2013). This raises some important questions. First, given Turkey's reservation to Article 27, what could the provision possibly have to say about the country's subsequent measures affecting Kurds' minority rights, such as the closure of privately operated schools teaching the Kurdish language (IHD Report 2016), the removal of bilingual Turkish-Kurdish street signs (Ahval News 2018), the shuttering of Kurdish language media outlets (Amnesty International 2017), and the solitary confinement of prisoners who use the Kurdish language during family visits (Tevgera Jinên Azad 2017)? Secondly and relatedly, was Turkey's derogation from Article 27 legally valid?

To begin with Turkey's reservation, it must first of all be noted that the UN HRC in 1987 accepted a reservation that purported to exclude Article 27 *in toto* (UNHRC, *H.K. v France* [1987] paras. 8.5–8.6). But the Committee's acceptance in that case was not based on any substantive reasoning beyond noting that the reservation was "unequivocal". More recent scholarship has engaged with the International Law Commission's 2011 *Guide to Practice on Reservations to Treaties*, which significantly advances international lawyers' understanding of the law of treaty reservations, and argues that there are plausible grounds for deeming Turkey's reservation invalid (Phillips 2019). It is not necessary to repeat that argument here; suffice it to say that if the argument is correct then Turkey's reservation is no obstacle to Article 27 providing legal grounds for challenging Turkey's severe backsliding in the field of Kurdish minority rights. Turning to Turkey's attempt to derogate from Article 27, in its *General Comment No. 29* the UN HRC notes that where certain rights are not listed in Article 4(2) of the ICCPR there are nevertheless "elements" of those rights that "cannot be made subject to lawful derogation under article 4" (UNHRC, General Comment No. 29 (2001) para.13). Article 27 is one such right, and the Committee is of the view that the elements of the right that are bound-up with the prohibition against genocide, the notion of non-discrimination in Article 4(1), and freedom of religion "must be respected in all circumstances" (UNHRC, General Comment No. 29 (2001) para.13/c). This can be read in a number of ways. First, it might mean that derogations from Article 27 are *prima facie* invalid. This is the stance adopted by the International Commission of Jurists (2018, 10). But this interpretation of the Committee's comments does not sit easily with the fact that Article 27 is not included in the list of non-derogable rights in Article 4(2). Instead, it is submitted that the Committee's comments clarify that it is precisely the most foundational elements of Article 27 that must be respected in all circumstances. Discrimination against members of minority communities (in the formal, limited sense), physical genocide of minorities, and abridgement of their freedom of religion are never lawful no matter how grave the threat to the life of the nation. Whether desirable or not, states may—in our view—lawfully derogate from the other aspects of Article 27.

Nevertheless, the other elements of Article 27 cannot be subject to derogation at will. As the Committee notes, there is a "legal obligation to narrow down all derogations to those strictly required by the exigencies of the situation" (UNHRC,

General Comment No. 29 (2001) para.6). Derogation measures must be strictly necessary to deal with the threat and proportionate to its nature or extent. And when one considers Turkey's restrictions on Kurdish cultural institutions and its destruction of cultural objects, it is difficult to see how much of it was either necessary to deal with the threats giving rise to the state of emergency or how it was proportionate to that aim. For instance, it requires a vivid imagination to envisage a scenario in which bilingual street signs or private schools teaching children the Kurdish language constitute even a partial threat – almost certainly not one that requires their total abolition. Furthermore, the almost complete closure of Kurdish media outlets was criticized by Minority Rights Group International (2016) in terms of Turkey's legal obligation to take positive measures in support of minorities and the UN's Special Rapporteur on the right to freedom of opinion and expression (2016) noted his particular concern about the "decimation" of Kurdish media despite attempts to justify it in terms of stability. Additionally, the UN OHCHR notes that the authorities were using machinery to raze objects of Kurdish cultural heritage to the ground *after* security operations against the PKK and its affiliates had taken place and *after* the local population had been forced to flee (UN OHCHR 2017, para.33). *Prima facie* this has all the appearances of a violation of Article 27 which was either unnecessary or, at the very least, disproportionate.

In short, during the state of emergency, Turkey's limited but significant progress in terms of Kurdish minority rights was rolled back, and this is open to legal criticism on Article 27 grounds notwithstanding Turkey's reservation and notwithstanding Turkey's derogation from the provision. There are, therefore, plausible grounds for concluding that certain measures taken during the state of emergency, which impacted upon the Article 27, right were not necessary or proportionate in the sense mentioned above.

5.4 The Crux of the Question: The Kurdish Struggle for Self-Determination

The right of self-determination, expressed in common Article 1 of the ICCPR and the ICESCR, may be characterized as both an *erga omnes* and *jus cogens* norm, which is to say that it is a norm owed to the international community as a whole and from which no derogation is permitted. For purposes of analytical clarity, this chapter differentiates between *individual* minority rights on the one hand, and the *group* right of self-determination on the other. The former right belongs to individual members of minority groups whereas the latter right belongs to "peoples" understood either as a corporate entity or a collection of individuals (Jones 2013).

In practice, however, there is a significant degree of overlap between the two norms. A group right to autonomy, for example, is a form of self-determination that might be desirable, or even necessary, for the maintenance and development of minority cultures and languages (OSCE 1999). Outside of the colonial context, the modern right of self-determination is only, at best, concerned with *external* self-determination (independent statehood) as an *ultima ratio* in exceptional cases of very severe human rights abuses and unrepresentative government (Raic 2002). But it is also widely recognized that self-determination has an *internal* aspect.[14] In short, internal self-determination is about the relationship between the state and the various communities (including minority communities) that together make up the whole "people" of the territory (Kingsbury 2000). It is less about automatic rights to particular outcomes for particular groups (secession, statehood, autonomy, and so on[15]) and more about finding ways of maximizing political, social, economic and cultural participation *within the framework of the state* and *in the context of the particularity of each claim.*

It is also widely recognized that the right of self-determination contains remedial elements (Canadian Supreme Court, *Reference re Secession of Quebec* [1998] para.124), which are aimed at mitigating the pathologies arising from international law's allocation of sovereignty around the globe and its failure to allocate it to arguably deserving groups (Macklem 2015). In practice, the right of self-determination therefore has the capacity to legitimize the disaggregation of state sovereignty to (for example) autonomous regions and to tie these constitutional rearrangements to a "normative universe" (Bell 2002) of international law, particularly when such rearrangements serve to offset the negative effects of state sovereignty on minority groups. As well as performing these *legitimizing* and *remedial functions*, the right of self-determination requires *inclusive processes of negotiation* when a minority group clearly expresses a desire to pursue constitutional change, such as the introduction of a territorial autonomy arrangement (Klabbers 2006).

In sum, the right of self-determination is ontologically grounded in the state system and seeks to "reconstitute the political normality of statehood" (Koskenniemi 1994). But it can validate important reorientations of relationships between minorities and the state (such as the introduction of a territorial autonomy arrangement), and it requires states to negotiate with representatives of minority communities in good faith. The right can therefore be used by oppressed minority groups to obtain normative support for their legitimate demands and to criticize governments that fail to take those demands seriously.

In terms of Kurdish self-determination, "pro-Kurdish" political parties have quite consistently called for some kind of territorial autonomy arrangement (Güneş 2009). To take a recent example, a former co-chair of the pro-Kurdish HDP has referred to the quasi-federal Spanish model of territorial autonomy as an example of the form of government that the HDP recommends (Demirtas 2015). There is, in fact, a more radical project called Democratic Confederalism, which forms a core part of the

[14]The Canadian Supreme Court notes that internal self-determination, understood as "a people's pursuit of its political, economic, social and cultural development within the framework of an existing state", is the usual way in which the right of self-determination is fulfilled. See, *Reference re Secession of Quebec* [1998] 2 R.C.S., para. 126.

[15]Recent scholarship argues convincingly that there is no direct right to autonomy under international law, see Nam and Fessha 2018, 530.

Kurdish self-determination claim (Jongerden 2017). In brief, this revolutionary project focuses on bottom-up grassroots democracy against the nation-state form, and on the empowerment of women (Öcalan 2013). But at least in the short to medium term, as a matter of revolutionary tactics, it appears to be compatible with something like the Spanish model.

The claim to territorial autonomy along broadly Spanish lines is clearly a far-reaching one. It goes beyond calls for non-discrimination and individual minority rights and demands a "thicker" measure of executive and legislative power. It is a call for a "right to be different" and to be given some space "to preserve, protect, and promote values which are beyond the legitimate reach of the rest of society" (Hannum 1990, 4). Given the self-determination framework outlined above, one can construct a strong normative argument that this particular claim in the particular historical and contemporary circumstances of Turkey garners strong normative support from the right of self-determination. The argument is that the construction of the Turkish state, followed by the ongoing attempt to forge a monolithic Turkish nation harnessed to the Turkish *ethnie,* has given rise to a range of negative pathologies. For the Kurds, this has involved severe cultural, political, economic, and social marginalization. Their language is being slowly killed (Hassanpour et al. 2012), their political parties are excluded and hobbled (Watts 2010), and their local economy has been deliberately underdeveloped (Yadirgi 2017). Moreover, the war with the PKK, brought on by the oppression of the Kurds, has claimed tens of thousands of mostly Kurdish lives (International Crisis Group 2011). All told, the Kurdish situation in Turkey is one in which "the legal and political ideal of territorial unity causes moral havoc and social, economic, and cultural injustice resulting in great suffering and endless strife for these entrapped peoples" (Falk 2000, 102). These pathologies—which are bound-up with international law's allocation of sovereignty and the way in which it legitimizes its use—need to be mitigated, and self-determination in the form of territorial autonomy is *one ingredient* in an overall solution.[16]

To return to the focus of this chapter, certain measures taken by Turkey during its state of emergency may be criticized on self-determination grounds. On a procedural level, the lifting of parliamentary immunity via Law No. 6718 led to a number of prosecutions against HDP members of parliament and exposed others to "the risk of excessive sanctions for speech related to their activity as Members of Parliament" (Venice Commission 2016, para.54). The political nature of some of these actions has been confirmed by the ECtHR. For example, the Court ruled that a former co-chair of the HDP was held in extended pre-trial detention for "the predominant ulterior purpose of stifling pluralism and limiting freedom of political debate" (*Demirtas v. Turkey* [2018] para.273). According to a third-party intervention in that case, this was part of a broader crackdown on opposition voices that was "wholly unjustified under international law" (Article 19 & Human Rights Watch

[16]Given the fact that roughly half of Turkey's Kurds do not live in the southeast, territorial autonomy arguably has to be complemented with some form of cultural autonomy.

2017, para.33). The CoE's Commissioner for Human Rights (2017, para.61) noted that the crackdown on legitimate representatives of the Kurdish people "disenfranchised millions of voters" and "reduced the scope of democratic debate". In terms of the right of self-determination, the post-coup-attempt crackdown on the HDP has made it significantly more difficult to advance legitimate Kurdish claims. As a mechanism for Kurdish political participation, representation at the national level is both an important aspect of internal self-determination *in its own right* and an important part of the *process* towards negotiating "thicker" forms of self-determination, such as autonomy. Alongside the earlier decision to end peace talks, this demonstrates that legitimate Kurdish claims are not being taken seriously. Thus, as well as being legally questionable on a variety of individual rights grounds (freedom of expression, the right to political participation, freedom of association) the attempt to hobble the HDP runs counter to the normative requirements contained in the right of self-determination.

As well as hobbling the HDP, Turkey also seriously undermined local Kurdish-run institutions. Turkey's heavily circumscribed power of local government (a limited form of administrative autonomy) has been used by pro-Kurdish parties to "try to establish an alternative Kurdish governmental presence and to construct a new Kurdish subject or collective community" (Watts 2010, 142). Important projects have been pursued in the cultural, political and economic realms in an effort to build towards demands for more substantial autonomy. However, in September 2016 Decree No. 674 altered the Law on Municipalities and paved the way for democratically elected municipal organs to be seized by government appointed trustees. More than 90 elected mayors affiliated with the Kurdish movement were removed (under the usual terrorism pretext) and replaced with government appointed trustees. This "suspension of local democracy"—as Human Rights Watch describes it—continued after the official end of the state of emergency with the removal of three elected Kurdish mayors in Diyarbakir, Van and Mardin (Human Rights Watch 2019).

Decree No. 674 was criticized by, *inter alia*, the Venice Commission (Opinion No. 888/ 2017) on certain individual rights grounds and on the basis of the European Charter for Local Self-Government. The criticism focused, among other things, on the fact that the replacement of elected officials with trustees was not necessary or strictly required by the exigencies of the situation. But the measures also ran counter to the normative requirements contained in the right of self-determination. Indeed, the limited administrative autonomy granted under Turkish law is likely (with improvements and augmentations) to be part of an overall solution to the Kurdish Question. In the Spanish model, for example, the state consists of democratic municipalities and provinces *as well as* self-governing communities (Spanish Constitution, Section 137). In fact, given the significant obstacles to achieving far-reaching territorial autonomy in Turkey any time soon (Kymlicka 2004), strengthened local governments (combined, perhaps, with some form of cultural autonomy) might be a more achievable short-term palliative. Throwing this into reverse—as Turkey has done—fails to take into account the normative requirements of the right of self-determination.

5.5 Conclusion

In this chapter we have mapped the impact of Turkey's widening state of emergency on the Kurdish minority and tested its derogation measures against the non-discrimination principle, minority rights, and the right of self-determination. Our overall conclusion is that certain measures taken during the state of emergency were unlawful or may be criticized on the grounds of minority rights and the right of self-determination.

Although the widening scope of Turkey's state of emergency (which goes far beyond threats directly linked to the coup attempt) is certainly questionable, the generally conservative international institutions responsible for interpreting and implementing human rights have afforded an exceptionally wide margin of appreciation to states when it comes to the legal requirements for triggering a state of emergency and determining its scope. Furthermore, although Turkey's Kurds have been forced to shoulder an intolerable burden during the state of emergency, it seems likely that any *prima facie* discriminatory treatment will not be classified as such due to the wide margin of appreciation afforded to states.

Whether or not Turkey's emergency measures are legally discriminatory, they can still be criticized on human rights grounds. Article 27 of the ICCPR applies to Turkey notwithstanding its reservation thereto and its derogation therefrom. Certain measures taken to erode Kurds' right to maintain and develop their own language and culture—such as the almost complete abolition of Kurdish-language media, the closure of private schools teaching the Kurdish language, and the removal of bilingual signs—were either unnecessary or disproportionate to meet the threat of terrorism.

The right of self-determination, contained in common Article 1 of the ICCPR and ICESCR, is usually fulfilled *internally*. It is about reorienting the relationships between minorities and the state in order to maximize political, cultural, social and economic participation. It also contains remedial elements that are supposed to mitigate the adverse consequences arising from how international law allocates sovereignty around the globe and legitimizes its use. The right also contains a procedural element, which requires states to take minority claims for constitutional reforms seriously. Within that framework, Turkey's Kurds can obtain strong normative support for some kind of autonomy, such as the disaggregation of sovereignty to autonomous regions. But by taking measures to hobble the pro-Kurdish HDP, Turkey has both undermined a key mechanism for Kurdish political participation at the national level *and* narrowed the available space for articulating legitimate Kurdish claims. Turkey has therefore signaled its ongoing refusal to take Kurdish demands seriously. Furthermore, by removing elected co-mayors and municipal officials and replacing them with centrally appointed trustees, Turkey has undermined a key pillar of the 'thicker' form of self-determination sought by the Kurds. Indeed, given the obstacles to securing a fully-fledged territorial autonomy regime any time soon, strengthened local governments represent a paving stone on the path to a meaningful and lasting self-determination arrangement to better manage (if not answer) the Kurdish Question.

References

Ahval News. 2018. *Kurdish Language Signs Removed from Diyarbakir* streets, April 2018.

Altiparmak, Kerem, and Senem Gürol. 2019. Turkey's Derogation of Human Rights under the State of Emergency: Examining its Legitimacy and Proportionality. *Austrian Review of International and European Law Online* 22 (1): 101–136.

Amnesty International. 2017. *Journalism is Not a Crime: Crackdown on media freedom in Turkey*, May 2017.

Arai-Takahashi, Yutaka. 2002. *The Margin of Appreciation Doctrine and the Principle of Proportionality in the Jurisprudence of the ECHR*. Intersentia.

Arnardóttir, Oddný Mjöll. 2003. *Equality and non-discrimination under the European Convention on Human Rights*. The Hague: Martinus Nijhoff Publishers.

Aydin, Hasan, and Koksal Avincan. 2020. Intellectual Crimes and Serious Violation of Human Rights in Turkey: A Narrative Inquiry. *The International Journal of Human Rights* 24 (8): 1127–1155. https://doi.org/10.1080/13642987.2020.1713108.

Bakircioglu, Onder, and Brice Dickson. 2017. The European Convention in Conflicted Societies: The experience of Northern Ireland and Turkey. *International & Comparative Law Quarterly* 66 (2): 263–294.

Barkey, Henri, and Graham Fuller. 1998. *Turkey's Kurdish Question*. Lanham: Maryland.

Bayir, Derya. 2013. Turkey, the Kurds and the Legal Contours of the Right to Self-Determination. *Kurdish Studies* 1 (1): 5–27.

Bell, Christine. 2002. *On the Law of Peace*. Oxford: Oxford University Press.

Bezwan, Naif. 2018. Addressing the Kurdish Self-Determination Conflict: Democratic Autonomy and Authoritarianism in Turkey. In *Democratic Representation in Plurinational States*, ed. Ephraim Nimni and Elçin Aktoprak, 59–82. Palgrave Macmillan.

Capotorti, Francesco. 1979. *Study on the Rights of Persons Belonging to Ethnic, Religious and Linguistic Minorities, UN Doc*. E/CN.4/Sub.2/384/Rev.1.

Codaccioni, Vanessa. 2018. The State of Emergency in France: Community Profiling and the Discriminatory Exception Regime. *Monitor Racism.*

CoE. 2016. *Memorandum on the Human Rights Implications of the Measures Taken Under the State of Emergency in Turkey*, Council of Europe Commissioner for Human Rights, Comm.DH 35, 7 October 2016.

Craven, Miles. 1996. The European Community Arbitration Commission on Yugoslavia. *British Yearbook of International Law* 66: 333–413.

David, Harris, Michael O'Boyle, Ed Bates, Carla Buckley, and Harris O'Boyle. 2009. *Warbrick Law of the European Convention on Human Rights*. Oxford: Oxford University Press.

Demirtas, Selahattin. 2015. The Middle East, the Kurdish Peace Process in Turkey, and Radical Democracy. *Turkish Policy Quarterly* 13: 27–33.

European Commission. 2019. *EU Turkey Progress Report 2019*. {COM(2019) 260 final}, 29 May 2019.

Falk, Richard. 2000. *Human Rights Horizons: The Pursuit of Justice in a Globalizing World*. New York: Routledge.

Green, Leslie. 1979. Derogation of Human Rights in Emergency Situations. *Canadian Yearbook of International Law/Annuaire canadien de droit international* 16: 92–115.

Güneş, Cengiz. 2009. Unpacking the 'Democratic Confederalism and Democratic Autonomy': Proposals of Turkey's Kurdish Movement. In *Autonomy as a Model for Minority Self-Government: From Theory to European and Middle Eastern Perspective*, ed. O. Akbulut and E. Aktoprak, 246–267. Brill.

Hannum, Hurst. 1990. *Autonomy, Sovereignty, and Self-Determination*. University of Pennsylvania Press.

Hassanpour, Amir, Jaffer Sheyholislami, and Tove Skutnabb-Kangas. 2012. Kurdish: Linguicide, Resistance and Hope. *International Journal of the Sociology of Language* 217: 1–18.

Henrard, Kristin. 2011. Boosting Positive Action: The Asymmetrical Approach Towards Non-Discrimination and Special Minority Rights. *Heidelberg Journal of International Law* 71: 379–418.

Human Rights Association (IHD). 2016. *Report on Recent Situation in the Kurdish Region of Turkey*, November 2016.

Human Rights Watch. 2016. *France: Abuses Under State of Emergency*, 3 February 2016.

———. 2017. *Turkey: Crackdown on Kurdish Opposition*, 20 March 2017.

———. 2019. *Turkey: 3 Kurdish Mayors Removed from Office*, 20 August 2019.

———. 2018. *Turkey: Normalising the State of Emergency*, 20 July 2018.

International Commission of Jurists. 2018. *Justice Suspended: Access to Justice and the State of Emergency in Turkey*, 2018.

International Crisis Group. 2015. *A Sisyphean Task? Resuming Turkey-PKK Peace Talks*, 17 December 2015.

———. 2011. *Ending the PKK Insurgency*, September 2011.

Jones, Peter. 2013. Groups and Human Rights. In *Human Rights: The Hard Questions*, ed. C. Holder and D. Reidy, 100–114. Cambridge: Cambridge University Press.

Jongerden, Joost. 2017. The Kurdistan Workers' Party (PKK): Radical Democracy and the Right to Self-Determination Beyond the Nation-State. In *The Kurdish Question Revisited*, ed. G. Stansfield and M. Shareef, 245–258. Hurst.

Klabbers, Jan. 2006. The Right to be Taken Seriously: Self-Determination in International Law. *Human Rights Quarterly* 28: 186–206.

Koskenniemi, Martti. 1994. National Self-Determination Today: Problems of Legal Theory and Practice. *The International and Comparative Law Quarterly* 43: 241–269.

Kurban, Dilek, and Haldun Gülalp. 2013. A Complicated Affair: Turkey's Kurds and the European Court of Human Rights. In *The European Court of Human Rights: Implementing Strasbourg's Judgments on Domestic Policy*, ed. Dia Anagnostou, 166–187. Edinburg University Press.

Kymlicka, Will. 2004. Renner and the Accommodation of Sub-State Nationalisms. In *National Cultural Autonomy and its Contemporary Critics*, ed. Eprahim Nimni, 137–149. Routledge.

Macklem, Patrick. 2015. *The Sovereignty of Human Rights*. Oxford University Press.

Mariniello, Triestino. 2019. Prolonged Emergency and Derogation of Human Rights: Why the European Court Should Raise Its Immunity System. *German Law Journal* 20 (1): 46–71.

McDowall, David. 2004. *A Modern History of Kurds*. London: IB Tauris.

Moeckli, Daniel. 2008. *Human Rights and Non-Discrimination in the 'War on Terror'*. Oxford University Press.

Nam, Nora Ho Tu, and Yonathan Fessha. 2018. Revisiting the Place and Use of Territorial Autonomy Under International Law. *International Journal on Minority and Group Rights* 25 (4): 530–560.

Nugraha, Yordan. 2018. Human Rights Derogation During Coup Situations. *The International Journal of Human Rights* 22 (2): 194–206.

Öcalan, Abdullah. 2013. *Liberating Life: Woman's Revolution*. International Initiative Edition.

Oeter, Stefan. 2018. The Kurds Between Discrimination, Autonomy and Self-Determination. In *Autonomy and Self-Determination: Between Legal Assertions and Utopian Aspirations*, ed. Peter Hilpold, 208–246. Edward Elgar.

Oraá, Jaime. 1992. *Human Rights in States of Emergency in International Law*. Oxford University Press.

OSCE. 2018. *Office for Democratic Institutions and Human Rights*, Expert Meeting Report, 27–28 October 2018.

———. 1999. *The Lund Recommendations on the Effective Participation of National Minorities in Public Life & Explanatory Note*, September 1999.

Pentassuglia, Gaetano. 2002. *Minorities in International Law: An Introductory Study*. Council of Europe Publishing.

Phillips, Thomas. 2019. The (In-) Validity of Turkey's Reservation to Article 27 of the International Covenant on Civil and Political Rights. *International Journal on Minority and Group Rights* 1: 1–28.

Raic, David. 2002. *Statehood and the Law of Self-Determination*. Brill.

Reidy, Aisling, Francoise Hampson, and Kevin Boyle. 1997. Gross Violations of Human Rights: Invoking the European Convention on Human Rights in the Case of Turkey. *Netherlands Quarterly of Human Rights* 15 (2): 161–173.

Ruys, Tom, and Emre Turkut. 2018. Turkey's Post-coup 'Purification Process': Collective Dismissals of Public Servants Under the European Convention on Human Rights. *Human Rights Law Review* 18 (3): 539–565.

Svensson-McCarthy, Anna. 1998. *The International Law of Human Rights and States of Exception: With Special Reference to the Travaux Preparatoires and the Case-law of the International Monitoring Organs*, 19. The Hague: Martinus Nijhoff Publishers.

Tevgera Jinên Azad. 2017. *Information Report on the State of Emergency and Violations of Women's Rights in Prisons*, November 2017.

Thornberry, Patrick. 1980. Is There a Phoenix in the Ashes? – International Law and Minority Rights. *Texas International Law Journal* 15: 421–444.

Turkut, Emre. 2019. Accommodating Security Imperatives v. Protecting Fundamental Rights: The Challenge of States of Emergency in the Context of Countering Terrorism in Turkey. *Security and Human Rights* 28 (1–4): 62–91.

UN Committee on the Elimination of Racial Discrimination. 2016. *Concluding Observations on the Combined Fourth to Sixth Periodic Reports of Turkey*, 11 January 2016.

UN Office of the United Nations High Commissioner for Human Rights. 2017. *Report on the Human Rights Situation in South-East Turkey July 2015 to December 2016*, February 2017.

Venice Commission. 2017. *Opinion on the Provisions of the Emergency Decree Law No. 674 of 1 September 2016*, Opinion No. 888/2017.

———. 2016. *Opinion on the Suspension of the Second Paragraph of Article 83 of the Constitution (Parliamentary Inviolability)*, October 2016, CDL-AD (2016)027.

Watts, Nicole. 2010. *Activists in Office: Kurdish Politics and Protest in Turkey*. University of Washington Press.

Wheatley, Steven. 2005. *Democracy, Minorities and International Law*. Cambridge University Press.

Yadirgi, Veli. 2017. *The Political Economy of the Kurds of Turkey: From the Ottoman Empire to the Turkish Republic*. Cambridge University Press.

Yeğen, Mesut. 1999. The Kurdish question in Turkish State Discourse. *Journal of Contemporary History* 34 (4): 555–568.

Yıldız, Kerim, and Susan Breau. 2010. *The Kurdish conflict: International Humanitarian Law and Post-Conflict Mechanisms*. Routledge.

Emre Turkut is a doctoral researcher at Ghent University and a member of the Ghent Rolin-Jaequemyns International Law Institute (GRILI). He previously held a Swedish Institute fellowship at Uppsala University. Emre's research covers a variety of fields within the domain of public international law and international human rights law, including derogation from human rights, state of emergency, human rights in the fight against terrorism, self-determination and remedial secession doctrine. He is a DAAD visiting fellow at the Hertie School's Centre for Fundamental Rights (2019/2020).

Thomas Phillips is a senior lecturer in law at Liverpool John Moores University. His research focuses on public international law, human rights law, Kurdish studies, and critical approaches to international law. His PhD—which he completed at the University of Liverpool—concerned the right of self-determination as it applies to the Kurds in Turkey, with a particular focus on mother tongue education an political participation. Thomas has also been involved in activities related to his research, including trial and election observation missions in Turkey at the invitation of the HDP.

Chapter 6
Justice and Development (AKP) Attitudes Towards the LGBTI Community in Turkey

Fait Muedini

Abstract In this chapter, I examine the history of Justice and Development Party (AKP) statements with regards to homosexuality and LGBTI based issues in Turkey. As I shall argue, a number of members of the AK party (including Recep Tayyip Erdoğan) have said quite problematic statements with regards to LGBTI community. These comments are in combination with government failures to fully support sexual minorities within Turkey. I will then compare these quotes to statements made by opposition parties in the country.

Keywords LGBTI rights · Turkey · AKP (Justice and Development) · Human rights

6.1 Introduction

Lesbian, Gay, Bisexual, Transgender, and Intersex (LGBTI) rights have come under increasing attack within Turkey in recent years. (Muedini 2019). Under Recep Tayyip Erdoğan and his Justice and Development Party (AKP) led government, the regime has said (and done) various things to suggest that they are not supportive of LGBTI rights, and actually view homosexuality as contrary to their values and beliefs. The lack of support for LGBTI individuals can be seen throughout the various aspects of government and civil society in Turkey. From a lack of clear language protecting sexual minorities as a marginalized group in the Turkish constitution, laws that can be interpreted to not protect the LGBTI community the same as others within Turkey, police actions against transgender and others, bans on Pride Marches in the country, to civil society attitudes regarding homosexuality and sexual minorities, conditions in Turkey are very challenging for sexual minorities.

In this chapter, I want to specifically focus on known attitudes of the ruling government (AKP) towards homosexuality and same sex rights. I argue that

F. Muedini (✉)
Department of International Studies, Butler University, Indianapolis, IN, USA
e-mail: fmuedini@butler.edu

H. Aydin, W. Langley (eds.), *Human Rights in Turkey*, Philosophy and Politics - Critical Explorations 15, https://doi.org/10.1007/978-3-030-57476-5_6

Erdoğan, and others within the Justice and Development party, have made their feelings known that they are not supportive of same sex rights, and view it as opposed to what they believe is Turkish and/or Islamic culture. In this chapter, I shall discuss the attitudes of Justice and Development Party (AKP) political leaders towards the LGBTI community in Turkey. I will be outlining the different comments made by AKP officials (at the local and national level) with regards to homosexuality and LGBTI rights. As I shall argue, government officials have—for years—continued trends of negativity towards same sex rights. AKP officials have said problematic statements against homosexuality for over a decade. Such comments are hurtful to the those who identify as LGBTI in Turkey, as well as show their lack of seriousness for complete equality and inclusivity. It should be noted that the LGBTI community are not the only ones whose rights are being oppressed in what has become an increasing authoritarian country, as "[c]ivil liberties in Turkey have grown as a concern for Western nations after an attempted military coup in July 2016. The ensuing crackdown resulted in more than 77,000 being formally arrested and some 160,000 people being dismissed from their jobs over alleged ties to the abortive putsch" (Sezer 2019). The country continues to move towards increased authoritarianism under the current regime. However, the scope of this chapter will specifically examine comments made by the AKP members related to LGBTI issues, as well as how this compares to other non AKP public figures. As we shall see, while some other non-AKP leaders have been vocal in their support of equality for all, the AKP has not offered serious support for same sex rights, and have actually added to the challenges the community faces within Turkey.

6.2 AKP Comments Against the LGBTI Community

The Justice and Development Party has been in power since 2002. In order to get a better picture of how the party on the whole has approached homosexuality and sexual minority issues in Turkey (based on public statements, but extended to the AKP's position, or also the lack thereof of comments by AKP members openly supporting same sex rights rights), It is important to at least briefly examine the history of LGBTI issues as it relates to the Justice and Development Party. Looking throughout the AKP's rule, the Justice and Development Party's history with regards to any support for LGBTI rights is one that has only deteriorated over time. As Yılmaz (2013) notes,

> The rise of the LGBT rights movement ironically coincided with the strengthening of conservative politics in Turkish political scene. Formerly excluded from the mainstream politics in Turkey, representatives of political Islam under the newly established Justice and Development Party (AKP) in the first half of 2000s seemed to be willing to cooperate with European institutions and human rights movements in Turkey to further democratization and extend rights and liberties. For this reason, despite the apparent ideological disharmony between the LGBT rights movement, which is positioned on the left of the political spectrum in Turkey, and the conservative ideology of the governing party, the LGBT rights movement stayed away from discourses that might make the political representatives of the

> conservatives, as the scapegoats of rampant homophobia and transphobia. Since, for many LGBT rights activists in early 2000s, the AKP was not the major obstacle against LGBT equality (135).

What has happened in recent years is that AKP officials began making very problematic statements with regards to same sex issues. There are a number of statements that one could point to in order to show the lack of respect that members of the AKP have for LGBTI issues. For example, "In 2010, then former state minister for family affairs, Selma Aliye Kavaf told Turkish newspaper Hurriyet, "homosexuality is a biological disorder, a disease ... something that needs to be treated." And, "[d]espite international condemnation, Mrs. Aliye Kavaf refused to retract her comments. Then in December of 2011, Interior Minister Idris Naim Şahin described homosexuality as a contributing factor to "an environment in where there are all kinds of dishonor, immorality, and inhuman situations" (SPOD et al. 2012, 6). The statements against homosexuality and the LGBTI community continued in 2012, where, in that year, "...Ankara mayor and member of the ruling Justice and Development Party Melih Gökçek spoke of homosexuality as contrary to Turkish culture; he remarked, "Each society has its own moral values. Especially for our Turkish society, it is not possible for us to be together with the gay culture in Europe. It is also not possible to approve of this. How we have been brought up, our brand of morality, our views are a little different. I hope to God that in Turkey there will not be a gay and there should not be" (Kaos GL et al. 2016). Along with these statements, "Türkan Dağoğlu, Istanbul MP and Deputy President of the Committee on Health, Family, Labor, and Social Affairs, stated in 2013 that "'LGBT' is a behavior that is outside the bounds of normality" (Kaos GL et al. 2016). While Dağoğlu condemned killings against transgendered individuals in a May 29th, 2013 speech to The Grand National Assembly of Turkey, in the same speech, Dağoğlu said that

> A woman marrying a woman, or a man marrying a man is not a right. On the contrary, it is a practice that leads to public corruption that presents itself as if it is favorable by reversing sexual constructs. I find the idea that we should consider the West modern as groundless. As we all followed through the media, the famous French historian Dominique Venner has committed suicide in Paris' famous Notre Dame Cathedral to protest the passing of the law that allows same-sex marriages. The protests against the passing of this law that's been held in France with the participation of thousands of people shows that the public opinion is not ready in developed countries including Turkey, and even in the most democratic countries (LGBTI News Turkey 2013).

Dağoğlu, with this statement, clearly sees homosexuality as a problem, and seems to suggest that being homosexual is something as part of the "Western modern" and thus different from culture domestically. Along with these comments, there are other statements made by AKP officials that also seem to be contrary to supporting homosexuality. For example, it was also in 2013 that Recep Tayyip Erdoğan himself made negative comments towards homosexuality, describing homosexuality as a "sexual preference" that was incompatible with the "culture of Islam" in Turkey" (Fox and Yalcin 2017). Such sentiments are dangerous for the LGBTI community, as many also feel marginalized within their own country.

The general position of AKP leaders regarding this issue has not seemed to change in recent years. For example, Çetin (2016) states that unlike some other political parties in Turkey, "The AKP has not yet taken up LGBTI topics, either in its charter or in its platform. The charter has a conservative character, which stresses "public morals and the propriety of the individual" as well as "national values". Çetin adds that "On the contrary, in the campaigns for the local and parliamentary elections in 2014 and 2015 AKP politicians have spoken out against LGBTI persons being nominated for political positions. The governing mayor of Ankara, Melih Gökçek, in an TV program in 2014, spoke against the idea of "a gay ever holding the office of mayor in Turkey" Similarly, President Erdoğan objected to the HDP nominating a gay candidate shortly before the parliamentary elections of 2015. This would not even be considered by his party" (18). In addition, it was also believed that the government cancelled a gay men's choir during the same year. Coogan (2019), when discussing this event, wrote about the experience in 2015, saying:

> I organized a tour of Israel and Turkey for the Boston Gay Men's Chorus, a first for any LGBTQ group in the region. The highlight of the trip was to be a final performance at Istanbul's state-of-the-art Zorlu Performance Center. Ending our five-city tour by singing on the main stage in a hall specifically designed to amplify the sound of acoustic performances would be the experience of a lifetime for our talented, but all-volunteer, ensemble.
>
> But after Turkey's leading daily ran a story about our upcoming performance — which prompted a rush on tickets four months before the date of our concert — I received a text from our tour company on behalf of Zorlu's management team asking if we could perform as the Boston Men's Chorus instead of the Boston Gay Men's Chorus. Of course, I said no. They cancelled our show.
>
> This move by Zorlu's owners was no small matter. We had already signed a contract and by breaking it, they were liable for substantial damages. In lieu of a lawsuit to recoup our losses, we required them to make substantial donations to Turkish LGBTQ organizations. We later learned that the order to cancel our performance came from Erdogan's office.

Erdoğan's position towards the LGBTI community and homosexuality has not improve in the years that have followed. In fact, one could argue that matters have only worsened for sexual minorities in Turkey. Part of the reason to believe this has to do with government's response to the Pride March. Beginning in 2015, and now in each subsequent year afterwards, authorities have worked to stop the Pride March from taking place. This first took place in 2015, and then in 2016. In 2017, "The annual Istanbul gay pride parade was cancelled for the third year in a row. . .on security grounds, and last week Erdoğan condemned the main opposition bloc, the Republican People's party (CHP), for a plan that would introduce a "gay quota" for employees in a local municipality. Erdoğan described the party as "waging war against the values of our nation" (Shaheen 2017). The government has continued to disallow the Pride March in Istanbul.

Again, much of this is driven by Erdoğan's use of religion to bolster support and popularity in Turkey. As Shaheen (2017) notes, "Erdoğan's critics have long accused the president, who once said that he wished to raise a "devout generation" of attempting to impose a morality rooted in Sunni Islam on a polarized society. The polarization has only increased in the aftermath of a failed coup attempt last year and an ensuing crackdown that has targeted both individuals complicit in the attempted putsch and dissidents more broadly" (Shaheen 2017). As noted in media reports,

> In what appeared to be a direct political attack, Erdoğan said the committee was in a city run by the main opposition Republican People's Party (CHP), which has repeatedly labelled him a "dictator" in recent months.
>
> "Their ties with the values of our nation have become so severed that in a district run by the CHP of a major city, a one-in-five gay quota is put forward for the local committee elections," Erdogan said in a televised speech.
>
> "When there is no moderation left in a party, no-one knows where it can lead them. Let them continue like this," he added in a speech to local Turkish officials (mukthars) where he often makes his toughest pronouncements.
>
> It was one of the first times that Erdogan, who regularly promotes family values, has even mentioned homosexuality in a speech, a topic he has generally steered clear of (The Daily Star 2017).

The government's negative views on LGBTI individuals has not changed as of late. In fact, it can be argued that their disdain for sexual minorities has only continued. For example, in recent years, the government has worked to stop the yearly Pride March. Following the 2019 Pride March, and the AKP's electoral loss in the mayoral elections for the city of Istanbul, government officials have continued their hateful comments against homosexuality and the LGBTI community. For example, as Özkazanç (2019) writes:

> By looking at the social media reactions and beyond one can reveal the novel ways in which homophobia and misogyny are articulated in the emerging anti-gender narratives in Turkey. We can also see how the nationalist and hetero-patriarchal anxieties are reflected in anti-gender politics. As a reaction to pro-Pride declarations, the Minister of Family, Zehra Z. Selcuk and KADEM, (Women and Democracy Association, a government's NGO) posted tweets which immediately triggered an anti-Pride campaign on social media under the hashtag "don't mess with my *ancestry* and "family is our everything". The tweets declared that the 'gay perversity' is an assault on the survival of the ancestry [*nesil* in Turkish] as well as on its religious and moral values. Yet surprisingly, most of the posts by pro-government people were condemning the female Minister and KADEM for their alleged collaboration and support for gender equality policies. By way of over-trumping the Minister, the tweeters forwarded the usual demands of the rising men's rights movement such as alimony payments, child custody, İstanbul Treaty and n. 6284 Law to protect women against violence. They claimed that the tolerance of what they call 'gay perversity' was the natural outcome of a government policy which has been unjustly favoring women at the expense of men. Moreover, they were eager to underline their firm conviction that that the promotion of homosexuality was part of a 'global conspiracy'.

The Turkish government has also carried out other policies that have discriminated against the LGBTI community. For example, in 2017, Mehmet Kiliclar --the governor of the city of Ankara, through written communication, said that the events were to be cancelled for the sake of "public order, prevention of crime, general health and morals"" (Alam et al. 2017). Of course, LGBTI human rights organizations in Turkey responded to this development, with Kaos GL and Pink Life issuing a statement that read: "Ankara governor's office's grounds for the omnibus ban, including the phrases 'protecting public health and morality,' 'social sensibilities and sensitivities,' 'public security' and 'protection of other people's rights and liberties' are clearly discriminatory. This decision legitimizes rights violations and discrimination against LGBTIs." They also said in the statement the following: "In our country where discrimination and hate based on sexual orientation and gender identity is rampant, it is the duty of national and local administrations to combat this discrimination and hate"" (Alam et al. 2017). The LGBTI community continues to suffer because of the actions of government officials. Their lives have negatively affected because of discriminatory attitudes against them.

6.3 Republic Party (CHP) and Same-Sex Rights in Turkey

Comparing the AKP's main political rival, the CHP, it is evident that the Republican Party has been much more supportive of LGBTI Rights in Turkey. This can be seen in their attempts to support constitutional changes to include sexual orientation as a specific category. As Engin (2015) notes: "The Republican People's Party's introductory bill criticized the Turkish constitutional law of equality and argued that the law is not holding up to the standards of the European Union and the United Nations clauses on prohibiting discrimination against LGBT individuals. Article 10 of the Constitution proclaims that, "Everyone is equal before the law without distinction as to language, race, color, sex, political opinion, philosophical belief, religion and sect, or any such grounds" [41]. Supporters of the proposed bill argue that "Article 10 and Article 70" of the Constitution of the Republic of Turkey, and "Article 5″ of the Labor Law should also broaden its categories to sexual minorities in order to reduce gender discrimination. Legal guarantees on behalf of sexual orientation and gender identity must be provided for LGBT individuals [40]" (845). Engin (2015) study of political party attitudes towards LGBTI rights in Turkey shows that the Republican People's Party (RPP/CHP) continued to advocate for complete equality. As noted in the work, ".

On behalf of the Republican People's Party (RPP), both deputies Toprak and Erdemir spoke in favor of the proposed bill. Erdemir stated:

> They could not find a place for my child in this huge world,' distinguished members of the parliament, these are the words of the mother of our citizen with a different sexual orientation who was murdered in September 2010 in Bursa. Today we are talking about opening a tiny space in this huge world to fit these parents' children. Is there a tiny space for the ones who have been murdered by 12 stab wounds, 40 stab wounds, or for the ones whose bodies have been inflicted by wounds that will not heal, whose wounded hearts will not heal [42]?

Erdemir (2013) then discussed the progress of LGBT rights in Turkey by saying,

> (...)The world is changing. Taboos are breaking. A better, freer, and more equal world is possible. Unfortunately, Turkey is not moving forward in the same speed as the Western systems in regard to freedom of gender expression (...) As Republican People's Party, we wish that in Turkey, we would not move with anger and hate. As we have also engaged in our election report; we are demanding the creation of a legal arrangement for the fight against discrimination and hate crimes as soon as possible. We want that, we hope that one day in the huge agenda of the assembly a tiny space and time will be created for hate crimes [42].

However, "Before Erdemir could finish his speech a deputy of the Justice and Development Party (JDP) Ibrahim Korkmaz interrupted Erdemir's speech three times by shouting, "What you are talking about is immoral". Korkmaz left the assembly room without hearing the rest of Erdemir's speech" (Engin 2015).

Other non-AKP individuals have also been supportive of including language to protect sexual minorities. Also, in 2015 during these discussions in parliament,

> The Peace and Democracy Party (PDP) deputy Ertugrul Kurkcu also expressed his supportive views of the Toprak's bill proposal by stating that, "There is a group of people who are pushed to the margins of society because of public bias, traditional behaviors, legends, and negative myths. Special precautions need to be taken in order to make them equal with the rest of the society. This is why this inquiry is necessary" [43]. In addition, Kurkcu argued that the state cannot protect people's rights if it neglects or denies the rights of certain groups. To support his point of view he argued:

> When we said, we are Kurds in Sisli and gays in Taksim during gay pride, media outlets propagandized against this said, "they are homos too". In truth, it would not have matter even if I were; however, the issue here is to ask for protection of the rights of homosexuals even if one does not consider himself as one. The day we protect the rights of those who are not like us, then we are going to see a real change in this country (...). Otherwise, things will stay the same. You will continue to stone homosexuals, and in places where you cannot stone them, you will insult them and leave the assembly room [43]."

Others, such as Selahattin Demirtaş, who was formerly within the former Peace and Democracy Party, and more recently the co-chair of the HDP (Hurriyet Daily News 2014) has also spoken on behalf of LGBTI rights in Turkey. In 2014, "Several associations representing the LGBT community have announced support for Peoples' Democratic Party (HDP) co-chair Selahattin Demirtaş in the upcoming presidential elections Aug. 10, emphasizing he was the only candidate to express his commitment to gay rights. The 12 associations, including Kaos GL, Pembe Hayat, Gender Identity and Sexual Orientation Studies Association (SPOD) and Hêvî LGBTİ Initiative, stressed Demirtaş had acknowledged the LGBT's place in society without "ifs and buts"" (Hurriyet Daily News 2014). LGBTI NGOs, in a statement noted that "We are making public that we support the candidate of the people and change in the presidential elections, Selahattin Demirtaş, who has made a call for a new life based on freedom, equality, fraternity and peace and who has defended human rights without making exceptions"." They added critique of other politicians, noting that ""'Being referred to as the 'other,' LGBTI's are pushed away from society due to their sexual identities, discriminated in education, health, work life, media and social benefits. Not only limited to this, they are subjected to every kind of oppression and violence, while their basic right to live is limited by hate speech and hate crimes"" (Hurriyet Daily News 2014).

Demirtaş has continued to be a staunch supporter of LGBTI Rights. For example, in 2015 he spoke about the dire conditions facing the LGBTI community in Turkey, saying that: "LGBTI individuals who are targeted, killed, repressed, or ostracized because of their sexual orientations and sexual identities are ignored by the system. LGBTIs' mere existence is seen as a crime. Homophobia and transphobia are fed. "New Life" calls for equal citizenship rights for all sexual identities to live free and honorable lives in society without fear of discrimination" (Engin 2015, 848). In fact, he and the HDP party continued to advocate equality during their recent campaigns; "While the HDP has its base of constituents in Turkey's minority Kurdish population, which makes up about 20 percent of the country, Demirtaş has broadened the party's appeal. Under his lead, the HDP has reached out to a variety of minority groups excluded by the socially conservative AKP such as environmentalists, LGBT rights activists and secular Turks" (Robins-Early 2017).

However, much to this has been to the ire of Erdoğan. For example, as Yackley (2015) notes, "the HDP's choice of unconventional candidates has drawn contempt from President Tayyip Erdogan, who has sharpened his rhetoric in recent weeks to rouse conservatives. Though not a candidate, Erdogan fears the HDP could endanger the majority enjoyed by the AKP, which he founded. He has railed against "atheists and Zoroastrians", "the Armenian lobby and gays" and parts of the Alevi community he accuses of being irreligious" (Yackley 2015). Thus, it is evident that there are many political officials in Turkey who have be vocal supporters of the LGBTI community. Sadly, a number of members of the AK Party have not been willing to advocate for complete equality of all individuals in Turkey; their statements clearly demonstrate that they do not view sexual minorities as having the same protections as other members of society.

6.4 Conclusion

In this chapter, I have discussed the sentiments AKP officials have taken towards homosexuality, and their views on LGBTI issues within Turkey. For many years, officials have said many problematic comments as it relates to sexual minority rights. These statements have done great harm to the LGBTI community. Sadly, these comments have not stopped, but rather, have continued as Erdoğan has increased what seems to be an increasing authoritarian hold on power. It is imperative that the AKP government stop their harsh treatment of the LGBTI community in Turkey, and grant them their full rights. This includes altering the constitution to include language that specifically protects sexual minorities. Continued hateful comments will only serve to further marginalize sexual minorities in the country. The LGBTI community continues to face various forms of discrimination.

References

Alam, Hande Atay, Hallam Jonny, and Cullinane Susannah. 2017. Turkish capital bans LGBT events. *CNN*, November 27, 2017. https://www.cnn.com/2017/11/20/europe/turkey-ankara-gay-rights/index.html.

Çetin, Zülfukar. 2016. The Dynamics of the Queer Movement in Turkey before and during the Conservative AKP Government. Working Paper, Research Group EU/Europe 2016/01, January 2016 SWP Berlin. https://www.swp-berlin.org/fileadmin/contents/products/arbeitspapiere/WP_RG_Europe_2016_01.pdf.

Coogan, Craig. 2019. *What the Fight for Gay Rights in Turkey Tells Us About America Under Donald Trump*. Commentary. WGBH. June 21, 2019. https://www.wgbh.org/news/commentary/2019/06/21/what-the-fight-for-gay-rights-in-turkey-tells-us-about-america-under-donald-trump.

Engin, Ceylan. 2015. LGBT in Turkey: Policies and experiences. *Social Sciences* 2015 (4): 838–858.

Fox, Kara, and Dilay Yalcin. 2017. 'They turn their backs' In *Turkey violent homophobia festers in Erdogan's shadow*. CNN, June 23, 2017. https://www.cnn.com/2017/06/23/europe/turkey-homophobia-violence/index.html.

Hurriyet Daily News. 2014. LGBT associations announce support for HDP candidate Demirtaş. Hurriyet Daily News. August 08, 2014. http://www.hurriyetdailynews.com/lgbt-associations-announce-support-for-hdp-candidate-demirtas%2D%2D70163.

Kaos GL, LGBTI News Turkey, and IGLHRC. 2016. Republic of Turkey. Human Rights Violations of LGBT Individuals in Turkey. Submission to the United Nations Universal Periodic Review. 21st Session fo the Working Group on the UPR. United Nations Human Rights Council. January-February 2015. https://ilga.org/wp-content/uploads/2016/02/Shadow-report-16.pdf.

LGBTI News Turkey. 2013. AKP'li vekil Türkan Dağoğlu homofobi'ye yenik düştü: LGBT denen durum normal dışı bir davranış! [AKP Parliamentarian Türkan Dağoğlu succumbs to homophobia: LGBT condition is a behavior that is outside the bounds of normality.] *LGBTI News Turkey*, August 9, 2013. https://lgbtinewsturkey.com/2013/08/09/akp-rebuttal-lgbt-motion/.

Muedini, Fait. 2019. *LGBTI Rights in Turkey: Sexuality and the State in the Middle East*. Cambridge: Cambridge University Press.

Özkazanç, Alev. 2019. *'Global gay conspiracy' and misogyny in Turkish anti-gender narratives*. Engenderings. The London School of Economics and Political Science. https://blogs.lse.ac.uk/gender/2019/08/05/turkish-anti-gender-narratives/.

Robins-Early, Nick. 2017. *Meet the HDP, The Pro-Gay, Pro-Women Kurdish Party Shaking Up Turkey's Politics*. Huffington Post. https://www.huffpost.com/entry/turkey-hdp-party_n_7537648. Accessed 6 Dec 2017.

Sezer, Murad. 2019. Istanbul's LGBT community holds small rally after march banned. *Reuters, June* 30: 2019. https://www.reuters.com/article/us-gay-pride-turkey/istanbuls-lgbt-community-holds-small-rally-after-march-banned-idUSKCN1TV0Q1.

Shaheen, Kareem. 2017. Turkish LGBTI activists condemn 'illegal' ban on events in Ankara. *The Guardian*, November 20, 2017. https://www.theguardian.com/world/2017/nov/20/turkey-bans-lgbti-events-ankara-public-order.

SPOD, Kaos GL, International Gay, and Lesbian Human Rights Commission (IGLHRC). 2012. Human Rights Violations of Lesbian, Gay, Bisexual, and Transgender (LGBT) People in Turkey: A Shadow Report. Submission to the 106th Session of the Human Rights Committee (15 October-2 November 2012). https://www2.ohchr.org/english/bodies/hrc/docs/ngos/IGLHRC_Turkey_HRC106.pdf.

The Daily Star. 2017. Erdogan takes aim at 'gay quota' on Turkish committee. *The Daily Star*, November 09, 2017. https://www.dailystar.com.lb/News/Middle-East/2017/Nov-09/425782-erdogan-takes-aim-at-gay-quota-on-turkish-committee.ashx.

Yackley, Ayla Jean. 2015. Gay, Christian, Roma election candidates show Turkey's changing face. *Reuters,* June 5, 2015. https://www.reuters.com/article/us-turkey-election-minorities/gay-christian-roma-election-candidates-show-turkeys-changing-face-idUSKBN0OL1BN20150605.
Yılmaz, Volkan. 2013. The New Constitution of Turkey: A Blessing or a Curse for LGBT Citizens? *Turkish Policy Quarterly.* 11 (4): 131–140. http://turkishpolicy.com/Files/ArticlePDF/the-new-constitution-of-turkey-a-blessing-or-a-curse-for-lgbt-citizens-winter-2013-en.pdf.

Fait Muedini holds the Frances Shera Fessler Professorship in the Department of International Studies at Butler University. He is also a Faculty Fellow at the Desmond Tutu Peace Lab at Butler University. Along with a number of other articles on Middle East politics, and also human rights, Muedini has published three books: *Sponsoring Sufism: How Governments Promote 'Mystical Islam' In Their Domestic and Foreign Policies* (Palgrave Studies in Religion, Politics, and Policy), *Human Rights and Universal Child Primary Education* (Palgrave Macmillan), and his most recent book entitled *LGBTI Rights in Turkey: Sexuality and the State in the Middle East* (Cambridge University Press).

Chapter 7
LGBTQ Rights in Turkey: Do Not Touch My Body!

Barbaros Sansal

Abstract This chapter provides the experiences of LGBTQ individuals who have been subjected to discrimination, physical abuse, and death in Turkey within the context of Turkey's attitudes towards LGBTQ members. This chapter narrates the story of Ahmet Yıldız, who is believed to have been killed by his father because he was gay; Hande Buse Seker, a sex worker, shot by a police officer who was a client of hers; and Hande Kader, a gay activist who was subjected to police violence and burned to death during the march of honor in 2015. Furthermore, the study includes the accounts of two laborers, one soldier, and one teacher. These stories of gay people suggest that all systems in Turkey are united in discriminatory policies against LGBTQ members, and that civil society organizations have been unable to protect gay rights. Even though the Turkish Constitution and the Universal Declaration of Human Rights, to which Turkey is a signatory, guaranteed equal rights, the rights of LGBTQ people have been, and will continue to be, abrogated until the country and its people develop a more enlightened and humane view.

Keywords LGBTQ rights in Turkey · Discrimination · Violation · Case study

7.1 Introduction

Although the twenty-first-century has witnessed numerous technological advances, societies are experiencing various issues related to sociological and human rights in addition to negative situations initiated by technology. Nevertheless, the widespread use of technology-based social media has been a factor in breaking the power of discrimination and has played a significant role in social change (Kongar 2019). As a result, with the courage to announce all kinds of infringements imparted by technology today, LGBTQ (Lesbian-Gay-Bisexual-Transgender-Questioning)

B. Sansal (✉)
Human Rights Activist, Ankara, Turkey

H. Aydin, W. Langley (eds.), *Human Rights in Turkey*, Philosophy and Politics - Critical Explorations 15, https://doi.org/10.1007/978-3-030-57476-5_7

individuals have begun to make their voices more audible. Discrimination against LGBTQ individuals has become more recognized thanks to videos, photos, and news, on social media, of infringement of their rights. However, some people in society still do not respect the sexual orientation of LGBTQ members. In recent years in Turkey, several studies have shown the bitter truth of the continued acts of violence that continue to be imposed on LGBTQ individuals (Engin 2015).

Continuous development of nations should not just address the technological aspects of society, but should further examine social problems as well. In order for a country to enter the category of a developed country, that nation must be open to technological developments and sensitive to social problems. Therefore, it is imperative for an integrated perception of development to be created.

The rise of the LGBTQ issue has become part of the structural change in the political organization of contemporary democracies and has risen to the forefront (Kulpa 2011). Among the developing countries considering these issues is the Republic of Turkey.

7.2 Violations Against LGBTQ Individuals in Turkey

Established after the collapse of the Ottoman Empire, the Republic of Turkey was driven toward a secular political state in order to minimize the influence of the religious groups. However, the tendency to politicize social, religious, or cultural issues has continued to this day. Moreover, the left-right conflict, the Kurdish issue, headscarf ban, and LGBTQ rights, which have been on the agenda in recent years, have not escaped politicization (Fishman 2013).

This situation has caused polarization. When the Justice and Development Party (AKP) was established in 2001, select members declared that homosexuals could not join the party (Arat and Carly 2017). Then in 2002, the AKP came to power and the nation entered a period of dynamic change. In the first years of AKP rule, regulations barring women from wearing the headscarf in universities were loosened, Kurds gradually gained the right to use their language in the public sphere, and average citizens started to challenge the official state narratives of history (Fishman 2013). AKP leader Recep Tayyip Erdoğan, in a TV program he attended in 2002, answered the question about homosexual rights and stated that the rights of homosexuals must be legally secured (Kaos/GL 2002). Contrary to the great hope that arose during this early period, the AKP did not take any effective steps for the rights of LGBTQ individuals, and some government officials made homophobic discourses (Amnesty International 2011).

Erdoğan has not spoken out publicly against LGBT rights despite his conservative family ideology and an increasingly oppressive climate in Turkey (The Guardian 2017). However, in February 2018, Ali Erol, the founder of Kaos Gay and Lesbian Cultural Research and Solidarity Association (Kaos GL), was arrested because of his social media posts (Kaos/GL 2018).

The Directorate of Religious Affairs (Diyanet İşleri Başkanlığı), a state agency that is in charge of the training and appointments of Muslim clergy and that provides various educational programs for the public, has issued several inflammatory circulars that indicate the scope and effect of fear and disgust pointedly. For example, on October 16, 2008, a circular claimed that homosexuality was a behavior disorder and that has been spreading in a scary way within society. . .homosexuality cannot be accepted. . . . [It] is against human nature, and it should be corrected without targeting homosexuals (United States Department of State – Bureau of Democracy Human Rights and Labor 2010).

Later, Selma Aliye Kavaf, who was the Turkish Minister of State at that time and responsible for Women and Family Affairs, stated that "homosexuality was a biological disorder, an illness, and should be treated" (Amnesty International 2011, 5). In response, the Turkish Medical Association (2010) said that Kavaf's statement was "contrary to contemporary scientific medicine and human rights." They continued, saying that Kavaf should resign due to this statement, which harbored the potential to increase homophobia and hate crimes in society; "We call on the government to engage with organizations of gay, lesbian, bisexual and transgender individuals and to support the fight against homophobia and hate crimes" (Turkish Medical Association 2010).

Contending that tolerance toward sexual and gender deviance does not equate to non-discrimination or freedom from persecution, this chapter examines Turkey in the first decade of the new millennium, at a particular juncture when overt violence against LGBT people coexisted with liberalization and reform (Arat and Carly 2017). However, the reform process in Turkey came to a halt in 2011 (Arat and Carly 2017). Over time, Turkey has developed a tumultuous relationship with human rights, including LGBTQ rights. Although Turkey is a signatory to the Universal Declaration of Human rights, after the failed coup attempt of 2016, it has regularly violated the first, second, third, fifth, and seventh articles, which guarantees the rights to life, liberty and security of person, free from torture or cruel, inhuman or degrading treatment or punishment, and equal protection under the law. Additionally, Turkey has not been among sponsors who have supported LGBTQ in the General Assembly. Turkey was not among the 85 signatories of the joint statement, Ending Acts of Violence and Related Human Rights Violations Based on Sexual Orientation and Gender Identity in 2011 (US Mission to International Organizations in Geneva 2011).

Despite this lack of attention, Kaos GL, Lambada Istanbul LGBTT Association, Black Pink Triangle LGBTT Association, Hevjin LGBTT, Purple Hand Eskişehir LGBT Formation and activities of associations such as the Pink Life LGBTT Solidarity Association have brought some improvements in LGBTQ rights for Turkey (Amnesty International 2013).

In Turkey, LGBTQ individuals are not privy to the same rights that heterosexual individuals have. Foremost, it is illegal for two individuals of the same sex to marry. Furthermore, the situation of transgender individuals can cause problems in public institutions. Article 136 of the Civil Code, states that "Each man and woman must submit an identity card and the sample of the registry, the document if the previous marriage has ended, and if it is small or limited, the written consent of the legal representative and the written medical certificate showing that there is no disability to marry" (Turkish Civil Law 2011). Hence, cases exist in which trans individuals are prevented from marrying, primarily based on health-related statements (Akpinar 2014).

In line with their conservative gender approach, AKP officials have not only ignored demands for the recognition and protection of LGBT rights but have employed a hostile political discourse that obfuscates non-heterosexual gender identities by framing them as illnesses and as a threat to society (Karakuş 2008). The Turkish Medical Association (2016) stated that the notion that homosexuality was against nature and was a temporary desire that becomes a habit and that was the result of an early brain development problems or a dysfunctional upbringing, was incorrect. Due to this perspective, the association has been criticized in some circles for normalizing homosexuality.

Additionally, in some instances, some health workers view homosexuality as a disease and discriminate on that basis. Article 125 of the Civil Servants Law prohibits "disgraceful and embarrassing acts and is used to dismiss civil servants for their sexual orientation (Amnesty International 2011).

Turkey has not established laws that would protect individuals against discriminations on the grounds of sexual orientation or gender identity. Often communities view non-heterosexual as being oppositional to "community morality," and approximately 89% of Turkish people regard homosexuality as a crime (Yılmaz 2012). Thus, LGBTQ individuals often find that housing, work, family, and education, among others, are not readily accessible (Bicmen and Bekirogulları 2014) This situation has further led to hate speech, and LGBTQ individuals often become sex workers because they cannot secure jobs in the public or private sector. Hence, sex workers, more specifically, transgender sex workers, make up a significant number of hate crime victims (Arat and Carly 2017).

Unfortunately, the lack of explicit legal protections for LGBTQ individuals has led to legal approval of acts of violence and discrimination. In this context, The LGBT Equal Rights Association for Western Balkans and Turkey has sought to build a common platform for advancing LGBTQ rights and advocating against discrimination. Although a non-discrimination legal policy is currently being developed by the government, whether the law will address discrimination based on sexual orientation and gender identity remains unclear.

Similarly, neither the Law on the Protection of Family (no. 4320, enacted in 1998) nor its revamped new version, the Law on Protection of the Family and Prevention of Violence against Women (no. 6284, legislated on March 8, 2012), have any references to sexual orientation and gender identity, despite the tireless efforts by LGBT advocacy groups that demanded the inclusion of the terms (Merlo et al. 2012). LGBT rights are likely to be ignored in the new constitution of the country, which has been negotiated intermittently for years at special intra-party parliamentary commissions (Merlo et al. 2012).

Burhan Kuzu, a prominent figure in the AKP, who as Chair of the Constitution Committee of Parliament, complained about excessive demands for rights: "There is no end to people's demands. . .Homosexuals, too, made some demands. . .Should we grant them just because they want them?" (Karakuş 2008).

Although the law protects freedom of expression and peaceful demonstration, the AKP government had no qualms over firing water cannons and rubber bullets in order to prevent the LGBT Pride Parade from taking place during the month of Ramadan. They argued that the parade would offend the sensibilities of pious Muslims (Hurriyet Daily News 2015).

Such discrimination violates fundamental principles of the Universal Declaration of Human Rights, to which Turkey is a signatory. This includes Article 21,[1] which indicates that everyone has the right to equal access to public service in his country and Article 23,[2] which provides that everyone has the right to work, free choice of employment, and just and favorable conditions of work (United Nations 1948), in the form of everyone's right to benefit from the public and the right to work defined.

When comparing Turkey with Europe and other developed countries, Turkey has been found to lag significantly behind many countries in terms of LGBTQ rights. In 2019, the International Lesbian, Gay, Bisexual, Trans & Intersex Association (ILGA) ranked 49 European countries on their LGBTI rights. Turkey ranked 48th; only Azerbaijan was ranked lower (ILGA-Europe 2019).

Sex workers in Turkey have been subjected to violence, and some of these homosexuals have been murdered (Human Rights Association 2017). Furthermore, hate speech against homosexuals in Turkey is prevalent and has promulgated the abuse of LGBTQ individuals and their rights. For example, in 2012, Okan Bayulgen asked the mayor of Ankara and AK Party member Melih Gökçek, "When we will be a gay mayor?" (Milliyet 2012). Gökçek answered, "Of course, we have our own way of life, we have customs. They (the Western world) are at a different point. We hope that in Turkey there won't, and there shouldn't be a gay mayor" was his answer (Kaos/GL 2012). In response, the Social Policies Gender Identity and Sexual Orientation Studies Association said: "We assert that Melih Gökçek's discourse with his "there won't, and there shouldn't be a gay mayor" statement is not a democratic attitude, and we want to underline that just like there can be a religious prime minister, there can be a gay mayor as well. We would gladly like to inform you that we are working in this direction" (Kaos/GL 2012). The Kaos/GL and Pink Life associations added that Lesbian, Gay, Bisexual, and Transgender (LGBT) existence is hard to ignore, and legitimization of discrimination and human rights violations against LGBT people have been sustained through ambiguous terms like "General Morality," "Turkish Family Structure," "Mores" and "Traditions" (Kaos/GL 2012; 2014).

According to ILGA EUROPE (2019), legal, political, and social environments affect a person's life, whether homosexual or heterosexual. Thus, the fact that elected representatives of the society engage in hate speech in the media, and the rights of

---

[1]Article 21/2: Everyone has the right of equal access to public service in his country.

[2]Article 23/1: Everyone has the right to work, to free choice of employment, to just and favorable conditions of work and to protection against unemployment (United Nations 1948).

homosexual rights are not guaranteed by law, undoubtedly causes citizens to develop negative attitudes towards homosexuals and consequently, degenerate their lives.

The inaugural Istanbul Pride March was held in Istanbul in 2003, and became more popular over the subsequent years. By 2011, the event attracted more than 10,000 people, and in 2014, more than 100,000 attended. In addition, the LGBT movement used the Gezi Park protests to increase the visibility of LGBT issues in Turkey. Therefore, for the first time, the LGBT movement was able to protest with other groups of civil society (Birdal 2015; Muehlenhoff 2019). However, in 2015, the police dispersed the parade using a water cannon, and, a year later, the march was banned for the safety of citizens and participants as officials said that the parade might disrupt the public order (BirGun 2016; Civil Rights Defender 2018). Unfortunately, these bans have continued to be imposed to the present time.

During the period of the state of emergency, declared due to the July 2016 coup attempt, arbitrary prohibitions were continued for meetings and demonstrations, as well as for most citizenship rights (Amnesty International 2018). The Pembe Hayat LGBT Solidarity Association claimed that Ankara Governor's Office imposed a ban on meetings and demonstrations following an anti-LGBTQ social media campaign conducted on Twitter for a film screening event that they organized (Human Rights Watch 2019). In response, Human Rights Watch issued a statement that fundamental rights had been violated (Aydin and Avincan 2020; Human Rights Watch 2019).

7.3 Methodology

This section provides the stories of human rights violations and violence in Turkey through the voices of LGBTQ members who have suffered persecution. These include Ahmet Yıldız, who was murdered because his family refused to accept his sexual orientation; Hande Buse Seker, a sex worker, shot by her client, who was a police officer; and Hande Kader, an LGBT rights activist and sex worker, whose life ended with fire. In addition, they include the experiences of a civil servant who was terminated while working in the Turkish Armed Forces and another who was working in the Ministry of National Education.

In Turkey, while some individuals have been victims of violence, other individuals have been killed, for identifying as gay (Bilginsoy 2015). Reports regarding homosexual individuals who have been subjected to violence or murder are not written or published frequently. However, the stories of the participants of this study were victims who became recognized in the media. Although the cases of these victims are still pending, there is no one to pursue additional cases other than select LGBTQ organizations. Hence, the participants agreed to participate in this study due to their situations being on the agenda for a given time, but recognize that they are now forgotten.

After gathering these stories, the LGBTQ activist and author of the chapter, presented and interpreted sections of violence from his own life within the framework of the Universal Declaration of Human Rights.

7.4 Victim Stories

7.4.1 Murdered Gay and Litigation Process in Turkey

7.4.1.1 Ahmet Yıldız Case

Ahmet Yıldız, the son of a couple from Urfa, left his partner İbrahim Can at home and went out to get ice cream on the night of 15 July 2008. He was 26 years old when his father, Yahya Yıldız, allegedly wounded him with 5 bullets. Although he tried to escape in his car, he lost control of the steering wheel and crashed into the wall of a pharmacy building. He was pronounced dead at the scene. After his family did not claim his corpse, his uncle retrieved it days later at the Yenibosna Forensic Medicine Institution.

The murder trial began on 8 September 2009, more than a year after Yıldız's murder. However, the person who brought suit was not someone from Ahmet's family or his partner İbrahim Can (because it is not allowed by law) – but by the Justice and Development MP Candidate, Ümmühan Darama, who was shot in the foot during the incident, and subsequently had his store shot at as a means of intimidation. To date, the trial has not had any significant developments, due to the runaway defendant, Yahya Yıldız, remaining at large. Lawyers and NGOs who have overseen the trial have complained of the slow process as well as officials' unwillingness to capture and arrest the murder suspect. Upon leaving one of the hearings, Ümmühan Darama's lawyer and Lambdaistanbul and SPoD volunteer attorney, Fırat Söyle, stated, "Along with the slow pace of the proceedings, there is no effort to catch the defendant."

The murder of Ahmet Yıldız is often characterized as the "first homosexual honor killing in Turkey." Therefore, this case will be a significant turning point in Turkey's judicial history with its procedures, handling, and conclusion. However, it would be naïve to think that Ahmet Yıldız was the first or only individual to be killed by a family member due to their sexual orientation. Unfortunately, Yıldız is one of multiple victims of family murders that have been unnamed and concealed.

Although the legitimization of the murder through custom and honor remains, the public interest in Ahmet Yıldız's murder was a result of a series of critical political actions that came together. The first is about the "coming-out" process that is painful for many LGBT individuals. Ahmet Yıldız chose to come out to his family despite the negative examples he had around him. He may not be the first person to be pressured, threatened, and killed by his family for coming out, but he is the most noted because his partner chose to be visible, chose to struggle, worked to keep the trial in the public eye, and talked to journalists.

Another contributing factor was the organized LGBT movement. Many LGBT associations requested to join the pending case as joint plaintiffs, and although they were rejected, they continued to follow the trail, to announce, and to call into the hearings (Kaos/GL 2017). Therefore, it is plausible to prescribe that visibility and organization are fundamental parts of this case.

In Turkey, the cases that the state operates "halfheartedly" on, like the one of Ahmet Yıldız, proceed very slowly, and may take several years. Consequently, for the decision-makers, this murder is deemed moral, if not legal, in the context of the "honor/custom." It is precisely for this reason that following the case of Ahmet Yıldız is essential for the LGBT movement which is working towards legislation on hate crimes (Sahan 2015).

7.4.1.2 Hande Buse Seker Case

Hande Buse Seker, a transgender woman born in 1994, made a living in the Alsancak district of İzmir working as a sex worker in a house she rented with her friends. On the night of January 8, 2019, she went out to find customers. Two people in a car approached her and stated that they wanted to be with her. However, one of the people in the vehicle became aggressive and threatening before driving away. After a while he returned, and following an amicable conversation, Hande agreed to terms with her customer, and they went to Hande's room. The other people at the house were in other rooms or in the hall at the time Hande engaged in an argument with her customer. The argument frightened Hande, who fled into the hallway. Unfortunately, the customer took pursuit and shot her. The attacker rejected requests for help, instead removing people from the area before shooting Hande again. Then he raped Hande's friend, a transgender woman who was in the room at the time and let her go. Before leaving, he raped Hande's body.

In contrast to other cases, due to the attacker being identified as a police officer, the prosecution quickly applied to the Magistrates' Court and ordered a confidentiality decision. Objections to the confidentiality decision by Hande family's lawyers were rejected. Furthermore, in seeking an investigation of the offending police officer, Hande's lawyers requested that the investigation be carried out by the gendarmerie and not by the police. However, these demands were also rejected. Although the perpetrator was arrested after the incident, the trial is still pending. During the first hearing, non-governmental organizations demanded to participate in the case, but their demands were rejected. Ultimately, the decision was made to close the hearings (Evrensel Gazetesi 2019).

7.4.1.3 Hande Kader Case

Hande Kader was a trans-gender female. Many knew Kader as a sex worker and an LGBTQ rights activist. Her friends last saw her while she was riding in a customer's vehicle in Harbiye during the first week of August 2016. They later learned that she was beaten, raped, stabbed, and killed, before her body was set on fire and left burning in the street (Kelley 2018). Those who were acquainted with her believed that she was killed due to her identity as a transgendered woman as well as an LGBTQ advocate. Although a suspect was arrested in the later stages of the investigation, no case has been filed yet, and the investigation file has been made confidential. At the time of this study, no indictment had been made.

Unfortunately, Ahmet Yıldız, Hande Buse Seker, and Hande Kader, all LGBTQ members, are only three of the gay people who have been murdered in Turkey. As *Huck Magazine* has reported, Turkey has a higher rate of trans-murder than anywhere else in Europe. Between 2008 and 2015, more than 40 transgender people were murdered (Rios 2017). The Red Umbrella Sexual Health and Human Rights Association, which works with sex workers in Turkey, recorded 520 incidents of hate crimes committed against trans people in Turkey (Kelley 2018).

Thus, while the safety of the Turkish people is generally limited, no security exists in any capacity for homosexuals. Within a country governed by a police state, a police officer can shoot someone who is not guilty. Furthermore, in cases where the perpetrator is a police officer, the prosecutor makes the file confidential. Within this context, it may be noted that judicial authorities watch out for each other, oppress people, disregard the grave situations experienced, and sign rights violations. In addition, neither the police nor the prosecutor endeavor to clarify events when the victims are gay, and non-governmental organizations, who could assist these individuals, are not permitted to join legal proceedings. Therefore, these behaviors abrogate the Universal Declaration of Human Rights, which states that all are equal before the law and are entitled without discrimination to equal protection of the law (Equal Rights Association (ERA) 2019). For example, the United Nations (1948), clearly stated in article 7, "all are equal before the law and are entitled without any discrimination to equal protection of the law. All are entitled to equal protection against any discrimination in violation of this Declaration and against any incitement to such discrimination." However, in a majority of the occurrences regarding LGBTQ members, the Turkish judicial system does not adequately aid the victims of these hate crimes. Moreover, because domestic remedies have not been exhausted, the European Court of Human Rights will not hear these cases. Hence, the lawlessness in Turkey, pertaining to the LGBTQ community, continues unabated.

7.5 The Constitutional Court Rejects Gay Military Service

An indictment was issued against a soldier who was involved in a homosexual relationship while he was not on duty. It was determined that he was to be punished under Article 153 of the Military Criminal Code.[3] Thus, a case was filed at the

[3]Article 153- A person who deliberately marries or maintains the bond of marriage or who maintains such a person, or insists on living permanently without any other person, such as husband

Military Criminal Court, and the soldier was expelled from the army. However, the defendant appealed the decision at the Military Court of Cassation. Subsequently, the Military Court of Cassation appealed to the Constitutional Court with the view that the applicable law was contrary to Article 10 of the Constitution regulating equality, and demanded the annulment of the article. The Constitutional Court determined that, pertaining to the duties of the Turkish Armed Forces, in order to protect national security, the characteristics of the military profession are considered, and therefore, the legal status of military personnel is not the same as the civilian population. Hence, on November 29, 2017, the court rejected the appeal with a majority vote.

7.5.1 The Constitutional Court Rejects a Gay Teacher

Z.A, a teacher of Religious Culture and Ethics, was expelled from his profession because he was a homosexual, and was dismissed from the civil service with the procedure of the High Disciplinary Board of the Ministry of National Education, dated 3/12/1998, because he sought homosexual relationships with those around him. Additionally, the applicant lost his case for the annulment of the decision. However, he applied to be a teacher again by benefiting from the registry amnesty that was later brought to the officers. However, in contrast to his peers, his application was rejected. Although he filed an administrative case against the refusal, the cases were rejected, prompting Z.A. to apply to the Constitutional Court (Istanbul Gercegi 2018). The Constitutional Court rejected the individual application, stating that the refusal for the readmission of the applicant to the profession was not his sexual orientation, but the decision was made in accordance to acts committed during his duty. The court said that the profession to which the applicant sought to be reappointed to was a teaching profession that included the education of primary school children. The teaching profession is closely linked to the healthy upbringing of children and the protection of their rights. In this context, the teaching profession has a more prominent position when it is considered that one interest that must be considered is the healthy upbringing of children and the protection of their rights. Therefore, those who want to work as teachers in the education of young children are subject to certain restrictions that other people are not. Therefore, the legitimacy of discrimination was established.

There following are countless human rights violations that I, Barbaros Sansal, have experienced. Some of them are as follows:

---

and wife, shall be sentenced to expulsion from the Turkish Armed Forces and to withdraw his rank on privates. Anyone who deals with a person in an unlawful manner or who makes this act voluntarily, even if the acts constitute another offense, is also punishable by the Turkish Armed Forces for removal from the Turkish Armed Forces and for the withdrawal of the rank of privates.

"In 1978, homosexuals became the targets of the Police Department in Istanbul. Day and night, in bars, baths, even tea gardens, the police carried out operations against suspected gay people, who were gathered up one by one. First, our identification papers were confiscated, and our hair was shaved, and then we were transferred to Zuhrevi Diseases Hospital for a health checkup. After being kept locked up for 2-3 days, we were taken to another center for a lung x-ray. Finally, we were put on the trains from Haydarpaşa Railway Station and deported to Anatolia. During that time, I lost half my teeth due to the torture I was subjected to in the Sansaryan."

"Four years later, in 1982, homophobia and violence continued to climb. This time the excuse for the abuse was AIDS. A group was picked up from a restaurant in Bodrum, a holiday resort, and taken to the central police station. Our profile, portrait, and height photographs were taken, and fingerprints were taken. Moreover, our ID papers were punched with staples. We were beaten at the same time, and the beaten caused a vertical hernia that I needed a prosthesis to be inserted years later. Those who were released from prison in those years received a punch hole in their identity papers, which meant that you were a criminal in the controls."

"I was a recognized political tailor and leading professional in 1990 while walking on the road, a blue police van suddenly approached me. A commander Ugur (pseudonym) forced me into the van. I was taken to one of the city's hills with three other officers in the vehicle. I was sexually abused at gunpoint in the dark. When I went to the police station to complain when they released me, I was further humiliated."

"In 2017, on a New Year's Eve, I uploaded a video on social media from my house in North Cyprus that focused on homophobia, radical Islam, bribery, pedophilia, zoophilia, and the destruction of social morality in a sarcastic satire. As a result, I was taken from North Cyprus illegally and then flown to Istanbul Atatürk Airport. Here, I was arrested by police officers and officials at the airport with heavy insults and threats. I was constantly subjected to homophobic and anti-Semitic psychological torture. I was not able to get medical help. At the end of 56 days, I was acquitted and released. And because the penalty limit was not enough, all the roads to the Constitutional Court or the ECHR were closed. I experienced substantial commercial losses as a result of the campaign to discredit me. So, I had to use most of my savings."

"I have been subjected to many acts of violence and threats like these. This has been in contravention to several parts of the Universal Declaration of Human Rights. For instance, Article 9 says that "No one shall be subjected to arbitrary arrest, detention or exile" and Article 12 says that "No one shall be subjected to arbitrary interference with his privacy, family, home or correspondence, nor to attacks upon his honor and reputation. Everyone has the right to the protection of the law against such interference or attacks."

"The legal system is the most fundamental fact guiding the functioning of the state mechanisms and the behavior of the citizens. As long as separatist attitudes towards homosexuals continue in the judicial bureaucracy, the rights of LGBTQ individuals will be fundamentally abrogated."

7.6 Conclusion

Turkey is a country of paradoxes. The people are trying to maintain their lives in a land in which the safety of life and property, freedom of expression and thought, and freedom of travel and worship are hindered. The country has become racist, nationalist, and sexist, and the nation is amidst a process in which the religious autocracy is being converted into dictatorship.

From justice to education in Turkey, serious problems are prevalent in all areas of the nation – ranging from the economy to the environment. Within the social climate, where systematic problems exist, taking effective steps to combat social problems is inhibited in the near term. However, when the narrated stories in this study are comprehended, then the context of justice in situations paralleling the participants, can be better understood. In Turkey, where job opportunities are limited, excluding homosexuals from the systems brings economic relief. Furthermore, within the justice system, judicial institutions watch out for each other and target homosexuals to use as scapegoats. Due to the exclusion of homosexuals in all systems, judicial authorities are not held accountable. Therefore, it is inevitable that the education system, which is devoid of empathy, will also turn against those who are not like it. At that point, all systems in Turkey will feed off each other and turn against homosexuals.

Consequently, gay rights in Turkey are much less protected than in the majority of today's world. The stories in the study are not yet punctuated. The stories presented above clearly demonstrate that Turkish state institutions have driven homosexuals from their ranks because of their homophobic perceptions. Such circumstances are antithetical to Article 23 of the Universal Declaration of Universal Rights to which Turkey is a signatory which addresses the right to work. The cases of LGBTQ activists and organizations are rejected, and the decisions of institutions are often arbitrary. The violation of the constitution and international conventions indicates that the state has committed numerous offenses for which they should be held accountable.

7.7 Recommendations

To better protect LBBTQ rights, the following should be done;

1. If the term" everyone" in the law does not cover homosexuals, then specific constitutional provisions should be added to protect gay rights.
2. Non-governmental organizations should be granted standing in order to participate in cases in which the plaintiffs have granted consent. In cases involving harassment, violence, and violation of rights, the scope of the investigation should be extended, and impartiality should be ensured.
3. National and international human rights organizations should be allowed to conduct sudden inspections to prevent violations of rights in detention centers. The government should consider the reports of these organizations. Judicial action must be taken against civil servants who violate human rights.
4. Government officials should abandon hate speech against homophobia and homosexuals.

5. Administrative measures that reject all forms of discrimination against homosexuals should be developed.
6. Practices that develop empathy should be made in educational institutions.
7. Studies should be made to overcome the perception that homosexuality is a disease or a crime.
8. The ban on pride marches should be lifted.
9. Work on rights violations against homosexuals should be increased. Statistical analysis of the collected data should be compared with developed countries. The result should be shared with the public.

These recommendations have been presented within the framework of universal human rights norms. Because respect is a matter of conscious, those who define homosexuality as a sin, crime, or sickness with disgust should develop empathy for homosexual individuals as human beings.

References

Akpinar, Aslıhan. 2014. Stigma and Discrimination Based on Sexual Orientation and Gender Identity. *Turkish Journal of Bioethics* 1 (3): 149–153.

Amnesty International. 2011. *Turkey 'Not an Illness Nor a Crime' Lesbian, Gay, Bisexual, and Transgender People in Turkey Demand Equality*. https://www.amnesty.org/download/Documents/28000/eur440012011en.pdf. Accessed 25 Sept 2019.

———. 2013. *Gezi Park Protests: Brutal Denial of the Right to Peaceful Assembly in Turkey*. https://www.amnesty.org/download/Documents/12000/eur440222013en.pdf. Accessed 02 Oct 2019.

———. 2018. *Amnesty International Report 2017/18 – The State of The World's Human Rights*. https://www.amnesty.org/download/Documents/POL1067002018ENGLISH.PDF. Accessed 02 Oct 2019.

Arat, Zehra F. Kabasakal, and Nuñez Carly. 2017. Advancing LGBT Rights in Turkey: Tolerance or Protection? *Human Rights Review* 18 (1): 1–19.

Aydin, Hasan, and Koksal Avincan. 2020. Intellectual Crimes and Serious Violation of Human Rights in Turkey: A Narrative Inquiry. *The International Journal of Human Rights* 24 (8): 1127–1155. https://doi.org/10.1080/13642987.2020.1713108.

Bicmen, Zümrüt, and Zafer Bekirogulları. 2014. Social Problems of LGBT People in Turkey. *Procedia-Social and Behavioral Sciences* 113: 224–233.

Bilginsoy, Zeynep. 2015. *Evaluating Hate Murders Based on SOGI in TURKEY: Shortcomings and Proposals*. http://lgbtinewsturkey.com/2014/11/30/infographic-hate-murders/. Accessed on June 5, 2015.

Birdal, Mehmet Sinan. 2015. Between the Universal and the Particular: The Politics of Recognition of LGBT Rights in Turkey. In *Sexualities in World Politics: How LGBTQ Claims Shape International Relations*, ed. Manuela Lavinas Picq and Markus Thiel, 124–138. Routledge.

BirGun. 2016. *LGBTI Onur Haftası basın açıklamasına da Valilik'ten 'hassasiyet' yasağı!*. https://www.birgun.net/haber/lgbti-onur-haftasi-basin-aciklamasina- da-valilik-ten-hassasiyet-yasagi-117478. Accessed 02 Oct 2019.

Civil Rights Defenders. 2018. *A State in Emergency – When Exceptions Become the New Norm*. https://crd.org/wp-content/uploads/2018/04 /CRD-6700-Rapport-Turkiet.pdf. Accessed 07 Oct 2019.

Engin, Ceylan. 2015. LGBT in Turkey: Policies and Experiences. *Social Science* 4: 838–858.

Equal Rights Association. 2019. *Türkiye*. https://www.lgbti-era.org/content/turkey. Accessed 11 Oct 2019.

Evrensel Gazetesi. 2019. *Hande Buse Şeker'in katledilmesiyle ilgili dava 13 Eylül'e ertelendi* [Hande Buse Seker's Trial is Postponed on September 13]. https://www.evrensel.net/haber/381680/hande-buse-sekerin-katledilmesiyle-ilgili-dava-13-eylule-ertelendi. Accessed 08 Oct 2019.

Fishman, Louis A. 2013. Turkey and LGBT Rights: A Historical and Global Perspective. *Turkish Policy Quarterly* 11 (4): 149–159.

Human Rights Association. 2017. *Human Rights Association 2016 Violations Report*. http://www.ihd.org.tr/wp-content/uploads/2017/04/2016_ ihd_t%C3%BCrkiye_ihlal_raporu.compressed.pdf. Accessed 08 Oct 2019.

Human Rights Watch. 2019. *Turkey: End Ankara Ban on LGBTI Events*. https://www.hrw.org/news/2019/02/14/turkey-end-ankara-ban-lgbti-events. Accessed 08 Oct 2019.

Hurriyet Daily News. 2015. *Turkish Police Crackdown on Gay Pride in Istanbul*. http://www.hurriyetdailynews.com/turkish-police-crack-down-on-gay-pride-in-istanbul-84673. Accessed 12 Oct 2019.

ILGA-Europe. 2019. *Country Ranking*. https://www.rainbow-europe.org/country-ranking. Accessed 09 Oct 2019.

International Lesbian, Gay, Bisexual, Trans & Intersex Association – Europe. 2019. *Annual Review of the Human Rights Situation of Lesbian, Gay, Bisexual, Trans and Intersex People in Europe*. https://www.ilga-europe.org/sites/default/files/2019/full_annual_review.pdf. Accessed 08 Oct 2019.

Istanbul Gercegi. 2018. *AYM'nin 'eşcinsel öğretmen' kararına iki üyeden karşı oy: Devletin cinsel yönelimi yoktur. [Supreme Court votes against two members of the gay teacher's decision. The state has no sexual orientation]*. https://www.google.com/search?q=google+translate&rlz=1C1CHBD_enUS756US756&oq=&sourceid=chrome&ie=UTF-8. Accessed 20 Oct 2019.

Kaos/GL The International Gay and Lesbian Human Rights Commission (IGLHRC) and LGBTI News Turkey. 2014. *Human Rights Violations of LGBT Individuals in Turkey*. https://ilga.org/wp-content/uploads/2016/02/Shadow-report-16.pdf. Accessed 10 Oct 2019.

Kaos/GL. 2002. *Erdoğan'ın Eşcinsel Hakları Sözü [Erdoğan's pledge of gay rights] [Youtube Video]*. https://www.youtube.com/watch?v=-bp6grWsIJA. Accessed 09 Oct 2019.

———. 2012. *The Mayor of Ankara, Melih Gökçek, Openly Discriminates Against LGBT People!* http://www.kaosgldernegi.org/news_detail.php?id=7478. Accessed 11 Sept 2019.

———. 2017. *Ahmet Yıldız davasında 24. duruşma 31 Ocak'ta [Ahmet Yildiz's 24th case is on January 31st]*. https://www.kaosgl.org/haber/ahmet-yildiz-davasinda-24-durusma-31-ocakrsquota. Accessed 11 Sept 2019.

———. 2018. *Co-founder Ali Erol has been Detained. LGBTI News Turkey*. https://lgbtinewsturkey.com/2018/02/02/kaos-gl-co-founder-ali-erol-has-been-detained/amp/?__twitter_impression=true. Accessed 01 Sept 2019.

Karakuş, Abdullah. 2008. *AKP'li Burhan Kuzu'dan Lisede Türban Tartışmasına Yanıt: Eşcinseller de eşitlik istiyor, verecek miyiz?* https://www.milliyet.com.tr/2008/01/28/siyaset/asiy. Accessed 10 Oct 2019.

Kelley, Laura. 2018. *Hande Kader, Transgender Woman Who was Raped, Beaten, Killed & Burned: 5 Fast Facts You Need to Know*. https://heavy.com/news/2018/01/turkish-transgender-activist-raped-killed-burned/. Accessed 10 Oct 2019.

Kongar, Emre. 2019. *Toplumsal Değişme Kuramları ve Türkiye Gerçeği*. Ankara: Remzi Bookstore.

Kulpa, Robert. 2011. LGBT Issues and the Queer Approach. In *21st Century Political Science: A Reference Handbook*, ed. John T. Ishiyama and Marijke Breuning, vol. 1, 856–865. Thousand Oaks: SAGE Publications.

LGBTI Equal Rights Association for Western Balkans and Turkey. 2019. *TURKEY. Belgrade, Serbia*. https://www.lgbti-era.org/content/turkey. Accessed 10 Sept 2019.

Merlo, Timothy, Supraja Murali, and Shana Tabak. 2012. *Human Rights Violations of Lesbian, Gay, Bisexual, and Transgender (LGBT) People in Guatemala: A Shadow Report*. New York: United Nations Human Rights Committee.

Milliyet. 2012. *Shocking Gay Question from Okan to Melih Gökçek!* http://www.milliyet.com.tr/gundem/okandan-melih-gokceke-sok-gay-sorusu-1523190. Accessed 10 Oct 2019.

Muehlenhoff, Hanna L. 2019. Neoliberal Governmentality and the (de) Politicisation of LGBT Rights: The Case of the European Union in Turkey. *Politics* 39 (2): 202–217.

Rios, Lorena. 2017. *Documenting the Violence Facing Turkey's Trans Community*. Huck. https://www.huckmag.com/art-and-culture/photography-2/documenting-violence-facing-turkeys-trans-community/. Accessed 01 Oct 2019.

Sahan, Idil Engindeniz. 2015. The Case of Ahmet Yildiz: Violation of the Right to Life. *LGBTI News Turkey*. https://lgbtinewsturkey.com/2013/09/17/ahmet-yildiz-murder/. Accessed 11 Oct 2019.

The Guardian. 2017. *Turkish Police Break Up Gay Pride Protest in Istanbul*. https://www.theguardian.com/world/2017/jun/25/turkish-police-break-up-gay-pride-protest-in-istanbul. Accessed 12 Oct 2019.

Turkish Civil Law. 2011. *Official Newspaper (Number: 24607)*. https://www.resmigazete.gov.tr/eskiler/2001/12/20011208.html. Accessed 26 Sept 2019.

Turkish Medical Association. 2010. *Kavaf'ın açıklaması bilimsel tıp ve insan haklarına aykırıdır [Kavaf's statement is contrary to scientific medicine and human rights]*. http://www.ttb.org.tr/haberarsiv_goster.php?Guid=66a40fc4-9232-11e7-b66d-1540034f819c. Accessed 15 Oct 2019.

———. 2016. *LGBTI Health for Physicians*. Turkish Medical Association Publications. http://www.ttb.org.tr/kutuphane/lgbti_ sagligi.pdf. Accessed 10 Oct 2019.

United Nations. 1948. *Universal Declaration of Human Rights*. https://www.ohchr.org/EN/UDHR/Documents/UDHR_Translations/eng.pdf. Accessed 08 Oct 2019.

United States Department of State – Bureau of Democracy Human Rights and Labor. 2010. *Turkey 2009 Human Rights Report*. https://2009-2017.state.gov/j/drl/rls/hrrpt/2009/eur/136062.html. Accessed 12 Oct 2019.

US Mission to International Organizations in Geneva. 2011. https://geneva.usmission.gov/2011/03/22/lgbtrights. Accessed 01 Oct 2019.

Yılmaz, Volkan. 2012. Political Threats and Opportunities in the LGBT Issue. *Bianet*, July 21.

Barbaros Sansal was born in 1957 in Turkey's capital Ankara as the child of Sungur Tekin Sansal and Guner Eczacıbaşı. He studied Business Management at Marmara University and mastered in design and chromatics at the Royal Academy of Arts in London, before becoming an apprentice to prominent fashion designer Yıldırım Mayruk. Besides being a fashion designer, Sansal is also known as an LGBT rights advocate and an anti-war activist. Barbaros Sansal hosted two TV programs on Turkish TV channels called "Pin" and "Safety Pin". He also wrote two books called "Printing Ink Lives on Newsprint" and "Fitting Room". He translated the book "101 things I Learned in Fashion School" written by Matthew Frederick and Alfredo Cabrera. Sansal gave lectures about the history of fashion at Marmara University and Ankara Baskent University.

Part III
The Rights of the Displaced

Chapter 8
Syrian Refugees in Turkey: (Un)Equal Opportunities in Education

Alia Hadid and Rabia Hos

Let us commit to quality education for all of the world's children. Financing education is the best investment we can make for a better world.
- Antonio Guterres, UN Secretary-General

Abstract The number of Syrian refugees seeking shelter in Turkey continues to rise as Syria enters its tenth year of violence. The ongoing crisis has resulted in more than 3.5 million registered Syrian refugees (UNHCR 2019). Although multiple social, economic, and security related debates have been studied by researchers in this field, the scope of this chapter focuses on the education of the Syrian refugees in Turkey. Despite the importance of such challenges, there is a much more pressing issue, which is providing education to all children who constitute 1.6 million Syrian refugees of which more than 430.000 are out of school (UNICEF 2018) in Turkey. In this chapter we provide a detailed review of the current situation of schooling Syrian refugee children in Turkey. We seek to investigate how Turkey responded to meet the Syrian refugees' educational needs and how the continuing efforts are still in violation of the basic human rights of refugees because around half a million of them are still out of school (Karasapan and Shah 2018). In the conclusion section, we end with a discussion of how the responses thus far have not improved despite the many years that had passed and how this is in violation of basic human rights.

Keywords Syrian refugees · Access to education · Human rights · (Un)equal opportunities · Turkey

A. Hadid · R. Hos (✉)
School of Education, University of Rhode Island, Kingston, RI, USA
e-mail: alia_hadid@uri.edu; rabiahos@uri.edu

H. Aydin, W. Langley (eds.), *Human Rights in Turkey*, Philosophy and Politics - Critical Explorations 15, https://doi.org/10.1007/978-3-030-57476-5_8

8.1 Introduction

In article 61 of the Law on Foreigners and International Protection, the word 'refugee' refers to:

> A person who owing to well-founded fear is unwilling to avail himself or herself of the protection of that country; or who, not having a nationality and being outside the country of his former residence as a result of such events, is unable or, owing to such fear, is unwilling to return to it, shall be granted refugee status upon completion of the refugee status determination process.

The number of Syrian refugees seeking shelter in Turkey continues to rise as Syria enters its tenth year of violence. The ongoing crisis has resulted in more than 3.5 million registered Syrian refugees (UNHCR 2019). For the first time, Turkey found itself confronted with the need to accommodate a huge number of refugees and without proper skills and systematic policies, there were many trial and error phases, which resulted in the current situation.

The enormous numbers of Syrian refugees burden Turkey's economy, cause housing problems and result in lower job opportunities for both Syrian and Turkish citizens (Carpio et al. 2015). Due to the government regulations of Syrians being considered "guests", many of them do not have access to legal authorization to work. The scarce resources for both Syrian and Turkish citizens in Turkey create a conflict as Bonacich's 1972 split labor market theory suggests. Given Turkey's struggles with job creation structurally, many Syrian refugees still remain "socially and economically vulnerable" (Zetter and Héloïse 2016, 179). Multiple social, economic, and security-related debates have been studied by researchers in this field. Despite the importance of such challenges, there is a much more pressing issue, which is providing education to all children who constitute 1.6 million Syrian refugees of which more than 430.000 are out of school (UNICEF 2018). Thus, this chapter will focus on the education of Syrian refugees in Turkey.

Receiving an education is one of the refugees' fundamental human rights as stated by the 1951 Refugee Convention (UNHCR USA 2019) given that education can help them build a better future and allow them to contribute to either their country of origin or their host country. Educating refugees is particularly crucial as it liberates them, provides them with opportunities, and promotes "understanding, tolerance and friendship among all nations, racial or religious groups…" (United Nations, para. 35, n.d.). Through education, refugees will be empowered to fully participate democratically in society, (Nie et al. 1996), promote tolerance, and co-exist peacefully with diverse individuals in society (Inglehart and Welzel 2005).

Challenges in accommodating Syrian refugee children in schools are not unique to Turkey. The same problem extends to Jordan and Lebanon where schools cannot accommodate the increasing number of Syrian refugee students. Thus, in Jordan, they were segregated and registered as part of a second shift (Krafft et al. 2018). Likewise, Lebanon did not resolve the problem since more than 250,000 children are still without schooling (Children on the Edge 2018).

In the past, much research focused on how the Turkish government responded to the education of the Syrian refugees in Turkey. However, not many people offered thorough solutions to the problems. In this chapter, we refer to UN documents, non-governmental organization (NGO) reports, and scholarly work to present an overview of the Syrian refugee education in Turkey. We seek to investigate how Turkey responded to meet the Syrian refugees' educational needs and how the continuing efforts are still in violation of the basic human rights of refugees because around half a million of them are still out of school (Karasapan and Sajjad 2018). In the conclusion section, we end with a discussion of how the responses thus far have not improved despite the many years that had passed.

8.1.1 Failed Attempts to Support Syrian Refugees in Turkey

The big influx of Syrian refugees to Turkey translates into increased challenges and a strain to Turkey's economy (Makovsky 2019). As such, Turkey needed international help to fund the education of Syrian children. In fact, several commitments were made during the Supporting Syria Conference in London, but donors failed to meet their promises (Human Rights Watch 2017). The chart below (Fig. 8.1) – (original figure as cited in Carlier 2018) shows the vast gap between how much funding is needed and how much is being provided, which indicates that many governments hosting refugees in the Middle East are falling short of meeting many of the refugees' basic needs (Human Rights Watch 2017).

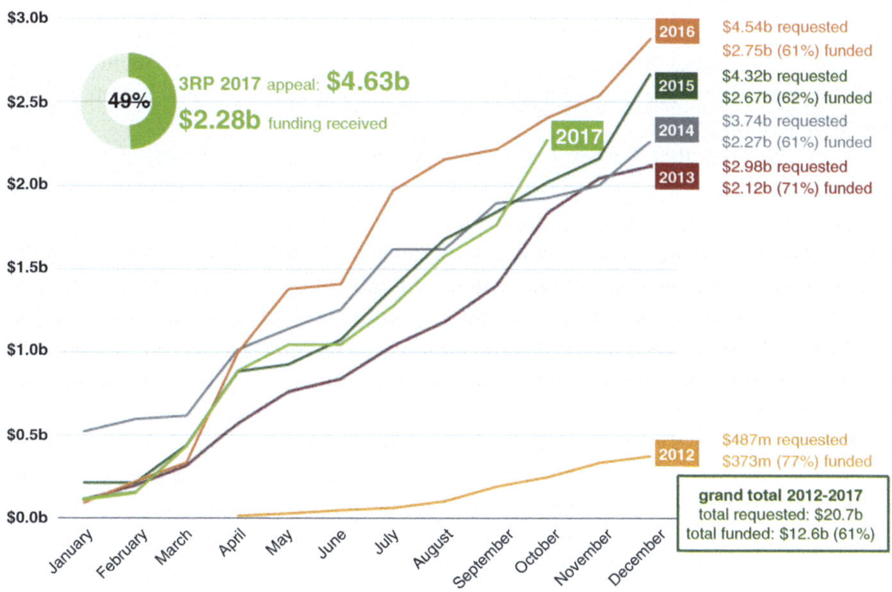

Fig. 8.1 KidsRights report 2018 (Carlier 2018, Fig. 1)

Ekinci (2016) reported that the European Union (EU) made an agreement with Turkey in 2016 stating it will offer 3 billion Euros to help it fulfill its financial obligations towards refugees, of which 500 million Euros will go towards education. However, officials state that this will only cover 10% of the needed expenses (Coşkun et al. 2017). Having received little support from international organizations has negatively impacted Turkey, particularly in the education sector due to the increasing demands for skilled teachers, larger institutions, and more school supplies and textbooks (Human Rights Watch 2017).

8.2 Literature Review

In this section, we highlight Turkey's efforts to cater to the needs of Syrian refugee children and examine what has been done. We then move on to discuss the many challenges it faces, which we divide into three main categories: lack of efficient educational opportunities, lack of funding, and attitudes.

Turkey has been exerting conscientious efforts to integrate Syrian refugees and provide them with opportunities for education. To this end, it has founded The Immigration and Emergency Education Department. Furthermore, in compliance with article 22 of the UN Convention on the Rights of the Child, Turkey strives to provide all children on its land with the benefits stipulated in the convention, that is set regulations that provide Syrian refugees with learning opportunities. Thus, in 2014, the Ministry of National Education (MoNE) published Circular 2014, which regulates the learning of foreigners on Turkish soil. This Circular allows Syrian refugees access to public schools, which are free of charge. The Circular has served some Syrian refugees well, but not all since those who do not have identification cards are not allowed to receive a diploma and are treated as guests (Human Rights Watch 2015).

Despite the law that Turkey had passed, many problems with lack of access to education still exist because of insufficient planning. Turkey had originally resorted to temporary solutions such as implementing temporary education centers in cities and camps because the government was under the impression that Syrians would leave as soon as the situation in Syria has improved, but the reality is that the crisis is ongoing, and Syrians are not going home any time soon (Hos and Cinarbas 2018). Turkey is still adhering to its short-term solutions, which has caused the situation to worsen. The problems need to be eradicated and to this end, Turkey must initiate some permanent solutions.

In their policy analyses of the Turkish government's response to the education of the Syrian refugees, Coşkun and Balamir (2018) categorized the response in three phases, the first phase between 2011–2013, the temporary stay phase, which is between 2014–2016, and finally the last phase from 2016-present, which plans to integrate Syrian children in Turkish public schools. As of the beginning of 2016, the number of children studying at temporary education centers was three times higher than the number of those going to Turkish public schools (Heyse 2016). Despite the continuous efforts to integrate Syrian refugee children in the Turkish education system, there are still 400,000 children out of school (Regional Refugee and Resilience Plan in Response to Syria Crisis 2019).

The Ministry of Education –Turkey – announced that the TECs will be closed by 2020 and will integrate Syrian refugee children into K-12 education in Turkey (Qaddour 2017). This is a much-needed approach; however, there is doubt regarding the implementation of this plan given the existing situation (Eryaman and Evran 2019). Considering that 2020 is soon coming to an end while multiple problems still persist, this seems a far-fetched dream that requires much work and dedication. Working to integrate Syrian refugee children does not only mean allowing them access to public schools, it goes far beyond that to include social, political, and cultural integration (Birman et al. 2008). The language barrier is one of the biggest problems for Syrian refugees (Aydin and Kaya 2019; Hos 2016; Taskin and Erdemli 2018). It renders them unable to communicate and learn and gives rise to many other problems. In the following section, we examine the obstacles that hinder the integration of Syrian refugee children, which can be divided into three main categories.

8.2.1 Lack of Efficient Educational Opportunities

This category includes several factors that the Turkish government should carefully consider and strategically implement.

Enrolling Syrian Refugee Children in Public Schools TECs were founded to end a period of interrupted schooling and enable Syrian children to learn despite the language barrier. As such, both the Syrian curriculum and Arabic were used (Emin 2016) to decrease the changes Syrian refugee children had to undergo and create opportunities for them to continue their education. However, TECs cannot secure a future for the Syrian children since they were not accredited by the Turkish government considering that the quality of education provided was lower than that in public schools (Aydin and Kaya 2019). Planning to shut down all TECs by the end of 2019 has negatively served the Syrian refugee children because that emphasized the temporary presence of those TECs and as such there were no efforts to develop them and that even affected the teachers who are worried about their future unemployment (Karakuş 2019).

Inability to Monitor Turkish Schools The education problem is not only limited to TECs but permeates the entire schooling system. Public schools have various problems that need to be resolved (Erdem et al. 2011). This comes as a result of the absence of an active role for MoNE. According to Icduygu (2015), MoNE is unable to oversee schools and provide support. In addition, Aydin and Kaya (2019) pointed out that MoNE has no policies regarding the assessment of Syrian refugees. Furthermore, it does not reach out to teachers to help them implement the existing policies. As such, teachers are left to improvise and do what they believe is befitting.

This creates a burden on teachers since their needs should be met if they are to efficiently cater to Syrian refugees and provide quality education. To ensure that Syrian refugees are receiving optimal education and are being taught according to a set standard, MoNE needs to implement several policies.

8.2.1.1 Teachers

Teachers constitute a major building block in the education system since they are in direct contact with the students and can have a great influence on them. MoNE, as indicated earlier, fails to equip teachers with the policies regarding teaching Syrian refugees and making education an equal opportunity to all (Hauber-Özer 2019). As such, teachers follow the sink or swim rule whereby they exert individual efforts to help Syrian refugees. Some try to learn Arabic to translate for students while others alter their style of teaching (Aydin and Kaya 2019). Such efforts reflect sincerity and a willingness to support; however, they are not enough to resolve the issue.

Another problem that teachers face is the presence of Turkish and Syrian students in the same classroom. Integrating Syrian children in Turkish classrooms is much needed but cannot take place without careful planning. Taskin and Erdemli (2018) narrate how teachers struggle trying to teach Turkish students the curriculum while trying to help Syrian students learn how to read and write. Attending to the needs of two different groups does not only cause the teacher to lag but also results in creating a gap since students are not working together towards the same goal.

To lessen the pressure on teachers, MoNE hired 5000 Turkish teachers to accommodate the needs of the increasing number of refugee students in schools. This seems like an important step towards remedying the present situation except that those teachers are young, inexperienced, and lack classroom management skills (Karakuş 2019). Furthermore, there is a gap between Syrian and Turkish teachers since the former receive support from UNICEF whereas the latter receive neither non-governmental organizations nor school administration assistance (Taskin and Erdemli 2018). To add insult to injury, there is a lack of communication between Turkish and Syrian teachers since they usually teach at different times of the day (Karakuş 2019).

8.2.1.2 Curriculum

Turkish schools often follow a secular framework as well as mixed-gender structures within the public education. In contrast, Syrian schools are gender-segregated and the curriculum is rooted in the religious beliefs (Sert 2016). Additionally, there are not any language learning courses in place to teach Turkish to Syrian refugees when they first enroll in the school, which is one of the biggest obstacles in the integration. Rather than providing additional language support, the whole language approach to "sink or swim" (Garcia 2013) would result in drop-outs, especially at the middle and secondary school level. In addition, Turkish textbooks are used to teach Turkish to

Syrians when there is a need for textbooks that teach Turkish as a second language (Taskin and Erdemli 2018). Like Jordan and Lebanon's efforts of schooling Syrian refugees, Turkey has had challenges with shortage of classroom space, lack of trained teachers and school personnel, cost of supplies, and uncertain funding (Visconti and Gal 2018).

Due to these issues, the integration of the refugees in Turkish public schools has been a challenge. Refugee integration is often recommended to be a mutual process where both the refugees and the host society need to put forth an effort (Eryaman and Evran 2019; Taylor and Sidhu 2012). For the host society, refugees' integration can be beneficial as they bring new knowledge and skills from their culture and through the exchange of culture and ideas, the dignity and rights of refugee children can be protected (Taylor and Sidhu 2012). Madziva and Thondhlana (2017) suggest three approaches to educating the refugees: a human capital approach that focuses on economic development, a human rights approach that focuses on basic human rights, and a social justice approach that allows the voices of marginalized groups to be heard (p. 945). Unfortunately, Turkey's response to the education of refugees hasn't really focused on any of these approaches.

8.2.2 Lack of Funding

The unavailability of adequate funding has led to a series of problems and has negatively impacted Syrian refugees' opportunities for education. One adverse effect is the unavailability of teaching materials and the inability to provide Syrian students with school supplies (Karakuş 2019). A second drawback is the inability to overcome the over crowdedness of schools and to have more classes to fit the new students. Extra classes require more money to pay teachers. As a result, teachers find themselves obliged to teach multi-level classes (Kaysili et al. 2019) where they have students that belong to different levels. This requires that teachers channel their attention and energy, which prevents them from creating an optimal learning environment. Moreover, financial issues greatly affect Syrian families' decision to support their children's education. Given the many hardships they face, they are forced to neglect education in their attempt to survive. Thus, boys try to take on jobs whereas girls marry at a young age (Karakuş 2019).

Facing economic hardships leads to an increase in drop-out in the higher grades (Fig. 8.2). A study by Coşkun et al. (2017) shows that educational enrollment both in schools and TECs dramatically decreases as students get older. Such low percentages imply that these students are not likely to pursue higher education, which can negatively impact their future and that of Turkey, as well.

TABLE 2. RATE OF SYRIAN REFUGEES' SCHOOLING BASED ON POPULATION AGE IN DIFFERENT GRADES					
	PUBLIC SCHOOLS	TECs	Total	Population	Schooling Rate
Pre-School (Age 5)	20.738	5.023	25.761	82.866	31,09%
1. Grade (Age 6)	70.451	5.280	75.731	80.807	93,72%
2. Grade (Age 7)	25.640	81.766	107.406	76.586	140,24%[8]
3. Grade (Age 8)	17.592	54.357	71.949	76.473	94,08%
4. Grade (Age 9)	13.504	40.048	53.552	70.561	75,89%
5. Grade (Age 10)	18.068	16.672	34.740	61.557	56,44%
6. Grade (Age 11)	7.048	22.681	29.729	62.408	47,64%
7. Grade (Age 12)	5.200	17.869	23.069	55.518	41,55%
8. Grade (Age 13)	3.714	15.005	18.719	53.032	35,30%
9. Grade (Age 14)	6.829	7.630	14.459	55.688	25,96%
10. Grade (Age 15)	2.189	9.020	11.209	55.002	20,38%
11. Grade (Age 16)	1.530	6.206	7.736	52.082	14,85%
12. Grade (Age 17)	999	9.290	10.289	50.459	20,39%
TOTAL	201.505	291.039	492.544	833.039	59%

Fig. 8.2 Data obtained from MoNE interview (Coşkun et al. 2017, Table 2)

8.2.3 Attitudes

Given the gravity of the situation, it has not been easy neither for Turkish nor Syrian people to coexist and build intercultural competence. Turkish people suddenly found themselves obliged to share their land, schools, and life with people whose language they cannot speak and who come with their set of political, economic, and psychological problems. This resulted in a feeling of hostility on the part of the Turkish people who considered that Syrian refugees lowered their chances of finding jobs and competed with them since the latter accepted lower rates (Kaysili et al. 2019). Tarman and Gürel (2017) also pointed out that attitudes change depending on where refugees are residing, that is the more refugees in the area, the higher the negative attitude:

> I may accept a refugee as my neighbor, but I do not think my neighborhood would accept it either. Because even my mother refuses to become neighbor to refugees. People do not know them, they regard them as thieves who are preoccupied with dirty works or whose women are engaged in different kinds of works. Consequently, they do not want the refugees to come. This affects my decision [M3] (p. 188).

A few negative incidents result in labeling an entire nation and having misconceptions that can affect how they communicate with one another. This is further evident in how they are perceived as a source of trouble in the areas where they live

(Erdoğan 2014). The public opinion has also affected how their children behave towards their Syrian peers at school (Aydin and Kaya 2019). This unfriendliness surpasses the school walls as a teacher reported hearing children repeat, "This is the Syrians' street; they will take our street now, then our house and our food, too!" (T3) (Karakuş 2019). This is a clear indication of the divide and that Syrians are not welcome, but rather considered as thieves. In addition, Turkey has specified designated areas for the resettlement of Syrian refugees (Jimenez 2019), which hinders their chances to work and integrate. Moreover, Turkey has a history of discrimination (Kaya 2009) as in the case of the Kurds who were not allowed to use their mother tongue and who were deprived of their rights (Kaya and Aydin 2014). A Turkish citizen expressed his opinion about having a Syrian refugee for a neighbor saying, "Turkish population is in a continuous decline already. They are back bone of the country...people's ethnicity has a big impact on how I see them. My priority is my own cognates. I favor those with the same origins with me. . ." [M2] (Tarman and Gürel 2017).

From a different perspective, Syrians who sought shelter in Turkey already have their set of problems and many of them need psychological support. Facing economic hardships in Turkey makes it difficult for them to prioritize education. In addition, living in overcrowded houses with people who have little interest in education does not promote an environment that is conducive to learning (Karakuş 2019). Furthermore, a lack of sense of belonging hinders their integration and ability to move forward (Gurer 2019). They blame the media for that saying:

> *The way Syrians are represented in the media leads the Turkish people to look at Syrians with fearful eyes. As a Syrian I feel bad, but I cannot blame them. If the media adopts a more positive approach, if success stories are given more space, it will greatly help to build social bridges between the two communities* (Memişoğlu 2018).

One way that Turkish educational policymakers can address the discrimination toward Syrian refugee children is to adopt a culturally responsive teaching (CRT) framework. CRT is defined as "using the cultural characteristics, experiences, and perspectives of ethnically diverse students as conduits for teaching them more effectively" (Gay 2010, 110). As the Turkish ministry of education is training teachers, they need to emphasize that teachers would best understand their students through a CRT lens and recognize the cultural and social realities of their lives. Once educators recognize that culture has a big role in the way students learn, they will be able to apply more CRT methods that would welcome students and instill a sense of belonging.

8.3 The Paradox of Welcoming Syrian "Guests"

The concept of hospitality has been the common reference that Turkish government had used since the beginning of the Syrian refugee crisis. Syrians were called "misafir" which translates into English as "guests". For the purposes of this chapter,

Stevens's (2015) Middle Eastern Refugee Protection Model is appropriate. Stevens (2015) states that the Middle East and North Africa categorize refugees based on their migration status. The categories that she refers to are refugees, emigrants, the exiles, the forgotten, and the asylum seekers. She argues that the concept of hospitality which is part of the culture is still the most common response to the refugee crisis in the Middle East, and Turkey too. There needs to be a shift from the hospitality mindset and the government must follow a well-structured plan to improve the education of Syrian refugee children.

Turkey's many attempts to welcome the Syrians have been short-lived. First, Turkey's open-door policy has saved thousands of lives and given hope to many. However, Turkey seems to be adopting a push and pull policy in its practices. First, it welcomes Syrian refugees and announces that it will help regulate their education. Later, we find TECs springing and more than eight years later, Turkey is still trying to find ways to integrate Syrian refugee students and provide them with opportunities for learning. This is an alarming indicator that so many children have not yet had proper education, which raises doubts about the future of the new generation.

As a candidate for the membership to the European Union, Turkey endorses the United Nations Convention on the Rights of the Child (CRC) (UN 1989). The aim of the CRC is to set guidelines that will protect the rights of the children in different areas such as education, health care, social services etc. However, CRC may not be a perfect system to follow since Freeman (2000) argued that it outlines the minimum standards that governments could adopt. Furthermore, there have been several incidents whereby countries breached children's rights (European Commission 2010). In fact, Lundy (2012) indicates that there is a gap between what CRC promises to achieve and what takes place in reality.

Turkey has been pushing to have all Syrian students in schools and provide them with an education by 2020. However, this does not guarantee that they will be receiving a fair education. Currently, there is much doubt about the schooling system and the future of those students (Taştan and Çelik 2017). Research shows that inequality exists on multiple levels in Turkey. For example, there is regional inequality (Ferreira and Gignoux 2010) whereby students have more advantages depending on where they reside. Gender inequality also exists since girls may be sent to different schools than boys, which can affect their education (Marks 2005). In fact, Özdemir (2016) accuses the Turkish education system of further widening the gap, which is alarming considering that those refugees have limited rights and are already underprivileged.

To comply with the different articles set by the convention, Turkey needs to take several measures: help Syrian refugee students overcome the language barrier, provide education under the supervision of skilled teachers, design a curriculum that acknowledges their culture and presence, eliminate discrimination, and take their psychological needs into consideration. Only when all these are put into place can we say that Turkey meets the standards set by the UN CRC (1989).

In the next section, we provide a discussion of our insights as language educators on how Turkey should be responding to meet the educational needs of the Syrian refugee children.

8.4 Discussion

More than 1.1 million Syrians are at the age of schooling (Stevens 2017). Of these, approximately 30 percent are in primary school, 30 percent are in middle school and 40 percent are in high school (Stevens 2017). The rate of non-school attendance of primary and secondary school children is 50% (Directorate of General Migration Management 2018). This number could be imprecise given that approximately half a million Syrian children were born in Turkey (Coşkun and Balamir 2018). Therefore, the temporary solutions that have been in place will not be functional and a permanent structure needs to be established to ensure that the future generation will not be robbed from their right to education.

Providing educational services for Syrian refugees should be a goal that the Turkish government strives to achieve. This is necessary given the ongoing instability in Syria and the unwillingness of many Syrians to return to their country (Kadi 2018). From our perspectives as educators in the field of language teaching and learning, we believe that Turkey hand in hand with the European Commission and NGOs need to conscientiously work to ensure that the educational rights of Syrian refugee children are being met. To this effect, they may consider some of the following solutions:

8.4.1 Encourage Turkish and Syrian Teachers to Join Efforts

On one hand, Turkish teachers cannot easily communicate with Syrian students because of the language barrier. They also face problems trying to teach a multi-level class to both Turkish and Syrian students. On the other hand, Syrian students are not familiar with the Turkish curriculum and standards and do not meet the required criteria (Karakuş 2019).

Encouraging Turkish and Syrian teachers to work together is likely to yield positive results. Syrian teachers can receive training at the hands of the more competent Turkish teachers and help ease the pressure while helping the Turkish teachers achieve more-CRT that allows for the inclusion of the Syrian students. Creating a culturally-responsive and sustainable environment will not only allow for the inclusion of refugee students but also Syrian teachers; thus, moving a step closer towards integration. In order to achieve sustainability on potential professional opportunities for teachers, higher education teacher preparation programs must offer courses on culturally responsive and sustaining pedagogies. Teacher education programs in Turkey often do not offer courses on multicultural education. Therefore, teachers are not ready to address the needs of diverse students. This lack of training on multicultural pedagogy results in teachers not being able to meet the social-emotional needs of refugee students (Taylor and Sidhu 2012). CRT starts with getting to know your students and developing meaningful relationships. The cultural differences should be seen as strengths that the refugee students bring into the classroom and embraced as a learning opportunity for the teachers as well as the Turkish students. Teachers should be mediators as Syrian refugee children build the necessary social and cultural capital to navigate the Turkish education system (Hos et al. 2019).

8.4.2 Provide Sufficient Funding

In talking about funding, the goal is to help Syrian refugees improve their standard of living and provide them with their most important needs. Thus, it does not matter who gets the funds as long as they are used to better the lives of Syrian refugees. Ironically, Taskin and Erdemli (2018) show that NGOs provide support to TECs but not to public schools. In contrast, MoNE supports public schools, not TECs. This shows a clear division between Turkish and Syrian teachers and those supporting organizations would rather provide funding to one party and not the other, regardless of the fact that they both cater to the same population. With funding from the EU, the establishment of the Conditional Cash Transfer Program for Education (CCTE) has increased the number of refugee children in schools. Through this program, Syrian families receive cash to keep their children in school (European Civil Protection and Humanitarian Aid Operations 2018). This is a positive start that needs to expand further to be inclusive of all refugee children. Providing funds for textbooks, school supplies, and other necessities will lessen the burden on parents who would rather spend money on their basic needs than worry about extra expenses for school.

Turkey with the help of different organizations should give parents incentives to send their children to school. First, they need to raise awareness about the importance of education and how it can greatly impact the children's future lives as well as that of their parents. In addition, special funds should be allotted to families that send their children to schools, which will lessen incidents of school drop-outs and help in lowering child labor and brides (Bircan and Sunata 2015). The economic situation is a major cause of not pursuing education as a mother states:

> *We would, of course, want to send him to school but who will work then? There is no father in the house. The rent, the bills. His younger brothers are going to school but my eldest son has to work. I would have wanted him to be educated too of course but the conditions necessitate this* (Coşkun et al. 2017).

Although there has been consistent funding support to Turkey, the funding has not been dispersed and allocated well. According to the 2019 progress report, sector funding in Turkey was 118 million USD for protection, four million USD for food security, 109 million USD for education, 16 million USD for health and nutrition, 325 million USD for "basic needs", and 54 million USD for "livelihoods" (Regional Refugee and Resilience Plan in Response to Syria Crisis 2019, 5). The funding allocated for education is not enough and does not cover the increasing expenses. Thus, the end result is that many refugee children do not go to school (Akar and Mustafa Erdoğdu 2019). Finally, most of the funding received by outside organizations is often limited to funding the camp schools, leaving the majority of the unschooled Syrian refugees out of school (Akar and Mustafa Erdoğdu 2019).

The current efforts to integrate Syrian refugee children into Turkish education has been a slow process without in-depth long-term planning and it is clearly violating the UN Convention, Article 29, Rights of the Child. United Nations has also created Sustainable Development Goals on Quality Education. The sustainable development, which should be implemented by 2030 include: providing girls and boys with complete free, equitable, and quality primary and secondary education; giving all girls and boys access to quality early childhood development, care, and preprimary education; eliminating gender disparities in education and ensuring equal access to all levels of education and vocational training for the vulnerable, including persons with disabilities, indigenous peoples, and children in vulnerable situations; building and upgrading education facilities that are child, disability, and gender-sensitive and providing safe, non-violent, inclusive and effective learning environments for all; and substantially increasing the supply of qualified teachers through international cooperation for teacher training in developing countries, especially the least developed countries and small island developing states. The current developments are too far-fetched from meeting the targeted goals of the sustainable development established by the U.N. Thus, there needs to be sanctions attached to not meeting the educational needs of the Syrian refugee children in Turkey.

Furthermore, in talking about the importance of providing education to refugees, we should not forget that it needs to be quality education in compliance with the human rights approach that views education as a basic right of all learners (Claude 2005). Defining quality education can be problematic since it can have different interpretations. Here, we reference Tikly's (2011) approach which includes the human capital approach; the human rights approach; and the social justice approach. Based on this framework, quality education arises from the interaction of the school, the home, and the wider education context. In discussing our population, this framework is violated on several levels. In discussing school, we have clearly pointed out the limitations of the infrastructure as well as the structured pedagogy. As far as home is concerned, books are not always available nor a good place to study. Finally, with respect to the wider education context, there are many breaches including lack of teacher development and the non-existence of an inclusive curriculum. As Dryden-Peterson (2016) asserts although refugees are increasingly able to access some form of education, universal access is "yet to be achieved" (479) due to challenges of non-citizenship and not having mechanisms of support in accessing education and fully participating in society.

8.5 Conclusion and Implications

This chapter has focused on the current educational system in Turkey and the various problems that arise due to its inability to accommodate the vast numbers of Syrian refugee children. Several impediments withhold Syrian children from transitioning into the Turkish educational system with the language barrier coming at the forefront.

This calls for a strategic plan whereby Turkey with the help of the UN, EC, and other NGOs exert concerted efforts to resolve the problem and abide by the article of the UN Convention on the Rights of the Child (CRC) (UN 1989). They need to come up with a terminal solution that has the welfare of Syrian children at heart. As educators in the field of language learning, we strongly believe that much focus should be given to language education as it counts as a stepping stone toward resolving other arising issues and that it should be in tandem with Rutter's (2006) call for a "welcoming environment, free of racism and violence" (p. 5).

The growing number of Syrian refugees resulting from an increase in birth rates suggests a growth in the challenges that Turkey will face. The pressure is heightening and unless a solution is found, the problem may get out of control. The current situation is that of many Syrian children not receiving an education or what is deemed an accredited education that will allow them to secure a good future. A few years from now, the numbers will multiply, and Turkey will be burdened with people who continuously worry about their source of income instead of becoming productive people who can repay the country that welcomed them and allow it to prosper and become a better nation.

References

Akar, Sevda, and M. Mustafa Erdoğdu. 2019. Syrian Refugees in Turkey and Integration Problem Ahead. *Journal of International Migration and Integration* 20: 925–940. *America*. Chicago: University of Chicago Press.

Aydin, Hasan, and Yeliz Kaya. 2019. Education for Syrian Refugees: The New Global Issue Facing Teachers and Principals in Turkey. *Educational Studies* 55: 46–71.

Bircan, Tuba, and Ulaş Sunata. 2015. Educational assessment of Syrian refugees in Turkey [Türkiye'deki Suriyeli mültecilerin eğitim değerlendirmesi]. *Migration Letters* 12: 226–237.

Birman, Dina, Sarah Beehler, Emily Merrill Harris, Stacy Frazier, Marc Atkins, Shanika Blanton, Louis Fogg, et al. 2008. International Family, Adult, and Child Enhancement Services (FACES): A community-based comprehensive services model for refugee children in resettlement [Uluslararası aile, yetişkin ve çocuk büyütme hizmetleri (YEMLER): Mülteci çocuklara yeniden yerleşimde toplum temelli kapsamlı bir hizmet modeli]. *American Journal of Orthopsychiatry* 78: 121–132.

Bonacich, Edna. 1972. A Theory of Ethnic Antagonism: The Split Labor Market. *American Sociological Review* 37: 547–559.

Carlier, Wannes. 2018. *The Widening Educational Gap for Syrian Refugee Children*. KidsRight Report 2018. https://reliefweb.int/report/turkey/widening-educational-gap-syrian-refugee-children. Accessed 21 Aug 2019.

Claude, Richard Pierre. 2005. The Right to Education and Human Rights Education. *International Journal on Human Rights* 2: 36–59.

Coşkun, Bezen, and Coşkun Gülçin Balamir. 2018. *Primary and Secondary Level Education Models in Migrant Integration: A Comparative Analysis of the Cases of Britain, Germany and Turkey*. Working Paper Series II, DEMIS.

Coşkun, Ipek, Celile Eren Ökten, Nergis Dama, Mümine Barkçin, Shady Zahed, Marwa Fouda, Dilruba Toklucu, and Hande Özsarp. 2017. *Breaking Down Barriers: Getting Syrian Children into Schools in Turkey*. İstanbul: Turkuvaz Haberleşme ve Yayıncılık A.Ş.

Del Carpio, Ximena V., and Mathis Wagner. 2015. *The Impact of Syrian Refugees on the Turkish Labor Market*. (World Bank Policy Research Working Paper 7402). https://data2.unhcr.org/en/documents/download/54522. Accessed on 22 Aug 2019.

Dryden-Peterson, Sarah. 2016. Refugee Education: The Crossroads of Globalization. *Educational Researcher* 45: 473–482.

Ekinci, Mehmet Uğur. 2016. *Türkiye-AB Geri Kabul Anlaşması ve vize diyaloğu*. Ankara: SETA Report.

Emin, Müberra Nur. 2016. *Turkiye'deki Suriyeli cocuklarin egitimi temel egitim politikalari (Education of Syrian Children in Turkey Basic Education Policies)*. Istanbul: SETA.

Erdem, Mustafa, Inayet Aydin, Murat Tasdan, and Ugur Akin. 2011. Educational Problems and Solutions in Turkey: The Views of District Governors. *Educational Management Administration & Leadership* 39: 242–256.

Erdoğan, M.Murat. 2014. *Türkiye'deki Suriyeliler: Toplumsal Kabul ve Uyum Araştırması*. Ankara: Hacettepe Üniversitesi Göç ve Siyaset Araştırmaları Merkezi.

Eryaman, Mustafa Yunus, and Sümeyye Evran. 2019. Syrian Refugee Students' Lived Experiences at Temporary Education Centres in Turkey. In *Education, Immigration and Migration: Policy, Leadership, and Praxis for a Changing World*, ed. K. Arar, J. Brooks, and I. Bogotch, 131–143. Bingley: Emerald Publishing Limited.

European Commission. 2010. Qualitative Eurobarometer: The Rights of the Child (Brussels, European Commission). *European Educational Research Journal* 15: 193–217.

Ferreira, Francisco HG, and Jérémie Gignoux. 2010. *Inequality of Opportunity for Education: The Case of Turkey*. Working paper (No. 4). http://siteresources.worldbank.org/INTTURKEY/1472541268836253913/22597335/InequalityOfOpportunityInEducation.pdf. Accessed 2 Sept 2019.

Freeman, Michael. 2000. The Future of Children's Rights. *Children and Society* 14: 277–293.

Garcia, Marcela M. 2013. Sinking in an English-Only Classroom. *Boston Globe,* May 23.

Gay, Geneva. 2010. *Culturally Responsive Teaching: Theory, Research, and Practice*. New York: Teachers College Press.

Gurer, Cuneyt. 2019. Refugee Perspectives on Integration in Germany. *American Journal of Qualitative Research* 3 (2): 52–70. https://doi.org/10.29333/ajqr/6433.

Hauber-Özer, Melissa. 2019. *Schooling Gaps for Syrian Refugees in Turkey. Forced Migration Review: Schooling Gaps for Syrian refugees in Turkey*. https://www.fmreview.org/sites/fmr/files/FMRdownloads/en/education-displacement/hauberozer.pdf. Accessed 5 Sept 2019.

Heyse, Kaya. 2016. *Kayıp Neslin Eşiğinde. Türkiye'deki Suriyeli Mülteci Çocuk ve Gençlerin Eğitime Erişimde Karşılaştıkları Zorluklar*. Açık Toplum Vakfı.

Hos, Rabia, and Halil Ibrahim Cinarbas. 2018. Learning to Teach in a Global Crisis: Teachers' Insights from a Temporary Non-Formal Refugee Education Project in Gaziantep. *Global Education Review* 5: 182–193.

Hos, Rabia, Kayon Murray-Johnson, and Amy Correia. 2019. Cultivating Capital for High School Newcomers: A Case Study of an Urban Newcomer Classroom. *Journal of Ethnic and Cultural Studies* 6: 1–13.

Hos, Rabia. 2016. Education in Emergencies: Case of a Community School for Syrian Refugees. *European Journal of Educational Research* 5: 53–60. https://www.eu-jer.com/EU-JER_5_2_53_Hos.pdf.

Human Rights Watch. 2015. *When I Picture My Future, I See Nothing: Barriers to Education for Syrian Refugee Children in Turkey*. https://www.hrw.org/report/2015/11/08/when-i-picture-my-future-i-see-nothing/barriers-education-syrian-refugee-children. Accessed 14 Sept 2019.

———. 2017. *Following the Money: Lack of Transparency in Donor Funding for Syrian Refugee Education*. https://www.hrw.org/report/2017/09/14/following-money/lack-transparency-donor-funding-syrian-refugee-education. Accessed 14 Sept 2019.

Icduygu, Ahmet. 2015. *Syrian Refugees in Turkey: The Long Road Ahead*. Washington, DC: Migration Policy Institute Press.

Inglehart, Ronald, and Christian Welzel. 2005. *Modernization, Cultural Change and Democracy*. New York: Cambridge University Press.

Jimenez, Krystell. 2019. Documentation and Recordkeeping Issues Affecting Refugees in Turkey: A Review. *Preservation, Digital Technology and Culture* 48: 69–84. https://doi.org/10.1515/pdtc-2019-0001.

Kadi, Samar. 2018. *Syrian Refugees Are Not Going Home Anytime Soon*. https://thearabweekly.com/syrianrefugees-are-not-going-home-anytime-soon. Accessed 20 Sept 2019.

Karakuş, Mehmet. 2019. Views of teachers and students on the problems of Syrian children in a refugee school in Turkey. *International Journal of Education & Literacy Studies* 7: 211–219.

Karasapan, Omer, and Shah Sajjad. 2018. *Syrian Refugees and the Schooling Challenge*. (Brookings Blog). https://www.brookings.edu/blog/future-development/2018/10/23/syrian-refugees-and-the-schooling-challenge/. Accessed 10 Sept 2019.

Kaya, Ilhan, and Hasan Aydin. 2014. *Pluralism, Multiculturalism and Bilingual Education* [Cogulculuk, Cokkulturlu, ve Ikidilli Egitim] Ankara: Ani Press.

Kaya, Nurcan. 2009. *Forgotten or Assimilated? Minorities in the Education System of Turkey*. London: Minority Rights Group International Press.

Kaysili, Ahmet, Ayşe Soylu, and Mustafa Sever. 2019. Exploring Major Roadblocks on Inclusive Education of Syrian Refugees in School Settings. *Turkish Journal of Education* 8: 109–128.

Krafft, Caroline, Maia Sieverding, Colette Salemi, and Caitlyn Keo. 2018. Syrian Refugees in Jordan: Demographics, Livelihoods, Education, and Health. In *Economic Research Forum Working Paper Series*, no. 1184.

Lundy, Laura. 2012. Children's Rights and Educational Policy in Europe: The Implementation of the United Nations Convention on the Rights of the Child. *Oxford Review of Education* 38: 393–411.

Madziva, Roda, and Juliet Thondhlana. 2017. Provision of Quality Education in the Context of Syrian Refugee Children in the UK: Opportunities and Challenges. *Compare: A Journal of Comparative and International Education* 47: 942–961.

Makovsky, Alan. 2019. Turkey's Refugee Dilemma: Tiptoeing Toward Integration. *Center for American Progress*. https://www.americanprogress.org/issues/security/reports/2019/03/13/467183/turkeys-refugee-dilemma/. Accessed 14 Sept 2019.

Marks, Gary N. 2005. Cross-National Differences and Accounting for Social Class Inequalities in Education. *International Sociology* 20: 483–505.

Memişoğlu, Fulya. 2018. *The Syrian Community in Turkey: Perspectives, Prospects, and Policies. Public Policy and Democracy Studies*. http://podem.org.tr/en/researches/the-syrian-community-in-turkey-perspectives-prospects-and-policies/. Accessed 14 Sept 2019.

Nie, Norman H., Jane Junn, and Kenneth Stehlik-Barry. 1996. *Education and Democratic Citizenship in America*. Chicago: University of Chicago Press.

Özdemir, Caner. 2016. Equity in the Turkish Education System: A Multilevel Analysis of Social Background Influences on the Mathematics Performance of 15-year-old Students. *European Educational Research Journal* 15 (2): 193–217.

Qaddour, Kinana. 2017. *Educating Syrian Refugees in Turkey*. Washington, DC: Carnegie Endowment for International Peace.

Regional Refugee and Resilience Plan In Response to the Syria Crisis. 2019. *2019 Progress Report*. http://www.3rpsyriacrisis.org/wpcontent/uploads/2019/08/Midyear2019.pdf. Accessed 15 Sept 2019.

Rutter, Jill. 2006. *Refugee Children in the UK*. London: McGraw-Hill Education.

Sert, Deniz. 2016. The Oxymoron of Perpetual Temporary Protection: Syrians in Turkey. *Migraciones Internacionales* 8.

Stevens, Dallal. 2015. *Refugee Protection in the Middle East and North Africa. Personal Collection of (Dallal Steven)*. Oxford: University of Oxford.

———. 2017. Asylum, Refugee Protection and the European Response to Syrian Migration. *Journal of Human Rights Practice* 9: 184–189.

Tarman, Bülent, and Davut Gürel. 2017. Awareness of Social Studies Teacher Candidates on Refugees in Turkey. *The Journal of Social Studies Research* 41: 183–193.

Taskin, Pelin, and Ozge Erdemli. 2018. Education for Syrian refugees: Problems Faced by Teachers in Turkey. *Eurasian Journal of Educational Research* 75: 155–178.

Taştan, Coşkun, and Zafer Çelik. 2017. *The Education of Syrian children in Turkey: Challenges and recommendations*. Ankara: Eğitim-Bir-Sen Stratejik Araştırmalar Merkezi.

Taylor, Sandra, and Ravinder Kaur Sidhu. 2012. Supporting Refugee Students in Schools: What Constitutes Inclusive Education? *International Journal of Inclusive Education* 16: 39–56.

The Edge in Lebanon. 2018. *Children on the Edge*. https://www.childrenontheedge.org/latest-stories/the-edge-in-lebanon. Accessed 16 Sept 2019.

Tikly, Leon. 2011. Towards a Framework for Researching the Quality of Education in Low-Income Countries. *Comparative Education* 47: 1–23.

UNHCR. 2019. *Operational Portal Refugee Situations*. https://data2.unhcr.org/en/situations/syria/location/113. Accessed 16 Sept 2019.

UNHCR, USA. 2019. *The 1951 Refugee Convention*. https://www.unhcr.org/en-us/1951-refugee-convention.html. Accessed 15 Sept 2019.

UNICEF. 2018. *UNICEF Turkey 2018 Humanitarian Situation Report, 24*. https://reliefweb.int/sites/reliefweb.int/files/resources/UNICEF%20Turkey%20Humanitarian%20Situation%20Report%20No.%2024%20-%20August%202018.pdf. Accessed 15 Sept 2019.

United Nations. 1989. *UN Convention on the Rights of the Child Geneva*. United Nations.

Visconti, Louisa, and Diane Gal. 2018. Regional Collaboration to Strengthen Education for Nationals & Syrian Refugees in Arabic Speaking Host Countries. *International Journal of Educational Development* 61: 106–116.

Yabancilar ve Uluslararasi Koruma Kanunu [Law on Foreigners and International Protection], Apr. 4, 2013 (most provisions in force on Apr. 11, 2014), Resmî Gazete [Official Gazette], No. 28615 (Apr. 11, 2013), http://www.mevzuat.gov.tr/MevzuatMetin/1.5.6458.pdf, archived at https://perma.cc/RQ3R-EWCV.

Zetter, Roger, and Ruaudel Héloïse. 2016. *Refugees' Right to Work and Access to Labor Markets – An Assessment*. (KNOMAD Working Paper). https://www.knomad.org/sites/default/files/2017-12/KNOMAD%20Study%201-%20Part%20II-%20Refugees%20Right%20to%20Work%20-%20An%20Assessment.pdf. Accessed 16 Sept 2019.

Alia Hadid, Ph.D. is currently teaching at the University of Rhode Island. She has a Ph.D. in Technology in Education and Second Language Acquisition from the University of South Florida. She has more than twenty years of experience teaching English as a foreign/second language. In her research, she focuses on refugees' experiences learning English online and their identities.

Rabia Hos, Ph.D. is an assistant professor of TESOL/Bilingual and Dual Language Education at The University of Rhode Island. After receiving her Ph.D. from University of Rochester in 2012, she was an assistant professor in the English Language Teaching Department at a Turkish university in Gaziantep, Turkey and participated in numerous research projects involving Syrian refugees until 2017. Her research focuses on the experiences of newcomer immigrant and refugee students with interrupted formal education (SIFE).

Part IV
State of Emergency (OHAL)

Chapter 9
Authoritarianization and Human Rights in Turkey: How the AKP Legitimizes Human Rights Violations

Mehmet Efe Caman

Abstract Turkey has gradually become an authoritarian regime. Numerous studies of Turkish politics consider Turkey a hybrid regime and have tried to understand how and why this regime change has happened. So far, however, there has been little discussion about the correlation between the authoritarianization of the country and its human rights situation. This chapter deals with the human rights situation in Turkey as a reflection of the authoritarian characteristics of the political regime, examines the existing correlation between the regime's character and its human rights practices as well as focuses on discursive justification strategies for the use of repression. It puts forward the claim that legitimation strategies have consolidated the regime and contributes to its durability. It is argued that Turkey's human rights policy is closely related to the general features of the current political regime as well as its trajectory from relatively well-functioning democracy to competitive authoritarianism, and the shift in its human rights policy happened through a legitimation construct of the "new Turkey". In other words, the deterioration of human rights was not only a result of the regime's transformation but also an instrument of regime consolidation.

Keywords Authoritarianism · Democracy · Human rights · Legitimation · Islamism · Purge

9.1 Introduction

Human rights are rights inherent to all people, regardless of race, sex, nationality, ethnicity, language, religion, or any other status. Human rights include the right to life and liberty, freedom from slavery and torture, freedom of opinion and expression, the right to work and gain an education, and many others. Human rights are a

M. E. Caman (✉)
Memorial University of Newfoundland, St. John's, Canada
e-mail: mecaman@mun.ca

H. Aydin, W. Langley (eds.), *Human Rights in Turkey*, Philosophy and Politics - Critical Explorations 15, https://doi.org/10.1007/978-3-030-57476-5_9

tremendously complex and far-reaching topic. They are closely interrelated with the process of democratization and the concept of the rule of law. The intimate relationship between the process of democratization, which is a systemic transformation leading to the rule of law, and the improvement of human rights standards require both processes to be considered together. The process of democratization and human rights improvements are usually not linear. In the case of Turkey, for example, it can be observed that the process is a battlefield between progressive vanguard forces and state-centered political elite that is devoted to the existing Kemalist "old state" and prioritizes "Realpolitik"-based security concerns. Although Turkey is a signatory to the fundamental conventions on human rights and its constitution guarantees upholding the protection of fundamental human rights for Turkish citizens, it has been unable to show stability in terms of maintaining and preserving these rights.

With the experience of a transnational democratization process since at least the Edict of Gulhane in 1836 and particularly since the first Constitutional Era of 1876 in the Ottoman period, Turkey has had a long history of seeking constitutional democracy, basic freedoms, and human rights. This history, however, has not ensured lasting standards for individual and human rights in Turkey. On the contrary, although democracy and individual and human rights were highly prioritized in Turkish domestic politics during the early Ottoman reforms, the implementation of individual and minority rights has been a challenge both in the Ottoman and Republican periods.

Turkey's aspiration for membership in the European Union (EU) has been an external factor that has influenced the Turkish democratization process. The Justice and Development Party (AKP) recognized this aspiration and deliberately integrated reform policy into their party program and policy practice. When the AKP came to power in 2002, it declared its aspiration to implement an intensive reform program to fulfill EU accession criteria (Karaveli 2016). The level of human rights in Turkey as of 2004 when the EU began negotiations for Turkish membership presents an example of how the deep penetration of political modernization and democratization in terms of the sophisticated organization of the state architecture provided the basis for further democratization. In this process, the role of the Turkish military and its "veto regime" had to be removed. The EU opened negotiations with Turkey in 2004 based on a recommendation from the Commission, deciding that Turkey fulfilled the minimal democracy and human rights standards of the EU, namely the Copenhagen political criteria. Considering the progress Turkey had achieved in this reform process and the level of democratization and improvement in human rights-related legislature and policy practices, it is difficult to understand the rapid decay and eventual collapse of the liberal constitutional democratic system and deterioration of human rights practices.

There are two parallel processes regarding the political system in contemporary Turkey. On the one hand, Turkey has gradually become an authoritarian regime (Onis 2012, 2015); on the other hand, it has transformed its political system from a parliamentary governance system to a de facto presidential one. These processes have transformed Turkey's political system from a democracy into an authoritarian regime (Somer 2016; Tansel 2018). And, more importantly, they have contributed to the unprecedented deterioration of the human rights situation in Turkey.

This chapter deals with the human rights situation in Turkey as a reflection of the authoritarian characteristics of the political regime. It does not aim to reconstruct and summarize the Turkish human rights situation chronologically. There are numerous publications by independent international human rights institutions that present the human rights situation in Turkey in their annual reports. This chapter, in contrast, examines the existing correlation between the regime's character and its human rights practices. It particularly focuses on discursive justification strategies for the use of repression. It is argued that Turkey's human rights policy is closely related to the general features of the current political regime as well as its trajectory from relatively well-functioning democracy to competitive authoritarianism, and the shift in its human rights policy happened through a legitimation construct of the "new Turkey". In other words, the deterioration of human rights was not only a result of the regime's transformation but also an instrument of regime consolidation. Legitimation can be understood in this context as a process of gaining support and seeking to guarantee active consent, compliance, obedience, or even mere toleration within the population (Gershewski 2013, 18). Edel and Joshua indicate when the security apparatus acts forcibly against certain groups, authoritarian governments often present the target as a threat to the public or the state (Edel and Joshua 2018, 883). Specifically, since the military coup attempt of 15 July 2016, the regime has purged hundreds of thousands of people, particularly public servants, to "cleanse all state institutions" of the targeted groups, so-called traitors and enemies (Kirby 2016). The purge that followed the 2016 coup attempt was symptomatic of the government's increasing authoritarianism. Repression is an important component of autocracies and involves actual or threatened use of violence against targeted groups. However, repression alone cannot enable the stability necessary for autocracies since it is costly and can have destabilizing effects in the long run (Davenport 2007). Thus, it is crucial to understand how the regime's justification mechanisms have functioned. In this chapter, it is argued that an important component of the AKP's successful restructuring of human rights policies and practices has been the legitimation of these policies and practices in the eyes of political elites including the opposition as well as the population through a legitimation construct of the so-called New Turkey. This authoritarian restructuring required the development of cohesiveness so that sacrifices by the population or concessions among elites could be expected temporarily. This chapter will not only describe what has happened but, more importantly, will answer how and why it has happened.

9.2 Democratization

Turkey signed the Universal Declaration of Human Rights adopted by the United Nations General Assembly in Paris, 1948. It was among the first group of countries that voted for and signed the Declaration. Moreover, Turkey is also among the

12 founder members of the Council of Europe from 1949 and, consequently, one of the 14 signatory nations to the Convention for the Protection of Human Rights and Fundamental Freedoms in 1950, which it ratified 4 years later. Yet, 'human rights practices' and violations as such did not come into the country's political agenda before the 1980s when authoritarianism and human rights abuses including torture and extrajudicial killings began to attract local and worldwide attention (Casier 2009, 3). Geopolitical and security policy considerations shadowed Ankara's human rights practices. Thus, the West turned a blind eye to Turkey's human rights record during almost the entire Cold War because of Turkey's significant role in the Western alliance. However, during the détente, particularly after the military coup of 1980, the Turkish human rights situation gradually became a European concern. Turkey's increasing motivation to join the European Community, especially after the official application of Turkey for full membership in 1987, created an effective conditionality in Turkish-European relations. After the Cold War and the foundation of the European Union (EU), the European integration process became a dynamic of transformation for post-communist east European countries, which helped those countries democratize their political systems and address their human rights situations. By 1991, when the Soviet Union collapsed and the Cold War officially ended, post-coup Turkey was still struggling with its democratization and human rights situation. In 1999, Turkey officially declared its political will to fulfill the Copenhagen Criteria (EU democracy and human rights standards), and it was accepted as an official EU candidate. It abolished the death penalty and reformed some human rights-related policy areas. However, as of 2002, when the AKP came to power, the human rights situation in Turkey was still the major obstacle to Turkey's further progress regarding its desired EU membership (Caman 2005, 230–236).

Despite its Islamist roots, the AKP did not appear like a political party with an Islamist agenda. On the contrary, it denied being an Islamist party and highlighted ideologically a moderate conservatism and advocated liberalization of the market economy and integration with Europe. Likewise, it promised democratization, the de-securitization of domestic and foreign policy, EU-orientation, transparency, accountability, the rule of law, limited government, pluralism, diversity and more freedoms as well as the promotion of universal human rights and the improvement of minority rights when it came to power in 2002 (Hale and Özbudun 2010, 20). More importantly, the AKP acted according to this political discourse as well. It accelerated the reform process and achieved considerable improvements.

Thereby, between 2002 and 2006, Turkey underwent profound changes that led to substantial progress in human rights and individual freedoms, political rights, the rule of law, and particularly civil-military relations. Like its predecessors, the AKP government enacted a series of legal reforms aimed at providing 'stability of institutions guaranteeing democracy, the rule of law, human rights and respect for and protection of minorities' (Casier 2009, 1). The level of democracy in Turkey in 2006 presents an example of how the deep penetration of political modernization and the sophisticated organization of the state architecture, especially in terms of the separation of powers and its manifestation in the constitutional design, promoted a basis for further democratization. As mentioned above, the full membership perspective in the EU played a significant role in this rapid and effective democratization process, since Turkey had to become more democratic and adopt the Acquis of the EU to accomplish the accession process for membership (Hale 2011, 331). Thus, when the EU Commission recommended accession talks with Ankara in 2004, it recognized the Turkish achievement and concluded that Turkey had fulfilled the EU's democracy criteria. The reforms and the new legal framework introduced as an extension of the democratization process and the judgments of the European Court of Human Rights (ECtHR) brought developments, at least on the normative level (Cinar and Sirin 2017, 133).

The reforms subordinated the military to elected political decision-makers, abolished the death penalty, extended civil rights, cancelled the hawkish-nationalistic military strategy in Kurdish politics and replaced it with a moderate political approach based on talks with elected representatives of Kurds. However, in the EU-adaptation process, the systemic protective elements of Turkey's political system, particularly the role of the military in the veto regime – a concept used by William Hale to describe the military's superiority in the Turkish political system – in which the military de facto had significant weight in the political decision-making process, especially for security-related policy fields, had to be removed (Hale 1994, 309). The pro-European military accepted the "demilitarization of the political sphere" since they considered this step as relevant to Turkey's further westernization and democratic improvement.

Erdogan and his AKP government were supported by almost all pro-democracy and pro-European forces in Turkish society including liberals, Kurds and the Gülen Movement. In terms of foreign policy, the Erdogan government's internal reform and growing economic capabilities have enabled the country to broadly de-securitize its foreign policy, to introduce an export-oriented foreign trade policy, to improve its bilateral relations with regional neighbours and to appear as a peace-promoter in the region. The EU-candidate status increased Turkey's prospects as a stable country and as the 17th largest economy in the world and attracted foreign investment.

9.3 Authoritarianization

There are two parallel processes regarding the political system in contemporary Turkey. On the one hand, Turkey has gradually become an authoritarian regime (Tugal 2016); on the other hand, it has transformed its political system from a parliamentary governance system to a de facto presidential one. These processes have transformed Turkey's political system from a democracy into an authoritarian regime. The question of whether Turkey can still be considered a functioning liberal democracy is no longer being asked since there is an extensive consensus in the literature that it is not. Instead, many observers of Turkish politics consider Turkey a hybrid regime and have tried to understand how and why this regime change has happened. Erdogan's Justice and Development Party (AKP) and Turkish right-wing nationalists of the MHP have been cooperating within the framework of a de-facto coalition since a military coup attempt on July 15, 2016. Turkey has been noticeably changing its regime since this coup attempt. However, the initial steps of democratic decay started much earlier.

The first step in the process of democratic decay was incontestably the Gezi Park protests. From the very beginning, Erdogan saw the Gezi Park protests as an existential threat to his personal power. Accordingly, the AKP government considered the Gezi Park protests, which began on 28 May 2013 and rapidly became a large-scale mass movement, a civilian coup attempt perpetrated by external and domestic forces trying to topple the government. Thus, the government reacted to the Gezi Park demonstrations with the arbitrary and abusive use of asymmetric force (Amnesty International 2013, 6). Through protests began peacefully, they soon escalated into violence. They resulted in injuries to both officials and protestors because of the asymmetric intervention of police due to the pressure brought about by the AKP (Amnesty International 2015; Human Rights Watch 2014). Expanding throughout Turkey, about three and a half million people conducted almost 5000 demonstrations (De Bellaigue 2013). During these demonstrations, 12 people died one of whom was Berkin Elvan, a 15-year-old child, more than 4000 people were injured, 5513 civilians were taken into the custody, 189 civilians were arrested, and hundreds were charged with terrorism.

The second step in the process of democratic decay was the 17 December 2013 corruption scandal. The AKP government was shaken when a corruption investigation accused high-ranking politicians and bureaucrats from Erdogan's closest circle of being involved in a corruption network (Freedom House 2014). A criminal investigation took place and 52 people were detained, among them Iranian businessman Reza Zarrab and the director of the state-owned Halkbank. Erdogan blamed the investigation on an *international plot* and accused the *Gülenists* of being the domestic perpetrator of this *civilian coup attempt.* He promised payback to the so-called instrument of this *international plot.* The government sacked the prosecutors involved in the investigation as well as numerous high-ranking police chiefs and changed the procedural regulations in the police force, forcing officers to inform their superiors of their investigations to stop similar, potentially ongoing corruption investigations (Freedom House 2015). Moreover, Erdogan increased his control over Turkish public and private media outlets to spread his manipulative narrative (international conspiracy, *parallel state*, *civilian coup attempt* against the elected government, etc.) (Amnesty International 2015). Moreover, numerous journalists were detained and accused of being a terrorist because of their news stories regarding the corruption operation of 17 December 2013 (Amnesty International 2015). He intervened in the ongoing judicial process to protect himself and those in his circle of power from justice.

The most critical milestone in the Turkish reverse-democratization process was, without a doubt, the military putsch attempt that took place on 15 July 2016. The crackdown on the coup attempt in July 2016 caused serious damages to Turkish society, resulting in 237 civilian deaths, and 2191 injures in Turkey (Amnesty International 2017). The scope of the State of Emergency was not limited to those who were involved in the attempted coup, and it turned into a "witch hunt" (Abramowitz 2018). Those who were not involved in the coup or any wrongdoing were discriminated against based on their political position. Dissidents, opponents and political parties, who did disagree with the policies of the AKP were labelled as terrorists and enemies of the state. The AKP used the "enemy" slogan in all of its rallies during their election campaigns (Abramowitz 2018). Both the gradually increasing authoritarian character of the regime and the transformation of the parliamentarian system into a presidential system have helped President Erdogan increase his competences and consolidate power. Thereby, Erdogan has succeeded in creating an excessive concentration of authority, which includes the subordination and control of the judiciary and the expansion of coercive bodies such as the Turkish intelligence service MIT,[1] the police force, the state bureaucracy and partially also the military. He has also succeeded in eliminating powerful and prominent party functionaries in the AKP. More importantly, he has been successful in obtaining the consent of citizens and elites.

After the constitutional amendments and formal introduction to the presidential system, he finally transformed the de facto regime into a presidential system with a lack of separation of powers and checks and balances. In accordance with his newly designed system, he gradually increased his already consolidated control by appointing his close confidants to key political positions, including his son-in-law Berat Albayrak, who became the minister of finance and treasury. Erdogan has utilized leverage gained from the post-coup-attempt era as a means to discharge his opponents in the Turkish public sector and replace them with his loyalists. He has wiped out the independent media, locking up pro-Kurdish lawmakers and journalists and hundreds of thousands of civil servants, academics, military, police, and judges on specious grounds of national security.

The optimism based on this fruitful democratization of Turkey and its analogous economic growth, however, was shaken and eventually broke down. The first milestones on the way to the breaking point of the deterioration of Turkish democracy were the outbreak of the Gezi protests in spring 2013 and the following corruption investigations against the inner circle of the AKP government in fall 2013. The Gezi protests triggered intolerance to criticism and increased the securitization of politics. High-ranking politicians and bureaucrats from Erdogan's closest circle were involved in the corruption scandal. Erdogan declared that the investigation that took place was a coup-attempt and accused the Gülen Movement and the West (particularly the USA) of being the masterminds of this plot. The government stopped the ongoing judicial process in exceeding its constitutional competences, and the prosecutors conducting the investigation process were discharged under dubious circumstances.

The scandal posed one of the major challenges of Erdogan's 12-year rule, leading three cabinet members to quit. Erdogan's response to tightening control over the Internet and banning Twitter for two weeks drew international criticism (Amnesty International 2015). Thousands of judges, prosecutors, police officers, and other public servants — most notably the officials leading the corruption investigations —

---

[1] *Milli IstihbaratTeskilati* (MIT).

have been reassigned or even dismissed, and the government has passed a law increasing government control of the judiciary. The High Council of Judges and Prosecutors (HSYK), which now answers directly to the justice minister, launched an investigation into the former deputy chief Istanbul prosecutor who led the corruption investigations until he was replaced weeks later. The executive branch of the government thereby violated the Turkish constitution and the constitutional order de facto extended its power deliberately, seized the power of justice gradually and thereby dismantled power-separating elements (the judiciary, Constitutional Court, Higher Election Board, etc.). These developments indicated a de facto regime change in Turkey, providing Erdogan with sweeping powers incompatible with the democratic rule of law and an open, pluralist society.

After this breakdown, Erdogan abandoned all his former associates – liberals, Kurds, his Islamic brothers from the Gülen Movement, and even the EU and Western allies. He suspended the Solution Process (negotiations with the outlawed "Kurdistan Workers' Party" PKK), launched a new course of action in Kurdish politics and initiated a military strike to undermine the snowballing positive perception of the pro-Kurdish Peoples' Democratic Party (HDP) (Human Rights Watch 2016b). Thereby, the AKP government used new Islamist-nationalist rhetoric to increase the AKP's decreasing votes. The heavy military offensive caused numerous civilian casualties in villages, towns, and cities. As a result, tens of thousands of Kurds left their homes, and entire towns and neighborhoods in Kurdish cities were destroyed (Human Rights Watch 2016a; Office of the United Nations High Commissioner for Human Rights 2017).

The gradual power seizure enabled Erdogan to control all key functions of the Turkish state apparatus (intelligence, the police force, the economy, foreign policy, the bureaucracy, etc.). Erdogan's power has been further strengthened by decrees issued by the cabinet under his chairmanship. After the military coup attempt and declaration of a state of emergency, Erdogan ruled by decree and bypassed the parliament. Therefore, the parliament has largely lost its ability to legislate. In this way, Erdogan paralyzed the parliament and seized its power. The far-right Nationalist Action Party (MHP) played an important role in paving the way in the reverse-democratization process. Erdogan's AKP and MHP have been cooperating within the framework of a de-facto coalition since the 2016 military coup attempt. Nevertheless, the leader of the MHP, Devlet Bahceli, and Erdogan did not get along well before. When Erdogan pursued a progressive peace policy with the PKK and the Kurdish movement in Turkey, Bahceli accused Erdogan and the AKP of treason. He also vowed to bring Erdogan to justice after the corruption scandal in 2013. It was Erdogan's radical policy change on the Kurdish issue that opened the path to reconciliation between Erdogan and Bahceli. The ultranationalist and far-right MHP welcomed this policy change for comprehensible reasons.

The left-wing Republican People's Party (CHP) was also pleased because the secular-nationalist (or left-nationalist) pillar in the Kemalist worldview that is still the main doctrine of the CHP dominated the party's position regarding the Kurdish issue. The CHP was also delighted to eliminate the Gülenists and were not eager to defend the rights of other democratic forces such as the liberals. For most CHP politicians or secular-nationalists, eliminating the Gülenists through an Islamist leader and his party was a fairly positive arrangement – even if the destruction of the constitutional order and democracy was a high price to pay for this objective. Turkish Kemalists of the CHP have never prioritized the basic minority rights of the Kurds. On the contrary, their positions regarding the Solution Process (negotiations with the PKK) were similar to those of the MHP.

The reason I call the current political system of Turkey a "regime" is simply that there are so many deviations from the Turkish constitution established in 1982 that this constitution has ceased to exist. What can be called the "constitutional architecture of the state" has been replaced by a new regime. This new political reality has not been approved by parliament, which means it is neither legal nor legitimate. The decision-making process of the executive branch, including its hierarchical order, has been altered without the necessary constitutional amendments. In other words, an unconstitutional and illegal systemic change has taken place.

The second process regarding the regime change in Turkey, as mentioned above, concerns the shift from a parliamentarian system to a presidential system. The constitutional amendments changed the previous state architecture and initiated an extraordinarily influential presidency including an institutional restructuring and reorganization of powers, which is in sharp contrast to the prior parliamentary system. Erdogan terminated the office of the prime minister, who used to be the head of the cabinet and the main political decision-maker of the executive according to the constitution of 1980. After the constitutional amendments and the formal introduction to the presidential system, Erdogan finally transformed the de facto regime into a presidential system with a lack of separation of powers and checks and balances.

In the new system, the president embodies the executive entirely and possesses excessive powers. He acquires, for instance, the power to appoint ministers without requiring a confidence vote from parliament, to make the budget and to appoint more than half of the members of the Constitutional Court (the highest court of the judiciary). Moreover, he also has the power to dissolve the parliament and declare states of emergency. Furthermore, the amendments empower the president to issue decrees that do not need conversion into law by the parliament.

The proposed changes have twofold influences in terms of checks and balances: on the one hand, they transfer numerous key powers traditionally held by the national assembly to the president, while on the other hand, they empower the president to determine the composition of the higher courts. As a result of this new constitutional framework, the safety mechanisms of checks and balances of the previous system have been decisively diminished in favor of the president, which subordinates the judiciary under the executive power of the president and legislature. Correspondingly, the Turkish parliament lacks a mechanism of advice on the appointment of ministers. Another example concerns the implementing of presidential decrees since the amended constitutional provisions do not sufficiently elucidate the procedures for the abrogation of presidential decrees.

9.4 Purge and the Human Rights Situation

31 decrees having the force of law were issued under a state of emergency until the Turkish government finally ended it on 18 July 2018. The state of emergency was used to consolidate severe government powers to silence critical voices and strip away fundamental rights and freedoms. The most serious deteriorations have included arbitrary detentions, abusive prosecutions, purged public servants, and a crackdown on media freedom and basic freedoms (Aydin and Avincan 2020; Human Rights Watch 2019).

Under the state of emergency, the president presides over the cabinet, which can pass decrees without parliamentary scrutiny or the possibility of appeal to the constitutional court. Many decrees passed contain measures that conflict with basic human rights precautions and Turkey's commitments under international and national law. The presidential decrees adopted since July 2016 have widened the scope of the original emergency to include measures against individuals who "belong to, connect to, or have contact with the *Fethullahist Terrorist Organization – FETO*" (Decree 668, of 27 July 2016) and public personnel who have "membership in, affiliation or connection with the *Fethullahist Terrorist Organization*" as well as the spouses and children of such persons (Decree 670, of 17 August 2016) (Office of the United Nations High Commissioner for Human Rights 2017, 11). In their brutal implementation, the decrees have caused all civil and political rights to disappear, including freedom of speech, freedom of the press, freedom of assembly, the ban on arbitrary detention, the right to the presumption of innocence, and others (Girdap 2020). Moreover, they enabled the creation of a police state by giving the bureaucracy a broad, lawless space in which to proceed with the extensive oppression. The decrees are not open to any judicial review, and they are not subordinated to the Constitutional Court. In addition, the Constitutional Court has been rendered inoperative through the de-facto cancellation of the constitutional order. These changes have eroded not only the fundamental civil rights of Turkish citizens based on the constitutional order but also the international responsibilities of Turkey on human rights, such as the right to a fair trial, the right to effective legal remedy and even the very basic right to protection of property (Aydin and Avincan 2020). Moreover, the Turkish regime detained numerous US and other Western citizens after the attempted coup and has been using them as bargaining chips. German journalist Deniz Yücel from the German daily Die Welt and US American Pasteur Andrew Craig Brunson, both of whom were prosecuted on charges of terrorism, espionage and conspiracy, were obvious examples of the control of the judiciary by the executive in Turkey since both Yücel and Brunson were released from prison after German and American governments negotiated with President Erdogan (Erdemir and Tahiroglu 2018).

After the military coup attempt, hundreds of pro-Western and pro-NATO admirals and generals (around 50 percent of all flag officers in the Turkish military) were jailed. Erdogan and many high-ranking Turkish officials frequently accused the US and other Western allies of being the mastermind of the attempted coup. Groups that were close to the deep state – above all, officers who opposed the Turkish military's pro-Western course – clearly gained the upper hand. Turkey's military replaced the NATO orbit with a new strategic partnership with Russia. Turkey and Russia signed a deal for Moscow to supply Ankara with S-400 surface-to-air missile batteries to deepen ties between the two countries.

The most crucial milestone in the Turkish reverse-democratization process was, without a doubt, the military putsch attempt that took place on 15 July 2016. The government was able to control and defeated the coup with the help of loyalist soldiers and police forces. President Erdogan exploited the attempted coup, which he called a "gift of God", to declare a state of emergency (Champion 2016). A purge based on 22 emergency decrees was enacted, bypassing parliamentary scrutiny and sidestepping the Constitutional Court's formal appeal procedure. The post-coup atmosphere allowed Erdogan to gain control of the Turkish media almost entirely. Since the attempted coup, 69 journalists have been convicted, 169 journalists remain in pre-trial detention and 148 journalists are officially wanted.

Parallel to this persecution policy, the regime shut down or sold off numerous oppositional media outlets to companies close to Erdogan's confidants. According to the 2018 Report of the UN Office of the High Commissioner for Human Rights, 570 lawyers were arrested, 1480 faced some kind of prosecution, and 79 were sentenced to long-term imprisonment. Moreover, approximately 34 bar associations were shut down on the grounds of alleged affiliation to a terrorist organization. The same document also reports that by the end of December 2017, 159,506 individuals had been arrested in relation to the emergency decrees. Furthermore, Erdogan signed several decrees enabling the closure of 15 universities, and the Board of Higher Education ordered a crackdown on academics in the wake of a failed military coup in July 2016 (The Inquiry Commission on the State of Emergency Measures 2018). Some universities and high schools were designated "terrorist organizations". Sources indicate that about 7000 academics have been dismissed from public universities under emergency decrees (Jacinto 2017). Many of those dismissed were prohibited from traveling abroad, as were their spouses and children. More than 15,000 schoolteachers were designated "terrorists" and lost their jobs and licenses to teach. Moreover, numerous institutions and people affiliated with the Gülen Movement were purged, their schools, universities and media outlets were plundered and seized without legal basis, and even their private properties were unlawfully confiscated (Human Rights Watch 2016c; Stockholm Center for Freedom 2018). During the purge, the government has confiscated and destroyed more than 300,000 books and, including textbooks (Bar'el 2019).

According to the annual report by Human Rights Watch, at least 2200 judges and prosecutors were imprisoned pending investigation, reportedly because their names appeared on a list of alleged Gülen supporters. With 3400 permanently dismissed for the same reason, their assets frozen, over one-fifth of Turkey's judiciary had been removed (Human Rights Watch 2017a).

The government has so far seized billions of US dollars' worth of property belonging to arbitrarily criminalized people without a court ruling, among which are multiple private companies and numerous schools and universities (Stockholm

Center for Freedom 2018). The government also appointed trustees to hundreds of local municipalities, most of which are located in Kurdish provinces (DBP Local Authorities Commission 2017; United States Department of State - Bureau of Democracy Human Rights and Labor 2019). Elected mayors of those municipalities were also dismissed without court rulings and arrested (Peoples' Democratic Party (HDP) 2019). Tens of MPs of the pro-Kurdish HDP, one MP from the CHP and 71 Kurdish mayors are still in prison (Piri 2019). The co-chairman of the HDP and a Member of Parliament, Selahattin Demirtas, has been in jail since November 2016 (Human Rights Watch 2017b).

Since 2015, approximately 400,000 Kurds have been displaced (Human Rights Watch 2017a). At least 1487 civil society organizations and 117 media outlets shut down during the state of emergency. After the 2016 coup attempt, Turkey became the biggest jailer of journalists in the world, a position it has maintained since, with up to 123 journalists and other media workers currently imprisoned either in pre-trial detention or serving a custodial sentence (Amnesty International 2019). According to Amnesty International, as of December 2018, the total number of detainees in prison without an indictment or pending trial is 57,000, over 20% of the total prison population. 44,690 people are in prison for "terrorism"-related charges. These include academics, journalists, political activists, lawyers, human rights defenders, and others caught up in a crackdown that has vastly exceeded the legitimate purpose of investigating and bringing to justice those responsible for the 2016 coup attempt (Amnesty International 2019).

9.5 Legitimation Strategies

To justify the purge and massive human rights violations, the regime has utilized effective legitimation strategies (missions). The missions in the case of Turkey are based on ideational narratives. The target audience or groups were not only AKP grassroots and the MHP but also the opposition parties the CHP, IYIP, and HDP. Even though the HDP has been securitized and largely excluded from legitimate politics, the main narrative of the regime such as "FETO" is being utilized by MPs and other HDP members in their public speeches or statements.

Erdogan has exploited the putsch attempt to mobilize Turkish society based on his discourse to "defend their country" against "internal traitors" or enemies of the state that attacked Turkey and were controlled like puppets by external nemeses to damage Turkey. This might be considered a good example of an "internal mission". The idea that Turkey is under attack is the main pillar of the entire mission-construct. The mission includes tracing and eliminating these domestic enemies to re-establish security and order. This process has been designated by Erdogan as a process of "cleansing" or "purifying" the state, its institutions, and society. Erdogan said: "We know they have not been completely cleansed. They are still present in our military, in our police force, in our judiciary"(Hincks 2016). The language Erdogan and his regime uses is genocidal. In fact, the social exclusion of the purged people as well as "exceptional treatment" in the purge such as depriving the targeted group of their constitutional rights violates internationally acknowledged law principles such as Sippenhaft[2] criminalization against the principle of the private penalty and the presumption of innocence, indicating a systematic policy. Without the justification and legitimation mechanisms utilized by the regime, these policies would be unimaginable.

To legitimize this mission, the regime generated a narrative towards the Gülen Movement, calling them: "perverts", "tape editors", "hashashins" (a medieval Islamic cult of assassins), "worse than Shiites", "viruses", "traitors", "spies", and members of "spy rings" and a terrorist organization. Erdogan's leadership cult, ethno-religious discourses, victimhood, and the promise of revanchism – on a national and international level – supported the acceptance of his mission and narrative. This narrative has been an effective instrument of the authoritarian police-state's mass persecution. A considerable extent of civil and military bureaucracy, including approximately 50 percent of all admirals and generals of the Turkish military, about 4000 judges and prosecutors, more than 9000 police officers, more than 8000 academics, 28,000 teachers, and more than 150,000 public servants, have been liquidated (Jacinto 2017). In domestic politics, Erdogan has pursued a policy of overthrowing the kind of opposition that questions the official narrative of the 2016 military coup attempt. Those who reject this narrative are labelled as Gülenist. This performance objective does not only include Gülen-affiliated individuals but also other opposition that question the government discourse regarding the coup; for instance, liberal democratic or social-democratic intellectuals and some Kurdish activists.

In domestic politics, Erdogan pursues a policy that overthrows every kind of opposition that questions the official narrative of July 15th, which accuses the Gülen Movement of being the organizers and perpetrators of the military putsch controlled by the United States and other Western states. Everybody who rejects this mission is considered a potential Gülenist. The mission has a formulated performance objective (eliminating Gülen movement followers and other opposition that questions the mission's legitimacy; for instance, liberal-democrat intellectuals, some Kurdish activists, etc.). One of the most noteworthy features of the mission is that it is presented as a "native" and "national" strategy. Accordingly, since he seized absolute power, Erdogan has presented himself as the reis[3] (chief). The "reis" is defined as a native and national[4] (*yerli ve milli*) leader of the Turkish people who executes the mission.

---

[2]A NAZI term for the idea that a family shares the responsibility for a crime committed by one of its members, justifying collective punishment.

[3]A similar title as "Fuhrer" or "Duce".

[4]Erdogan distinguishes politics that correspond with Muslim and Turkish people's values and politics that has its roots in foreign cultures or countries. He emphasizes that he is a native and national leader who acts according to his nation's expectations and is not controlled by foreign powers.

Erdogan himself has stated multiple times that they (he and the regime) would enter the "hiding places of the traitors". The great majority of the persecutions (that have targeted the aforementioned groups) are based on allegations not supported by solid evidence, and the principle of individual criminal responsibility has been violated systematically. Furthermore, human rights records have deteriorated severely due to the post-coup-attempt's systematic and massive purge, and the main oppositional parties (CHP and MHP) have accepted the discourse, the articulated "mission" and its ways and means. As regards the social democratic CHP, the state-centric roots as the founding party of the Kemalist secular republic and its left-nationalist ideological fabric commonly prioritized the securitization of sensitive policy areas such as identity politics or religion-state affairs. Thus, the regime narrative of massive destruction, elimination, and liquidation against the masses affiliated with the Gülen Movement (which is an Islamist movement) are broadly accepted by both CHP leadership and the party grassroots.

In regard to the far-rightist, ultranationalist MHP that, firstly, idealizes the state as the embodiment of Turkishness and, secondly, perceives both the Gülen Movement and all other pro-Western political forces (such as liberal-democratic intellectuals or members of the Kurdish movement who request minority rights and cultural autonomy) as alienated elements who have lost their national identity or (in case of the Kurds) never had it. In this context, the MHP also welcomed the mission of the regime towards targeted groups. However, regarding the level of cooperation with the regime that both political parties have demonstrated since the regime change, there are significant differences. Whereas the MHP actively supported the AKP group in parliament in almost all policy areas, the CHP – as the main oppositional party – did not give up its opposition against Erdogan's leadership and person, aside from his mission and the policies connected with it. In other words, the CHP concentrated its opposition on Erdogan's failures in the past, such as his close relationship and collaboration with the Gülen Movement.

According to the CHP's position, Erdogan and his government enabled the Gülen Movement to infiltrate key state institutions such as the military, judiciary, police, intelligence and other institutions. The CHP considers Erdogan and his party the political leg of the Gülen Movement (Küçükkaya 2018). They argue that Erdogan, thus, must pay the price for this mistake politically. The left-nationalist faction *ulusalci kanat* of the CHP dominates the post-coup-attempt era discourse in the party and, consequently, the CHP prioritizes state-security over massive and systematic human rights violations. This political orientation might sound surprising for a leftist (social democratic) party; however, publications are verifying the ideological deviations of Turkish leftist movements, first and foremost of the CHP tradition. Another significant difference between the CHP and Erdogan's leadership and regime concerns the critical position of the CHP towards the presidential system. The CHP criticized the presidential system from the beginning, with the main argument being that this system does not have sufficient checks and balances, and it would open the door to dictatorship. However, Erdogan and his AKP along with the MHP advocated for the presidential system with the argument that without strong leadership and the stability of a strong power center in the state hierarchy, the fight against internal and external enemies would fail.

The Islamist Erdogan and his AKP otherized the secularist CHP to generate a sense of belonging (us-feeling) among the AKP's Islamist, conservative and traditionalist grassroots. Erdogan uses the dichotomy of "native and national" political forces that are patriotic and loyal to their national/religious roots versus alienated political forces that ally with other ideas, values, and cultural ideologies. The first category includes Erdogan and his allies, whereas the latter comprises the CHP and the Kurdish movement (particularly including the pro-Kurdish leftist HDP). By doing this, Erdogan's mission manufactures a connection between the "objective mission" and its value system, whereby a political (and social-cultural) polarization is created that can be utilized to paralyze the opposition. He has used more nationalistic rhetoric in efforts to delegitimize the opposition. The regime portrayed Erdogan as the embodiment of the national will – a strategy that required delegitimizing the opposition as extremists and terrorists, dehumanizing and demonizing them and excluding them from the Turkish nation. His discourse particularly excluded ethnic and religious minorities, such as the Kurds, Alevis, Armenians, Jews, socialists, and secularists. Instead of confronting the absurdity of this dichotomy, the CHP has taken a more conservative position, moved more to the center and tried to demonstrate that it is indeed "native and national"; even more "native and national" than Erdogan's AKP and MHP. This has disarmed the CHP's capability to effectively resist the anti-democratic structures that have been permanently established in the political sphere. This rhetorical tactic has cornered the CHP to such an extent that any possible collaboration – even of a tactical and short-term nature – with the pro-Kurdish HDP has been incapacitated. This enhances the mission in terms of its justification and in generating consent to the authoritarian regime. Those are purposeful strategies that shape the political equilibrium in the regime, and, more importantly, the dialogue-form of political communication between the "native and national" forces and the others reproduces this balance and contributes to the durability of the regime.

9.6 Conclusion

This chapter discussed the human rights situation in Turkey as a reflection of the authoritarian characteristics of the political regime. It tried to understand how the justification mechanisms of the regime on human rights practices have functioned. Although Turkey is a signatory to the fundamental conventions on human rights and its constitution guarantees the upholding and protection of fundamental human rights for Turkish citizens, it has been not maintained or preserved these rights. When the AKP came to power in 2002, it declared its aspiration to implement an intensive reform program to fulfill EU accession criteria. The level of human rights in Turkey as of 2004, when the EU began negotiations for Turkish membership, presents an example of how the deep penetration of political modernization and democratization in terms of a sophisticated organization of state architecture promoted a basis for further democratization. Considering the progress Turkey achieved in this reform process and the level of democratization and improvement in human rights-related legislature and policy practices, it is hard to understand the rapid decay and eventually the collapse of the liberal constitutional democratic system and deterioration of human rights practices.

We particularly focused on discursive justification strategies for the use of repression. It is argued that Turkey's human rights policy is closely related to the general features of the current political regime and its trajectory from relatively functioning democracy to competitive authoritarianism. It is also argued that the shift in the human rights policy of the political regime happened through a legitimation construct of the "New Turkey". In other words, the deterioration of human rights was not only a result of regime transformation but also an instrument of regime consolidation.

Erdogan exploited the 2016 coup attempt to mobilize Turkish society based on his discourse of "defending their country" against enemies of the state or "traitors" controlled by external enemies. The idea that Turkey is under attack is the main pillar of the mission construct. The regime demonized the Gülen Movement, labelling it with a hateful narrative. It organized the purge based upon a mission of "cleansing the state" of this "domestic enemy". The 2016 coup attempt provided an opportunity for the regime to effectively utilize these ideational narratives in the domestic context (Yilmaz et al. 2019, 9). The Erdogan regime has managed to turn the 2016 coup attempt into a new "foundational myth" of the Turkish state to strengthen solidarity ties and instrumentalized it as an effective legitimation narrative (Von Soest and Grauvogel 2017, 290). This narrative resonated with the opposition, the CHP and IYIP, and partially with the pro-Kurdish HDP. The nationalist MHP is already an ally of the Erdogan regime, and they also supported this position. Apart from a marginal number of dissidents, the political parties including the MHP, the CHP (the main opposition party), the IYIP, and partially the HDP accepted the main discourse of the purge ("FETO"), which has been instrumentalized to legitimatize the authoritarianization of the regime. Thereby, the regime was able to purge large numbers of public servants, academics, journalists and other opposition including their family members. This legitimation has consolidated the regime and contributes to its durability.

References

Abramowitz, Michael J. 2018. Freedom in The World 2018: Democracy in Crisis. In *Freedom House*. https://freedomhouse.org/sites/default/files/FH_FITW_Report_2018_Final_SinglePage.pdf.

Amnesty International. 2013. *Turkey: Gezi Park Protests: Brutal Denial of the Right to Peaceful Assembly in Turkey*. https://www.amnesty.org/download/Documents/12000/eur440222013en.pdf.

———. 2015. *Amnesty International Report 2014/2015-The State of the World's Human Rights*. https://www.amnesty.org/download/Documents/POL1000012015ENGLISH.PDF.

———. 2017. *Amnesty International Report 2016/17- The State of the World's Human Rights*. https://www.amnesty.org/download/Documents/POL1048002017ENGLISH.PDF.

———. 2019. *Turkey: Amnesty International's Brief on the Human Rights Situation*. https://www.amnesty.org/download/Documents/EUR4497472019ENGLISH.PDF.

Aydin, Hasan, and Koksal Avincan. 2020. Intellectual Crimes and Serious Violation of Human Rights in Turkey: A Narrative Inquiry. *The International Journal of Human Rights* 24 (8): 1127–1155. https://doi.org/10.1080/13642987.2020.1713108.

Bar'el, Zvi. 2019. *Destroying Books and Jailing Dissidents: Erdogan's Cultural Purge Is in Full Swing*. Haaretz, October 7. https://www.haaretz.com/middle-east-news/turkey/.premium-keeping-dissidents-quiet-turkey-s-literary-cleansing-drive-knows-no-rest-1.7949072.

Caman, Mehmet Efe. 2005. *Türkische Außenpolitik nach dem Ende des Ost-West-Konflikts: außenpolitische Kontinuität und Neuorientierungen zwischen der EU-Integration und neuer Regionalpolitik*. Berlin: Wiss. Verl. Berlin. ISBN978–3–86573-104-3.

Casier, Marlies. 2009. Contesting the 'Truth' of Turkey's Human Rights Situation: State-Association Interactions in and outside the Southeast. *European Journal of Turkish Studies*, 10.

Champion, Marc. 2016. *Coup Was 'Gift from God'for Erdogan Planning a New Turkey*. Bloomberg. com, July 17. https://www.bloomberg.com/news/articles/2016-07-17/coup-was-a-gift-from-god-says-erdogan-who-plans-a-new-turkey.

Cinar, Özgür H., and Tolga Sirin. 2017. Turkey's Human Rights Agenda. *Research and Policy on Turkey*, 2:2, 133–143, https://doi.org/10.1080/23760818.2017.1350354.

Davenport, Christian. 2007. State Repression and Political Order. *Annuel Review of Political Science* 10: 1–23.

DBP Local Authorities Commission. 2017. *Demokratik Ekolojik Katilimci Kadin Özgürlükçü Yerel Yönetim Modeli Ve Bir Gasp Araci Olarak Kayyum Uygulamalari*. https://www.hdp.org.tr/images/UserFiles/Documents/Editor/DBP%20Kayyum%20Raporu.pdf.

De Bellaigue, Christopher. 2013. Turkey: surreal, menacing... pompous. *The New York Review of Books IX* (20): 30–34.

Edel, Mirjam, and Maria Josua. 2018. How Authoritarian Rulers Seek to Legitimize repression: Framing mass killings in Egypt and Uzbekistan. *Democratization* 25 (5): 882–900. https://doi.org/10.1080/13510347.2018.1439021.

Erdemir, Aykan, and Merve Tahiroglu. 2018. *Pastor Brunson is free. But the West Still Needs a Policy on Erdogan's Hostages*. The Washington Post, October 15. https://www.washingtonpost.com/news/democracy-post/wp/2018/10/15/pastor-brunson-is-free-but-the-west-still-needs-a-policy-on-erdogans-hostages/.

Freedom House. 2014. *Freedom in the World 2014*. http://freedomhouse.org/sites/default/files/FIW2014 booklet.Pdf.

———. 2015. *Freedom in the World 2015*. https://freedomhouse.org/sites/default/files/01152015_FIW_2015_final.pdf.

Gershewski, Johannes. 2013. The Three Pillars of Stability: Legitimation, Repression, and Co-optation in Autocratic Regimes. *Democratization* 20 (4): 13–38.

Girdap, Hafza. 2020. Human Rights, Conflicts, and Dislocation: The Case of Turkey in a Global Spectrum. *American Journal of Qualitative Research* 4 (1): 69–84. https://doi.org/10.29333/ajqr/8266.

Hale, William. 1994. *Turkish Politics and Military*. Routledge.

———. 2011. Human Rights and Turkey's EU Accession Process: Internal and External Dynamics, 2005–10. *South European Society and Politics* 16 (2): 323–333. https://doi.org/10.1080/13608746.2011.577953.

Hale, William, and Ergun Özbudun. 2010. *Islamism, Democracy and Liberalism in Turkey the Case of the AKP*. Oxon: Rutledge.

Hincks, Joseph. 2016. Here's a Time Line of the Insane Number of People Turkey's President Has Fired Since July 15. *Time,* November 23. https://time.com/4581070/turkey-erdogan-fired-dismissed-suspended-sacked-officials-total/.

Human Rights Watch. 2014. *Human Rights World Report 2014.* https://www.hrw.org/world-report/2014/country-chapters/.

———. 2016a. *Turkey: State Blocks Probes of Southeast Killings.* https://www.hrw.org/news/2016/07/11/turkey-state-blocks-probes-southeast-killings.

———. 2016b. *World Report 2016.* https://www.hrw.org/world-report/2016/country-chapters/turkey.

———. 2016c. Turkey: Court orders newspaper takeover. *Zaman latest critical voice.* https://www.hrw.org/news/2016/03/05/turkey-court-orders-newspaper-takeover.

———. 2017a. *Annual Report on Turkey.* https://www.hrw.org/world-report/2017/country-chapters/turkey.

———. 2017b. *Turkey: Crackdown on Kurdish Opposition.* https://www.hrw.org/news/2017/03/20/turkey-crackdown-kurdish-opposition.

———. 2019. *Lawyers on Trial Abusive Prosecutions and Erosion of Fair Trial Rights in Turkey.* https://www.hrw.org/report/2019/04/10/lawyers-trial/abusive-prosecutions-and-erosion-fair-trial-rights-turkey.

Jacinto, Leela. 2017. *Turkey's Post-Coup Purge and Erdogan's Private Army.* Foreign Policy, July 13. https://foreignpolicy.com/2017/07/13/turkeys-post-coup-purge-and-erdogans-private-army-sadat-perincek-Gülen/.

Karaveli, Halil. 2016. Erdogan's Journey: Conservatism and Authoritarianism in Turkey. *Foreign Affairs* 95: 121.

Kirby, Paul. 2016. *Turkey Coup Attempt: Who's the Target of Erdogan's Purge.* BBC, July 20. https://www.bbc.com/news/world-europe-36835340.

Küçükkaya, Aykut. 2018. *First CHP Report: AKP-FETO Brotherhood.* Cumhuriyet, April 9. http://www.cumhuriyet.com.tr/haber/english/956059/first-chp-report-akp-feto-brotherhood.html.

Office of the United Nations High Commissioner for Human Rights. 2017. *Report on the Impact of the State of Emergency on Human Rights in Turkey, Including an Update on the South-East.* https://www.ohchr.org/Documents/Countries/TR/2018-03 19_Second_OHCHR_Turkey_Report.pdf.

Onis, Ziya. 2012. The triumph of conservative globalism: The political economy of the AKP era. *Turkish Studies* 13 (2): 135–152. https://doi.org/10.1080/14683849.2012.685252.

———. 2015. Monopolising the Centre: The AKP and the Uncertain Path of Turkish Democracy. *The International Spectator* 50 (2): 22–41.

Peoples' Democratic Party (HDP). 2019. *The Trustee Regime in Turkey & Deniel of Right to Vote and Right to be Elected.* https://www.hdp.org.tr/tr/raporlar/hdp-raporlari/31-mart-sonrasi-kayyim-raporumuz/13727.

Piri, Kati. 2019. *2018 Report on Turkey.* European Parliament. http://www.europarl.europa.eu/doceo/document/A-8-2019-0091_EN.html.

Somer, Murat. 2016. Understanding Turkey's Democratic Breakdown: Old vs. New and Indigenous vs. Global Authoritarianism. *Southeast European and Black Sea Studies* 16 (4): 481–503. https://doi.org/10.1080/14683857.2016.1246548.

Stockholm Center for Freedom. 2018. *Free Thought Under Siege in Turkey: the Crackdown on Education.* https://stockholmcf.org/wp-content/uploads/2018/07/The-Crackdown-On-Education-in-Turkey_june_2018.pdf.

Tansel, Cemal Burak. 2018. Authoritarian neoliberalism and democratic backsliding in Turkey: Beyond the narratives of Progress. *South European Society and Politics* 23 (2): 197–217. https://doi.org/10.1080/13608746.2018.1479945.

The Inquiry Commission on the State of Emergency Measures. 2018. *Olağanüstü Hal İşlemleri İnceleme Komisyonu Faaliyet Raporu 2018.* https://ohalkomisyonu.tccb.gov.tr/docs/OHAL_FaaliyetRaporu_2018.pdf.

Tugal, Cihan. 2016. *The Fall of the Turkish Model.* London: Verso.

United States Department of State - Bureau of Democracy Human Rights and Labor. 2019. *Turkey 2018 Human Rights Report*. https://www.state.gov/documents/organization/289241.pdf%0Ahttps://mv.usmission.gov/wp-content/uploads/sites/212/HR-report-2018-Maldives-English.pdf.

Von Soest, Christian, and Julia Grauvogel. 2017. Identity, Procedures and Performance: How Authoritarian Regimes Legitimize Their Rule. *Contemporary Politics* 23 (3): 287–305.

Yilmaz, Ihsan, Mehmet Efe Caman, and Galib Bashirov. 2019. How an Islamist Party Managed to Legitimate its Authoritarianization in the Eyes of the Secularist Opposition: The Case of Turkey. *Democratization*. https://doi.org/10.1080/13510347.2019.1679772.

Dr. Mehmet Efe Caman earned his B.A.-M.A. and Ph.D. degrees at Augsburg University in Germany. He focuses on democratization and human rights as well as on Turkish politics in comparative politics and international political contexts. He is broadly interested in democratic decay, current human rights issues in Turkey and the political justification mechanisms of authoritarian regimes. He has published a book on Turkish foreign policy, numerous book chapters and scholarly articles in English, German and Turkish about topics related to his research areas. He is a professor at Memorial University of Newfoundland.

Chapter 10
Shunned and Purged: Turkey's Crackdown on the Hizmet (Gülen) Movement

Sophia Pandya, Brenda Oliden, and Ibrahim Aytac Anli

Abstract This chapter examines the reasons for which the Hizmet Gülen Movement (HGM) has become a primary target of Erdoğan, and offers analysis on the characteristics and strategies of conservative, authoritarian populism, and of the processes used to destroy the HGM network in Turkey and attempts to neutralize it abroad. It also sheds light on the human consequences of the purge, or crackdown, against the movement. This work is informed, in part, by scholarship on populist state-sponsored violence and the effects of collective trauma. The mechanisms by which Erdoğan has carried out his crackdown have been effective, and have had far-reaching consequences. These include firing people at random, seizing property, kidnapping, arbitrary arrests (without due process), promoting a climate of fear, silencing, scapegoating, and social and religious shunning (or "takfirism"). This qualitative research is shaped by participant/observation ethnographic methodology. Interviews were semi-structured in nature, collected via a mixture of purposive and snowball sampling, and were carried out from June, 2016, to July, 2018. Our goal was to interview those HGM participants that recently fled Turkey due to political oppression and/or fear of imminent arrest to seek asylum in the US. We asked informants why they had left Turkey, what their experiences were, and how those experiences impacted them and their families. Fethullah Gülen was also interviewed at his residence in Saylorsburg, Pennsylvania, on April 23, 2017.

Keywords Crackdown coup · Hizmet Gülen Movement (HGM) · Purge · Trauma · And human rights violations

S. Pandya (✉) · B. Oliden
California State University, Long Beach, CA, USA
e-mail: Sophia.Pandya@csulb.edu

I. A. Anli
Independent Researcher, Washington, DC, USA

H. Aydin, W. Langley (eds.), *Human Rights in Turkey*, Philosophy and Politics - Critical Explorations 15, https://doi.org/10.1007/978-3-030-57476-5_10

10.1 Introduction

Mithat Yolcu,[1] a Turkish 53-year-old former educational director, pulled out his handkerchief and wept, wiping his reddened nose, eyes, and fogged up black wire-rimmed glasses, when he recalled to me the anguish his wife went through when he was abruptly forced to flee Turkey in 2015. Now an asylum seeker in the US, he had feared imminent and arbitrary arrest for his involvement in the Hizmet Gülen Movement (HGM), also known as the Gülen Movement.[2] His wife suffers from muscular dystrophy, and having to take care of their children alone for months before joining him gave her stress, aggravating her condition. "She kept all her pain to herself until she arrived to the US," he expressed, choking up. "Many days she didn't have the strength to cook for the kids. The younger two were young and didn't understand why Dad was away," he added (personal communication, April 22, 2017). Mithat is only one of the thousands that have fled Turkey in the last few years to seek asylum, and many HGM participants that remain in Turkey risk social exclusion, financial difficulties, arbitrary arrest, and torture (Amnesty International 2018).

In the aftermath of the July 15, 2016 coup attempt, towards unifying Turkey under his rule and neutralizing those perceived as his opposition, President Recep Tayyip Erdoğan has taken advantage of pre-existing conditions to scapegoat HGM participants, thousands of whom have fled Turkey. Blaming them for the failed putsch, he furthered their broad ostracism, whereby even casual participants have been fired, rejected or reported by neighbors, friends and family members, sometimes jailed, and even tortured (Amnesty International 2018).

Hizmet (the Turkish word for service), is the name used by movement participants for the organization that was founded in Turkey in the 1960s by the Islamic cleric Fethullah Gülen (b.1938) (Pahl 2019, 11). The HGM is considered by its supporters (mainly outside of Turkey) to be a Sufi Muslim-inspired, humanitarian, civil society network of an estimated ten million participants, which has opened thousands of cultural and interfaith centers and science-focused schools in Turkey and around the globe. Scholar of Islamic studies Caroline Tee describes the movement's efforts towards creating a modernity inclusive of both piety and science. She writes, "Their ability to bridge this gulf is contingent largely on their willingness to engage with modern scientific education, and their considerable success in doing so, while retaining their ability to proactively project a pious Islamic identity" (2016, 58).

[1]For their protection and privacy, all names of those interviewed have been changed, with the exception of Fethullah Gülen.

[2]While the term "Gülen Movement" is more commonly used, here we choose to include the term the movement uses for itself, which is "HGM," towards a position of neutrality. The terms "Gulenist" and "Gulen Movement" are not preferred by those to whom those terms refer; using the term "Hizmet" alone can signal alliance or sympathy.

In Turkey today, however, many (if not most) believe it to be a secretive cult which harbors nefarious political goals, controls billions of dollars' worth of schools, institutions, and businesses; and schemes to covertly control the direction of the country. At the minimum, many believe the movement was well-poised to plan the coup attempt; circumstantial evidence points to member's involvement (Yavuz 2018). Political scientist Hakan Yavuz (2018) writes, "there is no question in my mind that the top leadership of the movement planned and carried out the coup" (p. 314). However, while the HGM's very success in Turkey likely laid the groundwork for its unpopularity in that country, according to the UK Foreign Affairs Committee, there is no conclusive evidence it attempted to carry out a coup (The UK's Relations With Turkey 2017). In fact, no one knows who planned and carried out the coup attempt, other than those involved. Critics, such as political scientist Joshua D. Hendrick (2013), have looked past altruistic or pious motives of the movement, instead arguing that the movement's goals are to promote Islamization, and to gain influence and power (in part, through financial gain). Religious studies scholar David Tittensor (2014) claims the movement has a history of defensive and secretive behavior, is considered a threat to Turkey's secularism, and holds endless self-promotional events; the latter somewhat contradicting its self-image as spiritual and humanitarian. However, he concedes the movement's behavior must be understood as a reaction to Turkish secularist hysteria regarding Islamic revivalism in that country.

Regardless of HGM's motives, behavior, or culpability—or lack thereof, this chapter examines the reasons for which the movement has become a primary target of Erdoğan, and offers analysis on the characteristics and strategies of conservative, authoritarian populism, and of the processes used to destroy the HGM network in Turkey and attempts to neutralize it abroad. It also sheds light on the human consequences of the purge, or crackdown, against the movement.

This work is informed, in part, by scholarship on populist state-sponsored violence and the effects of collective trauma. The mechanisms by which Erdoğan has carried out his crackdown have been effective, and have had far-reaching consequences. These include firing people at random, seizing property, kidnapping, arbitrary arrests (without due process), promoting a climate of fear, silencing, scapegoating, and social and religious shunning (or "takfirism").

Historian Rene Girard (1986) argues that collective violence against a "scapegoat" serves to assuage group tensions and thus unify the greater community. Indeed, political analysts Matthew N. Lyons and Chip Berlet (2016) also note, "Right-wing populism can act as both a precursor and a building block of fascism, with anti-elitist conspiracism and ethnocentric scapegoating as shared elements." These theories are both relevant towards understanding Erdoğan's Turkey.

Even before the coup attempt, it was not hard to foresee that violence against the HGM, separatist Kurds[3] (or those perceived as such), and others, would escalate in Turkey. According to psychologist Ervin Staub (1999), collective violence against a group is predictable. Indicators include a culture of authoritarianism, a homogenous

[3]The Kurds make up approximately 18% of Turkey's population (The World Factbook).

society, group trauma, and a "devaluation of a subgroup." He pens: "These ideologies usually identify a devalued, vulnerable group, often the scapegoated group and sometimes a historical antagonist, as an enemy that stands in the way of the ideology's fulfillment. The presence of such an ideology, leaders propagating it, and its wide appeal are all important sources of and indicators of potential violence" (Staub 1999).

Turkey exemplifies this type of socio-political climate due to the ongoing trauma of the loss of the Ottoman Empire a century ago. This trauma is epitomized by the term "Sèvres Syndrome," named after a post-WW I treaty that envisioned a partitioned Anatolia but which was never implemented (Montgomery 1972, 775). Sèvres symbolizes the culmination of existential threats against the Turkish nation by Western powers externally, and by a variety of minorities (Kurds, Armenians, etc.) internally (Nefes 2015). Unlike post-WW II Germany and Japan, Turkey failed to heal its trauma after the loss of empire. This has resulted in a dysfunctional social-political environment with no shortage of potential scapegoats and discourses of devaluation. Not a decade has passed in the history of modern Turkey without this paradigm manifesting itself against a minority community. In this case, this syndrome reappears in the form of violence on the part of Erdoğan government and his supporters, against the HGM.

Towards understanding this phenomenon, it is worth noting parallels with populist, authoritarian regimes from the past, which led to violence against subgroups. Political scientist Khatharya Um (2015) points out that although not right-wing, Pol Pot's populist Khmer Rouge was also characterized by a quasi-religious form of patriotism, "utopian ambitions," and "self-consuming paranoia" (p. 7). So was Nazi Germany. Manifestly xenophobic, obviously both the Khmer Rouge and the Nazis resorted to scapegoating, although on a genocidal scale. In Turkey, Erdoğan's current scapegoats are primarily members of the HGM, but also those in the Kurdish community perceived as separatists, Alevis (Champion 2016), journalists, and all others perceived as opposition. While the Turkish purge is not a genocide, Um's arguments speak to the effects of collective trauma and the mechanisms of fearmongering, relevant in Turkey's case.

Regarding collective trauma in general, psychologist Jack Saul (2014) offers insight on its consequences (such as PTSD, feelings of betrayal, etc.) on a given community; here we consider his ideas in light of the trauma experienced by the HGM. Psychiatrist Judith L. Herman's (2015) study of victims of collective trauma suggests paths to healing and recovery.

This qualitative research is informed in part by participant/observation ethnographic methodology, and shaped by grounded theory, in which data is collected and analyzed until themes emerge and theories about the data can be drawn (Charmaz and Mitchell 2001, 160). Grounded theory allows for "humanistic stories" (p. 162) to illuminate an issue, but also requires a process of contextualization and analysis (p. 170). The interviews were semi-structured in nature, collected via a mixture of purposive and snowball sampling, and were carried out from June, 2016, to July, 2018. Pandya's contacts with the movement helped find appropriate informants—our goal was to interview those in the HGM that recently fled Turkey due to political oppression and/or fear of imminent arrest to seek asylum in the US. Interviews were carried out in California and Washington, although one person residing in Arizona was interviewed via Skype. Twenty-nine people were interviewed in all, with 18 males and 11 females. All interviews, of approximately 1 h each, were carried out by either Pandya or Oliden. We asked informants to describe why they had left Turkey, their experiences of the purge, and how those experiences impacted them and their families. Fethullah Gülen was interviewed at his residence in Saylorsburg, Pennsylvania, on April 23, 2017. Four informants are of Kurdish descent, and the rest identify as ethnically Turkish. All but Gülen left Turkey in 2016 fearing political and religious persecution, although a few fled before the July 15 coup, anticipating imminent arrest. We have both emic and etic perspectives on the HGM: one author (Pandya) has interacted with the movement since 1999, another (Oliden) since 2015, and the third (Anli) has identified as a member of the movement since 1995.

10.2 Historical Context: From Collaboration to Conflict

Ironically, the HGM and Erdoğan's AKP (Justice and Development Party) collaborated together from around 2003 to 2011, shortly after the 2010 referendum on constitutional amendments, which ended judiciary-military tutelage and paved the way for a strong Erdogan presidency (Karaveli 2010).

The relationship deteriorated even more seriously in 2013. The years of collaboration created a mutually beneficial voting bloc composed of the religiously inclined. Through this alliance, the two actors joined efforts to curb the established power of the military elites (Butler and Friedman 2016). Inspired by Turkey's founder Mustafa Kemal Atatürk's (1881–1938) ideas, the Kemalists held power in Turkey for decades, discriminating against the overtly religious, and stifling religious behavior in the public sphere towards defending Atatürk's secularist legacy. For example, women were banned from wearing headscarves at universities or if employed in the public sector and non-state institutions until 2013, preventing many pious women from receiving an education or pursuing a career (Hart 2013).

The HGM is only one of many Sufi (mystical Islam) groups[4] that has suffered persecution in Turkey. While the movement may be considered to be a neo-Sufi order, it differs in many ways from traditional Sufi brotherhoods (Ergene 2008). While most Turks can trace their religious lineage back to a Sufi order, these brotherhoods were quashed by Atatürk who sought to curb their influence, breaking up the orders (*tarikatlar*) in 1925 (Hart 2013). Erdoğan's family is affiliated with Nakşibendi Sufism—he is currently part of the powerful İskenderpaşa community, rooted in the Nakşibendi order—and his own political authority is dependent in part on the AKP's coalition of religious orders. While theologically, the Nakşibendi order

[4]Sufism is a broad category, and is associated both with its classical forms, but also with popular religiosity, syncretism, indigenous beliefs, women's practices, magic, and healing. Perhaps because of the breadth of the term, its critics have portrayed it as regressive and superstitious.

advocates an inward mystical Sufi path, in Turkey, the İskenderpaşa order also works towards influencing politics and society. More a political Islamist than a mystical Sufi, Erdoğan's muscular form of Islam is deeply connected to that of the Muslim Brotherhood which he has long courted (Cornell 2015).

In 2003, when Erdoğan came to power, he promised reforms: to amend the Constitution toward safeguarding individual human rights, and to pursue inclusion into the European Union. In an interview with Gülen in Pennsylvania, the reticent cleric explained that Erdoğan had appeared to be moving in a positive direction, at first. "On the outside he gave the impression he was an honest, virtuous person with good morals, pious, concerned for an eternal life, and as if he had a deep connection with God. This image has been demolished," Gülen stated. Referring to Erdoğan's involvement in the December, 2013, Iran-Halkbank-Gold corruption scandal, Gülen added, "He began acting like a bandit, smuggling money here and there" (personal communication, April 24, 2017). It was alleged that key members of Erdoğan's government took bribes and colluded to trade natural gas for gold, circumventing US sanctions against Iran.

According to Gülen, he and Erdoğan never had a genuine union of hearts, despite their collaboration. HGM and AKP come from two distinct Islamic schools of thought with widely differing worldviews. The AKP has its origins in the ambitiously political Islamist movement of Milli Görüş (National Outlook), whereas the HGM pursues a "civil Islam" agenda which claims to be apolitical and emphasizes spirituality and civility (Tol 2014). Yet it is also possible to argue a certain level of convergence between the two during their decade of alliance. Examples include the AKP's earlier pursuit of moderation and the HGM's more overt involvement in politics (Ayan 2019). During their 8–10 years of alliance, the movement was able to build a large network of institutions (educational, media, health, and charitable) in Turkey, and Erdoğan's AKP-led government was able to remain in power. Jointly, both groups strengthened the ability for religious people to openly identify and behave as such, for the first time since the founding of the Republic.

However, this uneasy alliance become increasingly uncomfortable after the 2011 general elections. The AKP's landslide victory consolidated Erdoğan's power and initiated the erosion of checks and balances, eventually causing a derailment of Turkey from its reformist path (Öniş and Kutlay 2019). Probably the most straightforward expression of the AKP's majoritarian orientation came from Aziz Babuşçu, the party's Istanbul chairman. In a 2011 statement Babuşçu admitted "Those who were somehow [partners] of ours in the 10 years of our rule will not be partners for us in the next 10 years" (Turkish Ruling Party to Leave Liberals out 2013).

The government's harsh reaction to the Gezi Park protests embodied a watershed moment in Erdoğan's shift to authoritarianism. When a diverse group of Istanbulites including environmentalists, feminists, non-AKP Islamists, celebrities, and soccer fan groups demonstrated to save Gezi Park (a small park adjacent to Istanbul's Taksim Square) from being demolished and converted into a mall, they were later joined by larger crowds across the country who also demonstrated against government repression, police brutality, lack of freedom of press, environmental degradation, discrimination against the LGBT community, and Kurdish marginalization. While the catalyst for the Gezi Park protests was initially driven chiefly by an environment agenda, the wide-ranging motives of the protesters cannot be reduced to that (Özbudun 2014). Rather, the nationwide demonstrations expressed public outrage against the government's "moralizing intrusions into the citizen's way of life" (Göle 2013, 10). The protesters were met with water cannons, tear gas, and pepper spray. Gezi was not only a turning point in AKP's overall political orientation, but also a moment that reflected the deepening of the rift between Erdogan and Gülen. The latter took a critical position with regard to the government response to the crisis (Birnbaum 2013). On a June 23, 2013 video, apparently during a heated moment while discussing the Gezi Park issue and its repercussions, Gülen urged people to refrain from using the term *çapulcu* (looter), a label Erdoğan used incessantly to discredit the protesters (Fethullah Gülen: Çapulcu demeyin 2013).

In December 2013, when Erdoğan's son and other government officials were exposed as involved in the Iran-Halbank-gold corruption scandal, the president furiously accused the HGM of bringing the scandal to light in order to weaken his government. He resorted to Islamist conspiracy theories, implying the corruption investigation was an American-Israeli conspiracy against the AKP's rise as the leader of Muslim world (Yilmaz 2018). In a January, 2014, interview with the BBC, Gülen expressed his belief in the existence of governmental corruption in Turkey, and insisted he did not know "even 0.1% of them" when asked about those who carried out the operation associated with the scandal (Franks 2014). The feud worsened when Erdoğan, livid, retaliated by closing down hundreds of HGM-affiliated institutions. In 2015, despite a lack of evidence, the Turkish president officially designated the HGM as the "Fethullahist Terrorist Organization" ('FETÖ'), effectively neutralizing them in Turkey (Human Rights Watch 2016), and clearing the path for further arrests, seizures of media and educational institution, and the mounting social exclusion of its members.

Other than consolidating Turkey's conservative religious block and presiding over a relatively strong economy, Erdoğan's electoral success, like that of other right-wing nationalist politicians, is largely due to populist support. Erdoğan's populism—he has positioned himself as the hypermasculine *Devlet Baba* (Father of the Nation), who alone can "make Turkey great again" and save it from its supposed ubiquitous enemies— is a key facet of his ability to strengthen his authoritarian rule (Müller 2016). This reflects the established semi-divine image of the state in Turkish political culture, exemplified by the historic reverence of sultans as the "*zillullah fil ard*" (Arabic for God's shadow on earth).

Despite Erdoğan's graft scandal, after his 2014 bid to be Turkey's president (instead of prime minister), he emerged more powerful, due in part to his polarizing rhetoric, and relentless demonization of his opponents (Müller 2014). Even before Erdoğan won the April 16, 2017, constitutional referendum vote, which grants him near-dictatorial powers and consolidates his authority to rule by decree, he had already resorted to increasingly harsh methods to repress his opposition, especially targeting the HGM.

One compelling factor behind the movement's unpopularity among the Kemalist secularists is the HGM's former support for the ultimately discredited Ergenekon trials. These were criticized for being far from fair, and most of the 275 accused of belonging to Ergenekon, a secret, secular, ultranationalist organization also known as the "deep state," received lengthy sentences for their alleged crimes (including plotting against the state) in 2013, which were later overturned. Many felt that the trials were little more than a way for both Erdoğan and the HGM, then allied, to weaken their respective opposition (Vela 2013). However, these alliances shifted, as it become increasingly clear that Erdoğan considered Gülen and the movement to be his primary adversaries. Having already alienated the secularists, the HGM found itself lacking allies to support it in Turkey.

At a more abstract level, it is possible to argue that there are profound doctrinal reasons for both the Kemalist and the Islamist camps to harbor hostility towards the HGM. As for the secularists, the domestic as well as international achievements of the movement, without its members compromising their devout lifestyles, shook the foundations of the established Kemalist discourse that saw religiosity as antithetical to worldly success. Kemalists believe religious behavior should remain firmly in the private realm. The movement's success resulted in the privilege of the Kemalist elite being threatened by large segments of Turkey's urban middle class, and to the eventual erosion thereof. The HGM's gains, in part, had to do with its widespread engagement with non-Muslims. Gülen rejects the dichotomous Islamist worldview based on the medieval concepts of *dar al-Islam* (abode of Islam) versus *dar al-harb* (abode of war), and has instead proposed *dar al-hizmah* (abode of service) that suggests looking at the world as one single realm to serve fellow humans (Keleş and Sezgin 2015).

Immediately after the putsch attempt in Turkey, Erdoğan accused the HGM of masterminding the plot, and launched the purge, or *tasfiye* (Turkish for cleansing, liquidation, and purge), apparently in retaliation. Staub's model, which outlines factors predictive of impending collective violence, suggests violence was inevitable (Staub 1999). Erdoğan's strongman rule, Turkey's historical persecution and marginalization of minorities, the trauma and dishonor regarding the 1922 loss of the Ottoman Empire, and rampant Turkish paranoia of being "surrounded by enemies," all catalyzed to ripen conditions for violence. The Turkish president's framing of the HGM as a "parallel state," a "state within a state," and ultimately as a terrorist group, cast it as Turkey's primary enemy (Pandya 2017). He won the referendum vote in April, 2017, and as of May, 2017, his declaration that the state of emergency would go on indefinitely, left many feeling unable to breathe.

Describing the increasingly deep fault lines in Turkish society Gülen believes were created by Erdoğan, the cleric commented:

> Even if God were to send extraordinary help to heal hearts, they [governmental forces] have already divided Turkish society into segments, and each group views the others with enmity. Those [in power] are determined to dominate. They are determined not to surrender the places they now occupy, and they intend to use any treacherous means necessary to ensure that (Gülen, personal communication, 2017).

Gülen also pointed out that the ripple effect, created by each family hurt by the purge, would eventually reach millions of people, whose laments would eventually turn into prayers, compelling God to respond to the cruelty they had faced. "When this happens," he added sternly, those responsible for the purge "will regret what they have done" (Gülen, personal communication, 2017).

10.3 Neutralizing the Movement: Strategies of the Purge

After the failed putsch, Erdoğan lost no time suspending the European Convention of Human Rights, declaring a three-month state of emergency, which he extended repeatedly until July, 2018 (Kenyon 2018). After this was lifted, no steps were taken towards investigating or prosecuting the human rights abuses that took place during those years, and the climate of fear continues to impact many sectors of society, including journalists, human rights activists, and the judiciary. As of 2019, the court system is still not able to function independently (European Commission 2019). Additionally, the state of emergency was replaced with a security law until 2021, which grants his government similar powers (Butler and Küçükgöçmen 2018). Human Rights Watch (2019a, b, January 17) notes that despite the termination of the state of emergency: "Prolonged and arbitrary jailing of critics on bogus terrorism charges has become the norm in Turkey." Below we describe several of the means by which the Turkish government has attempted to deactivate the movement.

10.3.1 Human Rights Abuses

According to the United Nations Universal Declaration of Human Rights (UNUDHR) (General Assembly resolution 217 A), all people have the right to life, property, liberty, security of person, freedom of speech, freedom from arbitrary arrest and torture, the right to work, the right to seek an education, to have freedom of movement, and more. The Turkish government has violated all of the above since 2016. Amnesty International has labeled the purge "a crackdown of exceptional proportions" (Amnesty International 2016). Bizarrely, even the chairman of Amnesty International Turkey, Taner Kılıç, was detained on June 7, 2017 (Uras 2017). According to a movement-affiliated website, as of March, 2019, Erdoğan's AKP-led government has arrested over 85,000 people, and detained almost 500,000 (Turkey's Post-Coup Crackdown 2019). Most of those arrested or fired were affiliated with the movement, although other opposition groups, such as members of the Kurdish HDP (the Peoples' Democratic Party), have also been targeted. Without a doubt, those perceived as opposition found themselves acutely vulnerable to human rights abuses in light of Erdoğan's suspension of the European Convention of Human Rights, which allows him to rule by decree and his government to carry out ordinarily illegal activities against Turkish citizens. According to both Amnesty

International and Human Rights Watch, human rights abuses include torture, rape, beatings, and forced confessions (Amnesty International 2017; Human Rights Watch 2015). Many detainees are arbitrarily held, unable to contact attorneys or family members (Amnesty International 2017).

During political conflict, women in particular suffer from displacement, poverty, and sexual abuse (Roberts 2017). Those detained are vulnerable to strip searches, rape, and other demeaning treatment (Amnesty International 2018). A summary of the 2017 UN OHCHR report on Turkey states: "Turkish authorities reportedly detained some 100 women who were pregnant or had just given birth, mostly on the grounds that they were 'associates' of their husbands, who are suspected of being connected to terrorist organizations. Some were detained with their children and others violently separated from them" (United Nations Human Rights Office Of The High Commissioner 2018, 20). Over 700 babies and children are held in jail with their imprisoned mothers in inadequate conditions (Baby Accompanying Mother In Prison Joins 700 Other Kids Growing Up Behind Bars 2019). All of this violates the human right to be free from arbitrary arrest, unfair trials and detentions, torture, and "cruel, inhuman or degrading treatment or punishment." Article 25, in particular, notes that "motherhood and childhood are entitled to special care and assistance" (United Nations 1948). Obviously, this has not been granted.

10.3.2 Economic

Article 17 of UNUDHR holds that everyone "has the right to own property alone as well as in association with others, and that "no one shall be arbitrarily deprived of his property" (United Nations 1948). Yet the HGM, known for establishing schools, tutoring centers, and universities, lost billions when these were closed or taken over in Turkey by the government. Since the purge began, the Turkish government continued to shut down or take control of thousands of educational institutions. Almost 6000 academics have been fired from their positions without due process, most accused of links to the HGM (Human Rights Watch 2018). Additionally, over 130,000 teachers, academics, police, prosecutors, judges, and other public or civil servants were similarly sacked (Human Rights Watch 2019a). According to Amnesty International, those that lost their jobs due to the purge have suffered "professional annihilation," unable to work in public service at all. Many are forced to live off of their savings, or are supported by family members, and a few have gone on a hunger strike in protest (Gardner 2017). Those fired lost their medical and social service benefits, and if they lived in publicly-owned housing, they became vulnerable to government-ordered eviction (United Nations High Commissioner for Refugees 2018). According to many interviewees and human rights reports, the government has also resorted to seizing private businesses and freezing bank accounts and other assets (Ates 2016).

10.3.3 Kidnapping

Erdoğan's reach has extended far beyond Turkey. On March 24, 2017, the *Wall Street Journal* (WSJ) reported that former CIA director James Woolsey attended a meeting the previous summer, in which Michael Flynn (advisor to then candidate Donald Trump) and officials from the Turkish government discussed illegally kidnapping Gülen, who legally resides in Pennsylvania. A subsequent WSJ article published November 10, 2017, revealed that Special Counsel Robert Mueller investigated Flynn's alleged involvement in the kidnapping plot, for which Flynn was to receive up to 15 million dollars from the Turkish government (it has denied these allegations) (NY Daily News 2017). Although the plan to kidnap Gülen failed, Erdoğan, emboldened and empowered by his referendum success, continues to aggressively pursue HGM participants residing in Turkey and around the globe. HGM-affiliated businessman İhsan Aslan, academic İsmet Özçelik, and school principal Turgay Karaman, for example, were extrajudicially abducted by the Turkish government from Malaysia on May 2, 2017, surfacing in Turkey's jails nine days later (violating UNUHDR Article 9, the right to "liberty and security of person" (United Nations 1948). The UN has requested they been freed, as they were arbitrarily detained and deprived of a free trial (United Nation Human Rights: Office Of The High Commissioner 2019). Six Turkish citizens and participants of the HGM, residing in Kosovo, were "deported" in April, 2018, by Kosovo's secret service, clearly pressured by Turkey--but *without* the consent of Kosovo's Prime Minister (suggesting bribery) (Bytyci 2018). In a July 2018 interview, Turkey's Foreign Minister Mevlüt Çavuşoğlu admitted to the existence of the abduction campaign executed by the country's notorious intelligence organization MIT. Çavuşoğlu told CNN Turk that more than 100 individuals affiliated with the movement "have been brought back to Turkey" (Baykan 2018).

10.3.4 Spying and Reporting

In the Cambodian context, "spying and denunciations amplified the terror," and the survivors' anguish was intensified when what they had lived through went unacknowledged (Um 2015, 43). According to our informants, in Turkey, people report on their own neighbors for suspected "Gülenist" ties, lest they be suspected themselves. The long arm of the Turkish government has also created a global intelligence network to spy on its own citizens, monitoring the activities of HGM participants in Turkey and abroad (Kazem 2017). These acts on the part of the government violate the right to association and to freedom from discrimination. In particular, UNUDHR Article 12 states that all should be free from interference with "privacy, family, home or correspondence" and attacks on "honor and reputation" (United Nations 1948). In addition to conventional intelligence bodies, concerns have been raised by the Council of Europe regarding "reported cases of religious authorities allegedly spying on the Turkish community living abroad" (Council of Europe 2017, 16–17). Furthermore, Turkey's Directorate of Religious Affairs has briefed a parliamentary commission and admitted to its spying activities (Erdem 2016). Turkey's Directorate of Religious Affairs' (*Diyanet*) spying activities became subject of an investigation in Germany, resulting in police raids widely covered in German outlets (Germany Investigates Possible Anti- Gülen Spies 2017).

10.3.5 Controlling the Message

The Turkish government has also engaged in propaganda against the movement, using discourse to sway local and international opinions about the HGM, spending millions of dollars on its message. Inside Turkey, it closed or took over dozens of media outlets, which obviously grants Erdoğan the ability to shape, maintain, and control popular opinion regarding his enemies. Notably, it hired Robert Amsterdam, a Canadian attorney and a partner of London-based Amsterdam and Partners, and Michael Flynn, former US national security advisor, to spread anti-Gülen propaganda. In 2015, Amsterdam declared at a news conference in Washington that he was hired by President Erdoğan's government "to expose allegedly unlawful conduct by the Gülen network worldwide," focusing on a range of issues such as the movement's use of U.S. visas, members' political activities and educational operations (Pamuk 2015). Michael Flynn was paid at least half a million dollars to advocate for Turkey during Trump's campaign; in particular, to smear the HGM. The money worked. On Election Day, an op-ed written by Flynn was published, in which he referred to Gülen as "Turkey's Osama bin Laden," a "shady Islamic mullah" and a "radical Islamist" (Baker and Rosenberg 2017). Erdoğan has also hired several lobbying firms in the US (i.e. the Gephardt Group), funds a network of US-based NGOs to promote his agenda (i.e. the Turkish Heritage Organization and the Turken Foundation), and has links to multiple business organizations (i.e. MUSIAD USA, which is the US branch of the Independent Industrialists' and Businessmen's Association). He spent a staggering hundred million dollars to build the Diyanet Center of America Mosque in Maryland, which opened in April, 2016 (Russia Today 2016), bolstering his support among the Muslim-American community. His daughter, Sümeyye Erdoğan, gave a talk in December, 2016, at the annual Muslim American Society (MAS)- Islamic Circle of North America (ICNA) Convention, in which she told the American Muslims there that the movement was "'actually more dangerous' than ISIS" (Ross 2016). This type of attack appears to violate the right to freedom from attacks on "honor and reputation" (United Nations 1948).

10.3.6 Shunning and Takfirism

Shunning or social ostracism can be motivated by religious or ideological differences, and has been a destructive mechanism not only catalyzed by religious groups but also by nation states. Theologian Paul Griffiths (2010) points out that shunning can take the form of refusing contact with those previously in your group, or declining to share food, speech, space, or even a gaze. Shunning can lead to killing the other, or simply to "seek to remove the shunned from one's presence and thought, to make the shunned as if he or she were not" (p. 119).

The terrorist designation launched the social ostracism of movement participants in Turkey. After the coup attempt, the government was able to take "measures against individuals who 'belong to, connect to, or have contact with the Fetullahist Terrorist Organization' (Decree 668, of 27 July 2016) and public personnel who have 'membership in, affiliation or connection with the Fetullahist Terrorist Organization,' as well as the spouses and children of such persons (Decree 670, of 17 August 2016)" (OHCHR 2017, 11). This conflicts with UNUDHR Article 18, which safeguards "freedom of thought, conscience and religion," and with Article 20, the right to peaceful assembly and association (United Nations 1948). This designation has also created a justification for harassing defense attorneys of participants of the HGM, closing bar associations, and arbitrarily arresting and detaining those with even distant connections to the movement (OHCHR 2017).

Our interviewees described the loss of family, friends, occupations, and property, and even of their citizenship. Shunning within family units was also a dimension of Pol Pot's violence, leading to "people uprooted from support systems" (Um 2015, 30). Regarding the Khmer Rouge and its impact on social networks, Um (2015) writes, "Through state control over every aspect of social life, and manipulation of language and loyalty, violence not only unmakes the family but destroys relationality" (p. 30). In Cambodia, social ostracism was intended to cause "social death" (Um 2015, 46). Unfortunately, the various forms of violence meted out during the purge will have long-lasting damaging effects to the social fabric of Turkey as well.

One method of causing social death is through religious excommunication. The former head of Turkey's Diyanet, Mehmet Görmez, issued a religious degree in which he pronounced members of the HGM movement apostates (Doğan 2018, 56). The Diyanet is controlled by Erdoğan's AKP (Doğan 2018, 5). While the great majority of Muslims believe it is unacceptable to excommunicate another Muslim, also known as engaging in *tekfir* (the Turkish word for the Arabic *takfir*), the practice has roots that go back to the extremist Kharijites of the seventh century (Badar et al. 2017). Islamic history shows that such literalist movements grow in appeal during times of political and social uncertainty. The turmoil and disorder during the Crusades and Mongolian invasions are cited as key factors for the emergence of Ibn Taymiyyah's Salafi school (Hosseinzadeh 2015). More recently, the Egyptian twentieth century reformer, Sayyid Qutb, argued that most Muslims had fallen into a state of apostasy due to living in what he considered "non-Islamic" environments, and that to return to Islam they must live in *dar ul-Islam,* a "pure" Islamic state, where sharia law would be observed (Qutb 2006). He also believed in making use of *takfir* to excommunicate other Muslims, which would then make them permissible to kill them, as the (non-Muslim) enemy (Eikmeier 2007). In contemporary times, historian James L. Gelvin (2018) points out that *takfir* is a key strategy of ISIS (The Islamic State of Iraq and Syria). He further describes Abu Musab al-Zarqawi's deployment of *takfir* to spark violence between Sunnis and Shiites in Iraq. Turkish officials, then, try to justify their human rights abuses by first characterizing their enemies as non-believers, violating UNUDHR Article 12 regarding freedom from attacks on "honor and reputation" (United Nations 1948). Using *tekfir* in the Turkish context is a multi-layered accusation. It connotes both a betrayal of the faith of "Turkishness" or Turkish exceptionalism, and a betrayal of the form of Islam Erdoğan would like to promote. Political Scientist Ihsan Yilmaz (2018) writes: "The AKP elite has increasingly resorted to anti-Western ideology, takfirism, and conspiracy theories that simultaneously try to influence global *ummah* and the Turkish diaspora communities that predominantly live in the west." Yilmaz should know, the AKP-affiliated Islamist scholar Hayratttin Karaman issued a fatwa in which Karaman "takfired" him (p. 8).

10.4 The Human Consequences of the Purge

The Turkish government's derogation from the European Convention on Human Rights and International Covenant on Civil and Political Rights allowed it to suspend safeguards which were in place to prevent human rights abuses (Human Rights Watch 2016). Coupled with the state of emergency, this led to an extraordinarily oppressive climate across the country. The crackdown has had severe implications which have manifested in a variety of personal losses. To predict the long-term effects of the purge on members of the movement, it helps to consider the aftermath for other survivors of collective trauma. Substance abuse and domestic violence are common among the survivors of the Cambodian genocide (Um 2015). Regarding collective trauma in general, psychologist Jack Saul (2014) writes: "The mental health consequences of disaster are many and include depression, anxiety, post-traumatic health disorder (PTSD), physical health problems, chronic problems in living, interpersonal relationship, and financial stress, as well as the loss of resources such as actual and perceived social support (p. 1). Survivors also may suffer from a sense of betrayal, loneliness, a loss of security, ruptures in their relationships at every level, diminished ability to parent effectively, and a sense of alienation (Saul 2018, 5–6). Below are narratives that reflect, in part, the human cost of the purge.

10.4.1 Silenced: "I want to break the silence"

Without a doubt, Erdoğan has effectively used Foucauldian panopticon-like methods to create a climate of fear and silence, which together ultimately work to smother dissent. The Turkish Consulate routinely sends letters to those Americans involved in some way with a HGM-affiliated event, warning them that the movement is a terrorist organization.

In Turkey, even those who might feel sympathy for those affected by the purge cannot openly express it without fear of reprisal, or of others stigmatizing them as associated with the movement or other opposition groups. Sema, a HGM-affiliated professor in her thirties forced to leave Turkey, complained: "There is a complete silence regarding people's suffering. Life appears normal, but outside of Turkey people are afraid to go to the Consulate. You can't get anything done; passports are cancelled for nothing. It's ridiculous that people aren't talking about it. I want to break the silence" (personal communication, 2017).

Many of those interviewed described not being able to call relatives in Turkey, or even email them, for fear that the government would be recording the interchange and then arrest their families for being connected to "terrorists." For example, 26 year-old Fatih, a science teacher from Gaziantep, explained, "On the phone, I don't speak on the country's situation with my family. If they tag my family members as associated with a Hizmet follower, they will go to jail. In jail, people are dying, committing suicide" (personal communication, August 2, 2016). Like others, he does not feel safe to criticize the purge on social media, or by openly demonstrating against the government. This reflects lack of freedom of expression in Turkey, and fear of those in the movement outside of Turkey.

10.4.2 Shunned: "What Did We Do to Become Terrorists"

In many cases, friends and family member have distanced themselves from HGM participants or denounced them, either out of fear or anger. Tahsin's father was against his involvement in the movement even before the attempted coup, and at one point he disowned him, telling Tahsin, a 38-year-old HGM-affiliated director, that he was a traitor. Later, they reconciled, but according to Tahsin, "after the coup, the relationship became very tense again." Tahsin explained sadly, "My father told my brother that he lost his son to Hizmet and that he couldn't get his son back" (personal communication, May 19, 2017). Three months later, Tahsin's father died of a brain tumor.

Zeynep, a 37-year-old woman from Izmir, is married, and she and her husband share one cat. She narrated that before leaving Turkey, she had been a teacher and also worked in a government-run office, and volunteered for the movement. She left Turkey before the coup, but was scared she would not be able to leave safely. Her supervisor in the government-run establishment knew she was in the movement.

Zeynep explained that before she left, he warned her in an intimidating, menacing way: "Be careful, I know you" (personal communication, July 12, 2018).

Similarly, Elif's father supports the AKP, and was even a classmate of Erdoğan. A 39-year-old chemical engineer, Elif's family originates from the Black Sea region, but lives in Istanbul. Married with one child, she had to flee Turkey before finishing her PhD thesis. After the coup attempt she had the first argument with her father, who blamed the movement for the coup attempt, that she had ever had in her life. Upset, she asked him, "What did we [HGM participants] do to become terrorists?" She said that for her, the worst part of the purge was that she lost many of her relationships—her family and friends rejected her. She explained, "They used to think I was a good person, but now. . .suddenly I am a terrorist to them" (personal communication, July 12, 2017).

10.4.3 Loss of Turkishness: "I Didn't Come Here Because I Wanted To"

Those that managed to leave Turkey for abroad due to the purge, find themselves in permanent exile, unable to return to their families, lives, professions, and very identities, further inflaming their trauma. Movement participant refugees and asylum seekers are often unable to renew their passports or found that their passports have been revoked (including NBA player Enes Kanter) (Jenkins 2017). At the end of July 2016, the government had invalidated over 50,000 passports (Dearden 2016); that number has now reached 234,000 (Olağanüstü Hal(OHAL) 2019). This violates UNUDHR Article 15, which speaks to the right to a nationality and to freedom from arbitrary denial of one's nationality. It also violates Article 13: the right to freedom of movement, and to leave and return to one's country (United Nations 1948). On a trip to Nigeria in February 2017, a HGM-affiliated Turkish woman lifted her stateless baby for me (Pandya) to see, and she exclaimed: "No passport!" The child had been born in Nigeria and neither that country nor Turkey would grant him one. While HGM participants have found that their very identity as Turks has been negated, they also find their experiences of the purge denied by the Turkish government (Contradicting Earlier Remarks, Erdoğan Denies Existence Of Purge Victims 2016), and by those Turks, who, perhaps due to cognitive dissonance, choose not to see what is happening to their compatriots.

Fahri, a 36-year old jewelry businessman from Çorum, a province in the Black Sea region, also cried when he expressed to me why he left Turkey. Like many Turks, he was raised with intense feelings of pride and loyalty to his country, and leaving it was acutely painful for him. A strong, well-built man with a wife and small children, he added, weeping: "I love my country *too* much; I didn't come here because I wanted to. In October, 2015 the police detained nineteen people from my business. Six were arrested and accused of sponsoring terrorism, and were in prison for 52 days. I felt lots of pressure. One night at the door I heard, 'Knock, knock.' The kids were sleeping, but I got up and opened the door. I asked them who they were, and they said police officers. My wife began to cry and we hugged each other" (personal communication, July 11, 2017). Fortunately for Fahri's family, the police had made a mistake and were looking for someone else at that moment. However, they decided to flee Turkey for the US on the first flight out, bringing only 2500 dollars. He continued, "I escaped my country, but I wasn't guilty of any crime. I know that I had to flee, but I didn't know what my crime was" (personal communication, July 11, 2017). His wife, Yaprak, said Fahri cried for a week when he arrived. While the family safely resettled in California, Yaprak was diagnosed with breast cancer the following year.

10.4.4 Loss of Professional Identity: "Starting from zero"

Yaprak, 33, described her own experience. Formerly a banker, she explained: "It's like I'm starting from zero. It's always like I don't have anything from before, not even my photo albums. Like an incredible hand took us from Turkey and just put us here without anything" (personal communication, July 11, 2017).

Many refugees, like Yaprak, told me they felt disoriented at having to start over again, "from zero," which points to the repercussions of the denial of the right to secure personhood, nationality, and employment in Turkey. A Kurdish former vice-principal, Atilla, 39 years old, independently echoed what Yaprak had described, "It's like starting from zero in life. No job, no visa, no diploma. I'm surprised. It's like being a duck swimming with no direction. I'm depressed" (personal communication, August 3, 2016). He also had to step away from the interview for a few moments to compose himself, tears running down his face.

10.4.5 Physical and Mental Health Problems: "Every Day It Does Get Worse"

The dozens we interviewed have spoken of the loss of a sense of security, professional and personal identities, life plans, financial stability, and social networks—in many cases including family members. While a few sought psychological treatment, most did not—likely due to lack of resources, and the stigma associated with doing so in Turkish culture.

Fatih, suffers from stomach reflux because of his stress. Currently seeking asylum in Seattle, Washington, he told me, "I'm worried about genocide [in Turkey]. Now neighbors are reporting on their own neighbors. Police will come and arrest them, and no one knows what is happening and no one can say anything about when it will end." He complained, "Our own people hate us. I'm worrying about the future; what will they do? I turn on the news each day and I think this is the worse day, it can't get worse. But every day it does get worse. As a patriotic person, it is really, really hard to leave your country. But it's impossible right now. I can't believe the torture photos online" (personal communication, August 2, 2016).

10.4.6 Dishonor: "This Hurts the Entire Family"

In a Muslim, patriarchal country, an effective fear-creating tactic is to threaten the community's sense of honor. In general, Turkish men are tasked with protecting their wives and children; failing to do so is a dishonor. Many of the men interviewed wept when narrating their devastating inability to protect their wives during the purge. A recurring refrain was that they did not mind being arrested and even tortured, if it meant that their wives and children would remain safe. Since the purge, there has been an increase in the harassment of women in general—but clearly HGM women have been particularly targeted. On February 16, 2019, a movement-affiliated university student, Demirel, took part in a peaceful protest and was sexually assaulted by a police officer (Young Woman Lashes The Perverted Ways Of A Policeman Who Sexually Harassed Her During A Protest 2019). The Ankara police appeared to justify the assault by stating that her "father was a teacher who was dismissed from duty after the 2016 coup attempt," implying that her father was affiliated with the HGM and thus deserved the dishonor of his daughter's assault (Young Woman Lashes The Perverted Ways Of A Policeman Who Sexually Harassed Her During A Protest 2019).

Kader, a 32-year-old married Kurdish woman who worked as a college counselor, confirmed that the government targets women with arrest, mistreatment, and rape, for the express purpose of spreading fear. She said, "I think this is why they arrest pregnant women. Men can bear it, but women are more vulnerable. In jail those children don't see men, and when they are released, they are scared of men" (personal communication, July 12, 2018). Sometimes when the mothers and children are released from jail, the children are afraid of their own fathers, she added.

Her friend Zeynep agreed that the government tries to terrorize women and children first, in order to spread fear in society. She added, "This hurts the entire family. It makes the whole family and society scared. They arrested pregnant women, with babies, or small children. All of those children will never forget this situation, it doesn't matter how old they are. They lost their own freedom, they never got to see the sky, the stars, or even to play in a playground. There are kids in jail that have never been outside, they don't know what it looks like" (personal communication, July 12, 2018).

10.4.7 Interrupted Education

Because of the purge, PKK violence, and the government's denigration of educated people, many intellectuals and promising students have left the country, exacerbating Turkey's brain drain (Bucak 2016). Elif was trying to finish her PhD thesis at HGM-affiliated Fatih University, which was closed by the government after the failed putsch. Her thesis advisor was connected to another university, however, so there was still a small chance she could finish her PhD. Unable to return for her oral defense from the US, that advisor was afraid to continue working with her due to Elif's affiliation with the HGM. "We cut the relationship with my professor," she clarified, "My relationship with the university was cut. I tried to continue here [in the US] but I have a son who was two then, and it was too hard, I was depressed" (personal communication, July 12, 2018). Because of the fear of arbitrary detention, and closure of educational institutions (and deletion of students' records), many students have been unable to complete their education—violating the right to education.

10.5 Gülen on the Purge: "It Is Not That We Are Not Sad; Yes, We Are"

Gülen offered a philosophical interpretation of the ordeal his community is suffering through, reminding his followers to stay firm, remember their blessings from the Divine, and keep in mind that humans cannot understand all of God's actions. During our meeting (with Pandya), he quoted the following verses by the Turkish Sufi Saint İbrahim Hakkı (1703–1780): "In all His acts there is wisdom; God does not act without reason" (Gülen, personal communication, April 24, 2017). According to Gülen, God has favored HGM followers by spreading them throughout the world, giving them the opportunity to present "genuine, non-radical Islam, with an emphasis on interfaith dialogue." He went on to acknowledge that "when you get kicked, no one has the luxury to say that you are not hurt" (personal communication, April 24, 2017).

However, he vigorously maintained that many participants in jail right now were uncomplainingly content with their fate, as the Sufi tradition asks the devout to submit fully to whatever God wills. Yet, he conceded, "It's not that we are not sad; yes, we are." That level of oppression, he pointed out, "surely has some impact on the soul and the thought of a person." He also quoted an Ottoman poet, Keçecizade İzzet Molla (1785–1829): "I would endure suffering, O the light of my eye, but mine is a soul too, after all, it does get tired of suffering" (Gülen, personal communication, April 24, 2017).

Gülen also discussed solutions to the conflict in Turkey, and conflict in general. In a May 15, 2017 op-ed for the Washington Post, he stated he hopes for a new "civilian constitution" in Turkey, involving "all segments of society," and pointed out that

Kurds, Alevis, secularists, academics, journalists, and of course his own movement, have historically suffered persecution at the hands of the Turkish government. He also urged the West to help Turkey turn back towards democracy (Gülen 2017). While hate is the world's greatest problem, Gülen argued, the answer is education. He believes educational curriculum should offer strategies for interpersonal conflict resolution, and include a focus on the contributions the world religions have made towards addressing interpersonal conflict.

10.6 Global Ramifications

Erdoğan's march towards authoritarianism, and the purge as an enabling component of that, must be understood as reflective of the global rise of populist and nationalist politicians, which have recently included Donald Trump, Narendra Modi, Rodrigo Duterte, and others. Those who support conservative populists tend to fear globalization, immigration, intellectualism and the educated elite, and liberal social change. Some are even willing to throw liberal democracy and the protection of individual human rights under the bus in order to feel safe—they would rather trust the leader whose vision they share than work to safeguard individual human rights. As bystanders, they often turn a blind eye to the scapegoating taking place in their respective countries, or sometimes violently take part in it, perhaps because they believe it will make them more secure.

Clearly, Erdoğan benefits, for now, from the fearmongering he has unleashed. Additionally, he is leaning more towards Russia (which supplies most of Turkey's energy), and the Shanghai Cooperation Organization (Wang 2016), and away from the West and NATO. Even if Turkey remains a member of NATO, Erdoğan's behavior could set a precedent for other members, and he could paralyze "all decision-making and effectiveness" by working against NATO from within, as historian Michael Rubin (2017) argues. As Erdoğan becomes more dictator-like, he finds he does not need the West, Turkey's traditional ally. Some in the Arab world, pleased with his aggressive stance with Israel and accommodation of Syrian refugees— Turkey hosts almost four million refugees (United Nations High Commissioner For Refugees 2018) —is supportive of him. Strategically located and an influential player in the Middle East, losing Turkey will cost the West dearly.

Turkey also squanders much. The high number of educators, scholars, journalists, and businessmen currently incarcerated likely makes for some interesting jailhouse conversations, but also means thousands of students have lost their teachers and professors—a large percentage of Turkey's educated class. The HGM's network of educational projects focus on science, math, and technology, Gülen strongly emphasizes learning and teaching as part of one's religious duty. Many students have had to transfer schools or universities, or in some cases found their degrees no longer valid. With at least 123 journalists currently imprisoned, there is no free press in Turkey (Eski 2019). Since 2015, Turkey has earned the dubious distinction of being "the world's worst jailer," having jailed more journalists than any other country (Beiser 2018). Some of the businessmen who left took millions with them, although many lost their fortunes when their assets were seized by the government. Before the failed coup, the HGM also provided educational and charitable resources to the disadvantaged Kurdish communities in Southeast Turkey (Koç 2013). Crushing the HGM might have strengthened Erdoğan, but it robbed Turkey of valuable resources. Even more dangerous is that in the long term, the purge destabilizes Turkey, a country with a history of coups (1960, 1971, 1980, 1997, and failed coups in 2003 and 2016).

Finally, as a pointedly humanitarian group, the HGM has functioned as a buffer against more conservative or extremist forms of Islam. The very names of some of its US-based venues convey this: i.e., "Tolerance Foundation," "Peace Islands," and "Institute for Interfaith Dialogue." HGM activists, who espouse a relatively progressive Sufi form of Islam, counter the global influence of conservative Salafism through promulgating their own interpretation of the faith. Yet the movement does not generate this impact by prioritizing advocacy of an anti-radicalism agenda. Rather, the HGM's interpretation of Islam, and the resulting projects such interpretation inspires, narrows the space for a violent extremist mentality. That impact is not pursued but rather ensued, in a form of "deradicalization by default" (Keles and Sezgin 2015, 27–28). With a clear stance against extremism, the movement, by its sole existence, has served as a formidable barrier against Erdoğan's ambition to monopolize the arena of Islamic thought in Turkey and abroad. The tragedy is not only the violence carried out against those many (if not all) HGM-affiliated individuals who were unaware of any coup plot, but also the weakening of the movement's liberal, reformist, and democracy-supporting influence in the greater Muslim world.

10.7 Conclusions: "We Are Hopeful"

While those interviewed tend to tell me that prayer will heal them, it is unlikely that they will escape these wounds without earthly help as well, such as access to adequate basic resources (food, shelter) including mental health treatment. Judith L. Herman (2015) argues that healing for the victims of collective violence begins when the violence against them is halted, their needs are provided for, and the perpetrators and bystanders of the atrocities have been brought to justice. She also advocates that victims give testimony regarding their experiences, and find a "survivor mission," which can be shared by the traumatized group (Herman 2015, 181, 208, 209, 222). Obviously, until Erdoğan ceases his purge of the movement and removes the terrorist label he affixed to them, those with family members still in Turkey cannot safely speak out. For some, the price of participating in the HGM is simply too high, and they have left.

Shedding light on why and how Erdoğan's government has attempted to destroy the HGM and its institutions in Turkey and abroad also explicates the mechanisms of populism. Populism often leads to fascism, and fascists tend to find a vulnerable group or groups to sacrifice as scapegoats, which they frame as "the dangerous enemy of the people" and "the cause of all the country's problems" to garner support. In Erdoğan's case, he has committed multiple human rights violations. These include the arbitrary arrest of thousands of people, detaining people without just cause, seizing property and institutions, torture, defamation, denial of nationality, invasion of privacy, and using the weapons of intimidation to neutralize the ability of the movement to operate in Turkey. Even if the HGM or even a few dozen HGM activists *had* participated in the coup plot on July 15, 2016, that hardly justifies the arrest and torture of thousands of people, some of whom are only tangentially affiliated with the movement. The corollaries of all of this are grave, and include Turkey's shift away from liberal democracy and the West, its own future destabilization and loss of resources, and the undermining of a faith group that has much to offer. Safiye, 38, a HGM-affiliated teacher who worked in Ankara before fleeing to Seattle, told me: "I feel that we didn't deserve this. I have a feeling of injustice, that it's unfair. But we are hopeful" (personal correspondence, August 3, 2016).

Others interviewed also emphasized hopefulness and the opportunities of diaspora despite their trauma. Fatih, the science teacher and refugee in Seattle, commented (personal correspondence, August 2, 2016), "I'm sure the people in the Hizmet Movement can do great things in the US for humanity and for peace. My life purpose is to do something for humanity. I chose the movement because of this. I'm not sure I can achieve my life's purpose here. But if I get a chance, I'll try. Absolutely."

References

Amnesty International. 2016. *Turkey: State Of Emergency Must Not Roll Back Human Rights*. Https://Www.Amnesty.Nl/Actueel/Turkey-State-Of-Emergency-Must-Not-Roll-Back-Human-Rights.

———. 2017. *Turkey: Independent Monitors Must be Allowed to Access Detainees Amid Torture Allegations*. https://www.amnesty.org/en/latest/news/2016/07/turkey-independent-monitors-must-be-allowed-to-access-detainees-amid-torture-allegations/

———. 2018. *The Aftermath of the Failed Turkey Coup: Torture, Beatings and Rape*. Https://Www.Amnesty.Org.Uk/Aftermath-Failed-Turkey-Coup-Torture-Beatings-And-Rape.

Ateş, Hazal. 2016. *Turkey Takes Action To Freeze FETÖ Assets In 34 Countries*. Daily Sabah, August 16. Https://Www.Dailysabah.Com/Business/2016/08/17/Turkey-Takes-Action-To-Freeze-Feto-Assets-In-34-Countries.

Ayan, Arslan. 2019. An Ontological Reading Of Turkey's AK Party – Gülen Movement Conflict. *E-International Relations*, July 21. Https://Www.E-Ir.Info/2019/07/21/An-Ontological-Reading-Of-Turkeys-Ak-Party-Gulen-Movement-Conflict/.

Baby Accompanying Mother In Prison Joins 700 Other Kids Growing Up Behind Bars. 2019. *Turkish Minute*, May 10. Https://Www.Turkishminute.Com/2019/05/10/Baby-Accompanying-Mother-In-Prison-Joins-700-Other-Kids-Growing-Up-Behind-Bars/.

Badar, Mohamed, Masaki Nagata, and And Tiphanie Tueni. 2017. The Radical Application Of The Islamist Concept Of Takfir. *Arab Law Quarterly* 31 (2): 134–162.

Baker, Peter, and Rosenberg Matthew. 2017. *Michael Flynn was Paid to Represent Turkey's Interests During Trump Campaign*. The New York Times, March 10. Https://Www.Nytimes.Com/2017/03/10/Us/Politics/Michael-Flynn-Turkey.Html.

Baykan, Dildar. 2018. *Over 100 FETO Members Brought Back To Turkey: Cavusoglu*. Anadolu Agency, July 16. Https://Www.Aa.Com.Tr/En/Politics/Over-100-Feto-Members-Brought-Back-To-Turkey-Cavusoglu/1205603.

Beiser, Elana. 2018. *Hundreds Of Journalists Jailed Globally Becomes The New Normal*. Committee To Protect Journalists, December 13. Https://Cpj.Org/Reports/2018/12/Journalists-Jailed-Imprisoned-Turkey-China-Egypt-Saudi-Arabia.Php.

Birnbaum, Michael. 2013. *In Turkey Protests, Splits In Erdogan's Base*. Washington Post, June 14. Https://Www.Washingtonpost.Com/World/Erdogan-Offers-Concessions-To-Turkeys-Protesters/2013/06/14/9a87fff6-D4bf-11e2-A73e-826d299ff459_Story.Html.

Bucak, Selin. 2016. *Purge in Turkey Intensifies Brain Drain*. Financial Times, September 27. Https://Www.Ft.Com/Content/E7142eb6-7e90-11e6-8e50-8ec15fb462f4.

Butler, John, and Dov Friedman. 2016. *The Roots of Gulenist Power in Turkey: The Coup and After*. Foreign Affairs, August 2. Https://Www.Foreignaffairs.Com/Articles/Turkey/2016-08-02/Roots-Gulenist-Power-Turkey.

Butler, Daren and Ali Kucukgocmen. 2018. *Turkish Parliament Passes Security Law to Replace Emergency Rule*. World News, July 25. Https://Www.Reuters.Com/Article/Us-Turkey-Security/Turkish-Parliament-To-Vote-On-Security-Law-To-Replace-Emergency-Rule-Iduskbn1kf0p9.

Bytyci, Fatos. 2018. *Six Turks Arrested in Kosovo Over Gülen Links Extradited to Turkey: Anadolu*. Reuters, March 29. Https://Www.Reuters.Com/Article/Us-Turkey-Security-Kosovo/Six-Turks-Arrested-In-Kosovo-Over-Gulen-Links-Extradited-To-Turkey-Anadolu-Iduskbn1h51jl.

Champion, Marc. 2016. *Sectarian Tension Builds in Turkey as Erdoğan Crackdown Widens*. Bloomberg, July 19. Https://Www.Bloomberg.Com/News/Articles/2016-07-19/Sectarian-Tension-Builds-In-Turkey-As-Erdogan-Crackdown-Widens.

Charmaz, Kathy, and Richard G. Mitchell. 2001. Grounded Theory in Ethnography. In *Handbook of Ethnography*, ed. Paul Atkinson, Amanda Coffey, Sarah Delamont, John Lofland, and Lyn Lofland. Los Angeles: Sage Publications.

Contradicting Earlier Remarks, Erdoğan Denies Existence Of Purge Victims. 2016. *Turkish Minute*, October 22. Https://Www.Turkishminute.Com/2016/10/22/Contradicting-Earlier-Remarks-Erdogan-Denies-Existence-Purge-Victims/.

Cornell, Svante E. 2015. *The Naqshbandi-Khalidi Order and Political Islam in Turkey*. Hudson Institute, September 3. https://www.hudson.org/research/11601-the-naqshbandi-khalidi-order-and-political-islam-in-turkey

Council Of Europe. The Functioning Of Democratic Institutions In Turkey. 2017. *Council of Europe*, April 5. Http://Website-Pace.Net/Documents/19887/3258251/20170308-Turkeyinstitutions-EN.Pdf/Bbd65de5-86d4-466f-9bc1-185d5218bce7.

Doğan, Recep. 2018. The Usage of Excommunication (Takfir) in the Ideology of Justice And Development Party (The AKP), Political Islamists of Turkey. *Macrothink Institute* 6 (2): 54–68. https://doi.org/10.5296/Iss.V6i2.13290.

Eikmeier, Dale C. 2007. Qutbism: An Ideology of Islamic-Fascism. *Parameters* 37 (1).

Energy Minister: Gülenists Are More Dangerous Than ISIL Because They're Well Educated. 2016. *Turkish Minute*, October 7. Https://Www.Turkishminute.Com/2016/10/07/Energy-Minister-Gulenists-Dangerous-Isil-Theyre-Well-Educated/.

Erdem, Umut. 2016. *Diyanet Gathers Intelligence On Suspected Gülenists Via Imams in 38 Countries*. Hürriyet Daily News, December 7. Http://Www.Hurriyetdailynews.Com/Diyanet-Gathers-Intelligence-On-Suspected-Gulenists-Via-Imams-In-38-Countries-107028.

Erdoğan Opens $100mn Turkish Cultural Center In Maryland, Blasts US Elections' Islamophobic Rhetoric. 2016. *RT*, April 3. Https://Www.Rt.Com/Usa/338200-Erdogan-Diyanet-Islamophobic-Elections/.

Ergene, M. Enes. 2008. *Tradition Witnessing the Modern Age: An Analysis of the Gülen Movement*. Somerset: Tughra Books.

Eski, Beril. 2019. *Turkey: The World's Largest Prison for Journalists*. Amnesty International, May 3. Https://Www.Amnesty.Org/En/Latest/News/2019/05/Turkey-The-Worlds-Largest-Prison-For-Journalists/.

European Commission. 2019. *Turkey 2019 Report*. European Commission, May 29. Brussels. Https://Ec.Europa.Eu/Neighbourhood-Enlargement/Sites/Near/Files/20190529-Turkey-Report.Pdf.

Fethullah Gülen: Çapulcu Demeyin. 2013. *Radikal*, June 24. Http://Www.Radikal.Com.Tr/Turkiye/Fethullah-Gulen-Capulcu-Demeyin-1138930/.
Franks, Tim. 2014. Fethullah Gulen: Powerful But Reclusive Turkish Cleric. BBC News, January 27. Https://Www.Bbc.Com/News/World-Europe-25885817.
Gardner, Andrew. 2017. *Turkey: 'Professional Annihilation' of 100,000 Public Sector Workers in Post-Coup Attempt Purge*. Amnesty International, May 22. Https://Www.Amnesty.Org/En/Latest/News/2017/05/Turkey-Professional-Annihilation-Of-100000-Public-Sector-Workers-In-Post-Coup-Attempt-Purge/.
Gelvin, James L. 2018. *The New Middle East: Everything You Need to Know*. Oxford: Oxford University Press.
Germany Investigates Possible Anti-Gülen Spies. 2017. *DW*, February 15. Https://Www.Dw.Com/En/Germany-Investigates-Possible-Anti-Gulen-Spies/A-37557872.
Girard, René. 1986. *The Scapegoat*. Baltimore: The Johns Hopkins University Press.
Göle, Nilüfer. 2013. Gezi-Anatomy of a Public Square Movement. *Insight Turkey* 15 (3): 7–14.
Gülen, Fethullah. 2017. *Fethullah Gülen: The Turkey I No Longer Know*. The Washington Post, May 15. Https://Www.Washingtonpost.Com/Opinions/Global-Opinions/The-Turkey-I-No-Longer-Know/2017/05/15/Bda71c62-397c-11e7-8854-21f359183e8c_Story.Html.
Hart, Kimberly. 2013. *And Then We Work for God: Rural Sunni Women In Western Turkey*. Stanford: Stanford University Press.
Hendrick, Joshua D. 2013. *Gülen: The Ambiguous Politics of Market Islam in Turkey and the World*. New York: New York University Press.
Herman, Judith L. 2015. *Trauma and Recovery: The Aftermath of Violence-From Domestic Abuse to Political Terror*. New York: Basic Books.
Hosseinzadeh, Vahid. 2015. Salafism and Its Socio-Intellectual Foundations. *Humanities & Social Sciences Reviews* 3 (1): 34–37. http://Giapjournals.Com/Index.Php/Hssr/Article/View/242.
Human Rights Watch. 2015. *Turkey: Emergency Decrees Facilitate Torture, Reinstate Safeguards to Curb Abuse by Police. Human Rights Watch*, October 25. Https://Www.Hrw.Org/News/2016/10/25/Turkey-Emergency-Decrees-Facilitate-Torture.
———. 2016. *Turkey: Rights Protections Missing From Emergency Decree: Orders to Purge Civil Servants, Judges; Close Groups Down*. Human Rights Watch, July 25. Https://Www.Hrw.Org/News/2016/07/26/Turkey-Rights-Protections-Missing-Emergency-Decree.
———. 2018. *Turkey: Government Targeting Academics: Dismissals, Prosecutions Create Campus Climate of Fear*. Human Rights Watch, May 14. Https://Www.Hrw.Org/News/2018/05/14/Turkey-Government-Targeting-Academics.
———. 2019a. *Turkey: Events of 2018*. Human Rights Watch: World Report 2019. Https://Www.Hrw.Org/World-Report/2019/Country-Chapters/Turkey.
———. 2019b. *Turkey: State of Emergency Ends, But Not Repression: New System Expands President's Power*. Human Rights Watch, January 17. Https://Www.Hrw.Org/News/2019/01/17/Turkey-State-Emergency-Ends-Not-Repression.
Jenkins, Aric. 2017. *Enes Kanter Detained in Romania Over Canceled Passport*. Time Magazine, May 20. Https://Time.Com/4787350/Enes-Kanter-Detained-Romania-Airport-Turkey/.
Karaveli, Halil. 2010. Referendum Victory Opens the Way for Erdogan's Presidency. *Turkey Analyst* 3 (15) https://Www.Turkeyanalyst.Org/Publications/Turkey-Analyst-Articles/Item/224-Referendum-Victory-Opens-The-Way-For-Erdogans-Presidency.html.
Kazem, Hasnain. 2017. *Global Spying Network: Turkey's Worldwide Monitoring of Suspected Gülen Supporters*. Spiegal Online, March 31. Https://Www.Spiegel.De/International/Europe/Turkey-Spies-On-Suspected-Guelen-Supporters-Around-The-World-A-1141367.Html.
Keles, Ozcan, and Sezgin Ismail Mesut. 2015. *A Hizmet Approach to Rooting Out Violent Extremism*. Centre For Hizmet Studies. Https://Www.Hizmetstudies.Org/Assets/Docs/A-Hizmet-Approach-To-Rooting-Out-Violent-Extremism.Pdf.
Kenyon, Peter. 2018. *Turkey's State of Emergency Ends, While Erdoğan's Power Grows and 'Purge' Continues. NPR*, July 26. Https://Www.Npr.Org/2018/07/26/632307755/Turkeys-State-Of-Emergency-Ends-While-Erdogans-Power-Grows-And-Purge-Continues?T=1582981513403.

Koç, Dogan. 2013. Hizmet Movement's effects on PKK recruitment and attacks. *Turkish Journal Of Politics* 4 (1): 65–84.

Lyons, Matthew N., and Berlet Chip. 2016. *Populism as Core Element of Fascism*. Political Research Associates December 21. Https://Www.Politicalresearch.Org/2016/12/21/Populism-As-Core-Element-Of-Fascism.

Montgomery, Alfred E. 1972. VII. The Making of the Treaty of Sevres of 10 August 1920. *The Historical Journal* 15 (4): 775–787. https://doi.org/10.1017/S0018246x0000354x.

Müller, Jan-Werner. 2014. *Erdoğan and the Paradox of Populism*. Project Syndicate, August 11. Https://Www.Project-Syndicate.Org/Commentary/Jan-Werner-Mueller-Examines-The-Underpinnings-Of-The-New-Turkish-President-S-Political-Staying-Power?Barrier=Accesspaylog.

———. 2016. *Trump, Erdoğan, Farage: The Attractions of Populism for Politicians, the Dangers for Democracy*. The Guardian, September 2. Https://Www.Theguardian.Com/Books/2016/Sep/02/Trump-Erdogan-Farage-The-Attractions-Of-Populism-For-Politicians-The-Dangers-For-Democracy.

Nefes, Türkay Salim. 2015. Understanding Anti-Semitic Rhetoric in Turkey Through the Sevres Syndrome. *Turkish Studies* 16 (4): 572–587. https://doi.org/10.1080/14683849.2015.1084876.

Office Of The United Nations High Commissioner For Human Rights. 2018. *Report on the Impact of the State of Emergency on Human Rights in Turkey,* Including an Update on the South-East January – December 2017. Https://Www.Ohchr.Org/Documents/Countries/TR/2018-03-19_Second_OHCHR_Turkey_Report.Pdf.

Olağanüstü Hal(OHAL). 2019. *Ohalde Kaç Pasaport Iptal Edildi Kaç Kişi Tutuklandı*. Https://Www.Olaganustuhal.Com/Ohal/Haberler/Ohalde-Kac-Pasaport-Iptal-Edildi-Kac-Kisi-Tutuklandi/.

Öniş, Ziya, and Mustafa Kutlay. 2019. Global Shifts and the Limits of the EU's Transformative Power in the European Periphery: Comparative Perspectives From Hungary and Turkey. *Government and Opposition* 54 (2): 226–253.

Operational Portal Refugee Situations. 2019. *Total Registered Syrian Refugees*. Https://Data2.Unhcr.Org/En/Situations/Syria?Id=224.

Özbudun, Ergun. 2014. AKP at the Crossroads: Erdoğans Majoritarian Drift. *South European Society And Politics* 19 (2): 155–167. https://doi.org/10.1080/13608746.2014.920571.

Pahl, Jon. 2019. *Fethullah Gülen: A Life of Hizmet—Why a Muslim Scholar in Pennsylvania Matters to the World*. New Jersey: Blue Dome Press.

Pamuk, Humeyra. 2015. *Update1-Turkish Government Hires UK Law Firm to Probe Cleric's Global Network*. Reuters, October 26. Https://Www.Reuters.Com/Article/Turkey-Politics-Gulen/Update-1-Turkish-Government-Hires-Uk-Law-Firm-To-Probe-Clerics-Global-Network-Idusl8n12q3mv20151026.

Pandya, Sophia. 2017. The Roots of the Turkish Crisis. *Democracy* 43 (1).

Qutb, Sayyid. 2006. In *Milestones*, ed. A.B. Al-Mehri. Birmingham: Maktaba Booksellers and Publishers.

Roberts, Angela Raven. 2017. Women and the Political Economy of War. In *Women and Wars*, ed. C. Cohn. Cambridge: Polity Press.

Ross, Chuck. 2016. *Erdoğan's Daughter Tells US Muslims That Gülen Movement is 'More Dangerous' Than ISIS [VIDEO]*. Daily Caller, December 27. Https://Dailycaller.Com/2016/12/27/Erdogans-Daughter-Tells-Us-Muslims-That-Gulen-Movement-Is-More-Dangerous-Than-Isis-Video/.

Rubin, Michael. 2017. *Turkey's Turn Toward Russia*. National Review, August 25. Https://Www.Nationalreview.Com/2017/04/Turkey-Russia-Recep-Tayyip-Erdogan-Foreign-Policy-Nato-West/.

Saul, Jack. 2014. *Collective Trauma, Collective Healing: Promoting Community Resilience in the Aftermath of Disaster*. New York: Routledge.

Staub, Ervin. 1999. The Origins and Prevention of Genocide, Mass Killing, and Other Collective Violence. *Peace and Conflict: Journal of Peace Psychology* 5 (4): 303–336.

Tee, Caroline. 2016. *The Gulen Movement in Turkey: The Politics of Islam and Modernity*. London: I.B. Tauris.

The UK's Relations With Turkey. 2017. *House of Commons Foreign Affairs Committee,* March 25. *Https://Publications.Parliament.Uk/Pa/Cm201617/Cmselect/Cmfaff/615/615.Pdf.*

Tittensor, David. 2014. *The House of Service: The Gülen Movement and Islam's Third Way*. Oxford: Oxford University Press.

Tol, Gönül. 2014. *The Clash of Former Allies: The AKP Versus the Gulen Movement*. The Middle East Institute, March 7. Https://Www.Mei.Edu/Publications/Clash-Former-Allies-Akp-Versus-Gulen-Movement.

Turkey: The World Factbook. 2016. *Central Intelligence Agency*. Https://Www.Cia.Gov/Library/Publications/Resources/The-World-Factbook/Geos/Tu.Html.

Turkey's Post-Coup Crackdown. 2019. *Turkeypurge*. Https://Www.Turkeypurge.Com/.

Turkish Ruling Party To Leave Liberals Out. 2013. *Hürriyet Daily News,* April 2. Https://Www.Hurriyetdailynews.Com/Turkish-Ruling-Party-To-Leave-Liberals-Out-44082.

Um, Khatharya. 2015. *From the Land of Shadows: War, Revolution, and the Making of the Cambodian Diaspora*. New York: New York University Press.

United Nation Human Rights: Office Of The High Commissioner. 2019. *Arbitrary Detention and the Right to a Fair Trial: UN Experts Find Turkey Violated Human Rights*. ONHRC, May 29. Https://Www.Ohchr.Org/EN/Newsevents/Pages/Displaynews.Aspx?Newsid=24661&Langid=E.

United Nations. 1948. *The Universal Declaration of Human Rights*. Https://Www.Ohchr.Org/EN/UDHR/Documents/UDHR_Translations/Eng.Pdf.

United Nations High Commissioner For Refugees. 2018. *Turkey Factsheet*. United Nations High Commissioner For Refugees. Https://Www.Unhcr.Org/.

United Nations Human Rights Office Of The High Commistioner. 2018. *Turkey: UN Reports Details Extensive Human Rights Violations During Protracted State Of Emergency*. https://www.ohchr.org/EN/NewsEvents/Pages/DisplayNews.aspx?NewsID=22853&LangID=E.

Uras, Umut. 2017. *Turkey Arrests Head of Amnesty Over 'Gülen Links.'* Al Jazeera, June 7. Https://Www.Aljazeera.Com/News/2017/06/Turkey-Arrests-Head-Amnesty-Gulen-Links-170607054123709.Html.

Vela, Justin. 2013. *Analysis: Turkey's Divisive Ergenekon Trial*. Al Jazeera, August 13. Https://Www.Aljazeera.Com/Indepth/Features/2013/08/201381175743430360.Html.

Wang, Lina. 2016. *Will Turkey Join the Shanghai Cooperation Organization Instead of the EU?* The Diplomat, November 24. Https://Thediplomat.Com/2016/11/Will-Turkey-Join-The-Shanghai-Cooperation-Organization-Instead-Of-The-Eu/.

What Is Leading Turks To Deism?. 2018. *Ahval News,* April 21. Https://Ahvalnews.Com/Religion/What-Leading-Turks-Deism.

Yavuz, M. Hakan. 2018. Alternative Coup Scenarios? In *Turkey's July 15th Coup: What Happened and Why*, ed. M. Hakan Yavuz and Bayram Balci. Salt Lake City: University Of Utah Press.

Yilmaz, Ihsan. 2018. Potential Impact of the AKP's Unofficial Islamist Law on the Radicalization of the Turkish Muslim Youth in the West. In *Theological and Sociological Perspectives on Terrorism and Violent Extremism*, ed. Z. Keskin and F. Mansouri, 163–182. Singapore: Palgrave.

Young Woman Lashes the Perverted Ways of a Policeman Who Sexually Harassed Her During a Protest. 2019. *IPA News,* February 21. Https://Ipa.News/2019/02/19/Young-Woman-Lashes-The-Perverted-Ways-Of-A-Policeman-Who-Sexually-Harassed-Her-During-A-Protest/.

Sophia Pandya is a professor and department chair at California State University at Long Beach, in the Department of Religious Studies. Winner of the 2016 Advancement of Women Award at CSULB from the President's Commission on the Status of Women, she received her BA from UC Berkeley in Near Eastern Studies/Arabic, and her MA and PhD from UC Santa Barbara in Religious Studies. A Fulbright Scholar, she specializes in women and Islam, and more broadly in contemporary movements within Islam. Dr. Pandya has authored a book (2012), *Muslim Women and Islamic Resurgence: Religion, Education, and Identity Politics in Bahrain*, on Bahraini women and the ways in which globalization and modern education impacted their religious activities. Having carried out research in Turkey on several occasions, she is also the co-editor of a second published volume (2012), *The Gülen Hizmet Movement and its Transnational Activities: Case Studies on Charitable Activism.* Dr. Pandya has also published about the Hizmet movement and its relationship to the Kurdish community, "Hizmet Educational Institutions and the Kurdish Community: Assimilation vs. Identity Politics," and an article about family and gender in wartime Yemen, "The War Took Us Backwards": Yemeni Families and Dialectical Patriarchal Reordering." She is currently working on a book on the stories of Turkish refugees, and the meanings they find or construct from their ordeal.

Brenda Oliden received her Master's Degree from California State University at Long Beach in Religious Studies. Her emphasis was in contemporary Islam and diasporas. Ms. Oliden's research on the Syrian refugees placed her on the list of distinguished scholars and artists at her university. She conducted 5 months of independent, field research for her thesis in Jordan. Her thesis, titled, "The Syrian Refugees in Jordan: Negotiating Diasporic Identity Through Sacred Symbols," highlighted the desire for migrants to connect symbolically to their homeland while reinforcing their diasporic identity in their host land. Ms. Oliden has presented her research at several conferences. For example, she presented "Islam and Diaspora Negotiating New Centers" at the Pacific Coast Regional Conference of the American Academy of Religion (2014). Ms. Oliden has guest-lectured on several occasions, on subjects such as "Syncretism in Islam" and "Violence in Religion."

Ibrahim Aytac Anli received his BA degree in Economics from Istanbul University in 1999. Anli completed the MA program in Conflict Analysis and Resolution at Sabancı University, Istanbul in 2007. During the academic year of 2007–2008, he was a visiting graduate student at the Hebrew University of Jerusalem where he learned Hebrew and conducted research on conflict. Ibrahim Anli joined the Journalists and Writers Foundation's (JWF) Ankara office as diplomacy coordinator in 2010. In 2013 he became the secretary general of Abant Platform, JWF's Istanbul based forum of intellectuals, and worked at that position until he left Turkey in July 2016. During the academic year of 2016–2017, he was a full time lecturer and acting chair at the International Relations and Diplomacy Department of Ishik University in Erbil, Kurdistan Region of Iraq. Ibrahim Anli was an active member of Bosporus-Atlantic Association through 2006–2016, an Istanbul based civil society organization dedicated to improving Turkish-American relations through citizen diplomacy. He was also a board member of the Center for Peace and Conflict at the Istanbul Institute for Social, Economic and Political Research. Anli is currently a board member of the New York based Journalists and Writers Foundation and exectuive director of the DC based Rumi Forum. Anli was a regular contributor for the online edition of Istanbul based English daily Today's Zaman, writes on his independent blog, and has published articles in scholarly journals.

Chapter 11
The Cases of Dismissal Under State of Emergency (OHAL): The Right to a Fair Trial as a Human Right

Ufuk Yesil

Abstract After the coup attempt in Turkey on July 15, 2016, more than 125,000 public servants were dismissed from their professions without any concrete justification, and their names were published in lists announced by Decree-Laws associated with the state of emergency (Emergency Decree-Laws, Decree-Laws) along with the decisions that they would not be reinstated in the future. These individuals were accused of being members of a terrorist organization, and rights guaranteed by the European Convention on Human Rights (ECHR, Convention) were not afforded to them. Furthermore, the presumption of innocence was violated, and even their fundamental right to defend themselves was not granted. Because they were officially classified as terrorists, they became isolated from social life, and in practice, were sentenced to "civil death." This study focuses on the denial of fundamental rights, including that of a fair trial.

Keywords State of emergency · Decree-Law · Dismissal · Presumption of innocence · Right to a fair trial · Right to defense

11.1 Introduction

Based on Emergency Decree-Laws after the failed coup attempt in Turkey on July 15, 2016, and contingent on the decisions of the National Security Council (Milli Güvenlik Kurulu, NSC),[1] more than 125,000 persons who were alleged to be members of, or affiliated with, the so-called terrorist organizations, were dismissed

[1]The NSC has the mission of "informing the President about the recommendations on determination, identification and implementation of state's national security and providing the necessary coordination" by Article 118/3 of the Constitution of the Republic of Turkey (Altıparmak 2017a; Ardıçoğlu 2017).

U. Yesil (✉)
Independent Researcher and Human Rights Activist, Istanbul, Turkey

H. Aydin, W. Langley (eds.), *Human Rights in Turkey*, Philosophy and Politics - Critical Explorations 15, https://doi.org/10.1007/978-3-030-57476-5_11

from public office. Due to the Emergency Decree-Laws, 3122 institutions and foundations were closed (1748 associations and charitable foundations, 834 educational institutions, 49 health foundations, 109 student dorms and pensions, 15 private universities, 19 labor unions, union federations and confederations, 34 TV channels, 34 radio channels, 65 newspapers, 5 news agencies, 29 publishing houses, 19 journals) and 985 commercial businesses were transferred to the Savings Deposit Insurance Fund (Altıparmak 2017a).

People who have suffered as a result of grievances due to decisions related to the issuance of the Decree-Laws have applied to administrative institutions, the Constitutional Court, the European Court of Human Rights (ECtHR), and administrative and judicial authorities, for the nullification of the transactions. Very few of the applications to the administrative institutions were accepted, the decisions having been annulled (Bianet 2018). Applications to administrative courts and the Council of State have been rejected because the decisions were based on State Decree-Law, and as a result of this, no case could be filed against them (Altıparmak 2017b; Ardıçoğlu 2017; Kaboğlu 2017; Kaboğlu and Palluel 2018; State Council 2016). Additionally, applications made to the Constitutional Court were found to be inadmissible on the grounds of the failure to exhaust domestic remedies under the state of emergency (Remziye Duman 2017), and the applications made to the ECtHR were rejected because administrative, judicial and subsequent individual remedies, were not exhausted before the establishment of the State of Emergency Commission (Akif Zihni v. Turkey 2016; Altıparmak 2017b; Kaboğlu 2017; Kaboğlu and Palluel 2018). After the establishment of the Commission, applications were rejected because no applications were made to the Commission, which was an unprecedented reason for rejection (Altıparmak 2017b; Ardıçoğlu 2017; Gökhan Köksal v. Turkey 2017; Kaboğlu and Palluel 2018).

The definition of "membership, affiliation, contact and liaison with the structures, entities, and groups that operate against the national security of the state" in Emergency Decree-Laws is addressed in Turkish Criminal Code (Official Gazette 2004) as "membership in a terrorist organization" and in the Convention as "a criminal charge" (Albayrak 2013; Altıparmak 2017c). The crimes committed against the security of the state are regulated in Article 302 and the following articles of the Turkish Penal Code are subject to heavy penal sanctions. For a group or organization to be identified as a terrorist organization and for individuals to be identified as members of that organization, a final court decision must be made since the administrative committee of the NSC cannot legally make such a decision (Artuk et al. 2013; Özgenç 2017). With the issuance of the Decree-Laws related to terrorist organizations, as well as membership in those organizations, the principles embedded in the Turkish Criminal Code and the Convention were abandoned.

Hence, the Decree-Laws established processes without proper administrative actions, disciplinary procedures, or the right to a defense in a fair trial to those concerned (Aydin and Avincan 2020). This situation has led to much discussion and criticism. For example, the 2016 European Union Progress Report, the Venice Commission's Report (OHAL Önlemleri Sınırları Aştı 2016; OHAL Tedbirleri Anayasaya Aykırı! 2016), and the 2016 Human Rights Report of the United States

Department of Foreign Affairs (Cumhuriyet Gazetesi 2017), intensely criticized Turkey for the Decree-Laws.

The European Union Progress Report noted that these Decree-Laws had caused setbacks in the Judiciary, evidenced when one fifth of judges and prosecutors were dismissed after the coup attempt, action plans on implementation of fundamental rights to prevent violations of the ECHR were limited, and no progress was made in the field of justice and fundamental rights (European Commission 2016).

The Venice Commission Report emphasized that Turkish authorities had enough reason to declare a state of emergency after July 15, however, the measures the Turkish government had taken went beyond that which the Turkish Constitution and international law permitted. The measures taken in Turkey were geared toward the dismissal of public servants, not their suspension, and liquidating institutions, not controlling them. Although the verdicts of the Constitution in the proclamation of the state of emergency seem to be in line with European standards, the Turkish government used extraordinary powers to discredit individuals. Moreover, the mass dismissals of individuals lacked evidence. The expedited list preparation revealed that not even minimum assurances of due process were adhered to, and the dismissals were not open to judicial review by the ordinary courts. According to the Commission, the immense terminations by the state displayed powerful arbitrariness, and even if the assumption could be made that the Gülen network was behind the failed coup, those who were merely related to the network should not have been the targets of criminal and disciplinary action (Venice Commission Report 2017).

The 2016 Human Rights Report of the United States Department of Foreign Affairs indicated that the government closed press organizations and broadcasting corporations, raided media companies, dismissed more than 3000 judiciary members, and restricted judicial independence. Furthermore, the government linked hundreds of businesses to the Gülen Movement and confiscated their assets. The confiscated assets totaled more than fifteen billion dollars, and the closures included more than 195 media companies (Cumhuriyet Gazetesi 2017).

This study discusses whether the imposed sanctions were of a criminal nature, whether they were concerned with civil rights and whether they complied with the presumption of innocence, access to a court, and fair trial and defense rights in an independent court.

Although many articles of the Convention were violated as a result of the imposed sanctions, this study is confined to matters under the right to a fair trial. However, before examining explanations pertaining to this right, a brief overview provides insight into the compliance of Turkey's declaration of derogation from the Convention provisions with Article 15 of the Convention. This overview highlights similarities and differences between the measures of dismissal through the Emergency Decree-Laws and post-Communist public cleansing (lustration) procedures in the Central European countries.

11.2 Compliance of the Derogation Regime with the Convention

Matters on which particular emphasis are to be placed in this study are the appropriateness of derogation by Turkey from the Convention provisions on the basis of Article 15 of the ECHR on July 21, 2016 and which path the ECtHR would follow about that issue. In time of war or other public emergency threatening the life of the nation, any High Contracting Party may take measures derogating from its obligations under this Convention. These derogations must be in accordance with Article 15 of the Convention, with the exemption of Articles 2, 3, 4, and 7 of the Convention to the extent strictly required by the exigencies of the situation, provided that such measures are not inconsistent with its other obligations under international law (Önok 2016, 109).

Although the margins of appreciation of the contracting parties are widened by the declaration of the state of emergency, this does not mean that they can do anything. Since there are rights whose essence cannot be violated in such a period, when limiting rights and freedoms, they should be treated proportionately (Aksoy v. Turkey 1996; Cyber Rights 2017; Önok 2016, 136). For this reason, the restriction power of the state to the rights and freedoms is limited by international law. Accordingly, the limitation on rights and freedoms should only be to the extent strictly required by the situation. That is, the objective criterion for the measures to be implemented during the state of emergency is not the "*subjective assessment*" of the state implementing them, but the "*necessity.*" In other words, the measures taken during this period should be necessitated in order to eliminate the situation causing the state of emergency. Thus, derogation for reasons other than that purpose may be in violation of Article 18 of the Convention (Bayar 2013, 104; Harris et al. 2014, 643–644; Önok 2016, 119).

Another point regarding the compatibility of the Emergency Degree-Laws with Article 15 of the ECHR is that the obligation enshrined from the international law should not be breached. That is, introduced restrictions should be compatible with the international law and conventions to which Turkey is a party. The determination of this compatibility depends on the interpretation of the article according to universal standards (Önok 2016, 124).

In accordance with Article 15 of the ECHR, the relevant contracting party should notify Secretary-General of the Council of Europe of the measures taken and their reasons. However, the ECtHR has the power to evaluate the compliance of the measures taken with Article 15 of the Convention. In making this assessment, the Court examines the existence of an emergency situation threatening the life of the nation, whether the measures taken are to the extent required by the exigencies of the situation, and whether they constitute a violation of other obligations enshrined from international law. In other words, the court has the authority to examine the margin of appreciation for the existence of the circumstances of the measures. In exercising that authority, it reviews the nature of the rights subject to the measure, the circumstances leading to the measure, and the duration of the measure (Aksoy

v. Turkey 1996; Sevtap 2017, 116). Furthermore, following the state of emergency declared by the contracting parties, it is imperative to clear the following three points pertaining to the derogation from the Convention: the necessity of the derogation from the Convention, the proportionality between danger and measures taken, and how long the provisions of the Convention will be derogated.

A letter sent by Turkey to the Secretary-General of the Council of Europe made general notifications, but did not specify which articles it was derogating. Thus, there was a desire to retain the opportunity to make a separate derogation defense for each complaint (Önok 2016, 110). However, considering the ECtHR's past case laws (Aksoy v. Turkey 1996; Elçi and Others v. Turkey 2003; Nuray Şen v. Turkey 2003) pertaining to the derogation from the Convention and the case law that states that detentions made after July 15, 2016 are not in line with the exigencies of the situation (Alparslan Altan v. Turkey 2019; Şahin Alpay v. Turkey 2018; Mehmet Hasan Altan v. Turkey 2018), it is thought that it will reject the Turkish declaration of derogation in the case of dismissal. Furthermore, it will determine which regulations that are based on the Emergency Decree-Laws are contrary to the Convention (Türmen 2016, 13).

Considering its well established case laws, it is thought that the ECtHR will question the existence of three points relating to the measure of dismissal from public office: (1) Whether the derogation notice made by the government includes a dismissal from public office, (2) Whether the measure taken is required by the exigencies of the situation, (3) Whether the rights that cannot be derogated under Article 15/2 of ECHR are affected by the measure.

The derogation notice of the Government did not include that more than a hundred thousand public officials would be dismissed, nor that the measures in question went beyond the notice in terms of *ratione materiae* (Sakık and Others v. Turkey 1997, 39; Cyber Rights 2017). Furthermore, the Emergency Decree-Laws did not provide for a standard regarding what the criteria were, nor did they prove that the individuals were in contact with an organization deemed sufficient for dismissal from the profession. Moreover, none of the procedures relating to persons subject to a special investigation were followed, no personalization was made, and everyone who was dismissed was treated the same (Önok 2016, 136).

The measures in the study do not meet the criteria of being "*to the extent required by circumstances,*" which is the second element of the derogation of rights. As the United Nations Human Rights Committee has stated, the measures to be taken in the state of emergency should be exceptional and temporary. However, the members of the judiciary who are subject to the measures have been dismissed from public office completely, barred from performing public duties and almost left to "*civic death*" (Cyber Rights 2017; Human Rights Committee 2001).

Furthermore, the measures imposed are not in line with the "*requirements of the conditions*" in terms of the *ratione materiae*. The cause of the state of emergency is a coup attempt by a group of soldiers in the army, and there is no evidence that the dismissed public officers participated in this attempted coup or that they resorted to violence. Under these circumstances, it is not plausible to imply that the measure imposed by derogation of the fair trial principles is in accordance with Article 15 of the Convention (Cyber Rights 2017; Önok 2016, 137).

Moreover, the decisions of dismissal are in contravention of the prohibition in Article 15/2 of the Convention. For this reason, in accordance with this prohibition, it is not allowed to derogate at the time of a state of emergency from Article 7 of the Convention, envisaging that no punishment can be imposed without law. Nevertheless, concepts of "*connection*" and "*affiliation*" that were not existing in our legislation have been introduced with the Emergency Decree-Laws, issued after July 15. There is no clarity as to whether these concepts are subject to criminal or disciplinary investigation, nor is it clear what actions of people will be evaluated in this context (Judgement of TCC 1988; Özgenç 2017, 89).[2] Furthermore, since the NSC decisions are confidential, it is not possible for people to identify which structures and formations mentioned in these decisions are harmful to the national security of the state (Özgenç 2017, 84), and they are not included in any of the Emergency Decree-Law-Laws. Again, the persons were not informed about which structure they were in connection or affiliation with. Therefore, this approach has forced people to accept the blame and then formulate a defense related to that offence accordingly (Altıparmak 2017c, 6–7). An intervention that results in the termination of public office or the closure of institutions must have a basis in domestic law, and those persons it concerns should be able to access the law and foresee the consequences of

[2]*The administration has the authority to impose sanctions on those who are governed due to relationship of the administration. This authority, which is the source of disciplinary law, is used in areas regulated by law within the framework of the Constitution as well as in conditions determined by law. For sanctions, which are generally considered to be a disciplinary penalty, with the types, methods, reasons of application and consequences determined by regulatory procedures, the administration shall be authorized by the rules of procedure. Without legal determination and justification, the administration cannot, in its sole discretion, recognize that any conduct requires sanctions and cannot rule on this issue. Administrative sanctions are mandatory ones for the supervision of management's decisions and operations. Offences and punishments thereof can be imposed by law in accordance with the Constitution. While spontaneous crime and punishment were also determined to be acts of non-compliance or failure to succeed, the administration did not define non-compliance, nor did it disclose which actions would be considered 'non-compliance'. The concept of 'non-compliance', whose content is suitable for wide and varied interpretation, may cause inequality, contradiction and injustice based on differences of understanding, interpretation and evaluation in the implementation of the disciplinary penalties related to it. It gives the management a wide margin of appreciation that will turn it into arbitrariness at any time. In accordance with the principle of 'no crime/punishment without law (nullum crimen nulla poena sine lege), in a state of law, the definition of every act connected to criminal sanction must be made and the crimes must be revealed in a definite manner. The essence of the mentioned principle is that the law states, without doubt, what actions it prohibits, and accordingly its punishment is determined by the law. Article 38 of the Constitution entitled 'Principles relating to offences and penalties' provides that "No one shall be punished for any act which does not constitute a criminal offence under the law in force at the time committed; no one shall be given a heavier penalty for an offence other than the penalty applicable at the time when the offence was committed". The law under review not only created a violation of Article 38 of the Constitution by regulating a sanction of "non-compliance with the in-service training program" but also it did not specify which of the penalties would be imposed in which circumstances, and thus gave the administration a wide margin of appreciation and thereby, it is contradicted with paragraph 3 of Article 38 of the Constitution reads "Penalties, and security measures in lieu of penalties, shall be prescribed only by law.*

the intervention (Altıparmak and Akdeniz 2017a, 8; Mutlu et al. 2012, 100; Özpınar v. Turkey 2010, 52). However, the arrangements made with the Emergency Decree-Laws are not foreseeable for the intervention in question, and the concepts introduced are suitable to be interpreted in a way that includes all kinds of events.

Interfering in the professional and private lives of public officials with ambiguous statements, contrary to the principle of foreseeability, results in disproportionate consequences. Furthermore, there is no clarity as to whether the concepts introduced by the Decree-Laws are related to the private or professional lives of those concerned. Since public officials have an obligation to isolate themselves from groups that defy the constitutional order, there is no harm in punishing those who act contrary to this obligation. However, the punishment of persons with ambiguous and abstract concepts not found in the previous legal regulations, which give the administration an unsupervised and broad discretion on the violation of this obligation, is not compatible with the legitimate purpose pursued by the state (Al Nashif v. Bulgaria 2002, 119–124). Succinctly, the concepts that express the connections amongst the structures stated which aim to eliminate the constitutional order, should be revealed with objectivity and certainty that would be void of any doubt (Judgement of TCC 2016).[3]

[3]"*…In terms of administrative offences where the principle of No Punishment Without Law" is applied more flexible, it is not sufficient that the regulations relating to crimes and punishments are included only in the text of the law. …These arrangements should also be conducive to achieving a specific purpose in terms of content. In this respect, the text of the law should be written at a level that allows individuals to predict with certain clarity and certainty which concrete acts and facts are imposed by which legal sanction or linked to which outcome. Therefore, within a certain certainty, individuals should know which action is imposed by which legal sanction, and the consequences of the actions should be foreseen for them. Disciplinary penalties are legally regulated administrative sanctions imposed in the event of a breach of the code of conduct which appears in the form of doing or not doing, prescribed for the purpose of ensuring the proper conduct of public services. The duties, powers and responsibilities of those who carry out public services are restricted by public service and service requirements, and those who go beyond these limits are punished with disciplinary penalties provided for in the related laws. Disciplinary actions of members of the police are among the matters which must be stipulated by law in accordance with the above provisions of the Constitution. Although the law specifies the types of disciplinary penalties, the authorities authorized to impose disciplinary penalties and the procedure for, the only criteria introduced by the rule stipulating that disciplinary actions requiring the imposition of such penalty shall be established by statute is that "consideration of the importance and characteristics of the policing profession", no rule other than this was not included. As is, there is no legal guarantee for members of the police is available regarding disciplinary actions. The contested provision does not set out the general principles of disciplinary actions, nor does outline the framework, and nor does determine the acts that require disciplinary actions even if in general terms. Due to its mentioned characteristics, the contested provision which regulates that the acts and behaviors which require disciplinary action are regulated by the concerned regulation does not set out the acts subject to the penalty in the legal level and it does not allow individuals to predict with a certain clarity and certainty which legal sanction or outcome is connected to which concrete acts and facts. In this aspect, the provision is found to be contrary with "the principle of legality" enshrined in Article 38 of the Constitution and the principle of legal regulation enshrined in Article 128 of the Constitution.*

The Venice Commission stated that the Decree-Laws mentioned the relation, connection, membership, affiliation and contact. Hence, based on these comprehensive definitions which identify links to a criminal organization, people are dismissed from the profession. However, these criteria are determined by the administrative authorities who issue the Decree-Laws, but are not explained in judicial decisions. It further added that rather than being implemented with personalization, they are implemented based on evidence; that this connection may be subject to criminal investigation only if it is involved in the attempted coup; and that the investigative authorities should distinguish between those involved in illegal activities and those who sympathize or support the movement. Thus, implicating that terrorism charges will not be applied for acts before the July 15. Considering the aforementioned considerations, it is recommended that the wording in the Decree-Law be changed accordingly "*dismissal can only be ruled on the basis of the combination of de facto elements that clearly show that the public official acted in a way that objectively cast serious doubt on his loyalty to the democratic legal order.*" (Altıparmak and Akdeniz 2017a, 10; Muižnieks 2016, 21–22; Venice Commission 2017, 445–446).

Moreover, the actions taken and decisions rendered, based on the Emergency Decree-Laws, punished persons that it concerned, for conduct that occurred before the regulation was made, thereby violating the principle of non-retroactivity of crimes and punishments (Aydin and Avincan 2020). The most important indicator of this situation is that people who had not been subject to any disciplinary investigations related to their actions prior to the coup attempt, have been dismissed from their profession based on the Emergency Decree-Laws, for those actions (Gergerlioğlu 2019, 945; Sevdiren 2018, 131). In addition, the rendered decisions have had negative consequences on the careers of those involved and resulted in proactive consequences such as not being allowed to hold public office again, as well as the cancellation of gun licenses and passports.

However, the evidence and basis of the elements of the crime of membership or leadership to a terrorist organization, that is to be put forward against individuals, must be relevant after July 15, 2016. Furthermore, in accordance with the principles of the rule of law and legal security and the principle of individual criminal responsibility and principle of non-retroactivity of the crime and punishment (Council of Europe 1996), the persons concerned cannot be held responsible in the sense of criminal law for their activities prior to the date when the so-called "*Cemaat*" was declared a terrorist organization. In order for the crime of a terrorist organization to be committed, individuals need to provide support to a structure knowing that it is a terrorist organization and be willing to participate. Therefore, this crime cannot be committed by negligence. As stated by the Venice Commission and the Council of Europe Human Rights Commissioner, the date to be considered for the charge of terrorism is July 15, 2016. Activities prior to this date cannot constitute a basis for this crime, and persons who have nothing to do with the coup attempt cannot be punished for terrorism charges according to their activities prior to this date. In addition, criminal laws are interpreted broadly and arbitrarily, and legal activities are considered a crime. Moreover, sanctions imposed on persons result in a violation of the principle of no crime/punishment without law (nullum crimen nulla poena sine lege) (Sevdiren 2018, 133; S.W. v. The United Kingdom 1995). In brief, since the actions were taken and decisions were made based on the NSC decision, as well as with the Emergency Decree-Laws, they are not predictable, they have retroactive effects for the crimes and punishments, and they are incompatible with Article 38/1 of the Constitution, Article 7/1 of the ECHR. and Article 7/1 of the Turkish Penal Code.

11.3 The Emergency Decree-Laws vis a vis Cleansing (Lustration) Acts

In general terms, cleansing acts are specific laws scrutinizing whether public officers acted in concert with the regime, led to human rights violations and complied with their obligation to remain loyal to the Constitution (Horne 2009, 714). These laws commonly consist of two sections: matters, which are included in the first section and cleansing procedures, which are mentioned in the second section. These laws are aimed at the acts of constructive dismissals, thereby stipulating which matters would be examined in respect to individuals as well as how the cleansing would be carried out (David 2003, 388).

According to the "Guiding Principles" (Council of Europe 1996; Cyber Rights 2017) prepared by the Parliamentary Assembly of the Council of Europe (PACE), the measures to dismantle the heritage of former communist totalitarian systems in Eastern European countries should be in accordance with the principles of the rule of law. These principles are taken into account by the ECtHR and the Venice Commission. The dismissal measure should be limited to those who are responsible for the deterioration of public order and national security, or who perform such functions. That is, those who use public power to commit crimes that result in human rights violations (Cyber Rights 2017).[4]

[4]The guiding principles of the PACE provide that the following must be respected in the process of purification: A democratic state based on the rule of law has sufficient means at its disposal to ensure that the cause of justice is served and the guilty are punished and it cannot, and should not, however, cater to the desire for revenge instead of justice. It must instead respect human rights and fundamental freedoms, such as the right to due process and the right to be heard, and it must apply them even to those people who, when they were in power, did not apply them themselves (P. 4). These measures can be compatible with a democratic state under the rule of law if several criteria are met. Firstly, guilt, being individual, rather than collective, must be proven in each individual case. Secondly, the right of defense, the presumption of innocence until proven guilty, and the right to appeal to a court of law must be guaranteed. Revenge may never be a goal of such measures (P. 12). In addition to these, the following points should be observed: "***a.*** *Lustration process should be carried out by independent commissions established specifically.* ***b.*** *Lustration measures can only be used to reduce the serious threat posed to the democratic order by the person who uses his position to commit human rights violations or to obstruct the democratization process and only to that persons* ***c.*** *lustration cannot be used for punishing, paying or revenge purposes. Sentencing can be carried out as per the criminal laws and in accordance with the rules of Criminal Procedure.* ***d.*** *Lustration should only be applied in institutions such as law enforcement, security, intelligence and the judiciary, where there are good grounds for grave danger to human rights and democracy,*

Relative to the present case, the soldiers who attempted a coup, as well as the people who assisted the attempt, can be considered in this context. However, it cannot be mandated in a democratic society for people, other than those involved, to be dismissed and banned from holding public office again. The measure of dismissal from public office, which is applied without personalization, taking into account only the period in which the person has served and without any investigation of personal fault, is contrary to the ECHR (Adamsons v. Latvia 2008, 125; Altıparmak 2017d, 6). Since the procedures for the dismissal from public office is similar to the criminal law, the personal fault of those concerned must be investigated. The ECtHR found that all procedures covering all persons, regardless of the level of contact with the KGB, were contrary to the ECHR (Altıparmak 2017d, 6; Soro v. Estona 2015; Zickus v. Lithuania 2009, 33). Moreover, they were found to be in breach of the Convention. However, the persons who were dismissed had not committed a crime, nor had they caused a violation of human rights. Rather, they held differing opinions and beliefs or were members of an association, and by referencing the PACE principles, were asked if they were willing participants or if they were forced to cooperate with the communist regime (Altıparmak 2017d, 6; Aydin and Avincan 2020; Ivanovski v. Macedonia 2016, 117).

A recent judgment of the ECtHR on the matter is about Ukraine (Polyakh and Others v. Ukraine 2019). In the case giving rise to the judgment, the newly established government following Ukrainian President Viktor Yanukovych's resignation in 2014, enacted the *"Government Cleansing (Lustration) Act"* on the dismissal of different categories of civil servants. This Act paved the way for the dismissal of career civil servants (judiciary, police, intelligence etc.), as well as those who held important posts in the Communist Party, for at least one year between 2010 and 2014 when Yanukovych was president. It was aimed by the Act to dismiss public officers who facilitated, by their action or inaction, Yanukovych to usurp all powers, undermine national security and violate human rights (Art. 2). According to the Act, all officers working at those units would file a declaration with their superiors on whether they fell under the Act or not. Consequently, those who failed to do so were dismissed. Moreover, the names of those dismissed on the basis of the Act would be published in the Lustration Register, a publicly accessible online database maintained by the Ministry of Justice. Furthermore, persons who were dismissed would be banned from public service for a period of 5–10 years.

i.e. those who conduct and implement government policies and practices relating to internal security, and where human rights violations are ordered and/or committed. ***g.*** *Dismissal due to the lustration should not last more than 5 years, as changes in one's personal attitude and habits must be taken into account.* ***m.*** *In no way should a person be subjected to a process of lustration without granting all guarantees of a fair trial, including, but not limited to, the right to access to counsel (with legal assistance in cases where the person's condition does not allow), the right to oppose the evidence presented against him, the right to access all incriminating evidence, the right to present his own evidence, the right to an open trial if he wishes and the right to appeal to an impartial tribunal."*

Contrary to *"lustration acts"* previously enacted in Central and East European countries, the ECtHR noted that the Act did not solely target security officers in totalitarian regimes. Rather, it targeted all public officers in legitimate democratic institutions, thereby officers, including the applicants, were collectively held responsible for all wrongful practices carried out in Yanukovych's time, without any individualization. Furthermore, it emphasized that *"lustration acts"* could not seek the purposes of punishment or revenge. It concluded that the applied measures were not necessary in a democratic society, stating that the same aim could have been achieved with more lenient measures such as dismissing or appointing to less important posts, the individuals who had participated in crimes. Therefore upholding that there had been a violation of the applicants' right to respect for private life. The ECtHR included the following points in its judgment:

It is established by a number of international reports that Yanukovych's rule had a bad record in terms of rule of law and human rights, and this government had engaged in large-scale anti-democratic practices and corruption (par. 284–286). Accordingly, it could be argued that the new-coming government's will to deal with officers having worked under such a rule, had a legitimate purpose. Yet, this purpose was exceeded by the new government and therefore, it could not be inferred that the Act was in line with the pursued aim (par. 287).

Furthermore, given the President who enabled the law to be enforced had operated for 9 months under the terms of the former government, it is not plausible to understand how that goal, expected from lustration, could be achieved by cleansing officials at lower posts (par. 302).

However, it is unclear how the main criterion to work at least for 1 year from 2010 to 2014 was set, or why the period between 1991 and 2010 was excluded (par. 301). The applicants were expelled exclusively for occupying relatively high-ranking public positions in the period of 2010–2014. One of the applicants was accused of misconduct after his dismissal. However, there was not an investigation conducted at the time of his dismissal and therefore, could not be relied on for a justification of his dismissal (par. 305). Regardless, this did not alter the decision pertaining to his unjustified dismissal (par. 294).

Similarly, the Ukrainian government should have reasoned its claim that individualization was not possible under the circumstances of the state of emergency and the Russian occupation of Ukrainian territory. For this reason, even though the state of emergency was declared and this ground was put forward, the dismissal act was be applicable for 10 years and there was no indication that the need would remain throughout the 10-year period (par. 307).

By the same token, although convincing material evidence should have been provided in relation to the fact that the applicants had acted in breach of democratic principles of the state or that they were engaged in corruption (par. 296), the applicants' actions against national security, democratic governance, and/or the rule of law or human rights were not established. Therefore, there was no evidence that any of them had been involved in Yanukovych's alleged wrongful acts (par. 304). Moreover, their names were disclosed to the public even before they made use of their legal rights, and their appeals against the judgements took a long time (par. 308).

11.4 Comparison Between the Government Cleansing Act and the Emergency Legislative Decree-Laws

1. The Government Cleansing Act in Ukraine was applied to a limited number of public officers who worked within judiciary, police and intelligence units, as well as to those who had occupied important positions at the Communist Party. Regardless, 125 thousand public officers were dismissed irrespective of their professions, and thousands of institutions and establishments were closed down as a result of the Emergency Decree-Laws.

The government aimed solely to dismiss individuals, who by their action or inaction, undermined national security or violated human rights. However, the Emergency Decree-Laws used lists compiled through unknown means, and void of any criteria, to dismiss individuals from public service. Even though the ECtHR noted that arrangements such as cleansing acts could not pursue the aim of punishment and revenge (Council of Europe 1996), the implications of the provisions allowed for the dismissal of individuals involved in irregularities, as well as for reappointing them to less important posts. Furthermore, it stated that collectively holding certain individuals responsible for all wrongful actions, without individualization, and for dismissal from professions and other measures, the Emergency Decree-Laws were not applied restrictively to those individuals having taken part in the attempted coup. Moreover, more than a hundred thousand people were dismissed, without regard to whether they committed such an act, without individualization and without providing a right to defense. Therefore, the applied measure was manifested, not in the form of suspension, but direct dismissal from public service.

2. Although those expelled under the Government Cleansing Act were banned from public service for a period of 5–10 years, those dismissed under the Emergency Decree-Laws have been permanently banned from working in many private sectors in addition to being permanently banned from public service. For instance, they are prevented from acting as a public lawyer and mediator, and are restricted from working in the private sector as a result of having their permits, licenses and certificates revoked.
3. The names of those dismissed under the Government Cleansing Act were published in the Lustration Register, a publicly accessible online database maintained by the Ministry of Justice. In addition, the names of individuals, expelled with the Emergency Decree-Laws, were published in the Official Gazette. The publishing of the names is a breach of the presumption of innocence because it included their places of duty, registration numbers, dates of birth, identity numbers and even their fathers' names.
4. The ECtHR stated that it could not see how the goal expected from the lustration would be achieved by cleansing officials of lower levels, noting that the President, having signed the Government Cleansing Act into law, had worked for a while under the rule of the previous government. The aim of the emergency was, as mentioned in Article 1 of Emergency Decree-Law No. 667, to *"establish measures that must necessarily be taken within the scope of the attempted coup*

and fight against terrorism and to determine procedures and principles relating to these measures." Its justification was that *"measures to protect our democracy endangered by the attempted coup, the principle of the rule of law and rights and freedoms of our citizens were able to be effectively implemented"*.

Nevertheless, a number of matters governed by the Emergency Decree-Laws had nothing to do with the purpose, subject and reason of the state of emergency. For instance, forbidding marriage programs, amending procedure for appointing rectors, selecting members to the Court of Cassation and Council of State, establishing the Turkey Wealth Fund, the practicing of winter tire, and the closing of thousands of companies, associations, foundations, unions, television and radio channels, had no relevance to the exigencies of the state of emergency. In the same way, expelling more than a hundred thousand people who did not take part in the attempted coup from public service, also had nothing to do with the purposes of the state of emergency. Since those people, who served till the attempted coup, were dismissed from their professions without any disciplinary procedure being conducted respectively to them, in addition to a lack of concrete and convincing evidence having been brought against them, their individualization was impacted. However, it is unknown why any legal or administrative actions were not taken against them prior to the attempted coup, what changed with the attempted coup, and upon obtaining evidence, why such extensive actions were carried out. These are questions which lack any validated resolutions according to the Emergency Decree-Laws. In addition, even though measures to be taken in the period of the state of emergency must be limited to the exigencies of the situation, it is not possible to say that many of the measures taken with the Emergency Decree-Laws are proportionate (Kaboğlu and Palluel 2018, 8; Office for Democratic Institutions and Human Rights 2017).

5. The ECtHR did not accept matters raised by the Ukrainian government in relation to taking these measures without individualization. For example, the existence of the state of emergency circumstances and Russian occupation of its territory. It was not provided justification for why the dismissal actions would continue for the duration of the state of emergency instead of a period of 10 years.

Emergency Decree-Laws are applicable only during the period of the state of emergency, and arrangements made by those Decree-Laws automatically cease to exist when the state of emergency ends. This is the case because when the state of emergency is over, the grounds requiring the issuance of the Decree-Laws ceases. In other words, under the Emergency Decree-Laws, there are no provisions that would allow it to continue after the state of emergency. Nevertheless, most of the arrangements made by the Decree-Laws issued after June 15, were permanent. For example, the closed institutions and establishments were permanently closed down, and people were permanently dismissed from public service jobs (not just for 10 years), and were restricted in their ability to be working within various branches of the private sector as well. In this respect, the conditions in the Emergency Decree-Laws have grave and serious implications. Hence, even though the risk resulting from the attempted coup was eliminated in a very short time, it was not explained why the arrangements with the Decree-Laws for all fields of life were necessitated.

6. The ECtHR held to that the fact that, after the dismissal, an investigation would be conducted and accusations would be brought against one of the applicants. Regardless, this did not change the conclusion that these individuals were expelled without justification due to the lack of an investigation at the time of dismissal which thus meant it could not be relied on for the dismissal. The same applies to those who were expelled by the Emergency Decree-Laws. Furthermore, there were not any investigations against those people, matters that were claimed to be relied on for the dismissals were their legal and usual activities in the past, behaviors were being used as justification that were not identified as an offense, and offenses and punishments were retroactively interpreted, for procedures and decisions carried out or taken. Namely, the decisions and procedures, taken or carried out with the Emergency Decree-Laws, were devoid of any justification.
7. The ECtHR underlined in its judgment that the consequences of the Government Cleansing Act were very serious. Furthermore, although it should have been established accordingly with concrete evidence, that those concerned had acted in contravention of democratic principles, governance, security of the state, and the rule of law and human rights, no evidence to that effect was brought forward. For our country as well, the situation was no different. Instead of providing concrete evidence pertaining to real and legal people about whom a decision was made or procedure was taken or conducted, procedures were carried out and decisions were made based on terms like connection and affiliation, which has no meaning in disciplinary and criminal law.

As can be seen in the comparison above, circumstances leading to the adoption of the Emergency Decree-Laws and lustration acts are quite different. This is so, while the lustration acts are provisions adopted for normalization of conditions in social lives and for the sake of democracy and the rule of law, they were not the case in the declaration of the state of emergency in Turkey. Procedures and decisions, conducted or taken with the Emergency Decree-Laws, led to more serious consequences, and in view of the ECtHR judgments given in respect of previously Eastern European countries and now Ukraine, it is obvious that it would find more than a hundred thousand violations related to them. Foremost, those who were removed from their jobs with the Decree-Laws, and a weakening of the human rights record of our country.

11.5 Evaluation of the Processes and the Decisions Made Utilizing the State of Emergency Decree-Laws vis a vis the Right to a Fair Trial

Article 6 of the Convention addresses the right to a fair trial. Paragraph 1 states that "Everyone has the right to the right to ask for the verdict within a reasonable time by an independent and impartial tribunal established by law, which shall issue decisions on civil rights and obligations and on criminal charges against him." The presumption of innocence is included in Paragraph 2, and the right to defense is included in Paragraph 3.

The right to a fair trial aims at achieving a fair and equitable decision as a result of an objective trial by defining the rules of procedure relating to the proceedings, and in this respect is one of the fundamental elements of the rule of law (Harris et al. 2014; İnceoğlu 2013a). Article 6, Paragraph 1 of the Convention provides for the elements of the right to a fair trial. According to the Convention, these proceedings are to be carried out by an impartial and independent court that the law has established, within a reasonable time, and publicly and fairly. Moreover, the ECtHR stated that the right to a fair trial also covers certain rights that Article 6 does not address. These rights include the right to appeal and to access a court, the principles of an adversarial proceeding at trial, justification of decisions, effective participation in proceedings, the right to be present at hearings, and silence (Doğru and Nalbant 2012; Harris et al. 2014).

Article 6, Paragraph 2, prescribes the presumption of innocence, and Paragraph 3 provides for the minimum rights of a person who is charged with a criminal offense in relation to general principles of Paragraph 1 (Harris et al. 2014; İnceoğlu 2013a).

Although the scope of the right to a fair trial is limited to personal rights and obligations and criminal charges in the ECHR, such a restriction is not included in the Turkish Constitution. Furthermore, the scope of the right is not restricted. In other words, according to the Turkish Constitution, a violation of the right to a fair trial can be asserted (Doğru and Nalbant 2012; İnceoğlu 2013a). In the context of a fair trial, one concern is if a purported offence is of a criminal nature and whether a decision to dismiss someone constitutes a criminal sanction.

11.5.1 Does a Dismissal Decision Constitute a Criminal Sanction?

Determining whether a dismissal is an administrative or criminal sanction is a useful exercise because the law to be applied should be determined on this basis. If an action warrants a criminal sanction, then the application of the guarantees envisaged in the criminal proceedings related to this sanction should come to the forefront. On the other hand, if punishment is an administrative sanction, then this sanction can be applied legally without any conviction. The ECtHR can be utilized to make a determination on this issue, but does not consider the qualification in domestic law sufficient by itself. The concept of "criminal charges against the individual" in Article 6, Paragraph 1 of the Convention, as well as administrative imposed sanctions in connection with this concept, fall within the scope of criminal law regardless of the domestic law, and can examine whether the assurances of the right to a fair trial are afforded to a person.

The ECtHR, while determining the criminal nature of a potential sanction, checks for the classification of the proceedings in the domestic law, the nature of an offence, and the severity of the possible punishment. While determining the nature of the sanction for an offense, the ECtHR determines whether this sanction is directed at a particular group or generally, whether a sanction is made by an authority with the competence to make an executive decision (Engel et al. v. Netherlands 1976, 81–82; Öztürk v. Germany 1984, 53; Lutz v. Germany 1987, 5; Demicoli v. Malta 1991, 33; Bendenoun v. France 1994, 47; Benham v. UK 1996, 56; Steel et al. v. UK 1998, 48–49; Phillips v. UK 2001, 31; Pakozdi v. Hungary 2014, 20; Ramos Nunes de Carvalho e Sa v. Portugal 2018, 133),[5] whether it carries the purpose of punishment, and whether it is based on a crime determination (Altıparmak 2017d; Altıparmak and Akdeniz 2017a; Doğru and Nalbant 2012).

Although anyone may engage in criminal acts, disciplinary actions may solely be carried out by persons of certain qualifications. Disciplinary law is usually related to the internal functioning of an institution. The ECtHR considers the nature, duration, and mode of enforcement of the sanction imposed under the disciplinary law to determine whether some action is considered to be criminal (Campbell and Feel v. UK 1984; Doğru and Nalbant 2012; Engel et al. v. Netherlands 1976).

For example, in Poland, those who acted as agents of the KGB during the communist regime and who allegedly made false statements about their past, have not been fined and imprisoned. However, they were prohibited from working in the public sector, as well as most of the private sector and from engaging in any political activity. Although this prohibition is not considered as a criminal sanction in domestic law, the ECtHR considered that the proceedings applied were very similar to criminal proceedings. In assessing the nature of the alleged offence and the severity of the sentence imposed, the ECtHR decided these prohibitions constituted a violation of the right to a fair trial because those subject to such punishments had lost the ability to have a clean and spotless history that would be necessary in order to engage in many professions as a result of being labeled as unreliable and liars in public. In one particular case, a person who was subject to this process was unable to carry out particular duties for 10 years as a result of his dismissal from the profession

[5]Judgment of the ECtHR on Phillips v. UK, App. No 41087/98 on December 12, 2001 P.31; in a later decision it is indicated that "Since, failure to punish with imprisonment and relatively mildness of the sanction does not remove the classification of the crime to be punished, it is not an obstacle to the implementation of Article 6." ECtHR Grand Chamber judgment on Ramos Nunes de Carvalho e Sa v. Portugal, No. 55391/13, 57,728/13 and 74,041/13, Par. 133. 6 November 2018. In another decision, even if the amount is low the fine was aimed at deterrence and punishment and this aspect of the situation revealed the punishment. ECtHR decision on Öztürk v. Germany, No: 8544/79, Par. 53, 21 February1984. Engel et al. v. Netherlands decision, Application number (B. No): 5100/71, Pars. 81–82, 8 June 1976; Benham v. UK Grand Chamber Judgment, App. No. 19380/92, Par. 56, 10 June 1996, Bendenoun v. France Decision, App. No. 12547/86, Par. 47, 24 February1994, Par. 47; Lutz v. Germany Decision, Par. 5; Pakozdi v. Hungary Decision, App. No. 51269/07, Par. 20, 25 November 2014; Demicoli v. Malta, Decision App. No. 13057/87, Par. 33, 27 August 1991, Steel et al. v. UK, Decision, App. No. 24838/94, Pars. 48–49, 23 September 1998.

(Altıparmak 2017b; Altıparmak and Akdeniz 2017a; Bobek v. Poland 2006; Luboch v. Poland 2008; Matyjek v. Poland 2006).

When the process of dismissal by means of the Decree-Laws is considered in its entirety, these procedures clearly identify criminal sanctions, and thus those that the Decree-Laws affect should be given the guarantees inherent in criminal proceedings. First, the criminal nature of the alleged offences in Turkey were much greater than in Poland. Indeed, the actions leading to sanctions were "membership, affiliation, affiliation with, or liaison with, terrorist organizations or structures, entities or groups" that the National Security Council determined was acting against the national security of the state. In Turkey, membership in a terrorist organization is subject to severe criminal sanctions, as defined by Article 314 of the Turkish Penal Code. Finally, such an alleged crime does not carry with it a purely disciplinary offence. Moreover, the decision made was not merely about administrative sanctions; they formed the basis for detention decisions and were counted among the evidence for indictments and the reasons for the punishment of the persons. Thus, defendants should have been accorded the right to a fair trial because the actions taken were not disciplinary in nature, but criminal.

The Venice Commission indicated that the ECtHR was prepared to consider the imposed sanctions as criminal sanctions, in terms of their legal qualities and effects, due to the dismissal as a result of the Decree-Laws being markedly different from dismissals imposed as mere disciplinary measures. Thus, the guarantees of a fair trial, provided for in Article 6 of the ECHR, should be made available to the persons impacted (König v. Germany 2007; Venice Commission 2017).

11.5.2 Is a Dismissal Decision Within the Scope of Civil Rights and Obligations?

"Civil rights and obligations" are included in the scope of the right to a fair trial, as well as to criminal charges. The civil acceptance of a right under the ECHR depends on the existence of a dispute and its relevance in relation to the defensible rights and obligations under domestic law. In addition, although the civil rights of the Contracting States do not have the same meaning, Article 6 of the Convention covers civil rights (König v. Germany 2007; 6. Madde Rehberi 2013).

In principle, Article 6, Paragraph 1 of the Convention could be implemented for disputes concerning salary, compensation, allowance, career, and dismissal of civil servants related to working life, as well as civil debates in domestic law (Aire v. Ireland 1979; Altıparmak 2017b; Harris et al. 2014; Ivanovski v. Lithuania 2016; Rainys and Gasparavisious v. Lithuania 2004; Olujic v. Croatia 2009). Indeed, the Court held that Article 6 could apply in the application lodged by an unjustly dismissed embassy employee (Cudak v. Lithuania 2010), a judge against the disciplinary penalty imposed against him (Olujic v. Croatia 2009; Ramos Nunes de Carvalho e Sa v. Portugal 2018), a prosecutor against a presidential decree that ordered the appointment somewhere else (Zalli v. Albania 2011), and a decision by a customs director against his professional career (Fiume v. Italy 2009). Because of the special nature of the relationship between a public official and the state, the assurances recognized by Article 6 should be provided to the person concerned in such disputes (Vilho Eskelinen and Others v. Finland 2007).

For many years, the ECtHR did not consider applications for the reinstatement of public officials like soldiers and policemen engaged in occupations in the public service, unlawful dismissals or occupations that involved "special loyalty and trust," under Article 6 (Harris et al. 2014; Pellegrin v. France 1999; Vitkauskas and Dikov 2018). However, over time, case-law has evolved, and such cases were seen to be within the scope of Article 6.

The position now is that public employees must be considered under Article 6 unless they fall under the scope of the Eskelinen test. The test requires an "express exclusion" for public employees from bringing a private employment claim as a matter of national law, and that exclusion must be justified on objective grounds in the public interest (Olujic v. Croatia 2009; Sukut v. Turkey 2007; Vilho Eskelinen and Others v. Finland 2007). That is, it is normally insufficient to exclude the scope of Article 6 for a person who works in a position that uses authority granted by the public power, or who has a special loyalty and trust relationship with the state (Vilho Eskelinen and Others v. Finland 2007). In order to do so, the state must demonstrate that the incident is the result of the use of public power or be suspicious of the relationship of loyalty and trust (Çiftçioğlu 2012; Vitkauskas and Dikov 2018). In accordance with the Eskelinen criteria, the rule that obstructs the judicial remedy to the public official in domestic law must exist before the procedure in question (Baka v. Hungary 2016).

In its ruling on the dismissal of the President of the Court of Appeals by the Supreme Council of Judges, the ECtHR indicated that the application was a normal labor dispute since it pertained to the applicant's working life and salary, and thereby it concerned a "civil right" under the right to a fair trial (Denisov v. Ukraine 2018). In another judgment, the application of a judge who was sentenced to three different disciplinary punishments and suspended for 240 days as a result of combining the penalties imposed, the application of the Article 6 (legal part) was not disputed and the ECtHR evaluated the dispute under Article 6 at Grand Chamber (Ramos Nunes de Carvalho e Sa v. Portugal 2018). In another decision, an applicant, who had previously served as a judge of the ECtHR and was elected as the President of the Supreme Court for a period of 6 years, applied to the ECtHR, stating that he had no access to the court concerning the constitutional amendment, which resulted in the termination of his term of office two and a half years after his election.

The ECtHR developed two criteria to assess such cases. These were: (1) whether the national law expressly excluded access to a court of the post or category of staff in question, and (2) whether the exclusion is justified on objective grounds in the State's interest. The Court decided that Article 6, Paragraph 1, does not apply when these two conditions are met. According to the Court, the President of the Supreme Court was not expressly excluded from the right of access to a court. Indeed, Hungarian law explicitly provided for a right of judicial review in cases of dismissal.

This was in line with several (soft law) international and Council of Europe standards regarding the independence of the judiciary. Moreover, for national legislation excluding access to a court to have any effect under article 6, Paragraph 1, the legislation should be compatible with the rule of law, which is inherent to the Convention. Because the new legislation was directed against a specific person, and therefore is not an instrument of general application, the Court considered the legislation contrary to the rule of law. In this light, the conclusion was reached that national law expressly excluded access to a court. Therefore, the action did not meet the first of the Eskelinen criteria based on the facts (Baka v. Hungary 2016). Thus, based on precedent and facts, the dismissal procedures of the Decree-Laws do not meet the two elements of the Eskelinen test.

In addition, how the civil servants are expelled from the public service is regulated in detail in the Turkish Constitution, as well as the Civil Servants Law No. 657. Under Article 135/5 of the Law 657, the administrative, judicial remedy against the dismissal penalty is open. Even if it is assumed that a clear legal regulation exists that prevents the right of access to a court for a moment, the declaration by Decree-Law that accuses a civil servant of being a member of a terrorist organization without any defense (Article 129/2 of the Constitution), is in violation of the presumption of innocence (Article 15/2 of the Constitution). Additionally, no objective justification for dismissal from public office, without the ability to ever work in the public sphere again, exists.

In other words, charges against a person in relation to the criminal law, preventing access to a trial, and excluding appropriateness of this sentence from the judicial review, are against the presumption of innocence as well as the rule of law. Therefore, it is impossible to provide an objective reason for preventing access to the courts.

The argument can be made that public officials exercise part of the sovereign power of the State, and in this respect, a "special trust and loyalty" relationship exists with the State. However, this alone does not prevent them from benefiting from Article 6. The State must demonstrate that a sanction is imposed because of the use of public power or the relationship between loyalty and trust is endangered. The reason for the application of this measure against public officials was the failed coup attempt.

However, no evidence, documents, or information that exists for the more than 100,000 public servants who were involved. Hence, the loyalty and trust relationship between the State and these persons was compromised. In other words, no plausible reason or concrete evidence existed that resulted in the dismissal of the majority of the public servants who were alleged to be related to the coup attempt. Therefore, the imposed sanctions did not meet the second element of the Eskelinen test, which was that of "a special trust and loyalty" relationship.

In short, the dispute between public officials and the administration was a civil rights and obligations dispute, as well as an accusation against the person. As a result of these falling within the scope of Article 6 of the ECHR, all guarantees required under Article 6, Paragraph 3 of the Convention must be granted to the persons concerned (Çiftçioğlu 2012).

In the following section, additional elements of the right to a fair trial are discussed. They include: the lawfulness of the dismissal of public officials within the framework of the right to apply to the court; the right to be tried in an independent court; the right to a defense; and the presumption of innocence.

11.5.3 Access to the Courts and Independent Court Rights

Article 6 of the ECHR protects the right to a fair trial. This article protects the right to a public hearing before an independent and impartial tribunal within a reasonable time, the presumption of innocence, and other minimum rights for those charged in a criminal case. These include adequate time and facilities to prepare their defense, access to legal representation, the right to examine witnesses against them or have them examined, and the right to the free assistance of an interpreter (Doğru and Nalbant 2012; Ekinci 2014; Golder v. England 1975; Harris et al. 2014; İnceoğlu 2013a).

The right to apply to the court is regulated in Article 36 of the Turkish Constitution in domestic law. Article 36 states that "Everyone has the right to a fair trial by means of claim and defense as plaintiff or defendant in front of the judicial authorities by making use of legitimate means and ways." As can be seen from the text of the article, this right is explicitly regulated in the Constitution, and the law does not restrict the right to a fair trial (İnceoğlu 2013a).

Case law of the ECtHR notes that everyone must have the right to actual and effective access to courts for the determination of his personal rights and obligations (Geouffre de la Pradella v. France 1992). This right includes not only the right to bring proceedings before the first instance courts but also the right to appeal to the upper courts (Doğru and Nalbant 2012; Harris et al. 2014; İnceoğlu 2013a).

It is contrary to the concept of the right to a fair trial to exclude administrative actions and procedures that interfere with a personal right of the individual (Boden v. Sweden 1987). Moreover, according to the ECtHR, the state's exclusion of personal claims by the courts without any limitation or immunity to large groups on civil matters is incompatible with the principles of the rule of law and the imposition of personal claims before the court (Fayed v. England 1994). Again, ECtHR's case-law has put forward that disciplinary proceedings and dismissal cases should be brought before a competent court; otherwise, the acceptance of such actions would frustrate the right to access the court (Albert and Le Compte v. Belgium 1983).

The legal basis for the dismissal of public officials and the source of the dispute are the Emergency Decree-Laws. According to the Constitution (Art. 148/1), the Decree-Laws are outside of the purview of judicial supervision. After July 15, 2016, the cancellation cases brought by the Decree-Laws and those who were dismissed from public office were rejected by dozens of administrative courts on the grounds that "there is no administrative action to be canceled." (See, for example, Neyapilabilir.net). Several regional administrative courts upheld these decisions.

In addition, the Decree-Law No. 690 of April 29, 2017 addresses specific regulations under the state of emergency dealing with cases that are pending in the administrative jurisdiction. In instances in which a dispute arises between public officials and the administration, the executive body is given the power on how to conclude pending proceedings. However, this violates the rights of those concerned to have a hearing before an independent and impartial court (Golder v. England 1975; Stran Greek Refineries and Stratis Andreadis v. Greece 1994).

The right to access the court is understood as the right to access an independent and impartial judicial body established by law before a dispute arises. In the present case, the right to access the court had been violated because no such judicial body to be appealed existed at the time of the dispute. Furthermore, as stated in the Venice Commission Opinions dated 12 December 2016, the violation of the right to access the court had no relevance with suppressing the acts of violence leading to the state of emergency. The punishment of civil servants who had no involvement in the coup attempt, in breach of their right to access to court, was not a "type precisely required by the situation" as required by Article 15 of the Convention.

The right of access to court of those, dismissed from public office, was hindered. Additionally, the Commission on the State of Emergency Measure, which was established to consider applications about procedures and decisions based on the Emergency Decree-Laws and decide on them, is one of the biggest hurdles before their right to have access to a court. In a decision, the ECtHR reviews the possibility of an application to "*Police Complaints Authority*" and notes the important role played by the Secretary of State in appointing, remunerating and, in certain circumstances, dismissing members of the Police Complaints Authority. Therefore, it holds that it does not provide an effective remedy within the meaning of Article 13 (Khan v. the United Kingdom 2000; 46–47).

In view of its structure and formation, the Commission is also far from the standards set by the Venice Commission and the ECtHR. Since more than half of its members are appointed by the Council of Ministers who issue the Emergency Decree-Laws, the authority in this regard, shall be afforded to the President without any objective criteria. Considering the fact that the Minister of Justice is the chairman of the Council and the undersecretaries of the Ministry are natural members of the Council, although the two members are appointed by the HSYK, the impact of political will on designated members is unquestionable and it is unlikely that the Commission, which is affiliated to the executive body in all respects, will examine and make a fair decision on weighty, highly political matters (Altıparmak 2017a, 5; Altıparmak 2017c, 76–77).

Furthermore, there are no guarantees in Law No. 7075 that will enable its members to function impartially and independently. Although the heading of the article is "*the guarantees and rights of the members*", when paragraph "*e*" of the article is considered, it is evident that this is not the case at all. Accordingly, this is due to the threat that offices of members will be terminated by an administrative investigation, initiated by the Presidency (Amnesty International 2018, 13), and there is no requirement for a judicial investigation or court decision. That is, an investigation by the president regarding members should be sufficient to end the membership if an unwelcome decision is made. Again, the initiation of an investigation against members for crimes mentioned in Article 4/1-d of the law is subject to the permission of the President.

Similarly, the working procedures and principles of the Commission are set by the President, not by law. Since there are no legal guarantees on this issue, the initiative is entirely afforded to the Presidency. Furthermore, the secretariat service, which will sort and prepare the files for the Commission and thus face the heaviest workload, will be met by the Presidency and will become hierarchically subordinate to the Presidency. However, there is no guarantee in the law for persons working in the secretariat – these persons may be replaced by the President at any time without reason. Hence, the commission has no discretion and right to appeal on this matter (Altıparmak 2017a, 5; Altıparmak 2017c, 76).

Succinctly, the Presidency has the sole authority for the selection of the members of the commission, its working procedures and principles, its secretariat and the determination of the additional fees to be paid, as well as for all judicial and administrative investigations against its members. It is not possible for a commission that is subordinate to the president in all respects to be independent and impartial, to make objective decisions, and most importantly, to be accepted as an effective legal remedy, considering the criteria of the Venice Commission and the ECtHR (Altıparmak 2017a, 4–5; Altıparmak 2017c, 76–77; Ardıçoğlu 2017, 41).

Moreover, pursuant to the ECtHR's case-law, for a subsequently-established remedy such as the Commission to be effective, it should also be able to suspend the execution of this transaction which is alleged to be contrary to the ECHR, if it causes irreparable damages (Jabori v. Turkey 2000, 49–50). In addition, the remedy must provide adequate procedural safeguards for the identification of those responsible. The remedy shall be considered ineffective if those responsible for the resulting damages are prevented from being paid compensation, or if it is stated that they are irresponsible (Altıparmak 2017c, 80; Doğru and Nalbant 2012, 562–563; Harris et al. 2014, 580; İnceoğlu 2013b, 443).

In light of these statements, if the commission is evaluated;

1. In accordance with the Law No. 7075, the commission will accept or reject the application, and the "*acceptance*" decision is not of the nature of the "*annulment*" decision rendered by the administrative judicial authorities. While the annulment decision provides the opportunity to eliminate all the consequences from the moment the administrative process is performed, it has a retroactive and proactive effect whereas the acceptance decision has a proactive effect (Çağlayan 2016, 520). This implies that those interested will not be able to claim material and moral damages suffered in the period between the date of establishment of the administrative process and the date of the commission's acceptance decision (Amnesty International 2018, 23). The Commission has not been granted with any power in this regard. In addition, it is not possible to claim their damage by initiating a full remedy action pursuant to Article 12 of the Law No. 2577 on Administrative Procedure (İYUK). Furthermore, the possibility of the persons concerned to claim compensation has been eliminated with Article 10/1 of the

Law No. 7075. That is, those concerned shall neither be able to recover their damages by applying to the Commission nor by filing a full remedy action.

In short, the Commission does not have the authority and power to address the essence of the violation claims, to prevent the violation, to terminate if it is ongoing, to decide if it is terminated, or to decide on compensation for the damages of those concerned if they are not possible. Thus, for these reasons, it cannot be considered as an effective remedy.

2. It must be decided with the prescribed remedy whether the provisions of the ECHR have been violated (Harris et al. 2014, 583; Smith and Grady v. United Kingdom 1999). However, it is not possible for the Commission to decide whether the provisions of the ECHR have been breached. In accordance with Article 14/2 of the Communiqué Governing the Working Procedures and Principles of the Commission, the Commission's review shall be conducted in respect of the membership, affiliation, connection and contact of the persons concerned with the structures which are, or which are considered as terrorist organizations. This determination depends on the notification to the relevant person about which organization he has a connection with, and according to the notification, the person concerned is able to defend himself and has rights to procedural guarantees. However, since the Commission does not have the authority to examine the applications in accordance with the law or the Communiqué in accordance with the provisions of the ECHR, it is not possible to make available these guarantees to the concerned persons (Altıparmak 2017b, 7).

The Turkish Constitutional Court noted that "*As the decision of the Commission is subject to the judicial review, Article 36 of the Constitution provides the applicants with all guarantees of the right to a fair trial when the remedy is applied...since there is no regulation contrary to this, there is no reason in the trial that potentially prevents applicants from accessing the file, participating effectively in the case, having the opportunity to present and review their evidence*" (Altıparmak and Akdeniz 2017a, 3; Remziye Duman 2017, 43). As can be seen from the decision, the TCC, by ignoring the quasi-judicial nature of the commission stage, stated that the guarantees to be provided to those concerned shall only be made during the administrative judicial phase. However, it is not possible to accept such interpretation. If those concerned can have the guarantees during the trial stage, which they have within the scope of the right to a fair trial, why has a commission step been introduced? Even if the commission decides quickly, it is questioned why no arrangement has been made to allow those concerned to apply directly to the administrative judiciary when in fact, it is the right of the concerned to have access to the administrative judicial remedy, and therefore the right to a fair trial within 2–3 years (Altıparmak and Akdeniz 2017a, 9–10).

3. In accordance with the Law No. 7075, even if those concerned have an opportunity to file an action against the Commission decision before the administrative courts, to be determined by the HSYK, in such cases the supervisory power of the courts is limited. The lawsuit will be filed not to the annulment of the Emergency

Decree-Laws which resulted in the violations, but for the annulment of the Commission decision. That is, there is no possibility before the Administrative Court for the annulment of the Emergency measure which caused the violation. Again, those concerned have no possibility of compensation for damages either directly, or in conjunction with, the annulment case after the annulment decision by filing a full remedy action on the basis of this decision in accordance with Article 12 of the Code of Administrative Procedure. Since the transaction which caused the damage is not the transaction of the Commission, but the measure arisen from the Emergency Decree-Law, no full remedy action against this transaction shall be filed. Furthermore, the administrative courts do not have the opportunity to rule on compensation, as the rights of the concerned to claim compensation, have been abolished (Altıparmak 2017c, 84–85; Günday 2017, 38).

4. One hundred and twenty-five thousand public servants have been dismissed from their profession and thousands of institutions and organization have been closed down due to the Emergency Decree-Laws based on intelligence reports and intelligence concepts such as "*connection*" and "*affiliation,*" which were not previously in our legislation. This is executed without being able to find out the accusations or to which organization they are alleged to be a member of, and without showing any concrete evidence or reason based on personalization. Such decisions about real persons and legal entities having been taken, an offence was attributed and identified in the Criminal Code as "*membership of a terrorist organization.*" (Altıparmak and Akdeniz 2017a, 7; Altıparmak and Akdeniz 2017b, 74; Altıparmak 2017a, 6; Altıparmak 2017c, 76). Since the accusation is of criminal nature, all rights of those concerned under the right to a fair trial should be granted (Teixeira de Castro v. Portugal 1998, 9). In this context, pursuant to the principles of equality of arms and adversarial proceedings, those concerned should be notified or become knowledgeable about charges attributed to them, and should be able to put forward counter-evidence in order to make their defense, and if necessary, call a witness (Ruiz Mateos v. Spain 1990, 63). This is imperative because the raison d'etre of the right to a fair trial is to prevent the abuse of public authority (Altıparmak 2017a, 7; Altıparmak 2017c, 79; Coeme and Others v. Belgium 2000, 102).

However, the issues mentioned in the Law and the Communiqué regarding the examination of the Commission are far from those mentioned above. It is stated in these regulations that the Commission will make its examination only on the file content. Therefore, the applicants do not have the opportunity to call witnesses, to provide an oral defense, or to present documents, information and evidence to the file. Although the Commission is able to request all kinds of documents and information in accordance with Article 5 of the Law, the relevant institutions may not provide the required documents and information, saying that it remains within the scope of the state secret. In this case, the decision will be rendered according to the incomplete information in the file.

As can be understood from the above considerations, it cannot be said that it is an effective legal remedy (Amnesty International 2018, 20) since the Commission cannot present any of the rights granted by the right to a fair trial to those concerned and its formal review (Altıparmak 2017a, 6–7; Altıparmak 2017c, 77; Özgenç 2017, 89).[6]

5. The Commission also has no authority to suspend the execution of the transaction that caused this situation in the event of irreparable damage due it being contrary to the law. Moreover, the administrative courts, where a judicial remedy is introduced against the decisions of the Commission, do not have the powers to decide to suspend the execution due to the arrangement made by the Emergency Decree-Law No. 668. Perhaps one of the most important powers in the Commission and administrative courts is the power to suspend the execution. The transactions carried out and decisions made with the Emergency Decree-Laws are contrary to the law and have caused irreparable damages to more than a hundred thousand people and institutions. However, the fact that neither the Commission nor the administrative courts have such authority is another indication that the legal remedy introduced is not effective.
6. Although Article 40/3 of the Constitution envisages that any compensation paid by the State as a result of wrongdoings of public officers is to be reimbursed by the officer leading to the damages, pursuant to Article 4/4 of the Law No. 7075, Article 37 of the Law No. 6755 shall apply on the legal, administrative, financial and criminal responsibilities of the Commissioners regarding their decisions, duties and actions under their membership duties. Article 37 reads that "*The persons who have adopt decisions within the scope of quashing the coup attempt and terrorist acts carried out on 15/07/2016 and the acts which are in the continuation of these acts, who have carried out the decisions or measures, who have taken part in all kinds of judicial and administrative measures, the legal, administrative, financial and penal liability of the persons performing the duties due to such decisions, duties and acts shall have no criminal liability.*" Due to this arrangement, the fact that no liability can be assumed to the persons who cause harm by their actions is another indication that the introduced remedy is not

[6]Mr. Özgenç said that: "*the declaration of a state of emergency does not open the way for any sanctions to be imposed on persons without question. The most natural right of a person is to defend himself against any charges attributed to him. Even if he has committed a crime, regardless of the weight of the crime he has committed, even if he has been caught red-handed, it is necessary to grant the person with the right to defend himself in order to be able to impose sanctions against him for this reason. The decision on sanction without granting this right, even if the person is caught red-handed, should be lifted and an investigation process should be initiated accordingly. The commission established with the Decree-Law No. 685 has no such authority. The granting of an application to this commission cannot be substituted for the exercise of the right of defense. This remedy can be used after the sanction decision has been rendered and even after it has been implemented. However, the right to defend must be exercised before a sanction decision is rendered. Despite this situation, if the legal remedy is available and will be used, it is inevitable that the dismissal decisions not associated with a concrete crime be annulled.*".

an effective remedy (Türmen 2016, 13; Venice Commission 2017, 430).[7] However the Constitutional Court rejected an application for the annulment of Article 9 of the Emergency Decree-Law No. 667, which contains the first version of the provision and was later turned into law by the Law No. 6746 (Judgment of the Constitutional Court 2019).

11.5.4 As Per the Presumption of Innocence

The presumption of innocence is stipulated in Article 6, Paragraph 2 of the ECHR, and Article 38, Paragraph 4 of the Turkish Constitution. Article 6, Paragraph 2 of the Convention states; "Everyone charged with a criminal offense, is assumed innocent until proven guilty according to law," and Article 38, Paragraph 4 of the Turkish Constitution indicates "No one shall be considered guilty until proven guilty in a court of law."

Based on Article 15, Paragraph 2 of the Turkish Constitution, the presumption of innocence is a right that can only be suspended in exceptional cases as in the time of war, which is an indication of the importance attached to the presumption (İnceoğlu 2013a; Ormanoğlu 2016). In accordance with this principle, the burden of proof belongs to the state, and a person has no obligation to prove that he/she is not guilty (Barbera, Messque and Jabardo v. Spain 1988; Harris et al. 2014; Ormanoğlu 2016). Shifting the burden of proof to a defendant would constitute an infringement of the presumption of innocence (Harris et al. 2014; Telfner v. Austria 2001) To accept that public authorities have fulfilled the requirement for the burden of proof, strong evidence must demonstrate that an individual has committed a crime (Harris et al. 2014; İnceoğlu 2013a).

[7]TÜRMEN, State of Emergency, p.13; Venice Commission noted on the "Waiver of liability" *introduced by the Emergency Decree-Law that; "However, in the opinion of the Venice Commission, this clause sends a very dangerous message, especially as regards the waiver of criminal liability. This waiver may be understood as implying that the decree-laws directly authorize and command certain actions which should be otherwise considered as "crimes" under the Criminal Code of Turkey, or at least that they suggest to those committing these crimes in the exercise of their functions that they will not be persecuted. Furthermore, this waiver may be seen as removing any accountability for actions which are taken within the broad discretionary powers given by the Decree-Laws to various state institutions and officials. This, again, is a dangerous logic and contrary to the rule of law. A person may use his or her discretionary powers reasonably and bona fide. However, as it will be demonstrated below, the emergency Decree-Laws are formulated in excessively vague terms, giving almost unfettered powers to the state officials implementing them. This creates the risk of large-scale abuses, which cannot be tolerated in a State under the rule of law. Finally, this provision may be seen as waiving criminal liability ad personam – i.e. giving immunity to persons who "fulfilled their duties within the scope of this Decree-Law", even if those persons acted clearly in excess of their powers, or violated non-derogable human rights obligations (for example, ill-treated detainees). Even if this is not intended, it may be perceived as such. And given that some of the measures enacted by the Decree-Laws are supposed to remain after the end of the emergency period, this waiver of liability may also become a permanent feature of the Turkish legal order, which is clearly unacceptable".* Venice, p. 430.

As noted in Article 6, Paragraph 2 of the ECHR, a "Criminal charge" is a written notification to an individual by authorities that a crime has been committed. Criteria for infringement of the presumption of innocence have been established concerning whether an individual is indeed affected by the process and actions (Salabiaku v. France 1988). A violation of the presumption of innocence can be created by a court decision of public authorities, as well as news published in the press that a person is guilty (Doğru and Nalbant 2012; Harris et al. 2014; İnceoğlu 2013a; OHAL Tedbirleri Anayasaya Aykırı! 2016). As the Venice Commission noted, "Although the constitutional provisions on the proclamation of the state of emergency seem in line with European standards, the government has used extraordinary powers for defamation" (Venice Commission 2017).

In a recent decision, the ECtHR found Turkey in violation of the presumption of innocence because authorities issued a verdict in a disciplinary case referring to considerations of the criminal court that had not been finalized. The administrative proceedings resulted in a statement that the defendant was a member of the terrorist organization. The result of this decision was that an administrative penalty, based on a connection to an illegal organization, depended on a court decision that an organization could be classified as illegal. In other words, the disciplinary penalty to be imposed pursuant to this cause can only be validated with a court judgment. Punishment cannot be based on the past, so individuals cannot be penalized for a past relationship in accordance with Article 7 of the Convention on offenses and penalties. Thus, for any dismissal, a present relationship must be proven (Çelik (Bozkurt) v. Turkey 2011; Urat v. Turkey 2018).

According to the ECtHR, any decision made concerning a person without proving that the individual is guilty, or without recognition of the rights of the defense, heightens the impression that people were guilty. Therefore, the presumption of innocence was violated (Doğru and Nalbant 2012; Minelli v. Switzerland 1983). The Court did not see drawbacks in providing information to the public about the investigations and prosecutions being carried out. However, to prevent any manipulation about whether individuals were guilty or that would cause prejudice against them, the Court asked that the authorities to be more discrete with the information (Allenet de Ribemont v. France 1995; Maslarova v. Bulgaria 2019).

Similarly, the ECtHR, in another decision against Turkey, concluded that the state had violated the presumption of innocence because government authorities had announced a guilty verdict before the end of the trial. Although the security forces had not disclosed the names of the accused, their photos from which they could be identified, were distributed at a press conference (YB v. Turkey 2004). Likewise, a violation of the presumption of innocence can occur in instances in which an investigator or prosecutor expresses a public opinion that a crime has been committed before the judgment is made, or that states that the individual may be guilty even if the proceeding ultimately leads to a conviction (Affaire Kouzmin v. Russia 2010; Daktaras v. Lithuania 2001; Lutz v. Germany 1987; Matijasevic v. Serbia 2006; O. v. Norway. 2003; Sekanina v. Austria 1993; Panteleyenko v. Ukraine 2006).

Regarding the dismissal of the public officers, the relevant Emergency Decree-Laws contains only the following reason: "Members of terror organizations or organizations, structures, or groups addressed by the National Security Council of State as acting against the state or the ones related to members or affiliates of these organizations (those with their names included in the attached lists) are dismissed without any further procedures being required." Therefore, dismissal of public officers as a result of their names being on a list prepared by the executive branch, and by accusing them of being the members of a terrorist organization without a court decision finalized, clearly violated the presumption of innocence. According to Article 38, Paragraph 4 of the Constitution, "*No one shall be considered guilty until proven guilty in a court of law.*"

Under Article 15 of the Constitution, the presumption of innocence cannot be suspended even in the case of a state of emergency, except in times of war. Individuals and their groups cannot be declared guilty by Decree-Laws and legal regulations, and thus, cannot be convicted. Indeed, according to the Turkish Constitution, "*the exercise of sovereignty shall not be delegated by any means to any individual, group, or class. No person or organ shall exercise any state authority that does not emanate from the Constitution*" (Article 6, Paragraph 2). Considering the requirements of the presumption of innocence, only judicial decisions can convict a person. Pursuant to Article 9, "*Judicial power shall be exercised by independent and impartial courts on behalf of the Turkish Nation.*" Therefore, neither the executive nor the legislature have jurisdiction. Therefore, decisions by the National Security Council or Council of Ministers decisions cannot pronounce individuals or their groups as guilty, nor can they identify them as if they are sentenced.

Thus, the Emergency Decree-Laws violated the presumption of innocence for those who were dismissed, making it necessary for the Decree-Laws to be terminated. In brief, all measures should be returned to the conditions when no such violations (*restitutio in integrum*) occurred.

11.5.5 As Per the Right to Defense

The right to a fair trial, no matter how intense the public interest is, the inalienable rights, and assurances based on this right must be granted to individuals in cases of organized crimes, as well as the simplest ones, according to the ECtHR (Altıparmak and Akdeniz 2017a; Teixeira de Castro v. Portugal 1998). Additionally, Turkey's Constitutional Court found that "since there is no distinction between administrative and judicial punishments in Article 38 of the Constitution, disciplinary punishments are to comply with the principles suggested by this article" (Constitutional Court 2015).

Article 6 of the ECHR and Article 129, Paragraph 2 of the Turkish Constitution address the right to a fair trial. The opinions of the Constitutional Court on the issues ensure the application of these rights should occur both in administrative proceedings as well as criminal cases (Harris et al. 2014; İnceoğlu 2013a).

Article 129, Paragraph 2 of the Turkish Constitution, which regulates the disciplinary actions in administrative procedures, states that no disciplinary punishment can be made unless civil servants and other public officials are granted their rights to a proper defense. According to the ECtHR, inspectors must first hear cases. The inspectors' reports and witness statements should be forwarded to someone who is accused, and a superior authority must supervise the decision to prevent arbitrariness. Under the scope of this process, an individual must be given the right to present his/her opinions and argue against the charges made against him/her (Mutlu et al. 2012; Özpınar v. Turkey 2010).

No investigation of public officials with dismissal from the profession existed before the Decree-Laws. In addition, the actions requiring dismissal and how these actions are classified according to the Decree-Laws were not indicated. Evidence, information, and documents that did not exist at the time that the decision was made were later created to prove that the individuals were related to terrorist organizations. Because criminal charges were made against individuals by the Decree-Laws, all requirements of fair trial, that is, access to a lawyer, the ability to provide contradictory evidence to respond to charges, access to the evidence against the individual, and forwarding the evidence to the individual so-charged, should be granted to the person who was charged (Altıparmak and Akdeniz 2017a; Ruiz Mateos v. Spain 1993). However, none of these rights were fulfilled, and the most fundamental right of defense was not provided because the process was not administered properly, therefore the right of an individual to a fair trial was violated (Venice Commission 2017). Due to this, the Venice Commission noted that individuals should be given the right to assess the evidence against them and to defend themselves before a decision is finalized.

11.6 Conclusion

Following the failed coup attempt of July 15, 2016, in Turkey, more than 125,000 career civil servant were dismissed, and more than 3000 institutions and organizations were closed. Individuals dismissed from their jobs by the Emergency Decree-Laws were accused of being members of a terrorist organization without a trial, and they were tried for, or convicted of, this offense by the courts. In another words, charges within the meaning of criminal law were attributed to them and they were dismissed from office without any opportunity for reinstatement in the future. In brief, persons were accused and convicted by means of Decree-Law, and have been left to civil death as a result.

Although the charges against those individuals were "membership of a terrorist organization," the names of the organizations assumed to be terroristic were not in the annexes of the Decree-Laws. Those who were accused of being members of these terrorist organizations, or having affiliation with them, were branded as criminals, and they were forced to defend themselves against these accusations that accompanied their dismissal.

Because membership in a terrorist organization is considered a crime in domestic law, those that were dismissed from their jobs were somehow accused of this crime. Article 6 of the ECHR required the right to a fair trial before an independent and impartial tribunal, which they were denied. Additionally, because the names of the accused were clearly announced to the whole world as being a member of a terrorist organization, persons were sentenced to live as terrorists, stigmatized, and their recruitment, even in the private sector, has become almost impossible.

Furthermore, although the individuals were exposed to severe criminal charges and severe sanctions, they were not granted the rights that Article 6 of the ECHR provided including: the right of access to court, the right to be judged by independent and unbiased courts established by law, the presumption of innocence, the right to know the charges as soon as possible, the right to request the hearing of the charges face to face at a public trial, the right to have all kinds of facilities to prepare defense as well as to listen to the witnesses at a public trial, and to have the witnesses for listening under the same conditions. Therefore, the right to be judged fairly, is violated.

The current practices which run contrary to the principle of the rule of law are also contrary to Article 15 of the Convention. According to this article, "*measures strictly required by the exigencies of the situation*" can be put into action in the state of emergency. The actions taken under the Decree-Laws did not meet this threshold, and thus violated the Convention rights.

References

6. madde rehberi, adil yargılanma hakkı (medeni hukuk yönü). [Article 6, the right to a fair trial (aspect of civil law)]. 2013. Ankara: Avrupa Konseyi/Avrupa İnsan Hakları Mahkemesi Yayınları.

Adamsons v. Latvia. 2008, June 24. ECtHR. No: 3669/03.

Affaire Kouzmin v. Russia. 2010, March 18. ECtHR. B. No: 58939/00, Pars. 59–69.

Aire v. Ireland. 1979, October 9. ECtHR. B. No: 6289/73, Par. 21.

Akif Zihni v. Turkey. 2016, November 29. ECtHR. No: 59061/16.

Aksoy v. Turkey. 1996, December 18. ECtHR. No: 21987/93.

Al Nashif v. Bulgaria. 2002, June 20. ECtHR. No: 50963/99.

Albayrak, Mustafa. 2013. *Türk ceza kanunu, öz kitap* (12. bs.). [*Turkish penal code*] (12th ed.). Ankara: Adalet Yayınevi.

Albert and Le Compte v. Belgium. 1983, February 10. ECtHR. B. No: 7299/75, Par. 23.

Allenet de Ribemont v. France. 1995, February 10. ECtHR. B. No: 15175/89, Par. 41.

Alparslan Altan v. Turkey. 2019, September 9. ECtHR. No: 12778/17.

Altıparmak, Kerem, and Yaman Akdeniz. 2017a. *OHAL Komisyonu Karar Vermeye Başlıyor: Ama Nasıl?* [The State of Emergency Commission is Deciding: But How?]. Cyber Rights. http://privacy.cyber-rights.org.tr/wp-content/uploads/2017/09/OHAL_Komisyonu_Nasil_Karar_Verecek.pdf. Accessed 20 Feb 2020.

———. 2017b. *Barış İçin Akademisyenler: Olağanüstü Zamanlarda Akademiyi Savunmak* [Academics for Peace: Defending the Academy in Extraordinary Time]. İstanbul: İletişim Yayınları.

Altıparmak, Kerem. 2017a. *685 sayılı KHK ile kurulan OHAL Komisyonu etkili bir hukuk yolu mu?* [Is the OHAL Commission Established with Decree-Law No. 685 an Effective Remedy?]. İnsan Hakları Ortak Platformu. http://www.ihop.org.tr/wp-content/uploads/2017/03/%C4%B0nceleme-Komisyonu_OHAL.pdf. Accessed 20 Feb 2020.

———. 2017b. *AİHM'in OHAL komisyonu kararı sonrası BAK imzacıları* [BAK Signers After the Decision of the ECtHR Commission of the ECtHR]. Cumhuriyet Akademi. http://www.cumhuriyet.com.tr/haber/aihmnin-ohal-komisyonu-karari-sonrasi-bak-imzacilari-789806. Accessed 20 Feb 2020.

———. 2017c. Ölü doğan çocuk: 685 sayılı khk ile kurulan OHAL komisyonu [Stillborn Child: OHAL Commission Established with the Number 685]. *Ankara Barosu Dergisi* 2017(1):69–88.

———. 2017d. OHAL KHK'leri sivil ölüm mü demek [OHAL Decree-Law Means Civic Deaths Say]. *Bianet*. https://m.bianet.org/bianet/siyaset/178496-hal-khk-leri-sivil-olum-mu-demek. Accessed 20 Feb 2020.

Amnesty International. 2018. *Purged Beyond Return?*. https://www.amnesty.org.tr/public/uploads/files/Purged%20Beyond%20Return_Report_EN.pdf

Ardıçoğlu, M. Artuk. 2017. Olağanüstü hal işlemleri inceleme komisyonu işlemlerinin hukuki niteliği. [Legal Nature of the Emergency Commission Review Commission Operations]. *Ankara Barosu Dergisi*, 2017(2):26–57.

Artuk, Mehmet Emin, Ahmet Gökçen, and A. Caner Yenidünya. 2013. *Ceza hukuku genel hükümler* [General Provisions of Criminal Law]. Ankara: Adalet Yayınevi.

Aydin, Hasan, and Koksal Avincan. 2020. Intellectual Crimes and Serious Violation of Human Rights in Turkey: A Narrative Inquiry. *The International Journal of Human Rights* 24 (8): 1127–1155. https://doi.org/10.1080/13642987.2020.1713108.

Baka v. Hungary. 2016, June 23. ECtHR. B. No: 20261/12, Pars. 112–118.

Barbera, Messque and Jabardo v. Spain. 1988, December 6. ECtHR. B. No: 10590/83, Par. 77.

Bayar, Oya. 2013. Derogation Regime on Fundamental Rights and Freedoms in Emergency Management Procedures. In *European Convention on Human Rights and the Constitution*, ed. Sibel Inceoğlu. Ankara: Council of Europe Publication, Sen Matbaa.

Bendenoun v. France. 1994, February 24. ECtHR. No: 12547/86.

Benham v. UK. 1996, June 10. ECtHR. No: 19380/92.

Bianet. 2018. *701 Sayılı KHK İçin OHAL Komisyonu'na Başvuruda Son Gün* [Last Day to Apply to the State of Emergency Commission for Decree-Law 701]. http://bianet.org/bianet/hukuk/200498-ohal-komisyonu-na-basvuruda-son-gun.

Bobek v. Poland. 2006, October 24. ECtHR. B. No: 6876/01.

Boden v. Sweden. 1987, October 27. ECtHR. B. No: 10930/84, Par. 35.

Çağlayan, Ramazan. 2016. *İdari Yargılama Hukuku* [Administrative Jurisdiction Law].

Campbell and Feel v. UK. 1984, June 28. ECtHR. B. No: 781/77, Pars. 72–73.

Çelik (Bozkurt) v. Turkey. 2011, July 12. ECtHR. B. No: 34388/05.

Çiftçioğlu, Cengiz Topel. 2012. 2802 Sayılı Hâkimler Ve Savcılar Kanununa Göre Hâkim ve Savcıların Disiplin Soruşturmaları [Disciplinary Investigations of Judges and Prosecutors According to the Law No. 2802 on Judges and Prosecutors]. *Dokuz Eylül Üniversitesi Hukuk Fakültesi Dergisi* 13 (1): 127–157.

Coeme and Others v. Belgium. 2000, October 18. ECtHR. No: 32492/96, 32547/96, 32548/96, 33209/96 and 33210/96.

Constitutional Court. 2015, January 14. Numbered 2014/100 E and 2015/6 K.

Council of Europe. 1996. *Measures to Dismantle the Heritage of Former Communist Totalitarian Systems*. http://assembly.coe.int/nw/xml/XRef/Xref-XML2HTML-en.asp?fileid=16507&lang=en.

Cudak v. Lithuania. 2010, March 23. ECtHR. B. No: 15869/02.

Cumhuriyet Gazetesi. 2017. *ABD'den sert uyarılar* [Hard Warnings from the US].

Cyber Rights. 2017. *Additional Statement Expanding on the Complaints*. http://privacy.cyber-rights.org.tr/wp-content/uploads/2017/06/K%C4%B1sa_Aciklama.docx.

Daktaras v. Lithuania. 2001, January 17. ECtHR. B. No: 42095/98, Pars. 42–45.

David, Roman. 2003. Lustration Law in Action: The Movies and Evaluation of Lustration Policy in the Czech Author(s). *Law and Social Inquiry*, 28(2), Blackwell Press.
Demicoli v. Malta. 1991, August 27. ECtHR. No: 13057/87.
Denisov v. Ukraine. 2018, September 25. ECtHR. B. No: 76639/11, Par. 54.
Doğru, Osman, and Atilla Nalbant. 2012. *İnsan hakları Avrupa sözleşmesi, açıklama ve önemli kararlar (Vol 1)* [European Convention on Human Rights, Clarification and Important Decisions (Vol 1)]. Ankara: Legal Yayıncılık.
Ekinci, Ahmet. 2014. Anayasa Mahkemesi'nin bireysel başvuru kararlarında mahkemeye erişim hakki [The Right of Access to Court in Individual Application Decisions of the Constitutional Court]. *Gazi Üniversitesi Hukuk Fakültesi Dergisi* 28 (3–4): 821–848.
Elçi and Others v. Turkey. 2003, November 13. ECtHR. No: 23145/93-25091/94.
Engel et al. v. the Netherlands. 1976, June 8. ECtHR. No: 5100/71, Pars. 81–82.
European Commission. 2016. *Turkey 2016 Report.* https://ec.europa.eu/neighbourhood-enlargement/sites/near/files/pdf/key_documents/2016/20161109_report_turkey.pdf.
Fayed v. England. 1994, September 21. ECtHR. B. No: 17101/90. Par. 47.
Fiume v. Italy. 2009, November 6. ECtHR. B. No: 20774/05.
Geouffre de la Pradella v. France. 1992, December 16. ECtHR. B. No: 12964/87, Pars. 34–35.
Gergerlioğlu, Ömer Faruk. 2019. 2. Yılında OHAL'in Toplumsal Maliyetleri. *Mağdurlar İçin Adalet.*
Gökhan Köksal v. Turkey. 2017, June 12. ECtHR. No: 70478/16.
Golder v. England. 1975, February 1975. ECtHR. B. No: 4451/70, Par. 35.
Günday, Metin. 2017. *OHAL İhraç KHK'leri ve Hukuki Durum* [State of Emergency: Dismissal with Degree of Law and the Condition of Law]. Ankara Barosu Dergisi, Sayı: 2017/1, Ankara.
Harris, David John, Michael O'Boyle, Ed Bates, and Carla Buckley. 2014. *Harris, O'Boyle & Warbrick: Law of the European Convention on Human Rights.* Oxford: Oxford University Press.
Horne, M. Cynthia. 2009. International Legal Rulings on Lustration Polices in Central and Eastern Europe: Rule of Law in Historical Context. *Hukuk ve Sosyoloji Dergisi* 34 (3): 249.
Human Rights Committee. 2001. General Comment 29, States of Emergency (article 4), U.N. Doc. CCPR/C/21/Rev.1/Add.11.
İnceoğlu, Sibel. 2013a. Adil yargılanma hakki [Right to a Fair Trial]. In *İnsan Hakları Avrupa Sözleşmesi ve Anayasa kitabı [The European Convention on Human Rights and the Constitution]*, ed. S. İnceoğlu, 209–228. Ankara: Şen Matbaa.
———. 2013b. In *Etkili Başvuru Hakkı. İnsan Hakları Avrupa Sözleşmesi ve Anayasa [Effective Application Right. European Convention on Human Rights and Constitution]*, ed. Sibel İnceoğlu. Ankara: Avrupa Konseyi Yayınları, Şen Matbaa.
Ivanovski v. Lithuania. 2016, January 21. ECtHR. B. No: 29908/11, Par. 117.
Ivanovski v. Macedonia. 2016, April 21. ECtHR. No: 58812/15.
Jabori v. Turkey. 2000, Juli 11. ECtHR. No: 40035/98.
Judgement of TCC. 1988, August 19. Docket No. 1987/16, Decree No. 1988/8.
———. 2016, January 13. Docket No. 2015/85, Decree No. 2016/3.
Judgment of the Constitutional Court. 2019, Juli 24. No: 2016/205 E., 2019/63 K.
Kaboğlu, İbrahim Özden. 2017. OHAL komisyonu etkili başvuru yolu olabilir mi? [Can the State of Emergency Commission Be an Effective Application]. *Cumhuriyet Akademi*, July 26.
Kaboğlu, İbrahim Özden, and Christelle Palluel. 2018. İnsan hakları Avrupa hukuku bağlamında Türkiye'de olağanüstü hal [Human Rights in Turkey in the Context of European Law, Then the State of Emergency]. *Suç ve Ceza, Ceza Hukuku Dergisi* 2018 (1): 1–26.
Khan v. the United Kingdom. 2000, May 12. ECtHR. No: 35394/97.
König v. Germany. 2007, May 23. ECtHR. B. No: 5163/99, Par. 89.
Luboch v. Poland. 2008, Janury 15. ECtHR. B. No: 37369/05.
Lutz v. Germany. 1987, August 25. ECtHR. B. No: 9912/82, Pars. 50–64.
Maslarova v. Bulgaria. 2019, January 31. ECtHR. B. No: 26966, Pars. 40–46.
Matijasevic v. Serbia. 2006, December 19. ECtHR. B. No: 23037/04, Par. 49.

Matyiek v. Poland. 2006, May 30. ECtHR. B. No: 38184/03, Pars. 49–58.

Mehmet Hasan Altan v. Turkey. 2018, September 10. ECtHR. No: 13237/17.

Minelli v. Switzerland. 1983, March 25. ECtHR. B. No: 8660/79, Par. 28.

Muižnieks, Nils. 2016. *Memorandum on the Human Rights Implications of the Measures Taken Under the State of Emergency in Turkey*. Council of Europe Commissioner for Human Rights. https://rm.coe.int/ref/CommDH(2016)35.

Mutlu, Erdem İlker, Begüm Şermet, and Nil Merve Çelikbaş. 2012. Özpınar Türkiye davası [Özpınar Turkey Case]. *Hacettepe Hukuk Fakültesi Dergisi* 2012: 89–102.

Nuray Şen v. Turkey. 2003, June 17. ECtHR. No: 41478/98.

O. v. Norway. 2003, May 11. ECtHR. B. No: 29327/95, Pars. 33–41.

Office for Democratic Institutions and Human Rights. 2017. *Fair Trial Rights During States of Conflict and Emergency*. https://www.osce.org/odihr/317766?download=true.

Official Gazette. 2004. *Official Gazette* No. 25611, October 12. https://www.resmigazete.gov.tr/eskiler/2004/10/20041012.htm.

OHAL önlemleri sınırları aştı [OHAL Measures Have Exceeded Limits]. 2016. *Hürriyet Gazetesi, December 10*. http://www.hurriyet.com.tr/gundem/ohal-onlemleri-sinirlari-asti-40302365.

OHAL tedbirleri anayasaya aykırı! [OHAL Measures Contrary to the Constitution!]. 2016. *Cumhuriyet Gazetesi,* December 10.

Olujic v. Croatia. 2009, February 5. ECtHR. B. No: 22330/03, Pars. 36–43.

Önok, Murat. 2016. *State of Emergency Measures in the context of the European Convention on Human Rights*. Ankara: Panel on the Right of Defence in Turkey Governed by Decree-Laws, Turkish Bar Association Publications.

Ormanoğlu, Hatice Derya. 2016. Anayasal bağlamda ve Avrupa insan hakları sözleşmesi boyutuyla suçsuzluk karinesi [Presumption of Innocence in the Constitutional Context and in the Dimension of the European Convention on Human Rights]. *Ankara Üniversitesi Hukuk Fakültesi Dergisi* 65 (4): 2241–2276.

Özgenç, İzzet. 2017. *Suç örgütleri* (10th ed.) [Criminal Organizations (10th ed.)]. Ankara: Seçkin Yayıncılık.

Özpınar v. Turkey. 2010, October 19. ECtHR. B. No: 20999/04, Par. 77.

Öztürk v. Germany. 1984, February 21. ECtHR. No: 8544/79.

Pakozdi v. Hungary. 2014, November 25. ECtHR. No: 51269/07.

Panteleyenko v. Ukraine. 2006, June 29. ECtHR. B. No: 11901/02.

Pellegrin v. France. 1999, December 8. ECtHR. B. No. 2854/95, Pars. 64–71.

Phillips v. UK. 2001, December 12. ECtHR. No: 41087/98.

Polyakh and Others v. Ukraine. 2019, October 19. ECtHR. No: 58812/15.

Rainys and Gasparavisious v. Lithuania. 2004, January 22. ECtHR. B. No: 7435/01. 22 January 2004.

Ramos Nunes de Carvalho e Sa v. Portugal. 2018, November 6. ECtHR. No. 55391/13, 57728/13 and 74041/13, Pars. 199, 120, and 122.

Remziye Duman. 2017, July 20. B. No: 2016/25923. https://bedirhaber.com/aymden-70-bin-basvuruya-ret/.

Ruiz Mateos v. Spain. 1990, November 6. ECtHR. No: 12952/87.

———. 1993, June 23. ECtHR. B. No: 12952/87, Par. 63.

S.W. v. The United Kingdom. 1995, November 22. ECtHR. No: 20166/92.

Şahin Alpay v. Turkey. 2018, June 20. ECtHR. No: 16538/17.

Sakık and Others v. Turkey. 1997, November 26. ECtHR. No: 23878/94 to 23883/94.

Salabiaku v. France. 1988, October 7. ECtHR. B. No: 10519/83, Par. 42.

Sekanina v. Austria. 1993, August 25. ECtHR. B. No: 13126/87, Pars. 20–31.

Sevdiren, Öznur. 2018. Olağanüstü Hal Hukukunda Müebbet Kamu Görevinden İhraç Yaptırımının Cezai Niteliği (Criminal Character of Enforcement from Life of Public Service Under State of Emergency Law). Suç ve Ceza, Ceza Hukuku Dergisi, Yıl: 2018, Sayı: 2, İstanbul.

Sevtap, Yokuş. 2017. *Avrupa İnsan Hakları Sözleşmesi'nin Türkiye'de Olağanüstü Hal Rejimi Pratiği ve Anayasa Şikayetine Etkisi [The European Convention on Human Rights Regime*

Impact on Practice of Emergency and Constitutional Complaint in Turkey]. Ankara: Seçkin Yayınları.
Smith and Grady v. United Kingdom. 1999, December 27. ECtHR. No: 33985/95.
Soro v. Estona. 2015, September 3. ECtHR. No: 22588/08.
State Council. 2016, October 4. Decision of the 5th Office of the State Council, No. 2016/4076.
Steel et al. v. UK. 1998, September 23. ECtHR. No: 24838/94.
Stran Greek Refineries and Stratis Andreadis v. Greece. 1994, December 9. ECtHR. B. No: 13427/87.
Sukut v. Turkey. 2007, September 11. ECtHR. B. No: 59773/00.
Teixeira de Castro v. Portugal. 1998, June 9. ECtHR. B. No: 25829/94, Par. 26.
Telfner v. Austria. 2001, March 20. ECtHR. B. No: 33501/96, Pars. 18–20.
Türmen, Rıza. 2016. *OHAL Kararnamelerinin Hukuksal Sorunları* [The Legal Problems Under the State of Emergency]. Cumhuriyet Gazetesi, August 22.
Urat v. Turkey. 2018, November 27. ECtHR. B. No: 53561/09 and 13952/11, Par. 58.
Venice Commission Report. 2017. *Opinion*: On the amendments adopted by the Grand National Assembly on 21 January 2017 and to be submitted to a national referendum on 16 April 2017. https://www.venice.coe.int/webforms/documents/default.aspx?pdffile=CDL-AD(2017)005-e.
Vilho Eskelinen and Others v. Finland. 2007, April 19. ECtHR. B. No: 63235/00, Par. 62.
Vitkauskas, Dovydas, and Dikov, Grigoriy. 2018. *Avrupa İnsan Hakları Sözleşmesi Kapsamında Adil Yargılanma Hakkının Korunması, Uygulamacılar İçin El Kitabı* [Handbook for Practitioners on the Protection of the Right to a Fair Trial Under the European Convention on Human Rights]. Turkish translation by S. Cengiz. Ankara: Anayasa Mahkemesine Bireysel Başvuru Sisteminin Desteklenmesi Ortak Projesi Yayını.
YB v. Turkey. ECtHR. 2004, October 28. B. No: 48173/99, Pars. 46–50.
Zalli v. Albania. 2011, February 8. ECtHR. B. No: 52531/07.
Zickus v. Lithuania. 2009, April 7. ECtHR. No: 22652/02.

Dr. Ufuk Yesil completed his BA in Law at Selçuk University, and earned his Master's Degree at Gazi University, and received his doctoral degree in public law from Kırıkkale University. In 2005, the Republic has started his career as a prosecuting attorney, in addition, he worked as Secretary in General for the Court of Dispute which is one of the four high courts in Turkey. He was removed his position during a crack-down failed coup in July 2016 and has been arrested and jailed for 28 months. During the 28 months of his imprisonment, he has written two books on "State of Emergency (OHAL) Practices in the Context of Law and Human Rights", and another book that titled "and Evidence of Bylock Information in the Context of Law and Human Rights". Currently, he is working as an independent researcher and a human right activist.

Chapter 12
Intellectuals on Hunger Strike for Reinstatement to Their Job: The Case of the "Yuksel Resistance"

Acun Karadag and Nazan Bozkurt

Abstract The purpose of this chapter is to identify various human and constitutional rights violations in Turkey, and to demonstrate those violations in a systematic way. The data were collected through interviews, reports, and open-source media articles, written after a protest in Ankara named "We Want Our Jobs Back." The article also employs verbal histories of activists, including Acun Karadag, Nazan Bozkurt, and Mehmet Dersulu, and participant observations of activities in which the researchers have been involved since the beginning of the State of Emergency. Five people were interviewed for this study. The analysis of the data unveiled two themes: Violence and Unlawful Intervention, and Resistance and Determination. The findings were discussed and accompanied with photographs under these two themes. Furthermore, police brutality and excessive use of force are depicted in the photographs that were acquired from social media platforms. The conclusion reveals that the Turkish government violated fundamental human rights including the right to a fair trial, as well as the right to peacefully assemble and demonstrate. In addition, the Turkish police disproportionately intervened using unnecessary and extreme violence in cases in which Decree-Law victims were trying to exercise their Constitutional rights.

Keywords Human rights violations · Intellectuals · Hunger strike · Reinstatement · Yuksel resistance

---

A. Karadag (✉)
Human Rights Activist, Ankara, Turkey

N. Bozkurt
Human Rights Activist, Düzce, Turkey

H. Aydin, W. Langley (eds.), *Human Rights in Turkey*, Philosophy and Politics - Critical Explorations 15, https://doi.org/10.1007/978-3-030-57476-5_12

12.1 Yuksel Resistance in a Nutshell

Following the failed coup attempt on July 15, 2016, the Justice and Development Party (AKP) government declared a state of emergency in Turkey on July 21, 2016, for a period of 3 months. It was extended seven times for three-months each time, and was finally lifted on July 17, 2018 (Erem 2018). Throughout the two-years of the state of emergency, the government issued several unrelated enactments through decree-laws (DLs). The state of emergency, which was presented as a temporary measure after the failed coup attempt, allowed the government to begin immediately purging members of the Islamic group who were accused of plotting the coup attempt, from their government positions. Later, it was used as an opportunity to purge all the anti-government groups from public service (Kingsley 2017). In addition, the government passed a number of unrelated issues through DLs. With these DLs, more than 150,000 civil servants were dismissed from their jobs, the licenses of 21,000 private school teachers were revoked, more than 4400 prosecutors and judges were dismissed, and 3000 schools, dormitories and universities, as well as 189 media outlets, were closed down (Turkey's post-coup crackdown 2019).

Although the state of emergency lasted for only 2 years, it had significant impacts on the country's society and institutions due to it imposing restrictions on individuals' right to exercise numerous fundamental freedoms. Furthermore, human rights violations included reports of arbitrary killings, suspicious deaths of persons while in custody, forced disappearances, abuses, arbitrary arrests and detention of tens of thousands of persons, including opposition members of the parliament, lawyers, journalists, and foreign citizens (United States Department of State – Bureau of Democracy Human Rights and Labor 2019, 1).

Nuriye Gülmen, one of over 6000 academicians who were dismissed from their jobs by decree-laws during the state of emergency, started a protest with a simple but decisive demand, "I Want My Job Back," on Yuksel Street in the central Kizilay District of Ankara, Turkey's capital city. Other activists, such as Semih Ozakca, Acun Karadag, Nazan Bozkurt, Veli Sacilik, and Mehmet Dersulu, joined Gülmen at various times. However, the impact of their protest echoed across the country and abroad as a result of the broadcasts by foreign media, as well as the broadcasts of correspondents who had interviewed the activists. The Yuksel Protest/Resistance, named after Yuksel Street where the protest took place, has become a symbol of resistance against the human rights violations committed by the DLs issued during the State of Emergency. In this vein, this study examined the stories of activists Acun Karadag, Nazan Bozkurt, Merve Demirel and Mehmet Dersulu, as well as the rights violations and violence to which Nuriye Gülmen and Semih Ozakca, symbols of the resistance with their hunger strikes, and many other protestors, were exposed.

12.2 The Prominence of Yuksel Street in Ankara

The civil/political resistance that has taken place on Yuksel Street has symbolic importance. Ankara is the capital and the second-largest city of Turkey, with a population of slightly over 5.5 million people (Ankara Nufusu 2019). The Turkish National Assembly, all the central institutions of the State, including ministerial buildings, headquarters of the army, police, and intelligence, several other organizations of the government, headquarters of all political parties, and embassies, are located in Ankara. Therefore, it is the center of the bureaucracy and the political heart of the country.

Kizilay Square in Ankara, which is a five-minute walk from the Turkish National Assembly, is comparable to Times Square in New York City. Most political protests, demonstrations, and activities similar to "I Want My Job Back," customarily take place in or around this square. Yuksel is one of the major streets of the Kizilay District, located between the Square and the Turkish National Assembly compound. Traditionally, the street has been the meeting and gathering point of intellects, university students, political activists, and many others. Another factor of Yuksel Street that highlights its significance and symbolism in the context of political resistance, is the Human Rights Monument that is placed along the street. Sculptor Metin Yurdanur, a state-recognized artist, created the bronze-casted monument in 1990. This symbolic structure of art depicts a woman reading the Universal Declaration of Human Rights (UDHR) that is open in her hands (Shafak 2017). The Yuksel Resistance originally came out with the demand for fundamental human rights prescribed in the Universal Declaration of Human Rights and therefore, the location of the protests was aptly chosen provided the context of thousands of people who alleged that the state had violated their rights (see the data below).

12.3 How the Yuksel Protests Were Born and Gained Strength

Gülmen was dismissed from her job without any reason. Although there was not a case brought against her, she was arrested after participating in a hunger strike and tried on charges of membership of an anti-government organization (Amnesty International 2017; Human Rights Foundation of Turkey 2018; Kingsley 2017). After Gülmen was suspended from her position at Eskisehir Osmangazi University, she began her protest in front of the Human Rights Monument on November 9, 2016. The first day of the protest concluded as a result of the intervention of hundreds of police officers and the arrest of Nuriye Gülmen. Although she was repeatedly detained, Gülmen did not cease her protest. In fact, many individuals who were persecuted as a result of the DLs joined her. On November 14, Acun Karadag, a teacher who was dismissed from his job after 20 years of service, joined Gülmen's protest. It was after Karadag, who had begun her protest in front of her school, participated in the protest on Yuksel Street, that the street became the symbolic location of "We Want Our Jobs Back" (Human Rights Association 2017). On November 22, Semih Ozakca, who was dismissed from his public service job as an elementary teacher in the city of Mardin, joined. Another individual, Sociologist Veli Sacilik, had lost his right arm on July 5, 2000, when he was in the Jail of Burdur, as a result of the walls of the jail being demolished with construction vehicles during a police operation conducted against inmates. Upon his release, he began to work at the General Directorate of Population and Citizenship Affairs of the Ministry of Interior until he was dismissed with a DL. On January 13, 2017, Mr. Sacilik participated in the Gülmen protest.

Thousands of detentions were made, administrative fines were imposed, investigations were initiated, and charges were pressed during this sit-in protest. Law enforcement made 232 interventions, and more than 2000 detentions (Human Rights Association 2018). The judicial inquiries that were initiated against them and other activists participating in the protest included allegations of membership to a terrorist organization, violation of the Law on Meetings and Demonstrations No. 2911, and libel through social media. It was not solely the activists who were fined, but also those who applauded or video-recorded the protest and those who reacted against the police abuse. These imposed fines on the protesters were a significant amount, costing each of the active participants 500,000 Turkish Liras (approximately USD 100,000). In addition to the charges and imposed fines, police used pepper gas in the early days of the resistance to interfere with the right to peaceful protest in the region, which is one of the most central parts of Ankara (Human Rights Association 2017).

Reports indicated that the police resorted to several types of abuse on the protestors including: beating the participants, using intense pepper spray that affected the whole street, shooting plastic bullets directly targeting the protestors, holding them back-handcuffed in police cars for hours, and spraying them with water cannons (Human Rights Association 2017). The Ankara Chamber of Doctors conducted an analysis of the gas released by the police from the container named *Model 5,* and determined that it was poisonous and harmful to the protestors' digestive systems.

In addition, the right to a defense of the protestors was violated during this intervention. For example, 18 of the protestors' lawyers were detained before the first hearing of the cases, and 14 of them were later arrested and jailed. The protestors' head-counsel lawyer and chairman of the closed-down Progressive Lawyers Association, Selcuk Kozagacli, was one of those arrested (Human Rights Watch 2018).

The Justice and Development Party (AKP) formed the 67th government since 1923, on July 9, 2018, by gaining the support of 42.6% of voters. However, as Karadag and Sacilik stated in an interview, the majority of the people felt restless because of the government's oppressive policies implemented in response to the Yuksel Resistance, which lasted over 1100 days (Kaynak 2018).

Although the announced reason for the declaration of the state of emergency was the failed coup attempt, the decree-laws enacted during the state of emergency deprived citizens of their citizenship rights and prohibited them from association with others (Human Rights Association 2018). As determined during inspections by the officials from the Office of the United Nations High Commissioner for Human Rights, practices beyond the restrictions foreseen in the conventions regarding fundamental human rights and freedoms throughout the state of emergency occurred. Thus, those practices should be corrected (Human Rights Association 2018). The state of emergency was lifted after 2 years, however, the victimization of the dismissed civil servants continues.

Having started in Ankara, similar protests continued throughout many other provinces. For example, architect Alev Sahin started a sit-in protest in Duzce on January 30, 2017 (People's architect Alev Sahin started her sit-in protest at TMMOB 2018). Sahin continued her protest on Yuksel Street on certain days of the week, and in Duzce on others. In addition, several DL-victims, who were the main targets of the state of emergency and were accused of membership to a terrorist organization, supported the Yuksel Protest. One of them, Merve Demirel, was subjected to abuse during the time she was detained when she was sexually harassed and forced to remove her head cover (Gergerlioglu 2019b). In regard to of the victimization of people having different world views, Gergerlioglu (2019b) stated:

> No matter what the political views of DL victims are, I saw that they were mostly people who worked for the good of this country by making sacrifices. I call them patriots, let alone traitors, harmful or terrorists. From Gokhan Acikkollu, who was killed under crime, to hero teachers in the Yuksel Protest. (p. 924)

Succinctly, he noted that the victims were all patriots, but the government makes them appear otherwise.

Acun Karadag shared his knowledge with protestors and reassured them that he would never give up resisting (Karadag 2018, 2019). Therefore, as the protest grew, the protestors gained confidence and regularly shared their diaries in newspapers, in which they explained why they continued their resistance. In addition, they shared photos in their publications and on social media platforms and wrote articles and posts about how they were able to continue resisting in spite of the disproportionate force that law enforcement was applying.

In response to officials overlooking the protesting by academician Gülmen and teacher Ozakca, who became the symbols of the resistance against dismissals by DLs during the state of emergency, the two protestors led a hunger strike from March 9, 2017 until January 26, 2018, when the judicial remedy was adopted for rejections for their court trials of the Commission on State of Emergency Measures (Human Rights Association 2018). During this 324 days, Gülmen and Ozakca experienced significant weight loss and illness (Neither of them can walk 2017).

Gülmen and Ozakca were arrested on May 23, 2017, the 76th day of their hunger strike. The Human Rights Association (2018) said that their arrests were orchestrated in order to "silence the rising voices of the protestors who continued their protests uninterruptedly." Although Semih Ozakca was released in October 2017, Nuriye Gülmen was held under arrest until December 2017. Consequently, Gülmen was convicted of membership to the DHKP-C organization, but Semih Ozakca was acquitted of the same allegation (Amnesty International 2018).

Gülmen and Ozakca stated that although it was challenge to reinstate their rights, they remained motivated to take a stand against fascism, the decree-laws, and government oppression that occurred during the state of emergency (May Nuriye always laugh, May Nuriye always live 2017).

12.4 Hunger Strikes in Turkey

Historically, individuals who are deprived of their fundamental human rights, including refugees, captives, and minority groups who seek political, religious and social rights, have used hunger strikes as the "weapon of the weak" (Beynon 1996). Hunger strikes, which were first orchestrated by political prisoners in Russia in 1889 (Ratcliffe 1932) and by Gandhi's civil disobedience camping announcement for the beginning a "fast unto death" against British government in 1932 in India, have been observed a few times in the recent history of Turkey. Unfortunately, hunger strikes may end tragically. Four of the hunger strike cases in 1982, six in 1984, and 12 in 1996 resulted in deaths of the participants (Altun et al. 2004). The longest hunger strike in Turkey, conducted by political prisoners in 2000, ended in the deaths of 57 prisoners and 7 supporters (Turkey Country Report 2004). However, the most recent example in Turkish history was the hunger strike by Gülmen and Ozakca, which was not terminated as a result of their claims being met, but because they and other DL victims were allowed to apply for judicial remedy.

12.5 Legal Regulations

A key reason for the detentions and investigations of the protestors and their supporters was a result of individuals releasing information in the press or conducting meetings obtaining permission from the authorities. However, such obligations/regulations/practices do not exist in the related law, as will be seen below. Regardless, some provincial governors acted sharply in order to prevent such protests and prohibited meetings and demonstrations, by citing the state of emergency as justification for the prohibition (Human Rights Association 2018; Mazlum-Der 2018). Although not legally required, the Human Rights Association applied to the Governor's Office of Ankara to make a press release on Yuksel Street on the International Human Rights Day on December 10, 2017, but the application was rejected (Human Rights Association 2017).

The illegality of such a prohibition policy is embedded in national and international regulations. The Constitution of the Turkish Republic regulates the issue in Article 34 under the title of "Right to hold meetings and demonstration marches," which reads:

- Everyone has the right to hold unarmed and peaceful meetings and demonstration marches without prior permission.
- The right to hold meetings and demonstration marches shall be restricted only by law on the grounds of national security, public order, prevention of commission of a crime, protection of public health and public morals, or the rights and freedoms of others.
- The formalities, conditions, and procedures to be applied in the exercise of the right to hold meetings and demonstration marches shall be prescribed by law.

From the article, it can be inferred that: (1) everyone is entitled to hold peace meetings and demonstrations freely, (2) no prior permission is required, (3) meetings and demonstrations may only be prohibited by law on the grounds of the causes cited in the article, and (4) the required procedure may be regulated by laws, but no other types of regulations may be imposed.

The "law," referred to in the article of the Constitution, is the Law on Meetings and Demonstrations No. 2911 of 1983 (Law on Meetings and Demonstrations 1983). Article 3 of the law reiterates the regulation in the Constitution with a minor addition: Everyone has the right to hold unarmed and peaceful meetings and demonstration marches without prior permission for certain purposes that are not considered a crime by law. Therefore, the government must prove with concrete evidence that the purpose of the current or would-be meetings and demonstrations are "considered crimes by law" to be able to intervene or impose a prohibition. Furthermore, unless the government demonstrates such evidence, any prohibition would be constitutionally illegal.

Article 20 of the Universal Declaration of Human Rights of 1948 encompasses a similar principle: "Everyone has the right to freedom of peaceful assembly and association." Similarly, The European Convention on Human Rights of 1950 regulates the issue in the first clauses of its 11th Article, which are:

1. Everyone has the right to freedom of peaceful assembly and to freedom of association with others, including the right to form and to join trade unions for the protection of his interests.
2. No restrictions shall be placed on the exercise of these rights other than such as are prescribed by law and are necessary in a democratic society in the interests of national security or public safety, for the prevention of disorder or crime, for the protection of health or morals or for the protection of the rights and freedoms of others.

As evidenced, no significant difference exists between national and international principles pertaining to human rights. Therefore, in order for the government's prohibition of and intervention in the Yuksel Protests to be legal, the government must prove that the protests were made for reasons that constitute a crime according to the laws. However, the government's prohibition and intervention through its governors and law enforcement did not involve such legal grounds. Furthermore, no evidence exists that would have indicated that protestors acted in any inappropriate or criminal manner. They were pointedly protesting the Decree-Laws, according to which they were dismissed from their jobs, which is not plausible to categorize as a criminal act. Therefore, the conclusion can be made that the governors ignored the related laws and international conventions and violated citizens' rights.

In this context, this study will examine the stories of activists Acun Karadag, Nazan Bozkurt, Merve Demirel and Mehmet Dersulu, as well as the rights violations and violence to which Nuriye Gülmen and Semih Ozakca, symbols of the resistance with their hunger strikes, and many other protestors were exposed.

The research question focused on in this study is, "Which rights of public servants, who were victimized by Decree-Laws, were violated during the Yuksel Protest?" The importance of this lies with the notion that the findings may be generalizable to similar protests occurring in Turkey.

12.6 Methodology

A qualitative interpretive case study method was employed for data collection and analysis (Stake 2006; Yin 2014). This study emphasized the understanding and interpretation of human perceptions (Lincoln and Denzin 2005) of their actions into a broader system of meanings to which those actions belong. Therefore, a case study was appropriate to use because it allowed the researchers to examine one or more events or people in order to understand a topic, phenomenon, or problem (Creswell and Poth 2017). In order to collect data, the researchers employed in-depth interviews, open-ended interviews, direct observation, and written documents (Patton 2002). The researchers generated their reports by employing multiple data collection methods within a certain period of time (Baxter and Jack 2008). Thereby, conducting a qualitative case study enabled the researchers to discover a topic or problem in a real-life context, and by using a particular event (Creswell 2014).

12.6.1 Participants, Setting, and Procedures

Following the failed coup attempt on July 15, 2016, more than 120,000 public workers were dismissed from the jobs under the pretext of the state of emergency. The researchers of this study employed a case study in order to analyze and present the rights violations against Acun Karadag, Nazan Bozkurt, and other activists, who participated in the Yuksel Resistance. The Yuksel Resistance started with Nuriye Gülmen's "I Want My Job Back!" protest on Yuksel Street in Ankara in November 2016. However, as more activists began to attend, the slogan evolved into "We Want Our Jobs Back!"

Participants of this study are the public servants who initiated and maintained the *Yuksel Resistance*. Although hundreds of people were subjected to similar repercussions of the government throughout the course of this resistance; the participants were selected from among those who were most active and willing to participate in the study. Therefore, the researchers used the criterion sampling technique of purposive sampling. In criterion sampling, the sample is composed of persons, events, objects, or situations with specified qualifications pertaining to the problem (Stake 2006). The sample of this research consisted of Acun Karadag, Nazan Bozkurt, Merve Demirel and Mehmet Dersulu, and more significantly, Nuriye Gülmen and Semih Ozakca, whose hunger strikes became the symbol of the resistance, as well as others who occasionally supported the resistance.

The Yuksel Resistance started out with Nuriye Gülmen who became a world-renowned figure who was readily recognized and associated with the Gülmen and Ozakca's hunger strikes. However, although neither of these activists were able to participate actively in this study, they were aware that an academic study regarding human rights violations during the Yuksel Resistance would be conducted. Journalists from domestic and foreign press organizations had previously interviewed Gülmen and Ozakca during their hunger strike. Thus, the authors examined the human rights violations experienced by Gülmen and Ozakca through the observations of people who worked closely with them, interviews they made with journalists, and relevant document analyses.

The primary data collection methods utilized to gather stories and opinions of participants were observation, interview, and document analysis. Additionally, experiences, as well as opinions, were collected. An interview is the most preferred technique for collecting data in qualitative research that aims to obtain information about people's attitudes, opinions, and behaviors about past, present, or future (Harrell and Bradley 2009). However, observations are one of the most accurate and valid research techniques because the data obtained through observation reflect what people actually do, rather than what they say they do (Gillham 2008). Document analysis, another data collection technique, is frequently used in cases in which observation and interviewing is not possible. In such cases, written documents and visual materials related to the research subject are compiled and examined in order to obtain more detailed, objective, and detailed information (Yin 2014).

The selection of these three techniques was designed to increase the reliability, validity, and fortitude of the study. The researchers took advantage of the power of photographs, videos, and social media to inform the entire world about what was occurring on Yuksel Street. Although police video recorded the experiences of individuals in custody 24 h a day, outside electronic recording devices were forbidden in custody. Thus, the experiences of those who were detained was not shared with other activists until after they were released. This allowed all the violations against the victims to be shared with the public in the Yuksel Newspaper and on Yuksel TV [on Youtube]. Data collected via video recordings assists in increasing the validity and reliability of the study.

The case of this study is the Yuksel Resistance. We, the activists of Yuksel Resistance, used our own experiences, as well as publications about the Resistance, as the primary source of data for this study, thereby further increasing the validity of the study. The data set of this study consists of what we, the authors Acun Karadag and Nazan Bozkurt, have been experiencing personally, have directly observed, and have obtained through interviews with activists. In addition information on various cases and human rights violations was obtained from, and crosschecked through, media, human rights reports, interview texts, video recordings and photographs that have come out since the July 2016 coup attempt in Turkey. Regarding cases of detentions, police violence, and arrests, we interviewed victims and witnesses. The data we collected were examined and analyzed by us as well as by researchers both from Turkish and foreign universities. We detected common themes when we compared the analysis of the codes in the dataset with the themes each of us found. Then, we sent those codes and themes to the participants of the study. Corrections were made in response to the feedback received from the participants. Finally, the codes and final themes were sent to two social researchers at two different universities for outside checking.

12.7 Findings

An analysis of the multiple methods of data revealed two themes: *violence and unlawful inter*vention, and *resistance and determination*. This section examines the rights violations to which the Yuksel Protestors were exposed under those themes. Related parts of the statements of the protestors, from which those themes emerged, are referred to below:

12.7.1 Theme 1: Violence and Unlawful Intervention

Case 1: Acun Karadag

Karadag has made criticisms and comments against the government since her dismissal. In her story, Karadag mentions not only her own experiences, but also those from victims she spoke with or visually witnessed. It can be understood from this narrative that Karadag defends the rights of persons who have been dismissed or otherwise victimized after the coup attempt on 15 July 2016. Therefore, Karadag is perceived to be on the right track even though she is subjected to police violence almost every day. This is her story.

> When I was a teacher and a civil servant with 25 years of experience, I was dismissed with the Decree-Law No. 675 on October 29, 2016. Our names were listed and published in the Official Gazette. Neither I nor the other protestors who were dismissed like me know why we were dismissed. Although we were labelled in the DL list as "being affiliated with the terrorist organization," we do not know anything about the reasons, for which we were dismissed because we were not shown our files.
>
> The day after I was dismissed, I went to the school where I worked, but I was told that I was not allowed to get in. This procedure itself was a violation of human rights. We have employment security. According to the Civil Servants Law No. 657, they may not issue even a disciplinary sanction of reprimand without conducting an investigation. Decree-Laws

are regulations that function like laws, but in fact, are not laws. They may be used during states of emergency; however, they lose their validity as soon as states of emergency are lifted. The reason is that DLs are only used as measures against events that require a declaration of the state of emergency. The AKP, which claimed that there was a coup attempt on July 15, and therefore declared the state of emergency, could issue those decree-laws only after a coup attempt. In sum, they could issue decree-laws for emergencies to avoid waiting for the long procedure of passing laws.

How could a schoolteacher be related to the coup?

To cease people's support for those whose rights were violated, the AKP government said those who were dismissed were responsible for the killings and stated that those dismissed were related to terrorist organizations. However, for a civil servant to be dismissed in Turkey, he or she must have committed a serious crime that was substantiated by courts, and he must have been convicted. For all those reasons, dismissal by decree-laws is unlawful and a crime committed by the State.

I said on the day that I was dismissed that I would start a sit-in protest in front of my school and resist against the unlawfulness. For my first protest, I went to the front of the school, from which I had been dismissed with my daughter on November 14, 2016. That day police officers covered my mouth with their hands so that my address to my students would not be heard, and arrested me and those who supported my protest. They threatened my students, my teacher colleagues, and parents saying that they would get into trouble, and they would also be dismissed if they supported me. Everybody was scared of this threat and retreated.

I tried to go to my school and do my protest, but I was detained in the first five minutes. The detentions went on for 15 days. Some bulky officers approached and said: 'Get out of here, or we will arrest you.' Each time I told them that I was exercising my legal right to make a protest, and they had to go. Then I was detained. By appearance, they were stronger, but I was the one who was stronger. Although I stood in front of the school alone and with no weapon whatsoever, tens of officers came to arrest me. Once I asked an officer why they detained me because I had neither a weapon nor a bomb. He said to me: 'Your pen is more dangerous than weapons.' I responded: "My pen is dangerous for you and the government which you worship. I enlighten children and help them think."

The detentions lasted for 24 days. On the 25th day of my protest, on December 08, 2016, I went to the hospital for angiography. They took me under an emergency operation and placed a pacemaker. My heart health deteriorated after the 24-day long continuous intensive stress that I went through. Teacher Kazim Unlu, from the same union as mine, who [became] depressed about his dismissal, had a heart attack and died.

Many others have been lost over the last three years. More than 70 people committed suicide after they were dismissed. I was lucky because I was able to get an operation. I had to rest at home for a month after the surgery. I wanted to resume my protest in January 2017 and joined Nuriye Gülmen's protest of "We want our jobs back." I was wounded by police interventions during those protests and contracted some diseases (Fig. 12.1).

After I became involved in the Yuksel Protest, I participated for several months with Nuriye Gülmen, Semih Ozakca, Veli Sacilik, Mehmet Dersulu, and many others. Nuriye and Semih declared that they would start a hunger strike. We made a press release with parliament members at the Grand National Assembly of Turkey. As soon as we went out of the Assembly, Nuriye, Semih, and I were detained by the police division of counterterrorism. We were released four days later. The hunger strike started in this process, and we were prosecuted for membership to a terrorist organization.

Fig. 12.1 Acun Karadag's exposure to plastic bullets and pepper spray

The hunger strike created a reaction in the population, and masses came to the area of the Yuksel Protest. People increased in number, and then the government detained the hunger strike protestors claiming that we were trying to start a new Gezi Resistance. The Gezi Resistance, in which protests took place in 2013 against the government's decision to build a mall in the area of Gezi Park in Taksim, Istanbul, was their nightmare.

After the arrests of Gülmen and Ozakca, our protest area and all the roads around it were blocked by the police with anti-riot water cannon vehicles and barricades. All the protestors were detained. After we were released, we came near the water cannon vehicles and the iron barricades and said: 'No matter where you place your barricades, we will continue our protests in front of them.' In the course of time, we first had water cannon vehicles removed and then the barricades.

The police attacked us every day in order to prevent us from approaching the Human Rights Monument on Yuksel Street. However, we were determined to make two press releases daily, one at noon and one in the evening. We wanted to exercise our rights in Articles 26[1] and 34[2] of the Constitution that guarantees Freedom of Expression and the right to Peaceable Assemble and Demonstrate, respectively.

However, the provincial and district governors, as well as the judiciary, were all under the influence of the AKP in the country which had turned the country into a party-state. The Palace gave commands to the governor and made him issue a ban on protests. In legal terms, the police were breaking the law, and we were right. However, fascism was gaining strength in the country.

[1]See Article 26 of the Constitution; VIII. Freedom of Expression and Spreading Thought.

[2]See Article 34 of the Constitution; B. Right to Organize Meetings and Demonstrations.

The police exposed us to chemical gasses every day and ruthlessly shot plastic bullets towards different parts of our bodies. I received several medical reports for my bruised legs because of the plastic bullets so that I could submit them to the Human Rights Foundation of Turkey. We were taken to the police station when we were detained. Because we did not want to be taken to the police station, we were dragged on the ground, and our hair was pulled. This is why I had my hair cut very short, like a man. I also said that I would not grow it until the protest was over. Although they knew that I had a heart problem, they repeatedly sprayed gasses into my mouth and towards my eyes. After a year, I was diagnosed with asthma because of the gasses to which I was exposed.

Another one of the rights violations was harassment. I was exposed to harassment by one of the police chiefs during a police attack. When I complained to the people around me that the chief had grabbed my right breast, the police attacked me. They dispersed the people by spraying gas, prevented me from speaking by spraying gas towards my mouth and eyes. They pushed me to the ground and back-handcuffed me. I still have pain in my shoulders due to bursitis that developed because of back-handcuffing.

I cannot do hard work with my right arm. I filed a complaint against a police officer, but I was detained instead of him. I was [the one being] harassed, but a public action was initiated against me for calling the officer as harasser and pervert. My complaint about the harassment is still under examination in the prosecutor's office, and it has not been put in process for two years. We live in a country in which we are prosecuted for being harassed (Fig. 12.2).

Not being able to cope with the protestors, the government attempted to get rid of the problem by putting them under house arrest. My protestor friend, Nazan Bozkurt, and I were put under house arrest. Nazife Onay and Abidin Sirmawere were jailed after refusing electronic bracelets. Esra Ozakca, the wife of Semih Ozakca, could not leave home because

Fig. 12.2 The harassing police chief (left) taking vengeance against Acun Karadag after she filed her complaint

she was on a hunger strike. We wore an electronic bracelet for 25 days until Nazife Onay was arrested. In this process, Nazan Bozkurt violated the confinement many times by leaving her house. I did not go out for 25 days.

When Nazife Onay was arrested, I removed my bracelet and went to our spot of protest on Yuksel Street. Nazan Bozkurt was there, too, without removing her bracelet. I was detained and taken to court for removing the bracelet, with a request for arrest. I told the judge that I wanted my job back, I had not committed any crime that requires arrest, I would not turn my house into a jail and be my own guard, they may arrest me if they thought that I had committed a crime, and I would never take on the electronic bracelet again. The judge rejected the request for arrest, and we were able to get rid of the house arrest that day.

After the hunger strike was over, the police changed their methods. They did not take us to the police station now but released us after the medical check fining us 320 TL according to the Law on Misdemeanors. In other words, what they used to call "a terrorist activity" suddenly became a misdemeanor. It was not an arrest, but an act of frustration. Ultimately, the amount of the fines imposed on the protestors and the supporters exceeded two million TL (approximately USD 400,000). We did not pay the unlawfully-imposed fines.

I have been out on the streets since November 14, 2016, except for the periods I had an operation, and [while] I wore the electronic bracelet. I have been on the streets freezing in winter and getting soaked with sweat in summer. I have been detained, maybe, more than 1,000 times in the last three years. The fines they imposed on me exceeded 200,000 TL. The police raided my house four times. They seized my cell phone three times, and my computer, but they did not return them to me. My writings and photographs on my computer were all deleted, and I did not have their backups. I had to buy cell phones repeatedly. I was very severely affected financially. They also urged my neighbors to make complaints against me. The government tried to infamize me in every way it could think of.

Karadag continuously emphasized her story as follows;

"Some of those who were victimized by decree-laws and defamed by arbitrary detentions committed suicide. Teacher Canan, who had lived in the city of Denizli, was one of those victims. She was 40 years old and the mother of two children. She left everything behind and hanged herself with a rope she tied to the ceiling of her kitchen. People talked behind her back and said that her husband was in jail because of a 'FETO' investigation and dismissed. A mother never entrusts her children with anybody. A mother never dies by leaving her children behind. She was in such desperation that she did not even think about her children. Only three years ago, that woman was together with her students in a classroom. If someone had told her that she would commit suicide, she would probably have thought that he was insane. The AKP government turned the country into a huge graveyard with those who died and, more importantly, with a living death." "I, and all other public servants, have served this country and nation for years. Under the pretext of the coup attempt of July 15, our rights to work were taken without being able to defend ourselves. It was not only our jobs that we lost, but the AKP government completely eliminated the concepts of justice and law for Turkey after July 15. The government violated the Constitution, and many articles in laws were violated. It is more accurate to call the courts in the country as courts of the AKP, instead of courts of the State. The AKP courts may be persecuting the people and ignoring our rights; however, governments are temporary while states are permanent. The violators of rights shall be called to account, sooner or later."

Case 2: Merve Demirel

The Yuksel Protest has an essential role in reference to people's brotherhood. Merve Demirel, whose father had been dismissed for Gülen Movement (GM) related

Fig. 12.3 Yuksel protestor Merve Demirel being roughed up while being detained (Okatan 2019)

allegations, was detained while supporting the protest. A police officer roughed up Demirel, and this action was photographed (Fig. 12.3).

In general, women try to hide the harassment to which they have been exposed due to the shame that they feel. However, Demirel did not refrain from calling out that harassment as the shame of the perpetrator, not the victim.

Although the actions of the police officer became a hot button issue, the Ministry of Interior preferred to protect the officer and did not start an investigation. Her headscarf was removed during the detentions, violating her honor. Nevertheless, such treatments could not deter her from continuing her struggle. She said:

> I am a student who tries to adopt Selcuk Koazagacli's words into her life: 'What is divine is not the life itself, but to live with honor.' Although we attempted to exercise our Constitutional rights, we are always faced with attacks. They may hurt our bodies, but our consciences and inner worlds remain so clean and strong that their abuses and harassment cannot affect us. Their press releases are met with hatred by the people. They try to cope up with their disability to rule by trying to silence the people. It is their disgrace. Women's honor may not be affected by harassment. We can overcome abuses with the honor of people.

Case 3: Nazan Bozkurt

Bozkurt presented her story with several photographs in order to prove the occurrence of the violence that she, and those around her experienced, and stated why she was so persistent in the resistance. Bozkurt mentioned that submission to injustice was not acceptable. Although she had undergone eye surgery as a result of the violence she experienced, she emphasized that she would not give up the resistance despite her experiences. She believes that she will get her job and other rights back.

When I was a register with 10 years of experience, I was dismissed with the Decree-Law No. 683 issued on January 23, 2017, by being placed in the list of people affiliated with a terrorist organization. There was not even a single investigation against me. I applied to all the legal means available, but my requests were rejected. Legal remedies were eliminated, our petitions went unanswered, and our applications for vocational courses were rejected because we had been dismissed with decree-laws. It was nearly impossible for me to find a job, like all other decree-law victims, because my dismissal with a decree-law was entered into the system of social security. The Social Security Organization adds the annotation of *Dismissed with a Decree-Law* in the records of dismissed public servants to prevent them from working at other workplaces.

Even if I had found a job and worked, I would have lost all my social security premiums, which had accumulated through my 10 years of service. In the end, I decided that the most appropriate way to follow against all the injustice was to make myself heard, and I participated in the protest that had been going on for a couple of months. Nuriye Gülmen, who had been dismissed unlawfully like us, started her protest in front of the Human Rights Monument on Yuksel Street on November 9, 2016, to return to her job, which she liked so much.

On the first day of the protest, hundreds of police officers intervened on a woman whose only means of defense was the placard 'I want my job back!' in her hand, and detained her. After she was released, she did not give up her protest. Gülmen's protest had more and more impact on national and international media each day. Hundreds of people who were dismissed from their jobs, or [who] wanted to be together with the protestors, supported the Yuksel Protest. At this point, the objective was to make the State know about the unlawfulness of the dismissals we were exposed to and to get our jobs back.

Although we had a right to make press releases on Yuksel Street, the Governor's Office of Ankara arbitrarily banned our protests, and we were detained as soon as we started to make our press releases. We were abused and detained each time. I estimate that I was detained about 1,500 times. I was never arrested, but I was sentenced to house arrest. An administrative fine of 250,000 TL (approximately USD 50,000) was imposed. About 25 public actions were started against me for a violation of the Law on Meetings and Demonstrations, and I was acquitted of 8 or 9 of them. The other actions are pending.

My friends and I were detained twice with the allegation of membership to a terrorist organization and were sentenced to house arrest in one of them. The house arrest was lifted in the first hearing. I was exposed to intimidation methods like judicial control measures, the obligation to signing in at a police station, and prohibition from leaving the country. As long as I wanted my job back on Yuksel Street, I was exposed to all kinds of mistreatment and persecution, as were my friends. They pulled my hair, sprayed poisonous gas towards my eyes and mouth, kicked me on the ground, sexually harassed me, insulted my mother, changed my body into a target for their plastic bullets, slapped me in the face, attempted to choke me, and handcuffed me in the back. They did everything they could in terms of cruelty. My cheekbone got broken with a punch of a police officer on June 8, 2018. I had to have surgery not to be blind. A titanium prosthesis was placed under my left eye (Fig. 12.4).

I filed a complaint against the officer who did that, but the prosecutor explicitly protected the abuser and ruled for non-prosecution, deciding that 'He did his job.' I contested the decision, but it has not been concluded yet. Lastly, a police officer who applied abuse and harassment on us found two other officers as false witnesses and claimed that we insulted them. Therefore, Mehmet Dersulu and I were detained and brought before the judge after intensive abuse. We were sentenced to house arrest, again. Of course, we did not accept this unlawfulness or obey the decision.

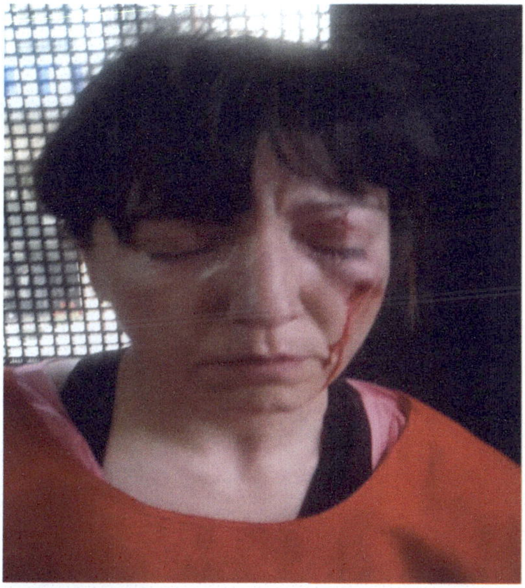

Fig. 12.4 Nazan Bozkurt's face after the police attack

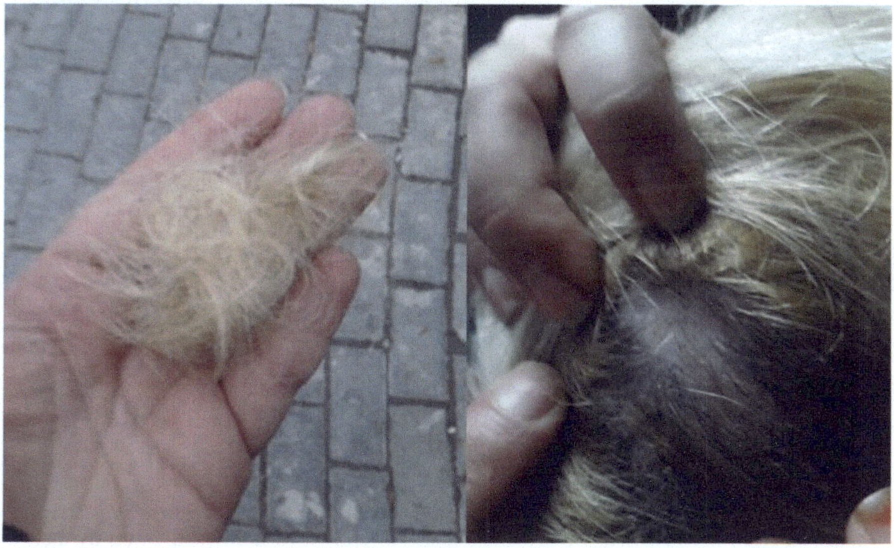

Fig. 12.5 Gulnaz Bozkurt's hair after the police attack

Besides, my elder sister, Gulnaz Bozkurt, was also dismissed from her job because she supported my lawful struggle. Because officers tore my sister's hair out. They bit her finger and tore the skin of her hand with their nails. She now works for a market and has filed an action against the officers who abused her. The action is pending (Fig. 12.5).

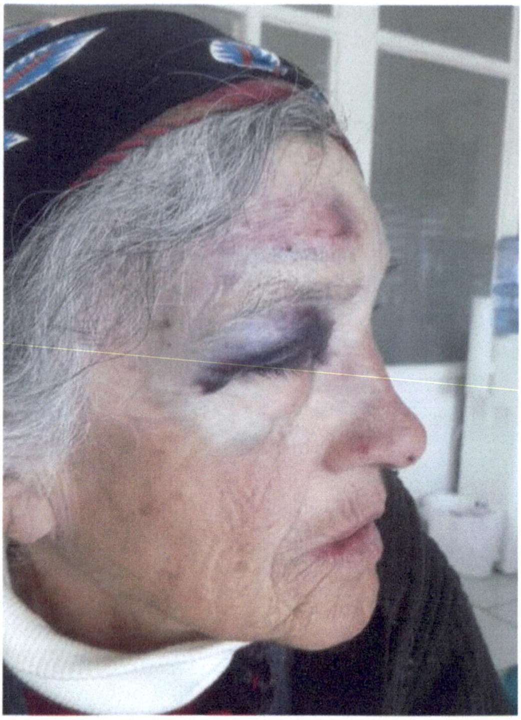

Fig. 12.6 Perihan Pulat after the police attack

Four female protestors, including me, were at the spot on the day my sister was abused. They sprayed pressure water on us from the special vehicle. I was pushed down by the first water attack. 76-year old Perihan Pulat was pushed behind her back, knocked off her feet, and fell. This photograph shows what her face was turned into (Fig. 12.6).

Case 4: Mehmet Dersulu

Mehmet Dersulu was one of the protestors who were exposed to the most intensive police harassment. Dersulu is one of the most active of the Yuksel insurgents. Almost every day, he acts in the square and is taken into custody. However, the story and pictures of Dersulu show that police detention often turns into abuse.

He narrates the abuse in the following words:

We continue resisting our honor against injustice. Once there is resistance against injustice, poverty, and hunger, there is always harassment by the system which generates them. They apply all types of oppression, violence and abuse to prevent us from being heard by the people. Because they do not tolerate our exercise of the most basic right of making a press release, they start their attacks as soon as we start our first sentences. They tell us not to resist while they are detaining us. More accurately, while they are kidnapping us because they do not follow the due process of detention. But we resist, and we will resist. We continue our resistance to be able to be heard for half a minute more in the face of the attacks we are exposed to twice a day. And we are exposed to harassment every time we resist.

The following words of Dersulu are especially crucial in terms of demonstrating the level of violence the police applied:

> During our press release at noon on the 484th day of the Yuksel Protest, we were subjected to abuse again. The harassment that day was very different from before. To say the least, that day's abuse was turned to total violence. While two or three officers were dragging me towards the detention vehicle, another police officer in civilian clothes or a riot control officer, I could not see then, continuously kicked me. I kept resisting to be heard for even a very short period of time. Before being pushed into the vehicle, I heard a riot control police chief commanding for my handcuffing. After I was shoved into the vehicle, undercover officers and riot control officers continued kicking me. Two undercover officers got into the vehicle and took me out of the vehicle dragging me on the ground. They also closed the door so that their colleagues in the vehicle could not interfere.
>
> This time, the violence turned into crime. They laid me down face downwards and continued kicking. An officer sat on my feet, another pushed me on my back, and a third one pressed against my neck with his knee while another abuse was pressing my head against the ground with his hand. Other abusers violently kicked my body wherever they found unoccupied. I had difficulty breathing, and shouting slogans was even more difficult. I had been exposed to harassment many times before, but I was met with such intense violence for the first time. For the first time in my life, my breath was not enough to shout slogans, and I shouted out of pain. After being back-handcuffed, I was thrown into the vehicle. I had such a terrible headache that I did not see anything because of pain. The abusive and cruel treatment officers also detained a supporter of ours. My dizziness and nausea continued until we arrived at the hospital.

Officers involved in the violence against Yuksel protestors knew that what they did was wrong and may end with their prosecution for their maltreatment. The intervention of the police was more of an act of abuse than pure intervention. Dersulu points out the worries of the police officers who got involved in the violence:

> The undercover and riot control officers, who had abused me, rushed into the hospital to cover up their guilt. After being held at the hospital for three hours for such examinations as tomography and x-ray, I left. The outcome of the day: swellings at five different locations on my head, wounds on both of my legs, pain in my wrist, and of course, my developing anger fed by our rightfulness against injustice and harassment. . . .

No matter what the government's police did, Mehmet Dersulu continued his resistance against dismissals (Fig. 12.7).

12.7.2 Theme 2: Resistance and Determination

Case 1: Nazan Bozkurt

In her words, the righteousness in resistance expressed her determination. Bozkurt also stated that as laborers whose jobs were taken away from their hands, they suffered significant financial difficulties. The insurgents believed that resistance was the only thing that scared the authorities. Below is her story.

> When I decided to join the protest, I found myself on Yuksel Street, where there were public servants who had been struggling for their jobs and honor. The first police attack I was

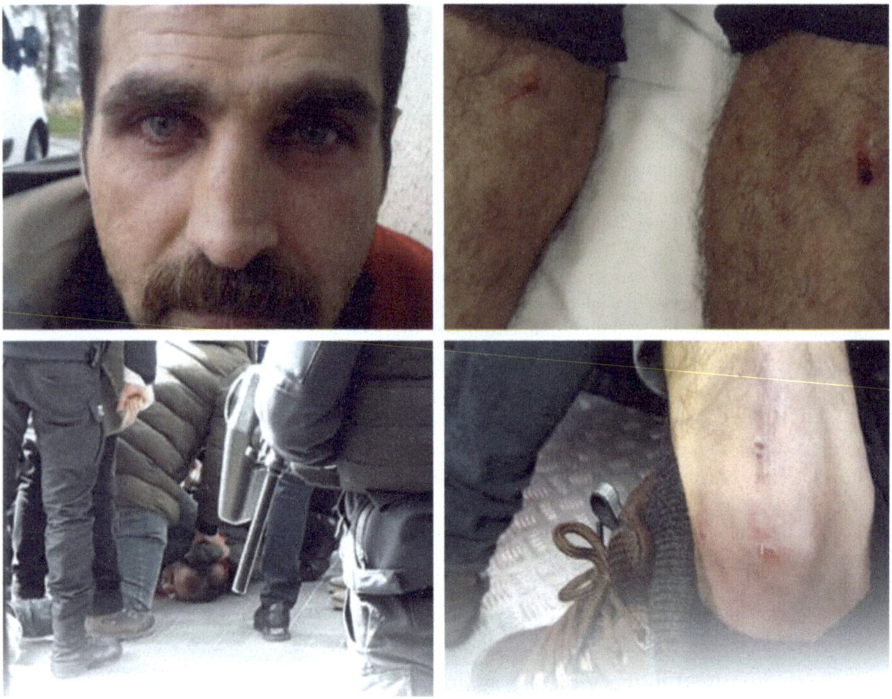

Fig. 12.7 Images of Mehmet Dersulu after police harassment

exposed to was during the folk dance that we played for the 100th day of the protest. I was still scared of police officers, and the attacks continued. Each time I faced fear more closely. Plastic bullets hurt really bad, but I overcame the pain. Just as the sound of the police's water cannon vehicle, I had to overcome this scary sound, too. When those vehicles are placed in front of you to spray water, you do not have such an option as running away.

I was equipped against all types of attacks, including back-handcuffing, gasses, punches, kicks, harassment, insults, etc. Then I realized that it was the government that was scared of the protestors. However, I was made aware of the hard punch on my eye on June 08, 2018, and that there was one other fear I had yet to overcome. For the first few seconds, some crazy thoughts came to my mind: 'They will kill us here, what should we do? To walk away. Never! They will go! We will never quit.' It was something that I would not have believed if someone had told me. What I had said to myself became real in only a few seconds. I realized that I was scared of death, but I was more scared of giving up. What I was scared of most was to be afraid and retreat. It is what empowered me against fascism.

The violations in police detention were clear violations of human rights. We were detained during police raids into our houses. Although the normal period of police custody was four days, the police took us before the judge and had the period unlawfully increased to 8 days. In this process, I met a young mother who was accused of being a GM member in the detention. She was crying out of breast engorgement because she could not breastfeed her baby. How can this unarmed mother, who was removed from her job under the pretext of the coup attempt, be affiliated with the failed coup attempt? She had to milk her breasts, but she endured the pain to keep her milk for her baby.

> We, protestors, were exposed to a number of acts of police abuse in detention. We declined the food and water we were given. Our lawyers were not allowed to bring sugar and water for us. Therefore, we remained hungry and thirsty for 8 days. Some of our friends passed out. When Acun Karadag fainted the last time, she would say: 'If something happens to me, you take care of my daughter Ipek.' We repeatedly asked officers to take us to the hospital, but they brought a doctor who had the same mentality as the police and did not want to transfer us to the hospital. At the end of this procedure, only one of us was arrested. We lacked food, water, and light in detention, although we were innocent.

Case 2. Acun Karadag

While the resistance was going on, Nuriye Gülmen and Semih Ozakca started a hunger strike, which made a great impact in the global media. He emphasized that the resistance would continue until the return of all the dismissed public laborers to their jobs and the injustice they suffered, not only for Acun Karadag but for the whole of the Yuksel insurgents. However, it is believed by the insurgents that no punishment in the law is strong enough to pay for the abuse suffered by the insurgents. He summarized the process and expressed his determination. Acun Karadag said:

> My insistence and determination in this protest are just as strong as they are right. I want the government to admit the injustice against me, and I want my job back. In fact, I want this nation to see that the fascist government is hostile to people and workers. No matter how long my struggle is, and no matter what it costs, it will last until I win. I will continue resisting and enlarging the street until we get rid of this fascist government and its derivatives.
>
> Yuksel Street ignited the resistance. It will continue, and the system of persecution of the AKP will collapse one day. . . . We can say that Yuksel Street became our hope in spite of all the negativities. The resistance started with Nuriye and went on with hunger strikes. The stage of hunger strikes was the point our resistance gained power because it became audible. But, especially after Nuriye and Semih were arrested, the period in which the de facto police harassment began for the protestors who did not go on hunger strike. They had no intention to give our jobs back, and they looked for ways to end the protest.
>
> It would be for the benefit of the government if we ended our hunger strike with the force of detentions and jail conditions, and we quit our resistance under the threat of detention, house arrest, and arrest. They hide their heads in the sand and thought that they had disappeared. But they were wrong. Neither the hunger strike ended under those conditions, nor did we quit our resistance. Our resistance continues. Either they will give our jobs back to us, or we will reveal them. I describe the fact that the resistance did not have a happy ending as the government's shooting itself in the leg. If they had been able to think abstractly, they could have foreseen what they would face and would have given our jobs back to us.
>
> It is as if the resistance is going on in its own course, but the reality is very different. We converted the positive opinion of many AKP supporters into negative opinions. Even those with fixed ideas about the rightfulness of the government say 'maybe' today. The happy ending is the time when this fascist government is overthrown.

Case 3: Nuriye Gülmen

Nuriye Gülmen, who started the resistance and was talked about by vast masses, was on the agenda of the world press. Several national and international journalists interviewed Nuriye Gülmen, Semih Ozakca, and his wife Esra Ozakca, who joined them for support. The protestors received tens of letters and messages every day while they were on hunger strike and were visited by thousands of supporters and students. The central theme of the interviews and the speeches they delivered during visits was to continue the resistance. While racing against time during the hunger strike, Nuriye Gülmen said:

> The fact that my health problems overtake the resistance may stimulate another motivation in people, but this is not what I want. While the hunger strike itself is political, reducing it to some health problems is very risky. This is what the State already does (Aktan 2017).

This is why Gülmen and Ozakca ended their hunger strike. They did so not because of the deterioration of their health conditions, but because the government decided to establish the state of emergency Commission to reconsider decisions of dismissals. Therefore, the conclusion can be reached that the resistance won. Combining the resistance and the gain, Gülmen uttered the following words and attracted attention to the need for collaborative work of all DL victims:

> More than 120,000 people were dismissed. This resistance is the fight of getting our jobs back, but civil servants are under a huge threat. We struggle for job security. After we started our hunger strike, dismissals became less frequent. I really think that it was a gain of resistance. The Decree-Laws have lost their legitimacy. One way or the other, they will take our job security away from us. While we struggle for the job security of contracted workers, civil servants lose theirs. Therefore, we need to act together. If we do not do anything, we will get buried in the dark. There is a government to be fought against in front of us. Semih used to say: 'Let us fight well and let us hope that it has a good ending.' There should be something we can bequeath to our children. Nobody should feel secure. We need to do something for our own future. People support us very nicely, but maybe we need to take an additional step. They should not think that they do something for us only, but everybody does something for himself. I am deeply grateful to those who support us.
>
> Nobody living in Turkey has assurance. When everything runs in its course for someone today, he may think that law and justice side with the rightful. However, all the systems may collapse in an instant. A free person may find himself in jail tomorrow for a reason he never learns. This is why everybody should consider this resistance as a struggle for the equality of the law and justice for all citizens (Pasayigit 2017).

Thinking in line with Gülmen, many protestors began their activities all around Turkey: Nazife Onay in front of Cevahir Mall, Istanbul; Engin Karatas in Bodrum; public servants in Aydin; Erdogan Canpolat, Sertac Okdemir, Ozkan Karatas and Cengiz Ugurlu in Malatya; Alev Sahin in Duzce; Mahmut Konuk and Cemal Yildirim in Ankara; Baris Bozkir in Didim, and many others.

Gülmen persisted in her hunger strike in spite of major weight loss and health problems. She expressed her persistence thusly:

> There are revolutionary rituals and traditions in Turkey. They never come to an end until reaching the ultimate result. In fact, our resistance is a continuation of those traditions. You want to get something, and you continue until you get what you want. You take the risk of paying all the cost, pay when necessary, and win in the end. It is impossible to gain rights otherwise in Turkey. You can take any movement in which people gained their rights as for example. This rule never changes. The activist is determined. He is assaulted but goes to the last point and so gains. Therefore, I have always had an idea of getting involved in a

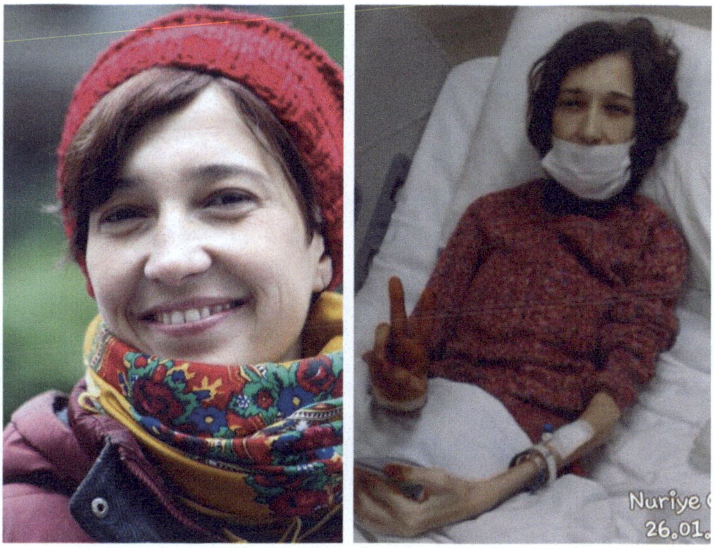

Fig. 12.8 Nuriye Gülmen before (left) and during (right) the hunger strike

> determined activity. I had the same opinion when I left home for the resistance. I did not go out for a one or two-day activity. I had done some research before. I had gone to a number of cities. I talked to anybody I could reach, including the academia, and especially those who had signed the Declaration of Peace, those who were dismissed in this process, and subjected to investigations. I met with them and talked to them about my opinion. I offered them to do something together. I spent one and a half months of mine with such efforts after I had been dismissed. Unfortunately, I did not come up with any concrete solution. This is why I had to start alone (Interview with Nuriye Gülmen 2017).

The struggles of Nuriye Gülmen that started the movement has proliferated change. After the termination of the hunger strike, the state of emergency, which had been declared in 2016, was lifted in 2018. Although the effects continue, the government may no longer hurt people with new Decree Laws (Fig. 12.8).

Case 4: Semih Ozakca

Semih Ozakca chose not to remain silent in the face of the rights violations that he had been exposed to. He started his hunger strike with Nuriye Gülmen and ended it for the same reason (Figs. 12.9 and 12.10).

Ozakca continued his determination in resistance despite the rights violations, harassment, detentions, and arrests. He gave hope to protestors with the following words:

> I offered information in detail to everybody. There were so many people who just passed by. We carried out this process with small movements and actions. The magnitude of the protest stems from this accumulation. To come up with such accumulation, it is required to put determination forward. You must be ready to pay its costs. If someone is determined to struggle and resist, then the cost must be paid. He must take the risk. Everybody should know that it was not something instantaneous, or an ordinary press release, but something historical. If it is a responsibility we were given by history and we have started resistance, it

Fig. 12.9 Semih Ozakca before the hunger strike (with his wife, Esra Ozakca)

Fig. 12.10 Semih Ozakca during the hunger strike

must end in victory. We won, and we have had so many gains. Why should we not take our jobs back? We have made so much sacrifice.

The resistance continues. Really, it continues in full force. I start every day by saying to myself: 'We have resistance today!' I feel the enthusiasm saying, 'Resistance is the most important of all!' and I am filled with hope. Even if there is only one person on Yuksel, only one person prays for us, or we receive only one letter, those are also parts of the resistance and very valuable.

Semih Ozakca and Nuriye Gülmen are not important for their names. There are some people seeking their own rights here. There is a framework having been established here. If we were not here, there would be others. It is absolute that there would be others. It is exactly the obstacle of the hegemon and the fear of capitalism. The resistance is an ideal, and it emerges in some way, either as your labor or culture, or as a matter of your honor. Being aware of all these, I have continued my resistance with the values which my people have given me, and my resistance continues. This resistance is only a drop for extremely beautiful days. This is what makes me happy most (Interview with Semih Ozakca 2017; Ozakca: They cannot get away by saying, 'We were deceived' 2017).

The resistance began with Nuriye Gülmen on Yuksel Street, grew in intensity with Acun Karadag, Semih Ozakca, Alev Sahin, Nazan Bozkurt, Veli Sacilik, Mehmet Dersulu, and many other protestors, and continues to grow.

12.8 Discussion and Conclusion

This study demonstrated the police violence during the Yuksel Protests as well as the rights violations, that a group of people who were exposed to the Decree-Laws, experienced during the State of Emergency that was declared after the failed coup attempt of July 15, 2016. The State violated numerous human and Constitutional rights of its citizens after the failed coup attempt (Amnesty International 2017, 2018; Civil Rights Defenders 2018; Gergerlioglu 2019b; Human Rights Association 2018, 2019; Mazlum-Der 2018; Stockholm Center for Freedom 2017a, 2017b; Tevgera Jinen Azad 2017; United States Department of State – Bureau of Democracy Human Rights and Labor 2017). Civil servants were dismissed from their jobs without proper defense, protested on Yuksel Street and were subjected to rights violations daily (Human Rights Association 2017).

Human rights violations often rose to the level of abuse in Turkey, especially during the State of Emergency that was declared in 2016. Hundreds of thousands of people were dismissed from their public service with no investigation, arbitrarily arrested, left to civilian death, subjected to abuse, crime, sexual harassment, and fines, and deprived of their rights to object (Gergerlioglu 2019a; Human Rights Association 2017). According to the Human Rights Association, 2278 people were subjected to torture and maltreatment within the first 11 months of the year 2017; 423 were subjected to beatings and other inhumane treatment, and 1855 were detained during meetings and demonstrations (Human Rights Association 2017). A Bureau of Democracy, Human Rights and Labor Affairs of the US State Department report showed that more than 300 arrestees had bruises, cuts and broken bones during the state of emergency (United States Department of State – Bureau of Democracy Human Rights and Labor 2017). The data covered only a part of the state of emergency period, and the state of emergency lasted eight more months after the data collection period. Furthermore, women were harassed while they were detained; and some detainees were forced and pressured into signing documents – they were threatened that their wives and children be raped if they did not cooperate (Office of the United Nations High Commissioner Rights for Human 2019; Stockholm Center for Freedom 2017a, b).

Other acts of maltreatment were providing detainees with minimal food rations and holding them under unhealthy conditions. Additional abuses were reported during the state of emergency including not providing enough water and food for detainees and not allowing them to use restrooms for long periods of time (Amnesty International 2017). Yuksel Protestors were detained almost daily, and on certain occasions, custody periods were deliberately extended; so much so, that it was extended up to 30 days for some victims during the state of emergency (Mazlum-Der 2018). The detention period, which was 30 days until January 23, 2017, imposed the violation of the presumption of innocence and the right to a fair trial. Those who were detained after the failed coup attempt were subjected to torture, including being physically abused, forced to adopt stress positions, and back-handcuffed (Aydin and Avincan 2020, Girdap 2020; Human Rights Association 2017). Furthermore, the police used plastic bullets and pepper spray, and on some occasions, real bullets, during the peaceful demonstrations. These measures caused severe harm to both police officers and protestors (Amnesty International 2016; Human Rights Watch 2014). However, such violations still continue and are increasing in intensity (Bozkurt 2019).

Certain public servants, who were first blacklisted by the state and then dismissed from their jobs without any investigation, decided to conduct protests daily. The determination, which arose from the three-year-long Yuksel Protests, ignited the spirit of struggle against the rights violations, inhumane treatment, and arbitrary applications in many parts of Turkey after July 15, 2016. Those who were dismissed or arrested under the cover of the GM as well as their relatives, began resisting in September 2019 (Yildirim 2019). However, they also received the same reactions, and were unlawfully detained and punished.

The effects of the state of emergency have been written into history, tainted with human rights violations. However, the violence imposed on protestors on Yuksel Street has been diminishing. Acun Karadag stated in her interview with Kaynak (2018) that the police barriers, placed when the protests first began, were later removed, and gave credit and recognition to the determination in the resistance. Furthermore, she asserted that the dismissed public servants would be returned to their jobs with this determination.

This study revealed that the arbitrary employment of DLs during the state of emergency caused human rights violations. The state of emergency was declared after the failed coup attempt in order to investigate and prosecute the forces that attempted to overthrow the government. However, it was not used for its true purpose. Thirty-seven DLs were adopted, the first of which was on July 23, 2016, and the last on July 09, 2018. The examination of those DLs shows that the government used the DLs for the following actions: dismissal of thousands of public servants without investigation, adopting new regulations for military schools and hospitals,[3] and providing immunity for those who worked against terrorist activities, even if they were civilians.[4] The government, which used the failed coup attempt as a pretext, tried to hold all the authority and sided against citizens in the opposition. The dismissed public servants were not from the military or the police, but were employed in public service jobs of the State, such as teachers and academia.

A second finding of the research is that the police violated the rights of citizens, with the support of the government, by not allowing them to exercise their constitutional rights. The dismissed public servants wanted to meet and stage demonstrations in line with Articles 26 and 34 of the Constitution; however, the police intervened in the protests each time. Acting as the authority in charge, governors violated the rights of citizens by prohibiting meetings and demonstrations in their assigned provinces.

Third, the police engaged in abusive behavior such as spraying water from water cannon vehicles, dragging women on the ground by pulling their hair, spraying pepper gas towards the faces of protestors, conducting beatings, back-handcuffing, laying protestors on the ground and applying pressure on their bodies, covering protestors' mouths, holding them in detention vehicles, sexually harassing them, and not allowing lawyers to provide sugar and water for detained clients.

Another finding of this study is that the public servants who were dismissed with DLs were also tagged in the national social security network intended to prevent them from obtaining future employment. This application was a clear violation of Article 23[5] of the Universal Declaration of Human Rights, which guarantees the right to work.

Finally, the protestors, whose rights were violated by being dismissed with DLs, and who were exposed to additional violations while trying to speak out about their victimization in peaceable street protests, never thought of quitting their resistance. Thus, the increase in violations against human rights not only provoked the protestors but increased their determination.

---

[3]Decree No. 669, Article 5.

[4]Degree No. 696, Article 121.

[5]Article 23.

1. Everyone has the right to work, to free choice of employment, to just and favorable conditions of work and to protection against unemployment.
2. Everyone, without any discrimination, has the right to equal pay for equal work.
3. Everyone who works has the right to just and favorable remuneration ensuring for himself and his family an existence worthy of human dignity, and supplemented, if necessary, by other means of social protection.
4. Everyone has the right to form and to join trade unions for the protection of his interests.

12.9 Policy Implications and Recommendations

The results of this study show that after the failed coup attempt of July 15, 2016 and the resultant decrees, the lives of citizens of the Republic of Turkey were darkened, and they were exposed to various forms of exclusion and harassment. For these abuses not to continue, for the country to return to order, and for lives to be restored, the authorities should surrender the attitudes that they have taken and consider the following suggestions:

1. Claims that public servants dismissed with DLs are affiliated with terrorist organizations should be proven by logical and concrete evidence.
2. The public servants who were dismissed with DLs and arrested should be released pending trial.
3. Public servants should be returned to their jobs during investigations. If their affiliation with terrorist organizations is proven with logical and concrete evidence, they should then be dismissed.
4. The criminal complaints made against police officers engaged in abusive behavior at Yuksel Street should be taken into consideration by public prosecutor's offices, and officers should be prosecuted.
5. Governors are not authorized to ban meetings and demonstrations. The governors who resort to banning meetings and demonstrations should be subjected to investigation.
6. The police should cease intervening in peaceful activities, meetings, and demonstrations, as well as applying harassment.
7. The prison sentences and fines imposed on DL victims should be cancelled.
8. All DLs should be cancelled, and the records of public servants cleared.
9. DLs victim should be compensated for material loses.
10. The government should apologize to them individually.

References

Aktan, Irfan. 2017. Nuriye Gulmen: I Wonder Where I Will Be 10 Years Later. *Gazete Duvar*, December 10. https://www.gazeteduvar.com.tr/yazarlar/2017/12/10/nuriye-gulmen-10-yil-sonra-nerede-olacagimi-cok-merak-ediyorum/.

Altun, Gurcan, Bulent Akansu, Betul Ugur Altun, Derya Azmak, and Ahmet Yilmaz. 2004. Deaths Due to Hunger Strike: Post-Mortem Findings. *Forensic Science International* 146 (1): 35–38.

Amnesty International. 2016. *Amnesty International Report 2015/16-The State of the World's Human Rights*. London. https://www.amnesty.org/download/Documents/POL1025522016ENGLISH.PDF.

———. 2017. *Amnesty International Report 2016/17- The State of the World's Human Rights*. London. https://www.amnesty.org/download/Documents/POL1048002017ENGLISH.PDF.

———. 2018. *Amnesty International Report 2017/18- The State of The World's Human Rights*. London. https://www.amnesty.org/download/Documents/POL1067002018ENGLISH.PDF.

Ankara Nufusu. 2019. https://www.nufusu.com/il/ankara-nufusu.

Aydin, Hasan, and Koksal Avincan. 2020. Intellectual Crimes and Serious Violation of Human Rights in Turkey: A Narrative Inquiry. *The International Journal of Human Rights* 24 (8): 1127–1155. https://doi.org/10.1080/13642987.2020.1713108.

Baxter, Pamela, and Susan Jack. 2008. Qualitative Case Study Methodology: Study Design and Implementation for Novice Researchers. *The Qualitative Report* 13 (4): 544–559.

Beynon, Joe. 1996. Hunger Strike in Turkish Prisons. *The Lancet* 348 (9029): 737.

Bozkurt, Nazan. 2019. Contributions of the Resistance, Courage. *Yuksel Newspaper*, Volume: 27.

Civil Rights Defenders. 2018. *A State in Emergency – When Exceptions Become the New Norm.* https://crd.org/wp-content/uploads/2018/04/CRD-6700-Rapport-Turkiet.pdf.

Council of Europe. 1950. *The European Convention on Human Rights*. Strasbourg: Directorate of Information. https://www.echr.coe.int/Documents/Convention_ENG.pdf.

Creswell, John W. 2014. *A Concise Introduction to Mixed Methods Research*. Thousand Oaks: SAGE.

Creswell, John W., and Cheryl N. Poth. 2017. *Qualitative Inquiry and Research Design: Choosing Among Five Approaches*. Thousand Oaks: SAGE.

Erem, Onur. 2018. The State of Emergency Is Over: Inventory of the Two-Year Process. *BBC*, July 19. https://www.bbc.com/turkce/haberler-turkiye-44799489.

Gergerlioglu, Omer Faruk. 2019a. *Social Cost of the State of Emergency in Its Second Year. Community of Justice for Victims.* https://www.raporlar.org/ikinci-yilinda-ohalin-toplumsal-maliyetleri-raporu/.

———. 2019b. *Merve Demirel and Her Father Are Our Guests in Live Cast* [Video podcast]. https://twitter.com/gergerliogluof/status/1154741354930552832.

Gillham, Bill. 2008. Observation Techniques: Structured to Unstructured. *Education Review/ Reseñas Educativas/Resenhas Educativas*.

Girdap, Hafza. 2020. Human Rights, Conflicts, and Dislocation: The Case of Turkey in a Global Spectrum. *American Journal of Qualitative Research* 4 (1): 69–84. https://doi.org/10.29333/ajqr/8266.

Harrell, Margaret C., and Melissa A. Bradley. 2009. *Data Collection Methods: Semi-Structured Interviews and Focus Groups*. Santa Monica: RAND National Defense Research Institute.

Human Rights Association. 2017. *Human Rights Association 2016 Report on Human Rights Violations*. Ankara: http://www.ihd.org.tr/wp-content/uploads/2017/04/2016_ihd_t%C3%BCrkiye_ihlal_raporu.compressed.pdf.

———. 2018. *Human Rights Association 2017 Report on Human Rights Violations: One year under the State of Emergency*. Ankara. https://www.ihd.org.tr/2017-insan-haklari-ihlalleri-raporu-ohal-altinda-gecen-bir-yil/.

———. 2019. *2018 Report on Human Rights Violations*. Ankara. https://www.insanhaklaridernegi.info/wp-content/uploads/2019/04/2018IHDYillikRapor_Sunum.pdf.

Human Rights Foundation of Turkey (Türkiye İnsan Hakları Vakfı). 2018. *TİHV Çalışma Raporu*. https://tihv.org.tr/wp-content/uploads/2019/07/%C3%87al%C4%B1%C5%9Fma-Raporu-2018_tihv.pdf

Human Rights Watch. 2014. *Human Rights World Report, 2014*. New York. https://www.hrw.org/world-report/2014.

———. 2018. *World Report, 2018*. New York. https://www.hrw.org/world-report/2018.

Interview with Nuriye Gulmen: "I am much happier than my first day". 2017. *5harfliler*. http://www.5harfliler.com/nuriye-gulmenle-roportaj-ilk-gunden-cok-daha-umutluyum-bugun/.

Interview with Semih Ozakca. 2017. *Meydan Newspaper*. https://meydanNewspaper.org/gundem/2017/11/aclik-eyleminin-232-gununde-semih-ozakca-ile-roportaj/.

Karadag, Acun. 2018. My Second Complaint to KESK and Egitim-Sen Union Members. *Yuksel Newspaper*, Sayı 13.

———. 2019. The Executive Board of Egitim-Sen Union Came to Speak with Me. *Yuksel Newspaper*, Sayı 17.

Kaynak, Ceren. 2018. Interview with Acun Karadag and Veli Sacilik: "If Their State of Emergency Will Continue, So Will Our Resistance!". *Gazetesolfasol*. http://www.gazetesolfasol.com/blog/acun-karadag-ve-veli-sacilik-ile-soylesi-onlarin-ohal-i-surecekse-bizim-de.

Kingsley, Patrick. 2017. In Turkey, a Hunger Strike Divides a Country in Turmoil. *New York Times,* June 1. https://www.nytimes.com/2017/06/02/world/europe/turkey-hunger-strike-erdogan.html.

Law on Meetings and Demonstrations. 1983. *Official Gazette*, October 8, (Sayı: 18185). http://www.mevzuat.gov.tr/MevzuatMetin/1.5.2911.pdf.

Lincoln, Norman, and Yvonna Denzin. 2005. *Handbook of Qualitative Research*. Thousand Oaks: SAGE.

May Nuriye always laugh, May Nuriye always live. 2017. *Meydan Newspaper*. https://meydanNewspaper.org/gundem/2017/12/roportaj-nuriye-hep-gulsun-nuriye-yasasin/.

Mazlum-Der (The Association for Human Rights and Solidarity for the Oppressed). 2018. *Report on Rights Violations During the State of Emergency*. https://drive.google.com/file/d/19HRL6VEBlQrGtLTi_dKqC6xvlW-hFwXS/view.

Neither of them can walk. 2017. *Sozcu Newspaper*, June 5. https://www.sozcu.com.tr/2017/gundem/ikisi-de-yuruyemiyor-1920268/amp/?__twitter_impression=true.

Office of the United Nations High Commissioner Rights for Human. 2019. *United Nations Human Rights Report, 2018*. https://www.ohchr.org/Documents/Publications/OHCHRreport2018.pdf.

Okatan, Derya. 2019. Young Women Harassed by the Police: It Is a Disgrace of the Police. *Artı Gerçek*, February 18. https://www.artigercek.com/haberler/polisin-taciz-ettigi-genc-kadin-utanc-polise-ait.

Pasayigit, Seyma. 2017. Nuriye Gulmen: We Were Concerned Mainly About Resistance, and It Continues. *Cumhuriyet Newspaper*, December 5. http://www.cumhuriyet.com.tr/haber/turkiye/880440/Nuriye_Gulmen__Bizim_icin_esas_olan_direnisti_ve_direnis_devam_ediyor.html.

Patton, Michael Quinn. 2002. *Qualitative Research & Evaluation Methods*. 3rd ed. Thousand Oaks: SAGE.

People's architect Alev Sahin started her sit-in protest at TMMOB. 2018. *Yuksel Newspaper*, Volume: 5.

Ratcliffe, Samuel Kerkham. 1932. Hunger Strike. *7 ENCYCLOPAEDIA Social Science*, 552.

Semih Ozakca: They cannot get away by saying, 'We were deceived'. 2017. *Sendika.org*, November 3. http://sendika63.org/2017/11/semih-ozakca-ile-soylesi-bir-adim-daha-attigimizda-kazanacagiz-454439/.

Shafak, Elif. 2017. Turkey's Future Is Moving Backward. *The New York Times*, September 19. https://www.nytimes.com/2017/09/19/opinion/turkey-islamism.html.

Stake, Robert E. 2006. *Multiple Case Study Analysis*. New York: Guildford Press.

Stockholm Center for Freedom. 2017a. *Jailing Women in Turkey – Systematic Campaign of Persecution and Fear*. https://stockholmcf.org/wp-content/uploads/2017/04/Jailing-women-in-Turkey.pdf.

———. 2017b. Mass Torture and Ill-Treatment in Turkey. https://stockholmcf.org/wp-content/uploads/2017/06/Mass-Torture-And-Ill-Treatment-In-Turkey_06.06.2017.pdf.

Tevgera Jinen Azad. 2017. Information *Report on the State of Emergency and Violation of Women's Rights in Prisons*.

Turkey Country Report. 2004. *Country Information & Policy Unit, Immigration and Nationality Directorate of Home Office, United Kingdom*. https://www.refworld.org/pdfid/40a887860.pdf.

Turkey's post-coup crackdown. 2019. https://turkeypurge.com/purge-in-numbers-2.

United Nations. 1948. *The Universal Declaration of Human Rights*. New York: United Nations Department of Public Information.

United States Department of State – Bureau of Democracy Human Rights and Labor. 2017. *Turkey 2016 Human Rights Report*. https://www.state.gov/documents/organization/265694.pdf.

———. 2019. *Turkey 2018 Human Rights Report*. https://www.state.gov/wp-content/uploads/2019/03/TURKEY-2018-HUMAN-RIGHTS-REPORT.pdf.

Yildirim, Cemal. 2019. *"Words Have a Meaning"* [Tweet]. https://twitter.com/cemalyldrm/status/1175742435659591680?s=03.

Yin, Robert K. 2014. *Case study Research: Design and Methods*. 5th ed. Thousand Oaks: SAGE.

Acun Karadag received his BA in History from Ankara University in 1992. She started to work as a translator at Military Strategic Studies Department in the General Staff of the Republic of Turkey. She translated many official documents of the War on Independence from Ottoman language to the modern Turkish language. She has been assigned to the Directorate of Museum of the Mausoleum Command. She reviewed the thousands of documents under construction in Anıtkabir (memorial tomb) one by one and created the Anıtkabir archive. In 1996, she started to work as a teacher at the Ministry of Education. In 2011, she was elected as a manager at Education and Science Workers' Union at Ankara Branch under the Confederation of Public Workers' Unions (KESK). She worked as a social studies teacher at Halim Sasmaz Middle School till October, 2016. On October, 2016, she was expelled from his job with the Decree Law no 675 after a crack-down failed military coup. In January 2017, she Remembering the Resistance of the "the Yuksel Resistance (Yüksel Direnişi)". Currently, she works as a freelance and human rights activist.

Nazan Bozkurt worked as a civil servant at the Cankaya Population Directorate, she wanted to apply for legal remedies many times after being expelled from my 10-year term with Degree Law (KHK No. 683) on 23 January 2017. She is a human rights activist and started to join the Yuksel Resistance initiated by people who has fired by Turkish government. She has been in this resistance for 2,5 years, she has been detained and arrested 1500 times.

Chapter 13
Human Rights Violations and Medicolegal Approach

Alper Keten

Abstract The United Nations Convention Against Torture defined torture as the infliction of physical or psychological harm by public officials or other persons acting in an official capacity. Torture and mistreatment are a matter of concern for the international society. In Turkey, the number of people directly exposed to torture is estimated at several million. The Turkish government declared a state of emergency on 20 July 2016 after an attempted coup d'état on 15 July 2016, and then extended it repeatedly. This state lasted for 730 days, until 20 July 2018. In this process, through ministerial decrees, 150,348 public servants including judges, prosecutors, state officials, teachers, bureaucrats, medical doctors, and academics were dismissed without any investigation. However, the assumption is most of these people were neither active in, nor aware of the coup attempt before 15 July 2016. In addition, 500.650 citizens were arbitrarily judicially investigated, and many associations, foundations, and media outlets were shut down. The study aims to discuss the medicolegal issues related to human rights violations in Turkey.

Keywords Torture · World Medical Association · Istanbul Protocol · Violations · Legal · Issues

13.1 Definition of Torture and Historical Background

Torture has various definitions. The Convention Against Torture of 1984 by the United Nations General Assembly defines torture as the severe physical or psychological harm caused intentionally by public officials. The Istanbul Protocol adopted the CAT definition and also described torture as the infliction of severe mental and/or physical pain on a person, with the aim of obtaining information from someone or from a third person, causing that person, or the third person, to make a confession,

---

A. Keten (✉)
Institute of Forensic and Traffic Medicine, Heidelberg University, Heidelberg, Germany
e-mail: alper.keten@med-uni.heidelberg.de

H. Aydin, W. Langley (eds.), *Human Rights in Turkey*, Philosophy and Politics - Critical Explorations 15, https://doi.org/10.1007/978-3-030-57476-5_13

punishing that person or the third person as a result of a crime that they have committed or are doubted to have committed, intimidating that person or the third one or forcing them to commit certain actions, when this action is committed by a public official or with the consent, command, toleration or complaisance of a public official or any person acting in an official capacity. The infliction experienced naturally as a result of legal sanctions is not included within the context of torture.

Torture is a method of oppression as ancient as humanity itself and has been used by the ones in power for millennia. In the modern era, it has been outlawed by most countries, but this could not prevent the practice of torture being committed secretly behind closed doors. Torture still exists as a serious problem in many countries in the world (Allden et al. 1996) including Turkey (Paker and Bugru 2016). Torture does not only aim to harm individuals physically and emotionally, but also sometimes aims to annihilating the will and honour of a whole society. As it contradicts with the meaning of our existence as humans and overshadows our hopes for a brighter future, it becomes a matter of concern for every member of humanity (Iacopino 1998; Istanbul Protocol 2004).

Even books guiding oppressors in the practice of torture have been published. The first known handbook for torturers was published by Malleus Maleficarum [The Hammer of Witchcraft] in 1486 (Peters 1986; The Malleus Maleficarum 1486). Starting in western societies, torture has become an indefensible issue since the middle of the Eighteenth century. Although it is prohibited on paper, it has continued to exist as a secret and dirty act of political violence practiced behind closed doors (Paker and Bugru 2016).

The right not to be tortured has been clearly and definitely stated in international law. The Universal Declaration of Human Rights (1948), International Covenant on Civil and Political (1976), Convention against Torture and Other Cruel, Inhumane or Degrading Treatment and Punishment (1984) clearly prohibit torture. The right not to be tortured has been pointed out in local conventions as well.

The United Nations have put forward different standards at a universally applicable level in order to provide people with adequate protection against torture and other cruel, inhumane or degrading treatment and punishment for years. Among those texts accepted by the Member States are:

- Standard Minimum Rules of Treatment Towards Prisoners (United Nations Congress 1955)
- Declaration of Protecting All Persons from Being Subjected to Torture and Other Cruel, Inhumane or Degrading Treatment and Punishment (General Assembly 1975)
- Codes of Conduct for Law Enforcement Officials (General Assembly 1979)
- Principles of Medical Ethics relevant to the Role of Medical Staff, Particularly Physicians, in Protection of Prisoners against Torture and Other Cruel, Inhumane or Degrading Treatment and Punishment, (General Assembly 1982)
- The Overall Principles for Protection of All People under any Form of Detention or Imprisonment (General Assembly 1988)
- Basic Principles for the Treatment of Prisoners. (General Assembly 1990)

Other human rights groups and institutions within the scope of the United Nations have also taken action to develop standards in terms of taking the responsibility of investigating all torture claims by the states in addition to developing standards for the prevention of torture.

The legal norms listed above determine the responsibilities that should be taken by states in order to provide protection against torture. Apart from these, similar rules were determined in local texts as well. Moreover, the fact that torture is prohibited has been clearly stated in many texts such as the Inter-American Convention To Prevent And Punish Torture (1985), African [Banjul] Convention on Human Rights and Rights of People, Rome Statute and European Convention for the Protection of Human Rights and Fundamental Freedoms (Can et al. 2019; Haar et al. 2019).

13.2 Torture from Medical Perspective

In international law, torture prohibition and prevention are incorporated into the education of medical staff, civil servants and other related staff and training them in terms of torture prohibition is the responsibility of the state.

13.2.1 World Medical Association Declarations and Other Ethical Texts

World Medical Association Declarations (WMAD): In many declarations by the World Medical Association (WMA), it is clearly stated that doctors are responsible for doing their best for their patients including prisoners and persons claimed to be guilty. This duty is stated frequently through the term professional independence, which requires doctors to remain faithful to the best medical treatment without considering the pressure potentially exercised over them (World Medical Association 1975, 1990, 1997).

The International Medical Ethics Rules of WMA emphasise that doctors have the responsibility of providing medical care in a professional and morally independent way, empathically and respectfully. This declaration puts an emphasis on the fact that medical staff are responsible for acting in the best interests of their patients.

WMA Tokyo Declaration (World Medical Association 1975) and the Declaration of Seoul on Professional Autonomy and Clinical Independence (World Medical Association 2008) state undoubtedly that doctors of medicine should insist on clinical independence when treating their patients. The International Nursing Council has set up similar rules for nurses. Another responsibility of medical staff is to support their colleagues who raise their voices against human rights violations. The contrary situation not only involves the risk of human rights violation and violating the declarations mentioned above, but also damages the reputation of the medical staff and is regarded as a serious professional abuse.

The Human Rights Directive of WMA (World Medical Association 1990) states that the national medical institutions should evaluate the condition of human rights in their countries and that doctors should not hide any evidence of mistreatment even if they fear retaliation. In the Hamburg Declaration published by WMA after the Human Rights Directive, the importance of collaboration in the struggle against torture and mistreatment has been emphasised (World Medical Association 1997).

In ethical and legal texts accepted by the Turkish Medical Association it is emphasised that the universal rules regarding human rights should be obeyed and there should be no discrimination towards patients (Can et al. 2019).

When these rules are considered as a whole in providing medical service, they should translate to compassionate, empathic care, not causing harm and respecting the patient's rights. Those are the main rules for all medical care professionals.

13.2.2 The Aim, Components, Goals and Methods of Torture

In studies conducted, nine possible aims of torture are listed. These are as follows: (1) obtaining information (2), raising a charge against a suspected offense by obtaining a confession (3), brainwashing (4), intimidating (5), dehumanising through isolation (6), vengeance or sadism (7), punishment (8), humiliation (9) and damaging one's personality (Paker 2000; Suedfeld 1990).

The components of torture have been listed by Suedfeld (1990) under four titles: debilitation, dependency, dread, disorientation. Keeping the person in a state of horror and exhaustion and breaking down their time-place-person orientation result in an acceptance that he is dependent upon the torturer. The torturer tries to demolish a victim's feelings of controllability and predictability.

When the objectives of torturers are analysed, it becomes apparent that they not only aim at the person of the victim but also (1) the family, relatives and friends of the victim (2) the political, ethnical or religious social group/identity that he is identified with and (3) the society in general. Torture starts with the victim and tries to intimidate and discipline the society as a whole. As a result of these practices, collaboration of the whole society in torture is enabled by labelling the victims and their identities, redrawing the borders of what is socially acceptable and forcing the general society to keep silent (Paker and Bugru 2016; Paker 2000).

13.2.3 The Aim of Examination, Treatment and Documenting

The general aim of investigating supposed torture and maltreatment practices is to collect and analyse data regarding the incidences and determine whether they really amount to torture. This enables:

- Determining the individuals committing torture and bringing them to justice;
- Justifying applications for political asylum;
- Analysing the circumstances around forceful confessions and providing the victims of torture with the opportunity of a fair trial
- Detecting geo specific torture practices. The medical evaluations can also be used for meeting the medical needs of the victims and as evidence in cases of human rights violations (Istanbul Protocol 2004).

13.2.4 Legislation Concerning Medical Treatment of Prisoners

In Article 3 in the European Convention on Human Rights (1950), it is pointed out that the state is responsible for guaranteeing that "No one shall be subjected to torture or to inhuman or degrading treatment or punishment." Furthermore, the European Convention on Human Rights states many times that people should be provided adequate and necessary medical service in the quickest, most efficient way possible.

In criminal law health-related problems may result in delaying or altogether cancelling the execution of imprisonment. However, the practices during and after the state of emergency in Turkey indicate a complete disregard for these positive legal norms. Hundreds of people were kept in prison although they were end-state cancer patients and women giving birth in jails has turned out to be a common occurrence. The points regarding the execution of punishment related to patients have been stated separately in the Turkish law system (Turkish Law No: 2004-5275, Footnote). None of these measures stated on paper have been practiced during and after the state of emergency in Turkey and law enforcement officials often intentionally refuse to provide access to necessary care.

In spite of such provisions in legislation, the European Committee for the Prevention of Torture and Inhuman or Degrading Treatment or Punishment (CPT) has concluded, that detainees have been denied access to adequate health services. The CPT has explicitly stated that prisoners have the right to benefit from necessary public or private medical services. (European Committee, CPT/Inf 2017) state of emergency in Turkey and law enforcement officials often intentionally refuse to provide access to necessary care.

Footnote; Law no: 5275: The purpose of this Law is to lay down the procedures and rules concerning the execution of penalties and security measures.

The CPT has also stated that medical check-up services including such aimed at detecting contagious diseases and psychological disorders should be provided at points of entry to the prisons, which is essential for detecting torture and maltreatment potentially experienced by the detainees before being taken to prison (European Committee, CPT/Inf 2017). The importance of providing prisoners with adequate healthcare, necessary medical treatment and social support has also been stated in the Nelson Mandela Rules (1955).

13.3 Istanbul Protocol (2004)

The Protocol, prepared by many scientists around the world and accepted by the United Nations, states how to manage the cases of torture and maltreatment. It also put forward both medical and legal requirements. It was prepared by 75 experts of medicine, forensic medicine, psychology and psychiatry, law and human rights, of 40 different organizations and from 15 countries.

The Istanbul Protocol underlines the importance of eyewitness testimony and the testimony of the torture victim themselves in the documentation of medical treatment in custody and cases of suspected torture. However, the absence of physical evidence should not be accepted as a disproval of possible torture practices since acts of violence do not necessarily leave a trace or scar. The forensic medical evaluations of the patients should be carried out objectively and fairly.

The Istanbul Protocol was created in order to protect individuals from torture and mistreatment and to hold the perpetrators responsible. Furthermore, this guide book was prepared with the aim of setting a standard for the states during investigation of torture and mistreatment.

It includes the principles and minimum standards for effective investigation and documentation of torture by the states. The conditions outlined by these principles can be summarised as follows: a fast, effective and full physical and psychological examination that is to be performed by an independent commission and shared with the victim's legal representatives if necessary.

The existence of psychological harm and various signs of stress especially resulting from trauma may cause the victim a fear of re-experiencing torture during an interview, physical examination and laboratory tests. Informing the victim about what will happen before a medical examination is thus a significant part of the process. Another point to consider is that the victims of exile and immigrants have left their native language, culture, family, friends, occupation and most everything that they are familiar with behind themselves, which makes the process more sophisticated, and may require professionals with specific knowledge and training.

The personal reaction of the victim towards the interviewer or translator and vice versa may also affect the interview process and therefore the investigation results.

During interviews a translator should be used if necessary. Even if the interviewer and the interviewee use a common language to a partial extent, the information obtained could be crucial to the investigation and therefore any misunderstanding should be avoided. The translator/s should be informed about the sensitivity of the task and the fact that everything they hear and translate during interviews should remain confidential. Informing translators about relevant trauma can be a real improvement in the translation process. They should also be instructed to translate the interviewee's words completely, not make reductions or assumptions and not have private contact with the interviewee. In some cases, translators show a tendency to not translate parts that they regard as unnecessary. The interviewer should always be in full control of the interview. Moreover, the interviewee should be assured that the information they give to the interviewers will not be abused neither by the researcher nor by the translator. A biased translator could potentially wrongly direct the victim or misrepresent or mistranslate their testimony, corrupting the entire interview process.

Whether the interviewer and the interviewee are of the same gender can also be important. Interviewees should therefore be given the choice to talk to a male or a female interviewer.

A multidisciplinary approach may often be needed in the investigation of torture and mistreatment. The victim may require to be referred to doctors of another medical speciality, psychologists, physical therapists or to consultants providing social advice and support. Doctors conducting medical examinations of potential torture victims should therefore have knowledge of local facilities and experts. The clinician should refer the patient to all medical examinations and evaluations that they regard as necessary (Istanbul Protocol 2004).

13.3.1 Interpreting the Findings

The physical findings regarding torture can vary in accordance with the biological condition and bodily built of the victim. When investigating cases of suspected torture all aspects regarding the physicality of the case – from a person's arms being handcuffed to the actual physical integrity of their body should be carefully examined. In recent years, methods that do not leave physical evidence in particular have been increasingly utilized. In the report it is of great significance to carefully analyse and interpret the results. It is also important to include in the report any relevant background/circumstantial information about the people conducting the examination themselves (Istanbul Protocol 2004).

13.3.2 Collecting Medical Evidence for Torture According to the Istanbul Protocol

In some cases, no physical or biological evidence of torture can be found. Findings of any other nature relating to possible torture and other kinds of mistreatment should not be excluded from a forensic report under any circumstances (Istanbul Protocol 2004).

13.3.2.1 Form of the Interview

The place of an interview and/or examination should be as secure and as comfortable for the interviewees as possible. Enough time should be devoted in order to conduct the interview and examination properly. Building trust and respect between interviewer and interviewee is most important.

The physicians are responsible for getting informed consent and they should not be exposed to pressure by law enforcement or other public officials. It should be stated that the person has the right to reject examination and the procedures should be arranged accordingly. Furthermore, it should be ensured that law enforcement representatives or other third persons should not be involved in the interview (Istanbul Protocol 2004).

13.3.2.2 Medical History

A complete medical history of the subject should be obtained, including any previous medical, surgical and psychological problems. Any injury before detention should be documented as such in the report. The process of obtaining medical history should be structured chronologically and the questions asked open-endedly.

Acute and chronical symptoms related to certain torture methods and limitations and the following recovery should be documented (Istanbul Protocol 2004).

13.3.2.3 Acute Symptoms

All possible harm occurring as a result of specific torture methods practiced upon a person should be analysed. The severity, frequency and duration of each symptom should be noted. Furthermore, the period in which the person is released from detention should be examined – whether the person was able to walk, had any injuries, had undergone an examination when he was released are all details that should be considered.

It should also be noted, that the observational skills of the detainee can be distorted because of the act of torture itself or its later effects (Istanbul Protocol 2004).

13.3.2.4 Chronic Symptoms

The disorders the person believes to have resulted from torture and mistreatment should be completely and carefully recorded. Although the effects of acute lesions cannot be detected until months or even years later, some symptoms such as scars from burns, skeletal deformations/malunion of fractures, tooth injuries, loss of hair and fibro myositis can become apparent. Along with frequent somatic complaints such as headache, backache, gastrointestinal symptoms, sexual dysfunction and muscle pain, psychological symptoms such as depressive disorders, anxiety, insomnia, reliving the past and difficulties in memory can be more frequently observed.

Additionally, diagnostics and imaging methods can be applied in the cases of possible torture and mistreatment. Magnetic resonance, computed tomography, and sometimes scintigraphic imaging methods can be of great importance, especially in view of the time elapsed after torture (Istanbul Protocol 2004).

13.3.2.5 Physical Examination

After obtaining the medical history of the victims, a detailed physical examination should be carried out. The consent of the patient should, again, be obtained. The patient should know that he/she is in control of the examination process and that he/she has the right to restrict or stop the examination at any time. The examiner should use all available means while carrying out the diagnosis. When it is impossible to carry out some diagnostic tests, those deficiencies should not affect the factual value of the report. If the clothes worn by the victim are the same as those worn during the alleged torture, they should be kept in evidence without being cleaned/washed, and the person should be provided with new clean clothes with other materials. The examination room should be adequately lit and equipped with all necessary medical supplies. When that is not possible, any deficiencies should be stated in the report.

Although it is often not possible to take pictures of lesions of the detainee resulting from torture, taking photos should be in general a routine part of the examination, as photo evidence can become important later in time. A detailed and complete physical examination should be carried out. Observable findings may not exist at first in some types of torture such as electric shock or blunt trauma and those findings can be detected in later examinations (Istanbul Protocol 2004).

13.3.3 The Psychological Evidence for Torture in the Istanbul Protocol

The significance of psychological evaluation has been emphasized in the Istanbul Protocol. The act of torture can pave the way for various physical and psychological problems. In many cases, only psychological findings exist, which makes psychological evaluation even more significant. Those psychological results can vary in accordance with personal characteristics (Franceschetti et al. 2019; Istanbul Protocol 2004; Johnson and Thompson 2008).

13.3.3.1 The Significance of Psychological Evaluation

The meaning attributed to torture is formed within the context of personality development and social, political and cultural factors. Psychological influences can vary according to torture methods. Furthermore, the psychological effects of torture can vary depending on the age, gender, education, faith, social circle etc. of the victim. For instance, the psychological results of mock executions are not the same as those of sexual abuse and it cannot be expected that isolating through solitary confinement will have the same psychological effects as physical torture methods. However, symptoms observed and documented in an orderly and systematic manner and the corresponding psychological reactions can be observed. Not all torture victims develop a diagnosable mental disorder. Nevertheless, many victims display serious affective reactions and psychological symptoms (Table 13.1).

The main psychiatric disorders associated with torture are Post-Traumatic Stress Disorder (PTSD) and major depression. The person-specific and wider cultural, social and political impacts of torture affect how people see and describe torture. As suggested by cross-cultural research, the most rational approaches to the evaluations of psychological and psychiatric disorders are phenomenological and descriptive methods. Reactions to trauma should be interpreted with the cultural context in mind (Engelhardt 1975; Kleinman 1986; Westermeyer 1985). Since the Second World War, considerable progress has been made in understanding the psychological effects of violence.

13.3.3.2 Diagnostic Classifications

Many symptoms of PTSD and depression can be seen among refugees coming from various ethnical and cultural societies and exposed to different types of torture (Allden et al. 1996; Kinzie et al. 1990; Mollica et al. 1993). In a cross-cultural study the World Health Organization draws special attention to the fact that people from different cultures can react differently to different methods of torture. In this

Table 13.1 Common psychological reactions and symptoms; Holtan (1998)

Reliving the trauma
Physical complaints: headache, backache, muscle/joint pain
Avoidance and affective bluntness
Sexual dysfunction
Hypervigilance
Psychosis: delusions, hallucination, strange thoughts and behaviours, illusions and misperceptions, paranoia persecution delusions, psychotic disorders
Symptoms of depression
Drug addiction
Impaired self-image and restricting future expectations neuropsychological dysfunctions
Dissociation, depersonalisation and atypical behaviours

Table 13.2 Diagnostic classifications (American Psychiatric Association 2013; WHO 2016)

Depressive disorders
Post-traumatic stress disorder
Permanent personality change
Drug use and addiction
Other diagnoses (Generalised anxiety-, panic-, acute stress-, somatoform-, bipolar affective disorder, disorders connected with an ordinary medical condition and phobia).

respect, it is stated that the symptoms concerning victims living in different cultural contexts may differ even though some symptoms exist similarly in different cultures (Table 13.2).

13.3.3.3 Psychological/Psychiatric Evaluation

Psychological evaluations can provide significant evidence for abuse that the victims of torture are exposed to. The general aim of psychological evaluation is to detect the level of consistency between the story of torture told by the person and the physical and psychological findings of the evaluation process.

Being aware of the idioms related to disturbances in the language through which culture specific syndromes and symptoms are stated is of great importance both in terms of carrying out the interview and in terms of formulating clinical observations and conclusions. Ideally, a translator from the same culture as the victim will know the language, traditions, religion and other beliefs that should be kept in mind during the interview. In order to reduce the risk of resurrecting a past traumatic experience, the clinician should approach the interviewee with empathy and understanding of their cultural background. Behaving in accordance with strict "clinic objectivity" rules used with some psychotherapy styles in which the clinic doctor is passive and generally avoids speaking is not appropriate. The clinicians should display a supportive/non-judgemental approach towards the interviewee (Table 13.3).

13.3.4 Children and Torture

Torture is an absolutely unacceptable act of violence in any case, but when it is directed at children, it becomes an unfathomable tragedy. Torture on minors is a big global problem, yet accurate data is hard to come by (Otter et al. 2013; Quiroga 2012).

Cases of children being exposed – directly or indirectly – to torture should be handled differently than cases involving only adults. A child's reaction to torture can vary in accordance with his/her age, stage of development and cognitive skills. The younger the child, the bigger the influence of the caretakers on how the child interprets and handles the traumatic experience (von Overbeck 1998). Considering

Table 13.3 The points of psychological/psychiatric evaluation (Istanbul Protocol 2004; Rothbaum et al. 1992; Sutker et al. 1991)

Introduction	Who referred the potential victim to the interview, summary of supplementary sources (i.e. medical, records etc.), methods of evaluation
Story of torture and maltreatment, psychological complaints available	Potential victim's recollection of the torture, infliction/pressure, deterritorialization (immigration and asylum), other traumatic experiences
Post-torture story	In this step of evaluation, information about current living conditions is obtained
Pre-torture story	History of personal development, of education, job/profession, past trauma
	Cultural and religious background should be examined
Medical story, past psychiatric story	
Story of drug use and addiction	
Examination of mental condition	
Evaluation of social performance	Trauma and torture can directly or indirectly affect one's ability of earning a living
The use of psychological tests and question forms	The victims of torture can have difficulty in stating their experiences and psychological symptoms verbally. In some cases, it may be useful to utilise questionnaires
Clinical observation	While obtaining clinic observation in order to document psychological evidence of torture, the physical and psychiatric findings should be evaluated together and their correlation with torture and mistreatment should be determined
Suggestions (in consistency with relevant findings)	When appropriate, settlement of legal issues, asylum and treatment

this delicate situation in which children can find themselves, the United Nations (1990) Convention on the Rights of the Child emphasizes the need to protect them from any sort of harm and violence. The Istanbul Protocol also highlights the importance of investigations into cases of torture involving children being handled by people with appropriate expertise (paediatricians, child psychologists and psychiatrists etc.) (Otter et al. 2013).

The caretakers have an especially significant role in cases of children below the age of three who have been exposed to torture or witnessed it. It is of great significance to demonstrate a protective and reassuring attitude (Grappe 1995). Being exposed to or witnessing torture in childhood or adolescence can lead to many different consequences (Grappe 1995; Piaget 1977). Thus it is very important to develop guidelines specific to the investigation of cases of alleged torture and mistreatment involving children (Otter et al. 2013). Recent human rights violations in Turkey have affected children both directly and indirectly. Minor can be faced with the consequences of their parents losing their jobs in mass dismissals, being forced to move within Turkey or even abroad. Children might have to overcome extreme obstacles, from dangerous border- and river crossings to the challenge of

Table 13.4 The reactions in children

Bedwetting, losing control of intestinal motility
Difficulties in falling asleep, sleep disorders, heightened startle response
Fear of darkness and going to the bathroom alone
Becoming introvert, emotional restrictions, nervousness
Difficulties in focusing and attention
Display of sexual behaviours incompatible with his/her age and show somatic reactions
Anxiety symptoms such as feeling of futurelessness, anger attacks, uncontrolled crying and eating problems
Fears non-existent before the traumatic event and aggressive behaviours
Exaggerated fear of foreigners, separation anxiety, panic, overexcitement

integration into a foreign country, at a very delicate age and such cases have to be handled very professionally and carefully (Kaplan et al. 2016).

13.3.4.1 Clinic Evaluations

The leading psychological consequence of torture is Post-Traumatic Stress Disorder. Clinic observation is crucial for the diagnosis. The symptoms observed in children are presented in the table (Sironi 1995) (Table 13.4).

13.3.4.2 The Role of the Family

The family of a child victim of torture has the main role in how these consequences are handled. The unity of the family and the roles of the parents in the family can play a big role in children being influenced negatively. Negative attitudes such as overprotectiveness or attributing children parental roles can be observed (Istanbul Protocol 2004).

13.4 Minnesota Protocol

Deaths can not only take place due to natural reasons during detention, but also can occur as a result of suicide, murder, execution and during revolts (Erkol et al. 2006; Fazel and Benning 2006; Hammet et al. 2002; Karaarslan et al. 2014). In different parts of the world, undocumented or undiscovered, illegal, arbitrary and extrajudicial execution take place. In order to detect and prevent this, a guide to post-mortem examinations was needed. A model protocol (The Minnesota Protocol 2017) regarding legal investigation of illegal, arbitrary and extrajudicial executions was prepared and accepted in 1989 as a result of extensive studies (Hammet et al. 2002). Within the context of this protocol, it is obligatory to examine prison deaths and make an effective evaluation (Erkol et al. 2006; Hammet et al. 2002).

The Minnesota Autopsy Protocol involves rules guiding the investigation of all death cases occurring suddenly, unexpectedly or suspiciously or as a result of violence. In this protocol, the actions to be taken during the different stages of the investigation by specialists of law, medicine and forensic science are listed and an exemplary autopsy protocol is presented. In this model autopsy protocol, the algorithm to be followed during crime scene investigations and autopsy processes is illustrated (The Minnesota Protocol 2017). During the autopsy process, it is stated in detail that the time and place of the autopsy and the people taking part in the process should be noted; the autopsy itself should be recorded in detail; a radiological examination should be made; trauma indications should be detected during external examination; the internal examination should be made in a way complementary to the external examination and adequate histopathological and toxicological analyses should be made (The Minnesota Protocol 2017).

According to the exemplary protocol, during a crime scene investigation forensic practitioners and medical researchers should have the right to enter into the area where the dead body is. Examination of the medical records regarding the case is of great significance.

In an autopsy it is important not only to record all protocol-related data, but also note the identity, expertise, role in the particular case and, if applicable, the political and governmental affiliation (i.e. if they are U.N. or NGO-representatives) of the members of the autopsy team.

Well-taken photographs are also of great significance for the precise documentation of autopsy findings. The photographs should be in colour (transparent or negative/print), be of adequate definition and be appropriately lit, and be of a professional quality. The whole body should be x-rayed and dental films should be taken. The necessary radiological imaging should be evaluated in detail.

If any kind of anomaly, trauma evidence and bleeding becomes apparent when the nose and ears are examined, it should be noted. The evaluation of bleeding or trauma changes throughout the examination of tympanic membranes is of great significance. In cases where a sexual assault is suspected, all relevant organs should be examined. Speculum should be utilised in order to examine vaginal walls. Samples of oral, vaginal and rectal liquid should be taken and appropriately stored.

The back, hips, arms and legs should be incised systematically (including wrists and ankles) and potential deep injuries should be carefully evaluated. Hair, blood and tissue samples should also be taken for toxicological examinations.

Any lesions observed during the autopsy and their formation mechanism should be reported in detail and no outside influence on the examination should be permitted (The Minnesota Protocol 2017).

13.5 The Present Situation of Torture in Turkey

According to 2017 numbers of the United Nations High Commissioner for Refugees, it is known that there are more than 70 million people who were forced to displace because of war, oppressive regimes and similar conditions in or outside their countries and the rate of exposure to torture among those people alternated between 5% and 35%. It is predicted that 3–20 million people among those are victims of torture (Basoglu 1992; Paker 2003; UNCHR 2017). However, more victims of torture still live in their countries where they are still exposed to it. In Turkey alone, the number of people exposed directly to torture is assumed to be several million (Turkey's post-coup crackdown 2019).

On July 15, 2015 President Erdogan and the Turkish government ended the peace process with ethnic Kurdish groups fighting for independence. After an alleged coup d'etat attempt on July 15, 2016, a state of emergency was announced on July 20, 2016. It lasted until July 20, 2018 and was characterized by systematic persecution of everyone opposed to and critical of the government. During this process with 32 decree laws over 732 days, 150.348 public servants including judges, prosecutors, state officials, teachers, bureaucrats, medical doctors, and academics were dismissed from their jobs without any kind of evidence or investigation. Additionally, judicial investigations were carried out of 500.650 citizens among whom 96.885 were arrested, and many associations, foundations, and media outlets were shut down (Turkey's post-coup crackdown 2019).

Furthermore, the number of children between the ages of 0–6 in prisons is stated to be 743. They are the children of those arrested during the state of emergency (Daglar 2019; Turkey's post-coup crackdown 2019).

These processes have been effective in leading to social fear and pressure. Moreover, there are also children who have been forcefully put in children's care homes, although they have parents or relatives to take care of them. This is another humanitarian tragedy and is used as an instrument of fear and pressure. State media has also broadcasted examples of torture and mistreatment, in many cases trying to justify them, which has spread fear in society. This should be handled as an example of mass torture.

Because of the dire situation in Turkey, many academics, journalists, teachers and doctors left and claimed asylum or refuge. Their main destinations are other European countries due to their geographic closeness. In Europe, Germany has the highest number of these refugees. People are known to use the Evros River in order to cross from Turkey to Greece. Many people including women and children have died while attempting this dangerous route. These tragedies have been extensively covered by the media, with pictures of the dead bodies of innocent children on the front pages.

13.5.1 The Evaluation of Practices Regarding Detention and Jailing Process in Turkey

Hundreds of thousands of people in Turkey are presumed to have been detained. A number of evidence that there was exposure to torture and mistreatment during these detention procedures is available (Aydin and Avincan 2020). Having an essential role in the prevention of torture and maltreatment, forensic science specialists were dismissed en masse from their jobs (105 forensic science experts and assistants, 20% of all forensic science specialists) (Keten 2020). This way, medical professionals were threatened into complicity. In a study conducted by the authors of this section, the detention process of forensic science specialists who were subjected to such practices and would be able to carry out the medicolegal evaluation of torture and maltreatment practices competently was investigated. Participants were asked questions regarding the treatment steps specified in the Istanbul Protocol. Seventy two percent of these specialists stated that they were exposed to psychological or physical torture. The images presented through media in relation to experiences during detention processes reveal just how dramatic the situation is – it can be regarded as mass torture. People have been suppressed and intimidated, which is a feature of oppressive regimes (Keten and Abaci 2020).

Following the traumatic experiences of Turkey during the state of emergency, many academics, journalists, teachers and doctors left and became refugees. In our previous study devoted to that group, 79 (39.1%) of the participants were teachers, 27 (10.8%) were academicians, 10 (4%) were doctors, 27 (10.8%) were law enforcement/army officers, 16 (6.4%) were businessmen, 14 (5.4%) were lawyers or prosecutors/judges, and 17 (6.8%) belonged to other professions. 46 (18.4%) participants stated that they were exposed to physical torture during a detention process. 186 (74.4%) cases pointed out that they were subject to psychological violence and mistreatment (Keten et al. 2020a).

Their testimony reveals that no attention was paid to the proper and humane use of handcuffs. Although it is regulated that handcuffing a person with their arms on their back should be used only under some special conditions, it was de-facto used as a way of insulting the detainees and deliberately causing them discomfort or pain. In a study conducted by Kantarcı et al., participants stated that the use of zip ties made them feel inhuman. It is an undeniable fact that the improper use of handcuffs by law enforcement officers has a negative psychological effect upon people (Kantarci et al. 2013; Singh et al. 2005; Vorbrüggen and Baer 2007).

Furthermore, both metal handcuffs and zip ties are known to cause lesions of the epidermis and dermis or handcuff neuropathy (Avsar et al. 2015; Grant and Cook 2000; Stone and Laureno 1991). The states are unequivocally responsible for protecting the health and security of people in detention. However, 78.6% of the participants suggested that they were not allowed to get medical support.

It was found that people in prison had difficulties in accessing health services because of health problems (Aydin and Avincan 2020). As previously mentioned, even detainees suffering from serious chronic conditions were kept in prison, despite legal provisions allowing for their premature release or imposing special measures on them like house arrest or moving them to medical facilities until their diseases reach their late stages and become irreversible (Aydin and Avincan 2020).

Additionally, it becomes apparent that in many cases standard detention procedures were not carried out properly. What is even more disturbing, the arrests of many people resemble a kidnapping more than an official detention. Some people were taken from in front of their homes and forced into unmarked vans and cars. Others were intentionally arrested in wide open spaces with many members of the public and the press present in acts resembling a publicity stunt.

These cases were revealed as a result of pressure from the Council of Europa and the victims' families not being informed in any way for months or even years are a powerful example of the scope of arbitrary practices in Turkey. While in Turkey itself there is no debate on torture, international organisations and experts have been working on the subject and publishing related materials.

The US-Based human rights organisation, Human Rights Watch (HRW), for instance, has published a report titled 'Turkey: Renewed Torture in Police Custody, Abductions'. The 43-Page report drawing, among other sources, from witness testimony, has detailed 11 cases of torture and 5 cases of abduction by government forces. Some victims who were held in custody while awaiting trial, report being transferred from detention centers to police stations without their families being informed, being held there for up to 6 weeks and tortured with the aim of forcing a confession. Some victims also reported being subjected to rape, sexual abuse through the use of different objects including bottles and torture by means of electricity while in custody. The respective evidence was reportedly shared by legal representatives, family members or through social media (HRW 2017).

It is pointed out that the Turkish Ministry of Justice refused to comment. The UN Special Rapporteur on Torture Nils Melzer has also referred to the widespread allegations of torture in Turkey, emphasizing that the state should take the necessary measures to prevent and punish torture. The report states that these atrocities are committed by special teams within the structures of the police and gendarmerie (UN 2016).

Torture and mistreatment in Turkey are not only confined to power structures, ordinary civilians have been increasingly exposed to it and they have been presented to them as acceptable. Supporters of cruelty and torture have been encouraged among other things by the fact that organised crime leader Sedat Peker was able to say in his speech, referring to the academicians who had signed the "Peace declaration", "We are going to make you bleed and shower in your blood!" and not face any consequences (Odatv 2016).

This and similar occurrences demonstrate how physical violence has come to be seen as a standard custodial procedure in Turkey, with very few victims able to speak out (Girdap 2020).

The Stockholm Center for Freedom (2017) reports that people have faced torture and rape threats not only directed at them, but also at their family members and relatives, including their parents, partners and children. The Center's findings highlight the massive dimensions of this humanitarian tragedy in Turkey.

13.5.2 The Evaluation of Medical Treatments Regarding Detention and Imprisonment Processes

In one of our previous studies, participants were asked questions regarding the treatment steps pointed out in the Istanbul Protocol and the results suggested that examinations during the state of emergency in Turkey were not conducted and reported in accordance with the Istanbul Protocol. Torture and maltreatment still continue to be a massive humanitarian disaster. It was found out in the reports that many examinations took place in mass, in halls, police stations or sports halls. Moreover, it was found out that law enforcement officers observed over and pressured the medical/forensic staff while they were preparing their reports, which immediately deems these questionable (Keten et al. 2020b).

Among the cases of death in custody was that of teacher GokhanAcikkollu, who was under arrest for 13 days following the attempted coup d'etat. He claimed during medical check-ups while in custody that he was subjected to violence but no measures were taken. He suffered from diabetes mellitus and panic attacks. After being briefly hospitalized following two panic attacks, he was brought back to detention, where he was again subjected to torture. He died in custody and while the official autopsy report mentions that he had a heart attack, possible torture was not investigated. Prof. Sebnem Korur Fincanci, who is President of the Turkish Human Rights Foundation and a forensics expert concluded after his investigation into the case that Acikkollu died of a heart attack as a result of torture. He was buried in a cemetery designated for 'traitors' (Cumhuriyet 2018).

There are many more similar examples of unacceptable treatment in custody. The facts that claims of torture and maltreatment in police custody are not investigated according to the Istanbul Protocol and post-mortem examinations do not conform to the Minessota Protocol are major obstacles in the way of justice.

13.5.3 The Evaluation of Migration and Mental Influence

Post-traumatic Stress Disorder (PTSD) can be defined as a wide scope of specific symptoms which start after encountering or witnessing an excessively traumatic event in DSM-V such as a death or a death threat, excessive injury or a condition threatening the bodily integrity of a person (American Psychiatric Association 2013).

Cases of PTSD in people who have fled Turkey because of human rights abuses during and after the state of emergency after the failed coup attempt have been studied in Germany. Post-Traumatic Stress Disorder being a condition observed frequently after a physical or mental trauma, in our study it was prevalent at a potential rate of 88%, which is much higher than the rates usually found in studies conducted on participants of migration waves from Turkey to Germany before. This result can be explained with the professional and social positions lost by those people; however, more studies should be conducted to evaluate this situation (Keten et al. 2020c).

13.6 Conclusion

Presently, torture and mistreatment are prohibited in universally accepted human rights documents and mechanisms for the prevention and investigation of torture practices have been established. The International Committee for the Prevention of Torture continues to exercise control and pressure upon state parties in this regard. However, the reports published by the committee regarding Turkey, especially in the last few years, indicate that torture and other violent occurrences are still practiced commonly during detention and those methods are used both against ordinary prisoners and terror suspects. With regards to Turkey, negligence of torture prohibition was stated to be an essential human rights problem as far back as the 1990s. With the state of emergency declared in 2016, those practices have become even more common. The most important role in the prevention and documentation of torture belongs to medical staff, who are subjected to both national and international legislation as well as professional ethical standards. Respecting these is both their professional and humanitarian duty. For this reason, when claims regarding torture and maltreatment and prison conditions are considered, it is of great importance to follow internationally established standards as defined in protocols such as the Istanbul and Minnesota Protocols. The dedication of the international community and medical, judicial and forensics professionals is crucial in the fight against torture, cruel and degrading treatment. Multidisciplinary and multinational collaboration is essential in preventing these inhumane practices observed throughout history.

Appendix

The Methods of Torture according to the Istanbul Protocol

(a) Blunt trauma, such as a punch, kick, slap, whipping, a beating with wires or truncheons or falling down;
(b) Positional torture, using suspension, stretching limbs apart, prolonged constraint of movement, forced positioning;
(c) Burns with cigarettes, heated instruments, scalding liquid or a caustic substance;
(d) Electric shocks;
(e) Asphyxiation, such as wet and dry methods, drowning, smothering, choking or use of chemicals;
(f) Crush injuries, such as smashing fingers or using a heavy roller to injure the thighs or back;
(g) Penetrating injuries, such as stab and gunshot wounds, wires under nails;
(h) Chemical exposure to salt, chilli pepper, gasoline, etc. (in wounds or body cavities);
(i) Sexual violence to genitals, molestation, instrumentation, rape;
(j) Crush injury or traumatic removal of digits and limbs;
(k) Medical amputation of digits or limbs, surgical removal of organs;

(l) Pharmacological torture using toxic doses of sedatives, neuroleptics, paralytics, etc.;
(m) Conditions of detention, such as a small or overcrowded cell, solitary confinement, unhygienic conditions, no access to toilet facilities, irregular or contaminated food and water, exposure to extremes of temperature, denial of privacy and forced nakedness;
(n) Deprivation of normal sensory stimulation, such as sound, light, sense of time, isolation, manipulation of brightness of the cell, abuse of physiological needs, restriction of sleep, food, water, toilet facilities, bathing, motor activities, medical care, social contacts, isolation within prison, loss of contact with the outside world (victims are often kept in isolation in order to prevent bonding and mutual identification and to encourage traumatic bonding with the torturer);
(o) Humiliation, such as verbal abuse, performance of humiliating acts;
(p) Threats of death, harm to family, further torture, imprisonment, mock executions;
(q) Threats of attack by animals, such as dogs, cats, rats or scorpions;
(r) Psychological techniques to break down the individual, including forced betrayals, accentuating feelings of helplessness, exposure to ambiguous situations or contradictory messages;
(s) Violation of taboos;
(t) Behavioural coercion, such as forced engagement in practices against the religion of the victim (e.g. forcing Muslims to eat pork), forced harm to others through torture or other abuses, forced destruction of property, forced betrayal of someone placing them at risk of harm;
(u) Forcing the victim to witness torture or atrocities being inflicted on others.

References

Allden, Kathleen, Charles Poole, Supang Chantavanich, Khin Ohmar, Nyi Nyi Aung, and Richard F. Mollica. 1996. Burmese Political Dissidents in Thailand: Trauma; and Survival Among Young Adults in Exile. *American Journal of Public Health* 86 (11): 1561–1569.

American Psychiatric Association. 2013. *Desk Reference to the Diagnostic Criteria From DSM-5*. Philadelphia: American Psychiatric Publishing.

Avsar, Abdullah, Erdem Okdemir, Ramazan Karanfil, Alper Keten, Omer Kaya, and Tuba Akkus. 2015. Medico-Legal Examination of Custody and Evaluation of the Lesions Related to Plastic Handcuffing. *The Medical Journal of Mustafa Kemal University* 6 (23): 8–11.

Aydin, Hasan, and Koksal Avincan. 2020. Intellectual Crimes and Serious Violation of Human Rights in Turkey: A Narrative Inquiry. *The International Journal of Human Rights* 24 (8): 1127–1155. https://doi.org/10.1080/13642987.2020.1713108.

Basoglu, Metin. 1992. Introduction. In *Torture and Its Consequences*, ed. M. Basoglu, 1–22. New York: Cambridge Press.

Can, İsmail Özgür, Yakup Gökhan Doğramacı, and Ümit Ünüvar. 2019. Istanbul Protocol. In *Tıp Hukuku*, ed. Z.Z. Erkol and Y.G. Doğramacı, 72–79. Ankara: Türkiye Klinikleri.

Cumhuriyet Gazetesi. 2018. *Gözaltında işkence sonucu ölen Gökhan öğretmen, 1.5 yıl sonra 'pardon' denilerek görevine iade edildi*. http://www.cumhuriyet.com.tr/haber/turkiye/935144/Gozaltinda_iskence_sonucu_olen_Gokhan_ogretmen__1.5_yil_sonra__pardon__denilerek_gorevine_iade_edildi.html. Accessed 28 Feb 2018.

Daglar, Ali. 2019. *Türkiye'nin hapisteki çocukları... 700 çocuk neden cezaevinde, nasıl bir hayatları var?*. https://www.independentturkish.com/node/27266/haber/t%C3%BCrkiyenin-hapisteki-%C3%A7ocuklar%C4%B1-700-%C3%A7ocuk-neden-cezaevinde-nas%C4%B1l-bir-hayatlar%C4%B1-var. Accessed 13 May 2019.

Engelhardt, H. Tristram. 1975. The Concepts of Health and Disease. In *Evaluation and Explanation in the Biomedical Sciences*, ed. H.T. Englehardt and S.F. Spicker, 125–141. Holland: D. Reidel Publishing Co.

Erkol, Zerrin, Bora Büken, Rıza Yılmaz, and Hayri Erkol. 2006. Prison Deaths in Kahramanmaras City. *Turkish Journal of Forensic Medicine* 20 (3): 18–23.

European Committee for the Prevention of Torture and in Human or Degrading Treatment or Punishment CPT/Inf (2017) 5-part.

European Convention on Human Rights. 1950. Convention for the Protection of Human Rights and Fundamental Freedoms. Aricle 3, Rome. https://www.echr.coe.int/Documents/Convention_ENG.pdf.

Fazel, Seena, and Ram Benning. 2006. Natural Deaths in Male Prisoners: A 20-Year Mortality Study. *European Journal of Public Health* 16 (4): 441–444.

Franceschetti, L., F. Magli, V.G. Merelli, E.A. Muccino, A. Gentilomo, F. Agazzi, D.M. Gibelli, et al. 2019. The Effect of the Medico-Legal Evaluation on Asylum Seekers in the Metropolitan City of Milan, Italy: A Pilot Study. *International Journal of Legal Medicine.* 2019 (133): 669–675.

General Assembly Resolution 3452 (XXX) of 9 December 1975, Annex, Arts. 2 and 4; See Official Records of the General Assembly, Thirtieth Session, Supplement No. 34 (A/10034), p. 91.

General Assembly Resolution 34/169of 17 December 1979, Annex, Art. 5; See Official Records of the General Assembly, Thirty Fourth Session, Supplement No. 46 (A/34/46), p. 186.

General Assembly Resolution 37/194 of 18 December 1982, Annex, Principles 2–5; See Official Records of the General Assembly, Thirty-Seventh Session, Supplement No. 51 (A/37/51), p. 211.

General Assembly Resolution 43/173 of 9 December 1988, Annex, Principle 6; See Official Records of the General Assembly, Forty-Third Session, Supplement No. 49 (A/43/49), p. 298.

General Assembly Resolution 45/111 of 14 December 1990, Annex, Principle 1; See Official Records of the General Assembly, Forty-Fifth Session, Supplement No. 49 (A/45/49), p. 200.

Girdap, Hafza. 2020. Human Rights, Conflicts, and Dislocation: The Case of Turkey in a Global Spectrum. *American Journal of Qualitative Research* 4 (1): 69–84. https://doi.org/10.29333/ajqr/8266.

Grant, Arthur C., and Albert A. Cook. 2000. A prospective Study of Handcuff Neuropathies. *Muscle & Nerve* 23 (6): 933–938.

Grappe, Michel. 1995. *La guerre en ex-Yougoslavie: un regard sur les enfants réfugiés. Psychiatrie humanitaire en ex-Yougoslavie et en Arménie: face au traumatisme*, 89–106. Paris: PUF.

Haar, Rohini J., Karen Wang, Homer Venters, Satu Salonen, Rupa Patel, Tamaryn Nelson, Ranit Mishori, and Parveen K. Parmar. 2019. Documentation of Human Rights Abuses Among Rohingya Refugees from Myanmar. *Conflict and Health* 16 (13): 42. https://doi.org/10.1186/s13031-019-0226-9.

Hammett, Theodore M., Patricia Harmon, and William Rhodes. 2002. The Burden of Infectious Disease Among Inmates of and Releases from US Correctional Facilities. *American Journal of Public Health* 92 (11): 1789–1794.

Holtan, Neal R. 1998. How Medical Assessment of Victims of Torture Relates to Psychiatric Care. In *Caring for Victims of Torture*, ed. J.M. Jaranson and M.K. Popkin, 107–113. American Psychiatric Press: Washington, DC.

Human Rights Watch (HRW). 2017. *Police Torture and Abductions Turkey*. https://www.hrw.org/report/2017/10/12/custody/police-torture-and-abductions-turkey.

Iacopino, Vincent. 1998. Treatment of Survivors of Political Torture: Commentary. *The Journal of Ambulatory Care Management.* 21 (2): 43.

Istanbul Protocol. 2004. *Manual on the Effective Investigation and Documentation of Torture and Other Cruel, Inhuman or Degrading Treatment or Punishment. Professional Training Series No. 8/Rev.1.* Geneva: Office of The United Nations High Commissioner For Human Rights.

Johnson, Howard, and Andrew Thompson. 2008. The Development and Maintenance of Post-Traumatic Stress Disorder (PTSD) in Civilian Adult Survivors of War Trauma and Torture: A Review. *Clinical Psychology Review* 28: 36–47.
Kantarcı, Muhammed Nabi, Eyüp Kandemir, Gürol Berber, Mustafa Bastürk, and Sebnem Korur Fincanci. 2013. Evaluation of Plastic and Metal Handcuff-Related Injuries Under Custody in Medical Examinations. *Türkiye Klinikleri. Tip Bilimleri Dergisi* 33 (2): 360.
Kaplan, Ida, Yvonne Stolk, Madeleine Valibhoy, Alan Tucker, and Judy Baker. 2016. Cognitive assessment of refugee children: Effects of trauma and new language acquisition. *Transcultural Psychiatry* 53 (1): 81–109.
Karaarslan, Bekir, Mehmet Cengil Aslan, Alper Keten, Ömer Lütfi Özkan, Onur Eyisoy, Mehmet Karasu, Ahmet Büyükçelik, and Ahmet Aslan. 2014. Minnesota Autopsy Protocol Autopsy Performed According to the Evaluation of the Prison Death: 13 Case Report. *Journal of Forensic Medicine* 28 (3): 294–301.
Keten, Alper. 2020. Evaluating the Experiences of Detained Turkish Forensic Medicine Specialists. Torture. (In press)
Keten, Alper, and Ramazan Abaci. 2020. Evaluation of Medical Examination of Forensic Medicine Specialists During/After Detention Within the Scope of Istanbul Protocol. *Journal of Forensic and Legal Medicine*. https://doi.org/10.1016/j.jflm.2020.101921.
Keten, Alper, Ramazan Abaci, and Nicolakis Johannes. 2020a. *The Medicolegal Evaluation of Detention Procedures During the Recent State of Emergency in Turkey*. California: American Academy of Forensic Science Annual Scientific Meeting.
———. 2020b. *Evaluating Medico-Legal Examinations of Turkish Detainees During the Recent State of Emergency in Turkey Within the Scope of the Istanbul Protocol*. California: American Academy of Forensic Science Annual Scientific Meeting.
———. 2020c. *The evaluation of Psychological Trauma of Individuals Escaped from Turkey due to Human Rights Violations: Post-traumatic Stress Disorder*. California: American Academy Of Forensic Science Annual Scientific Meeting.
Kinzie, J. David, James K. Boehnlein, Paul K. Leung, Laurie J. Moore, Crystal Riley, and Debra Smith. 1990. The Prevalence of Post-traumatic Stress Disorder and Its Clinical Significance Among Southeast Asian Refugees. *The American Journal of Psychiatry* 147 (7): 913–917.
Kleinman, Arthur. 1986. Anthropology and Psychiatry: The Role of Culture in Cross-Cultural Research on Illness and Care. In *World Psychiatric Association (WPA) Regional Symposium, Psychiatry and Its Related Disciplines*. Copenhagen: WPA.
Mollica, Richard F., Karen Donelan, Svang Tor, James Lavelle, Christopher Elias, Martin Frankel, and Robert J. Blendon. 1993. The Effect of Trauma and Confinement on the Functional Health and Mental Health Status of Cambodians Living in Thailand-Cambodia Border Camps. *JAMA* 270 (5): 581–586.
Nelson Mandela Rules. 1955. https://www.un.org/en/events/mandeladay/mandela_rules.shtml.
Odatv. 2016. *Sedat Peker, Akan kanlarinizda dus alcagiz*. https://odatv.com/akan-kanlarinizda-dus-alacagiz-1301161200.html.
Organization of American States. 1985. Inter-American Convention to Prevent and Punish Torture, OAS Treaty Series, No. 67. https://www.refworld.org/docid/3ae6b3620.html. Accessed 17 Feb 2020.
Otter, Joost Jan, Yolba Smit, Loreine B. dela Cruz, Önder Özkalipci, and Resmiye Oral. 2013. Documentation of Torture and Cruel, Inhuman or Degrading Treatment of Children: A Review of Existing Guidelines and Tools. *Forensic Science International* 224 (1–3): 27–32.
Paker, Murat. 2000. *Subjective Meaning of Torture as a Predictor in Post-Torture Psychological Response. Dissertation project*. New York: New School for Social Research.
———. 2003. Boğazımızdaki yumru: Türkiye'de işkence. *Birikim* 172: 10–22.
Paker, Murat, and Burcu Bugru. 2016. Review of The Studies Conducted on The Psychology of Torture Survivors in Turkey. *Türk Psikoloji Yazıları* 19: 76–92.
Peters, Edward. 1986. *Torture*. Oxford: Basil Blackwell.
Piaget, Jean. 1977. *La naissance de l'intelligence chez l'enfant*. Neuchâtel: Delachaux et Niestlé.
Quiroga, Jose. 2012. Torture in children. 2009;19(2):66–87. Erratum in Torture. 2012;22(1):68.

Rothbaum, Barbara Olasov, Edna B. Foa, David S. Riggs, Tamera Murdock, and William Walsh. 1992. A Prospective Examination of Post-Traumatic Stress Disorder Rape Victims. *Journal of Traumatic Stress* 5 (3): 455–475.

Singh, Sonal, Khagendra Dahal, and Edward Mills. 2005. Nepal's War on Human Rights: A SUMMIT HIGHER THAN EVEREST. *International Journal for Equity in Health* 4: 9.

Sironi, Francesca. 1995. On Torture un enfant, ou les avatars de l'ethnocentrisme psychologique. *Enfance* 4: 205–215.

Stone, Donald A., and Robert Laureno. 1991. Handcuff Neuropathies. *Neurology* 41 (1): 145–147.

Suedfeld, Peter, ed. 1990. *The Series in Clinical and Community Psychology. Psychology and Torture*. Washington: Hemisphere Publishing Corp.

Sutker, Patricia B., Daniel K. Winstead, Z. Harry Galina, and Albert N. Allain. 1991. Cognitive Deficits and Psycho-Pathology Among Former Prisoners of War and Combat Veterans of the Korean Conflict. *The American Journal of Psychiatry* 148: 62–72.

The Law on The Execution of Penalties and Security Measures. Law No. 5275. 2004. https://www.tbmm.gov.tr/kanunlar/k5275.html.

The Malleus Maleficarum (The Witch Hammer), First Published in 1486. http://www.malleusmaleficarum.org/.

The Minnesota Protocol on the Investigation of Potentially Unlawful Death. 2016. Office of the United Nations High Commissioner for Human Rights, New York/Geneva, 2017.

The Stockholm Centre for Freedom SCF. 2017. *Mass Torture and Ill-Treatment in Turkey 2017*. https://stockholmcf.org/wp-content/uploads/2017/06/Mass-Torture-And-Ill-Treatment-In-Turkey_06.06.2017.pdf.

Turkey's Post-Coup Crackdown. 2019. www.turkeypurge.com.

UNCHR The UN Refugee Agency. 2017. *Global Report*.

United Nations. 1984. *Convention Against Torture and Other Cruel, Inhuman or Degrading Treatment or Punishment*. https://www.ohchr.org/EN/ProfessionalInterest/Pages/CAT.aspx.

———. 1990. Convention on the Rights of the Child Adopted and Opened for Signature, Ratification and Accession by General Assembly Resolution 44/25 of 20 November 1989 Entry into Force 2 September 1990, in Accordance with Article 49.

———. 2016. Preliminary Observations and Recommendations of the United Nations Special Rapporteur on Torture and Other Cruel, Inhuman and Degrading Treatment or Punishment, Mr. Nils Melzer on the Official visit to Turkey–27 November to 2 December 2016.

United Nations Congress. 1955. On the Prevention of Crime and the Treatment of Offenders.

von Overbeck. 1998, January. Famillesvictimes de violences collectives et enexil: Quelle urgence, quelmodèle de soins? Le point de vue d'une pédopsychiatre. *La Revue Française de Psychiatrie et de Psychologie Médicale* 14: 35–39.

Vorbrüggen, Meike, and Hans U. Baer. 2007. Humiliation: The Lasting Effect of Torture. *Military Medicine* 172 (12): 29–33.

Westermeyer, Joseph. 1985. Psychiatric Diagnosis Across Cultural Boundaries. *American Journal of Psychiatry* 142 (7): s. 798–s. 805.

World Health Organization. 2016. *International statistical Classification of Diseases and Related Health Problems. – 10th revision, Fifth Edition Cenevre*. Geneva: WHO.

World Medical Association Considering the Declaration of Hamburg. 1997. *Calling on Physicians to Protest Individually Against Ill-Treatment and on National and International Medical Organizations to Support Physicians in Such Actions*.

World Medical Association Declaration of Tokyo. 1975. *Guidelines for Physicians Concerning Torture and other Cruel, Inhuman or Degrading Treatment or Punishment in Relation to Detention and Imprisonment*.

World Medical Association Declaration. 1990. *Considering the Resolution on Human Rights adopted by the World Medical Association in Rancho Mirage*.

World Medical Association Declaration of Seoul. 2008. on Professional Autonomy and Clinical Independence.

I am Assoc. Prof. Dr. Alper Keten. I am a medical doctor. After having medical degree from Çukurova University Medical Faculty (in Adana, Turkey, 2005), I got specialty degree from Hacettepe University Medical Faculty, in Ankara, Turkey. In 2010, I studied in Toronto University as a visiting scientist. After graduated from Hacettepe University, I had worked in the Council of Forensic Medicine, I have experience in forensic pathology and clinical forensic medicine cases such as human right violations, child abuse and neglect. I am a talented and dedicated medical professional. Besides my practical experience, I performed several academic studies and published many papers in respected journals.

When I was working as Assoc. Prof, in Hacettepe University Forensic Medicine Department, I immigrated from Turkey to Germany because of the increasing political pressure, antidemocratic government pressure and human right violations. I have been studying at Heidelberg University Hospital Institute of Forensic and Traffic Medicine since October 2018.

Part V
Social and Economic Rights

Chapter 14
Right to Education: Challenges and Issues Under the Justice and Development Party Era

Uzeyir Ogurlu and Koksal Avincan

Abstract The right to education has been recognized as a human right by several international conventions. The Constitution of the Republic of Turkey also protects the right to education. However, the government ruled by the AKP since 2002, has failed to protect and fulfill this right for all. Education in one's mother tongue, compulsory religious education, and a teaching recruitment system have been among the most debated education rights. However, the date of July 15, 2016, was a turning point in the history of violation of human rights in the Republic of Turkey, after a failed coup attempt. The controversies and violations of human rights became exacerbated after the failed coup attempt with a massive purge of dissidents. Thousands of teachers were dismissed, and thousands of public and private schools, dormitories, and unions were closed as part of the crackdown. This chapter examines the violations of education rights in Turkey under the AKP era, especially after the July 15 failed coup attempt, in the light of international agreements on rights to education.

Keywords Human rights · Right to education · K-12 education · The Justice and Development Party

14.1 The Right to Education

It is broadly accepted that education has an impact on the development of humanity as a whole and on the human personality of individuals. Thus, education is crucial for ensuring the quality of life. Education has been recognized as a human right in

U. Ogurlu (✉)
University of Wisconsin-Stevens Point, Stevens Point, WI, USA
e-mail: uogurlu@uwsp.edu

K. Avincan
A Doctoral Student and Human Rights Activist at Florida International University, Miami, FL, USA

H. Aydin, W. Langley (eds.), *Human Rights in Turkey*, Philosophy and Politics - Critical Explorations 15, https://doi.org/10.1007/978-3-030-57476-5_14

Table 14.1 International agreements on the right to education

Conventions
European Convention for the Protection of Human Rights and Fundamental Freedoms (Council of Europe 1952a)
UNESCO Convention against Discrimination in Education (UNESCO 1960)
European Social Charter (Council of Europe 1961)
International Covenant on Civil and Political Rights (The United Nations General Assembly 1966a)
International Covenant on Economic, Social and Cultural Rights (The United Nations General Assembly 1966b)
Convention on the Elimination of All Forms of Discrimination against Women (The United Nations 1988)
African Charter On Human And People's Rights (African Union 1981)
ILO Convention 169: Indigenous & Tribal Peoples Convention (International Labour Organization 1989)
Convention on the Rights of the Child (UNICEF 1989)
African Charter on the Rights and Welfare of the Child (Organization of African Unity 1990)
Declaration of Minimum Humanitarian Standards (UN Commission on Human Rights 1994)
Council of Europe Framework Convention for the Protection of National Minorities (Council of Europe 1995)
Additional Protocol to the American Convention on Human Rights, Protocol of San Salvador (Organization of American States 1998)
Charter of Fundamental Freedoms of the European Union (European Union 2000)

many international agreements, as shown Table 14.1. The right to education falls under the protection of many international constitutions as well (Gok and Ilgaz 2011). Signing these agreements requires these nations to accept obligations and respect the right to education. States are obliged to put forth efforts to ensure these rights, using their maximum capacities. Therefore, providing education to everyone is part of basic human rights. Violations of education rights result in infractions of international laws. Article 26 of the Universal Declaration of Human Rights (1948) articulated the right to education as "Everyone has the right to education" (UN General Assembly 1948). In addition to that, Article 26 states that:

- Primary education shall be compulsory and available free to all;
- Secondary education in its different forms, including technical and vocational secondary education, shall be made generally available and accessible to all by every appropriate means, and by the progressive introduction of free education;
- Fundamental education shall be encouraged or intensified as far as possible for those persons who have not received or completed the whole period of their primary education;
- The development of a system of schools at all levels shall be actively pursued, an adequate fellowship system shall be established, and the material conditions of teaching staff shall be continuously improved.

All of these conventions in Table 14.1 address common education rights, emphasizing that education should be for everyone, and directed to the full development of the human personality. It should also strengthen respect for human rights and fundamental freedoms. They also mentioned the rights of parents to choose the kind of education suitable for their children. Turkey is a party to most of these international conventions. The right to education is recognized by Article 42 of the Turkish Constitution, which states that "no one shall be deprived of the right of learning and education" (Türkiye Cumhuriyeti Anayasası 1982).

The right to education is also a citizenship right. Education as a citizenship right has become a crucial issue in the restructuring of Western democracies' school systems. Education as a parental civil right has been regarded as a central theme. But in addition to this, the right to education is a social right. For example, Marshall (1950) points to educational institutions as being specifically important for the distribution and upholding of social rights. Education as a social citizenship right is seen as a central prerequisite for the exercise of one's civil and political rights. Habermas (1992) also points out that the educational system can be seen as crucial to the development of the communicative rights that are central to political participation. This development is also well-argued by Gutmann and Thompson (1998) when they stress the democratic purpose of education is that 'schools should aim to develop their students' capacities to understand different perspectives, communicate their understandings to other people, and engage in the give-and-take of moral argument with a view to making mutually acceptable decisions' (Gutmann and Thompson 1998).

States are required to make education available, accessible, acceptable and adaptable to all, regardless of race, sex, language, religion, social class, and political or other opinions (Tomaševski 2006). Turkey has one of the youngest populations among members of the Organization for Economic Co-operation and Development (OECD), which calls for more attention to education rights (OECD 2005). It is crucial to provide educational access to this young population; a large population that puts education on the agenda as a priority. Although both quality and equity of education are a challenge in Turkey, rights to education have been retrogressing especially in recent years. As a striking example, since the establishment of the European Court of Human Rights (ECHR) in 1959, eighteen education rights violation decisions were given by the ECHR among the 47 European Council countries, and 7 out of eighteen were against Turkey; the most convicted country among all 38% (European Court of Human Rights 2020). This chapter examines the violations of education rights in the Justice and Development Party (AKP) era. To this end, an overview of the discourse shift of the AKP government and transformation of education under the AKP was completed, and language and religion-based education rights violations were scrutinized. It then analyzed violations of the right to education after the failed coup attempt, due to the fact that the crackdown has led to a chilling effect on all human rights in Turkey. After the crackdown, the AKP also radically restructured the teaching recruitment system, which is the foundation of the educational system. Thus, this chapter also reviews the teaching recruitment system from the right to education point of view. Higher education is beyond the scope of this chapter since it focuses on what has happened in PreK-12 education in the AKP era.

14.2 The AKP Government: Shifting from Democratic Values to Authoritarianism

The Justice and Development Party was founded in 2001 and became the ruling party in 2002 under the leadership of Recep Tayyip Erdogan. Since then, the AKP has been in power for the longest period in Turkish multi-party political history. In the beginning, the aim of the ruling party was to increase democratic and universal values, integrate laws with European standards, and increase prosperity in Turkish society (Karaveli 2016). However, the AKP's reform movement lasted until 2007 (Yilmaz and Bashirov 2018), focusing on strengthening its power and seizing the state in its second term from 2007 to 2011 (Somer 2017).

After 2011, Islamism and authoritarianism started to increase in the discourse of the AKP (Somer 2014). The AKP restricted freedoms, such as the media, and became intolerant of the opposition (Somer 2017). The crackdown on the coup attempt in July of 2016 caused severe damage to Turkish society, resulting in about 300 civilian deaths and more than 2000 injuries (Akkemik et al. 2019; Amnesty International 2017). After the failed coup, a state of emergency was declared by the government. During the state of emergency, hundreds of thousands of people suffered human rights violations (Aydin and Avincan 2020), such as arbitrary deprivation of the right to work, freedom of movement, torture, and other ill-treatment and arbitrary detentions (Office of the United Nations High Commissioner for Human Rights 2017). This failed coup has had a significant adverse effect on happiness, trust, and life satisfaction in the country (Akkemik et al. 2019). Thus, the shift from democratic discourse to authoritarianism in the AKP has brought about infringements on human rights, including the right to education. An overview of the educational system under the AKP would help readers better understand the breach of educational rights in the country.

14.3 The Education System in Turkey: The Drastic Transformation in the AKP Era

Ever since the founding of the Republic of Turkey, the education system has undergone a lot of changes. One of the reasons for its instability is that education has served as a battleground between factions in the country, especially the secular factions backed by left-wing parties and the army, and conservative religious factions recently advocated by the AKP (Makovsky 2015). The education system has been highly centralized, which has led to an escalation in the wrestling match between political and social wings. The Ministry of National Education (Milli Eğitim Bakanlığı, MEB) is responsible for deciding the school curricula, approving textbooks, paying teachers, maintaining school buildings, and allocating financial aid.

In Turkey, compulsory public education is free of charge and begins at age six, lasting through the 12th grade. As a result of the battle between groups, the secular faction, with the help of the military in 1997, changed the school system and mandated eight years of compulsory elementary education, followed by three years of optional secondary school. As this new system was launched, Imam-Hatip middle schools (religious schools) were closed as a part of the new system (Lüküslü 2016).

The primary officially established purpose of Imam-Hatip schools was to train imams and preachers in order to meet the religious needs of the people. They are generally gender-segregated schools. In addition to a general academic curriculum, the program of Imam-Hatip schools contains extra courses on various Islamic topics such as the Quran, Islamic law, Interpretation of the Quran, Hadith, and Islamic studies (Milli Eğitim Bakanlığı Talim ve Terbiye Kurulu Başkanlığı 2018). Only Sunni Islam perspectives related to Islamic religion are taught in these schools. By 1997, they had enrolled one in ten students in these schools. There has been a controversy that Imam-Hatip schools have been the voter base for the Islamist movement recently represented by the AKP (Ayata 1996). Considering this controversy, in 1997, the military-influenced government closed Imam-Hatip middle schools and restricted admission to colleges of graduates from Imam-Hatip schools. Thus, the introduction of eight years of compulsory education and new regulations for college admission led to a sudden and serious decline in the popularity of Imam-Hatip schools.

As a counterattack, the AKP introduced new legislation extending compulsory education 12 years and splitting it into three levels of four years each (4 + 4 + 4 system) in 2012. This system has given the AKP an opportunity to open more religious schools. Religion and religious topics then started to become a focus on education more than ever before (Kaya 2015a).

Preschool education is not compulsory in the country. In the 4 + 4 + 4 system, primary education consists of the first four years of schooling (grades 1–4), followed by a middle school education for another four years (grades 5–8). Then, high school education lasts a duration of four years (grades 9–12). After primary school, students have two different tracks: regular middle school and Imam-Hatip Schools. The high school level consists of academic, vocational and religious schools. Students attending vocational schools can earn a certificate in different fields, such as electricity, accounting, and health, or other technical areas. There are also selective academic and vocational schools, such as science high school or Anatolian high schools. Students must take a highly competitive and centralized exam at the eighth-grade level in order to get accepted into these selective high schools based on their scores (Ulutaş and Çıkrıkçı 2019).

Educational systems are built to improve students' performance in the country. Keeping in mind that academic achievement is influenced by various factors, not solely policies of the government, as far as academic success in the country is concerned, it overall seems to not be promising. Based on the Program for International Student Assessment (PISA) results, Turkey has remained below the OECD average in reading, mathematics, and science. PISA tests 15-year-old students from all over the world in reading, mathematics, and science every three years (OECD 2017). The last test was done in 2018, but the results have not yet been released. Turkey participated in PISA in 2003 for the first time. Although the scores have fluctuated by years, the position of Turkey remained mostly unchanged. Turkey has been far below the average of participated countries. For example, according to the PISA report for 2015, Turkey is the second from the bottom among 36 OECD countries in mathematics, science and reading (OECD 2017).

In addition to academic success, educational systems should consider the welfare of students. Children are the most affected group when it comes to education rights. Issues and challenges in education and society can have a negative impact on the well-being of children. Turkey appears to have issues in terms of students' welfare. For instance, for the first time ever, PISA 2015 analyzed students' well-being and their sense of belonging at school. Turkish students had the lowest score on well-being and a sense of belonging at school among 28 OECD countries (OECD 2017).

During the AKP era, the Minister of National Education has changed leadership more than any other ministry, having been assigned to seven different individuals. Excluding the current minister, none of them came from the field of education. This frequent change of ministers has led to frequent structural changes in the education system because each minister tried to change the system established by his predecessor. This attempt has caused instability in education. As an example, six different systems for the central entrance exam for high schools were adopted by the AKP government. There has not been a preliminary study on these changes to discern why they have been ineffective, nor has there been any transition period between the different systems (Eğitim Reformu Girişimi 2017). A recent study has shown that education administrators also pointed out the recent structural changes as the main problem of the Turkish educations system (Karakütük and Özdogan Özbal 2019). Thus, frequent radical structural changes in the AKP era has caused instability in education, which leads to failure in providing the right to education for all in the country.

14.4 Language-Based Education Rights Violations

It is a basic human right for one to use the language they are most proficient in (Ogechi 2003). Receiving an education in one's mother tongue is guaranteed by international agreements, including Article 13 of the Council of Europe Framework Convention for the Protection of National Minorities as cited in Council of Europe (1995), Article 5 of the UNESCO Universal Declaration on Cultural Diversity as cited in UNESCO (2001), and Article 8 of the European Charter for Regional or Minority Languages as cited in Council of Europe (1992). These agreements emphasize learning the mother tongue and receiving an education in that language. Considering the importance of the mother tongue in education, failing to provide this vital right can lead to a violation of the right to education. The conflict with the Kurdish minority in southeastern Turkey has been an important issue in local education (Kaya and Aydin 2013). Ethnicity and language can create a large gap in school achievement, especially in reading and science because speaking another language at home can impede understanding Turkish (Batyra 2017).

In 2012, after the introduction of the '4 + 4 + 4' education system, the AKP government added "Living Languages and Dialects" to the curriculum as an elective course for two hours per week (Dogan and Aydin 2019). Just after this decision, a few colleges in southern Turkey opened programs about Kurdish Language and Literature to meet the needs of teachers for this course. Students and parents were willing to select these programs in the schools attended by Kurdish children. For instance, in the 2012/2013 academic year, 28.587 students wanted to take this elective course, almost all in Kurdish and its dialects. This number increased by 53.000 in the 2013/2014 academic year and reached 83.344 in the 2014/2015 academic year (Kaya 2013). However, the abstention of colleges in Kurdish teacher training, and the lack of sufficient graduates of Kurdish language teaching hindered the further provision of these elective courses in schools, even though a considerable number of students selected this course (Göçer 2017). Thus, this small but important step could go no further.

The AKP changed the policy on the Kurdish language after its big setback in the 2015 election (Inal 2018). In 2015, the pro-Kurdish party triumphed over the AKP in Southern Turkey. After this policy change, teachers who speak Kurdish in schools have struggled with the administration. For instance, a primary school teacher, Medeni Oruç, underwent a disciplinary investigation by his school administration because he spoke Kurdish in school (Eğitim ve Bilim Emekçileri Sendikası Van Şubesi 2019). In 2019, Mardin Artuklu University made a decision to shut down the Institute of Living Languages (Bozarslan 2019). Table 14.2 shows the number of students the universities accepted for the Kurdish Literature program. Looking at these numbers, a downtrend each year can be seen in the number of students getting into these college programs.

In 2018, the Ministry of Education announced the intent to recruit 20.000 teachers, but just three out of 20.000 were instructors in the Kurdish Language. In 2019, this number declined to zero out of 20.000. The numbers of teachers teaching in Kurdish and its dialects can be seen in Table 14.3.

After the July 15 coup attempt, the government shut down some Kurdish teaching centers and associations that were opened to teach Kurdish and its dialects including KÜRD-DER (Kurdish Cultural Research Center), KURDİ-DER (Kurdish Cultural Research and Development Association) and Istanbul Kurdish Institute (677 Sayılı

Table 14.2 The number of students who get into Kurdish literature programs in colleges

University	2012	2013	2014	2015	2016	2017	2018	2019
Mardin Artuklu University	36	47	57	41	31	41	41	26
Muş Alpaslan University		41	47	41	31	41	31	36
Bingöl University		41	52	41	31	41	41	31

Note: Reprinted from "ÖSYS Yükseköğretim Programları ve Kontenjanları Kılavuzu" by *Ölçme, Seçme ve Yerleştirme Merkezi Başkanlığı (Measuring, Selection and Placement Center)*, 2012, 2013, 2014, 2015, 2016, 2017, 2018, 2019

Table 14.3 Number of hired teachers of living languages in years

Years	Total hired teachers	Number of hired teachers of living languages
2014	4.000	18
2015	52.000	22
2016	48.506	38
2017	20.127	3
2018	19.099	3
2019	19.914	0

Note: Reprinted from the *Ministry of National Education*

Kanun Hükmünde Kararname 2016). In addition, some private schools where Kurdish was the instructional language were shut down by force. Some Kurdish TV and radio channels were also terminated by the government (Kamer 2016; Karabağlı 2016).

Although the AKP government had taken positive steps toward education in Kurdish at the time it came to power, recently it seems that these gains have been destroyed, one by one. One of the reasons why the AKP has stepped back from providing education in one's mother tongue, is the loss of support in the southern part of the country, as seen in the June 2015 election (Inal 2018).

14.5 Belief-Based Education Rights Violations

The right to freedom of belief is also among the fundamental rights stipulated by many international conventions. According to the UN Human Rights Committee (1966a), forcing students who have different beliefs and religions to take religious courses, or do not want to select religious courses and compulsory religion lessons, is a violation of basic human rights. Turkey's education system mandates all students to take Religious Culture and Moral Knowledge in primary and secondary schools. The course focuses on teaching Sunni Hanafi Islam, and no other Islamic factions, in spite of the fact that Alevis' beliefs are different from Sunni Islam.

After the Sunnis, Alevis are the second-largest religious group in Turkey. Although the exact number is not known, it is estimated that they comprise about 25% of the population scattered throughout the country (Paul and Seyrek 2014). The systematic exclusion of, and discrimination against, Alevi citizens has been a chronic human right violation since the republic of Turkey was founded (Erdemir 2018). The Directorate of Religious Affairs only employs and serves Sunni Muslims, since Alevi's beliefs and places of worship have no legal status. As a residual effect from the AKP's revolutionist term, the AKP started a new initiative called "Alevi Openings" in 2008 to solve the ongoing problems of Alevi citizens. Alevi Openings involved a few workshops with Alevi community leaders. Similar to Kurdish language initiation, The Alevi Opening also failed and even led to more marginalization of Alevi citizens (Erdemir 2018). Constituting Turkey's second-largest religious community, Alevis have protested against this Religious Culture and Moral Knowledge course (Yilmaz 2018). Only Christian and Jewish children are exempt if their parents submit a petition and document their beliefs (Kaya 2012). Although the European Court of Human Rights (European Court of Human Rights 2007) has decided that compulsory religious education is a violation of the right to education in Turkey, the AKP has not made effort towards eliminating this violation yet.

After the AKP came to power, religious high schools became the central element in the Turkish education system. With the 4 + 4 + 4 system, elective courses related to religion include the Holy Qur'an, Life of the Prophet Muhammad and Fundamental Religious Knowledge. Some religious courses have been compulsory without the consent of the students in many schools (Kaya 2015b). A Religious Culture and Morals course has been added to the central placement exam from middle school to high school (Millî Eğitim Bakanliği Ortaöğretim Kurumlarina Geçiş Yönergesi 2018).

Under the AKP, the number of Imam-Hatip schools (religious schools) has increased exponentially. In the 2012/2013 academic year, students in these schools numbered 94.467. By the end of the 2016/2017 academic year, this number had increased seven times, reaching 651.954. In the same period, the number of students in religious high schools had also increased from 380.771 to 645.318 (Eğitim ve Bilim Emekçileri Sendikası 2017a; Stockholm Center for Freedom 2018). Also, one-third of the MEB budget for education investment was allocated to religious education, increasing the share of religious education by 68% (Çepni 2017). The transformation of regular schools into Imam-Hatip Schools resulted in the registration of some students without their or their parents' consent (Eğitim ve Bilim Emekçileri Sendikası 2019). For example, the Minister of National Education stated that 48 students were placed in Imam-Hatip high schools without their consent in 2014 (Kasap et al. 2014). In addition, some non-Muslim students were placed in Imam-Hatip schools, along with Armenian and Jewish students (Ceyhan 2014; Koca 2014; Makovsky 2015). These attempts to place religious schools and classes in the centerpiece of the educational system, and to increase the overall weight of religion classes in the assessment of a student's academic performance, are perhaps the most visible indicators of a failure to guarantee the right to education for all.

14.6 A Crack-Down After the Failed Coup on July 2016: The Peak of Educational Rights Violations in Turkey

Recent enforcements and applications are a serious setback for education rights especially after July 15, 2016. This date has become a monumental turning point in the history of the Republic of Turkey. On this date, turkey faced a fourth coup attempt, when a section of the Turkish military launched a coordinated operation in several major cities to take down the government. In a matter of hours, the government declared victory over the troops that had taken part. Two hundred forty-six people were killed and 2.194 others were injured (Human Rights Association 2017) Even though July's coup attempt gave rise to serious questions as to who the organizers behind it were, the sinister incident cost hundreds of thousands of people their homes and jobs, tens of thousands their freedom, and hundreds their very lives.

In addition to these costs, the incident was used as justification for transforming the administrative system of the entire country (Advocates of Silenced Turkey 2019). The violations and victimizations were carried out under the excuse of the July 15 coup attempt (Aydin and Avincan 2020). Controversies and violations of human rights were exacerbated after the coup attempt, with a massive purge of suspected coup plotters and dissidents. Education became the most affected branch of the state. The Ministry of National Education dismissed 40.000 staff, most of them teachers (Office of the United Nations High Commissioner for Human Rights 2017). In other words, after the crack-down, 36% of all purge victims were educators, which totaled more than even military officers (Eğitim ve Bilim Emekçileri Sendikası 2017b). In addition to that, according to statistics of the Ministry of Justice, the number of detainees and convicted students reached approximately 70.000 which is the highest rate of incarcerated students in the history of the Turkish Republic (Şimşek 2017).

After the failed coup attempt, the Ministry of Education suspended more than 55,000 staff, including 34,493 teachers (The Inquiry Commission on the State of Emergency Measures 2018), and revoked the licenses of 22,474 teachers at private education institutions using emergency decrees (Stockholm Center for Freedom 2018; United States Department of State Bureau of Democracy 2017). This included around 10,000 teachers in the southern part of the country, over 90% were Kurdish or were working in cities of predominantly Kurdish residents (Office of the United Nations High Commissioner for Human Rights 2017).This license revocation deprived them of the right to work as teachers for the rest of their lives. These dismissals also deprived the dismissed teachers of other rights, such as serving on commissions and boards as well as obtaining other licenses and passports.

As of December 2017, the number of private schools closing across Turkey had reached 1069, including 87 pre-schools, 274 primary schools, 306 middle schools, and 402 high schools. In addition, 301 tutoring centers were also shut down (Stockholm Center for Freedom 2018). Approximately 140.000 students were affected by the overnight shutdowns (Stockholm Center for Freedom 2018; Ülkütekin 2016). Students had to leave their now-closed schools and find others.

The government destroyed thousands of books from libraries across the country. The Minister of Education stated that 301.878 books were destroyed after the crackdown coup (Flood 2019; Kandiyoti and Emanet 2017). Of note, 848 student dorms, 20 journals or magazines, and 29 publishing companies were shut down (Stockholm Center for Freedom 2018; The Inquiry Commission on the State of Emergency Measures 2018). The government also shut down all military schools, including war academies, military high schools and high schools for non-commissioned officers following the coup attempt. Tens of thousands of military students were victimized in the process, and they have not been given compensation for their grievances (Gergerlioğlu 2019).

In addition, the education unions, Aktif Eğitimciler Sendikası with 18.000 members, and Pak Eğitim İşçileri Sendikası with 24.002 members were closed (T.C. Aile, Çalışma ve Sosyal Hizmetler Bakanlığı 2016a, b; The Inquiry Commission on the State of Emergency Measures 2018). Article 5 of the International Labor Organization (ILO 1989) 158 states that union membership and political opinion cannot be a valid reason for dismissal from a job. Dismissals of educators have been made on the basis of union membership. The government canceled the green and gray passports of some educators that were given after a certain length of service. Since regular passports cannot be canceled, these passports were invalidated as if they had been lost (Eğitim ve Bilim Emekçileri Sendikası 2017c). Thus, freedom of travel was violated by the government which had been guaranteed by the Constitution of the Republic of Turkey and international conventions (Council of Europe 1952b; Türkiye Cumhuriyeti Anayasasi 1982).

Thousands of people had been taken into custody and subjected to judicial procedures. There are no statistical data available as to how many teachers ended up in jails, but it is estimated that around 20.000 were in pre-trial detention centers (Stockholm Center for Freedom 2018). National and international human rights associations reported that after the July 15 failed coup attempt, human rights violations climbed significantly in Turkey; torture and ill-treatment under custody and in prisons emerged as significant problems (Aydin and Avincan 2020). For instance, The Office of High Commissioner for Human Rights Reports (OHCHR) noted the use of torture and ill-treatment in custody, including severe beatings, threats of sexual assault and actual sexual assault, electric shocks and waterboarding by police, gendarmerie, military police and security forces (Office of the United Nations High Commissioner for Human Rights 2018).

There has been an increase in the number of suspicious deaths in Turkey, most in Turkish jails and detention centers. Published on January 25, 2019, the Stockholm Center for Freedom (SCF) has compiled 126 cases of suspicious deaths and suicides in Turkey after July 15 (Stockholm Center for Freedom 2019). Fourteen of these suspicious deaths were of teachers. As a dramatic example, a history teacher, Gökhan Açıkkolu, died as the result of torture while under police custody. Even though his chronic illness was detected, he remained in custody. The abuse continued even after his death. The authorities tried to bury him in a special cemetery called the "Traitors Cemetery" that was built after the failed coup. The authorities also did not want to allow religious rituals to be performed for him. After his death, officials declared that Gökhan Acıkkollu was innocent of being a supporter of the coup (Stockholm Center for Freedom 2018). In another case, Halime Gülsu was an English teacher who died in jail because she was denied the necessary treatment for a chronic disease she has been suffering from since childhood (Stockholm Center for Freedom 2018). In addition to basic human rights abuses, these suspicious deaths of teachers can put current teachers in fear. They cannot teach effectively; the free play of ideas is limited; the free inter-human exchange is stifled; without these exchanges, there can be no full development of the human personality. Education is not only about physics and math—it is about values of openness, trust, caring, fairness.

Instead of securing access to education, after July 15, the Turkish government carried out some school closures during the school day. Many students were not even allowed to take their textbooks, which were later thrown out into the street (Anadolu Agency 2017; Demirören News Agency 2017). Since those schools were private, some students who were poor had been successful in getting scholarships to those schools. The status of those students has remained unclear (Yilmaz 2016). They have had struggles in finding other private schools or have had to attend public schools. As a disadvantaged group, prisoners desiring training were prohibited from participating in exams offered by education or public institutions during the state of emergency (Mazlum-Der 2018). Some students, especially those whose parents were dismissed, had issues in enrolling in public schools. Some parents had to hide their dismissal from the school administration because they feared the abuse and bullying of their children. Some private schools refused to enroll these children shortly after the coup attempt (Stockholm Center for Freedom 2018).

All these unjust applications, torture, and ill-treatment by the AKP government prove that after July 2016, violations of basic human rights including the right to education has reached their peak. They also show the severity of setbacks for education rights. It also does not seem that these human rights violations have been decreasing in the country, even after three years passed have passed.

14.7 Teaching Recruitment System

Teachers are the backbone of an education system. Assigning competent and well-skilled teachers is vital for protecting the right to education. The AKP caused severe damages to the teacher recruitment system with the recent changes to the system. The new system endangers the right to education. Teacher recruitment and assignment used to be based on performance on a set of centrally-administered multiple-choice exam: KPSS (Public Service Personnel Selection Examination). Candidates were then assigned to schools based on their test scores and school preferences. Each year, a base score was established, which had to be achieved in order to become a public school teacher. After July 15, the government made changes to the teacher recruitment system. The government built a system based on interviews, with no accountability in principal and teacher recruitment (Eğitim ve Bilim Emekçileri Sendikası 2018a). The new interview committee was composed of three members who were supervisors in the MEB (Sözleşmeli Öğretmen İstihdamına İlişkin Yönetmelik 2016). These supervisors were assigned by the government, so their objectivity is debatable. For instance, Deniz Eren Demir, who scored the highest points on the KPSS among physics candidates was eliminated by 54 points in the interview. He claimed that he did not know why he was eliminated even though he knew all the interview questions (Ertürk 2019). This injustice in evaluation is not limited to Deniz Eren Demir. There are many examples of those candidates who had very high points but failed the interview (Ağbaba 2019; Öztürk 2019). When candidates asked the interview committee the reasons why they were eliminated, the committee did not give any official explanation. Some were told they were eliminated just because of a "security investigation", but there is no official or legal requirement for this to pass the interview (Öztürk 2019). Nevertheless, the State Council mandated the use of video recording during interviews, but this decision was not implemented by the interview committee. It has been claimed that some targeted questions were intended to label the candidates in terms of their political ideas, such as; "who is Reis?" (Reis is the nickname that AKP supporters call Erdogan), "What do you think about Reis?", "What columnists or newspapers do you follow?" (Sağlar and Yarkadaş 2016). The Council of State found that some articles of the recruitment interview regulations were unlawful (Danıştay 2015). However, the government implemented new regulations in order to continue the interview-based system.

A recent study shows those same teacher candidates stated that the interview questions were not suited to the MEB Interview Evaluation Form, and also caused high anxiety in candidates (Tonbul and Ağaçdiken 2018). Although there is a serious teacher shortage, due to the lack of adequate appointments, an average of 17 out of every 100 teachers who took the KPSS between 2003 and 2017 were appointed; the remaining 83 unemployed teachers either took the exam again or now work in other fields (Eğitim ve Bilim Emekçileri Sendikası 2018b). Some teacher candidates committed suicide because they were not assigned by the government. As of 2018, in two years, 42 teacher candidates committed suicide because they were not appointed as teachers or could not find jobs (Karabağlı 2018). Karakütük and Özdoğan Özbal (2019) pointed out that administrators in education also complained about disregarding the qualifications in the assignment of teachers and administrators. These numbers show that the quality of the recruiting system has decreased since the coup attempt, and the government has established a recruitment system that is being misemployed by the authorities in order to hire their own supporters, instead of those with the right professional qualities.

14.8 Conclusion

All states, especially those who signed the aforementioned international agreements, must put forth an effort to ensure the right to education for all children. As a human right, the right to education is crucial in order to support the security, stability, and permanence of democracy and all other human rights in society. Considering violations of the right to education in the AKP era, the AKP views education as a threat to their power. The AKP government has fallen behind in protecting the education rights stated by international agreements. When the AKP came to power, it appeared to have an attitude towards human rights and democracy that included education in one's mother tongue, or Alevi Opening. However, these attempts were motivated by political interest, rather than by a sincere commitment to human rights. Once they saw that this attempt did not bring about more votes, they easily quit that initiative in favor of nationalist discourse. In other words, the AKP effectively has taken advantage of the language of human rights in order to consolidate power. The problems of Turkey's education system, including quality and equal access, are further exacerbated by the policies of the AKP government. Especially after 15 July, the Turkish government has seen severe lapses in the right to education. The government has failed to make education accessible, acceptable and adaptable for all people in the country. In fact, the outcomes of ongoing issues and challenges in education under the AKP government may worsen in the future.

References

677 Sayılı Kanun Hükmünde Kararname [Decree Law No. 677]. 2016. *Resmi Gazete* (Sayı: 29896), November 22. https://www.resmigazete.gov.tr/eskiler/2016/11/20161122-1.htm

Advocates of Silenced Turkey. 2019. *The So-called Coup Attempt.* https://silencedturkey.org/wp-content/uploads/2019/07/So-Called-Coup-Attempt-july-15-erdogan-human-rights-violations.pdf.

African Union. 1981. *African Charter on Human and Peoples' Rights*. Banjul: African Union. http://www.unesco.org/education/pdf/34_72.pdf

Ağbaba, Veli. 2019. KPSS'de derece yapanlar 'Reis' sorusuyla eleniyor. *Artı Gerçek,* January 26. https://www.artigercek.com/index.php/haberler/kpss-de-derece-yapanlar-reis-sorusuyla-eleniyor

Akkemik, K. Ali, Gerçek Çiçek, Charles Yuji Horioka, and Yoko Niimi. 2019. The Impact of a Failed Coup d'état on Happiness, Life Satisfaction, and Trust: The Case of the Plot in Turkey on July 15, 2016. *Applied Economics Letters*: 1–5, Vol. 2019-10.

Amnesty International. 2017. *Amnesty International Report 2016/17: The State of the World's Human Rights.* https://www.amnesty.org/download/Documents/POL1048002017ENGLISH.PDF

Anadolu Agency. 2017. *FETÖ ile irtibatlı 5 okul kapatıldı.* https://www.timeturk.com/feto-ile-irtibatli-5-okul-kapatildi/haber-780668

Ayata, Sencer. 1996. Patronage, Party, and State: The Politicization of Islam in Turkey. *The Middle East Journal* 50: 40–56.

Aydin, Hasan, and Koksal Avincan. 2020. Intellectual Crimes and Serious Violation of Human Rights in Turkey: A Narrative Inquiry. *The International Journal of Human Rights* 24 (8): 1127–1155. https://doi.org/10.1080/13642987.2020.1713108.

Batyra, Anna. 2017. *Gender Gaps in Student Achievement in Turkey: Evidence from the Programme for International Student Assessment (PISA) 2015.* Aydin Dogan Vakfı. https://aydindoganvakfi.org.tr/static/media/images/files/PISA_ENG.pdf

Bozarslan, Mahmut. 2019. Artuklu Üniversitesi'nden 'Yaşayan Diller Enstitüsü'nü Kapatma Kararı. *Amerikanın Sesi*, August 15. https://www.amerikaninsesi.com/a/artuklu-unversitesiden-yasayan-diller-enstitusunu-kapatma-karari/5043115.html.

Çepni, Ozan. 2017. Aslan payı imam hatibe. *Cumhuriyet,* November 8. http://www.cumhuriyet.com.tr/haber/egitim/861762/Aslan_payi_imam_hatibe.html

Ceyhan, Tuğba. 2014. Nabi Avcı: 200 bin öğrenciyi istediği halde İmam Hatip'e yerleştiremedik. *Star,* September 3. https://www.star.com.tr/guncel/nabi-avci-200-bin-ogrenciyi-istedigi-halde-imam-hatipe-yerlestiremedik-haber-934934/

Council of Europe. 1952a. *Protocol 1 to the European Convention for the Protection of Human Rights and Fundamental Freedoms*. https://www.refworld.org/docid/3ae6b38317.html

———. 1952b. *The European Convention on Human Rights*. Strasbourg: Directorate of Information. http://www.echr.coe.int/Documents/Convention_TUR.pdf.

———. 1961. *European Social Charter*. https://www.refworld.org/docid/3ae6b3784.html

———. 1992. *European Charter for Regional or Minority Languages*. https://www.refworld.org/docid/3de78bc34.html

———. 1995. *Framework Convention for the Protection of National Minorities*, Council of Europe Treaty Series 157. Strasbourg: Council of Europe.

Danıştay (Council of State). 2015. *19 Şubat 2015 tarihli 2015/1537 Nolu Karar*. https://www.danistay.gov.tr/upload/guncelkarar/24_04_2015_060405.pdf

Demirören News Agency. 2017. *İzmir'de özel bir lise 'FETÖ' bağlantısı gerekçesiyle kapatıldı*. http://www.diken.com.tr/izmirde-ozel-bir-lise-feto-baglantisi-sebebiyle-kapatildi/

Dogan, Fadime, and Hasan Aydin. 2019. Initial Development and Validation of the Multilingual Education Scale. *International Journal of Educational Reform* 28 (4): 376–389. https://doi.org/10.1177/1056787919856743.

Eğitim Reformu Girişimi (Education Reform Initiative). 2017. *Liselere geçişte yeni sistem ve nitelikli ortaöğretim için yol haritası*. http://www.egitimreformugirisimi.org/wp-content/uploads/2017/03/TEOG_BilgiNotu.07.12.17.web_.pdf

Eğitim ve Bilim Emekçileri Sendikası (Education and Science Workers' Union). 2017a. *2017/2018 Eğİtİm Öğretİm Yili Başında Eğİtİmİn Durumu Raporu*. http://egitimsen.org.tr/wpcontent/uploads/2017/09/E%C4%9Fitimin-Durumu-Raporu-13-Eyl%C3%BCl-2017.pdf

———. 2017b. *Eğitim Sistemi Alarm Veriyor, Bedelini Eğitim Emekçileri ve Öğrencilerimiz Ödüyor!*. http://egitimsen.org.tr/wp-content/uploads/2017/10/E%C4%9Fitim-Sistemi-Alarm-Veriyor-Sunum.pdf

———. 2017c. *Ohal ve Khk'lerin Eğitim ve Bilim Emekçilerine Etkileri*. http://egitimsen.org.tr/wp-content/uploads/2017/07/OHAL-ve-KHKlar%C4%B1n-E%C4%9Fitim-ve-Bilim-Emek%C3%A7ilerine-Etkileri-Raporu-son.pdf

———. 2018a. *MEB Öğretmen Atama Politikalarını Gözden Geçirmeli, Öğretmen Açıkları Derhal Kapatılmalıdır*. http://egitimsen.org.tr/meb-ogretmen-atama-politikalarini-gozden-gecirmeli-ogretmen-aciklari-derhal-kapatilmalidir/

———. 2018b. *2017–2018 Eğitim Öğretim Yılı Sonunda Eğitimin Durumu*. http://egitimsen.org.tr/wp-content/uploads/2018/06/E%C4%9Fitimin-Durumu-Raporu-7-Haziran-2018.pdf

———. 2019. *2018–2019 Eğitim Öğretim Yılı Başlarken Eğitimin Durumu Raporu*. http://egitimsen.org.tr/okullar-sorunlarla-aciliyor-ama-kararliyiz-bu-yil-ogretmenlerin-ders-yili-olacak/

Eğitim ve Bilim Emekçileri Sendikası Van Şubesi (Education and Science Workers' Union- Van Branch). 2019. Kürtçe konuşan Eğitim Sen'li sürgün edildi. *Yeni Özgür Politika Gazetesi*, June 25. http://yeniozgurpolitika.net/kurtce-konusan-egitim-senli-surgun-edildi/

Erdemir, Aykan. 2018. The Limits of Erdoğan's "Nation". *The Begin-Sadat Center for Strategic Studies*, Paper No. 724. https://besacenter.org/wp-content/uploads/2018/01/724-Limits-of-Erdogans-Nation-Erdemir-final-1.pdf

Ertürk, Ali Ekber. 2019. KPSS Türkiye birincisiydi mülakatta elendi. *Sözcü Gazetesi*, February 11. https://www.sozcu.com.tr/2019/gundem/turkiye-birincisiydi-mulakatta-elendi-3473558/

European Court of Human Rights. 2007. *Case of Hasan and Eylem Zengin V. Turkey (Application no. 1448/04)*. https://hudoc.echr.coe.int/eng#{%22itemid%22:[%22001-82580%22]}

———. 2020. *Overview 1959–2019 ECHR*. https://www.echr.coe.int/Documents/Overview_19592019_ENG.pdf

European Union. 2000. Charter of Fundamental Rights of the European Union. *Official Journal of the European Union C83* 53: 380. Brussels: European Union.

Flood, Alison. 2019. Turkish Government Destroys more than 300,000 Books. *The Guardian*, August 6. https://www.theguardian.com/books/2019/aug/06/turkish-government-destroys-more-than-300000-books

Gergerlioğlu, Ömer Faruk. 2019. 2. Yılında OHAL'in Toplumsal Maliyetleri. *Mağdurlar İçin Adalet*.

Göçer, Atalay. 2017. Seçmeli Kürtçe Dersi Anadilinde Eğitim Talebinin Neresinde? *Bianet*, February 21. http://bianet.org/bianet/insan-haklari/183827-secmeli-kurtc
Gok, Fatma, and Deniz Ilgaz. 2011. The Right to Education. In *Human Rights in Turkey*, ed. Zehra F. Kabasakal Arat, 123–136. Philadelphia: University of Pennsylvania Press.
Gutmann, Amy, and Dennis F. Thompson. 1998. *Democracy and Disagreement*. Cambridge, MA: Harvard University Press.
Habermas, Jürgen. 1992. *Between Facts and Norms: Contributions to a Discourse Theory of Law and Democracy*. Cambridge: The MIT Press.
Human Rights Association. 2017. *Violations of Human Rights in Turkey in 2016*. https://euromedrights.org/wp-content/uploads/2018/04/ihd_rights_violations_turkey-2016.pdf
Inal, Kemal. 2018. Akp döneminde Kürt dili politikalari. *Eğitim Bilim Toplum Dergisi* 16 (61): 97–151.
International Labour Organization (ILO). 1989. *Indigenous and Tribal Peoples Convention*, C169, C169. https://www.refworld.org/docid/3ddb6d514.html
Kamer, Hatice. 2016. Diyarbakır'da Kürtçe eğitim veren Ferzad Kemanger okulu kapatıldı. *BBC*, October 10. https://www.bbc.com/turkce/haberler-turkiye-37608054
Kandiyoti, Deniz, and Zühre Emanet. 2017. Education as Battleground: The Capture of Minds in Turkey. *Globalizations* 14 (6): 869–876.
Karabağlı, Hülya. 2016. KHK'lar Kürtçe dil öğreten okulları ve dernekleri vurdu. *T24 Bağımsız İnternet Gazetesi*, December 4. https://t24.com.tr/haber/khklar-kurtce-dil-ogreten-okullari-ve-dernekleri-vurdu,374790
———. 2018. CHP'li Kaya: Son iki yılda 42 öğretmen atanamadığı için hayatına son verdi. *T24 Bağımsız İnternet Gazetesi*, April 18. https://t24.com.tr/haber/chpli-kaya-son-iki-yilda-42-ogretmen-atanamadigi-icin-hayatina-son-verdi,608120
Karakütük, Kasım, and Ece Özdoğan Özbal. 2019. Eğitim Yöneticilerinin Yaşadiklari Sorunlar İle Sorun Çözmede Kullandiklari Teknikler. *Milli Eğitim Dergisi* 48 (223): 33–60. https://dergipark.org.tr/en/pub/milliegitim/issue/48112/608614.
Karaveli, Halil. 2016. Erdogan's Journey: Conservatism and Authoritarianism in Turkey. *Foreign Affairs* 95: 121.
Kasap, Selma, Yıldız Aktaş, Ferdi Türkten, and Kadir Karakuş. 2014. İmam hatibe tercihsiz 45 kişi yerleştirildi. *Anadolu Agency,* September 12. https://www.aa.com.tr/tr/egitim/imam-hatibe-tercihsiz-45-kisi-yerlestirildi/122700
Kaya, Nurcan. 2012. Türkiye'nin eğitim sisteminde azınlıklar ve ayrımcılık: Kavramsal çerçeve ve temel sorunlar. In *Ayrımcılık: Çok Boyutlu Yaklaşımlar İçinde*, ed. K. Çayır ve MA Ceyhan. İstanbul: İstanbul Bilgi Üniversitesi Yayınları.
Kaya, Esra. 2013. İşte "Seçmeli Kürtçe"nin Türkiye haritası. *Hürriyet Gazetesi,* February 6. http://www.hurriyet.com.tr/gundem/iste-secmeli-kurtce-nin-turkiye-haritasi-22534618
Kaya, Ayhan. 2015a. Islamisation of Turkey Under the AKP Rule: Empowering Family, Faith and Charity. *South European Society and Politics* 20 (1): 47–69.
Kaya, Nurcan. 2015b. *Discrimination Based on Color, Ethnic Origin, Language Religion and Belief in Turkey's Education System*. Istanbul: Tarih Vakfı.
Kaya, Ilhan, and Hasan Aydin. 2013. *Türkiye'de anadilde eğitim sorunu: Zorluklar, deneyimler ve iki dilli eğitim modeli önerileri*. İstanbul: Ukam.
Koca, Gönül. 2014. Gayrimüslimlere imam hatip şoku. *Hürriyet Gazetesi,* August 24. http://www.hurriyet.com.tr/gundem/gayrimuslimlere-imam-hatip-soku-27062894
Lüküslü, Demet. 2016. Creating a Pious generation: Youth and Education Policies of the AKP in Turkey. *Southeast European and Black Sea Studies* 16 (4): 637–649.
Makovsky, Alan. 2015. *Re-educating Turkey: AKP Efforts to Promote Religious Values in Turkish Schools*. Washington, DC: Center for American Progress.
Marshall, Thomas Humphrey. 1950. *Citizenship and Social Class*. The Syndics of the Cambridge University Press.
Mazlum-Der (The Association for Human Rights and Solidarity for the Oppressed). 2018. *OHAL Dönemi Hak İhlalleri Raporu*. https://drive.google.com/file/d/19HRL6VEBlQrGtLTi_dKqC6xvlW-hFwXS/view

Millî Eğitim Bakanlığı Ortaöğretim Kurumlarına Geçiş Yönergesi (Ministry of National Education Directive on Secondary Education Institutions). 2018. https://www.meb.gov.tr/meb_iys_dosyalar/2018_03/26191912_yonerge.pdf

Milli Eğitim Bakanlığı Talim ve Terbiye Kurulu Başkanlığı (Head Council of Education and Morality). 2018. *İmam Hatip Ortaokulu Haftalık Ders Çizelgesi*. https://ttkb.meb.gov.tr/www/haftalik-ders-cizelgeleri/kategori/7

OECD. 2005. *Basic Education in Turkey*. OECD Publishing. https://www.oecd.org/education/school/39642601.pdf

———. 2017. *PISA 2015 Results (Volume III): Students' Well-Being*. Paris OECD Publishing.

Office of the United Nations High Commissioner for Human Rights. 2017. *Un Human Rights Report 2017*. https://www2.ohchr.org/english/OHCHRreport2017/allegati/Downloads/1_Whole_Report_2017.pdf

———. 2018. *Turkey: UN Report Details Extensive Human Rights Violations During Protracted State of Emergency*. https://www.ohchr.org/EN/NewsEvents/Pages/DisplayNews.aspx?NewsID=22853&LangID=E

Ogechi, Nathan Oyori. 2003. On Language Rights in Kenya. *Nordic Journal of African Studies* 12 (3): 277–295.

Ölçme, Seçme ve Yerleştirme Merkezi Başkanlığı (Measuring, Selection and Placement Center). 2012. *ÖSYS Yükseköğretim Programları ve Kontenjanları Kılavuzu*. https://dokuman.osym.gov.tr/pdfdokuman/2012/OSYS/2012OSYSKONTKILAVUZ.pdf

———. 2013. *ÖSYS Yükseköğretim Programları ve Kontenjanları Kılavuzu*. https://www.osym.gov.tr/TR,876/2013-osys-yuksekogretim-programlari-ve-kontenjanlari-kilavuzu.html

———. 2014. *ÖSYS Yükseköğretim Programları ve Kontenjanları Kılavuzu*. https://dokuman.osym.gov.tr/pdfdokuman/2014/OSYS/Tercih/2014-OSYSKONTKILAVUZU14072014.pdf

———. 2015. *ÖSYS Yükseköğretim Programları ve Kontenjanları Kılavuzu*. https://dokuman.osym.gov.tr/pdfdokuman/2015/OSYS/2015-OSYSKONTKILAVUZU15072015.pdf

———. 2016. *ÖSYS Yükseköğretim Programları ve Kontenjanları Kılavuzu*. https://www.osym.gov.tr/TR,12454/2016-osys-yuksekogretim-programlari-ve-kontenjanlari-kilavuzu.html

———. 2017. *ÖSYS Yükseköğretim Programları ve Kontenjanları Kılavuzu*. https://www.osym.gov.tr/TR,13263/2017-osys-yuksekogretim-programlari-ve-kontenjanlari-kilavuzu.html

———. 2018. *ÖSYS Yükseköğretim Programları ve Kontenjanları Kılavuzu*. https://www.osym.gov.tr/TR,15240/2018-yuksekogretim-programlari-ve-kontenjanlari-kilavuzu.html

———. 2019. *ÖSYS Yükseköğretim Programları ve Kontenjanları Kılavuzu*. https://www.osym.gov.tr/TR,16858/2019-yuksekogretim-programlari-ve-kontenjanlari-kilavuzu.html

Organization of African Unity. 1990. *African Charter on the Rights and Welfare of the Child*. CAB/LEG/24.9/49. https://www.refworld.org/docid/3ae6b38c18.html

Organization of American States. 1998. *Additional Protocol to the American Convention on Human Rights in the Area of Economic, Social and Cultural Rights ("Protocol of San Salvador")*. https://www.refworld.org/docid/3ae6b3b90.html

Öztürk, Mustafa. 2019. MEB, mülakat, mağduriyet, şikayet. *Karar Gazetesi*, February 9. https://www.karar.com/yazarlar/mustafa-ozturk/meb-mulakat-magduriyet-sikayet-9204

Paul, Amanda, and Murat Demir Seyrek. 2014. *Freedom of Religion in Turkey: The Alevi Issue*. Brussels: European Policy Centre.

Sağlar, Fikri, and Barış Yarkadaş. 2016. Öğretmenleri fişleyen sorular Meclis'e geldi. *Sözcü Gazetesi*, October 3. https://www.sozcu.com.tr/2016/egitim/son-dakika-haberi-milli-egitim-bakani-ismet-yilmazdan-tam-gun-aciklamasi-1431467/

Şimşek, Hüseyin. 2017. Cezaevlerindeki öğrenci sayısı açıklandı: Tarihin en yüksek mahkûm sayısı. *BirGün*, September 11. https://www.birgun.net/haber/cezaevlerindeki-ogrenci-sayisi-aciklandi-tarihin-en-yuksek-mahk%c3%bbm-sayisi-178725

Somer, Murat. 2014. Moderation of Religious and Secular Politics, a Country's "Centre" and Democratization. *Democratization* 21 (2): 244–267.

———. 2017. Conquering Versus Democratizing the State: Political Islamists and Fourth Wave Democratization in Turkey and Tunisia. *Democratization* 24 (6): 1025–1043.

Sözleşmeli Öğretmen İstihdamına İlişkin Yönetmelik (Regulation on Employment of Contracted Teachers). 2016. *Resmi Gazete* (Sayı: 29790). http://www.resmigazete.gov.tr/eskiler/2016/08/20160803-22.htm

Stockholm Center for Freedom (SCF). 2018. *Free Thought under Siege in Turkey: The Crackdown on Education.* https://stockholmcf.org/wp-content/uploads/2018/07/The-Crackdown-On-Education-in-Turkey_june_2018.pdf

———. 2019. *Suspicious Deaths and Suicides in Turkey – Updated List.* https://stockholmcf.org/suspicious-deaths-and-suicides-in-turkey-updated-list/

T.C. Aile, Çalışma ve Sosyal Hizmetler Bakanlığı (Ministry of Family, Labor and Social Services). 2016a. *4688 Sayılı Kamu Görevlileri Sendikaları Ve Toplu Sözleşme Kanunu Gereğince Kamu Görevlileri Sendikaları İle Konfederasyonların Üye Sayılarına İlişkin 2016 Temmuz İstatistikleri Hakkında Tebliğ.* https://www.ailevecalisma.gov.tr/media/1240/2016-kamu-gorevlileri-sendikal-istatistikler.pdf

———. 2016b. *İşçi Sayıları ve Sendikaların Üye Sayıları Hakkında Tebliğler.* https://www.ailevecalisma.gov.tr/media/1260/2016_ocak_6856-5.pdf

The Inquiry Commission on the State of Emergency Measures. 2018. *Olağanüstü Hal İşlemleri İnceleme Komisyonu Faaliyet Raporu 2018 [Disaster Recovery Commission Annual Report 2018].* https://ohalkomisyonu.tccb.gov.tr/docs/OHAL_FaaliyetRaporu_2018.pdf

The United Nations. 1988. Convention on the Elimination of All Forms of Discrimination against Women. *Treaty Series*, 1249, 13.

The United Nations General Assembly. 1966a. International Covenant on Civil and Political Rights. *UN General Assembly*, Treaty Series, 999, 171. New York, NY. https://www.refworld.org/docid/3ae6b3aa0.html%20/

———. 1966b. International Covenant on Economic, Social, and Cultural Rights. *UN General Assembly*, Treaty Series, 999, 171. New York, NY. https://www.ohchr.org/Documents/ProfessionalInterest/cescr.pdf

Tomaševski, Katarina. 2006. *Human Rights Obligations in Education: The 4-A Scheme.* Nijmegen: Wolf Legal Publishers (WLP).

Tonbul, Yılmaz, and Yunus Ağaçdiken. 2018. Öğretmen adaylarının görüşlerine göre sözleşmeli öğretmenlik mülakatındaki soruların incelenmesi. *E-Uluslararası Eğitim Araştırmaları Dergisi* 9 (2): 46–63.

Türkiye Cumhuriyeti Anayasası (The Constitution of the Republic of Turkey). 1982. *Resmi Gazete* (Sayı: 17863 (Mükerrer), November 9. http://www.mevzuat.gov.tr/MevzuatMetin/1.5.2709.pdf

Ülkütekin, Deniz. 2016. 140 bin öğrenci açıkta kaldı. *Cumhuriyet Gazetesi,* July 26. http://www.cumhuriyet.com.tr/haber/egitim/574219/140_bin_ogrenci_acikta_kaldi.html

Ulutaş, Seher, and Nükhet Çıkrıkçı. 2019. Opinions on the Impacts of the TEOG System from Teachers Whose Courses Are Not Included in the TEOG Exam. *Eğitimde ve Psikolojide Ölçme ve Değerlendirme Dergisi* 10 (1): 68–79.

UN Commission on Human Rights. 1994. *Minimum Humanitarian Standards.* https://www.refworld.org/docid/3b00f0157c.html

UN General Assembly. 1948. *Universal Declaration of Human Rights.* https://www.refworld.org/docid/3ae6b3712c.html

UNESCO. 1960. *Convention Against Discrimination in Education.* Paris: United Nations Educational, Scientific and Cultural Organization.

———. 2001. *UNESCO Universal Declaration on Cultural Diversity.* https://www.refworld.org/docid/435cbcd64.html

UNICEF. 1989. *Convention on the Rights of the Child.* https://www.ohchr.org/documents/professionalinterest/crc.pdf

United States Department of State – Bureau of Democracy Human Rights and Labor. 2017. *Turkey 2016 Human Rights Report.* https://www.state.gov/documents/organization/265694.pdf

Yilmaz, Şule. 2016. Kapatılan okulların öğrencileri çözüm arıyor. *pervinkaplan.com,* July 24. http://www.pervinkaplan.com/detay/kapatilan-okullarin-ogrencileri-cozum-ariyor/1272

Yilmaz, Ihsan. 2018. Populism, Erdoganism, and Social Engineering Through Education in Turkey. *Mediterranean Quarterly* 29 (4): 135–146.

Yilmaz, Ihsan, and Galip Bashirov. 2018. The AKP after 15 Years: Emergence of Erdoganism in Turkey. *Third World Quarterly* 39 (9): 1812–1830.

Dr. Uzeyir Ogurlu currently teaches at the University of Wisconsin-Stevens Point. He has developed programs for gifted students and their parents including leadership development, global citizenship, and peace education. His interests are talent development, creativity, gifted students, human rights and diversity in education. He is a tireless advocate of human rights.

Koksal Avincan is currently a doctoral student and researcher at Florida International University. He served as a research assistant at Yildiz Technical University, Istanbul, Turkey from 2014 to 2016. He received his Master's degree in Computer Science from Computer Science Department of Yildiz Technical University, Istanbul, Turkey. He received his B.Sc. degree in Computer Science from Istanbul University. His research interests include Human Rights, Wireless Sensor Networks, Internet of Things, Security, and Privacy. He has published some articles, and has had many conference presentations. He speaks several languages including Kurdish(Kurmanji), Turkish, English, and German.

Chapter 15
Academic Freedom and Living in Exile: Experiences of Academics in Turkey

Hasan Aydin, Viktor Mak, and Kristina Andrews

Abstract Academic freedom within educational institutions is imperative for the scholarship of academics as well as for the promotion of progressive societies. Therefore, when academic freedom is threatened, a plethora of factors inhibit research and scholarship within universities that hinder the advancement of science and knowledge, and that impacts society. This qualitative phenomenological research study sought to explore the experiences of academics who left Turkey, their reasons for leaving, and their process of integrating into new societies. In addition, it aimed to understand their perceptions of academic freedom in Turkey before and after the July 16, 2016 coup attempt. Fifteen Turkish academics and scholars were purposively selected for this study. Data from multiple sources, including semi-structured individual interviews, focus group interviews, and field notes, were analyzed. To increase the validity and reliability of the study, the researchers triangulated the data, bracketed themselves, and used member checking and outside readers. The findings of the study indicated that most participants self-identified as apolitical but found themselves victims of a political system in which their academia brought brutal and unjustified repercussions. The events following the coup attempt extinguished their academic freedoms and human rights in Turkey. Consequently, the academic and personal struggles and pressures forced them to flee and become refugees or exiles on a quest to re-establish their lives, identity, and academia in a new country. Their experiences before and after the coup expose the atrocities and unjust and traumatic outcomes that were a result of their identity as highly educated scholars and advocates for a more democratic and peaceful society. Hence, this study reveals the political ramifications on academic freedom and scholarship in Turkey and how this has impacted universities and scholars.

H. Aydin (✉)
Department of Curriculum, Instruction, and Culture, Florida Gulf Coast University, Fort Myers, FL, USA
e-mail: haydin@fgcu.edu

V. Mak
Human Rights Activist and Independent Researcher, Budapest, Hungary

K. Andrews
Florida Gulf Coast University, Fort Myers, FL, USA

H. Aydin, W. Langley (eds.), *Human Rights in Turkey*, Philosophy and Politics - Critical Explorations 15, https://doi.org/10.1007/978-3-030-57476-5_15

Keywords Academic freedom · Living in exile · Violations · And qualitative phenomenology

15.1 Introduction

In recent years, academic freedom has come under attack in several countries with leaders who have autocratic tendencies. In Hungary, Prime Minister Viktor Orbán has banned certain disciplines and made it impossible for some universities to operate. In Putin's Russia, similar Western-style universities are under attack. Yet, perhaps some of the most egregious violations of academic freedom, in terms of scale and impact, have originated in Turkey. It is essential to understand academic freedom and its history in Turkey to understand these violations and their impact.

15.2 History of Academic Freedom in Turkey

Academic freedom does not have an agreed-upon definition, and its application and understanding are always nuanced by local context and history. Instead of positive definitions, often attempts to define academic freedom have focused on examples of when it has been violated, such as professors being fired for researching certain topics or signing petitions, when universities are shut down or face restrictions, or when students are harassed. Yet, it is vital to have a comprehensive definition that delineates the term. This chapter relies primarily on a definition by Seggie and Gokbel (2015), which builds on a 1998 UNESCO-IAU declaration, and defines academic freedom as:

> *the freedom of members of an academic community, comprised of scholars, teachers, and students, who pursue their scholarly activity within a framework determined by that community. It includes freedom of expression, learning, teaching, and research, as well as university autonomy and individual rights and freedoms, such as job security and the right to participate in decision making processes.* (Seggie and Gokbel 2015, 10)

Kandiyoti and Emanet (2017) used the same definition when discussing the Turkish case study, affirming it is an appropriate approach to the topic in this context. In its essence, academic freedom guarantees that members of an academic community can pursue knowledge and truth unhindered by political or economic pressures.

Despite this definitional confusion, Turkey has signed numerous international accords acknowledging the autonomy of universities and the right of academics. Even after the widespread attacks on academic freedom and research that began in 2016, the Turkish government signed the 2018 Paris Bologna Communiqué, in which it "committed to promoting and protecting academic freedom and institutional autonomy, as well as the social responsibility and civic engagement of higher education institutions and their members" (European Higher Education Area 2018, 1; European University Association 2019, para. 5). Hence, many of the domestic and international NGOs, such as Human Rights Watch, have called on Turkey to honor the commitments that it has made pertaining to academic freedom.

Yet, despite these formal commitments to ensuring academic freedom, Turkey has a dark history when it comes to protecting it. Violations date back to the 1930s and typically follow extraordinary political events - such as coups. In 1960, 147 faculty were dismissed after a military junta with the justification that their presence blocked the necessary reforms at universities. Their dismissal generated outcries that the purge was motivated by ideological and political considerations (Weiker 1962). As Baser et al. (2017) recounted in the 1960s and 1970s, universities in Turkey played a crucial and vibrant role for debates between the political left and right. However, the 1980s coup and the military rule afterward established the Higher Education Council (YÖK), which centralized control over autonomous universities and produced a detrimental effect on academic freedom. The YÖK is still in effect today and continues to centralize further the administration of universities (Kandiyoti and Emanet 2017).

The July 15, 2016 coup attempt, plotted out against Erdoğan and the AKP government, was a propelling agent to obliterate democratic gains and improvements in academic freedoms at the beginning of the twenty-first century (Aktas et al. 2019; Ozkirimli 2017; Ozturk 2018). Moreover, the coup attempt has been recognized as producing the greatest sociological consequences, as well as being the most significant damaging incident to influence the Turkish legal and political life (Ozturk 2018; Scholar's Rights Watch 2018). In the aftermath of the coup attempt, the AKP closed more than 2341 universities and organizations with the implementation of decree no. 667, issued on July 23, 2016 (Baser et al. 2017; Freedom for Academia 2018). Consequently, over 110,778 (Scholar's Rights Watch 2018) scholars and civil servants lost their jobs based on alleged associations with the Gülen Movement, or liberal groups (Ozkirimli 2017). Although some universities remain open and functioning, they are currently under the regulations and supervision of the YÖK whose interests rest in upholding the autocratic policies of the Erdoğan government and therefore, impose limits to liberties for research and speech in academia (Aktas et al. 2019; Baser et al. 2017; Ozturk 2018).

Turkey's state of emergency decree-laws that were published after the July 15 coup attempt created a "legal" basis for unlawful judicial and political practices (Scholar's Rights Watch 2018) by allowing the president and cabinet to act independently of parliament when developing new laws or restricting and suspending citizen's rights and liberties (Ozturk 2018). These rights and liberties included scientific and artistic freedoms formerly upheld in accordance with the constitutional democracy and international human rights conventions (The Science Academy Report 2017). Additionally, the ruling party removed civil workers and academics from their positions, closed universities and governmental organizations, and seized powers to unlawfully judge and socially pressure those whom they accused of initiating dissenting views. Violating citizen's rights signifies the decimation of liberal and democratic constructs and eviscerates scholars' potential to be valuable contributors to the scientific growth and democratic proliferation of the Turkish State.

Due to these recent political events and developments, academic freedom in Turkey is threatened at universities and other academic institutions and scholarly organizations (Aktas et al. 2019). With an emphasis on establishing state interests through a patrimonial approach over fundamental rights and freedoms of its citizens (Ozkirimli 2017; Ozturk 2018), dissenting thoughts and expressions towards authorities are not tolerated (Aktas et al. 2019). This was established to silence the voices and research of academics who pursue radical ideas intended to contribute to the nation's welfare (Cole 2017). These academics, who include scientists, military personnel, members of the judiciary, engineers, doctors, teachers, government workers, and scholars are perceived as a threat to the survival and homogenization of the Turkish state unless they agree to support and promote the interests and of the ruling elite (Ozturk 2018; Scholar's Rights Watch 2018; The Science Academy Report 2018). Hence, academic freedom within the universities and scholarly communities have become limited or exterminated.

The observations and definitions of academic freedom strive to be universal. However, in the Turkish context, it is more complicated. For example, Seggie and Gokbel (2015) explored the tension between the fidelity and loyalty of professors who are civil servants and the space for dissent and criticism that academic freedom guarantees them. How closely should professors be bound by the official ideology of the state? Because scholars are civil servants in Turkey, the degree that their obligations to the state could impede or influence their scholarships, publication, and teaching, is debated (Seggie and Gokbel 2015).

Although the early years of the 2010's saw some progress in academic freedom, students and faculty continue to be governed by laws developed after the military coup. Often, the debate in Turkey surrounding academic freedom is limited to discussing university autonomy. However, as defined above, academic freedom is much broader than university autonomy. For a detailed analysis and presentation of expansion and contraction of academic freedom in Turkey, see Seggie and Gokbel (2015), and for a detailed chronological analysis of higher education laws and waxing and waning of academic freedom, see Kandiyoti and Emanet (2017).

15.3 Importance of Academic Freedom

Academic freedom serves an important role, both in the functioning of a university, the development of science and knowledge, and in society itself. There is instrumental and material value to academic freedom, in so far that some theorists propose that scientific inquiry can only truly flourish when academics and universities are guaranteed their autonomy. Furthermore, a university's ability to govern itself is contingent upon its scholars and researchers possessing the liberty to participate in free inquiry and critical and open discourse, without interference, and without repercussions (Seggie and Gokbel 2015). Yet, its value goes beyond the material one. Theorists such as Judith Butler (2017) have stated that without academic freedom, a university cannot exist. Without the right to pursue knowledge unimpeded by political and economic considerations, a university is reduced to a building where teaching and learning happens, but under the close supervision of the state. Therefore, universities must be protected against threats to academic freedom (Seggie and Gokbel 2015) and maintain a capacity in which democratic thinking and diversity of thought (Cole 2017; Ozturk 2018) are recognized, encouraged, and fostered (Aktas et al. 2019).

Theorists such as Cole and Butler have argued that academic freedom plays a vital role in how a democratic society functions. Therefore, academic freedom serves as the critical component of liberal democracy, as it depends on individual liberty and freedom of expression (Cole 2017). It gives space to people to explore ideas, develop new theories, understand their societies better, and engage with them in critical ways. It is in this context that attacks on academic freedom should be seen. In an era of backsliding democracy, where civil liberties, freedom of speech and media are undermined, academic freedom is another pillar of democracy that governments with centralized and autocratic tendencies are eroding. Hence, when academic freedom and free inquiry are obliterated within a university, the democratic ideals and principles of individual liberties will cease to exist, threatening the existence of a liberal democracy both inside and outside the university (Cole 2017; The Science Academy Report 2018).

15.4 Literature Review

Academic freedom in Turkey has significant implications for research, academics, scholars, and society. In Turkey, political events have significantly impacted the operations of universities and organizations, as well as the lives of citizens and those currently living in exile or as refugees. There are a variety of factors that have imposed life changes for academics and scholars who were maintaining their living, raising their families, and establishing their careers in Turkey before and after the July 15, 2016 coup attempt. This literature review presents an analysis of previous findings of researchers, academics, NGOs, and governmental organizations that play a significant role in academia during this dynamic era in Turkey's history. These include Academics for Peace and the Peace Petition, the repercussions of signatories and academics as a result of their expression of dissent, their research projects, or their role in government or academia. Additionally, it presents the literature about living in exile, the psychological and physical impacts of authoritarian governments, the importance of research and the role of universities in society, and previous reports of experiences of Turkish academics and scholars.

15.4.1 Academics for Peace and the Peace Petition

According to Scholar's Rights Watch (2018), only hours after the July 15 coup attempt, was the signing of the Academics for Peace Petition in January 2016 by 1128 academics from 89 universities. The petition was organized by a group of academics named "Academics for Peace," which had initiated petitions in 2012, to encourage a resolution to the Turkish-Kurdish conflict. The group aimed to cast light onto the failed approach of creating peace and serving as a knowledge hub on conflict resolution and peace-building. The petition demanded the Kurdistan Workers' Party (PKK) and the Turkish state cease violence against Kurdish populated areas and criticized the Turkish state for violating its laws and international treaties (Baser et al. 2017; Ozturk 2018).

Although the signing of the petition was not unlawful (Aktas et al. 2019; The Science Academy Report 2017), standing up peacefully for democratic and moral values did not come without a price, and would result in life-transforming experiences for the academic signatories of the Peace Petition (Cole 2017; Ozkirimli 2017). The petition received a violent and hostile reaction from President Erdoğan. He perceived the petition as treason and terrorist propaganda and responded by ordering the judiciary and university administrations to take action and to punish the signatories (Abbas and Zalta 2017; Aktas et al. 2019; Baser et al. 2017; Ozkirimli 2017; Ozturk 2018). Thus, the Turkish Higher Education Council, the YÖK and Turkish constitution moved to dismiss, arrest, impose charges, and/or imprison the signatories, as well as to place them on a "blacklist" that prevented them from acquiring employment in the public and private sector (Aktas et al. 2019; Baser et al. 2017; Cole 2017; Ozkirimli 2017). Consequently, the signatories became subject to smear campaigns and personal repercussions for their actions, as well as to being ostracized by colleagues who supported Erdoğan. In addition, under the state of emergency decrees, they had multiple restrictions imposed including confiscation or cancellation of their passports, confiscation of personal property, loss of access to public housing, loss of freedom of speech, right to a fair trial, and protection of privacy, loss of any titles, removal of pensionary rights, and the inability to attend professional scholarly conferences (Aktas et al. 2019; Aydin and Avincan 2020; Baser et al. 2017; Ozkirimli 2017; The Science Academy Report 2017). This harsh crackdown against academics was the first time that counterterrorism rhetoric was used against scholars (Baser et al. 2017). The procedures against the Academics for Peace only indicated the direction into which the government would go in the coming years. Overall, the priority for the Erdoğan regime became silencing critical voices.

The arrests, initiated by order of President Erdoğan, began the morning after the July 15, 2016 coup attempt (Scholar's Rights Watch 2018). Ozturk (2018) reported that a total of more than 41,000 people who were accused of being associated with the coup attempt had been jailed, and around 59,000 more were facing investigation. It was also reported that 16,000 women and 700 children had been imprisoned for being accused of assisting the coup (Baser et al. 2017; Scholar's Rights Watch

2018). However, under the state of emergency laws, those who were dismissed were denied a trial, and those arrested were denied the right to appeal (Aktas et al. 2019). In addition to facing dismissal, arrest, and jail, academics were subject to having their homes raided by police (Scholar's Rights Watch 2018).

In February 2020, it was reported that Turkey had requested the extradition of 750 people from 101 different countries in a global crackdown of Gülen supporters and followers (Turkish Minute 2020). In addition to these persons, they have requested the extradition of Fethullah Gülen, who is currently residing in Pennsylvania in the United States. Thus far, 2411 of the accused individuals who have already had their trial, have been given a life sentence, 1558 were sentenced to 14 to 20 years in jail, and various high criminal courts acquitted 2648. The former ruling AKP deputy stated that more than one million people have been accused of being associated with the Gülen Movement and have been or are currently being investigated (Turkish Minute 2020).

The hundreds of thousands of people who lost their livelihoods as a result of accusations of being associated or assisting with the coup attempt in 2016, being a member of a terrorist organization, and unlawful practices during the state of emergency, included soldiers, police officers, scholars, teachers, judges, university staff, and journalists (Aktas et al. 2019; Ozturk 2018, Scholar's Rights Watch 2018). Their situations were exacerbated by the lamentations of their families being affected (A.K. 2018; Aktas et al. 2019), the loss of contact with former colleagues, and physical and verbal threats (Ozturk 2018). Hence, the academics became fully conscious of the repercussions that speaking out against the current political regime's autocratic and patrimonial agenda would entail. The result was intense, negative physical, psychological, and emotional impacts resulting from the stresses such as having to abandon their students (Ozkirimli 2017), torture in prisons, and loss of research opportunities (Aydin and Avincan 2020; Freedom for Academia 2018).

15.4.2 Academics in Exile after Crack-Down Coup of July 2016

After the failed coup attempt in July of 2016, Erdoğan cracked down on 15 private universities and more than 1500 schools with their dormitories, and centers of learning that were associated with the Gülen Movement. All 1576 deans from all universities in Turkey were forced to resign, and a travel ban was imposed on all academics. All of those affected were dismissed on allegations of being members of a terrorist organization or undermining the national security of the state. None were afforded any procedural rights or confronted with any evidence to justify such allegations and dismissals, and no charges have been brought. The official reasoning was the accusation that the followers of Fethullah Gülen organized the coup, a Muslim cleric living in the United States (Siegel 2017). However, Gülen denied

Table 15.1 Scholars at risk applications for assistance

Period	Applications
Sept. 2013–Aug. 2014	1
Sept. 2014–Aug. 2015	1
Sept. 2015–Aug. 2016	209
Sept. 2016–Aug. 2017	438
Sept. 2017–Aug. 2018	211
Sept. 2018–Aug. 2019	226

Source: Provided via email after inquiry

any involvement. A Human Rights Watch report (2018) estimated the number of faculty dismissed after the coup at 5800. Hence the crackdown after the coup attempt did not just target academics but entire institutions and their autonomy.

Scholars at Risk (SAR) serves as the network and hub for academics being pressured by governments. It hosts the most extensive repository regarding attacks on academic freedom. Estimates from 2018 from SAR stated that 1236 Turkish university employees and students had been detained, and 8535 employees fired. The dismissal from university also includes a ban on all public sector jobs as well as a ban on international travel, which limits the ability of dismissed academics from applying for positions abroad (Aktas et al. 2019). Many academics who been fired also faced persecution under false charges, abuse, torture, and jail time (Aydin and Avincan 2020). Table 15.1 shows data from Scholars at Risk pertaining to the number of academics who lost their jobs at public and private universities and applied for assistance.

According to data compiled by BBC's Turkish service, at least 23,427 academics were dismissed from government and private jobs, lost their tenure/rights, or lost their jobs due to the closure of their universities in the year following the coup in Turkey. This number includes about 15,000 research assistants from the OYP (graduate assistantships) program, which lost their status.

15.4.3 University and Research

Universities provide unrestricted opportunities for scholars and their students to engage in dialogue and discourse that critically analyzes and synthesizes multiple viewpoints to develop new ideas and theories for scientific and societal advancement that works in the best interest of all persons and societies (Seggie and Gokbel 2015). Furthermore, academic freedom provides job security and ensures liberties to conduct research, to publish, to teach and to learn, that is imperative to the autonomy of an institution and its scholars (Aktas et al. 2019; Seggie and Gokbel 2015). However, the events from the 2013 coup, and time leading up to and beyond the attempted July 15, 2016 coup, negatively impacted academic freedom in the classroom due to students who would report their activity or expressions to the university board, resulting in the professors monitoring how they conducted their class as well as the material they presented. In addition, the professors avoided going to their university at times other than for office hours and teaching times (Aktas et al. 2019). Therefore, when scholars do not have the freedom of thought and expression to develop critical thinking in their students, or while conducting research, as a result of decimated university autonomy, academic freedom has been extinguished (The Science Academy Report 2017).

Since the July 15th coup attempt, academics in and from Turkey have experienced difficulties pertaining to conducting, publishing, and sharing their research and continuing their scientific activities (Aktas et al. 2019). Publishers hesitate to publish their books and articles due to the researchers' connections to Decrees with Force of Law [Kanun Hükmünde Kararname] (KHK) investigations; some scholars were ejected from editorial boards of refereed journals; authors have withdrawn their names to avoid being associated with a researcher who is under investigation; journals have been warned not to publish dismissed academics works, and others had their proposals rejected due to being "blacklisted." Regardless, although some may experience feelings of shame and have a loss of motivation from being dismissed, others must continue their work under reduced circumstances, such as participating in street academics or work under anonymously (Aktas et al. 2019).

Academics who are currently living in exile exist and operate under a variety of experiences and circumstances. Some have been able to secure employment at universities, but work under the looming uncertainties of retaining their positions or are free solely to serve in a limited capacity – experiencing restrictions of being banned from teaching classes or being isolated from academic circles at their institution (Özdemir et al. 2019). Moreover, some are identified further as being "victims" to be saved or as "damsels in distress," having to provide their traumatic and dramatic stories for public distribution, in order to obtain funds that assist academics in exile or to bring attention to their suffering for improved humanitarian policies (Özdemir 2018; Özdemir et al. 2019). Therefore, although they are not subject to the constraints of the Turkish autocratic political regime policies, it may be perceived that their current scholarship and academia are still limited concerning their academic freedom. Moreover, it positions them as refugees or asylum seekers rather than academics and scholars (Özdemir 2018). However, the accomplishments of today's academics in exile may indicate that they experience more liberty to exhibit their scholarship in the locations to which they are exiled in than if they had remained in Turkey (Özdemir et al. 2019). Hence, while the scholars may do well adjusting to their host country's language, culture, and social lifestyles, they experience threats to their identity and belonging in the academic community (Özdemir 2018). Therefore, their quests to continue their scholarship and academia highlights their resiliency and dedication to advocate for social change and scientific advancement.

15.4.4 Civil Death

According to Özdemir et al. (2019), "totalitarian regimes have long used exile as a political method of expelling whole communities for the purpose of enforcing total domination" (p. 7). Since President Erdoğan came into power, Turkey has experienced the largest wave of exile in the nation's history (Özdemir 2018). The culmination of obstacles and struggles prompted the academics to identify their personal and professional condition as a "civil death" due to losing their civil rights and freedoms (Aktas et al. 2019; Ozturk 2018). In response to this "civil death," many of the persecuted academics felt their only reprieve and hope for a better life was to leave or escape Turkey. Thus, they deserted their homeland in search of opportunities and intellectual refuge in Western countries (Özdemir et al. 2019). For some, this meant risking their lives to cross the border to live freely, continue their academic pursuits (AK 2018). After leaving or escaping, they relied on their network of colleagues to assist in supporting them financially as well as providing or finding a place to reside, which was usually temporary (Mutluer 2020).

Lack of trust in former friends, family members, and colleagues, and fear for their personal safety are two significant barriers that academics from Turkey are facing. They are critical factors in the decisions of the scholars to leave or escape their homeland (Aktas et al. 2019). The exiled academics felt they were being watched and electronically monitored by supporters of President Erdoğan (Aktas et al. 2019; Times Higher Education 2017). Furthermore, being made aware that their phones were wiretapped, their social media accounts were being monitored, their homes were being raided, and citizens were being asked to report to officials, the academics acquired feelings of insecurity for themselves and their families (Aktas et al. 2019). Moreover, there were reports of Gülen supporters being jailed, abused, and tortured as well as threats and evidence of arrests and detainment for those who expressed dissent (Aktas et al. 2019; Aydin and Avincan 2020). Therefore, the scholars took precautions regarding to whom they talked and the content of their discussions, maintaining a low profile in the interest of their safety as well as their family's safety. Although some scholars were fortunate to be able to take their spouses and children with them, some had no choice but to leave them behind in Turkey. When sharing their experiences, fear is evidenced when they insist on remaining anonymous for their safety, as well as the safety of their loved ones. Unfortunately, the fear they experience due to being a target of the autocratic Turkish government, under the rule of Erdoğan, has implications for inhibiting their freedom of speech and hence, their academic freedom (Baser et al. 2017).

This chapter explores the experiences of academics who have left Turkey. It aims to understand how these academics saw academic freedom in Turkey before and after the coup, seeks to understand their decision to leave, and seeks to understand their process of integration into their new societies. The research questions guiding this study are as follows:

1. What were the experiences of academics and scholars before and after the July 15, 2016 coup attempt that prompted them to flee or escape Turkey?

2. How did the academics and scholars from Turkey perceive academic freedom before and after the July 15, 2016 coup attempt?
3. What implications did the events and repercussions of the events before and after the July 15, 2016 coup attempt have on academics and scholars' quests to re-establish their academic and personal livelihood in their new societies?

15.5 Theoretical Framework

To make sense of the experiences and stories of the academics reported, this chapter relies on the framework of exile provided by Edward Said. Said characterizes exile as the "unhealable rift forced between a human being and a native place" and highlights that exile is "irremediable secular and unbearably historical." Scholars such as Cohen (2002) and Clifford (1994) have used Said's work to make sense of the diaspora experience; by Ahmed (2013) to explore the complexity of identity in the post-colonial era, and by Chambers (2008) to explore issues of migration and identity. This chapter uses it as a framework to make sense of experiences of Turkish exiled academics.

Said outlines that the conditions for exile do not arise naturally, and it is one group of human beings who are responsible for creating the conditions that another group must flee from. While examining this topic of exiled Turkish academics, it is easy to forget this. At the microscale, listening to the experiences of fear, desperation, and need to rebuild lives, the reader is easily consumed by the pain and small joys of the subjects. At the macro scale, the reader can be astounded by the magnitude of the purge of 2341 institutions and organizations that have been shut down and the 110,778 civil servants who have been fired since the July 15, 2016 coup attempt (Scholar's Rights Watch 2018). Yet, beyond both these narratives, it is easy to forget that there are people responsible for this undue suffering. These forces are the result of political choices and decisions makers. Said reminds us to reflect upon this responsibility (Said 2013).

15.6 Methodology

This study employed a qualitative phenomenology approach (Moustakas 1994) to explore, describe, interpret, and situate the means by which 15 Turkish academics living in exile made sense/meaning of their experiences before and after being fired or removed from their professional positions as a result of politically motivated attacks on academic freedom from Turkey's political regime. According to Merriam (1988), "Qualitative researchers are interested in understanding the meaning people have constructed, that is, how they make sense of their world and the experiences they have in the world" (p. 6). The purpose of qualitative research is to understand and explain participant meaning (Creswell 2013; Morrow and Smith 1995; Van

Manen 1990) through the exploration of human experience, capturing the essence of participant experiences, and giving a voice to previously untold stories. Phenomenology explains the essence of lived experience by reflecting on the values of the experiences on an individual's inner perceptions of change. Furthermore, it motivates an inner reflection to validate the participant's perceptions of their experiences (Moustakas 1994; Van Manen 1990). Thus, a cohesive relationship exists between phenomenology and a study exploring the impact of being an academic living in exile due to their academic identity.

The purposive sample was comprised of 15 Turkish academics and scholars living in Turkey, Germany, the United States, Greece, Canada, and the Netherlands. The participants were selected because they had all obtained their master's and/or Ph.D. degrees in the United States or the United Kingdom and were employed at an educational institution or other organizations within Turkey before the time of the July 15th' 2016, coup. In addition, they were all suspended or fired from their positions without justification and suffered personal and academic persecution and emotional duress as a result of the actions of the political regime in Turkey either before and/or after the coup attempt. Two of the participants who were members of the Academics for Peace were fired due to their alleged links with the Gülen Movement. However, others who were fired were not directly linked with the Gülen Movement. Instead, they had bank accounts with Bank Asya, or they sent their children to private schools, which were affiliated with the Gülen Movement. The participants included 12 males and three females ranging in age from 36 to 53, who were professors in law, medicine, criminal justice, education, and engineering, or who were lawyers, medical doctors, freelancers, government employees, police officers, and civil servants. Fourteen were married with children, and one was single.

Ethical issues were recognized (Creswell and Poth 2018), and attempts were made to minimize or eliminate any potential violations. Institutional Review Board (IRB) approval was obtained before data collection, and consent forms were provided to participants before the interviews. The anonymity of the participants was preserved by removing any personal identifiers and assigning each participant a numerical identifier. Participants were informed that they would be participating in the study and were explained the purpose of the study. Due to the sensitive nature and emotional aspects of the study, the researchers were conscientious in maintaining the anonymity of participants in addition to ensuring that no ethics or participant requests were violated.

Multiple methods of data collection included semi-structured individual interviews, focus group interviews, and field notes taken during the interviews. The semi-structured interviews and focus group interviews consisted of open-ended questions focused on the academic's perception of academic freedom as human rights in their professional position before and after the coup of July 15th, 2016. Interviews were employed to gather data that would describe the meaning of the academic's lived experiences during exile (Czarniawska 2004) through the interpretation of their stories. As Brinkmann and Kavale (2015) stated, "the qualitative research interview is described as attempts to understand the world from the subjects' point of view, to unfold the meaning of their experience, to uncover their lived world" (p. 3). The interviews were audio-recorded on an external device as well as on a Skype recording app. The interviews were transcribed, and a copy of the interview was shared with the participants for member checking. Upon completion of the study, the audio recording files were deleted, and the transcripts will remain in a locked cabinet. To increase the validity of the study, the researchers triangulated the data from the multiple methods to develop a rich, detailed text that accurately detailed the essence of the participants' experiences.

The data analysis was conducted according to Moustakas' (1994) analytical framework. First, the interviews were transcribed. Then, the transcripts were read and re-read by the researchers to identify themes and develop significant statements. These statements were compiled with verbatim examples to compose a structural description that exposed the essence of the academic's experiences (Creswell and Poth 2018; Van Manen 1990). We sent out the analysis section with themes and participants' quotations to interviewees for feedback and comments to confirm the credibility of the information and the narrative account and to systematically check the data (Creswell and Miller 2000). Thus, rich descriptions were developed to express the essence of the experiences of Turkish academics living in exile before and after being fired or removed from their professional position as a result of Turkey's political regime. The researchers bracketed themselves and used member checking, outside readers, and thick, rich descriptions in order to ensure the validity and reliability of the research process (Merriam 2009).

15.7 Findings

15.7.1 Apolitical Orientation and Uncertainty of Job Loss

The findings of the study indicated that although most participants stated their apolitical behavior before the coup, a few noted that their research (e.g., Kurdish culture, religion, Syrian refugees, language) could be perceived as a particular political stance. Regardless, they found themselves a victim of a political system in which their academic and attempts to advance their fields brought brutal and unjustified repercussions. The academics who participated in the study were successful within their fields and respected in the international academic community for their quests to seek truth and knowledge. Furthermore, according to the data collected, they believed that the search for truth and knowledge were the greatest contributors to being blacklisted or targeted and ultimately removed from their professorial or scholarly positions. As one participant expressed:

> *We were heroes before, you know, almost heroes – US-educated people, holding higher administrative positions, teaching at the universities, bringing change to the country, saving millions of liras of dollars because of those practices that were modernized and innovative.* (Male Participant 11)

However, after the 2016 coup attempt, the experiences of the study participants revealed atrocities to academic freedom in Turkey as well as catastrophic academic and personal events and situations of academics. Furthermore, their voices are charged with uncertainty and speculation about the reasons they were suspended from their positions and why they were limited or prevented from conducting their research. The events that unfolded after the July 2016 coup attempt illuminated the remarks of President Erdoğan and further supported the lack of reason or justification for the mass suspensions, firings, and arrests of the scholars. A few participants referenced Erdoğan's statement about the coup attempt. One said:

> *'This coup is a gift from God'* . . . (participant voice on the statement): *now he has an excuse to fire, put the people in jail, abuse, persecuted.* (Male Participant 10)

They viewed the perception of the coup being a "gift from God" as an unjust and autocratic approach intended to instill fear in people and enable Erdoğan's regime to disregard laws and policies that would protect citizens.

15.7.2 Academic Freedom Before and After July 2016 Coup Attempt

In this study, eight of the academic participants believed there was academic freedom in terms of what could be researched and taught in classes in Turkey before the coup attempt in July 2016. However, seven of them believed that it did not exist at any time after the 2013 corruption operations. Those seven participants noted incidences in which they became aware of government spies/reporters in university classrooms, censoring of class material and interference in scholarly research. However, all the participants believed that academic freedom in Turkey was obliterated as a result of the 2016 coup attempt. As a result, due to the lack of civil protection and access to human rights, an array of pressures and threats were placed on the participants.

Those who were able to maintain or secure a teaching position post-coup attempt became aware of students or intelligence persons who were sitting in their classroom and who were monitoring course content and instruction. One participant stated:

> *And I always [reminded] my students of the importance of democracy, the importance of freedom of thought, the importance of freedom of expression. But sometimes students, some supporters of the current ideological party, were not happy about this kind of discussion.* (Male Participant 6)

These students would report any occurrences or teaching that they found to be threatening to the Erdoğan government policies, to the university board or government officials. As a result, the study participants in this situation stated that they were compelled to self-censor their course materials as well as their method of content delivery because if course content were not altered, then there were reprimands, repercussions, or firings. Furthermore, they were shunned by colleagues, referred to as terrorists, and ultimately forced to resign or were fired.

One participant made a note of the shutdown of entire universities and organizations, including hospitals that were accused of being associated with the Gülen Movement. As stated by one of the participants:

> *My university, which was one of the country's top medical schools, along with its state-of-the-art research hospitals, was looted with fabricated charges. Administrative staff and academic cadres were persecuted, exiled, and imprisoned. A board of trustees was appointed by the Erdoğan government to "put things in order(!)"* [Emphasis original] *while the university was already functioning perfectly. The new board sank the entire institution on purpose. The looting was done so blatantly and politically that they did not hesitate to put everything to the sack and allocate them for the benefit of their supporters. The topnotch medical school of the country is now serving as the center of Erdoğan's AK Party in one of the largest metropolitan cities.* (Male Participant 14)

The closures of these academic and scholarly facilities had implications for the freedom of expression and freedom of speech, most notably in terms of research. At the universities, the professors had to submit their research proposals to university boards comprised of persons appointed by the Erdoğan government. Therefore, their research proposals were denied. Their only option for obtaining permission to conduct research was to write their projects in a manner that supported the Turkish government. In addition to these obstacles in promoting and conducting scholarly research, the academics expressed several occurrences when publishers would not accept their completed work, graduate students were not allowed to cite the academics, or Erdoğan government supporters in administrative positions demanded that they be listed as the author of the study. One participant's experience was:

> *I think most of my masters and doctoral students . . . they cite your work, and the dissertation committee says, 'oh, remove his name from the list.' What? His work is done. This is his work. 'No, remove his name.' So, it's really kind of like a genocide. It's hatred, it's racism, it's ignorance.* (Male Participant 10)

Another participant shared:

> *He was very bad. He asked me to put his name on my articles. It was like a joke, and he understood that I didn't like that, and a month later, I was fired.* (Male Participant 3)

15.7.3 Academic Pressures/Need to Escape

The following statement from a participant succinctly summarizes the struggles and pressures of the study participants:

> *Imagine yourself; you were labeled as a terrorist, put in jail, dismissed from a job, and then not allowed to work, not allowed to travel abroad to find a job. Your family applies for financial help because normally the state has to, and does, help families who need social support, social benefit. But when we were in jail, our wives went to the authorities and asked for social benefit, and then they were denied. Our assets were frozen, we could not sell our houses – earned outright – and then we could not sell our cars, and then our bank accounts*

were frozen. We had nothing in hand to survive. You're in jail, your wife and your children have no money and nothing to survive. This has a great negative impact on the psychology of your wife and children. And my wife, unfortunately, developed certain health problems out of all this stress. And recently, one of my children, you know, developed a serious health problem because of the accumulation of all those stress and anguish and agony. She had to be hospitalized . . . for months. Just because of those troubles she had been exposed to. This is the worst thing for me. It is hard to explain, your little child has been exposed to extreme atrocities . . . and it went on for 4 or 5 years. Separated from father with no income and pressure from their peers. Even from their teachers in class . . . their approach is like 'you are the children of terrorists.' And then, the youngest and most fragile member of my family has been unable to take it anymore, and she had to be hospitalized with a serious diagnosis. (Male Participant 13)

The July 15, 2016 coup attempt was not a milestone for the government's atrocities, but the pressure had begun long before. The study participants found themselves placed in a position in which they had no future or opportunities in Turkey in the 2 years preceding, or the years following the 2016 coup attempt. With limitations imposed on their passports and a travel ban put in place, no or limited income, inability to secure employment, being labeled as a terrorist, threat of arrest, threats to family members, isolation from academia and society, and having their bank accounts and property appropriated, the participants realized they needed to flee or escape Turkey. How they left varied from one participant to another. However, most of them faced significant risks for them and their family in deciding to flee. Furthermore, due to the risks, threats, and uncertainties, some participants left with their families while others had to leave their spouses and children behind. One participant explained these dangers:

If you get caught with your wife, they (the government) put you in prison, and they sent your children to a state institution, and they mistreat them because they call them 'the children of terrorists.' There are horrible cases. They do it on purpose to make you come back and surrender or simply hurt you. (Male Participant 11)

Another participant explained the struggle with familial responsibilities:

I don't consider myself a brave person in that sense because I have kids. I'm not alone, so I cannot make a sudden decision of like, I'm doing this, you know. I couldn't make such an extreme decision of like I'm leaving everything. (Female Participant 15)

Unfortunately, friends, extended family members, and police may be colluding with the Erdoğan government, making it a risk for the subject participants and their family to trust anyone. Therefore, the participants experienced intense psychological pressures and trauma out of concern and worried about their loved ones back in Turkey.

Seven of the participants had been arrested and taken into custody while others made mention of colleagues or academic acquaintances who had been arrested or detained. The participants who were detained stated the conditions were unfavorable and deplorable and had seen, or heard of, other detainees being subject to inhumane and torturous treatment. One participant shared:

You have no rights. They get all your human rights. You have no right to talk to an attorney. You cannot get your medication. You get no food, no water, and that place that provided you for 3–4 people; they put over 30 people in one room. And they're telling you, they're using dirty words like, and you don't know what you have done. Why are you here in custody? Why are you being jailed? (Male Participant 10)

Furthermore, those who were arrested did not have validated accusations against them (e.g., being a terrorist), or had no accusations against them. Exacerbating the unethical treatment and events surrounding their imprisonment and accusations, the courts consisted of members of the Erdoğan regime. These participants noted that they were informed that all accusations could be dropped if they admitted fault and stated that they would support Erdoğan. One participant explained:

This is precisely what the police told everyone who was detained. They were saying it was so easy for you to get out of that door. Just tell us what you know, just mention your regret. They just asked people to mention regret, remorse. But I did nothing to remorse. I did nothing wrong. For example, I did nothing wrong to show remorse. I wouldn't do anything that I would remorse. (Female Participant 12)

Participant 12 further stated:

They said, 'make a choice, you are going to choose either them or us.' And they used the state power against any people who did not pledge allegiance to them. If you don't pledge allegiance to me, then you are from them, they said. (Female Participant 12)

However, to maintain their integrity, they did not give in to the demands of stating that they support the regime.

15.7.4 Living in Exile: Struggles and Looking Ahead

The dangers of the journeys and finding themselves as refugees in a new country accompanied by the emotional burdens of concerns for their family's safety caused them to experience significant psychological stress. Additional stressors included trying to adjust to new cultures, losing their identity, inability to secure employment, and inability to continue their research that was intended to make improvements or advancements in their homeland within their area of study. Some of the participants referred to these stresses as the consequences of the social genocide they were subjected to.

The findings of the study revealed that one of the greatest struggles is the loss of their identity. The participants said that living as a refugee or in exile after escaping from their homeland was social genocide. As one participant explained:

Because when people are in jail, you lose your freedom, but you have your identity. You are still you, you have your title, you have your friends, you have your country, you have your relatives, but when you leave your country, you lose everything, identity, relatives, family, your language and your culture. That's why in a foreign country, especially for first years it is so difficult. (Male Participant 2)

Furthermore, in addition to losing their identity, they struggle to find a new identity without 'belonging' to a new country. Each new place brings a need to learn and adjust to new culture and language, and thus a need to form a new and unfamiliar identity. Children get their share of this feeling of alienation in different ways. As one participant stated:

> *It is a trauma for many kids. You put your entire life in a backpack, leave everything behind one night holding your child's hand, and hit the road to an unknown world. There is no room for your child's best toy in that backpack. You tell lies of hope or play 'the game of silence' with your child on the road. They set up a whole new life in a foreign country too, and you do not even know its costs to them and how it will reflect in their personality and future. I know very sad cases. Children pay a much heavier price. When you see it, it hurts you worse than all atrocities you personally have endured.* (Female Participant 01)

The findings of the study reveal that none of the participants had a desire to return to Turkey to live. One participant stated:

> *Lost country for me. Sad because it's our motherland and has lost hope for it.* (Male Participant 2)

The participants whose spouses, children, and extended family still reside in Turkey would like to return for a visit. However, it was unanimous that it will take some time for Turkey to get back on the rails and for them to return to their homeland without feeling the threat of being arrested and jailed. One participant mentioned these struggles:

> *I haven't seen my wife and kid for roughly four years. I don't know when I will be able to see them. There is no estimation about when I will see them ... Just because of me, she* [my wife] *is suffering over there.* (Male Participant 2)

The participants miss their homeland and their family/extended family. Unfortunately, the risks are too significant to return at this time. Therefore, although the struggles of living as a refugee or in exile are difficult, establishing a career outside of Turkey enables them to continue their work as academics and offers the opportunity to resettle.

The study participants' expressions and statements illuminated the empathy and compassion they bear for all other persons. Being individuals who endured hardships and who were stripped of all material wealth and status, they overwhelming expressed the desire to ensure that all persons acquire and secure human rights. Moreover, they expressed a desire to seek avenues in which they could assist others in situations similar to theirs, as well as those who experience variations of extenuating challenges. Most of the participants continue to have a strong desire to remain apolitical, focusing instead on working for the good of humanity and identifying measures and means to use their experiences to prevent similar atrocities. Several of the participants also noted that it was their belief and trust in God that provided continual strength and help during their experiences, and was ultimately what will bring about the desired outcome. In addition, the participants expressed deep feelings of gratitude to those who assisted them in escaping, securing a dwelling place in a foreign land, protection during hiding, and connections (for some) to secure a position in their new nation. One participant expressed:

> *We had to stay strong, and we stayed strong, and we will stay strong. We will never submit to a dictator, never. This is what our faith orders us to do.* (Female Participant 12)

The findings of this study from the events in Turkey from 2014 to present express the emotions and experiences of academics living in exile or as refugees as a result of the political regime in Turkey. As individuals who hold master's and Ph.D. degrees, they did not perceive their work as political or advancing social change, instead they were "*trying to do great science*" and conduct research to pursue the truth. It is critical to note the ethical and moral obligation of scholars and academics such as one study participant stated,

> *We cannot leave the realities of life, but we must have another life as scholars, which we cannot expect from other people who didn't study. So, we have this responsibility, and I see that's more important than healing today's wounds. But to prevent this for a long time and the future.* (Female Participant 15)

Furthermore, pertaining to the fabricated allegations against scholars and academics, one participant noted:

> *The intellectual became a terrorist.* (Male Participant 10)

Therefore, the events in Turkey from 2014 to the present were a hindrance to academic freedom, and sometimes a detriment, not only to their personal lives but to what they commit their living to in working to promote positive change for their local as well as the global society.

15.8 Discussion and Conclusion

The 2013 corruption scandal in Turkey in which several members of cabinet ministers were accused of bribery, corruption, fraud, and money laundering, was believed to have initiated the making of lists and investigations into the works and lives of the academics. The Turkish government under President Erdoğan may have felt threatened by the academics who were educated in the United States under democratic principles and posed a threat to the power structure of Turkey. Hence, the government began to target and impose extraordinary restrictions against those they identified as public dissidents, enemies of the state, and to the greatest extreme terrorists, due to their accusations of being associated with or members of the Gülen Movement.

The findings of the study showed that while some individuals felt they had academic freedom before the July 15, 2016 coup attempt, none of them believed they had academic freedom after the coup attempt. The participants identified themselves as victims of a political system in which their academic attempts to advance their fields and seek truth and knowledge brought brutal and unjustified repercussions. Their voices were charged with uncertainty and speculation about the reasons they were suspended from their positions and why they were limited or prevented from conducting their research. The definitions of academic freedom support the academics' perceptions of the loss of academic freedom. Academic freedom guarantees that members of the academic community can pursue knowledge and truth unhindered by political or economic pressures (Kandiyoti and Emanet 2017).

Furthermore, when the academic community is limited in their freedom of expression, learning, teaching, and research, they no longer have academic freedom (Butler 2017; Cole 2017; Seggie and Gokbel 2015; Summak 2008). The government spies/reporters who were present in the university classroom interfered with and threatened academics' ability to pursue, practice, and advocate democratic principles. To promote critical thinking and advocate for freedom of expression, teachers must create a classroom environment where students feel safe to engage in debates and panels (Angelo 1993; Dirkx 2002; Minnich 2003; Seggie and Mabokela 2006). These violations of academic freedom were evident when the participants felt compelled to self-censor their course material and method of content delivery because not complying would result in reprimands, repercussions, or firings.

At the universities, professors were required to submit their research proposals to university boards that consisted of government-appointed officials. Unless their proposals were supportive of the Turkish government, they were denied. Moreover, they struggled to find publishers who would accept their completed work or allow them to be cited or listed as authors. Academic freedom serves as a platform upon which individuals can be free to express themselves and explore new ideas/knowledge to develop new theories in order to advocate and promote a better society without political interference (Butler 2017; Cole 2017; Summak 2008; Ozturk 2011). Therefore, the lack of civil protection and access to human rights pertaining to freedom of expression placed pressures and threats on the participants when their academic freedom was impeded. Furthermore, the censoring of research by government officials and the shutdown of entire universities and organizations, including hospitals, interfered with the autonomy of academics and universities and hindered valid scientific inquiry. According to the World University Service (1988), the right to education is a cultural right that guarantees an individual's freedom to engage in scientific inquiry for teaching and learning. The findings are further supported by scholars who recognize the destruction of academic freedom in turkey as extinguishing freethinking and independent institutions in order to fashion a society of pliant citizens (Kandiyoti and Emanet 2017; Tekdemir et al. 2018).

The findings of the study revealed travel bans and restrictions that were placed on academics who were attempting to conduct research and publish. A bulletin produced by International Association for Media and Communication Research (IAMCR 2016) supported these findings, indicating that Turkish researchers would not be able to attend the annual International Association for Media and Communication Research in Leicester, the United Kingdom due to travel restrictions imposed on academics working with or for Turkish Universities. The bulletin further stated that teacher licenses were revoked, and 15,200 state education employees were suspended from their positions. Furthermore, it explicitly noted that academic freedom had been violated by the government of Turkey, and alluded to the financial burden the Turkish colleagues would be bearing.

The Academics for Peace group, comprised of academics, began petitions that attempted to bring a peaceful resolution to the Turkish-Kurdish conflict (Tekdemir et al. 2018). The findings of our study revealed that the participants who signed the Peace Petition and who also associated with the Gülen Movement were prosecuted and jailed. This was supported by previous researchers who highlighted the firings, personal consequences, and imposed criminal charges of Academics for Peace group who signed the petition (Abbas and Zalta 2017; Ahval 2018; Cole 2017; Tekdemir et al. 2018). This crackdown on academics illuminated the threat the Turkish regime perceived those who were associated with criticizing the government.

The reported findings of the pressures of the July 15, 2016 coup attempt was supported by scholars who signified that it produced more significant sociological consequences than all of the former military movements in the history of the Turkish Republic (Scholar's Rights Watch 2018). The findings of the study revealed that pressures occurring as a result of events and experiences before and after the 2016 coup attempt prompted the participants to flee or escape Turkey. These pressures included: travel bans, passport restrictions, no or limited income, inability to secure employment, being labeled as a terrorist, threat of arrest, threats to family members, isolation from academia and society, having their bank accounts and property appropriated, and the inability to trust friends, extended family members, and police who may be colluding with the government. Those who felt pressure before the 2016 coup attempt are supported by Seggie and Gokbel (2015), who described a depressed academic freedom climate that resulted from politically sensitive periods as a result of previous coups. In addition, those who felt the pressures after the 2016 coup attempt was supported by evidence in other studies in which academics were reportedly removed from their teaching positions (Ahval 2018; Aktas et al. 2019; Human Rights Watch 2018).

Furthermore, it was reported that hundreds of thousands of people lost their livelihoods as a result of invalid allegations against them of being members of a terrorist organization, being associated with the Gülen Movement, or working with oppositional forces to overthrow the Erdoğan government (Girdap, 2020; Scholar's Rights Watch 2018). Similarly, a study by Tekdemir et al. (2018) described the human rights violations brought about by the 2016 coup attempt, elaborating on the political tension and unrest that threaten the academic freedom of academics and reduced the quality of living for those who were accused of being associated with oppositional forces to the Erdoğan government. Moreover, the study mentioned the climate of fear that permeated the universities and prompted instructors to censor their teaching and course content.

The findings of the study indicated the unfavorable and deplorable conditions and inhumane or tortuous treatment by those who had been arrested and taken into custody. Furthermore, those who were detained did not have validated accusations against them and were informed that all accusations and charges could be dropped if they were willing to admit fault and support Erdoğan. However, in order to maintain their integrity, they did not give in to the demands of the regime.

The findings of the study highlight the struggles of living as a refugee or in exile, of which some of the participants referred to as social genocide. The participants are psychologically burdened by a loss of their identity, concerns for family and friends back in Turkey, stressors of trying to adjust to new cultures, their inability to secure employment, and their inability to continue their research in their homeland. These findings are supported by Mphahlele (1994), who noted the considerable psychological impact that refugees are subject to as a result of the ongoing situation in their homeland. Moreover, the author highlighted the state of homelessness that deprives a person of a sense of belonging and results in feelings of insecurity and immeasurable duress. However, although the struggles of living as a refugee or in exile are difficult, establishing a career outside of Turkey enables them to continue their work as academics and offers the opportunity to resettle. Therefore, the struggles of the academics in this study are reflected in the framework of exile in which an irreparable separation is formed between an individual and their homeland due to political factors (Said 2013). Said's framework further outlines the micro-scale of the exile experience consisting of the fear, desperation, and rebuilding, to the macro scale of the magnitude of the imposed purge, including the shutdown of educational institutions and firings of educators/researchers. Fortunately, the struggles of the academics are recognized by many groups, including several non-governmental organizations, the Human Rights Association, Amnesty, and Scholars at Risk Network. These organizations seek to assist academics who are living as refugees or in exile in order to assist them in resettling in their new country (Tekdemir et al. 2018).

This study sought to describe the meaning of Turkish academics' lived experiences after the July 15, 2016 coup attempt. Furthermore, it aimed to understand how these academics perceived academic freedom before and after the coup attempt, sought to understand the reasons for them to flee or escape from Turkey, and to understand the struggles and processes of integrating into their new societies. The academics experienced a loss of academic freedom, a loss and violation of their human rights, and, thus, profound psychological stresses as a result of personal and professional/academic persecution. The participants were forced to flee or escape from Turkey to avoid being detained and put in prison while continuing their research or from previous academic endeavors. Living as refugees or in exile, with or without their spouses and children, has brought about a significant number of hardships and which they continue to endure. However, amidst being falsely accused of being members of associations or organizations working against the Erdoğan government, being depleted of material and financial means, and being forced to leave their homeland and loved ones, the academics in our study are motivated to maintain their integrity while striving to find new opportunities in their new countries.

References

A. K. 2018. Exile. *APH Project.* APH and Advocates of Silenced Turkey. Retrieved from https://silencedturkey.org/wp-content/uploads/2019/05/Exile-may1st.pdf. Accessed 25 Feb 2020.

Abbas, Tahir, and Anja Zalta. 2017. 'You Cannot Talk About Academic Freedom in Such an Oppressive Environment': Perceptions of the We Will Not Be a Party to This Crime! Petition Signatories. *Turkish Studies* 18 (4): 624–643.

Ahmed, Sara. 2013. *Strange Encounters: Embodied Others in Post-Coloniality.* Abingdon-on-Thames: Routledge.

Ahval. 2018. *Dismal State of Academic Freedom in Turkey Described by HRW.* https://ahvalnews.com/academic-freedoms/dismal-state-academic-freedom-turkey-described-hrw.

Aktas, Vezir, Marco Nilsson, and Klaus Borell. 2019. Social Scientists Under Threat: Resistance and Self-Censorship in Turkish Academia. *British Journal of Educational Studies* 67 (2): 169–186. https://doi.org/10.1080/00071005.2018.1502872.

Angelo, Tom A. 1993. A 'Teacher's Dozen': Fourteen Research-Based Principles for Improving Higher Learning in Our Classrooms. *AAHE Bulletin* 45 (8): 3–13.

Aydin, Hasan, and Koksal Avincan. 2020. Intellectual Crimes and Serious Violation of Human Rights in Turkey: A Narrative Inquiry. *The International Journal of Human Rights* 24 (8): 1127–1155. https://doi.org/10.1080/13642987.2020.1713108.

Baser, Bahar, Samim Akgonul, and Ahmet Erdi Ozturk. 2017. Academics for Peace in Turkey: A Case of Criminalizing Dissent and Critical Thought via Counterterrorism Policy. *Critical Studies on Terrorism* 10 (2): 274–296. https://doi.org/10.1080/17539153.2017.1326559.

Brinkmann, Svend, and Steiner Kvale. 2015. *Interviews: Learning the Craft of Qualitative Research Interviewing.* 3rd ed. Thousand Oaks: Sage.

Butler, Judith. 2017. Academic Freedom and the Critical Task of the University. *Globalizations* 14 (6): 857–861.

Chambers, Iain. 2008. *Migrancy, Culture, Identity.* Abingdon-on-Thames: Routledge.

Clifford, James. 1994. Diasporas. *Cultural Anthropology* 9 (3): 302–338.

Cohen, Robin. 2002. *Global Diasporas: An Introduction.* Abingdon-on-Thames: Routledge.

Cole, Jonathan R. 2017. Academic Freedom as an Indicator of a Liberal Democracy. *Globalizations* 14 (6): 862–868.

Creswell, John W. 2013. *Qualitative Inquiry and Research Design: Choosing Among Five Approaches.* 3rd ed. Thousand Oaks: Sage Publications.

Creswell, John W., and Cheryl N. Poth. 2018. *Qualitative Inquiry and Research Design: Choosing Among the Five Approaches.* 4th ed. Thousand Oaks: Sage Publications.

Creswell, John W., and Dana L. Miller. 2000. Determining Validity in Qualitative Inquiry. *Theory into Practice* 39 (3): 124–130. https://doi.org/10.1207/s15430421tip3903_2.

Czarniawska, Barbara. 2004. *Narratives in Social Science Research.* Thousand Oaks: Sage Publications.

Dirkx, John M. 2002. Using Groups Effectively in Collaborative Learning. In *Approaches to Active Learning in Adult Education: Tips, Strategies and Techniques for Teaching Adults*, ed. John M. Dirkx and Sean Courtney. Washington, DC: American Association of Adult and Continuing Education.

European Higher Education Area. 2018. *Paris Communiqué*, May 25. http://www.ehea.nfo/Upload/document/ministerial_declarations/EHEAParis2018_Communique_final_952771.pdf.

European University Association. 2019. *Academic Freedom in Turkey: EUA Calls for the Liberation of Former Rector Murat Tuncer*, November 26. https://eua.eu/news/428:academic-freedom-in-turkey-eua-calls-for-the-liberation-of-former-rector-murat-tuncer.html.

Freedom for Academia. 2018. *6-Month Interim Report: The Short-Term Effects of the Large-Scale Purges Carried Out by the AKP Government on the Research Output of Turkey-Based Academics.* Retrieved from http://www.freedomforacademia.org/the-short-term-effects-of-the-large-scale-purges-carried-out-by-the-akp-government-on-the-research-output-of-turkey-based-academics-2/.

Girdap, Hafza. 2020. Human rights, conflicts, and dislocation: The case of Turkey in a global Spectrum. *American Journal of Qualitative Research 2020* 4 (1): 69–84. https://doi.org/10.29333/ajqr/8266.

Human Rights Watch. 2018. *Turkey: Government Targeting Academics Dismissals, Prosecutions Create Campus Climate of Fear.* Retrieved from https://www.hrw.org/news/2018/05/14/turkey-government-targeting-academics.

International Association for Media and Communication Research. 2016. *Turkey: Academic Freedom Threatened.* https://iamcr.org/news/travel-ban.

Kandiyoti, Deniz, and Zühre Emanet. 2017. Education as Battleground: The Capture of Minds in Turkey. *Globalizations* 14 (6): 869–876.
Merriam, Sharan B. 2009. *Qualitative Research: A Guide to Design and Implementation*. San Francisco: Wiley.
———. 1988. *Case Study Research in Education: A Qualitative Approach*. San Francisco: Jossey-Bass.
Minnich, Elizabeth K. 2003. Teaching Thinking: Moral and Political Implications. *Change* 35 (5): 18–24.
Morrow, Susan L., and Mary Lee Smith. 1995. Constructions of Survival and Coping by Women Who Have Survived Childhood Sexual Abuse. *Journal of Counseling Psychology* 42: 24–33.
Moustakas, Clark. 1994. *Phenomenological Research Methods*. Thousand Oaks: Sage Publications.
Mphahlele, Ezekiel. 1994. Africa in Exile. In *Altogether Elsewhere: Writers on Exile*, ed. Marc Robinson, 120–128. Boston: Faber and Faber.
Mutluer, Nil. 2020. *I Am Not a Refugee. I Am a Scholar in Exile*, January 24. Berlin University Alliance. https://www.berlin-university-alliance.de/en/impressions/171102-nil-mutluer/index.html.
Özdemir, Seçkin Sertdemir, Nil Mutluer, and Esra Ozyürek. 2019. Exile and Plurality in Neoliberal Times: Turkey's Academics for Peace. *Public Culture* 31: 2.
Özdemir, Seçkin Sertdemir. 2018. Pity the Exiled: Turkish Academics in Exile, the Problem of Compassion in Politics and the Promise of Dis-Exile. *Journal of Refugee Studies*: 1–17. https://doi.org/10.1093/jrs/fey076.
Özkirimli, Umit. 2017. How to Liquidate a People? Academic Freedom in Turkey and Beyond. *Globalizations* 14 (6): 851–856. https://doi.org/10.1080/14747731.2017.1325171.
Ozturk, Ahmet Erdi. 2018. Lack of Self-Confidence of the Authoritarian Regimes and Academic Freedom: The Case of Istar Gozaydin from Turkey. *European Political Science*. https://doi.org/10.1057/s41304-018-0170-y.
Ozturk, Sevin. 2011. Üniversite özerkliği göstergeleri üzerine bir değerlendirme [An Evaluation on University Autonomy Indicators]. *Eğitim Bilim Toplum* 4 (16): 114–145.
Said, Edward W. 2013. *Reflections on Exile: And Other Literary and Cultural Essays*. New York: Granta Books.
Scholar's Rights Watch. 2018. *The Day-To-Day Weakening of the Rule of Law in Turkey – 2: The Assault on Academia*, March 18. Retrieved from https://scholarsrightswatch.org/wp-content/uploads/ReportOnAcademics-English-1.pdf
Seggie, Fatma Nevra, and Veysel Gokbel. 2015. *From Past to Present: Academic Freedom in Turkey*. Ankara: SETA.
Seggie, Fatma Nevra, and Reitumetse Obakeng Mabokela. 2006. Impact of Secularism on Undergraduate Core Curriculum: Perceptions of Turkish Students and Faculty Members. *Education & Society* 24 (2): 67–86.
Siegel, Robert. 2017. *Cleric Accused of Plotting Turkish Coup Attempt: 'I Have Stood Against All Coups*, July 11. National Public Radio. https://www.npr.org/sections/parallels/2017/07/11/536011222/cleric-accused-of-plotting-turkish-coup-attempt-i-have-stood-against-all-coups?t=1581689411365.
Summak, M.Semih. 2008. Academic Human Rights and Freedoms in Turkey. *The Educational Forum* 62 (1): 32–39. https://doi.org/10.1080/00131729708982678.
Tekdemir, Ömer, Mari Toivanen, and Bahar Baser. 2018. Peace Profile: Academics for Peace in Turkey. *Peace Review* 30 (1): 103–111.
The Science Academy Report. 2017. The Science Academy Report on Academic Freedoms 2016–2017. *Bilim Akademisi*, August 9. Retrieved from www.bilimakademisi.org.
———. 2018. The Science Academy Report on Academic Freedoms 2017–2018. *Bilim Akademisi*, October 13. Retrieved from www.bilimakademisi.org
Times Higher Education. 2017. Turkish Academics, Still Fearful in Exile. *Inside Higher Ed*. https://www.insidehighered.com/news/2017/09/28/Turkish-academics-remain-fearful-exile.

Turkish Minute. 2020. *Latest figures show 26,862 people in jail over Gülen links: Ministry*. Retrieved from https://www.turkishminute.com/2020/02/21/latestfigures-show-26862-people-in-jail-over-gulen-links-ministry/.

Van Manen, Max. 1990. *Researching Lived Experience: Human Science for an Action Sensitive Pedagogy*. London/Ontario: Althouse Press.

Weiker, Walter F. 1962. Academic Freedom and Problems of Higher Education in Turkey. *Middle East Journal* 16 (3): 279–294.

World University Service. 1988. The Lima Declaration of Academic Freedom and Institutional Autonomy of Higher Education. *The 68th General Assembly of World University Service Meeting*. Lima, Peru.

Hasan Aydin earned his Ph.D. from the University of Nevada, Reno in 2011. Dr. Aydin is a Professor of Multicultural Education in the Department of Curriculum, Instruction, and Culture at Florida Gulf Coast University. His scholarship focuses on multicultural education, bilingual education, Kurdish language and cultural rights, human rights, social justice, diversity and equity in education, educating refugee students, citizenship education in a global context, and international education. Dr. Aydin's research cuts across local, national, and international contexts, and he has conducted research with and prepared educators in countries such as Germany, Turkey, Romania, Mongolia, and Nigeria. He is the author of several books, has published numerous articles, and has had many conference presentations. Dr. is also a founding editor and editor-in-chief for the *Journal of Ethnic and Cultural Studies* and the *American Journal of Qualitative Research*, and an associate editor for the *Journal of Intercultural Education.* In 2018 and 2019, he was awarded a College of Education a professorship for his research, contributions, and publications. Dr. Aydin received the Human Right Educator Award from the United Nations Human Rights Florida in 2019. In addition, in 2019, Dr. Aydin received an outstanding research award from The Marquis Who's Who Publication Board. Dr. Aydin also served a program chair for American Educational Research Association (AERA)-2020/SIG: Multicultural/Multiethnic Education: Theory, Research, and Practice.

Viktor Mak completed his undergraduate degree at Colgate University in New York state in the fields of Global Studies and Philosophy. He returned to his native Hungary to study at Central European University, just as Prime Minister Orban began his campaign to oust the University from the country. Seeing first-hand the devastation that attacks on academic freedom have on communities and individuals, he dedicates his time to fighting back and understanding such tendencies.

Kristina Andrews received her BA in Biology and MS in Education from the University of Wisconsin – River falls. Currently, she is working on her doctoral degree in Curriculum, Instruction, and Culture and a Graduate Research Assistant at Florida Gulf Coast University. She is co-founder and co-advisor for the Youth for Human Rights International Organization at Florida Gulf Coast University. Her research focuses on multicultural education, diversity, social justice, human rights, and global citizenship education. Andrews has published several articles in peer-reviewed journals and has presented at national and international conferences, including AERA. She has served as a reviewer and an editor for international peer-reviewed journals and conference papers.

Chapter 16
The Effects of Democratic Regression on Turkish Economy and the Brain Drain

Zeliha Ozdogan

Abstract Turkey, once promised a hope for democracy, has returned back to an autocratic state in the last decade. In 2013, Turkey increased its authoritarian grasp with the Gezi Park protests, and brutally reacted to the eruption of the corruption scandal involving the highest-level politicians and officials. Later, the peace talks with Kurdish groups was halted. The state oppression expanded to persecute followers of the Gülen Movement, to thwart every opposition in the country, and to eradicate the checks over the government's executive power. As a result, Turkey has drastically plummeted to the bottom ends of the lists in the international indexes of democracy and human rights. Meanwhile, Turkey's economic stability has stalled, numerous freedoms including the property rights were disrespected and violated, while many intellectuals and scientists have fled from the country. After discussing some theoretical ideas about the nexus of political and economic development, this chapter presents the path of the Turkish economy in the last decade and explores the effects of democratic regression on the economy, particularly in the areas of property rights and brain drain.

Keyword Turkish economy · Autocracy · Human rights · Brain drain · Corruption

16.1 Introduction

From a bright country with an encouraging future, Turkey has plummeted to the lower echelons of global democracy indexes over the last decade. After seizing top political positions since 2002, Erdogan has lost his balance and epitomized Lord Acton's famous political maxim, "Power corrupts and absolute power corrupts absolutely." While this chapter is about economic impacts of Turkey's political degradation, particularly in the areas of property rights and brain drain, this chapter

Z. Ozdogan (✉)
Penn State Harrisburg, Middletown, PA, USA
e-mail: zzo12@psu.edu

H. Aydin, W. Langley (eds.), *Human Rights in Turkey*, Philosophy and Politics - Critical Explorations 15, https://doi.org/10.1007/978-3-030-57476-5_16

equally presents and discusses the political and economic happenings as they are tightly intertwined.

The immutable nature of the relationship between politics and economics have enormously attracted the rationalists and others who have been trying to formulize directions of causality (Bilecen and Kibis 2012). The relationship between politics and economy; and more specifically democracy and economic development is a highly contestable issue (Pereira and Teles 2011). There are immense studies supporting various and opposite hypotheses. Many scholars argue that economic development produces a middle class which drives social mobilization which in turn leads to political mobilization and then to a democracy (Heo et al. 2001; Lipset 1959, 1993; Schumpeter 1950; Skocpol 1979; Moore 1966). Berger, to support this idea reports the existence of "numerous cases of non-democratic market economies" (1992, 9). On the other hand, non-democratic markets do not have prospects in the long run. In fact, non-democratic countries managed dominantly by dictators' decisions rather than institutional rules do not provide stable environments for economic development.

> *Though experience shows that relatively poor countries can grow extraordinarily rapidly when they have a strong dictator who happens to have unusually good economic policies, such growth lasts only for the ruling span of one or two dictators. It is no accident that the countries that have reached the highest level of economic development and have enjoyed good economic performance across generations are all stable democracies.* (Olson 1993, 572–573)

Market economies, through their aptitude to expand their business and entrepreneurial autonomy, constitute a big pressure for democratic development. From this perspective, market economies are necessary but not sufficient for political development. (Diamond et al. 1990). Acknowledging the reductionism and simplicity of drawing a direct relationship between the economy and political outcomes, Moore (1966) emphasizes that the level of exploitation among the socioeconomic classes, an indispensable byproduct of economic development, impacts political development. To Moore (1966), what happens in the economic domain differentiates socioeconomic classes. When upper class' exactions are more than their contribution to the welfare of the lower class, the lower class infuriates. The infuriated class with a certain level of resources (i.e. "bourgeois") is the key group in the rise of democracy. Therefore, to Moore "*No bourgeois, no democracy*" (1966). Economic development which is equated to a well-functioning free market brings about democracy if free market is able to create a solid bourgeois class.

On the contrary, Olson argues that the emergence of economic development is contingent upon a peaceful order which can be established only in healthy polities. In the absence of peaceful order, even if the absolute ruler exhibits respect to the property and contract enforcement rights of the people, nobody can be certain of the continuity of his/her respect to their rights. In fact, "history provides not even a single example of a long and uninterrupted sequence of absolute rulers who continuously respected the property and contract-enforcement rights of their subjects" (Olson 1993, 572). For example, the anti-democratic systems such as the caste system in India and apartheid in South Africa produced inefficiency and hampered economic development in those countries (Olson 1993). In contrast, elimination of such discriminative and failed polities has fostered the economic growth (Heckelman 2007).

"No societies can work satisfactorily if it does not have peaceful order." (Olson 1993, 567). In the absence of peaceful order, the property rights are not secured, and entrepreneurship is discouraged. Nevertheless, democracies ensure civil liberties, property rights and entrepreneurial autonomy. Democratic institutions provide ground for economic development (Sirowy and Inkeles 1990). Democracies prevent the leaders to exploit state resources. Furthermore, democracies have rule of law and impartial judiciary, which prevent individual entrepreneurs from nepotism, corruption, arbitrary contract breaches, unfair competition, and other forms of illegitimate and unlawful exactions. Hence, in democracies the investors and consumers have confidence in the market mechanism enforced and guarded by the rule of law and impartial judiciary. Having such confidence, individuals securely exercise their property rights, make long-term contracts, establish businesses, invest and innovate (Acemoglu and Robinson 2012), establish trust funds, and make long term plans for their businesses, savings, and investments. It is not surprising that the information technology revolution was started in the US, where fundamental rights and contract enforcement is prevalent. In contrast, in failed political systems, individuals do not even have the confidence to keep their liquid assets and savings in local currencies or use national banks for their monetary transactions. In countries with failed political systems, the individuals tend to invest in undocumented and black markets, as it is the safest way of securing their businesses from uncertainties of the autocratic policies.

> *Not surprisingly, then, capital often flees from countries with continuing or episodic dictatorships (even when these countries have relatively little capital) to the stable democracies, even though the latter are already relatively well supplied with capital and thus offer only modest rates of return.* (Olson 1993, 572)

Political arrangements shape economic development, and democracies providing inclusiveness bring economic prosperity (Acemoglu et al. 2012; Olson 1982). Admitting the correlation between democracy and economic development, some empirical researches propose that the causal direction between them is not linear. This is better understood by examining the nuances and complexities in operationalizing the economic development and democracy, as well as incorporating the effect of the contingent factors. These factors include the level of democratic consolidation (Pereira et al. 2011), the timing of development, geophysical factors, economic development strategies, international political factors, domestic institutional factors, and world-system position (Heo and Tan 2001, 469). For Turkey, while talking about international institutions, European Union and International Monetary Fund (IMF) are probably the mostly cited ones on daily news and scholarly articles. The next section is about the role of those institutions in political and economic development of Turkey.

16.2 Effects of the International Institutions, Reforms and Turkey's Recent Economy

The European Union (EU) is an important institution with a notable impact on political development of the countries pushing for its membership. Turkey's desire to join the EU started in 1959 when it applied for associate membership of the EU. In other words, Turkey's political development has been affected by the EU policies by fits and starts in the last 60 years. EU aims to align Turkey's commercial interests including easier access to the European market "with the imperative to democratize" (Goodman 2018). Thus, the EU accession process has been a crucial instrument for political development of Turkey in such a way as to contribute to the political order of its near and far neighbors and to the integration to the international economy (Kirisci and Toygur 2019).

The EU has exerted pressure on Turkey for reforming the country's policies and legislation in various areas such as judiciary, civil rights, political rights, and so forth. The EU's pressure has accelerated Turkey's reforms during the periods when Turkey had a desire to integrate to and cooperate with the outer world. In periods when Turkey has opted to become a politically inward state, it has neglected the EU's pressure for harmonizing its legislation and policies. Turkey, in its recent history, has had politically inward periods when it is governed by military junta and more autocratic governments.

Turkey, as part of harmonizing its policies has reformed the state apparatus in various areas. The reforms were at an accelerated pace after the customs union agreement between Turkey and the EU came into effect in December 1995 (Kirisci et al. 2015). The customs union requires Turkey to harmonize its legislation with EU regulations related to the domestic market, government procurement and contracts, financial institutions, exports, tariffs, human rights, among others. In addition, Turkey's EU accession process led to reforms in various areas. The reforms include improving property rights for minorities, abandoning penalties for criticizing the national identity, abandoning the military courts, improving protection for women and children victims of crimes, improving workers' union rights, allowing public servants to unionize, allowing the Kurds and other minorities to broadcast and educate in their languages, ending the long standing state of emergency in Eastern provinces of the country, restricting the National Security Council's authority over performing arts and, radio and TV broadcasting, delegating the Constitutional Court as an appeal court for the violation of individual rights, and increasing respect to human rights set by the European Convention of Human Rights, as well as respect to the decisions of the European Court of Human Rights (Acemoglu and Ucer 2015).

Turkey came close to EU membership more than ever in the 2000s, not only because of the accelerated EU harmonization process, but also because of Turkey's economic reforms imposed by the International Monetary Fund (IMF) and the World Bank upon Turkey's financial crisis in 2001. Turkey, during the 2001 financial crisis asked IMF assistance to overcome the crisis. The IMF's recommendations enabled Turkey to reform economic and financial institutions which had many structural problems rooted at the inception of the Republic of Turkey established from the ruins of the Ottoman Empire.

Turkey was founded in 1923 when the Ottoman Empire's economic and political structure, along with its population had been devastated. There were no adequate middle-class and wealthy entrepreneurs to revitalize the economy (Aktas 2017). The one-party regime established dominantly a state-planned economic structure. This structure has involved many state-owned businesses (Aktas 2017). The state-owned businesses and the planned economy which might have been the only option to initiate the economy at the inception of Turkey, created its own rules and institutional culture to maintain hegemony of political or state-linked elites over the economy. In this new institutional culture, concepts such as free market, independent central bank, transparency of the government procurement process, impartiality in hiring to state-owned businesses and state institutions, accountability of the political elites, among others were nonsense. The state which owned many businesses, became the largest employer not only in service, but also in the industrial sector. The state had enormous power over redistributive policies. The state-controlled economy had been supported by a one-party regime until the 1950s, and military governments and pragmatic political elite after 1950s.

The liberal economic policies and free market was largely introduced in the late 1980s. This increased the weight of the market economy in Turkey's mixed economic system, but it did not solve the structural problems such as the weaker fiscal responsibility and the aforementioned problems in the Turkey's economic structure.

IMF, when it was called to save Turkey's collapsed economy in 2001, recommended Turkey to reform some of its structural deficiencies. As part of the IMF imposed reformation process, Turkey disciplined its budgetary and procurement processes, introduced transparency to the corrupted government spending, increased Central Bank independence, and established an authoritative and independent Monetary Policy Committee (Ozdogan 2009). The Central Bank's policy transition from fixed exchange rate regime to flexible exchange rate regime after the 2001 crisis is particularly important for minimizing the politicians' influence and manipulation power in Turkey where foreign exchange rate is an important monetary transmission channel (Ozdogan 2009, Butkiewicz and Ozdogan 2014). In fact, the prior knowledge of foreign exchange rate was the key element of the rentier economics where certain people who illegitimately acquired such knowledge from corrupted politicians and the bureaucrats earned enormous profits from the arbitrage.

The reforms in the post-2001 period involve several important legislations which contributed to fiscal and budgetary discipline including restrictions of the off-budget expenditures. One of the primary legislations passed in the aftermath of the 2001 crisis included the Public Procurement Law which replaced its archaic predecessor passed in 1930s that was amended many times to facilitate and legitimize the corruptive procurement practices. In addition, there are two important legislations: The Public Finance and Debt Management Law (PFDM) and the Public Financial Management and Control Law (PFMCL) passed in 2002 and 2003, respectively. These legislations aimed at improving accountability and transparency in fiscal policies and practices, as well as budgetary expenditures. The PFDM's objective was to bring all central government borrowings and guarantees under strict rules, and to impose reporting requirements on all debts and guarantees. The PFMCL's objective was to "set the main framework of the fiscal management system, by establishing 'principles and merits, multi-year budgeting, budget scope, budget execution, performance management and strategic planning, internal control, accounting, monitoring and reporting.'" (Acemoglu et al. 2015).

The 2001 post-crisis reforms came into fruition in the late 2000s: Turkey was able to lower the persistently high inflation and controlled it, lowered the corruption, improved the economic performance, stabilized and strengthened the economic growth, and gained public confidence which diminished the influence of military tutelage over politics and economy (Airado et al. 2004; Ozdogan 2009).

The reforms in its essence, while reducing the role of individual discretion, strengthened the institutional framework within which economic activities are carried out (Acemoglu et al. 2015). The strengthening institutions raised hope on the EU membership, while attracting FDI. Turkey's reforms in the early 2000s demonstrates the ability of an emerging economy with weak institutions to rapidly reform and evolve under the heavy pressure of economic crisis which left no option to the country other than reforming itself to save its political and economic system from the collapse and bankruptcy Turkey's reforms in the early 2000s demonstrate the effect of the heavy pressure of economic crisis on a country's ability to rapidly reform and evolve into a well-oiled economic system with strong institutions (Acemoglu et al. 2015).

Turkey's strong economic and democratic performance continued with a significant pace until 2007 with AKP ruling the government since 2002. The inflation rate fell from between 60% to90% on average in the 1990s, to single digits, and output was stabilized in the 2002–2007 period (Ozdogan 2009). The average economic growth was more than 7% in this period, about half of which was from the total factor productivity growth (Acemoglu et al. 2015). During this period, private investment and share of manufacturing in GDP rose significantly; the economic growth expanded its base from major industrial cities to other Anatolian cities which is bidirectionally related to declining income inequality and the convergence of living standards between the traditionally industrial and rich cities and the other parts of the country; middle class expanded; the gap between the eastern and western provinces' accessibility to public services, education and welfare was contracted; and public service expenditures rose significantly in the previously neglected parts of the country (Acemoglu et al. 2015). The AKP's policies to invest more in the previously neglected areas had strong political motivation, as those areas have been considered as the AKP's vote depots. Providing more welfare services in those areas widened and consolidated the AKP's support in those areas.

The reform process started to lose its pace after 2007 and was reversed in the early 2010s. The reversal of the reformist era was marked with the weakening of institutions, increasing corruption, erosion of impartiality in justice and contract enforcement, erosion of democratic gains, and halting and reversing of the EU accession process.

After 2007, the Foreign Direct investment (FDI) dropped, and private debt has steadily grown to the extent that it exceeds the public debt, while the public debt has steadily decreased. In the post-2007 period, the economic growth has still been at an acceptable rate (i.e. around 5%). Yet, this growth has not been robust, as it has relied on domestic consumption and the explosion of the construction sector funded by private debt and easy loans, and the FDIs that fled from the countries that were victims of the 2008 economic crisis (Rodrik 2015). "This strategy typically bears fruit as long as finance is cheap and available. But it comes at the cost of accumulating fragility and increased vulnerability to reversals in financial market sentiment. It often ends up in crisis as the funds dry up." (Rodrik 2015). Coincidentally, after winning another national election in 2007, the Erdogan regime started to reveal its authoritarian regime both economically and politically. Erdogan's pressure on the supposedly independent Central Bank to lower the interest rates was one of the visible signs of a reversed Erdogan who wanted control the institutions that had gained autonomy at the initial years of his regime. Erdogan's attempts to control these institutions has gradually been increased in the following years. Meanwhile, the government constantly asserted that the 2008 global financial crisis did not affect Turkey because of their strong leadership. The Erdogan regime also asserted that Turkey's economic contractions and building economic pressure that led to inflation in 2008 were fabricated by traitors and foreign powers.

JDP leadership ... [claimed that]... the economic growth and prosperity was only endangered by domestic traitors and international conspirators who are trying to stop Turkey from becoming a world super-power. Divisive and hatred rhetoric was increasing the tension in the country once again, after a period of 7–8 years of political stability, economic prosperity, and seemingly social inclusiveness (Aktas 2017, 179).

Government officials and bureaucrats everywhere were trying to convince the world that the financial system was robust, but at the same time were failing to explain why Turkish government was not able to borrow with long-term instruments, or why more than half the country's debt was short-term. (Aktas 2017, 179).

The relative stagnation in economic performance after 2007 can be traced back to structural problems exploited by the corrupted leadership. The AKP leadership, after ruling for about 7 years and solidifying its position by strong voters' support, started to reverse the reforms to facilitate and legalize their exploitation of state resources. One striking example of how the post-2001 reforms have been reversed is the multitude of amendments to the Procurement Law which came into force in January 2002. The law was amended 186 times within the 187 months period of the AKP ruling (Gokdemir 2017). Each amendment has added and expanded exemptions and derogations to the original legislation. In the 2010s, giant expenditures were exempted from the scope of the Procurement Law; the defense, security, and State Housing Development Administration (TOKI) were only a few of the sectors spending billions of dollars with almost no control mechanism over their expenditures. The exemptions to the legislation provide ground for the corruption. In fact, Turkey's largest corruption scandal erupted in December 17th, 2013. The Minister of the Environment and Urbanization supervising the TOKI was caught taking parts of deals involving billions of dollars of illegitimate gains through the corrupted land and construction deals, as well as gold smuggling.

16.3 Corruption and Prevailing Autocracy During AKP

On Dec. 17, 2013, Turkey was shaken by the police raids that resulted in the detention of the then Prime Minister (and current President) Erdogan's inner circle including the sons of three now-former ministers, general director of a state bank, a mayor and high-profile young businessmen with close ties to Erdogan and the government. The young businessman, Reza Zarrab, an Iranian-descent Turkish citizen, was accused of managing a network used to smuggle gold into Turkey and to launder at least 87 billion euros to circumvent international sanctions against Iran. Mr. Zarrab allegedly bribed ministers, their sons and public officials to keep his network running. According to the prosecutors' findings, Zarrab had allegedly distributed hundreds of millions in bribes. The police raided the houses of suspects (the sons of the ministers and general manager of a state bank) and found millions of US dollars in cash at the safety cases and shoe boxes in the suspects' homes.

The December 2013 investigation had many important figures including many cabinet ministers, and others. Reza Zarrab (a.k.a. Riza Sarraf after his name-change) was one of the two central actors of the investigation. Zarrab was later arrested in Florida on March 19, 2016 because of the same crimes (and several others). He was accused by the New York District Attorney office for "engaging in conspiracies to defraud the United States, to violate the International Emergency Economic Powers Act, to commit bank fraud and to commit money laundering" from at least in or about 2010, up to and including in or about 2015, according to the superseding indictment prepared on March 30, 2016 by the prosecutors in the US District Court-Southern District Court of New York (Raymond 2016). Mr. Zarrab pleaded guilty and testified on how he bribed Erdogan's inner circle as part of a billion-dollar scheme to smuggle gold for oil in violation of United States sanctions on Iran. Mr. Zarrab also accepted to cooperate with the authorities. Meanwhile, Erdogan's other bureaucrat, Mr. Hakan Atilla, the Deputy President of the public bank, Halk Bank, was arrested in New York in 2016 because of his facilitator role as one of the heads of the bank through which Zarrab used while laundering his money. Mr. Atilla was later sentenced to prison in the US for 32 months. The Zarrab case, as well as Italian Bologna prosecutor's investigation about Mr. Bilal Erdogan, the President Erdogan's son, who was alleged to bring one billion Euros in cash to Italy, confirms once again that the AKP leadership's corruption is real, and not conspiracy fabricated by Turkish judiciary and law enforcement.

The [then] Prime Minister Erdogan realized that the investigation would extend to him and reveal his corruption. A recording which became public (on social media) in March 2014 revealed that the then Prime Minister Erdogan called his son just after the raids on December 17, 2013 and asked him to move all cash out of Erdogan's residence (Day 2016). (Erdogan's home was not raided because he was the Prime

Minister with legislative immunity). Instead of resigning, Erdogan immediately intervened the investigation through several immediate means. First, he removed all possible investigators from their posts. Secondly, he amended the regulations about the procedure and authorization of criminal investigations in the country. Thirdly, he appointed the judges and prosecutors who closed the investigation by ruling all suspects innocent. Fourthly, his prosecutors stopped the second wave of the December 17 operation, launched on December 25th, 2013, which involved Erdogan's son as well as other members from his inner circle. Erdogan's reaction did not stop there. He started to redesign entire state institutions in the following months and years and launched a historical repression which Erdogan called as the "witch hunt" in the aftermath of December 2013. On July 15, 2016, A fabricated coup attempt provided justification to Erdogan to increase his authoritarianism. Just several hours after the declaration of the sham coup, Erdogan's regime dismissed 3400 judges and public prosecutors, tortured them, and jailed them without due process of law. In a matter of months, the number of judicial members dismissed reached about 4400, which comprised about half of the judiciary. In addition, two third of the military elite, one fourth of the national police force (i.e. 40,000 police officers including almost all provisional chiefs), nearly 7000 academicians, and about 100,000 others; were dismissed from their jobs, detained, tortured, and jailed. As of today, thousands of judges, public prosecutors, journalists, police chiefs, and military generals are in solitary confinement for years. This is a result of the paranoia embedded in the Erdogan regime, supposing that either they criticized Erdogan or that they have the potential to open or support investigation against Erdogan.

The AKP regime's oppression in the post-2013 period is historically unique because it imprisoned almost half of the members of the judiciary in a matter of days. It is an eradication of judicial independence and impartiality which is the most important component of democracy. Indeed, without impartial judiciary, it is impossible to have a well-functioning democracy with free elections, accountable politicians, and free individuals who exercise their fundamental rights without fear.

On the other hand, the corruption scandal that erupted in 2013 does not reflect the whole picture of corruption and autocratic oppression in Turkey. Turkey has a long history of oppression since its inception. Various societal fragments were oppressed in different periods of its history. Alawites, religious sects, leftists, Armenians, non-Muslim minorities, Muslim majorities (Sunnis), Kurds, Sufis, and recently Gülen Movement followers have been oppressed in different periods of Turkey's history.

The Gülen group, which is an international social movement focused on educational, and peace activities all around the world has been harshly targeted by the Erdogan regime since 2013 and have been declared as the number one enemy due their reaction to Erdogan's corruption.

Kurds, over the last several decades have been accepted as another major enemy. AKP, after steering Turkey's several decade long oppressive policies towards Kurds, continued to implement the same or similar policies under the excuse of counterterrorism. Failing to distinguish several hundred gunned terrorists from the millions of innocent Kurds, Turkey has had a long history of oppression towards Kurds. Turkey's fight against Kurds costed tens of thousands of lives, hundreds of thousands of prison sentences, evacuation of about 400 villages, and forced immigration towards the cities in the last several decades.

In the summer of 2013, AKP leadership found another enemy: environmental activists who simply wanted to protect the little green space, Gezi Park, in the heart of Istanbul against AKP's rentier policies which basically included cutting the trees and building a shopping mall. The AKP regime showed its authoritarian face by using excessive police force such as burning the peaceful protesters' tents, jailing them, launching judicial action, using hateful rhetoric, and accusing the protesters of treason and cooperating with international conspirators. In addition, the media, majority of which is sponsored and managed by AKP leadership started a massive slandering campaign against anyone defending nature in Gezi Park.

16.4 Analysis of the Economy, Corruption, and Autocracy

Turkey has had long history of oppression and autocracy. For the scope of this paper, I examine the autocratic period under AKP. The autocratic AKP regime has maintained the country's economic growth and expanded the state's redistribution policies to the lower economic class who have always been the AKP's vote base. AKP's redistributive policies, and AKP's "political economy of welfare" (Somer 2016) which includes providing five million "green cards", free and unlimited passes to all public health services, expansive food and fuel (i.e. coal for heating) assistance to millions of poor people in provinces where the majority voted for AKP in the elections, among others are typical populist policies exhibited by an autocratic and paternalistic regime. In fact, "any individual who has autocratic control over a country will provide public goods to that country because he has an "encompassing interest" in it." (Olson 1993, 569).

Erdogan assumes that his position is analogous to the owner of all wealth in the country. Accordingly, Erdogan has incentive to improve the economic performance of the country. In other words, better economy provides Erdogan with the opportunity to extract maximum surplus from the wealth and use it for his own purposes (Olson 1993). Accordingly, AKP leadership has carefully managed the economy until December 2013 in order to reap the rewards of maximum surplus from the well managed and growing economy. Turkey's economy became stabilized and robust by the end of the 2000s. Therefore, Economic growth was free from serious contractions, investors and other people had confidence that their property rights were respected and protected by the state, contract enforcement was impartial, and FDI was increasing.

Erdogan's approach to management of Turkey's economy changed when his multibillion-dollar corruption was revealed in December 2013. The eruption of the corruption scandal, for the first time, reminded Erdogan that he might not have thoroughly thought about the long term, and that his rule might come to an end.

Immediately, Erdogan's management style took a drastic turn into increased brutality and greed in his autocratic style. As a result, in the post-2013 period, the Erdogan regime eliminated the independence of judiciary by jailing almost half of them (i.e. nearly 4500 judges and public prosecutors as well as tens of thousands of clerks and other judicial and investigative officers), jailing opposition politicians (i.e. the Kurdish party leaders, the Kurd mayors, etc.), jailing hundreds of journalists criticizing AKP and its leadership, and seizing all media outlets criticizing Erdogan, as well as implementing many other draconian policies. From one perspective, Erdogan in the post 2013 period has disclosed that he had broken his promise which he intrinsically had made through the democratic election process within which the elected officials were accountable to the public. Indeed, this is an expected behavior from an autocrat as it was argued by Olson (1993).

> … the promise of an autocrat is not enforceable by an independent judiciary or any other independent source of power, because autocratic power by definition implies that there cannot be any judges or other sources of power in the society that the autocrat cannot overrule. Because of this and the obvious possibility that any dictator could, because of an insecure hold on power or the absence of an heir, take a short-term view, the promises of an autocrat are never completely credible (p. 571)

From Olson's point of view, the positive economic indicators in autocracies do not have much value in predicting the future of economic environment. The three factors including the absence of independent judiciary, absence of an heir, and presence of insecurity such as the possible revealing of his/her corruption lead an autocrat to ruin the security of the economic environment through confiscating assets, and disrespecting property and other rights. In fact, in Turkey, at least two of those factors came together in the last years. First, Erdogan's regime eradicated the independent judiciary. "Impunity and weak administration of justice" is the number one, most significant human rights problem in Turkey according to the US Department of State (US DoS 2014, 1). Second, the December 2013 corruption investigation provided great insecurity to corrupted politicians when their multibillion-dollar corruption enterprise was revealed. The third factor in Olson's theory is the absence of heirs. Erdogan has had a plan for dynastic succession, as it has been evident by appointment of his daughter and son-in-law to the top positions. Erdogan appointed his young daughter with no experience as his chief consultant in the later stages of the 2000s. In addition, Erdogan assigned his son-in-law, a young man with only several years of experience as a CEO of a multibillion dollar company owned by Erdogan's close friend who has huge contracts from the government, as the Minister of Energy and then the Minister of Finance and Economics.

16.5 Impacts of the Democratic Regression on the Property Rights

> *Whenever an autocrat expects a brief tenure, it pays him to confiscate those assets whose tax yield over his tenure is less than their total value. This incentive plus the inherent uncertainty*

of succession in dictatorships imply that autocracies will rarely have good economic performance for more than a generation. (Olson 1993, 567)

Erdogan realized that his time horizon is less than he initially predicted and felt uncertainty over his tenure and succession when the police detected that he was the mastermind behind a multibillion-dollar criminal network. Then he reacted to the police/judicial investigation with a typical autocratic reflex. He started a witch hunt involving victimization of at least a million human lives through torture, murders, jailing, dismissals from office, abrogation of the mine and other contracts, freezing bank accounts, depriving of individuals from their retirement benefits, and asset confiscations.

The Erdogan regime's first large scale attack on private property started with the seizure of Bank Asya in 2015. The number of the companies seized skyrocketed after the sham coup orchestrated to provide a "God given gift" in Erdogan's words, to purge his opponents primarily including the Gülen Movement followers. In the 2016–2018 period, according to Turkey's official numbers, over 1000 companies were confiscated. Those companies include some of Turkey's largest conglomerate corporations such as Kaynak Holding, Koza Holding, Boydak Holding, Naksan Holding, and Dumankaya Holding, as well as others. Those companies have billions of dollars in assets and equities. Table 16.1, copied from the report prepared by the US based organization, Advocates of Silenced Turkey, indicates the magnitude of asset values of some companies and individuals seized.

The combined value of big companies confiscated by the AKP regime is estimated at $11.5 billion at the time of the bogus coup in July 2016 (A Predatory Approach 2018). This value does not include the confiscated assets of "19 unions, 15 private universities, 49 hospitals, … 189 media outlets, 1,419 foundations and another 2,271 education companies" (A Predatory Approach 2018), and the assets, savings, retirement benefits, and properties of tens of thousands of individuals who were jailed for their affiliation with the Gülen Movement, an international social movement focused on education, peace, and humanitarian aid in Africa and other poor countries.

Turkey's General Directorate of Land Registry stated that a total of 6700 properties owned by the followers of the Gülen Movement were transferred to government control (A Predatory Approach 2018). This number does not include the other thousands of properties still under the full control of Erdogan regime's trustees, and the properties confiscated and auctioned off by the local authorities and courts.

The confiscation procedure starts with the National Intelligence Organization's profiling of companies and individuals. Being a member of the Gülen Movement, or any form of association with a business owned by an individual or charity affiliated with the Gülen Movement is more than enough of a reason for profiling. Then, the individual profiled is arrested by local police. The court, either the Criminal Court, or the Penal Judge of Peace Court prepare a seizure order for the companies, properties and all other assets owned by the profiled individual. The Penal Judge of Peace Court is an innovation by Erdogan's regime. Those judges have "extraordinary power" and are appointed based on their loyalty to the Erdogan regime (US Department of State

Table 16.1 Some of the largest companies/assets seized by the Turkish Government (A Predatory Approach 2018)

Company	Assets seized by Turkish Government
Boydak Holding	TL 7.8 billion in assets, a turnover of TL 3.8 billion, TL 5.8 billion in equities
Dumankaya Group	Had investment plans of over TL 1.5 billion in 2016
Naksan Holding	TL 6.8 billion in assets, a turnover of TL 1.2 billion, TL 1.3 billion in equities
Bank Asya	Total assets amounted to almost 1% of Turkey's $800 billion banking industry
Çetin Şaşmaz	Had 302 real estate properties
Ali Kervancı	He donated $34 million to the Nizamiye Külliyesi in South Africa
Hakan Şükür	TL 200 million in assets
Kaynak Holding	Had annual turnover of TL 1.5 billion
Uğur Group	850 sales locations and 240 service centers in 5 continents and 142 countries
İsmet Akil	Million-dollar projects including large construction companies in Antalya
Ömer Faruk Kavurmaci	CEO of Aydinli group representative of Pierre Cardin, Cacharel, and US polo in Turkey
Fi-Yapı	Multi-million-dollar construction projects in Istanbul
İnanlar Construction	Yearly turnovers of TL 600 million
Süvari Clothing	Yearly turnovers of TL 150 million
Faruk Güllü	One of the largest baklava makers in Turkey with nearly 70 stores
Çetin Tekdemir	Komagene Chee Kofta (Turkish fast food brand) with 900 branches in Turkey
Orkide Holding	2013 turnover was TL 1 billion

2014). Those judges have enormous power to decide arrest, search and seizures even before starting the judicial investigation, and without evidence other than the profiling report prepared by the intelligence agencies. For example, a single judge, in a matter of minutes. Prepared an order to freeze and seize all assets of Kaynak Holding with 8000 employees, and Boydak Holding which has about 13,000 employees, without trial and without indictment. Moreover, the case assignment to a Penal Judge of Peace Court is not random, so it violates the basic principles of law such as the natural judge doctrine. There is no vertical appeal mechanism for the orders of those judges. The appeal mechanism is horizontal, so the appeal is filed to another Penal Judge of Peace Court. In order to complete the full control of judiciary, the Erdogan regime restricted the number of judges to a compact number. For instance, they appointed only six Penal Judge of Peace Court in the Ankara Court House where about 1000 judges and prosecutors were employed in 2014.

The confiscation procedure, after issuance of the judge order, is followed by the appointment of the trustees to the company. The company is then transferred to the government-controlled Savings Deposit Insurance Fund (TMSF). The TMSF auctions off the company through false deals to the JDP affiliated businessmen who are closely affiliated with Erdogan's family. Meanwhile, the owner of the company is convicted and imprisoned so in many cases, he/she is unable to take the case to international institutions.

The asset confiscations do not have any legitimate or legal basis, just like many other persecutions committed by the AKP regime toward Gülen Movement followers, Kurds and activists among others. The asset confiscations, freezing of saving accounts, depriving individuals of their pensions and retirement benefits, dismissal of about a hundred thousand government employees from their jobs and threatening private businesses from hiring those dismissed employees are only some examples of the Erdogan regime's persecutions in the economic domain. The persecution clearly violates property as well as other fundamental rights set by both local legislations and international agreements.

The Erdogan regime's economic persecution violates Article 1 of the Protocol to the European Human Rights Convention, Article 17 of the Universal Declaration of Human Rights, and Article 35 of Turkey's Constitution. The mentioned provisions of all three documents explicitly protect property right of individuals (Constitution 2019; European Convention 2010; Universal Declaration 2019).

Article 17 of the Universal Declaration of Human Rights states that "(1) Everyone has the right to own property alone as well as in association with others. (2) No one shall be arbitrarily deprived of his property." This article was crafted after framers reflected upon the Nazis stripping Jewish properties during the Holocaust (Universal Declaration 2019).

> *This is yet another right included in reaction to the atrocities of the Holocaust, when property was confiscated from Jews and others, often to enrich Nazi officials. European Jews were stripped of billions of dollars' worth of cash, artwork, houses, businesses and personal belongings. "Hitler's Final Solution was not only an act of genocide: it was also a campaign of organized theft," says one writer.* (Universal Declaration 2019)

In addition to the violation of Article 17, the Erdogan regime's economic persecutions violate Articles 23 which states that, "everyone has the right to work, to free choice of employment, to just and favorable conditions of work and to protection against unemployment", as well as Article 29, which prohibits arbitrary infringement of exercising the rights set by the Universal Declaration of Human Rights.

Turkey ratified both the Universal Declaration of Human Rights, and the European Human Rights Convention (EHRC). According to Article 90 of the Turkish Constitution, international agreements ratified by the state have the force of law.

> *Article 90 – International agreements duly put into effect have the force of law. No appeal to the Constitutional Court shall be made with regard to these agreements, on the grounds that they are unconstitutional. In the case of a conflict between international agreements, duly put into effect, concerning fundamental rights and freedoms and the laws due to differences in provisions on the same matter, the provisions of international agreements shall prevail.* (Constitution of The Republic 2019).

Turkey's Constitutional Court, in its decision on February 7th, 2008, confirmed the application of Article 90 in regard to the EHRC. The Court stated that EHRC "had become a part of domestic law, so that the provisions of the Convention are of qualified law and that the judgments of the European Court of Human Rights are binding." (A Predatory Approach 2018).

16.6 Impacts of the Democratic Regression on the Brain Drain

The negative impacts of autocracy are countless. One striking impact of Turkey's autocracy is the brain drain, which was notably accelerated after 2015. The Turkish Statistical Agency reported that 113,326 people immigrated from Turkey in 2017. It was a 63% increase on the previous year.

The intellectuals and well skilled human capital have been fleeing Turkey for decades, even when the regime was more democratic. However, the primary factors driving the brain drain is different for the autocratic period than times of democracy. While brain drain was driven by constrained economic opportunities in the past, it has been driven by the political repression since 2015. A news report on Turkey's talent and money drain summarized these factors, "fear of political persecution, terrorism, a deepening distrust of the judiciary and the arbitrariness of the rule of law, and a deteriorating business climate, accelerated by worries that Mr. Erdogan is unsoundly manipulating management of the economy to benefit himself and his inner circle" (Gall 2019).

The general profile of people who fled Turkey is the young (i.e.24–30 years old) and educated people who live in cities. In addition, many millionaires left Turkey. Turkey is third when it comes to losing its millionaires. In 2017; more than 5000 millionaires left Turkey for other countries (Her 100 Gencten 2019).

A survey revealed that 95% of Turkey's youth desire to study abroad, and three fourths of Turkish youth receiving education abroad do not want to return to home (Her 100 Gencten 2019). The primary reason for not returning to Turkey is a lack of free speech, while insufficient economic opportunities comes second (Elveren 2018; Her 100 Gencten 2019).

The repression impacts the daily lives of academicians. For example, faculties do not enjoy some freedoms in their classrooms because they are worried about being reported by their students (Raphelson 2018). Once some excerpts from the recordings are cherrypicked and propagated through the state-controlled media (Lowen 2017), the faculty can face severe punishments including imprisonment.

In Turkey, 1128 Turkish academicians signed a petition called "The Academics Declaration for Peace" in 2016. Within weeks, alongside the support of many well-known academicians all around the world, the number of signatures reached 2212. The government quickly reacted against the peace declaration by launching a judicial investigation and accusing the signatories of terrorism. Eventually, 404 Turkish academicians that signed the peace declaration were dismissed from their jobs, and hundreds of them were prosecuted.

The total number of academicians dismissed from their job was 6081 from 2016 to July 2018. The number of academicians that applied to the UK based Council for at Risk Academics tripled (Her 100 Gencten 2019). In addition, 698 academicians from Turkey have applied to the US based Scholars at Risk organization to find a safe position abroad (Lowen 2017).

The dismissals of more than 6000 academicians have had significant effects on Turkey. The positions left open after the dismissals of the academicians have been filled by people who express their unconditional admiration to the country's leader and his perverted conservative ideology. This brings monolithic thinking into the higher education institutions and fosters the dogmatic ideologies in the campuses. "The 19th century British statesman and prime minister, Benjamin Disraeli, said: A University should be a place of light, of liberty and of learning. Instead, a Turkish university in the 21st century is a place of darkness, of suppression and of highly questionable learning." (Bekdil 2018).

16.7 Conclusion

Autocracy is callous with respect to human rights. In the current episode of autocracy in Turkey, corruption and property rights violations have prevailed, and disrespect to human capital has become salient. Several billion-dollar companies have been confiscated since 2013 and the Erdogan regime is showing no signs of slowing down.

Several groups, including primarily Gülen Movement followers and Kurds, have been the victims of countless occasions of several injustices, such as deprivation of human rights, unreasonable dismissals from professions, asset confiscations and retirement benefits among many other injustices. In doing so, Turkey has violated many fundamental rights set by both local legislations and international agreements including The Protocol to the European Human Rights Convention, and the Universal Declaration of Human Rights. Turkey, as a result, has suffered several economic consequences, as well as losing a concerning amount of intellectual strength and human capital, yet continue to show no intentions of putting an end to its draconian policies.

References

"A Predatory Approach to Individual Rights: Erdogan Government's Unlawful Seizures of Private Properties and Companies in Turkey". 2018, November. *Advocates of Silenced Turkey*. https://silencedturkey.org/a-predatory-approach-to-individual-rights-erdogan-governments-unlawful-seizures-of-private-properties-and-companies-in-turkey

"Her 100 gençten 95'i, yurt dışında okuma ya da çalışma derdinde". 2019. https://www.ibailetisim.com/default.asp?sayfa=yazi&id=47. Accessed 1 Nov 2019.

Acemoglu, Daron, and James A. Robinson. 2012. *Why Nations Fail*. New York: Crown Publishing Group.

Acemoglu, Daron, and Murat Ucer. 2015. *The Ups and Downs of Turkish Growth, 2002–2015: Political Dynamics, the European Union and the Institutional Slide*, NBER working paper no. 21608. Cambridge, MA: National Bureau of Economic Research.

Airado, M. K. Dervis, D. Gros, F. Ozatay, F. Bayar, and Y. Isik. 2004. Stabilizing the Stabilisation. EU-Turkey Working Papers, No. 7. *Center for European Policy Studies.*

Aktas, Elvan. 2017. The Rise and the Fall of the Turkish Economic Success Story under AKP (JDP). *Contemporary Islam* 11: 171–183. Springer.

Bekdil, Burak. 2018, December 19. *The Great Turkish Brain Drain*. https://www.gatestoneinstitute.org/13434/turkey-brain-drain. Accessed 1 Nov 2019.

Berger, Peter L. 1992. The Uncertain Triumph of Democratic Capitalism. *Journal of Democracy* 3 (3): 7–16.

Bilecen, Halil, and Eyyub Kibis. 2012. Economic Growth and Democracy in Turkey. *Yonetim Bilimleri Dergisi* 10 (20): 137–155.

Butkiewicz and Ozdogan. 2014. Financial Crisis, Monetary Policy Reform and the Monetary Transmission Mechanism in Turkey. *Middle East Developmental Journal* 6 (1): 66–83. Taylor and Francis.

Constitution of The Republic of Turkey. 2019. *The Republic of Turkey*. https://global.tbmm.gov.tr/docs/constitution_en.pdf. Accessed 1 Nov 2019.

Day, Michael. 2016, February 17. *Bilal Erdogan: Italy Names Turkish president's Son in Money Laundering Investigation Allegedly Connected to Political Corruption*. http://www.independent.co.uk/news/world/europe/bilal-erdogan-italy-investigates-turkish-presidents-son-over-money-laundering-allegedly-connected-to-a6879871.html. Accessed 1 Nov 2019.

Diamond, Larry, Juan José Linz, and Seymour Martin Lipse. 1990. *Politics in Developing Countries: Comparing Experiences with Democracy*. Boulder: Lynne Rienner.

Elveren, Adem Y. 2018. *Brain Drain and Gender Inequality in Turkey*. Palgrave Macmillian.

European Convention on Human Rights. 2010. *Council of Europe*. https://www.echr.coe.int/Documents/Convention_ENG.pdf. Accessed 1 Nov 2019.

Gall, Carlotta. 2019, January 2. Spurning Erdogan's Vision, Turks Leave in Droves, Draining Money and Talent. *New York Times*. https://www.nytimes.com/2019/01/02/world/europe/turkey-emigration-erdogan.html. Accessed 1 Nov 2019.

Gokdemir, Gurcan. 2017. *Ihale Kanunu 187 ayda 186 kere degistirildi*, May 19, 2018. https://www.birgun.net/haber/ihale-kanunu-187-ayda-186-kere-degistirildi-216485. Accessed 1 Nov 2019.

Goodman, Peter S. 2018, Aug 18. The West Hoped for Democracy in Turkey. *New York Times*. https://www.nytimes.com/2018/08/18/business/west-democracyturkey-erdogan-financial-crisis.html. Accessed 22 August 2020.

Heckelman, Jac. 2007. Explaining the Rain: The Rise and Decline of Nations after 25 Years. *Southern Economic Journal* 74 (1): 18–33.

Heo, Uk, and Alexander C. Tan. 2001. Democracy and Economic Growth: A Causal Analysis. *Comparative Politics* 33 (4): 463–473.

Kirisci, Kemal, and Ilke Toygur. 2019. Turkey's New Presidential System and Changing West. *Brookings*. https://www.brookings.edu/wpcontent/uploads/2019/01/20190111_turkey_presidential_system.pdf

Lipset, Seymour. 1959. Some Social Requisites of Democracy: Economic Development and Political Legitimacy. *American Political Science Review* 53 (1): 69–105.

Lipset, Martin S. 1993. Reflections on Capitalism, Socialism & Democracy. *Journal of Democracy* 4 (2): 43–55.

Lowen, Mark. 2017, December 27. Turkey Brain Drain: Crackdown Pushes Intellectuals Out. *BBC*. https://www.bbc.com/news/world-europe-42433668. Accessed 1 Nov 2019.

Moore, Barrington Jr. 1966. *Social Origins of Dictatorship and Democracy*. Boston: Beacon Press.

Olson, Mancur. 1982. *The Rise and Decline of Nations: Economic Growth, Stagflation, and Social Rigidities*. New Haven: Yale University Press.
———. 1993. Dictatorship, Democracy, and Development. *The American Political Science Review* 87 (3): 567–576.
Ozdogan, Zeliha. 2009. *Monetary Transmission Mechanism in Turkey*. Ph.D. Dissertation (University of Delaware).
Pereira, Carlos, and Vladimir Teles. 2011. Political Institutions, Economic Growth, and Democracy: The Substitute Effect. *The Brookings*. https://www.brookings.edu/opinions/political-institutions-economic-growth-and-democracy-the-substitute-effect/. Accessed 1 Nov 2019.
Raphelson, Samantha. 2018. *Turkish Government Crackdown Forces Intellectuals to Flee*. https://www.wfae.org/post/turkish-government-crackdown-forces-intellectuals-flee#stream/0. Accessed 1 Nov 2019.
Rodrik, Dani. 2015, April. 16. Turkish Economic Myths. Dani Rodrik's Blog. http://rodrik.typepad.com/dani_rodriks_weblog/2015/04/turkish-economic-myths.html. Accessed 22 August 2020.
Raymond, Nate. 2016, March 21. *U.S. arrests Turkish businessman accused of evading Iran sanctions*. Reuters. https://www.reuters.com/article/us-usa-iranzarrab/u-s-arrests-turkish-businessman-accused-of-evading-iran-sanctions-idUSKCN0WN295. Accessed 22 August 2020.
Schumpeter, Joseph A. 1950. *Capitalism, Socialism and Democracy*. 3rd ed. New York: Harper and Row.
Skocpol, Theda. 1979. *States and Social Revolutions*. Cambridge University Press.
Sirowy, Larry, and Alex Inkeles. 1990. The Effects of Democracy on Economic Growth and Inequality: A Review. *Studies in Comparative International Development* 25: 126–157.
Somer, Murat. 2016. Understanding Turkey's Democratic Breakdown: Old vs. New and Indigenous vs. Global Authoritarianism. *Southeast European and Black Sea Studies* 16 (4): 481–503. Routledge.
Universal Declaration of Human Rights at 70: 30 Articles on 30 Articles – Article 17. 2019. *United Nations Human Rights*. https://www.ohchr.org/EN/NewsEvents/Pages/DisplayNews.aspx?NewsID=23932&LangID=E. Accessed 1 Nov 2019.
US DoS, Turkey 2014 Human Rights Report. 2014. *US Department of State*. Available at: http://www.state.gov/documents/organization/236798.pdf (2016, May 05). Accessed 1 Nov 2019.

Dr. Zeliha Ozdogan is an Assistant Teaching Professor of Economics at Penn State Harrisburg. She received her Ph.D. degree in Economics from University of Delaware. She held a faculty position at North American University and served as MBA program director. She also worked as Senior Statistical Analyst and Director of Business Analytics at a media measurement company for several years. She teaches Economics and Business Analytics courses. Her research interests include work within the fields of Monetary Economics, Economic Development, Financial Crises and Quantitative Business Analysis. She works the impacts of financial crises on the economic development and Monetary Transmission Mechanisms of the countries.

Chapter 17
Neoliberal De-Development in Turkey and the AKP's Socioeconomic War on the Counterhegemony

Victoria Araj and Arin Y. Savran

Abstract The purpose of this chapter is to explore how and why Turkey's leading Justice and Development Party (AKP) embarked on a process of neoliberal de-development against dissenting classes and groups as part of a strategy to establish national hegemony. The chapter also discusses some of the counterhegemonic resistance posed by different subaltern (mainly Kurdish) groups against the AKP's growing efforts to monopolize the socioeconomic, the social, and the political spectrum. We argue that under AKP rule, de-development has gone beyond indigenous Kurdish de-development to include a number of former or new subordinate classes. Their quest for cultural hegemony was accompanied by extreme force, violence and human rights violations to suppress dissenting actors, thereby widening Turkey's democratic deficit. The chapter concludes that while counterhegemonic resistance against the AKP's intensified de-development, neoliberalism and authoritarianism remains afloat, it has in recent years suffered serious blows after which recovery will be painfully slow and extremely difficult unless more critical consciousness grows among traditionally AKP voters.

Keywords De-development · Hegemony · Counterhegemony · AKP · Turkey · Kurds

17.1 Introduction

Several studies on the politics of Turkey's Justice and Development Party (AKP), long under the leadership of current President Recep Tayyip Erdogan, have addressed its monopolization of power and rising authoritarianism as well as the

---

V. Araj (✉)
Women in International Affairs Network, London, UK

A. Y. Savran
University of Gothenburg, Gothenburg, Sweden

H. Aydin, W. Langley (eds.), *Human Rights in Turkey*, Philosophy and Politics - Critical Explorations 15, https://doi.org/10.1007/978-3-030-57476-5_17

resulting deterioration of democracy, including impediments on basic rights and freedoms (Onis 2012, 2015; Somer 2016; Tansel 2018; Tugal 2016). This chapter enriches these studies by reconnoitering the importance and centrality of the neoliberal[1] development and de-development of the country's socioeconomic structures as part of the Islamic-rooted AKP's quest for domestic and regional hegemonic power. Therefore, the purpose of this chapter is to explore the evolution of the de-development of subaltern (especially Kurdish) space in Turkey on both the national and regional level and to also discuss the resistance against the AKP's attempts at hegemonic dominance.

In section one; we discuss the AKP's authoritarian neoliberal development policies and the emerging counterhegemonic resistance from the subaltern against the commodification of the commons, gentrification of homes, privatization of the Turkish economy and human rights violations. Section two analyses the AKP power bloc's intensified de-development and authoritarian practices as well as the use of extreme force to maintain public consent and repress subaltern agency, thus widening the democratic deficit. We then conclude this section with an examination of where this leaves the prospects of counterhegemonic resistance in Turkey, particularly after the July 2016 attempted coup d'état, the 2017 presidential referendum and the 2019 municipal elections.

17.2 Background and Theory

The concept of *de-development* was originally coined and applied by Sara Roy (2007) to Israel's colonial, socioeconomic relations within the Occupied Palestinian Territories. She defined the process of de-development as

> . . .the policies imposed to thwart meaningful (socio)-economic development (despite some periods of limited growth). . .(that deprive or rid) the economy of its capacity and potential for rational structural transformation and (prevent) the emergence of any self-correcting measures. (foreword in Turner and Shweiki 2014, x)

Turner and Shweiki elaborate on Roy's theory to explain that this "dismemberment of an indigenous economy by a dominant one" not only distorts economic potential, but also distorts the progressive transformation of society too (2014, 3).

The de-development process in Turkey against the Kurdish populace began after the fall of the Ottoman Empire 1913 when a Turkish nation-state began to take form and eventually founded in 1923 (Yadirgi 2017, 58). Turkish nationalists envisioned a strong Westernized nation-state, identifying territorial unity as the top securitizing objective. As such, the large Kurdish population in East and Southeast Anatolia

[1]Borrowing from Harvey, we broadly conceptualize *neoliberalism* as a theory of political economy, which advances the idea that "human wellbeing can best be advanced by liberating individual entrepreneurial freedoms and skills within an institutional framework characterized by strong private property rights, free markets, and free trade" (2005: 2).

(ESA) or Kurdistan (used interchangeably here), was considered a potential threat to the future of the Republic. In a recent study of the political economy of the ESA, Veli Yadirgi (2017) notes that this perception resulted in a long-term trajectory of oppression of Kurds through the denial of their existence and suppression of their self-determination rights using brute force. According to Yadirgi, this was accompanied by the impairing of the productive capacity and sustainable growth of Kurdish society, also known as indigenous de-development. The early Turkish Kemalist ruling elite's de-development of Kurdish areas was driven by a quest to establish a cultural hegemonic leadership that would be nearly impossible to challenge.

Unlike Yadirgi, we expand the scope of the de-development theory to include the Turkish subaltern. Thus, de-development in the Turkish case also halts "the formation of vital sustainable political and economic alliances... between the dependent society and the international system generally" (Roy 2007, 33). Therefore, we argue that under the AKP government, de-development has gone beyond indigenous Kurdish de-development to include a number of former or new subordinate classes, in what Tuğal has termed as an "act of war against the subaltern" in Turkey (2016, 28). The subaltern includes several groups on the periphery of Turkish society (e.g. Christians, Roma, Kurds, Alevis, lower-middle class, workers, peasants, leftists, trade-unionists, women, Afro Turks, refugees, and LGBTQ's). Arguably, it also now includes certain liberal middle-class Turks who were previously privileged during the Kemalist decades but have in the twenty-first century been excluded from sociopolitical and economic processes (though in terms of class they maintain many of their past socioeconomic privileges). The AKP policy of de-development has resulted in the halting of the exchange of social capital between these groups supplemented by the denial of their socioeconomic activity. This has included impediments on the right to work and traditional resource extraction and livelihoods; legal and physical barriers to the provision and receipt of welfare; the securitization of public spaces; and aggressive urbanization resulting in the dispossession and displacement in society.[2]

To understand the politics behind these rights violations, Gramsci's theory of hegemony is a useful conceptual tool. Hegemony is a theory of *coercion*, but first and foremost it is a theory of *consent* (Gramsci 1971). Consent involves "a leading social group securing the (active or passive) 'consent' of other social strata, rather than unilaterally imposing its decrees upon unwilling subjects" (Thomas 2013, 21). Hegemony is when the supremacy of a particular social group or elite is successfully established through domination and force via the state machinery within political society (coercion that is) but, more importantly, through the consent of the populace

[2]The centrality of the indigenous aspect of de-development cannot be emphasized enough, yet, de-development can transcend ethno-political structure to ensure the peripheralization of subaltern groups.

located in civil society (e.g. schools, media, churches/mosques, trade unions and other non-state socio-cultural practices). Civil society and political society in turn "mutually reinforce each other to the advantage of certain strata, groups, and institutions" (Buttigieg 1995, 6). Civil society is therefore a sphere of hegemony but also where organized class resistance, with the help of intellectuals, could emerge as it forms the main space for the vivid exchange of ideas and tools (Gramsci 1971).

Hegemony, then, according to Gwyn Williams is, "an order in which a certain way of life and thought is dominant, in which one concept of reality is diffused throughout society, in all its institutional and private manifestations, informing with its spirit all tastes, morality, customs, religions and political principles, and all social relations, particularly in their intellectual and moral connotations" (quoted in Femia 1975, 30–31). Hegemony relies more on "subtle mechanisms of ideological integration, cultural influence or even psychological dependency, than upon the threat of censure or violence" (Thomas 2013, 21). Although hegemony depends on consent, consent should not be mistakenly equated with free will. As Buttigieg puts it, "consent is manufactured, albeit through extremely complex mediums, diverse institutions, and constantly changing processes" (1995, 7). One could argue that coercion and consent do not always involve violence or lead to authoritatian rule, but for Gramsci, the focus was on fascist rule. As such, there exists what Karl Marx famously termed a "false consciousness" in society andhegemony is intrinsically connected to consciousness, essentially a false sense or public order. To Gramsci (1971), intellectuals have an important role to play in breaking false consciousness and can do so by mobilizing a counterhegemonic force. A counterhegemony is, then, "the process by which subordinate classes challenge the dominant hegemony and seen to supplant it by articulating an alternative hegemony" (Hunt 1990, 312). Theoretically and practically, the alternative is not always a positive or democratic one either.

The AKP case study emulates that of many neoliberal semi-peripheral states in the capitalist world economy. Hegemony is central to maintaining the authority of state and non-state extraction and capital exchange in an increasingly competitive environment, ensuring the protection of the capital accumulation of the expanding petit-bourgeoisie and bourgeoisie. The global neoliberal hegemonic order was framed as "the only way" to modernize and enrich Turkey. Compounded by the support of the Bretton Woods institutions and the European Union (EU), this global intellectual hegemony led to the "de-legitimization of social critique, dissent . . .(and the) intellectual disarmament and disempowerment" of alternative polities and ideologies worldwide (Gosovic 2000, 447). Alternative political orders that addressed historical structures of oppression against for example Kurds and other indigenous groups, and which challenged neoliberal prescriptions, were in Turkey framed as security threats against status quo.

17.3 The AKP's Authoritarian Neoliberal Development Policies and the Emergence of Subaltern Resistance

The origins of the AKP power bloc can be traced back to the Sunni Turkish religious countermovement against years of strict secularism under the Kemalist regime. Nationalism, protectionism, and conservative values characterized the main Islamic religious party in Turkey of which the AKP founders broke away from and founded their own, more liberal and globalist, political party in August 2001. In November 2001, they stunningly won the national elections in Turkey and formed the first majority government for over a decade. The AKP's convenient marriage between neoliberalism and moderate Islamic values was an attempt by the global hegemony and growing religious economic middle class in Turkey to consolidate the Chicago School's economic order in Turkey and the wider Middle East (Tugal 2016). To Gürcan and Peker (2015), this reconfiguration of society accompanied by the proletarianization of the Turkish lower strata would define a new era of economic order in Turkey. Key to the consolidation of this neoliberal economic order was the rise in consumerism as a uniting force of the pious and secular masses. The AKP, who themselves surfaced from the central Anatolian religious subaltern, incorporated rather than blocked the ruling secular elite into their power bloc. Instead of dethroning them and trying to block their power, they allied with the center-right, liberals and other conservatives and convinced them their moderate religiosity was the end to the "Islamist threat" that previously emerged due to the 1979 Iranian revolution and imperiled secular Kemalists for years (De Leon et al. 2009). Indeed, to Gramsci (1971), a hegemonic project can only be successful if its broad enough, meaning that it cannot just be based on the views of pious, conservative Turks who make up the majority of AKP constituents. Some aspects of the interest and ideology of other subordinate groups must be included to create an *incorporative hegemony*, which for example included the Kurds' quest for rights and recognition (earning the AKP a high number of votes from the ESA).

The new historic bloc of post-Islamist business-owners[3] under the AKP reshaped economic relations through pulling back the state and allowing the private sector an expanded role (Dagi 2013). They pushed forward a massive economic liberalization policy with the aim of penetrating and reorganizing of society through altering economic relations, made possible through the subordination of the periphery (as well as the reproduction of old subordinations). Lindberg (2001) explains that

[3]Bayat explains the evolution of Turkey's Islamists into post-Islamists: "following a phase of experimentation, the appeal, energy and sources of legitimacy of Islamism were exhausted even amongst its once ardent supporters" (2013: 8). Therefore, the upcoming Islamist cadre, the young educated elite, began trying to change the movement from within for the modern era. They attempted to merge religious discourse with human rights discourse, the practice of faith as a practice of freedom and liberty and promote pluralistic ideals rather than the singular authoritative voice of past Islamic revolutions. The key ontological shift they underwent was to understand the practice of religion as individual choice rather than religion as collective responsibility (Bayat, 2013).

a state extracts and uses resources to sustain itself through either blocking or mobilizing social groups. The AKP centered its hegemonic consolidation through its development policies by rewarding consensual stakeholders via public spending. This is characteristic of a developmentalist state, where revenues are spent on the management of society and mobilization of social groups for state purposes (Hall 1999; Lindberg 2001). Social groups can be organized and empowered within the framework of the state through education and socialization, economic management and control, support to civil organizations and administration of state functions by semi-autonomous groups. This is how state polities reproduce their power through socioeconomic development. Thus, a formation of "infrastructural power" (Mann 2012), creates a bargaining relationship in which a society penetrated by the state through resource extraction and use, can feedback inputs, leading to an integrated state polity, or as Gramsci (1971) terms it, an *integral hegemony*. The AKP initially developed a neoliberal hegemony within Turkish society through a combination of consent and coercion without resorting to direct violence. To protect the new power bloc's neoliberal capital and its gains, the state apparatus became bound up with those of the dominant economic class (Femia 1993).

The AKP's swift rise to power was a political earthquake. Thanks to a solid power base amongst civil and political society as well as promises of economic growth, EU membership and equality between all citizens, they won 34.28% of the vote in November 2002 and later gained nearly 50% of the vote share in 2007. This was, "the formation of the most hegemonic bloc in Turkish history. The top academics, the most revered public intellectuals, many activists and a large proportion of the popular classes had become one with the regime, even if they attributed contrasting meanings to their adherence" (Tuğal 2016, 94). As explained in Araj, through neoliberalism, "the more embedded a state polity becomes in the international economy, the more alliance-building it will become in order to encourage international investment and free flows of capital. In turn, the more power it is able to wield as it actively opens the political system to layers of other polities who will thereby have a stake in maintaining the status quo" (2018: 167). Thus, opposition movements and parties found it increasingly challenging to mobilize against the government. It was problematic to argue with modernism, stable government, democratization, liberal Islam and economic success (Tuğal 2016).

Both domestically and abroad, Turkey's deregulated economic growth during the AKP's first decade was frequently heralded as a neoliberal success story. The AKP worked with the IMF and the EU to privatize public enterprises such as Türk Telecom, the Turpas oil refinery, Erdemir steel and iron producer (Türkmen 2008), focusing heavily on energy and natural resource businesses. Privatization revenue amounted to $30.6 billion (Morvaridi 2013). In turn, privatization and the opening up for investment led to a gargantuan increase of foreign direct investment. In 2002, the number of active companies was 498, by 2011 this figure was 25,927. Foreign capital was worth $1.5 billion in 2002 and sharply increased to $22 billion in 2007 (Morvaridi 2013; Tuğal 2016). This led to a stabilization of inflation, but the AKP were unable to close the trade gap. Exporters remained dependent on the import of capital and were harmed by the tech-negative pressure of import substitution. This meant that the Turkish economy became highly dependent on procuring from abroad (particularly for energy imports) and vulnerable to a possible slowing of capital flows (Tuğal 2016, 121). As such, dependency on, and embeddedness within the neoliberal international economy furthered the need for maintaining vertical power subordination and the consent of the masses.

The early laudation of the AKP's neoliberal development model was based on its ability to prevent large-scale dissent through poverty reduction, marketization and consumption culture, thus gaining and ensuring the consent of a broad stratum of Turkish voters. The government increased state-spending on the welfare system and significantly improved it, impressing the public who for years complained of slow and inadequate public services. The absolute poverty rate dropped from 26% in 2002 to 17.7% in 2007. Nevertheless, fiscal tightness ensued, and social expenditure was still well below the OECD average in 2007 at 19.2% of GDP. Yet, the AKP succeeded in cultivating the myth that that those who work hard and honestly would achieve higher standards of living and modernity. Although the government increased state funds for health services, more increasingly social welfare was provided by a number of private actors close to the AKP, creating the myth of and consent for the "generosity" of a brand of Islamic neoliberalism amongst the public (Morvaridi 2013). Faith-based organizations sympathetic to the AKP began to fill the welfare gap so as not to lose the power bloc's penetrative consent within society (ibid.).

The reduction in poverty rates and the philanthropic activities by private actors increased electoral support for the party in the crucial national and municipal elections of 2007, 2009 and again in 2011. Such philantrophic efforts by Islamic charities were especially visible in the majority-Kurdish ESA where poverty levels remain extremely high compared to the rest of the country, particularly the western region which continues to be the primary benefactor of Turkey's financial wealth (Bugra and Candas 2011). However, the AKP's market-oriented social policy only plugged the gap in the weak Turkish welfare system, thereby failing to address unequal social relations and distribution of resources (Morvaridi 2013). Then, between 2007 and 2011, at the height of the global financial crisis, the AKP cut healthcare expenditure, raised the retirement age, depressed wages, curtailed unions and limited strikes. The suppression of workers' rights intensified under this economic system.

Government spending in the Turkish education sector grew steadily between 2002 and 2011. In addition to private and international investment, in 2011 this amounted to 34 billion Turkish Lira, or 15% of the national budget (The Business Year 2011). A fundamental process between 2002 and 2011 was the expansion of early years education. Access to kindergartens became widespread throughout the country, bringing about a 22% increase in enrolment in 2009–2010 from 2008–2009. The number of universities also increased under the first two AKP governments, with the number of universities doubling between 2006 and 2011. This was due to fiscal incentivizing of the founding of private universities by various individuals and organizations, especially the Islamic Gülen Movement. Turkey hosted 20,000 foreign students in 2011, many from Africa and Central Asia. Despite increasing access to education and improved quality, concerns were raised by educational experts regarding the use of socialization and bias discourse within the education system that increasingly aligned with a Turkish-Sunni-Islamic ideology (Lüküslü 2016, 638). These programs alienated many younger students, especially those minorities of Alevi and non-Muslim background. Hegemonic formations are based around the values of the dominant group that bring together potentially antagonistic social actors (Gramsci 1971). Yet, the Alevis, who constitute a large group in Turkey (possibly about 20%), could not accept an AKP Sunni Islamic value-based political and educational program.

Power struggles became common throughout the state bureaucracy, not just between the religious and the secular, but also between management and workers[4] over their employment rights and pay. A particular problem that arose, noted by Gürcan and Peker (2015) on the precariousness of work contracts, was a marked increase in part-time work from 6.6% in 2002 to 11.7% in 2011. Aside from this, "at least a third of the total workforce in Turkey is informally employed, and stands as disorganized and isolated from the rest of the working population... and only 9.21 percent of the work force is unionized, which corresponds to 1,001,671 people" (Gürcan and Peker 2015, 5). Many in the casual workforce were employed in the fast-growing construction sector as the AKP put urban redevelopment, or put differently, the control and reproduction of space, at the center of its neoliberal developmentalist program.

Turkey's urban development program was led by the Mass Housing Administration (TOKI) under the authority of central government, acting in various roles such as constructor and planning authority, gaining the lead in both private and public projects. The AKP gave an entirely new role to TOKI which often gives building contracts to companies with close ideological or family relations to the AKP elite (Cavusoglu and Strutz 2014, 151). In 2002, the construction sector represented 4.5% of the country's labor market, growing to 5.9% in 2007. The construction industry grew year on year during that period by 22% (Cavusoglu and Strutz 2014, 141). The construction sector was no longer represented by a group of small and middle-size companies but instead "monopolised by a few large constructors and developers with close ties to the regime" (ibid.). Waldman and Caliskan note that "in 2002 there were 43,430 new construction projects, in 2006 this had ballooned to 114,204" (2017, 151). This growth, largely in the private sector, was supported by government deregulation. As such, between 2002 and 2007, 78 laws were passed by parliament with regards to non-commodified public spaces (Waldman and Caliskan 2017). This included central government authorization of the termination of public licenses on public property. Thus, the regime began privatizing "large state-owned stock of former industrial and public buildings, forests, rivers and informally urbanized land" as well as expropriating property in inner city *gecekondu* neighborhoods through TOKI and its "urban renewal" projects (Cavusoglu and Strutz 2014, 141).[5] Through the passing of the Law on the Transformation of Disaster-Risk Areas, TOKI was

[4]The weakness of the state bureaucracy meant international corporations could get away with treating workers inhumanely without repercussions. Between 2002 and 2011, 5213 workers died due to occupational injury (Tugal 2016: 147).

[5]*Gecekondu,* or "landed at night", neighborhoods are slum like settlements of unregistered housing on public property. These emerged in urban centers as part of the proletarianization of Turkey's rural workforce in 1960s and onwards, which supported the increasing migration of cheap labor to

granted the authority to declare any building as "at-risk", which was the case in many *gecekondu* neighborhoods. The occupant was forced to choose between giving it up to the municipality or knocking the house down at their own expense (ibid. 147). The forced expropriation of property in *gecekondu* areas by TOKI (often in cooperation with private sub-contractors) was launched under the pretext of providing earth-quake safe and regulated home ownership to the working class, with the hope of expanding hegemonic consent amongst those who historically had no stake in neoliberalism. As Cavusoglu and Strutz note, "while spatial policies used to be a method to *strengthen* [sic] hegemony, the AKP's neoliberal hegemony is *constituted* [sic] through their use of space" (2013, 143). The incredible drive to build (mostly apartment blocks, shopping malls and mosques) has enriched the government-allied construction section, generating huge revenues of income but also integrating citizens into the neoliberal ideology through property relations. According to Gramsci (1971), this is essentially how hegemony becomes solidified. Hegemony is not culture or ideology per se but refers to the material basis of these.

Ex-*gecekondu* residents around the country were offered new accommodation (usually kilometers away from the inner-city areas where many of them worked) if they paid towards the increased value of their new homes in monthly instalments. Yet, this proved highly problematic as this offer was not extended to those with formal rental contracts in the neighborhoods, and many residents could not meet the financial demand of the instalments so they peddled their entitlement documents to property speculators (Waldman and Caliskan 2017). There was a massive lack of citizen consultation and accountability for the planning and construction process. Essentially, these were gentrification projects with the purpose of making profit through displacing inner-city *gecekondu* residents to the outskirts of Istanbul and building luxury accommodation for middle class service workers in their place.

Urban redevelopment had solidified Turkey's place as a MINT economy open to foreign investment and an industrial hub of the global economic market. Although, on the domestic front the novel form of governance that the AKP implemented, supplemented by the Europeanization process, led to a reconstitution of the cleav-ages of Turkish political society as new alliances, power blocs and hierarchies emerged. The winners of the early years of the AKP tenure included the so-called Gülen Movement[6] that were more or less clandestine under the capstone Kemalist state and the rising economic force of the pious Anatolian middle class. The AKP managed to maintain a myth of the spoils of neoliberal Islam emancipating the young and the poor. They accomplished this through gentrification and metaphoric symbolism of Ottoman wealth in urban spaces and public discourse, which in turn-built consent and loyalty for the AKP state polity. The government were able to mitigate the grievances of the lower strata as inequality grew, through new urbanism

Turkey's cities even though the state was unable to provide housing for them (hence the initially illegal *gecekondu* settlements).

[6]The "Gülen Movement" commonly refers to the followers of US-based Turkish Islamic scholar Fethullah Gülen and the various services the movement offers globally in areas of education, media, health etc.

and politically targeted welfare initiatives and infrastructure development. Through a combination of neoliberal globalism and post-Islamism, the AKP managed to form a new social consciousness as well as to exercise its rule through a high level of public consent based on a new, relatively stable social system that came at a cost of increasing authoritarian practices and human rights violations. Yet, the AKP's rising Big Brother control and stiffling of rights, particularly after 2011, were also causing massive resentment among large segments of the populace.

17.4 Public Dissatisfaction and Resistance

The enormous amount of effort, time and energy put in by the AKP elite, under the iron leadership of Recep Tayyip Erdogan, to establish national hegemony was indeed remarkable. No other Turkish political party has managed to achieve what the AKP did in just a few years' time. Their achievements can be understood as a *passive revolution*, which Gramsci (1971) terms as the gradual takeover of a ruling class. However, hegemony needs constant nurturing and it can therefore be adeptly described as "an active process involving the production, reproduction, and mobilization of popular consent" (Hunt 1990, 311). Recognizing this, a counterhegemonic force may emerge to disrupt such control by the historic or hegemonic bloc mobilizing those with grievances through socialization, recruitment, interest articulation and interest aggregation. While there is considerable public support for the AKP, they have not gained complete consent from the populace. There is widespread dissatisfaction with not only urban policies but a range of other policies and discourses targeting the marginalized and disempowered. For example, many women across the country are wary of the AKP's attitudes towards women and traditional gender roles. They were frustrated with then Prime Minister Erdogan's religiously influenced statements that "defined women in terms of reproduction, homemaking, and nurturing functions", calling for women to give birth to at least three children to grow the country's future economy (Eslen-Ziya and Erhart 2015, 474). In another example, the Kurdish political movement was, overall, dissatisfied with the government's half-democratic political reforms, arguing they did not sufficiently address Kurdish demands of full cultural and linguistic rights and political liberalization.[7] Added to this, many secular and pious Kurds did not appreciate the AKP's attempt to use religious discourse to discredit the Kurdish movement and aim to replace Kurdish identity with religious identity (Sarigil and Fazlioglu 2013; Yavuz and Ozcan 2015). The AKP was accused of failing to comprehend the complexity behind the Kurdish question as well as stirring up nationalist sentiments amongst Turks instead of exerting genuine, pluralist politics and ending the violent conflict with the PKK.

[7]Immediate Kurdish demands remained ignored, such as the abolition of the village guard system that had sowed deep intra-Kurdish divisions, Kurdish medium instruction in education, and reduction of the 10% parliamentary threshold to allow diverse political access and representation.

It was not until the Gezi Park protests of May and June 2013 that millions of people of various social, cultural and economic backgrounds came together on the streets and on social media to express their rage against the increasingly authoritarian, interventionist and destructive Islamic-conservative neoliberal policies. The Gezi uprising initiated when a group of environmentalists gathered to protest the local authorities' decision to demolish a public park near the famous Taksim area of Istanbul. Instead, a mosque and a shopping mall was to be built – an ironic symbolism of the AKP integrated model of post-Islamism and conservative neoliberalism. Though soon enough, a small protest quickly turned into a massive transclass uprising by different subaltern groups in alliance against the neoliberal economic, political, cultural and ideological domination by the AKP and Erdogan, as argued by others too (Arat 2013; Gençoğlu Onbaşi 2016; Tugal 2013). The Gezi protests brought together such groups as workers, the middle class and lower middle class, students, the unemployed, artists, intellectuals, leftists, Kurds, environmentalists, feminists, LGBTQs, anti-capitalist Muslims and many other ordinary people with no prior experience of political protest (Eslen-Ziya and Erhart 2015; Gurcan and Peker 2015; Turam 2015). The protests were not a "middle class" uprising as was frequently portrayed, but led by "secularly oriented educated youth, wage-workers and service sector employees" (Gurcan and Peker 2015, 338).[8] The uprising was extraordinary in demonstrating the meaning of civic participation, inclusion and collective action by various (some opposing) groups "rising above their ideological and identarian differences" (Turam 2017, 186). These protests were unprecedented in modern Turkey in terms of the speed of escalation, duration, number of participants and the geographic space reached. According to official figures by the Turkish Interior Ministry, there were demonstrations in 80 out of 81 provinces with over 3,600,000 people participating in a staggering 5532 protest actions (cited in Gencoglu Onbasi 2016, 273).

The Gezi protests created large, passionate debates at home and abroad about where Turkey's frail democracy was heading. The protests spread from Istanbul to various cities in the country quite fast but gradually subsided towards the end of June and ultimately failed to institutionalize itself, a crucial step for a counterhegemony's success. Crucially though, the protests inspired a critical mass consciousness, which as mentioned is central to Gramscian theory (Gramsci 1971). Although the major protests were over, the resistance was not. As Eslen-Ziya and Erhart explain

> Once the protests were over, the movement continued with 'neighborhood forums' operating according to the principles of direct democracy and anti-government discourse. These forums were also referred to as 'people's assemblies' where hundreds gathered together in parks around Turkey to discuss social issues such as women's rights, animal rights, or

---

[8]Gürcan and Peker mention two surveys conducted by respected Turkish think-tanks GENAR and KONDA that outline the socioeconomic background of protesters. According to GENAR's survey in the Taksim area in June 2013 when protests continued, 53.8% were wage-earners, 24.1% students, and 10.8% unemployed. KONDA's survey took place around the same time and noted the figures 52%, 37%, and 6% respectively.

> unequal distribution of wealth. They discussed and criticized the current policies and tried to come up with strategies for systematic political change (2015, 476).

In this way, the Gezi protestors attempted to reclaim the public space that was increasingly denied to them (through rapid urbanization plans) but also to build up their resistance against the coercive state apparatus via bottom-up democratic practices. Such local assemblies and forums are considered critical to citizen empowerment in the literature on radical democracy (Bookchin 2015; Cohen and Fung 2004; Passerin d'Entrèves 1992). Therefore, as people organized against the AKP's increasingly undemocratic and unequal policies, a serious counterhegemonic challenge emerged. The AKP's discursive reaction to the Gezi protests as a mixture of a foreign and domestic conspiracy reveals both its fear of a counterhegemonic resistance as well as its shallow understanding of democracy (Alpan 2014). The AKP under Erdogan's leadership has always had a "two steps forward, one step back" approach that undermined democratization. In other words, whenever the AKP government moved towards consolidating democracy, cultivating minority rights, the rule of law, and shifting civil-military relations, it simultaneously acted in utter contradiction to such positive growth. This was frequently evidenced through Erdogan's increasingly divisive and nationalistic rhetoric since 2008 and onwards (Cicek 2011; Gençoğlu Onbaşi 2016). Yalvaç explains that "through the hegemonic bloc concept Gramsci demonstrates how a temporary alliance between social classes is established around a set of hegemonic ideas or 'dominant ideology' (2016, 8)." In this case, neoliberalism having certain environmental or social trade-offs that are inevitable sacrifices for a modernizing state.

Despite obvious shortcomings, the political left initially tolerated the AKP because of its record in promoting positive political reforms in the early 2000s, ending the Kemalist military tutelage, and attempting to address Kurdish grievances through legal reforms and the Democratic Opening between 2009 and 2011. However, the shocking experiences of the Gezi uprisings led to a serious period of reflection among both Turkish and Kurdish liberals and the wider socialist left. As a result, in the summer of 2013, some of them came together and decided to form a political alliance under the Peoples' Democratic Party (Turkish acronym HDP). Spearheaded by pro-Kurdish political elements, together this alliance was to jointly address the Kurdish case and the democratic deficit that characterized Turkish state-society relations. It is worth noting that the HDP's formation was encouraged by the imprisoned Kurdish leader Abdullah Ocalan, who wished to see the Kurdish national movement shift from a war of maneuver to a war of position, that is, to continue an ideological struggle via non-violent means together with different democratic segments of Turkish society (Bar-On 2015).

Through an inclusive and clearly anti-Erdogan policy, the HDP managed to expand its support base to include more liberal and left-wing Turks, minorities such as Armenians, as well as more religious-conservative Kurds (including Sunni Zazas) who normally voted AKP. Many of the HDP members and politicians possessed significant experience of Kurdish activism and thus were closely connected to the local, grassroots level. This was critical for the empowerment of the HDP, portraying parallels with the post-Marxist theory that, "empowerment focuses on 'bottom-up' social mobilization in society as a challenge to hegemonic interests within the state and the market" (Mohan and Stokke 2000, 249).

Turkey's struggle between the democratic and inclusive ideals of the left and the neoconservative, capitalist pursuits of the governing right-wing establishment rapidly intensified after the formation of the HDP. The conflict between the two sides was played out on the streets, the media, through elections, through arbitrary applications of the law and through violent conflict. The counterhegemonic forces have significantly disrupted the status quo and undermined the leadership of the AKP by creating a *crisis of authority* (Gramsci 1971) in the June 2015 national elections, when the HDP managed to pass the unusually high 10% parliamentary threshold. This resulted in the HDP becoming the third largest political party, but more importantly, in the AKP losing its parliamentary majority and thereby delaying Erdogan's plans for transforming Turkey's parliamentary system into an executive presidency. During these elections, many Turks (of mostly liberal background) voted for HDP and there were different explanations for this. A key reason, we argue, was that the HDP managed to some extent penetrate through false consciousness and to make people aware of their subordinated position in society and the dangers of AKP hegemony. Resistance is after all consciousness of one's subordinate position in society in hierarchical society (Gramsci 1971). Importantly, since counterhegemony requires "reworking" parts of the existing hegemony and existing discourses (Gramsci 1971), the HDP focused on developing a highly democratic agenda that included acceptance of the pious, conservative voters, despite being a largely secular party. In this way, they were able to attract a considerable number of Sunni Kurdish (both Kurmanj and Zaza) AKP voters, tipping the political balance in favor of the HDP in the ESA and greatly alarming the AKP. Democracy was the discourse all Turkish parties historically made use of, but it was always presented as the goal, never the means. Yet, the HDP managed to convince a large segment of society that it could lead the resistance and fight for real democracy, even if many Turks remained skeptical about the nature of its relationship with the PKK. When the HDP entered parliament in 2015, the sociopolitical struggle of the democratic opposition in general, and that of the Kurds in particular, became massively empowered. The HDP was not only leading the counterhegemonic bloc, but now assumed the position of the leading intellectuals and the revolutionary party able to break the political hegemony of the dominant bloc of the AKP and President Erdogan. The early transclass activism and social mobilization that the Gezi uprisings displayed and later the HDP represented, seriously intimidated the AKP authorities and the neoliberal elite. The election results of June 2015 were seen by many observers as a Kurdish victory, a leftist victory and/or a subaltern victory. The response from the government was the expedition of the de-development process in order to gradually obliterate any political and non-political future democratic opposition, including through the use of armed conflict with Kurdish rebels.

17.5 The AKP Expedites the De-Development of the Subaltern Classes

Due to the nature of the threats to state security emerging from reactionary segments (including from the wider region), the AKP altered its form of power reproduction by shifting their focus from consent to coercion. The AKP, and particularly the current President Erdogan, developed a strong need to reassert hegemony and power across the country, and even in the wider geographical region, in order to stay in power. Economic development was no longer the government's main priority. Instead a nationalist and militarized security discourse became mainstreamed. The state became an engine for de-development and threat mitigation rather than human agency and rights protection, or democracy and sustainable development. Erdogan largely succeeded in framing democratic and/or Kurdish resistance as an existential threat to the Turkish state and part of some grand Western conspiracy to destabilize Turkey or an attempt by the "seculars" to return to the oppression of the Kemalist era.

17.5.1 Regional De-Development

Despite Turkey's massive economic growth since the early 2000s, little has changed in the Turkish Kurdistan region in terms of better health, education, employment and business opportunities, except for those willing to toe the line. Since the founding of the Turkish republic, eastern Anatolia has suffered "widespread poverty and deprivation" due to historically discriminatory economic policies, forced migration, and violent conflict (TESEV 2008). Studies have highlighted that, compared to their Turkish counterparts, Kurds experience higher levels of income poverty, unemployment, illiteracy (especially among women) and infant mortality, including lower levels of educational opportunities and educational performance (e.g. shortage of teachers, large classes, lack of mother-tongue medium instruction) (Aydin 2005; Icduygu et al. 1999; Koc et al. 2008; Yalcin Mousseau 2012). The ESA has the lowest per capita income in the country; 54% lower than the national average and a striking 70% lower than Istanbul (Yadirgi 2017, 245). At the same time, before the arrival of Syrian refugees, Kurdish laborers made up a significant majority of the working class and the urban poor living in *gecekondu* houses (Park 2012, 83), particularly those in the construction sector but most still work in the agricultural sector. Others are seasonal laborers on mainly Turkish-owned fields in the west and north and work for low wages under difficult and arbitrary circumstances, often living in tents and their children missing out on school.

The decades long war with the PKK[9] contributed heavily to the internal displacement and forced migration of at least a couple of million Kurds to the western party

[9]It should be clarified though that before the war with the PKK broke out in the 1980s the ESA was already economically underdeveloped with weak infrastructure, lack of manufacturing industry and little public investments.

of Turkey. Many also migrated because of the lack of employment opportunities as well as large-scale "development" projects such as the GAP (Southeastern Anatolia Project) river basin building, which has already displaced thousands of people. According to Yadirgi, who refers to a government memorandum, part of the GAP project's purpose was to prevent Kurdish deportees (primarily from the republican era) living in the country's west returning to their lands in the southeast (2017, 256). The building of the Ilisu Dam as part of GAP is set to wash away the 12,000 year old settlement of the southeastern town of Hasankeyf and with that a vital part of the region's history of early human settlements, putting around 80,000 more people at risk of displacement (Letsch 2017). Furthermore, the Turkish army's counterinsurgency campaign in Kurdistan since the late 1980s has included burning down forests, fields and other resources that supported local living, causing large-scale environmental destruction and ecological imbalances that still have not been adequately addressed (Morvaridi 2004; Van Etten et al. 2008).

There are great regional inequalities and disparities in public investments in Turkey and the ESA particularly stands out (Sönmez 2016; Yadirgi 2017). Between 2002 and 2007, the biggest investments in the ESA were in the energy sector but in light of the extremely low level of industrialization and wage labor in this region, such energy production has little value to the region, especially since most of it (69%) is consumed outside of the ESA (Yadirgi 2017, 253). The Kurdistan region is rich in water and energy resources and subterranean and terrestrial riches, but the vast profit made from these resources were not flowing back into the same region (TESEV 2008). The chronically low level of investment in transportation and communications (mere 8%) is particularly indicative of the state's continued policy of de-development in the region as typically investments in communications and transport generally have a positive correlation with economic growth (Haque and Kim 2003). In addition, as Yadirgi mentions, even between 1999 and 2004 when there was a long PKK ceasefire and a highly calm period, the growth and investments in the ESA changed only marginally (2017, 245).

Although most of Kurdistan at large is agrarian, there has been an unequal distribution of land ownership since Ottoman times with no significant agricultural land distribution reform to date. Although in a much lesser scale compared to in the past, feudal relations still exist in the ESA where wealthy Kurdish *aghas* maintain their traditional role as large commercial landowners with close ties to the central government, regardless of who is in power (Morvaridi 2004). *Aghas* have been accused of land-grabbing by displaced Kurdish villagers who have attempted to return to their villages. Kurdish villagers attmepting to return faced other obstacles such as conflict (e.g. landmines), harassment from soldiers, and a general lack of socioeconomic opportunities. These marginalized people felt further disenfranchised when then Prime Minister Erdogan promised the large Kurdish landowning elite that their wealth would be protected (Yadirgi 2017, 258), presumably in exchange for their continued electoral support to the AKP. In this climate of violence, forced migration, and marginalization, Kurdish and other farmers suffered from a "repression of agricultural incomes, decrease in agricultural subsidies and the sectoral terms of trade turning against agriculture" with devastating impact on the cultivation of crops and raising of livestock (ibid. 2017, 248).

Between 2008 and 2015, there were attempts at engaging in political dialogue with the PKK and its incarcerated leader Abdullah Ocalan. Despite many positive overtures, in the summer of 2015, the peace talks between the Turkish authorities and the Kurdish PKK movement collapsed. The parties were once again engulfed in violent conflict, or what might be termed a civil war with more than a thousand dead per year (Savran 2018). The war brought about detrimental consequences to human life, local economic activity, and on the material environment in Kurdistan. The war became the AKP government's official excuse for the vast acceleration of state violence, including arbitrary arrests, clamp downs on rights groups, restrictions on basic freedoms, media censorship, and military-territorial control in Syria and Iraq. Through the ruse of security, the AKP now allied with the ultranationalist Nationalist Movement Party (Turkish acronym MHP) and extended Turkish military operations as well as devastating curfews in the ESA.

This gruesome urban war with the PKK further intensified de-development in the region through such extreme measures as emergency rule, arbitrary imprisonment, restrictions of movement and access, property destruction, and gross human rights violations according to detailed UN reports (UN News 2017). The excessive use of force by the Turkish military led to a completely shocking demolishment of places towns like Cizre (Cizîr), Nusaybin (Nisebîn), and Diyarbakır's (Amed) ancient Sur district (a UNESCO World Heritage Site), resulting in over 200,000 people's internal displacement (adding to the already large figure of Kurdish IDPs). As the fighting in Sur escalated, pro-government news outlets were frequently encouraging the governmentor TOKI to begin urgent expropriation due to the "slums" and "crime" in the area. Similar excuses were used in the gentrification projects in Istanbul's Tarlabaşı, Sulukule, Okmeydanı, 1 Mayıs, and so on. Additionally, the government expropriated the land and churches of Armenian and Syriac/Assyrian communities in Sur, which had previously been restored by the pro-Kurdish local council, to enable new mass construction in otherwise protected historical heritage sites (Yenginsu 2016). In this respect, the former and popular mayor of Sur, Abdullah Demirbas (2004–2014), described the ulterior motivations behind the destruction of the town as an attempt by the hegemony to create "an impoverished, obedient people who are domesticated and whose will to resist is broken" (Lepeska 2016). In other words, the government weakens political opposition and chases lucrative construction deals at the same time.

17.5.2 National De-Development

The deliberate de-development process described above was not limited to the Kurdish populace, but gradually also became a nationwide process. This became particularly apparent after the attempted *coup d'état* carried out by a small fraction of the Turkish armed forces on 15 July 2016. The putschists' attempted coup failed, however, and the AKP remained in power. Though the AKP were now given further pretext for their socioeconomic war on the subaltern and their peer rivals, notably the Islamic Gülen Movement led by its founder Fethullah Gülen. The Gülen Movement were firmly accused by the AKP of orchestrating the coup. As a consequence, mass purges of hundreds of thousands of Gülen-accused sympathizers, media, universities, and organizations from state institutions and civil society accelerated enormously. Thousands more were either thrown in prison or moved or sought asylum abroad. However, although the Gülenists had, like the post-Islamist AKP, turned from a marginalized movement to a ruling elite class, this clash between them was a hegemonic battle (as hegemonic leadership is never automatic!) that paid little attention to the human rights or human needs of the subaltern.

Central to the AKP's maintenance of power – following HDP challenges to their electoral hegemony, the attempted July 2016 coup, the regional spillover of violence and the reignition of the Turkey-PKK conflict in July 2015 – was the systematic suppression on any form of dissent. On the national level, this systematic suppression is characterized by two streams of coercive activity. The first is the targeted nation-wide suppression of key counterhegemonic Turkish and Kurdish activists or those suspected of support for the Gülen Movement through arrests and purges. The second stream of coercive activity is the deliberate de-development of the Turkish public sector and civil society through a structural war against security, education and health providers, hospitals, schools, universities, the ambulance service, the police service, third sector providers, the professionals and clients of these services and the unions and associations that represent them. This broad umbrella of organizations and citizens have become recipients of the AKP's determined deinstitutionalization and externalization as a form of collective punishment as the AKP builds a new pattern of authority based on fear, rather than passive consent (Araj 2018).

The resulting emergency law and crackdowns since the attempted coup led to a sector-wide de-development of education services. Yet, as reactionary and counterhegemonic threats to the AKP's hegemony emerged, the anesthetizing ability of educators began to diminish (Freire 2000). An important moment that reflected the shift in the education sector to embrace the rise of an alternate discourse to war was when in January 2016, 2000 higher education staff signed a petition labelled, "We will not party to this crime", to condemn the rise in violence against the Kurds as well as to call for an end to the war with the PKK (Rea 2016). Under the umbrella of Academics for Peace, they became an easy target for the AKP's purges of the education sector and were amongst the first to experience the evolving coercive nature of political/civil society relations in Turkey. In September 2016 onwards, 463 of the petition signatories were accused of being "terrorist" sympathizers and permanently lost the right to travel, their teaching posts and their teaching licenses (Benos et al. 2017). This was then followed by the suspension of 15,700 education workers, 1500 university faculty deans, and the annulment of 21,000 teacher's licenses in the private sector (Farooq 2016; Rea 2016). Many schools and universities were shut down for short and long-term periods. Around 20 allegedly Gülen-linked universities and 1043 Gülen-linked private schools were closed down permanently, suddenly leaving about 200,000 students without educational institutions (Farooq 2016).

This represented a case of de-development on two levels. The first, the prevention of the right to work for tens of thousands of skilled workers, denying their productive contribution to the collective and individual economy. This also had spillover effects to the rest of society in terms of family cohesion and mental health of those who had lost stable incomes (Agos 2017; Scholars at Risk 2016). There was an increase in suicide rates among dismissed academic staff and also hunger strikes launched by a few in protest against their dismissal (European University Association 2017). Despite the fear of arrest and loss of work, many education workers have not ceased to resist the de-development process. In Kocaeli University, the university that was the first casualty of AKP deinstitutionalization, 19 of the academics who were discharged from their academic posts at the institution formed an educational solidarity academy where they held critical pedagogic lessons in the student union (KODA) in September 2016 (Agos 2017).

Nonetheless, it was not only teachers, their networks and social capital that were blocked by the AKP's coercive methods, but also the dissemination of knowledge and knowledge itself. Online learning and social media platforms such as Wikipedia, Twitter, YouTube and other websites were frequently blocked by the order of the AKP government (European University Association 2017). One of the new civil society organizations that was founded as part of the counterhegemony was Internet access monitor Turkey Blocks. Turkey Blocks began recording the Turkish state's violations of Internet access and increasing censorship since September 2015. For example, in Fig. 17.1, they noted that with regards to the Twitter platform, in the second half of 2016 "Turkey once again led globally in the number of content takedown requests by court order" (Turkey Blocks 2016a).

In 2016 Turkey Blocks reported shutdowns of Facebook, Twitter, YouTube, WhatsApp, Skype and Instagram through throttling: the purposeful slowdown of access to these sites, which also coincided with a government ban on the use of VPN services in Turkey. These sites, aside from being used to transfer information, spread news and keep in touch, are also disproportionately used by many small-scale entrepreneurs. Their client base, advertising potential and other business practices are all accessed through social media and therefore are reliant on it to make any money on a given day. Naturally, it is also used by activists and ordinary citizens to organize

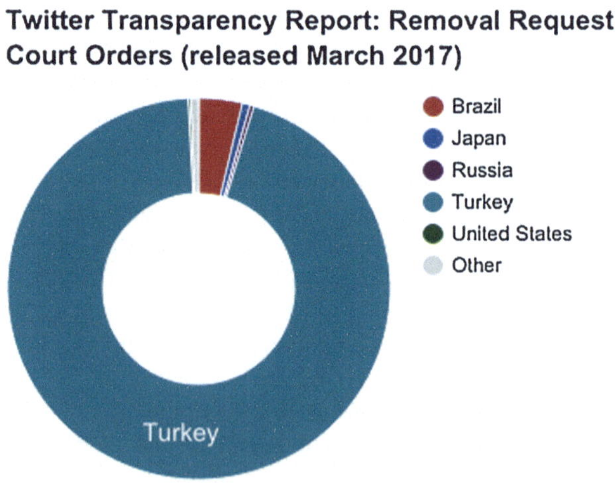

Fig. 17.1 Turkey leads in social media censorship: new Twitter transparency report (Turkey Blocks 2017)

and rally. This deliberate form of censorship can be understood as a form of collective punishment against the subaltern or the dissident classes.

Internet shutdowns in the ESA have had a direct de-development impact on the health sector in the region, where patient records, addresses, and other vital information is stored on cloud. This reportedly prevented "the supply of medical supplies to patients and crippling infrastructure" (Turkey Blocks 2016a). Thus, it is evident how the policies contributing to the steady de-structuring of one sector, impact the potential for structural growth in other sectors. Continued restrictions on the ICT sector could accelerate the process of decline across the Turkish periphery and social system.

The de-development process of the health sector is characterized by the state-led campaign of "terror and punishment" against thousands of health professionals (Benos et al. 2017). The AKP's erosion of the education sector, has also had a trickling effect to the health sector, as many academic physicians doing important research were dismissed or suspended. There was also a purge of medical international NGOs from Turkey (Benos et al. 2017). In 2015, the Turkish Medical Association reported an increase of state violations of Article 3 of the Geneva Convention in the Kurdish region due to the reigniting of the PKK-Turkey conflict. These violations have included direct assaults on health professionals, institutions and ambulances. Incidents noted included the loss of life of three health workers, the closure of pharmacies and hospitals due to curfew and increased violence, the entrance of armed security personnel and vehicles into spaces where emergency healthcare was being provided, the arrest/kidnapping of medics, and acts of physical violence by police forces on nurses and doctors (Turkish Medical Association 2015).

The challenges to the security and sovereignty of the Turkish state represented by the July 2016 attempted coup was used as a pretext to solidify the AKP's monopolization of power and win its "war of position" (Gramsci 1971). In order to win the war of position, or secure their hegemony, aside from growing authoritarianism and the suppression of basic freedoms, the AKP launched a deliberate strategy of de-development to suppress the subaltern, ensuring their subordinate social positions remained unchanged.

17.6 The Counterhegemony Today

The security dilemma that emerged from the 2016 coup and the reignition of the Kurdish PKK conflict served the AKP in maintaining its hegemony through expounding fear among the public. The AKP and President Erdogan at the forefront, framed threats to their ruling power as threats to national security itself. It was not a novel or unseen tactic, but it was a successful method since after they lost their majority in June 2015, they regained it when new elections were held November 2015 and old AKP voters returned and hardline nationalists turned to the AKP instead of the MHP. As Buzan states, a level of threat can present the pretext for a government to overturn dissent and manufacture consent (1991, 338).

However, centering the Gramscian idea of hegemony, Femia states that to build that unity "there must be a substratum of agreement so powerful that it can counteract the division and the disruptive forces arising from conflicting interests" (1981, 39). The manipulation of threat perception is what enables a state to maintain power (Buzan 1991). Erdogan chose the military approach because he believed he needed the support of hardline nationalists to achieve his broader political agenda, that is, to strengthen his presidential powers and to remain in power for another decade or more. Overall, this false consciousness that the AKP and Erdogan have so carefully crafted over the years, presenting themselves as the true "saviors" of Turkey, has actually been quite difficult for the counterhegemony to break. Yet, the Turkish opposition has persisted in the face of increased authoritarianism and political suppression.

In 2017, the main opposition party the Republican People's Party (Turkish acronym CHP) and its leader Kemal Kilicdaroglu led what they called the Justice March – a huge 25-day march from Istanbul to Ankara joined also by HDP members, other smaller opposition groups, journalists, intellectuals, writers and of course hundreds of thousands ordinary people. The event received broad national media coverage. It was an unusual but important show of unity of the opposition (Yilmaz et al. 2019). To the Kurdish political circles, the CHP remains problematic since it has largely pursued its traditional policies of Kemalist statism. It has failed to truly incorporate a wider social stratum into their party nor have they offered any concrete democratic and inclusive shifts in their political discourse. Thus, a broad, more inclusive, centre-left bloc has yet to emerge since Gezi. According to Isikara et al. (2016), "a left-wing push for a broad, independent democratic front against 'national unity' is not viable at the moment. If the Left cannot find a common line (and effective tactics) soon, it will be in serious trouble."

As for the HDP, the last few years have proved extremely difficult for the party. The powerful President Erdogan has set out to destroy it, both materially and through rigorous political propaganda, to prevent the transfer of intellectual social capital to the periphery. Its former co-leaders Selahattin Demirtas and Figen Yüksekdag and many other parliamentarians, party members and party activists are still detained or imprisoned. This has had a disastrous impact on the already fragile foundation of the counterhegemonic alliance. The party made a tactical decision when in the 2019 municipal elections it did not put up any candidates in major Western cities but decided to tacitly back the CHP opposition instead. In Istanbul, this made it possible for the CHP candidate Ekrem Imamoglu to win the mayoral title against the former AKP prime minister Binali Yildirim (Yilmaz et al. 2019).

Imamoglu's win was an extremely important political turning point and moral boost for the counterhegemonic forces in the country. In some urban centers' nationalists, socialists, liberals and conservatives united for the first time to challenge the AKP at the ballot boxes. Recently another initiative sparked the interest of commentators, the media have (at the time of writing) reporting on rumours a new political party potentially being created by former AKP heavyweights: former

President Abdullah Gül, former Prime Minister Ahmet Davutoglu, and former Deputy Prime Minister Ali Babacan that will be "true to the founding principles" of the AKP (Kirisci 2019). They would indeed form a formidable opposition against the AKP but there is currently much secrecy around it – Erdogan has warned "certain individuals" not to commit "treason" (ibid.). The establishment of such a party is likely to attract many AKP voters who are uncomfortable with the way the political climate has deteriorate. But the real question is whether they would seek alliance with the current counterhegemonic forces, in particular the CHP and HDP.

The international community has done little to halt the widening democratic gap in the country, mostly due to geopolitical concerns and trade ties with Turkey. The EU leadership has failed or refused to offer proper support to the democratic opposition in Turkey. They have turned a deaf ear to recent human rights violations, which is largely in relation to the refugee deal brokered by the EU and Turkey in 2015 and a fear of the implications of Erdogan's potential removal from power.[10] The former, yet highly popular and charismatic, HDP co-leader Demirtas stated in an interview that the HDP had given up calling for support from European political leaders but instead called upon the *people* of the EU to lobby their leaders to support democracy and human rights in Turkey (Güven 2018).

Further hope is attached to the youth of Turkey. Many of the activists and street protestors of Gezi in 2013 were largely comprised of young people. In the 2015 June national elections, a majority of those between the ages of 18–32 voted for the HDP (Araj 2018). During the presidential referendum of 2017, Erdogan lost the vote among the same demographic with a wide 5 point margin (Cagaptay 2018). Neoliberalism compounded by increased authoritarianism has not led to the employment and other opportunities first promised to this generation by the AKP. As of 2019, youth unemployment rate was around 25% (Trading Economics 2019). The purges and de-development of the recent years has violated the educational rights of many young people as well as affected their rights in the workplace (Starr 2018). As Turkey's economic crisis deepens and young people feel increasingly distant to the AKP, left-leaning opposition and civil society groups might just be able to seize a political opportunity to form a counterhegemonic bloc. It remains to be seen if those eligible to vote in the next elections of 2023 can become a solid democratic counterhegemonic force. What is certain though is that the AKP has lost its popularity of the old days and it is increasingly losing voters.

[10]In return for housing Syrian refugees within Turkey's borders, the EU gives billions of euros to the Turkish government each year.

17.7 Conclusions

This chapter has traced parts of the neoliberal development and de-development of the leading Justice and Development Party (AKP) in Turkey by framing it in a Gramscian perspective of *hegemony*. We argue that the neoliberal policies of the post-Islamist AKP governments were designed to establish national and regional hegemony through various development and de-developmental processes. Although we used the two terms separately, development and de-development can be understood as two sides of the same coin. The chapter explored in its first section Turkey's de-development, and the resistance against the AKP strategy of gaining (passive) *consent* that culminated with the Gezi uprisings in 2013. These uprisings would shape the counterhegemonic forces to come (e.g. the formation of the pro-Kurdish HDP bloc). The second section, then, analyzed the intensification of the AKP's de-development, which went hand in hand with rising authoritarianism, weakening of electoral democracy and fundamental freedoms, and the constraints to the public sphere through what is known as *coercion* in Gramscian theory. As counterhegemonic groups tried to disrupt the AKP's societal consent (e.g. the HDP's electoral win in 2015), the AKP government and President Erdogan reacted even more forcefully and accelerated the de-development process. The social and political condition of Turkey has declined markedly with strong features of dictatorship, intolerance and a lack of respect for the rule of law and due process. Many intellectuals, academics and left-wing activists continue to flee the country. The resistance against the AKP's politics advanced fiercely but in recent years has suffered near defeat after extremely harsh methods of suppression employed by the state. Despite aims to monopolize power and eliminate resistance through the use of militarized security discourses and measures, the counterhegemonic forces remain active and are slowly gaining strength – aided by a more politically conscious and continuously decreasing AKP voter base.

References

Agos. 2017. *Story of Academics Who Stay to Resist*. Retrieved from: http://www.agos.com.tr/en/article/18536/story-of-academics-who-stay-to-resist. Accessed 14 Sept 2019.

Alpan, Başak. 2014. AKP's "Conservative Democracy" as an Empty Signifier in Turkish Politics: Shifts and Challenges after 2002. *2nd European Workshops in International Studies (EWIS)*, 1–15.

Araj, Victoria D. 2018. *The Turkish Model, the Double-Security Dilemma, and the Political Reproduction of State Polities in the Middle East*, Doctoral dissertation, University of Bradford.

Arat, Yeşim. 2013. Violence, Resistance, and Gezi Park. *International Journal of Middle East Studies* 45 (4): 807–809.

Aydin, Zulkuf. 2005. *The Political Economy of Turkey*. London: Pluto Press.

Bar-On, Tamir. 2015. *From Marxism and Nationalism to Democracy: Abdullah Öcalan's Synthesis for the 21st Century*. https://kurdishissue.wordpress.com/2015/04/25/1-140/. Accessed 15 Sept 2019.

Bayat, Asef. 2013. *Post-Islamism: The Changing Faces of Political Islam*. Oxford: Oxford University Press.

Benos, Alexis, Chiara Bodini, Hannah Cowan, David McCoy, Penelope Milsom, and David Sanders. 2017. Defending Academic and Medical Independence in Turkey. *Elsevier 390* (10095): 645.

Bookchin, Murray. 2015. *The Next Revolution: Popular Assemblies and the Promise of Direct Democracy*. London: Verso.

Bugra, Ayşe, and Aysen Candas. 2011. Change and Continuity under an Eclectic Social Security Regime: The Case of Turkey. *Middle Eastern Studies* 47 (3): 515–528.

Buttigieg, Joseph A. 1995. Gramsci on Civil Society. *Boundary* 2, 22 (3): 1–32.

Buzan, Barry. 1991. People, states and fear. Hemel Hempstead: Harvester Wheatsheaf.

Cagaptay, Soner. 2018. *To Save Turkey's Democracy, the Country's Opposition Must Offer Erdogan a Grand Bargain*. https://warontherocks.com/2018/01/save-turkeys-democracy-countrys-opposition-must-offer-erdogan-grand-bargain/. Accessed 15 Sept 2019.

Can Gürcan, Efe, and Efe Peker. 2015. A Class Analytic Approach to the Gezi Park Events: Challenging the "Middle Class" Myth. *Capital & Class* 39 (2): 321–343.

Çavuşoğlu, Erbatur, and Julia Strutz. 2014. Producing Force and Consent: Urban Transformation and Corporatism in Turkey. *City* 18 (2): 134–148.

Cicek, Cuma. 2011. Elimination or Integration of Pro-Kurdish Politics: Limits of the AKP's Democratic Initiative. *Turkish Studies* 12 (1): 15–26.

Cohen, Joshua, and Archon Fung. 2004. Radical Democracy. *Swiss Journal of Political Science* 10 (4): 23–34.

Current Situation in the Turkish Higher Education Sector. 2017. *European University Association*. http://www.eua.be/activities-services/news/newsitem/2017/05/15/current-situation-in-the-turkish-higher-education-sector. Accessed 19 Sept 2019.

Dagi, Ihsan. 2013. Post-Islamism à la Turca. In *Post-Islamism*, 71–103. Oxford: Oxford University Press.

De Leon, Cedric, Manali Desai, and Cihan Tuğal. 2009. Political Articulation: Parties and the Constitution of Cleavages in the United States, India, and Turkey. *Sociological Theory*. Blackwell Publishing Inc, 27(3), 193–219.

Eslen-Ziya, Hande, and Itır Erhart. 2015. Toward Postheroic Leadership: A Case Study of Gezi's Collaborating Multiple Leaders. *Leadership* 11 (4): 471–488.

Farooq, Umar. 2016. Post-coup purge will Affect Turkey's Education Sector for Decades. *LA Times*. http://www.latimes.com/world/europe/la-fg-turkey-education-purge-2016-story.html. Accessed 19 Sept 2019.

Femia, Joseph. 1975. Hegemony and Consciousness in the Thought of Antonio Gramsci. *Political Studies* 23 (1): 29–48.

———. 1993. *Marxism and Democracy*. Oxford: Oxford University Press. https://doi.org/10.1093/0198279213.001.0001.

Freire, P. 2000. *Pedagogy of the Oppressed*. Continuum. https://www.bloomsbury.com/us/pedagogy-of-the-oppressed-9780826412768/. Accessed 25 Sept 2019.

Gençoğlu Onbaşi, Funda. 2016. Gezi Park Protests in Turkey: From 'Enough is Enough' to Counter-Hegemony? *Turkish Studies* 17 (2): 272–294.

Gosovic, Branislav. 2000. Global Intellectual Hegemony and the International Development Agenda. *International Social Science Journal* 52: 447–456.

Gramsci, Antonio. 1971. *Selections from the Prison Notebooks*. Trans. Q. Hoare and G. N. Smith, Ed. Q. Hoare & G. N. Smith.. New York: International Publishers.

Güven, Banu. 2018. Demirtas: Europe is Letting Turkey's Opposition Down. https://www.dw.com/en/demirtas-europe-is-letting-turkeys-opposition-down/a-43986216. Accessed 27 Sept 2019.

Hall, Martin. 1999. *Constructing Historical Realism: International Relations as Comparative History*. Lund University: Lund Political Studies.

Haque, M. Emranul, and Dong Heon Kim. 2003. *Public Investment in Transportation and Communication and Growth: A Dynamic Panel Approach*. University of Manchester, School of Economic Studies.

Harvey, David. 2005. *A Brief History of Neoliberalism*. Oxford University Press. https://global.oup.com/academic/product/a-brief-history-of-neoliberalism-9780199283279?cc=gb&lang=en&. Accessed 28 Sept 2019.

Hunt, Alan. 1990. Rights and Social Movements: Counter-Hegemonic Strategies. *Journal of Law and Society* 17 (3): 309–328.

Icduygu, Ahmet, David Romano, and Ibrahim Sirkeci. 1999. The Ethnic Question in an Environment of Insecurity: The Kurds in Turkey. *Ethnic and Racial Studies* 22 (6): 991–1010.

Isikara, Guney, Alp Kayserilioglu, and Max Zirngast. 2016. Turquía. Del golpe fallido al contragolpe. *Viento sur: Por una izquierda alternativa* 147: 13–19.

Kirisci, Kemal. 2019. *Is Democracy Dead in Turkey? The Re-run of Istanbul's Mayoral Race will Tell*. Retrieved from https://www.brookings.edu/blog/order-from-chaos/2019/05/10/is-democracy-dead-in-turkey-the-re-run-of-istanbuls-mayoral-race-will-tell/. Accessed 13 Sept 2019.

Koc, Ismet, Attila Hancioglu, and Alanur Cavlin. 2008. Demographic Differentials and Demographic Integration of Turkish and Kurdish Populations in Turkey. *Population Research and Policy Review* 27 (4): 447–457.

Lepeska, David. 2016. *The Destruction of Sur: Is This Historic District a Target for Gentrification?* https://www.theguardian.com/cities/2016/feb/09/destruction-sur-turkey-historic-district-gentrification-kurdish. Accessed 12 Sept 2019.

Letsch, Constanze. 2017. Turkey's 12,000-Year-Old Hasankeyf Settlement Faces Obliteration. https://www.theguardian.com/world/2017/aug/29/turkeys-12000-year-old-hasankeyf-citadel-faces-obliteration. Accessed 12 Sept 2019.

Lindberg, Staffan I. 2001. Forms of States, Governance, and regimes: Reconceptualizing the Prospects for Democratic Consolidation in Africa. *International Political Science Review International Political Science Review* 22 (2): 173–199.

Lüküslü, Demet. 2016. Creating a pious generation: Youth and Education Policies of the AKP in Turkey. *Southeast European and Black Sea Studies* 16 (4): 637–649.

Mann, Michael. 2012. *The Sources of Social Power*. Cambridge: Cambridge University Press.

Mohan, Giles, and Kristian Stokke. 2000. Participatory Development and Empowerment: The dangers of localism. *Third World Quarterly* 21 (2): 247–268.

Morvaridi, Behrooz. 2004. Resettlement, Rights to Development and the Ilisu Dam, Turkey. *Development and Change* 35 (4): 719–741.

———. 2013. The politics of philanthropy and welfare governance: The case of Turkey. *The European Journal of Development Research* 25 (2): 305–321.

Onis, Ziya. 2012. The Triumph of Conservative Globalism: The Political Economy of the AKP Era. *Turkish Studies* 13 (2): 135–152. https://doi.org/10.1080/14683849.2012.685252.

———. 2015. Monopolising the Centre: The AKP and the Uncertain Path of Turkish Democracy. *The International Spectator* 50 (2): 22–41.

Park, Bill. 2012. *Modern Turkey – People, State and Foreign Policy in a Globalized World*. Abingdon: Routledge.

Passerin d'Entrèves, Maurizio. 1992. Hannah Arendt and the Idea of Citizenship. In *Dimensions of Radical Democracy: Pluralism, Citizenship, Community*, ed. C. Mouffe, 145–168. London: Verso.

Rea, Jeannie. 2016. Advocate: Newsletter of the National Tertiary Education Union. *National Tertiary Education Union*. https://www.nteu.org.au/women/article/Turkish-education-sector-purged-%28Advocate-23-03%29-19192. Accessed 21 Sept 2019.

Roy, Sara. 2007. *Failing Peace: Gaza and the Palestinian-Israeli Conflict*. London: Pluto Press.

Sarigil, Zeki, and Omer Fazlioglu. 2013. Religion and Ethno-Nationalism: Turkey's Kurdish Issue. *Nations and Nationalism* 19 (3): 551–571.

Savran, Arin Y. 2018. *Why Peace Processes Fail: A Conceptual Analysis of the Peace Talks Between Turkey and the Kurdistan Workers' Party (PKK), 2009–2015*, Doctoral dissertation, University of Bradford.

Scholars at Risk. 2016. *SAR urges Expression of Support for Turkey's Threatened Higher Education Sector – Scholars at Risk.* https://www.scholarsatrisk.org/2016/07/support-for-turkeys-higher-education/. Accessed 21 Sept 2019.

Somer, Murat. 2016. Understanding Turkey's Democratic Breakdown: Old vs. New and Indigenous vs. Global Authoritarianism. *Southeast European and Black Sea Studies* 16 (4): 481–503.

Sönmez, Mustafa. 2016, May 23. *Regional Inequalities in Turkey not Easing.* http://www.hurriyetdailynews.com/regional-inequalities-in-turkey-not-easing%2D%2D99507. Accessed 12 Sept 2019.

Starr, Stephen. 2018. *Turkey's youth: The Last Hope for Democracy?.* https://www.thenational.ae/world/europe/turkey-s-youth-the-last-hope-for-democracy-1.742398. Accessed 26 Sept 2019.

Tansel, Cemal Burak. 2018. Authoritarian Neoliberalism and Democratic Backsliding in Turkey: Beyond the Narratives of Progress. *South European Society and Politics* 23 (2): 197–217.

TESEV. 2008. *A roadmap for a Solution to the Kurdish Question: Policy proposals from the region for the government.* https://www.tesev.org.tr/wp-content/uploads/report_A_Roadmap_For_A_Solution_To_The_Kurdish_Question_Policy_Proposals_From_The_Region_For_The_Government.pdf. Accessed 21 Sept 2019.

The Business Year. 2011. 'Head of the Class', *The Business Year.* https://www.thebusinessyear.com/turkey-2011/head-of-the-class/review. Accessed 14 Sept 2019.

Thomas, Peter D. 2013. Hegemony, Passive Revolution and the Modern Prince. *Thesis Eleven* 117 (1): 20–39.

Trading Economics. 2019. *Turkey Youth Unemployment Rate.* https://tradingeconomics.com/turkey/youth-unemployment-rate. Accessed 22 Nov 2019.

Tuğal, Cihan. 2013. *Resistance Everywhere: The Gezi Revolt in Global Perspective.* https://sociology.berkeley.edu/sites/default/files/faculty/tugal/Cihan%20Tugal,%20NPT-Gezi%20Revolt.pdf. Accessed 21 Sept 2019.

———. 2016. *The Fall of the Turkish Model: How the Arab Uprisings Brought Down Islamic Liberalism.* London: Verso.

Turam, Berna. 2015. *Gaining Freedoms: Claiming Space in Istanbul and Berlin.* Stanford: Stanford University Press.

———. 2017. Split City Versus Divided staTe in Turkey: Contrasting Patterns of Political Opposition to AKP's Authoritarianism. *Contemporary Islam* 11 (2): 185–199.

Turkey Blocks. 2016a. *Facebook, Twitter, YouTube and WhatsApp Shutdown in Turkey.* https://turkeyblocks.org/2016/11/04/social-media-shutdown-turkey/. Accessed 16 Sept 2019.

———. 2016b. *New Internet Shutdown in Turkey's Southeast: 8% of Country Now Offline Amidst Diyarbakir Unrest.* https://turkeyblocks.org/2016/10/27/new-internet-shutdown-turkey-southeast-offline-diyarbakir-unrest/. Accessed 16 Sept 2019.

———. 2017. Turkey Leads in Social Media Censorship: New Twitter Transparency Report – *Turkey Blocks.* https://turkeyblocks.org/2017/03/21/turkey-leads-social-media-censorship-new-twitter-transparency-report/. Accessed 16 Sept 2019.

Türkmen, Füsun. 2008. The European Union and Democratization in Turkey: The Role of the Elites the European Union and Democratization in Turkey: The Role of the Elites. *Human Rights Quarterly* 30 (1): 146–163.

Turner, Mandy, and Omar Shweiki. 2014. Introduction: Decolonizing the Study of the Political Economy of the Palestinian People. In *Decolonizing Palestinian Political Economy*, 1–9. London: Palgrave Macmillan.

UN News. 2017. *Turkey: UN Report Details Allegations of Serious Rights Violations in Country's Southeast.* https://news.un.org/en/story/2017/03/553062-turkey-un-report-details-allegations-serious-rights-violations-countrys. Accessed 21 Sept 2019.

Van Etten, Jacob, Joost Jongerden, Hugo J. de Vos, Annemarie Klaasse, and Esther C.E. van Hoeve. 2008. Environmental Destruction as a Counterinsurgency Strategy in the Kurdistan Region of Turkey. *Geoforum* 39 (5): 1786–1797.

Waldman, Simon, and Emre Caliskan. 2017. *The new Turkey and Its Discontents*. Oxford: Oxford University Press.
Yadirgi, Veli. 2017. *The Political Economy of the Kurds of Turkey*. Cambridge: Cambridge University Press.
Yalcin Mousseau, Demet. 2012. An Inquiry into the Linkage Among Nationalizing Policies, Democratization, and Ethno-nationalist Conflict: The Kurdish Case in Turkey. *Nationalities Papers* 40 (1): 45–62.
Yalvaç, Faruk. 2016. A Historical Materialist Analysis of Turkish Foreign Policy: Class, State, and Hegemony. *Uluslararası İlişkiler Dergisi* 13 (52): 3–22.
Yavuz, M. Hakan, and Nihat Ali Özcan. 2015. Turkish Democracy and the Kurdish Question. *Middle East Policy* 22 (4): 73–87.
Yenginsu, Ceylan. 2016. *Turkey's Seizure of Churches and Land Alarms Armenians*. https://www.nytimes.com/2016/04/24/world/europe/turkeys-seizure-of-churches-and-land-alarms-armenians.html. Accessed 21 Sept 2019.
Yilmaz, Ihsan, Mehmet Efe Caman, and Galib Bashirov. 2019. How an Islamist Party Managed to Legitimate Its Authoritarianization in the Eyes of the Secularist Opposition: The Case of Turkey. *Democratization*: 1–18.

Dr. Victoria Araj is a political analyst and activist for the rights of refugees and a mentor with the Women in International Affairs Network. Previously, Araj was a visiting fellow at Sabanci University, with the European Commission and was the commissioning editor for the Program on Civil-Military Relations in Arab States at the Carnegie Middle East Center. Araj holds a PhD in Peace Studies from the University of Bradford, UK. Her research focuses on security, authoritarianism and development in Palestine and Turkey.

Dr. Arin Y. Savran completed her PhD in Peace Studies at the University of Bradford in 2018 and is currently based with SND at the University of Gothenburg, Sweden. She was previously a Visting Scholar at Trinity College Dublin at Belfast and a Scholar-in-Residence at the Kroc Institute for International Peace Studies, University of Notre Dame, Indiana. Her research interests include the Kurds, peace processes, civil wars, social justice and radical democracy.

Part VI
Women and Children Rights

Chapter 18
Imprisoned Women and Children in Turkey: Human Rights Violations Under the State of Emergency

Ömer Faruk Gergerlioğlu

Abstract This chapter examines the violations of rights committed against women and children during the State of Emergency (OHAL) which was declared immediately after the coup attempt on July 15, 2016. Although it officially lasted for two years, its impacts continue. Narrative analysis was employed in this study. The narratives of 44 victimized women and children were included, and data were gathered through messages sent to social media accounts, letters received, social media communications, as well as face-to-face interviews. The themes of ostracism, civil death, torture, and persecution arose from the data. The findings of this research indicate that the coup attempt of July 15 was used as a pretext to eliminate a group of people. Furthermore, the data showed that the women and children in question had nothing to do with the coup attempt, but were victimized for their alleged ties with the Gülen Movement (GM). These women were exposed to all types of human rights abuses including arrests (even and commonly during pregnancy or postpartum period), detention, harassment, intimidations, job dismissals, threats, ostracism, the inability to find accommodations, the inability to find work, economic difficulties, illnesses, psychological problems, forced displacement, forced separation from loved ones, abortion, suicide and death, and torture. Moreover, women generally experienced those victimizations with their children.

Keywords Human rights violations · State of emergency (OHAL) · Women · Children · Torture

Ö. F. Gergerlioğlu (✉)
Parliament Member for Peoples' of Democratic Party (HDP), Grand National Assembly of Turkey, Çankaya, Turkey
e-mail: omerfaruk.gergerlioglu@tbmm.gov.tr

H. Aydin, W. Langley (eds.), *Human Rights in Turkey*, Philosophy and Politics - Critical Explorations 15, https://doi.org/10.1007/978-3-030-57476-5_18

18.1 Introduction

The Republic of Turkey declared a State of Emergency after the 2016 coup attempt (BBC 2016). Contrary to the common belief in the beginning that it would last only three months, the State of Emergency lasted for two years, exposing hundreds of thousands of people to civil death (Amnesty International 2018). Civil death denotes that a person has been stripped of so many of her or his civil and political rights that it is as if she or he were dead. Although 2019 marked a year since the State of Emergency was suspended officially, its negative impacts and sanctions on victims remain in effect. Hundreds of thousands of people who were in opposition to the government were subject to judicial and administrative proceedings after the coup attempt, even though no legal evidence existed against them at all.

During and after the State of Emergency period, thousands of people were dismissed from their jobs, detained, arrested, forced to emigrate, tortured, abducted, committed suicide, discriminated and ostracized by society or deprived of their right to education (Amnesty International 2018; Gergerlioglu 2019a; Tanrikulu 2019; Tevgera Jinen Azad 2017). For most of the people who were forced to live with constant fear and trauma, pre-existing health problems emerged, and deaths occurred (Gergerlioglu 2019a). According to Gergerlioglu (2019a) and Tanrikulu (2019), children who have been separated from their mothers and/or fathers, developed psychological and physical disorders due to the trauma and fear to which they had been exposed.

Considering the records of maltreatment, torture, rape, disappearance and murder cases of persons while under arrest, the costs of the State of Emergency to human welfare is alarming (Tevgera Jinan Azad 2017). The practices of the State of Emergency have either directly or indirectly affected a large part of the society; however, women and children were perhaps those who were affected the most. Therefore, this study explores the experiences and challenges that women and children have experienced as victims of the State of Emergency since it was declared.

18.2 Violence and Inventory of the State of Emergency

Violence against women and children, as well as violations of their rights, are among the most dynamic topics of discussion around the world (Radford and Stanko 1991). Among the topics discussed are gender discrimination, cultural oppression, economic deprivation, sexual abuse (harassment-rape-pornography), forced detention and abduction, slavery, murder, beating, child prostitution, victimization, mutilation, forced labor, underage marriage, and structural violence, such as inequitable educational opportunities (Bunch 1990; Chapman 1990; MacDonald 2013). Unfortunately, almost all the above-mentioned violations have occurred in Turkey (Amnesty International 2017). Every day, reports of child abuse, murders of women, or atrocities perpetrated on those detained because of alleged membership in the Gülen Movement, reach the social media (Gergerlioğlu 2019a).

Violence and human rights violations against women and children took on a darker dimension after the declaration of the State of Emergency in Turkey. Women who were victimized during the State of Emergency due to allegations of having ties with terrorist organizations are still labeled as terrorists, and their children as offspring of terrorists. As a result of this labeling, various violations of human rights have taken place (Amnesty International 2017; Girdap 2020). Women were dismissed from their jobs, ostracized and left by their families and society, became homeless, detained, tortured, harassed, arrested, separated from their children, experienced economic difficulties, and deprived of social rights (Aydin and Avincan 2020). In addition, their husbands were arrested, their property was confiscated, their freedoms were restricted (through restrictions on their passports, etc.); their children were separated from parents, left unattended, discriminated and harassed by peers, experienced psychological and physical problems or were forced to live with constant fear and trauma (Gergerlioglu 2019a; Tanrikulu 2019).

The Platform for Rights and Justice issued a report on the state of emergency entitled the Violations of Rights and Social Aspects in Post-15 July 2016 State of Emergency." The report highlighted the grievances experienced after the coup attempt, especially economic troubles and suicide attempts. In a survey of 2,173 people, including 630 women, who were victims of the state of emergency, the report revealed that 16.7% of the people being detained in prisons are considering suicide, making suicide plans or have attempted suicide (The Platform for Rights and Justice 2017). However, the Stockholm Center for Freedom reported difficulties in assessing the actual suicide rate among those who had been detailed. They stated that although the "53 alleged suicide cases SCF has been able to document may suggest a pattern of impunity in Turkey's prisons and detention centers (some are unofficial holding centers), it is likely that they represent only a partial picture in the terrible drama being played out in Turkey" (p. 7). (Stockholm Center for Freedom 2019).

The Republic of Turkey is a member of the United Nations, and therefore it must comply with the provisions of the Universal Declaration of Human Rights which is the first and most comprehensive United Nations document on human rights. Considering the human rights violations that women and children have experienced at the hands of the government and the police, correctional officers, judges, prosecutors, and other officials, the conclusion can be reached that articles 3, 5, 9, 11 and 17, of the declaration of Human Rights have been violated. These articles of the Declaration stipulate that;

1. Everyone has the right to life, liberty, and security of person (Article 3).
2. No one shall be subjected to torture or cruel, inhuman or degrading treatment or punishment. (Article 5).
3. No one shall be subjected to arbitrary arrest, detention, or exile (Article 9).
4. Everyone charged with a penal offense has the right to the presumption of innocence until proven guilty according to the law in a public trial at which he or she has all the guarantees necessary for his defense (Article 11/1).

5. No one shall be arbitrarily deprived of his property (Article 17/2) (Universal Declaration of Human Rights 1948).

Moreover, in addition to the violations of these fundamental rights, female victims of the State of Emergency reported horrible abuses. Detainees in official and clandestine detention centers were subjected to distress and strip searches, and threatened with rape (Amnesty International 2017; Gergerlioglu 2019a). Unfortunately, rapes, the threat of rape and sexual assaults were only part of the maltreatment and intimidation that thousands of arrestees and prisoners experienced after the failed coup attempt on 15 July 2016 (Amnesty International 2017). Some male detainees were threatened with being forced to witness the raping of their spouses and children if they refused to sign certain documents (Stockholm Center for Freedom 2017). In addition, women faced serious sexist and harassing treatment by law enforcement officers during house raids and detentions (Tevgera Jinen Azad 2017).

These events were evidence that the Declaration on the Elimination of Violence Against Women, that the Republic of Turkey adopted as a member of the United Nations in 1993, was ignored in the aftermath of the State of Emergency. This declaration had condemned violence against women in all its forms, including gender-based violence acts that resulted in "physical, sexual or psychological harm or suffering to women" (p. 2). Furthermore, the declaration pronounced that states should create policies that would eliminate violence against women and punish individuals who committed acts of violence against women (United Nations Declaration on the Elimination of Violence against Women 1993). Thus, the human rights violations that occurred during and after the State of Emergency indicate that the Republic of Turkey has disregarded the requirements of the Declaration.

In addition to physical mistreatment, arbitrary detention was among the leading human rights violations that women and children suffered during and after the State of Emergency. In Turkey, the number of inmates in prison increased significantly across the board after the declaration of State of Emergency. According to data that the Turkish Institute of Statistics (TÜİK) released, in 2015 there was a total of 183,770 inmates, of which 177,262 were male and 6,508 were female; in 2017 there was a total of 232,340 inmates, of which 222,444 were male and 9,896 were female; and in 2018, there was a total of 265,000 inmates, of which 254,665 were male and 10,335 were female (TÜİK 2017–2018). These numbers indicate a 52% increase in the number of female inmates and a 30.2% increase in the number of male inmates in a one-year period from 2017 to 2018.

Compounding the problems caused by increased incarcerations, the limited capacity of prisons is another major problem in Turkey, causing misery (Aydin and Avincan 2020; Tevgera Jinen Azad 2017). In response, the European Committee for the Prevention of Torture and Inhuman or Degrading Treatment or Punishment (CPT) has advised that Turkish authorities should limit the number of persons sent to prison or adopt policies designed to overcome prison density issues (Council of Europe 2018; Stockholm Center for Freedom 2017).

As of December 2017, about 600 pregnant women were estimated to be in Turkish prisons while another 100 were in custody (Human Rights Watch 2018; Office of the United Nations High Commissioner for Human Rights 2018; Stockholm Center for Freedom 2017). According to Article 16 of Turkey's Law on Execution of Punishments No. 5275, the imprisonment of women who are pregnant or who are not six months past the date of the birth of their child should be postponed (Law on Execution of Punishments No. 5275 2004). Furthermore, according to Human Rights Watch (2018), women and children should not be imprisoned without evidence. However, in Turkey, women and children have received prison sentences or have been arrested in the investigation phase (Stockholm Center for Freedom 2017). In these cases, a violation of the Execution Law has occurred. The women who were persecuted as a result of the noncompliance to the criminal justice system ranged from 18 to 80 years of age (Stockholm Center for Freedom 2017).

Even though capacity and the concomitant limited resources accompanying the capacity issue related to prison populations negatively affect all detainees, the impacts of these limitations are considerably worse for women who are in prison with their babies. The situation has become so dire that women take turns using the limited numbers of beds on which to sleep, and babies experience developmental problems as a result of not being able to crawl on the solid grounds in prisons (Gergerlioglu 2019a). Mothers and children who are exposed to such inhumane and degrading practices are at risk of health problems and death. According to Tevgera Jinen Azad (TJA) (2017), the transfer of female prisoners to hospitals without female staff, having to sit side-by-side with male prison guards, and traveling long distances, leads to sexual violence for women and children. In addition, another major issue is the lack of experts who can professionally handle the specific problems of female detainees.

Generally speaking, female prisoners suffer more emotional distress than do male prisoners (Quaker Council for European Affairs 2007). This is mainly because women, who are incarcerated away from their homes and families, cannot maintain family ties (Bastick and Townhead 2008; Council of Europe 2009). Particularly stressful for women is leaving their children behind. Therefore, many women in prison face a series of difficulties that may directly or indirectly hinder the social and emotional development of their children. Consequently, infants living in prison with their mothers or living outside away from them are known to be at risk of developing aggressive behavioral problems (Sleed et al. 2013).

The Bangkok Rules, which the United Nations adopted in 2010, is a set of 70 rules for the humane treatment of women, designed to address the special needs of female prisoners and highlight the differences between male and female prisoners that are often ignored (Philips and Harm 1998). The rules cover a variety of issues including admission procedures, healthcare, humane treatment, search procedures, and children who accompany their mothers into prison (UN General Assembly 2010). These rules stipulate that children held with detained mothers should never be considered as detainees, and the environment in which they are detained should be as close as possible to the outside world (Office of the United Nations High Commissioner for Human Rights 2018). Specifically, the rules read that "prison services must provide for the full range of needs of children in prison with their mothers, whether medical, physical or psychological. As these children are not prisoners, they should not be treated as such" (UN General Assembly 2010, 9). Unfortunately, in most women's prisons in Turkey, children staying with their mothers are not considered as separate individuals, and must share their mother's living space and conditions (Gergerlioglu 2019a).

Currently, 865 children are known to be living in Turkish prisons with their mothers (Gergerlioglu 2019b). Compounding this atrocity for nearly all of these children is the imprisonment of their fathers who face the same charges as their mothers. Some children whose parents are both in detention, but who are not in jailed with them, live either with their relatives or in government institutions. Consequently, some children are separated from their siblings as well as their parents (Gergerlioglu 2019a).

Even though the severity of the grievances that the State of Emergency has caused, appears to have declined to a certain degree towards the end of the third year, arrests, extrajudicial executions, and civilian massacres are continuing (Gergerlioglu 2019b). Article 17 of the Turkish Constitution reads: "No one shall be subjected to torture or ill-treatment; no one shall be subjected to penalties or treatment incompatible with human dignity" (para 1). Therefore, the current situation indicates that these provisions have lost their meaning for the Turkish government.

18.3 Methodology

The research design employed in this qualitative research was narrative analysis, which is an approach that involves the analyzing of the narrations of people regarding the actual events they have experienced (Andrew et al. 2008). According to Moen (2008), narrative analysis allows a large enough scope in which to evaluate the interactions among people over time and place, and the ability to analyze personal experiences that involve continuous change and progress. Narrative analysis covers the beliefs, values, and interactions of participants and allows them to comprehend their experiences about certain events through narration (Reid et al. 2005).

The sources of the data used in this research were as follows: letters and direct messages sent to official social media accounts from women who were victimized during and after the State of Emergency period, and from their relatives; notes taken during face-to-face interviews with the women participating in Decree Law (DL) platforms (platforms formed by people who were dismissed from their jobs or whose rights were abridged by Decree Laws); anecdotes from semi-structured interviews and news media; and reports and surveys prepared by institutions and people. In addition, the researchers occasionally met with the victimized women and children during the research period, spent time with them, and closely followed their victimization.

The research examined the experiences of women and children who were victimized due to allegations of affiliation with the coup attempt or terrorist organizations after the failed coup attempt in 2016. At the first stage of the research, the research group formed codes by listening to and reading the inputs in detail. In the second stage, members of the research group gathered and determined the themes through a comparison of the categories they provided from those codes. The themes that appeared were ostracism, civil death, torture, and persecution. The analyses revealed that the themes of ostracism and civil death, and torture and persecution, should be handled together. Additionally, the related news media was searched.

The participants of this study were women and children who were victimized during and after the State of Emergency period and reported their victimization. Thousands of e-mail messages and statements were received daily from the State of Emergency victims, each of which enumerated human rights violations. One researcher is a parliamentary deputy of the People's Democratic Party. Another researcher, who is an attorney, is also a human rights activist, and shared all reports of events that have been shared with her in her social media account pertaining to human rights violations.

This chapter included the narratives of 44 women and children, who experienced more severe victimization than others. Thus, this research used purposeful sampling. According to Maxfield and Babbie (1998), the selection of a sample in purposeful sampling depends on a researcher's knowledge about the population or the purpose of the research. The language of the interviews, incoming messages, and letters were all in Turkish. Hence all data collected were transcribed and translated into English. Finally, two experts edited and confirmed the language.

Multiple data sources (triangulation), including interviews, documentation, and letters and text messages from participants, were used for data analysis in order to increase the validity and reliability of the research. The cogency method, which is used in qualitative research for reliability, concerns the determination of the accuracy of the data by researchers (Sandelowski 1986). Another method that increases plausibility is data triangulation. Triangulation requires each researcher to analyze the data individually, and then collaboratively compare the results that emerged (Johnson 1997). In this study, four groups, each comprised of four experts, read the data used in the research and formed themes individually. Then, members of the groups shared their themes and determined the common themes that appeared. The experiences of the participants were not included in the dataset without being verified.

The dataset consists of the information received from women and children gathered from their experiences between July 20, 2016, and August 14, 2019. The research was limited to the narratives of 44 people. The participants of the study either stated that they were living in fear, or their narrations indicated that they had lives full of fear. Therefore, the participants generally provided information about their status from bogus accounts. However, they were assured that their credentials would never be shared with third parties. Implementing a data collection method that removed increased risks or threats to the participants enabled them to narrate their experiences in absolute freedom.

18.4 Findings

In this section of the study, the violation of rights that the 44 women and children experienced during and after the State of Emergency are discussed within the framework of the themes that emerged from the analysis of the data. The themes are ostracism, civil death, violence, and persecution. The hardships that these victims experienced are based on those four concepts. Examples of the victimizations of the participants are presented below.

18.4.1 Ostracism and "Civil Death"

The word "ostracism" means being excluded and not being accepted to a place or community (Kelimeler 2019). The cases of ostracism will be examined under the terms isolation, social stigma, labeling, social stress or polarization, and not being accepted to a community. Viewed in isolation, the phrase "civil death" has little meaning; however, seen from the perspective of the participants of this study, "civil death" conceptually meant unemployment, the deprivation of rights, and public disgrace.

The interviews with the State of Emergency/DL victims, as well as their messages and letters, suggest that all the victimized citizens felt ostracized, and that they had been left to die a civil death. Indeed, during the interviews, one participant said:

> We are being treated as if we are second-class citizens in our own country. There are no jobs, food, or medical services. We may not benefit from State services. And they do not allow us to leave. What shall we do? Die?

Another participant emphasized that she felt ostracized and, as a result, experienced psychological problems:

> I felt greatly humiliated. I felt so sad. I cried a lot. We were ostracized by the people around us. We have had financial problems since my husband was dismissed from his job and jailed. My husband has been in jail for 16 months. My child and I have had psychological problems. We do not have any income now. My child and I are in a fix.

One participant said that her experience went beyond mere ostracism:

> When I was dismissed from my job, I was pregnant for 9 months, and I had a difficult delivery. I was interviewed at the courthouse when my daughter was 40 days old. My husband, his elder brother, sister-in-law, and I were all dismissed. My husband, his elder brother, and sister-in-law were arrested. Although I knew that I was completely innocent, I got scared by every ring of the doorbell or the phone. I was thinking that I was losing my psychological health. My husband found a very hard job for a little wage. We started to live in a city that I did not know at all. We have been ostracized and labeled.

Another participant noted how much psychological trauma her children experienced due to being ostracized, in addition to the inhumane treatment to which she had been exposed:

> Only Allah and I know what we went through, what we were exposed to, and what we saw. We were staying at the government housing. Masked police officers entered our house abruptly with long-barreled weapons in their hands at 5 am while we were sleeping. They called us to put our hands up before we could say anything. Since my husband did not want to be seen in his pajamas by the officers, he tried to get his clothes on quickly in the bedroom. However, the officers did not wait and entered the bedroom, incapacitated him on the ground, and rear-handcuffed him. He was still in his underwear. Because of this case, which happened before the eyes of my children, they had psychological problems. We were also ostracized where we lived. My children are still receiving psychological treatment. My husband could not use his hands for four months after he went to jail.

Another participant referred to the stress she had due to ostracism and stated that she could not even enjoy having a baby, for whom she had waited for such a long time. To make matters worse, she had to stay alone with her 7-month old baby after her husband's incarceration.

One participant summarized the dreadful experience of being ostracized in the following words:

> Everybody around became "prosecutors," and we become "suspects." We were declared "members of an armed terrorist organization," even though we had nothing to do with weapons. Our relatives forgot that they were related to us, but they suddenly became founders of a political party. Even the purest feelings were split into two. We were badly ostracized. They became such people that they would kill and impale us if they caught us alone, and they have yet to change. Some people forgot the sin of killing a human being. Children cried, "mommy and daddy," and mothers cried, "my little one." Everyone had her own grief in disguise behind her own door because a society that was very much willing to kill us emerged if we went out. Whenever the word "FETÖ" was mentioned, all eyes turned to us.

Victims agreed that people looked at them with hatred and treated them viciously.

The victims of the State of Emergency who were impacted most significantly were the children (Gergerlioglu 2019b). One mother discussed the role of a teacher in her children's ostracism by his friends, and offered an example of how educational institutions act outside their missions. The father of the child had been linked GM or labeled as a FETÖist, and his teacher ostracized and humiliated him by saying before his friends: "It is [sometimes] necessary to strangle people at birth."

One child victim of the State of Emergency stated that his educational life was severely damaged by the negativities to which he was exposed and that he had developed psychological problems as well. He said:

> ... My father looked for a job and could not find one for a long time. Since my mother had chronic lung disease, we had difficulty covering her hospital and medication expenses. My mother had a doctor at a hospital, which was later closed by a decree-law. We could not see him anymore, and we had to go to private hospitals since there was not enough care at State hospitals. My sibling and I had to leave our school, which was closed by a decree-law and experienced the stress of adaptation to a new school during our high-school and university placement period. My sibling was diagnosed with an anxiety disorder and has been getting psychiatric support and antidepressant medication.

All participants commented that their children had experienced psychological problems. One participant suggested that her victimization was multidimensional, including ostracism, economic problems, and psychological disorders. She said:

> My husband became unemployed. Since a trustee had been appointed at his workplace, he had not been able to receive his salaries for 6 months. We could not pay our credit cards. We were socially ostracized. Our children's friends cut off their relationships. Our families did not protect us. We had to move. We spent all our savings. We were worried by every doorbell ring, thinking that it was the police. My children, and especially my daughter, got depressed. My husband's detention that started three months ago was the last drop of persecution. I have been trying to survive with my two daughters away from my hometown. My daughter says she does not feel secure. My neighbors do not know about the developments and think that my husband and I split. Those are the things that come to my mind first.

One major issue that the individuals who were ostracized and left to civil death lamented, was that the justice mechanism ran differently than the global norms. The following is one of the comments made about this issue:

> Being declared a traitor and ostracized by society is more than enough. It was disgusting that the principal of the school where I worked told me with humiliation that I was fired. Being taken from my house by the police for an investigation is disgraceful.... As well as I could learn on the national media, even those who shoot children playing in a park are released in this legal system. My husband was in jail for the same allegations, and I had an 11-year old son alone at home. I do not understand why such a legal system kept me in detention for a night. It was irritating that the judge at the Court of Peace shouted at us continuously: "Did the President not warn you?" I did not understand what crime I was warned. I did not commit any crime.

This comment demonstrates that society and the State saw victims of the State of Emergency/DL as criminals who committed more severe crimes than harassment, rape, theft, and blood-shedding terrorism, and responded accordingly. Another participant explained rights violations, how she was sentenced to civil death, and why she did not count on the justice mechanism by stating:

> My husband was suspended on April 26, 2017 and remained suspended for about 15 months. During this period, no judicial or administrative procedure was conducted, or no investigation was initiated. He was dismissed from his job by the Decree-Law No. 701 on July 8, 2018, with no reason offered. We have been psychologically affected deeply during this period. We had to move out of the government housing in 15 days and started to live with my parents-in-law. I have a son and am pregnant for 5 months. We have been ostracized by the circle we lived in. We cannot find jobs. Since we were dismissed by decree-laws, they do not employ us. We have financial problems. We are completely isolated from society. We strive to hold on to life discontentedly and desperately. We no longer have expectations from life. We do not count on justice in Turkey at all. We are worried about our future. My husband has gotten more irritable and is always restless. He does not enjoy life and prefers to stay alone most of the time. I am worried about him, too. The peace of our family has been broken.

According to Gergerlioglu (2019b), prohibitions were imposed on victims of the State of Emergency for working, starting a business, and providing licenses and certificates in the public and private sector. Victims who could not secure jobs suffered through substantial economic hardships. One participant stated that, when she applied for employment, the employer refused her, saying: "If we employ you, they will close down our company, and you cause other employees to lose their jobs."

This statement suggests that fear has spread over all regions of Turkish society, implicating that many State of Emergency victims who lost their jobs because of decree-laws cannot find jobs due to being labeled. In essence, it may be habitual for employers to have such fears, and media releases of some government officials and bureaucrats may be presented as evidence. For example, Osman Zabun, Isparta Provincial president of the AK Party, stated that citizens should not be worried about "what so many people will do" and added:

> They may polish shoes and work as porters. With all due respect, they should thank Allah if they can pay for the price of the pain they have caused to this nation, with such little suffering. This is not a simple act of coup. It is the attempt to start a civil war and a massacre in the country. If we thought of "what people will eat" in the face of such an attempt, it would be unconscionable. Let them eat tree roots. They should expect the help of the power groups and countries for which they made Turkey prone to invasion. This country has nothing to give them (İstanbul Gerçeği 2016).

Such expressions are a clear depiction of how much ostracism the State of Emergency victims were exposed to; that they were abandoned to a civil death; and why citizens who were not involved in any part of the issue were afraid of being seen with the victims. Similarly, Nihat Zeybekci, Minister of Economy at the time, delivered the following speech (Haberturk 2016):

> You know that there is a saying: "I wish I died." We will punish them in such a way that they will beg for death, let alone be executed. We will make them beg. We will put them in such jails, and they will serve their sentences in such holes that they will never see the sun as long as they breathe. They will never hear human voices again. They will beg for being killed. This punishment will be worse than execution.

Many other bureaucrats and government officials made similar speeches that tried to lead people to ostracize the mass declared as FETÖists and abandon them to civil death. Regarding this issue, one participant made the following statement:

> My husband and I had filed for a divorce before I was dismissed from my job, and a month after the dismissal, we got divorced. I suddenly lost both my job and my husband. I suffered a lot as a lonely and unemployed woman who stayed at a rental apartment and had no savings. I am still suffering. I am getting by, partly with my family's support and partly with the money I earn from temporary work that I find. However, we do not have any future assurance. We live only for the day. My older son's classmates treated him as a "son of terrorists" at his high-school senior class last year because of his parents' dismissal, and he could not make his selections at the university placement test. Since he could not get well prepared, his test score was not enough for the schools in the city where we were residing, and we did not have enough money to send him to universities in other cities. He had to retake the exam this year. Some of my family members quit calling me on the phone for the fear that my phone is wiretapped. They keep away from me to avoid any possible harm they may face for contacting me. On the other hand, some continue their same relationships with me as in the past. But the greatest disappointment was that I was left to civil death after being labeled as a terrorist without being investigated after struggling for 21 years to lead my students to the good and the respect for their homeland and the Creator. I cannot stand that. I did not deserve it. I am not even the last person to cause harm to her country. While I was a teacher loved by her students, I suddenly became one who hides her past. Not being able to talk about my past in the circles I got involved in converted me into a bag of nerves. I cannot even recognize myself. I cry every time and everywhere. The whole burden of life is on my shoulders. I live only because I have to, and I struggle for my children.

In addition to such ill-treatment, the State of Emergency victims experienced restrictions of their "human and citizenship rights" in several fields. All had restrictions imposed on employment or going abroad and were given a disparaging label. How fundamental rights may be restricted during the State of Emergency is explained in Article 15 of the Turkish Constitution (2016), which reads:

> In times of war, mobilization, and the State of Emergency, the exercise of fundamental rights and freedoms may be partially or entirely suspended, or measures derogating the guarantees embodied in the Constitution may be taken to the extent required by the exigencies of the situation, as long as obligations under international law are not violated.

As can be deduced from the article, restrictions of rights imposed during the State of Emergency have two necessary conditions: not violating international law and being proportional to exigencies of the situation. What occurred in Turkey violated international law. Pursuant to Article G of the European Social Charter, the rights and principles set forth in the Charter may only be subject to restrictions by law (not by State of Emergency decrees) in a democratic society for the protection of rights and freedoms, or for the protection of public interest, national security, public health, or morals. The European Council adopted the European Social Charter in 1996, which Turkey ratified on October 6, 2004. Furthermore, according to Article 90 of the Turkish Constitution, the Charter has the force of law in domestic law. Thousands of people were dismissed from public service through the State of Emergency/DLs or were imprisoned without a trial or being able to present a defense.

Although the State of Emergency was lifted in 2018, its effects and applications still ripple throughout the country. Therefore, those practices that doom people to a civil death in defiance of the universal principles protected by international law should be terminated, and the rights of victims should be reinstated.

In addition to exclusion and civil death, the theme of torture and persecution was revealed in the study. Within the scope of the theme of exclusion and civil death, participants presented how they were excluded from society and how it evoked their emotions. Their experiences of torture and persecution, both psychologically and physically, as well as how they were persecuted by state authorities, are shared concurrently.

18.4.2 Torture and Persecution

The second theme that emerged from the data was torture and persecution. The statements of participants, human rights reports prepared within the last three years, and news from the media, reported that many persons, including women and children, experienced torture and persecution (Amnesty International 2018; Aydin and Avincan 2020; Gergerlioglu 2019a; Stockholm Center for Freedom 2017; Tevgera Jinen Azad 2017; Office of the United Nations High Commissioner for Human Rights 2018). Thus, the lives of many people were devastated due to the torture and persecution they were subjected to during and after the State of Emergency (Aydin and Avincan 2020; Gergerlioglu 2019a).

Such persecution included abduction. For example, seven people were abducted by authorities in February 2019, however, the calls from their wives and other relatives seeking information about their status have gone unanswered by government officials. A report on social media read:

> Salim Zeybek was abducted in Edirne before his wife and two children. They were taken to separate vehicles. Zeybek's wife and children were taken to Ankara by unidentified people. Those people said: "We are the State. You should not talk about it to anybody."

In another instance, the police abducted six men. On July 26, 2019, the police informed four of the wives of persons who had been abducted that their husbands were in detention at the Division of Counter-Terrorism of the Ankara Police Department. However, the whereabouts of the remaining two persons remained unknown. Fortunately, four people were allowed to contact their wives while they were being detained at the Counter-Terrorism Division of the Ankara Police Department. However, they said that they did not request counsel and asked their wives to close their social media accounts. Thus, it can be inferred from their behavior that they were under threat, and the police wanted to scare the women. Confirming these assumptions were the opinions of the spouses of the kidnapped persons during the interviews.

In August 2019, the relatives of Yusuf Bilge Tunc, who had been abducted, reported that they could not reach him. Although his relatives found his private car, he has not been heard from since then. In addition, Gokhan Turkmen has also disappeared. Gokhan Turkmen's wife voiced her desperation, "We have not heard from my husband for 175 days. We have yet to receive the phone call that we have been expecting. Would you empower our voices, which are very weak now?" It is unknown where those people are, and their wives and children continue to live in fear.

Although I, as a researcher, have repeatedly submitted a motion to the parliament and asked questions to the Minister of the Interior, he has not yet made a statement.

Abduction cases are not limited to men. The suffering revolutionist Ayten Ozturk, who was abducted from Lebanon and exposed to torture at the Division of Counter-Terrorism of the Ankara Police Department for 6 months, went through offers enough evidence to perceive the extent of violence against women during the State of Emergency.

Ayten Ozturk was the first woman known to be tortured in TEM (Guven 2019). Ozturk described all the tortures that she was subjected to. She was handcuffed for about 25 days, calculating the number of days according to the breakfasts that was provided to her. She was repeatedly raped with an electric baton, and her body was shocked. She said that when she passed out, her head was pushed into a bowl full of water. She was tied to the wall and stripped naked, and was exposed continuously to promises of beatings and curses. In addition, Ozturk added that when she was arrested and taken to prison, inmates counted 898 scars on Ozturk's body (Guven 2019).

She alleged in her 12-page defense that a torture center existed in Ankara and it was where she was tortured for months.[1] In spite of these horrifying allegations, officials abstained from making any statements.

Saturday Mothers, who had been searching for relatives who were kidnapped years before the State of Emergency, were subjected to police violence when they used their constitutional rights to attempt to learn where their children were.

Another practice to which women were exposed during the State of Emergency was the purposeful infliction of fear. The statement of the following participant shows that she was exposed to psychological violence, fear, and persecution. She said:

> My husband was not home when they came over to our house to arrest him because he did not want to surrender and facilitate what tyrants wanted to do. One of the officers told me that they would arrest me on behalf of my husband if I did not find him. I told him that it was not fair, and I wanted to see the written order they had. Then the officer responded: "There is no order, but I can easily get it from the prosecutor. It is no big deal." As a result of my resisting attitude, they made a detailed search in the house and left without detaining me. I was scared that my child would stay unattended if I got arrested. Ten months later, I was arrested due to the statements I made during my husband's hearings. Police officers forced me to align others. At the courthouse, both the prosecutor and the judge told me that I would be released in the case that I benefited from showing remorse and revealed the names of some people, and I would stay in prison for a tiny portion of the imprisonment I would be sentenced to. Even though I repeatedly said that I would have admitted my crime if there had been any, I was subjected to the same treatment again and again.

The statements of the participants also indicated that they were threatened with the mistreatment of their children. One participant said, "My husband was subjected to unimaginable types of torture. He was threatened with our children and me. Those threats were of an ignoble type and with sexual content."

People may or may not be a criminal, but the threats, violence, and persecution are a grave violation of their rights. Even if a person in detention has, in fact, committed a certain crime, his wife or children do not deserve to be subject to such threats. The mother of one victim explained the difficulty of the situation in which she found herself:

> My daughter was arrested. My son-in-law has been in jail for 2 years. Their child has been able to see his father only during visiting days since he was born. This is another family tragedy. The authorities must be very happy now. They have ruined another child's life.

Another person who has been arrested with her baby during the State of Emergency was Ayşe Teacher. Ayşe Teacher was imprisoned with her baby for saying, "Children should not die", but was released after a while. Although Ayşe Teacher and her baby had been persecuted, after being released, she said, "we've always been behind our words. Our words are our honor. I will repeat it anytime, anywhere. Children don't die; mothers don't cry. No child's hair should be damaged." She said that she would continue to live in line with her beliefs without submitting it.

[1]Please see https://www.patreon.com/posts/27624554

Although the number of women who have been convicted in Turkey is made public, how many of them are mothers remains unknown. However, the written and e-mail messages in this dataset indicate that most of them have children. The pain that a woman under arrest suffers doubles in the case in which she is a mother. One mother used the following words to express her thankfulness to Allah for the condition she was in after listening to the story about a baby she met when she went to jail to visit her husband:

> My husband had been in jail for about a year. I went to jail for a non-contact visitation. While I was waiting in the waiting hall after my application, the puzzled looks of a baby attracted my attention. The baby was sitting on a table and looking around timorously. While I was playing with the baby, I asked the baby's grandmother why he looked around like that. At that time, the mother approached us and said: "My baby and I had stayed in jail in another city for four months. We were released yesterday. We have come here to see my husband." When I asked her why they were jailed in another city, she said: "When I talked about violations of rights to which I was exposed to a columnist, the public prosecutor learned about it, and then exiled me to a jail outside this city." After listening to their story, I decided that my victimization was not so grave and thanked Allah for that.

After the fear empire was created due to the State of Emergency that was announced after July 15, it was clear that the government would not tolerate the exercise of the constitutional rights of the citizens. For example, although the mother of Yüksel Resistance, Veli Saçılık, was dragged by law enforcement officers for several meters during the resistance, she could not file a lawsuit against the police. Regarding the situation Sacılık expressed his indignation with the experience by stating, "We're in the defendant's chair, while the defendant's chair is supposed to have cops."

The messages and statements received for this dataset revealed that the effects on those arrested and detained and the effects on their relatives may remain with them until they die. Some had completely lost hope. For example, a woman, whose husband was in jail in a city away from where they reside, had an accident on the way to the jail for visitation and lost two daughters, her father, and mother-in-law. The father, who was in solitary confinement, went through major trauma, and continuously called the names of his deceased children from the window of his cell. Despite the cries of the mother who was heavily injured and hospitalized, her husband was not released. Another mother who was dismissed by a Degree Law (DL) committed suicide after she returned from visiting her husband in jail, leaving two children behind.

Some messages and letters in the dataset demonstrate that the extent of cruelty during the State of Emergency period went beyond logic. For example, consider Sezen Atas, who was the wife of a martyred sergeant. She was pregnant for 8 months during her husband's funeral and attended the funeral in a wheelchair because she could not stand. Atas was arrested for the second time in July 2019, despite having a 2.5-year old child. However, after reactions on social media, she was eventually released.

Some of the messages and letters received confirm that the cruelty that took place during the State of Emergency defied logic. For example, Sezen Ataş is the wife of a martyr petty officer. She was 8 months pregnant when she attended the funeral of her late husband. Despite being a single mother of a 2.5-year-old child, in July 2019 she was detained for the second time. Fortunately, she was later released as a result of reactions on social media. However, the state had not refrained from treating the wife of a person the state identified as a martyr poorly.

Unfortunately, many women and children who were exposed to torture and persecution had illnesses. For example, Mrs. Canan Utangac was taken to jail after she went through a series of operations. First, she was accidentally burnt and then broke her spinal cord as a result of falling from the bed. These injuries placed her in a challenging situation when she was in the Sincan Jail. She required the use of a toilet bowl because of the burns on her body. However, the jail room lacked one and thus this intensified her victimization. Unfortunately, even in such a circumstance, she was not released. Furthermore, it is known that women arrestees who require operations decline them because they recognize that they will be returned to jail after the operations. A teacher who was dismissed by a Decree Law was detained while she was pregnant and started bleeding. Nevertheless, she was arrested and sent to jail. Tragically, she lost her health because of what she went through, and her baby died in the womb.

Another fatal case is that of Nesrin Gençosman. A relative of the young girl who died passed away for a while because she knew that Nesrin was being sought, but she was innocent and thought she might be mistreated. Regardless, she was arrested by the police. Due to the adverse conditions of the prison, she contracted pneumonia. However, the transfer from prison to the hospital was delayed, and her medication was withheld. After suffering from a heart attack, she was finally taken to hospital where she was diagnosed with acute pericarditis, acute myocarditis, pneumonia, and respiratory failure. Despite her failing condition, her lawyers barely succeeded to get her released from the Erzurum 3rd Assize Court. Tragically, Nesrin died in pain at a young age. Although this incident echoed in social media for days, the authorities did not make any statement. In October 2019, Gençosman's older sister was arrested for helping relatives in prison.

In addition to the attitude of government officials, inhumane treatment of jail officials marked the State of Emergency period. For example, Mrs. Gulden Asik, who was in Bandirma M-Type Penitentiary Institution, lost her 7-week old baby in-utero and had to undergo a surgery. She was released from the hospital one day after the surgery and taken back to jail. She noted the following conversation between a guard and a commander, which she witnessed: "Since the commander had just taken over the duty, she asked about the condition of the baby. The female officer responded: "Sir, it is too young. Only a 7-8- week old piece of garbage."

A relative of a convict shared the following observation and showed how female inmates are subjected to persecution:

> Female inmate A.G., who was staying in Tekirdag Jail, knocked on the door and called the guard. A female guard came to the door and asked what the inmate wanted. The mother inmate asked for baby food. The guard went to the canteen and returned with a box of baby food, but it was not the correct one. The mother said: "This food is not appropriate for my baby; it is for older children." Then the guard got angry, said, "You are too much nagging"

and threw the food to the mother. The mother said to the guard: "Do not be rude!" Then the jail administration considered those words as "assault and threat against an official," and she was sentenced to 10-day solitary confinement.

Some children who stayed with their mothers developed severe health problems. Inmate Rabia Tay stays with her 2-year old son Tunahan who has autism, in Sincan Jail, and inmate Bahar Altun stays with her daughter Ebru who has Down Syndrome, in Trabzon Jail (personal letter from participant). These two children are identified as having special needs, but courts have rejected requests for release.

Some women found out that they were being sought by the police right before they delivered their babies in the hospital. Thus, some of them were detained with their babies after delivery, and some of them were arrested. Relatives of these victims sent us photos of the mothers after delivery as well as photos of police officers who waited at the door of delivery rooms. The photos often showed that the officers were displeased with what they were doing and were acting out of fear due to orders that they had been given. An email from a female teacher confirmed this conclusion:

> Police officers arrested a mother and a father who were both teachers and got dismissed by a decree-law in a district in the Aegean Region. However, their three children, ages of 3, 5, and 8, stayed behind at home unattended. One of the officers felt sorry for the children and called the public prosecutor to ask for his permission to leave the mother at home. The prosecutor refused the request by saying, 'Did they ask me when they became terrorists?' It was evening when the parents were being taken outside their apartment. The oldest child rushed to the door of the lift and said to the mother: "I wish you had taught me how to cook pasta so that I can feed my siblings!"

The police officer who was involved in this event could not sleep until morning and cried because of the tragedy.

Although some women crossed the wall of fear and reported their status to the competent units, others remained mute. The State of Emergency is full of stories of fear, sin, violation of rights, and anti-democratic attitudes. For example, a letter of English teacher, Halime Gülsu, who lost her life as a result of the discomforts she had been arrested while complaining to Prime Ministry Communication Center (BİMER) from her prison, demonstrates this. She, as a person who had devoted her life to her students, was portrayed as a terrorist.

Some of the victims, who do not desire to surrender to the Erdoğan regime, left Turkey and continued their lives as refugees (Gurer 2019). However, these victims are having great difficulty as well. Consider a video shared on the social media about teacher Esma who left everything she had behind and crossed the Evros River with her 3 children. In the video, she talked into the camera, with her baby in her arms, and wished for salvation for all the victims. Meanwhile, two of her children were crying, saying, "Mom, I am freezing." According to information received, Teacher Esma died abroad and left her children motherless. This is how another woman narrated her story of attempted to escape from the country:

> My husband and I had been in disguise for 1.5 years in order not to surrender to the Erdoğan regime. When it became unbearable to live like that, we decided to leave the country. However, we were caught by the Turkish police at the border of the Edirne province.

> When they began beating my husband, I shouted. One of the officers hit me in the head with the grip of his weapon. I fell with the impact of the hit. After my husband saw this, he started to scream to the officers to leave me, but the officers continued applying force. Then followed detention and arrest. (Letter from participant)

The State of Emergency/Degree Law victims were dismissed from their jobs, prohibited from leaving the country by restrictions imposed on their passports, left to rot in jails, suffer from hunger and ostracism, and watch their children suffer psychologically.

Many universities abrogated the rights of arrestees to take exams during the State of Emergency period. Some universities expelled them without taking their petitions regarding their current statuses into consideration. The rights to education of most of the State of Emergency victims were revoked. Although many messages regarding this issue were received, the following can be considered as the cornerstone in terms of perceiving the extent of the victimization in education:

> I was a student at a university in Istanbul before the coup attempt. I had submitted my thesis proposal after making a great effort; however, after the coup attempt, none of the professors wanted to work with me. They refused my proposal for a number of reasons and made life miserable for me. In the end, when one of the professors had to work with me, I prepared a new proposal and submitted it to him. He said he liked it very much and signed it. Two more professors in my committee also liked my proposal and signed it. After a month, I went to university to submit my thesis progress report. During my presentation, one of the jurors forced me too much and asked questions. Although I answered all the questions logically, she was not satisfied. They asked me to go out, made their decision about me and called me in. They had made a negative decision. Both my thesis advisor and the member of the committee threatened me in the room. The member said to me: 'Your husband was dismissed from his job. Now, bring us a document from the State of Emergency Commission showing that you are not related to the GM. You cannot graduate unless you bring us this document. If you bring this document, I will take care of your thesis, help you graduate and put your gown on you with my own hands' When I said, "Now, shall we put the thesis aside and talk politics?" to the professor, he said "Yes." I said to him, 'My husband was dismissed, but he will acquit one day. Even if my husband is a criminal, the principle of individual criminal responsibility prevails. You may not judge me for that." My words irritated the professor so much that he shouted at me and showed me the door. Then he used his political power and had me expelled from my school, which I loved and for which I had made too much effort.

The participant's words indicated that relatives of the State of Emergency/Decree Laws were also persecuted, excluded, and their educational rights were taken away from them. However, according to Article 20 of the Turkish Penal Code, the responsibility for penalties is personal. Nobody can be held responsible for anyone else's actions. In addition to this, it is seen that the violent massacres have been made in the universities known as the science center due to political differences.

18.5 Discussion and Conclusion

The aftermath of the failed July 15, 2016 coup attempt is full of disgraceful events for the Republic of Turkey. The data collected in this research are evidence of the fact that a country massacred its own people. According to Gergerlioglu (2019a), 98.7% of the victims of the State of Emergency had an educational level of college and up. In addition, 83.9% of the victims have thought about leaving the country (Gergerlioglu 2019a). Such an exodus will represent a tremendous socio-economic and socio-cultural loss for the country. The victims of this persecution desire to go abroad because they were experiencing “civil death” (revocation of their well-earned diplomas, dismissal from their jobs, employers’ reluctance to employ them because of the warnings at entry to the social security network, lack of safety of life due to detention-arrest, threats and torture).

Among the 48-member states of the Council of Europe, Turkey had the highest rate of increase in the number of jails and ranked 9th in the total number of jails in 2017 (Tevgera Jinen Azad 2017). The construction of new jails continues unabatedly (Sözcü 2019), and it is evident that the increase in jail constructions is because of the overcrowding after the coup attempt of July 15. Although the State of Emergency lasted 2 years, the violations of rights have continued even after the State of Emergency was dissolved, and thousands of people, including women and children, have been sent to jails and prosecuted while under arrest. Even national and spiritual holidays are made unbearable for this ostracized part of the society.

The coup attempt on July 15 was converted into a political coup by the government; all constitutional violations were legalized, and pretexts were used to maneuver out of the law through the adoption of decree-laws (Tevgera Jinen Azad 2017). Throughout this period, positive legal norms were violated, the presumption of innocence was ignored, arrests were conducted without the prosecution having to prove its allegations, and victims had to prove their innocence (Gergerlioglu 2019a). The violations were increased to such an extent that prosecutors and judges continued the prosecution and disregarding whether the accused were sick, pregnant, mothers, elderly, or children (Human Rights Association (IHD) 2018). The Office of the United Nations High Commissioner for Human Rights (2018) documented at least 50 women who delivered their babies immediately before or after they were detained or arrested. According to the Human Rights Association (2019) data, the number of critically sick inmates in Turkey stands at 458. In addition to the difficulties those people have in reaching health services, serious problems are faced in providing medical evaluation reports from the Institution of Forensic Medicine because the institution is not independent or impartial (Human Rights Association (IHD) 2019).

The State of Emergency was declared on July 20, 2016, immediately after the coup attempt of July 15 and remained in force for two years. Even though officials had stated that the reason for the declaration of the State of Emergency was to take security measures against the coup attempt, the data collected for this particular research indicates that the victims prosecuted during the State of Emergency, and after, were convicted of either plotting coup or membership to a terrorist organization. Thus, the government used the coup attempt as a pretext to wipe out a particular group of the population (Amnesty International 2017). However, according to the Human Rights Association (2019), those who are not considered to constitute a serious or concrete threat against national security must be excluded from security measures. In total, about 612,347 people were investigated between July 2016 and July 2018, which was the State of the Emergency period (United States Department of State – Bureau of Democracy Human Rights and Labor 2018). Many of those people were arrested for alleged affiliation with the Gülen Movement (United States Department of State – Bureau of Democracy Human Rights and Labor 2018). Noteworthy, is that a considerable portion of them are women.

The evaluation of the data revealed the themes of ostracism, civil death, torture, and persecution. The victims were either ostracized by their families and social circles or had a perception that they were ostracized by the government. In addition, all the victims believed that they were left to a so-called "civil death" as a result of the ostracism. In addition, according to Amnesty International (2016–2017), people who were allegedly affiliated with the Gülen Movement went through serious torture and maltreatment practices during detention and arrest processes. Some victims developed intense, long-lasting psychological problems (Gergerlioglu 2019b).

Of the 31 Decree Laws that were adopted during the State of Emergency, 15 involved provisions concerning the dismissal of public servants such as academicians, teachers, and doctors. During the two years of the State of Emergency period lasted, 136,049 public servants were dismissed from their jobs (The Inquiry Commission on the State of Emergency Measures 2018), and their names were announced in the Official Gazette as terrorists without finalized judicial decrees. The assets of 965 companies and 107 people in 43 provinces were transferred to the Saving Deposit Insurance Fund (MAZLUMDER 2018). The victims who lost their jobs could not obtain employment due to the labeling. The data suggests that the women were under stress because of being unemployed and struggling against economic problems, in addition to the torture were subjected to.

The findings of this chapter demonstrate that, while all the victims continued their lives in fear, the process was harsher for the women and children. Female and child victims stated that they were subjected to systematic torture. The Office of the United Nations High Commissioner for Human Rights (2018) reported that at least six cases women were arrested while they were visiting their husbands in jail, and their children were left unattended.

18.6 Recommendations

The data collected for the research demonstrate that social strain has prevailed since the failed coup attempt in 2016, and the social costs may continue to increase if the strain is not eliminated. Considering the findings from the data, the Turkish government should consider the following suggestions and put them into practice:

1. All the allegations of maltreatment and torture must be investigated; the investigations must be supervised by national and international mechanisms, and due process must be followed.
2. Criminal investigations must be initiated immediately against officials who have been found to have committed torture, and they must be prosecuted in accordance with universal law.
3. The provisions of Article 16 of the Law on Execution of Punishments No. 5275 must be immediately put into practice, and women being unlawfully held in jails must be released immediately.
4. The women and children who experienced psychological trauma during the State of Emergency period must be provided with psychological assistance.
5. The conditions for the children under arrest, together with their mothers, must be improved in terms of nutrition, education, counseling, and toys.
6. Because strip searches of women in jails comprise inhumane treatment, this practice must immediately be terminated.
7. The gender-specific needs of women inmates, and the child-specific needs of the children who stay with them must be taken into consideration.
8. Sick patients must be released immediately.
9. Pregnant and postpartum women and those who have children, must be interviewed without being detained.
10. In most instances, inmates who are mothers must be allowed the alternative of house-arrest during the prosecution stage.
11. The conditions of jails in Turkey must be improved in accordance with the standards that the European Committee for the Prevention of Torture and Inhuman or Degrading Treatment or Punishment (CPT) has determined.
12. The victims who were dismissed must be returned to their jobs if their connection with the coup attempt is not substantiated.
13. The necessary regulations must be adopted to make all the judicial institutions operate outside political influence and within universal legal norms.
14. Because no legal mechanisms defend the rights of the victims of the State of Emergency in Turkey, the applications made by the State of Emergency victims to the European Court of Human Rights must be examined in an expeditious manner.
15. In addition to the suggestions listed above, damages caused in Turkey by the State of Emergency in economic, social, political, scientific, and intellectual realms must be determined, and effective remedial methods must be determined.

References

Amnesty International. 2017. *Amnesty International Report 2016/2017: The State of The World's Human Rights*. London: London Amnesty International UK. https://www.amnesty.org/download/Documents/POL1048002017ENGLISH.PDF.

———. 2018. *Amnesty International Report 2017/2018: The State of The World's Human Rights*. London: London Amnesty International UK. https://www.amnesty.org/en/latest/research/2018/02/annual-report-201718/.

Andrews, Molly, Corinne Squire, and Maria Tamboukou. 2008. *Doing Narrative Research*. Thousand Oaks: SAGE Publications.

Aydin, Hasan, and Koksal Avincan. 2020. Intellectual Crimes and Serious Violation of Human Rights in Turkey: A Narrative Inquiry. *The International Journal of Human Rights* 24 (8): 1127–1155. https://doi.org/10.1080/13642987.2020.1713108.

Azad, T.J. 2017. *Information Report on the State of Emergency and Violation of Women's Rights in Prisons*.

Bastick, Megan, and Laurel Townhead. 2008. *Women in Prison: A Commentary on the UN Standard Minimum Rules for the Treatment of Prisoners*. Geneva: Quaker United Nations Office. https://www.peacewomen.org/sites/default/files/HR_Prisoners_QUNO_2008_0.pdf.

BBC. 2016. *Türkiye'de olağanüstü hallerin tarihi* [Date of the extraordinary circumstances in Turkey]. https://www.bbc.com/turkce/haberler-turkiye-36852284.

Bunch, Charlotte. 1990. Women's Rights as Human Rights: Toward a re-vision of Human Rights. *Human Rights Quarterly 12* (4): 486–498.

Chapman, Jane Roberts. 1990. Violence Against Women as a Violation of Human Rights. *Social justice 17*: 2. (40 (1990): 54–70.

Constitution of the Republic of Turkey. 1982. https://www.tbmm.gov.tr/anayasa/anayasa_2018.pdf.

Council of Europe. 2009. *Annual Penal Statistics Space 1*. http://www.coe.int/t/dghl/standardsetting/cdpc/bureau%20documents/PC-CP(2011)3%20E%20 %20SPACE%20I%202009.pdf.

———. 2018. Committee for the Prevention of Torture. Report to the Turkish Government on the visit to Turkey carried out by the European Committee for the Prevention of Torture and Inhuman or Degrading Treatment or Punishment (CPT). https://rm.coe.int/168079457a.

Gergerlioglu, Omer Faruk. 2019a. 2. Yılında OHAL'in Toplumsal Maliyetleri [Costs of State of Emergency]. *Mağdurlar İçin Adalet I*. https://magdurlar.myfreesites.net/2-yilinda-ohal-i%CC%87n-toplumsal-mali%CC%87yetleri%CC%87.

———. 2019b. Düşünme Vakti: KHK'lıların Hali [Time to Think: State of Emergency]. https://youtu.be/LlhVqV88mCM.

Girdap, Hafza. 2020. Human Rights, Conflicts, and Dislocation: The Case of Turkey in a Global Spectrum. *American Journal of Qualitative Research 4* (1): 69–84. https://doi.org/10.29333/ajqr/8266.

Gurer, Cuneyt. 2019. Refugee Perspectives on Integration in Germany. *American Journal of Qualitative Research 3* (2): 52–70. https://doi.org/10.29333/ajqr/6433.

Guven, Cevheri. 2019. Ankara'daki işkence merkezinde 6 ay işkence gören Ayten Öztürk her şeyi anlattı. *Bold Medya,* June 14. https://boldmedya.com/2019/06/14/ankaradaki-iskence-merkezinde-6-ay-iskence-goren-ayten-ozturk-herseyi-anlatti/.

Habertürk. 2016. Nihat Zeybekçi: Lağım fareleri gibi ölecekler. https://www.haberturk.com/gundem/haber/1275177-nihat-zeybekci-lagim-fareleri-gibi-olecekler.

Human Rights Association (IHD). 2018. *World Children's Day: Children are Children with their rights*. https://ihd.org.tr/en/wp-content/uploads/2018/11/IHD-2018-Report-on-Rights-of-the-Child-in-Turkey.pdf.

———. 2019. *IHD 2018 Report on human rights violations in Turkey*. https://ihd.org.tr/en/ihd-2018-report-on-human-rights-violations-in-turkey/.

Human Rights Watch. 2018. *World Report, 2018*. New York: Human Rights Watch. https://www.hrw.org/world-report/2018.

Istanbul Gercegi. 2016. *AKP'li İl Başkanı'ndan ihraç edilen memurlara: Ağaç kökü yesinler* [The Officials Who Were Expelled from the AKP's Provincial Chairman: They Were Allowed to Eat Tree Roots]. https://www.istanbulgercegi.com/akpli-il-baskanindan-ihrac-edilen-memurlara-agac-koku-yesinler_111050.html.

Johnson, Burke R. 1997. Examining the Validity Structure of Qualitative Research. *Education 118* (3): 282–292.

Kelimeler. 2019. *Dışlanmak Nedir?* (What is the ostracizatio). https://kelimeler.net/D%C4%B1%C5%9Flanmak-kelimesinin-anlami-nedir.

Law on Execution of Punishments No. 5275.2004. *Ceza ve Güvenlik Tedbirlerinin İnfazı Hakkında Kanun*. http://www.mevzuat.gov.tr/MevzuatMetin/1.5.5275.pdf.

MacDonald, Morag. 2013. Women Prisoners, Mental Health, Violence and Abuse. *International Journal of Law and Psychiatry 36*: 293–303.

Maxfield, Michael G., and Earl R. Babbie. 1998. *Research Methods for Criminal Justice and Criminology*. Belmont: West/Wadsworth.

Mazlumder. 2018. *OHAL Dönemi Hak İhlalleri Raporu* [Report of Violations of the State of Emergency]. Istanbul: Solidarity Association for Human Rights and the Oppressed. https://drive.google.com/file/d/19HRL6VEBlQrGtLTi_dKqC6xvlW-hFwXS/view.

Moen, Torill. 2008. Reflections on the Narrative Research Approach. *International Journal of Qualitative Methods* 5 (4): 56–69.

Office of the United Nations High Commissioner for Human Rights. 2018. *Report on the Impact of the State of Emergency on Human Rights in Turkey, Including an Update on the South-East* (March). https://www.ohchr.org/Documents/Countries/TR/2018-03-19_Second_OHCHR_Turkey_Report.pdf.

Phillips, Susan D., and Nancy J. Harm. 1998. Women Prisoners: A Contextual Framework. *Women Therapy 20* (4): 1–9.

Quaker Council for European Affairs (QCEA). 2007. *Women in Prison: A Review of the Conditions in Member States of the Council of Europe*. Brussels: Quaker Council for European Affairs. http://www.qcea.org/wp-content/uploads/2011/04/rprt-wip1-main-en-feb-2007.pdf.

Radford, Jill, and Elizabeth Stanko. 1991. Violence Against Women and Children: the Contradictions of Crime Control Under Patriarchy. In *The Politics of Crime Control*, ed. K. Stenson and D. Cowell, 186–202. London: Sage Publications.

Reid, Shyanne, Helene Berman, and Cheryl Forchuk. 2005. Living on the Streets in Canada: A Feminist Narrative Study of Girls and Young Women. *Issues in Comprehensive Pediatric Nursing 28* (4): 237–256. https://doi.org/10.1080/01460860500396906.

Sandelowski, Margarete. 1986. The Problem of Rigor in Qualitative Research. *Advances in Nursing Science 8*: 27–37.

Sleed, Michelle, Tessa Baradon, and Peter Fonagy. 2013. New Beginnings for Mothers and Babies in Prison: A Cluster and Randomized Controlled Trial. *Attachment & Human Development 15* (4): 349–367.

Sözcü. 2019. *9 milyar lira yatırımla 48 yeni cezaevi geliyor* [Investment of 9 Billion Pounds Comes to 48 New Prisons]. https://www.sozcu.com.tr/2019/gundem/9-milyar-lira-yatirimla-48-yeni-cezaevi-geliyor-4562242/.

Stockholm Center for Freedom. 2017. *Jailing Women in Turkey – Systematic Campaign of Persecution and Fear*. Stockholm. https://stockholmcf.org/wp-content/uploads/2017/04/Jailing-women-in-Turkey.pdf.

———. 2019. *46 Purge Victims Have Died by Suicide in Post-coup Crackdown: Report*. Stockholm: https://stockholmcf.org/46-purge-victims-have-died-by-suicide-in-post-coup-crackdown-report/.

Tanrikulu, Sezgin. 2019. *Düşünme Vakti: KHK'lıların Hali* [Time to Think: State of Decree]. [Video]. https://www.youtube.com/watch?v=EmJgQzSOdKE.

The Inquiry Commission on the State of Emergency Measures. 2018. *Olağanüstü Hal İşlemleri İnceleme Komisyonu Faaliyet Raporu 2018* [Disaster Recovery Commission Annual Report 2018]. https://ohalkomisyonu.tccb.gov.tr/docs/OHAL_FaaliyetRaporu_2018.pdf.
The Platform for Rights and Justice. 2017. *Rapor: OHAL tutuklularının yüzde 16'sı intiharı düşündü* [Report: 16 percent of prisoners consider suicide under State of Emergency]. https://www.dw.com/tr/rapor-ohal-tutuklular%C4%B1n%C4%B1n-y%C3%BCzde-16s%C4%B1-intihar%C4%B1-d%C3%BC%C5%9F%C3%BCnd%C3%BC/a-41945448.
TÜİK (Türkiye İstatistik Kurumu (Turkish Statistical Institute)). 2017–2018. http://www.tuik.gov.tr.
UN General Assembly. 2010. United Nations Rules for the Treatment of Women Prisoners and Non-Custodial Measures for Women Offenders (the Bangkok Rules): note/by the Secretariat, 6 October 2010, A/C.3/65/L.5. https://www.refworld.org/docid/4dcbb0ae2.html Accessed 27 February 2020.
United Nations. 1948. *Universal Declaration of Human Rights*. https://www.ohchr.org/EN/UDHR/Documents/UDHR_Translations/eng.pdf.
———. 1993. *Declaration on the Elimination of Violence Against Women*. https://www.un.org/documents/ga/res/48/a48r104.htm.
United States Department of State – Bureau of Democracy Human Rights and Labor. 2018. *Turkey 2017 Human Rights Report* https://www.state.gov/reports/2018-country-reports-on-human-rights-practices/turkey/.

Omer Faruk Gergerlioglu received his medical doctor degree from Anadolu University in 1990. He worked several years as a medical doctor at various hospitals in different cities in Turkey. Dr. Gergerlioglu has been elected as a director Kocaeli Brach of the Association for Human Rights and Solidarity for the Oppressed (MAZLUMDER), Istanbul based non-governmental human rights organization in 2003. In 2007, he has been elected as a general director for MAZLUMDER. He has been published many articles and reports on human rights issue in Turkey. Currently, he is elected parliament member for Peoples' of Democratic Party (HDP) and he is a member of human rights inquiry Committee for the Grand National Assembly of Turkey.

Chapter 19
Trauma of Turkish Women and Children in an Era of Political Unrest

Vonya Womack

Abstract The chapter Turkish Women and Children in an Era of Unrest highlights through a series of vignettes drawn from interviews conducted by the author how recent developments in the Justice and Development Party (AKP)/Hizmet Gülen Movement (HGM) split has affected women and children's rights. While recognizing violations of women's and children's rights has been present for some time, the author limits her discussion to one particular group, the HGM Turkish women and children caught in the web of persecution perpetrated by Erdogan's policies initiated after the July 15, 2016 coup attempt. The chapter explores human rights violations, displacement, and individual and communal trauma. Through family stories, the author explores political, ethical, psychological, and cultural factors impacting refugee Turkish women and children. Reports of this trauma can potentially awaken the global community to action understanding the plight and resilience of the human spirit of these Turkish women and children.

Keywords Hizmet Gülen Movement · Trauma · Political unrest · Displacement · Human rights violations

19.1 Introduction

The violation of basic human rights, insecurity and the threat of violence often lead to trauma and victimhood. This is manifest in the current purge of Gülen Movement sympathizers or others in Turkey at odds with Erdogan's government. Often Turkish women and children are the recipients of gross injustices during these turbulent times. This chapter will illustrate and analyze the plight of Turkish women and children and address how to secure their futures through assistance and healing.

V. Womack (✉)
Cabrini University, Radnor, PA, USA
e-mail: vonyawomack@gmail.com

H. Aydin, W. Langley (eds.), *Human Rights in Turkey*, Philosophy and Politics - Critical Explorations 15, https://doi.org/10.1007/978-3-030-57476-5_19

Although concerns about the rights of women and children are and have been important in various sectors of Turkish society at different times, this chapter will focus on one particular group, the Hizmet Gülen Movement (HGM), whose rights have been under threat in recent years. HGM is used throughout this chapter to identify this group. The author offers the reader a series of vignettes that illustrate the ordeals of Turkish women and children associated with HGM and ways to help them address and assist them in their plight. This chapter does not address the sum total of women's experience in Turkey.

But first, what is the background leading up to the Turkish exile in Greece? Turkish President Recep Tayyip Erdogan blamed Fethullah Gulen for the 2016 coup attempt and consequently professionals and their families sympathetic to HGM found themselves targets. In Erdogan's crackdown these persons were frequently labeled as terrorists and subject to informant's reporting their activities and whereabouts. This was the case of Ahmet, his wife Fatma and their three children. As Ahmet, a medical professor at a top university in Turkey, sat in his prison cell in Ankara he had little word regarding his wife, Fatma, and three children who were in Greece. His only solace was that they had made it safely across the border after a harrowing escape. He worried continually about how they might best fend for themselves in their new environment and he reflected deeply on the events that had led up to his family's current circumstances.

When Recep Tayyip Erdogan took the oath of office in August 2014 he become the 12th president of Turkey. Political opposition including professionals and career politicians feared that even after a lower than expected vote of 52%, Erdogan would pursue his own agenda thus exercising tighter control of government (Orucoglu 2015).

An example of this can be seen in the April 2017 Constitutional Referendum vote abolishing the post of prime minister making the presidency an executive post with broad sweeping powers. An additional reform package amended 15 laws, further restricting the independence and control of the judiciary. Amnesty International (2019) also cites use of vague terminology such as "terrorist activities" as a pretext for criminalizing acts such as insulting the President.

Ahmet and Fatma and a few of Ahmet's colleagues and their wives at an unnamed medical university were openly advocating for democratic reforms, thus ushering in a new day for Turkish citizens. They had high hopes since Turkey began aspiring to achieve European standards promoting more democratic ideals. But after the coup attempt of July 15, 2016, that advocacy came under excruciating attack. Erdogan blamed Gülen as the orchestrator of the coup and then began to arrest anyone associated with HGM as well as anyone opposed to leadership. He subsequently declared a state of emergency and suspended the European Convention of Human Rights. He ordered the closure of 180 media outlets and Gülen schools (Amnesty International 2018).

Even Ahmet and Fatma began to worry that any personal criticism of the government by private citizens might place them on the radar of police censors. Their worries came to fruition sooner than expected when an informant complained to university officials and possibly to the police about Ahmet's support for Fethullah Gülen and opposition to Erdogan's policies. Because of this complaint Ahmet was jailed for a day, fired from his job at the university, and at his court date he was sentenced to six years in prison for disloyalty and his association with Gülen's Movement.

In retrospect, Ahmet blamed himself for not seeing clearly all the personal implications of these events as they were unfolding. As an avid follower of political events, he took special notice during Erdogan's corruption scandal that *Zaman News* withdrew support for Erdogan's agenda and the Justice and Development Party (AKP). The government shut down *Zaman News* and accused them of espousing terrorist agenda blamed largely on the followers of the HGM.

Muhammed Fethullah Gülen, a Turkish Islamic scholar born in 1941 in Erzurum, Turkey, who philosophically and practically advocated a centrist political agenda while embracing democratic modernity. He initiated an international faith- based organization known as the HGM. The word *hizmet* means service in Turkish. Today there are between five and ten million followers of the movement around the world. As a result of HGM, schools, foundations and other initiatives quickly took root in approximately 1500 schools in 80 countries. There are 140 HGM schools in 26 states in the USA. In Turkey HGM has founded hospitals, charities, banks, a publishing house, newspapers, and radio and television stations (Markoe 2016).

Ahmet and a number of his associates were attracted to Gülen's philosophy and theology. They shared the common values of strong ethical conduct, progressive education, civil society, and religious tolerance. Ahmet and Fatma's attraction to Gülen's values came with great cost to the family. As of 2018, Fatma and three children sit idly by in refurbished factory quarters in Greece lacking the fine amenities of their fashionable home in Turkey while Ahmet remains in a Turkish prison (V.S. Womack, personal communication, August 17, 2018). These events have left Fatma traumatized and insecure. She has learned of a relative in Germany who might assist her if she can locate there. But since immigration policies in Germany and other European nations are tightening as of late 2019 (Gurer 2019), Fatma's plight is increasingly dire.

Hundreds of families associated with HGM have not fared well. Frequently, families are separated with the arrest of a father as in Ahmet's case. Wives and mothers have little choice but to flee with their children before they too are incarcerated. As of October 2019, the plight and persecution of sympathizers with HGB residing in Turkey, most of whom are professionally educated persons, is relatively unknown to the outside world. However, this "hidden" reality of human rights violations perpetuated by Erdogan's government has not been widely publicized in the national press (Amnesty International 2018).

19.2 Human Rights Violations

The fundamental universal rights of human beings that cannot be abrogated by political authority include the right to life, liberty, education, equality before the law, right of association, freedom of speech, information, religion, movement and nationality (Kabasakal Arat 2017, United Nations Human Rights Office of the High Commissioner(OHCHR) 1989). Unfortunately, there are vast differences between theory and practice and all too often practice results in gross violation of human rights. International law does not often have the will or wherewithal to enforce accountability. According to the Stockholm Center for Freedom (2019), Turkey has attacked its own judicial and court system in the name of terrorism by arresting lawyers whose critical role it is to protect the rights of everyday citizens. Without due representation no one is safe and intellectuals including members of the teaching, medical, and law professions become primary targets (Aydin and Avincan 2020). Major contractors and leaders within oppositional political parties often become targets for arrest as well. Amnesty International (2019) reports that by the end of 2018 over 20% of the prison population were detainees following the crackdown of the 2016 coup. Over 120,000 public sector workers were arbitrarily dismissed from their jobs charged with "terrorist" links.

As mentioned in the introduction, Erdogan's pretexts for arrests and harassment by the police were exacerbated by proclamations of national emergency that he then prolonged indefinitely but canceled in July, 2018. Ahmet is a case in point since he was arrested on hearsay, suspended from his job as a medical doctor and incarcerated, and charged with disloyalty to nation. Other accounts on a larger scale have been documented. According to Butler and Toksabay (2016) over 10,000 Kurdish teachers were fired September 8, 2016 under a clause of national emergency issued by Erdogan for alleged links to terrorist groups. Such grandiose political actions clearly instill incredible fear and violate human rights and fundamental freedoms.

Moyn (2018) maintains that despite significant progress in the recognition of human rights, the tide may be turning placing human rights in jeopardy. This is attributed to the rise of radical populism and nationalism that diminishes respect of civil liberties in parts of the world in recent decades. Turkey is one among other countries that illustrate this. When the political state creates an atmosphere of fear it seeks to silence dissent and consolidate its power. If a government goes to the extreme of jailing women, it creates societal angst where no one is safe. In the chaos women and children, feeling powerless to control their destinies, are stripped of their dignity and fall victim to human rights abuses (Stockholm Center for Freedom 2017). This is the case of Turkish women, children, and extended families of HGM.

19.3 Rights of Children

The preamble, The Convention on the Rights of the Child in 1989, adopted by the United Nations General Assembly and available through the United Nations Human Rights Office of the High Commissioner (OHCHR), states the following:

> Convinced that the family, as the fundamental group of society and the natural environment for the growth and well-being of all its members and particularly children, should be afforded the necessary protection and assistance so that it can fully assume its responsibilities within the community,

> Recognizing that the child, for the full and harmonious development of his or her personality, should grow up in a family environment, in an atmosphere of happiness, love and understanding,
>
> Considering that the child should be fully prepared to live an individual life in society, and brought up in the spirit of the ideals proclaimed in the Charter of the United Nations, and in particular in the spirit of peace, dignity, tolerance, freedom, equality and solidarity.

Upon closer examination, this preamble asserts the primacy of the family and the protection and well-being of the child within its community. Further, it asserts preparation for life within a nurturing environment. Unfortunately, children of parents involved in the HGM can claim none of these autonomous family rights under current circumstances.

19.4 Displacement and Trauma

Let us define displacement and trauma and place within context of our discussion. The International Organization for Migration (2019) defines displacement as adapted from Guiding Principles on Internal Displacement, the "movement of persons who have been forced or obligated to flee or to leave their homes or places of habitual residence, in particular as a result of or in order to avoid the effects of armed conflict, situations of generalized violence, violations of human rights or natural or human made disasters" p. 1. SAMHSA (2014), defines trauma as "an event, series of events, or circumstances that is experienced by an individual as physically or emotionally harmful or life threatening and that has lasting adverse effects on the individual's functioning and mental, physical, social, emotional, or spiritual well-being" (p. 7). These two key definitions undergird an understanding of individual and communal trauma and healing.

19.4.1 Individual and Communal Trauma and Healing

The author finds healing can occur when opportunities are provided for traumatized persons to share their stories. This is supported by Guribye et al. (2011) who indicate that by sharing narratives persons can reconstruct meaning for their very existence and perhaps modify or better cope with the trauma they are experiencing. Such communal practice lightens isolation and loneliness and increases the group's ability to mobilize resources providing hope and healing in the process.

Three crucial aspects to all treatments of traumatic stress include safety for the individual, processing and integrating the trauma for the individual and re-engagement with the larger community. Without these key principles, in place, a successful process of trauma work cannot happen (Kaminer and Eagle 2010).

19.4.2 Factors Impacting Refugees

There are multiple complex factors that impact refugees. Among these factors are political, ethical, psychological, and cultural considerations. These factors are important to discuss since they are evidenced in the vignettes that follow.

The first time human security received prominent attention, according to Suhrke (2003), was when the United Nations Development Program report in 1993 urged that individual security become a central focus of international relations. This is an important political consideration since individual, group, and community security has held priority.

Frost (2003) identifies the problems of refugees as primarily ethical rather than solely religious, cultural, legal and political. The ethical structure Frost assumes is that all refugees have rights within a global civil society. Given both of these arguments of individual security and the ethic of contribution and rights, we can imagine a radical new paradigm for upholding individual rights of refugees. That is, they should be able to "move about global society freely" (p. 126). Such an accommodation with attention to fundamental human rights moves in the direction of protecting individual human rights, thus diminishing trauma for refugees.

In a comprehensive study by (Bryant et al. 2018), researchers found that the world's refugees, most of whom are children and adolescents, suffer an increased prevalence of psychological disorders some of which are associated with the severity of trauma carried by their caregivers and by harsh parenting methods. According to the Refugee Health Technical Assistance Center (RHTAC) (2014), many refugees have experienced stressful events before being forced to flee. During the escape process, refugees are separated from family members, experience loss of livelihood, imprisonment and fear. While in transition or in resettlement, women and children often experience high stress levels due to lack of resources and money for rent or lack of resettlement agencies to help them process paperwork. In some instances, fathers have been separated from their families because of imprisonment. Another reason for separation is that they seek asylum and employment in another country in preparation for uniting their families, all of which are evidenced in the following vignettes.

When interviewing and interacting with Turkish women and children, the author has noticed the significance of listening intently to them especially as they process their grief for what has been lost and as they express their fear for what is ahead. Their trauma is characterized by anxiety over safety of family members in prison, fear of being followed, and in some cases frustration in trying to understand and master a new language.

The National Child Traumatic Stress Network (NCTSN) (n.d.), funded by the U.S. Department of Health and Human Services reminds providers to attend to engagement and cultural considerations as important first steps when working with refugee children. Drozdek and Wilson (2007) recognize the value of the "real world" for healing and recovery of traumatized refugees. An individual's experience within an event may vary from individual to individual and how an individual responds may determine whether it is a traumatic event. The effect (s) of the event "may range from hyper vigilance or a constant state of arousal, to numbing or avoidance" and can affect a person detrimentally. The authors also propose several key principles of working with traumatized persons. The safety principle is of highest priority. Without physical and psychological safety for the traumatized person, a caretaker has little advantage to administer help. Trustworthiness and transparency are essential to building an ethic of care. An ethic of care includes peer support, collaboration and mutuality, empowerment, voice and choice. When persons are no longer targets of persecution, entry into a new society calls for resilience and rejection of victimization. As oppressed persons are empowered to contribute to the personal well-being of family, community, and civil society, they begin the healing process and recognize that new rights and obligations are to be gained in the process.

19.5 Stories from Refugee Mothers

Seven illustrative vignettes are based on interviews conducted in 2018 and 2019 by the author in Greece and Germany with refugee mothers from Turkey. She used an informal interview to record their stories. All interviews were recorded with permission from the interviewees. An interpreter translated conversations and later the author transcribed each interview. Interviews were spontaneous and informal in accordance with Masten and Powell (2003) who champion this process especially with traumatized individuals. All interviews were held on a voluntary basis in safe locations. All names were changed to ensure anonymity. Interviewees were invited to respond to the prompt, "Tell me your story." Each vignette is labeled by number and pseudonyms.

Vignette 1 Ali and Zehra
Ali and Zehra are a professional couple with two preadolescent children, Arda and Yasemin, ages six and nine respectively. Zehra, a pulmonologist, and Ali a neurologist, fled Turkey to Germany at a moment's notice when they learned they were targeted for arrest when an informer, a neighbor, took a phone photo of a children's magazine published by a HGM associated press with Ali and Zehra's postal address on the cover. This informer forwarded a copy to the local police implicating them as supporters of the HGM. After the attempted coup, Erdogan had declared national emergency targeting supporters of Gülen as terrorists. Citizens were encouraged to report suspicious behavior by notifying their local police precinct.

With only a couple of hours to pack some clothes and nothing else, Ali and Zehra and children were able to purchase airfare to Germany before authorities could arrest them and confiscate their passports. They were literally a few hours ahead of having their passports nullified or revoked. They had to leave the full value of their house, cars and other assets behind. With their financial assets frozen by the government, they now await next steps uncertain about their refugee status and their futures (V.S. Womack, personal communication, August, 17, 2018).

Vignette 2 Canan
The world turned upside down for Canan and her husband Baris after the July coup attempt. As a high school art teacher specializing in painting and drawing at a HGM school. Baris was a social studies teacher who worked for the department of education. Both Canan and Baris were well respected veteran teachers with 16 and 20 years of experience respectively. Canan learned through her colleagues that the government had shut down her school because of its HGM ties. Immediately Baris was laid off from his position as a supervisor in the department of education. Concerned but not expecting the worst, Canan and Baris and their two children, Ali and Fatma, went on summer vacation, but returned to chaos when they soon discovered that children in their apartment complex were forbidden to play with their children. While the neighborhood kids sought each other's company they now were derided with taunts of "We don't want to play with you because you are 'dirty GM's' (dirty Gülen Movement kids)!" This created so much anxiety and pressure on the children that the family moved to a different house to remove them from their home neighborhood.

Canan continued her story by relating how her husband returned one morning to check on their apartment that they had temporarily vacated, only to find that it had been ransacked. Baris knew this would lead to his likely arrest so he went into hiding. The police notified Canan that Baris needed to stop by the police station to answer some questions. Canan and Fatma were staying with an aunt while Ali was staying with his grandmother so he could continue to attend school. In the meantime the police continued to badger the family, demanding that Baris surrender. Although Canan did not know where Baris was hiding, the adults in the family instructed the children to tell those who asked about their father to say, "I have no idea!" Given their devotion to their father, this created tremendous anxiety for Fatma and Ali. Four months later Baris showed up accompanied by a friend. Canan almost did not recognize him because he had lost considerable weight, was quite disheveled, and had severe pneumonia. He needed to see a doctor but could not. Canan confided "we were able to find a doctor through some friends who wrote a prescription in my aunt's name so we could go to the pharmacy and buy his medicine." Canan and Baris were able to stay with her aunt for a year with Baris never leaving the house. They were able later to rent a house in Istanbul under an assumed name, but were under pressure to keep a low profile. Baris was able to get some work as a painter in nearby apartments, although he was painfully aware that because of GPS devices, it was safer to travel only using side streets. Canan created some handicrafts to make ends meet. Life became unbearable and Baris suggested the family flee to Greece. Canan was adamantly opposed to the idea but finally relented. The family successfully navigated the Evros River ending up in Athens as their final destination. Canan, with a twinkle in her eye, stated "Now that I have been helping some of the kids and moms here how to draw I am slowly starting to draw and paint myself, and this has been therapeutic and it makes me feel much better" (V.S. Womack, personal communication, July 23, 2019).

Vignette 3 Emine

Mehmet attended college at a university in Indonesia and met Emine while on summer vacation in Turkey. They got married and moved to Indonesia for a short time, after which Mehmet worked as a teacher in Papa New Guinea. In the interview, Emine stated that Mehmet has always worked as a teacher, having taught at HGM schools in Australia, Malaysia, and the Philippines. They returned to Turkey so he could teach in a HGM school there, while Emine took a job in a public school. Emine related in the interview that she was discriminated against as a public school teacher, since it became known that Mehmet taught at a HGM school. Knowing that they were at risk for being arrested because for their support of the Gülen Movement, they arranged to escape by boat to Greece in hopes of going to Germany or Switzerland. They had all their belongings packed, but the very morning they were to leave, police arrived at their doorstep and arrested Mehmet. He was detained for four months for alleged terrorist activity. Right after his release they prepared things again for escape. This time their plan was successful. After a three month stay in Athens, Mehmet traveled on to Switzerland to ask for asylum while Emine remained in Athens with her two little girls. Emine confided to the interviewer, "It doesn't matter for us as long as we have freedom and receive human dignity." Emine lamented that she has been unable to get work in Greece and that her neighbors are unfriendly. She was even accosted by a man as she was passing by a bar. She is now unable to pay rent for her apartment, and hopes to move in with another mother like herself whose husband is also seeking residency in another country. She confided "It's hard to live with other friends because kids have problems living together. My girls are important to me and I realize every small change or adjustment is now a trauma to them. They don't have a sense of belonging." Her five year old went around the house taking pictures of all their things because she said, "We just came here, where are we going now?" Emine stated, "each move is more challenging, we don't have our own space, we now need to live with other people" (V.S. Womack, personal communication, July 24, 2019).

Vignette 4 Asli

Berk and Asli are parents of Hakan, 6, Ceran, 3, and Yonca, 1. Both were employed as teachers at a HGM school in Turkey. The family experienced a harrowing escape from Turkey to Greece after being continually harassed by the local police. They fled under a cloud of darkness, walking six hours to meet a boat only to find that the boat contained another family. Berk and Asli decided placing two families in one small boat would too risky so they decided to wait for the smuggler to return, a promise he faithfully fulfilled. Once they arrived on Greek shores they walked to the police station where officials referred them to a refugee facility. Later they arranged to move to Germany on the eve of Ramadan. They had been targeted by Turkish police because their names appeared on a five year old bank transaction from Bank ASYA, a Gülen funded bank that Erdogan deemed to be a terrorist supported bank in disfavor of the Erdogan regime (Fuchs Ebaugh 2009). (V.S. Womack, personal communication, July 23, 2019).

Vignette 5 Hafsa

Hafsa, an elementary school counselor, has two boys, Hakan age six, Ibrahim age nine, and a daughter, Asli, age twelve. Zeki, her husband, was imprisoned in Turkey soon after the coup. Hafsa and her children were harassed in Turkey before fleeing to Greece. As a school counselor Hafsa learned first-hand before her escape, that some of the older students at her school were facing threats of jail time by authorities if they didn't inform on their parents. Her children have been out of school now for the last two years, and are now occasionally acting out, anxious, and restless. Hafsa is not alone with her responsibility for her own children. She and other mothers try to hold some semblance of school for their children. These mothers can't get jobs, although they do seek to help each other. They did not know each other previously. Hafsa described the process she experienced when she arrived in Greece by indicating that she and the children were assigned to a barracks like building that served as a detention center. Their living quarters were like jail cells. Rats were a problem and days were filled with anxious thoughts and many rumors about their futures (V.S. Womack, personal communication, July 23, 2019).

Vignette 6 Anta

Anta worked as a tailor but relied mostly on her husband Alican's income as a religious instructor in a public school where he had taught for the past 20 years. Anta and Alican had been married for 25 years and had three young adult children. One day Alican arrived at school to find that he had been suspended pending further investigation regarding his involvement with the HGM. Within days he was fired because he had downloaded a ByLock Application, an act that implicated him as associated with the HGM. Life changed drastically for Alican and his family. For two years he hid out in Turkey occasionally slipping home under the cover of darkness to spend a night at home. Other times he and Anta would agree to meet in the middle of a crowd. His children tried to help out as they could. Several of Anta's relatives including her father and two older brothers turned against the family and dissociated themselves from Anta and her family while two other siblings provided both financial and psychological support.

Life for Alican became unbearable in Turkey so he rented a jet ski, dressed as a tourist, and escaped to Greece. From Greece he eventually landed in Italy, and then was able to seek asylum in Switzerland, his goal. He knew that Switzerland had the reputation of being the safest place where he could reunite with Anta, and possibly his young adult children. Switzerland was also attractive because of its high standard of living and education system. Unfortunately, Anta and her youngest son are still in Greece while the two older siblings remained in Turkey. Anta despairs that her family has fallen apart (V.S. Womack, personal communication, July 23, 2019).

Vignette 7 Ria

Ria, a school counselor, came under suspicion when her principal questioned her about what she was teaching her students while in counseling sessions. An inspector interrogated the entire school staff regarding their political loyalties, with the goal of identifying any Gülen supporters. Ria was pregnant at the time, and gave birth a week before the coup. When Ria was arrested for aligning with the HGM, she received a short jail sentence, but was taken to jail with her infant who was only a few weeks old. Right after the coup, Ria and her husband Pazir had their names published in a local newspaper. Because of this they were subsequently stripped of their jobs. Pazir was completing a Ph.D. dissertation. His work was discredited and he feared arrest. His fears were confirmed when officials knocked on their door in the middle of the night to arrest him. Pazir and Ria's infant daughter was 6 months old and another daughter was 6 years old at the time. Ria had to continually explain to her 6-year old that her Daddy was on an important mission working for an important cause. She did not want to experience the humiliation of visiting Pazir in jail because officials would search everything, including the baby's diapers. Often, visitors had to wait over six hours in order to see a prisoner, with no seats available. It was common for prison officials to relocate prisoners to distant cities, which they justified by claiming space in the local prison was unavailable. He was finally released. Ria tried to continue relationships with some of her students who had serious needs of their own, and used a ByLock app on her phone to check in on them. Government officials were suspicious of anyone using a ByLock since it was created by a person in HGM and it was a custom for HGM people to use it and have it on their phones. Ria's arrest came when they asked her to report to the police station for questioning. Her father went with her but his appeals were ignored. She was immediately detained and placed in a mixed cell of men and women where she remained for five days. When her court date arrived she was released with a caveat that she would need to wear an ankle meter and adhere to a provision that she would only be allowed to venture 50 yards beyond her house. With hours to spare, she and Pazir fled to Greece. Ria wants to remain hopeful. She said, "we have been here for a while now and education is really important to us so I'm trying to show my family the beautiful side that there are better days to come" (V.S. Womack, personal communication, July 23, 2019).

19.6 Themes from the Vignettes

A closer analysis and view of each of the vignettes reveals the incredible impact stress, fear, and trauma has upon families. Perpetuated through structural violence, the Turkish purge deprived people of their rights to meet basic needs. Women and children are the most vulnerable and suffer physically, emotionally and spiritually (Yoder 2005). Continuous trauma occurs when mothers are stranded in apartments with little or no money to pay rent and when children are shuffled from household to household. Fear of the unknown and sudden changes of norms and laws also adds to the trauma.

One common theme in the vignettes is fear. Fear produces a freezing response especially when a combination of terror and helplessness occurs. The idea of constantly being hunted, like an animal, of having to look over one's shoulders constantly creates intense insecurity. When children are frustrated by uncertainty this creates special needs leaving them with an overwhelming sense of insecurity. Some mother's reported that they experienced a sense of death, that a certain trauma event signaled death, leaving little hope for survival. Others highlighted the Post-Traumatic Stress Disorder (PTSD) of one's inability to shake off anxiety and depression.

19.7 Summary and Analysis

Volkan (2018) states that the most complex traumas are deliberately caused by others. When Erdogan's purge occurred, large-group trauma directly impacted the HGM community among other groups including Kurds, Alevis, Leftists also vilified by the government. The family vignettes identified in this discussion strongly suggest that the trauma created by the Erdogan purge continues to create situations of insecurity and fear. One question then is how can reports of this trauma potentially awaken the global community to bring about empathy and understanding and resilience of the human spirit? Yesmin, the art teacher in Vignette 2, found purpose by sharing her art skills with her community in exile. She also found purpose, relief, and meaning by teaching children and mothers how to draw and by reflecting, "I am slowly starting to draw and paint myself and this has been therapeutic and it makes me feel much better."

References

Amnesty International. 2018. *We need to talk about Turkey.* https://www.amnesty.org/en/latest/campaigns/2018/04/turkey-human-rights-defenders-under-attack/.

———. 2019. *Turkey: Amnesty International's brief on human rights situation.* https://www.amnesty.org/en/documents/eur44/9747/2019/en/.

Aydin, Hasan, and Koksal Avincan. 2020. Intellectual Crimes and Serious Violation of Human Rights in Turkey: A Narrative Inquiry. *The International Journal of Human Rights* 24 (8): 1127–1155. https://doi.org/10.1080/13642987.2020.1713108.

Bryant, Richard A., Ben Edwards, Mark Creamer, Meaghan O'Donnell, David Forbes, Kim L. Felmingham, Derrick Silove, et al. 2018. The effect of post-traumatic stress disorder on refugees' parenting and their children's mental health: A cohort study. *The Lance Public Health.* https://doi.org/10.1016/S2468-2667(18)30051-3.

Butler, Daren, and Ece Toksabay. 2016. Turkey suspends thousands of teachers, wages biggest campaign against Kurds. *Reuters*, September 8. https://news.yahoo.com/turkey-suspends-thousands-teachers-wages-biggest-campaign-against-173726565.html.

Drozdek, Boris, and John P. Wilson. 2007. *Voices of trauma: Treating psychological trauma across cultures.* New York: Springer.

Frost, Mervyn. 2003. Thinking ethically about refugees: A case for the transformation of global governance. In *Refugees and forced displacement: International security, human vulnerability, and the state*, ed. E. Newman and J. van Selm, 109–129. New York: United Nations University Press.

Fuchs Ebaugh, Helen Rose. 2009. *The Gulen Movement: A sociological analysis of a civic movement rooted in moderate Islam*. New York: Springer.
Gurer, Cuneyt. 2019. Refugee perspectives on integration in Germany. *American Journal of Qualitative Research* 3 (2): 52–70. https://doi.org/10.29333/ajqr/6433.
Guribye, Eugene, Gro Mjeldheim Sandal, and Brit Oppedal. 2011. Communal proactive coping strategies among Tamil refugees in Norway: A case study in a naturalistic setting. *International Journal of Mental Health Systems* 5: 9. https://doi.org/10.1186/1752-4458-5-9.
International Organization for Migration. 2019. *Key migration terms* [adapted]. https://www.iom.int/key-migration-terms.
Kabasakal Arat, Zehra F. 2017. Political parties and women's rights in Turkey. *British Journal of Middle Eastern Studies* 44 (2): 240–254. https://doi.org/10.1080/13530194.2017.1281575.
Kaminer, Debbie, and Gillian Eagle. 2010. *Traumatic stress in South Africa*. Johannesburg: Wits University Press.
Markoe, Lauren. 2016. Religion news service. *USA Today*, July 21.
Masten, Ann S., and Jenifer L. Powell. 2003. A Resilience Framework for Research, Policy. Resilience and vulnerability: Adaptation in the context of childhood adversities.
Moyn, Samuel. 2018. *Not enough: Human rights in an unequal world*. Harvard: Harvard University Press.
National Child Traumatic Stress Network (NCTSN). n.d. *Refugee trauma types*. Rockville: NCTSN e-Bulletin. https://www.nctsn.org/what-is-child-trauma/trauma-types.
Orucoglu, Berivan. 2015. How president mastered the media. *Foreign Policy Magazine*. Washington, DC: FPGroup. https://foreignpolicy.com/2015/08/12/how-president-erdogan-mastered-the-media/.
Refugee Health Technical Assistance Center. 2014. *Traumatic experiences of refugees*. Boston: Newsletter.
Stockholm Center for Freedom. 2017.Jailing Women In Turkey: Systematic Campaign Of Persecution And Fear. https://stockholmcf.org/wp-content/uploads/2017/04/Jailing-women-in-Turkey.pdf
Stockholm Center for Freedom. 2019. Turkey continues to prosecute journalism while ignoring fair trial principles: Report – Stockholm Center for Freedom. https://stockholmcf.org/more-than-26000-people-investigate.../.
Substance Abuse and Mental Health Services Administration (SAMHSA). 2014. *SAMHSA's concept of trauma and guidance for a trauma-informed approach*. Rockville: HHS Publication. https://store.samhsa.gov/system/files/sma14-4884.pdf.
Suhrke, Astri. 2003. Human security and the protection of refugees. In *Refugees and forced displacement: International security, human vulnerability, and the state*, ed. E. Newman and J. van Selm, 93–108. New York: United Nations University Press.
United Nations Human Rights Office of the High Commissioner (OHCHR). 1989. *Convention on the rights of the child*. Geneva: OHCHR. https://www.ohchr.org/en/professionalinterest/pages/crc.aspx.
Volkan, Vamik D. 2018. *Immigrants and refugees: Trauma, perennial mourning, prejudice, and border psychology*. London: Karnac Books.
Yoder, Carolyn. 2005. *The little book of trauma healing*. New York: Good Press.

Vonya Womack is Executive Director of Refugees Unknown Stories Untold (RUSU) and a Human Rights Activist. She is an author, international presenter and key note speaker. A committed advocate for women and children and those who have experienced trauma as refugees. Vonya is an active contributor to public service messaging that supports human rights. Previously she was the Director of the Center for Global Learning and a business professor at Cabrini University (PA). Through her work she has developed leaders globally as well as developed study abroad programs for students. Her research expertise are leadership practices and sustainable models in current and post conflict zones, developing models to promote governance and public policy changes in conflict regions, women's and children's rights and the power of protest in North African regions. With over 20 years of corporate experience, Vonya brings her passion in this area to her teaching and her scholarship focusing on creating strategies to assist mothers and young women in re-establishing their life and leadership. She has an MS from the University of San Francisco where her thesis was on Conflict Resolution and Mediation for Business Administrators and a B.S. from Eastern Mennonite University.

Part VII
Foreign Policy Initiative: A Case Review

Chapter 20
Turkey's Accession to the European Union in Context of Its Human Rights Violations: Observations of a Journalist from Brussels

Gülsüm Alan

Abstract The year 1999 is considered a turning point in Turkey's path to European Union membership, as this was the year in which Turkey's European Union candidacy application was officially approved. Brussels, stating that Turkey sufficiently met the political criteria, made the decision to begin accession negotiations in 2005. Negotiations hit several political barriers, including the Cyprus issue. After 2011, Ankara quickly moved away from the European Union's human rights values. After the failed coup of 2016, the European Parliament, seriously concerned about the rule of law, media freedom, and the fight against corruption, recommended suspending EU accession negotiations with Turkey. Brussels said Ankara was moving away from the norms of the European Union and that no new chapter could be opened until the situation was resolved. Turkey has been a member of the Council of Europe since the 1950 assessments. The Council of Europe, which contains the European Court of Human Rights, has no organic ties with the institutions of the European Union. One of the most critical indicators of Turkey's commitment to European values is its membership in the Council of Europe, of which the European Court of Human Rights is a part. Although the Court has no organic ties to the EU, the Court often takes a stance on human rights violations within the borders of Council of Europe members, including Turkey, whose record of human rights violations has deteriorated since the July 15, 2016 failed coup. For its part, the European Union has considered Turkey's stance against the Court's assessments and evaluations.

In this context, this study examines Turkey's relations with the European Union during three periods – the 1990s, 2000s, and 2011.

Keywords European Union · Human rights violations · EU membership · Turkey

G. Alan (✉)
Euronews, Brussels, Belgium
e-mail: gulsum.alan@euronews.com

H. Aydin, W. Langley (eds.), *Human Rights in Turkey*, Philosophy and Politics - Critical Explorations 15, https://doi.org/10.1007/978-3-030-57476-5_20

20.1 Introduction

On July 31, 1959, Turkey applied for an association with the European Economic Community (EEC). The Council of Ministers of EEC accepted Turkey's application but held official membership in abeyance until Turkey's circumstances permitted an official association. The ensuing negotiations resulted in a formal agreement that was signed on September 12, 1963, and entered into force on December 1, 1964 (Billion 2008). In 1987, Turkey, pending the completion of the transition period envisaged in the Ankara Agreement, applied for full membership, but this request was not accepted. A Customs Union Agreement between the EU and Turkey entered into force on January 1, 1996.

December 1999 is considered to be a turning point for Turkey. Turkey's European Union membership application was officially approved as a result of the Helsinki Summit, which was held from the 10th to 11th of December. Accession negotiations to join the European Union began on October 3, 2005, pursuant to the decision (Magnien and Lazarovici 2019). However, due to the political objections by member states and the Cyprus issue, the accession process came to a deadlock.

EU-Turkey interactions have long since become a "love-hate" relationship. Although Turkey has had strong ties with members of that body, the country has struggled for years to become a member of the European Union. Turkey began negotiations in 2005, but serious human rights violations led to a loss of hope for full membership. Today, Turkey has seemingly abandoned the path of reforms that the EU has insisted upon, with thousands of victims of human rights violations and abrogation of fundamental freedoms (Amnesty International 2017; Aydin and Avincan 2020).

The former President of the European Commission Jean-Claude Juncker, on several occasions in recent years, has said that "Turkey is moving away from the European Union." Many reports on human rights violations were prepared and published (Radosavljevic 2017). On March 13, 2019, the 2018 European Parliament report on Turkey has been adopted by a vote of 370 to 109. The report noted:

1. That the Ministry of Religious Affairs applied pressure to the opponents of the Turkish intelligence organization,
2. The closure of 160 press organizations,
3. Violation of the rights of human rights defenders, including LGBT groups,
4. The "imprisonment for no reason" of Osman Kavala (civil society and business leader) and Selahattin Demirtas (former chairman of the HDP),
5. Consideration of asylum applications to the European Union countries,
6. 38 people lost their lives, and many people were sent to prison for protesting the poor working conditions of people in a 2015 protest,
7. A peaceful solution should be found to issues in southeastern Turkey,
8. A severe retrogression in terms of freedom of expression, freedom of assembly and freedom of property,
9. The use of methods such as harassment, kidnapping, secret follow-up surveillance, and notification tip lines,

10. Illegal abduction operations and unlawful extradition of 101 Turkish citizens from 18 countries,
11. The use of Interpol (red notices) to target Turkish opponents, human rights defenders, and journalists, and
12. A deep concern about the detention of 150,000 people for allegations of terrorism and the arrest of 78,000 people, and, in most cases, proceedings were conducted without conclusive evidence.

An EU-Turkey Association Council meeting was held in Brussels on 15 March 2019 (European Council 2019). The main agenda of the meeting, which aimed to reconsider neighborly relations, was human rights violations, anti-terrorism, customs union, migration, energy, visa liberalization, and security. In a joint press conference held in the European Council, the former High Representative of the Union for Foreign Affairs and Security Policy Federica Mogherini spoke about human rights violations in Turkey. Mogherini stated that the dismissal of judges and prosecutors posed a threat to the independence and impartiality of the law (Alan 2019). She also said that most cases against detainees were processed without definite evidence (Alan 2019).

Turkey said that it did not want to cut ties with the European Union, and the European Union is not in favor of ending Ankara's candidacy despite human rights violations in recent years. Due to human rights violations, European Union officials have contended that these violations have driven Turkey away from the EU. However, Turkey's Foreign Minister Mevlut Cavusoglu has insisted Turkey is "decisively moving towards membership" in the EU on July 7, 2016 (Cavusoglu from visa liberalization description 2016).

If Turkey complies with making the necessary reforms in democratic values and the rule of law, then the nation would stand closer to the European Union. However, as of today, Turkey stands closer to Russia and China regarding fundamental rights and freedoms. Depending on a rapprochement, an imbalance exists in Turkey's relations with the European Union. Turkey's European Union accession demands, the attitudes regarding this process request, and the action that has caused a movement away from the negotiations are considered in the chapters. The last 30 years of EU-Turkey relations will be discussed. In this context, the Council of Europe, which is not a European Union institution, has had a significant impact on the process. Turkey has been a member since 1950. Today, the Council of Europe has 47 member countries, including Russia. The best-known body of the Council of Europe is the European Court of Human Rights, which enforces the European Convention on Human Rights.

In this study, Turkey's EU membership process involves three periods: 1990–2000; 2000–2011; and 2011–2019. In each section, the European Commission, the European Parliament, and the European Council are taken into consideration. The reports of the Council of Europe will also be considered.

20.2 1990–2000: Turkey-EU Relations

20.2.1 The Council of Europe's View of the Kurdish Question

Working closely with European Union institutions, the Strasbourg-based Council of Europe published a report on June 3, 1998, entitled *South-East Turkey and North Iraq*. The Socialist group member who wrote the report was Swiss parliamentarian Ruth-Gaby Vermot-Mangold (Vermot-Mangold 1998).

The report strongly condemned the Turkish army's evacuation and the burning of villages that Kurdish citizens inhabited. The report further stated that the Turkish army was mostly responsible for the severe increase in human rights violations and the marginalization of human rights defenders. Turkish authorities have so far denied the charges. The report stated that 3185 villages were evacuated and burned, and 364,742 Kurdish citizens were victimized (Vermot-Mangold 1998). Representatives of the Council of Europe expressed great concern about the increase in the number of Kurdish-origin refugees and illegal immigrants trying to flee to European Union countries. The Council of Europe called on Turkey in the 1998 report to withdraw the army from the region and increase the social and economic development of the southeast.

According to the report, the number of village guards that the government employed to fight against the PKK of Kurdish origin had reached 50,000, and the report raised considerable concern about human rights violations (Vermot-Mangold 1998). Although the Turkish military denied the accusations, the European Court of Human Rights found the Turkish Army guilty of burning houses in villages in two different cases (Vermot-Mangold 1998).

These activities had consequences across the country as citizens of Kurdish origin, migrated (Vermot-Mangold 1998). The report stated that the population of Diyarbakır exploded from about 380,000 in 1990 to about 1.5 million in 1997 in some measure because of displaced villagers (Vermot-Mangold 1998). About three million Kurds migrated to Istanbul, Turkey (Vermot-Mangold 1998). In this context, the years between 1990 and 2000 clearly stand out as the biggest obstacle in Turkey's EU accession process because of the Kurdish problem (Dunér and Deverell 2001). By definition of the Kurdish issue, the recognition of the Kurdish identity and a solution to the displacement problems will not be easy to find (Dunér and Deverell 2001).

20.2.2 Customs Union Agreement Between the European Union and Turkey

Turkey-EU relations became unsteady after the September 12, 1980, military coup in Turkey, when these relations became officially frozen (Timeline: A History of Turkish Coups 2016).

On April 14, 1987, pending the completion of the transition period envisaged in the Ankara Agreement, Turkey applied for membership, but this request was not accepted. To join the community, Turkey was to make improvements in social and political fields to open membership negotiations.

The Customs Union between Turkey and the EU entered into force on January 1, 1996. The Customs Union is one of the most critical stages of the integration target for partnership relations with the European Union. At the Helsinki Summit of the European Union on December 10–11, 1999, the European Union formally approved the membership application of Turkey (Republic of Turkey Ministry of Commerce 2018). On December 17, 2004, at the Brussels Summit held on December 16 and 17, the European Council welcomed the "decisive progress made by Turkey in its far-reaching reform process and expressed its confidence that Turkey will sustain that process of reform. Furthermore, it expects Turkey to actively pursue its efforts to bring into force the six specific items of legislation identified by the Commission" (Council of the European Union 2005, 5).

20.3 Between 2000–2011: The Political Process in Turkey

20.3.1 European Union: The Reform Era in Turkey

The European Commission and the European Parliament publish annual reports on countries that are formal candidates of the European Union. The reports concerning Turkey began to be published in 2000, in which a snapshot of the country's economic, political, and social affairs is taken, and the steps to be taken, and reforms to be made in the context of human rights violations are discussed. The aim is to enable candidate countries to fulfill the Copenhagen Criteria, including respect for fundamental rights and freedoms and economic conditions.

Since 2000, Turkey had been undergoing changes in its political, economic, and cultural life (Keyman and Düzgit 2007). These changes were manifested mainly in the areas of democratization and its consolidation, and the restructuring of state–economy relations in a way that created sustainable economic growth and development. Moreover, several serious attempts emerged to make Turkish foreign policy more active, constructive, and democratic, to create a more rights-based citizenship regime, and to overcome the existing regional, economic, political, and cultural discrepancies and uneven development (Keyman and Düzgit 2007). During this period, Turkey had begun making all kinds of reforms as the European Union had demanded.

On November 3, 2002, general elections were held in Turkey, the AKP (Justice and Development Party) won the election, taking 34.3% of first-time voters. Founded just a year earlier, the party portrayed itself as pro-Western and advocated a liberal market economy with membership in the European Union. Controversies over whether the party remains committed to secular principles enshrined in the Turkish constitution have dominated Turkish politics since 2002 (Gauthier 2016).

Additionally, some experts drew attention to the traditional power of the Turkish army and stated that this Westernization would not be possible. Indeed, Hale noted that "The armed forces have played a crucial role in Turkish politics for many years hardly needs repeating here. In a tradition going back to the Ottoman era, military officers regard themselves as the bedrock of the state and, in the republican era, the guardians of Kemalist modernism" (Hale 2003, 112). Nonetheless, at the December 16–17, 2004 Brussels Summit, Turkey was found to have sufficiently met the political criteria, indicating the decision to start negotiations on October 3, 2005, and the membership process was launched.

Countries wishing to become a member of the European Union must abolish the death penalty to fully guarantee the protection of fundamental rights and freedoms. On January 15, 2003, Ankara signed the 6th Protocol to the European Convention on Human Rights, which calls for the abolition of the death penalty in "peacetime." In 2003, the Parliament ratified this protocol. The abolition of the death penalty in all circumstances was adopted. On 7 May 2004, Turkey adopted a constitutional amendment that repealed the death penalty altogether. The death penalty was also removed from the law. In this context, the death sentence of PKK leader Abdullah Öcalan that had been given on the grounds of "establishing and managing an armed terrorist organization" on 29 June 1999, was turned into imprisonment for life after the abolition of the death penalty in 2004.

20.3.1.1 Copenhagen Criteria

To start negotiations, Turkey had to comply with the Copenhagen criteria set by the EU in 1993(Council of the European Union 1993). The aim was to guarantee democracy and the rule of law, human rights, protection of minorities, and respect for minorities in EU candidate member states. Meeting the Copenhagen political criteria and respect for international human rights obligations aimed to establish good neighborly relations. Since November 2002, the AKP has confirmed its commitment to the reform process in the EU accession process.

When the European Union formally initiated accession negotiations with Turkey, the resolution of the Kurdish problem entered a new phase (Gunter 2007). The Copenhagen criteria required the stability of institutions guaranteeing democracy, formal rule of law clauses, human rights, and protection of minority rights to be instituted for membership in the Union (Gunter 2007).

In 2006, the European Commission published a report on Turkey's candidacy, which noted that "overall, there has been some legislative progress in the reform of public administration. Implementation of reforms adopted in previous years continued. Further efforts are needed in the area of decentralization" (p. 7). The report went on to note that "The recent reform environment for civil society organizations has led to positive developments. Especially since the adoption of the new Law on Associations, non-governmental organizations have been making their voices relatively better and better organized. There is a variety of organizations in Turkey, including approximately 80,000 registered associations and several hundred unions and chambers (including vocational and professional associations) (European Commission 2006, 16).

With respect to religious freedoms, the report noted that "In general, freedom of worship continues to be respected. However, no progress can be reported on the difficulties faced by non-Muslim communities. In addition, Alevis continue to face discriminatory practices" (p. 16).

In addition, the report said, "The level of participation of women in the parliament and in local representative bodies remains very low and prevailing discrimination exists in the labor market. Participation by women in the workforce is among the lowest in OECD countries" (European Commission 2006, 19).

The report also found that in terms of children's rights, the right to education for children is particularly problematic in some areas, especially for girls. To solve the problem of low school enrollment, enrollment campaigns should be continued and strengthened to increase school participation, especially in rural areas of the Southeast (European Commission 2006).

The European Commission's 2008 Turkey report noted that bilateral trade with Turkey was 100 billion Euros in 2006, making the nation the seventh largest trading partner. Overall, the report noted that limited progress has been made in the area of fighting corruption and that corruption was still prevalent (European Commission 2008).

20.3.1.2 Expressing the Desire to Enter the EU

In the first two to three years of the AKP's government, the negative attitudes towards Turkey began to wane. Positive texts were published in international circles because the government expressed the desire for Turkey's accession to the EU in a clear and unambiguous manner, and the country's leadership said the nation was to make the needed reforms. Indeed, President Erdoğan had implemented some of the reforms that Brussels demanded. In doing so, Erdoğan gave the world an image of a country that was making great efforts to improve and was determined to do so.

In 2003, the Turkish parliament denied permission for the stationing of US troops on Turkish territory as part of the preparation for the war against Iraq. A draft law allowing 62,000 US troops to use Turkey as a base for invading Iraq failed to gather the necessary absolute majority. This action damaged bilateral relations. Consequently, the United States held up aid to Turkey (Leicht and Schwarz 2003).

20.3.1.3 2005: The EU's Green Light to Turkey's Candidacy

Erdoğan emerged as a leader in support of the European Union, and Turkey began to be called a Muslim democracy and negotiations for full membership began on October 3, 2005. However, progress has been slow, and of the 35 Chapters necessary to complete the accession process, only 16 had been opened, and one had been closed by May 2016. During this period, the Armenian genocide issue was raised by

France, and later the EU accused Turkey of human rights violations in the aftermath of the crackdown following the failed coup attempt in 2016. On 26 June 2018, the EU's General Affairs Council stated that "the Council notes that Turkey has been moving further away from the European Union. Turkey's accession negotiations have, therefore, effectively come to a standstill, and no further chapters can be considered for opening or closing" (Michael 2018).

20.3.1.4 Only 16 of the 35 Chapters Were Opened, and the Human Rights Chapter Could Not be Opened

Turkey's EU accession negotiations are being conducted over 35 chapters, covering almost every area of social life. To date, only 16 of the 35 chapters have been opened for negotiation, one of which, Science and Research, has been temporarily closed. As of September 2015, the EU Council and Cypriot administration blocked 14 Chapters. Of these, Cyprus blocked Chapter 23 "Judiciary and Fundamental Rights" and Chapter 24, "Justice, Freedom, and Security (Chislett 2015).

After opening and closing the chapter on Science and Research in 2006, the European Union froze the opening of 8 chapters, citing the failure to implement the Ankara Protocol on Cyprus. However, in a good period of Turkey-EU relations, between 2007 and 2010, 12 chapters were opened (Magnien and Lazarovici 2019).

In 2007, the European Commission's annual report on Turkey said that the negotiations could last at least 10–15 years. However, in November 2008, the European Union noted the revival of Turkey's economy, saying that this revival was an essential step for European Union membership.

In May 2012, Stefan Füle, the former European Commissioner for Enlargement and European Neighbourhood Policy, visited Ankara and said that a positive agenda mechanism was launched to revive the deadlocked negotiations. Egemen Bağış, former minister for EU Affairs and chief negotiator of Turkey in accession talks with the European Union from 2009 to 2012, said: "We are entering a new era and we hope that we will accelerate the accession negotiations" (Sengul 2015). The aim was to establish working groups for the removal of blockages in front of chapters and making the reforms that Turkey must implement. On 1 July 2012, Cyprus assumed the rotating EU presidency, and Turkey said it would not participate in all meetings at the EU level during the Cyprus presidency.

20.3.2 Council of Europe: Corruption Is One of the Biggest Problems in Turkey

The Council of Europe's Group of States Against Corruption (GRECO) released a report on March 10, 2006, including information about corruption in both the public and private sectors in Turkey (Council of Europe 2006). The report states that corruption has caused foreign investors to back down and that a link existed between organized crime and corruption cases (Council of Europe 2006). In 2005, the World Bank and the European Bank for Development and Reconstruction (BERD) decided that organized crime and corruption incidents were concentrated in the business sector (Council of Europe 2006).

20.4 Turkey's Distancing from the EU Between 2011 and 2019

20.4.1 Stern Warning to Turkey from the European Union

On May 18, 2013, protests erupted to contest the urban development plans for Istanbul's Taksim Gezi Park. In the early morning of 28 May and 31 May, police used tear gas against a small number of environmentalists to stop their protest and burned down their tents in order to allow the bulldozing to continue. As a result of these police attacks in Taksim Square, more than 100 people were injured, and several of them incurred serious injuries (Ezikoglu 2014).

Supporting protests and strikes took place across Turkey, protesting a wide range of concerns at the core of which were issues of freedom of the press, expression, assembly, and the government's encroachment on Turkey's secularism. The action, which included more extensive demands, spread to other cities. The world press watched the protests closely. As a result of these events, one police officer and six people were killed (Ezikoglu 2014).

A 2013 European Commission report on Turkey harshly condemned the government's actions. The report said that although there were few protesters who resorted to violence, the demonstrations were generally peaceful. In some cases, the police used excessive force against the demonstrators. Six people were killed, including one police officer, and thousands were injured, some of them very severely. More than 3500 people were detained in the protests spreading to almost the whole country, and at least 112 of them remained in detention by a judicial decision and were arrested on suspicion of membership to a terrorist organization (European Commission 2013).

20.4.1.1 Corruption Operation Between 17 and 25 December

The corruption operations as known *Graft Probe* that took place between 17 and 25 December 2013 in Turkey was considered to be a breaking point in Turkey's political and social life between the Justice and Development Party (AKP), led by President Recep Tayyip Erdoğan, and the Gülen Movement, led by Fethullah Gülen (Turkey corruption inquiry: eight arrested 2013).

In the corruption operation on December 17, 89 people were detained, including Barıs Güler, son of Interior Minister Muammer Güler, Salih Kaan Cağlayan, son of Economy Minister Zafer Cağlayan, and Reza Zarrab, a Turkish businessman of Iranian origin. The detainees were charged with bribery, abuse of office, bid rigging, and smuggling.

20.4.1.2 EU-Turkey Agreement on Asylum Seekers

In 2016, a deal was struck between the EU and Turkey in the ad-hoc alliance against the refugee crisis. Under this plan, every refugee who had crossed into Greece illegally could be sent back to Turkey. In return, legal Syrian refugees would be accepted into the EU. The United Nations High Commissioner for Refugees was to assist in the repatriation of asylum seekers, and the EU covered all costs. (Collett 2016; Gogou 2017). Priority was given to women and children and to those who had not previously entered Greece illegally. For every Syrian refugee the EU would send back across the Aegean, a Syrian in Turkey would be given a new home in Europe (Rankin 2016a). However, the number of Syrians who can be rehoused in Europe from Turkey has been capped at 72,000, far short of the 108,000 a year recommended by international aid agencies, if the EU is to do its fair share. The EU's relocation scheme was to be stopped once more than 72,000 people have been settled in Europe, amid concerns among some EU members of an open-ended commitment (Rankin 2016a). The European Commission promised 6 billion euros of financial aid for refugees in Turkey. The European Commission announced that 5.6 billion was paid. However, President Erdoğan spoke of only 3–4 billion (European Council 2016).

20.4.1.3 July 15, 2016 Coup Attempt

On the evening of July 15, 2016, a "coup attempt" was made in Turkey. President Erdoğan, who dialed into a television channel with video from his phone, called for people to take to the streets. Thousands of people went out into the streets with Turkish flags and climbed onto the tanks. There was a clash between Erdoğan supporters and opponents of Erdoğan.

Following the failed coup, Erdoğan targeted the Gülen Movement blaming them for the coup attempt. Thousands of people were taken into custody immediately after the coup; Turkey's Justice Minister called this a "big cleansing." French Foreign Minister Jean-Marc Ayrault defended Turkey's post-coup state of emergency but said the "only thing we can repeat is our commitment to the rule of law, our commitment to fundamental freedoms" (Gunes 2016). Ayrault also warned Erdoğan not to use the failed coup as a "blank cheque" to silence his opponents. Konings (2018) argued that the failed military coup and its aftermath moved Turkey faster and further away from the EU standards. Under the state of emergency, fundamental human rights were being ignored on an unprecedented scale, and authoritarian amendments to the constitution were passed.

EU: Turkey Had Already Created Lists

Johannes Hahn, the EU commissioner dealing with Turkey's membership bid, said that the swift rounding up of judges and others after a failed coup in Turkey indicated the government had prepared a list beforehand (Bartunek 2016).

The European Union, especially in an economic and political sense, did not interfere in the internal affairs of the country because it expects that its members and candidate countries will solve their own internal problems through reforms. In the European Commission's 2016 report on Turkey, it condemned the coup attempt, but urged the government to observe the highest standards in the rule of law and fundamental rights, given that expulsions raised many questions (European Commission 2016). However, the mass detentions, arrests, and expulsions brought along many question marks.

The European Commission also noted that the Anti-Terrorism Law, in its scope and definitions, was not aligned with the acquis, and the implementation of the law raised severe concerns about fundamental rights. They said that Anti-Terrorism Law and the Turkish Penal Code must be brought in line with ECHR jurisprudence without reducing the capacity of Turkey in the fight against terrorism. In practice, the principle of proportionality must be respected (European Commission 2016).

The report also noted the decline of judicial independence. It noted significant changes to the structure and establishment of the Supreme Courts that were of grave concern and were not in line with European standards. Based on their alleged links to the Gülen Movement, judges and prosecutors continued to be removed from their jobs and, in some cases, were arrested. This situation worsened following the coup attempt of July, when one-fifth of judges and prosecutors were expelled, and their assets were frozen (European Commission 2016).

European Parliament Suspends Negotiations with Turkey

After the tremendous pressure created by the coup attempt and because of negotiations with Turkey concerning the migratory agreement, the European Parliament (EP), called for a temporary suspension of accession negotiations with Turkey (European Parliament 2016). Turkey reacted angrily after the European Parliament urged governments to freeze EU membership talks in a powerful symbolic vote that heightened tensions and could have endangered the landmark migration deal. The Turkish Prime Minister, Binali Yildirim, dismissed the vote as being of no importance but warned that ties with the EU were already strained. "We expect EU leaders to stand up against this lack of vision," he said. "The EU should decide whether it wants to continue its future vision with or without Turkey" (Rankin 2016b).

Cuts in EU Aid to Turkey

Turkey's European Union candidacy had degenerated to the point at which Brussels cut their funding (Emmott 2017). In October 2018, a European Parliament resolution cut 70 million Euros in EU aid to Turkey, which was confirmed by a majority vote. The lack of progress in the areas of democracy, human rights, and the rule of law was cited as the reason for the interruption of the financial aid called IPA (Instrument for Pre-Accession Assistance). The decision to cut funds was made for the first time against a candidate country (Flausch 2017).

Erdoğan: We Made a Mistake by Abolishing the Death Penalty

After the July 15 coup attempt, the President of Turkey, Recep Tayyip Erdoğan, said that if the parliament approved the death penalty, he would not oppose the re-implementation of it (Erdoğan: If the Parliament makes a death sentence, I will approve 2016). On March 18, 2017, Erdoğan made a speech before the April 16 referendum on the extension of his powers as president. "Martyr families should not be upset. Parliament will do what is necessary to bring the death penalty again." He stated that he would "sign" for the execution of the death penalty without a second thought.

The abolition of the death penalty in Turkey in 2014 fulfilled the Copenhagen criteria to become a member of the European Union. The re-implementation of the death penalty in Turkey in this context would mean the end of Turkey's European Union candidacy. In this context, President Erdoğan has stated in the past that "Democracy is like a train; when you reach your destination, you get off the train."

20.4.1.4 Fears After the Break of the EU-Turkey Association Council Meeting

The European Parliament called for the formal suspension of membership on March 15, 2019, in a tense atmosphere. Speaking after a meeting with the European Union High Representative for Foreign Affairs and Security Policy, Federica Mogherini said that dialogue would continue with Turkey (European Parliament 2019a).

The main agenda of the meeting, which reconsidered neighborly relations, was on human rights violations, anti-terrorism, customs union, migration, energy, visa liberalization, and security. The Association Council Meeting was attended by Turkish Foreign Minister Mevlüt Çavuşoğlu and the European Union High Representative for Foreign and Security Policies Federica Mogherini and EU Commissioner for Enlargement Johannes Hahn.

"The EU is Concerned About Human Rights Violations"

In a joint press conference held at the joint press conference following the 54th EU-Turkey Association Council held on March 15, 2019, High Representative/ Vice-President Federica Mogherini began voicing the concerns of the European Union about human rights violations in Turkey. Mogherini said the dismissal of judges and prosecutors poses a threat to the independence and impartiality of the law. She also said that most of the cases against detainees were processed without clear evidence (European Union 2019).

"We are Waiting for the Opening of the Chapters"

Foreign Minister Mevlut Cavusoglu has said that Turkey remains committed to joining the European Union. Cavusoglu stated that they expect the chapters to be opened within the scope of membership negotiations. "Our agency is conducting studies needed on the judiciary and fundamental rights," he said. Cavusoglu added that Turkey would not remain indifferent to the criticism of the European Union but said that the European Union should avoid hypocritical behavior (Alan 2019).

20.4.1.5 The European Parliament's 2019 Report on Turkey: Corruption, Repression, Human Rights Violations Are Criticized

The report said that Turkey emphasized that the fight against corruption must be continued, human rights violations must be addressed, violation of the rights of LGBT groups, including human rights defenders, must be eliminated and the arbitrary imprisonment of Osman Kavala and Selahattin Demirtas must be condemned. In addition, the report expressed concern about poor working conditions for workers that led 38 people to lose their lives in the construction of the new Istanbul Airport, and 31 people, including a union leader are currently in jail for protesting against poor working conditions. The report addressed the conditions in the south-east of Turkey and the serious allegations of human rights abuses and stressed the need for urgency in resuming a credible political process leading to a peaceful resolution (European Parliament 2019b).

20.4.1.6 Demand for Democratic Reforms

The report of Kati Piri, Turkey rapporteur for the European Parliament, calling for the suspension of EU accession talks with Ankara, was adopted on February 20, 2019, by the European Parliament Committee on Foreign Affairs and was later approved by the Parliament's general assembly (Turkish Minute 2019). The report called for the immediate and unconditional release of several prominent opposition figures and expressed concern over violations of human rights in Turkey (Piri 2019). "The European Union should formally suspend accession talks with Turkey after it crossed a red line by instituting a new constitution giving President Recep Tayyip Erdoğan sweeping executive powers," Piri said in an interview with the Peace and Justice Platform. The report left the door open for the upgrading of the 1995 Customs Union between Turkey and the EU, should democratic improvements take place. Ankara responded to the European Parliament's call quickly with the ruling Justice and Development Party spokesperson Ömer Çelik commenting that the decision was "worthless, null and disreputable" (News About Turkey 2019).

20.4.1.7 The EU Sanctions Were Approved to Cyprus: Turkey Will Cut off Funding

On July 15, 2019, the European Union (EU) announced its decision regarding the sanctions taken against Turkey with concerning drilling in the eastern Mediterranean. EU foreign ministers who met in Brussels decided to reduce the pre-accession assistance to Turkey for 2020 by €145.8 million. They also suspended negotiations on an aviation agreement and halted high-level bilateral talks between the two countries. Finally, they invited the European Investment Bank — the EU's not-for-profit lending institution to review its lending activities in Turkey, which amounted to €358.8 million in 2018 (Tidey 2019).

20.5 Council of Europe: Turkey Has the Most Prisoners in the ECHR's History

In 2018, the European Court of Human Rights (ECHR) stated that the country most frequently cited or condemned for violations of freedom of expression was Turkey. According to the Court's 2018 data, Turkey was judged to have violated the substance of the European Convention on Human Rights concerning the protection of freedom of expression numerous times. With 68 convictions that were found to be in contravention to different paragraphs of Article 6 for the right to a fair trial, Turkey was followed by Russia with 53 (European Court of Human Rights 2019).

20.5.1 Turkey & the Council of Europe's Group of States against Corruption

In 2019, the Council of Europe's Group of States against Corruption (GRECO) published a report on Turkey highlighting a continuing lack of progress on improving the transparency of party funding and preventing corruption among MPs, judges, and prosecutors. GRECO's initial evaluation of Turkey's efforts to criminalize different types of bribery and improve the transparency of party funding, published in April 2010, included a total of 17 recommendations to the authorities. The current report, which was the 7th assessment of Turkey's progress on implementing those recommendations, concluded that the results that have been achieved so far are still insufficient. The report noted that no code of ethical conduct exists for MPs, and other shortcomings also must be addressed, like the transparency of the legislative process as well as integrity training and counseling for MPs.

GRECO stressed that the underlying reasons behind its recommendations for the judiciary remain the fundamental structural changes that have weakened judicial independence and led the judiciary to appear even less independent from the executive and political powers than before (Council of Europe 2019).

20.5.2 Report on Turkey Can Not be Published Without the Consent of Ankara

According to the European Committee for the Prevention of Torture and Inhuman or Degrading Treatment or Punishment (CPT), the findings gathered during visits to prisons in Turkey in 2016 will not be published due to the absence of government approval.

In April 2016, The CPT paid an official visit to the F-type High-Security Closed Prison, located on the island of İmralı, to examine the conditions of detention of the Kurdistan Workers' Party (PKK) leader Abdullah Öcalan. A second visit was made to several major Turkish prisons in İstanbul and Ankara in August 2016 to inspect the treatment and conditions of those detained in connection to the failed coup attempt on July 15, 2016. CPT President Mykola Gnatovskyy had stated that, even though he "wants to discuss the findings," he cannot comment on the report due to Ankara's decision (Turkish Minute 2017).

20.5.3 Lawyers Report to UN

On January 24, 2019, the Law Society of England and Wales in the United Kingdom and 10 other law societies across Europe issued a Joint Declaration concerning the breakdown of the Rule of Law and severe threats against the Independence of Judges, Lawyers, and Prosecutors in Turkey to mark the Day of the Endangered Lawyer (The Law Society 2019).

The report noted that at least 594 lawyers had been arrested, 1546 prosecuted, and 216 convicted in Turkey since the attempted coup in July 2016. Many have been arbitrarily detained, and others are targeted with spurious allegations of support for terrorist organizations. The declaration went on to call for the government of Turkey to guarantee judicial independence, ensure that lawyers could practice their craft in accordance with Articles 5 and 6 of the ECHR, and end the persecution of lawyers.

On 23 May of 2019 which was the alert day for the independence of justice in Europe, Magistrats Européens pour la Démocratie et les Libertés (MEDEL) bemoaned what was occurring in Turkey. MEDEL noted the "orchestrated and premeditated campaign to completely destroy the independence of the Judiciary and the Rule of Law. Since the attempted Coup d'état of July 15th, 2016, all Judges, Prosecutors and Lawyers who had struggled continuously for an independent justice have been persecuted, arrested, dismissed and have seen their property seized without any previous due process and with absolutely no guarantees of defense" (MEDEL 2019).

They noted that YARSAV, the free Turkish association of Judges and Prosecutors, a member of MEDEL, had been administratively disbanded and its President, Murat Arslan (winner of the 2017 Vaclav Havel Human Rights Prize), dismissed and arrested, has been convicted in January 2019 and sentenced to 10 years of imprisonment, after a process in which all basic international standards of a due criminal process were infringed (MEDEL 2019).

As Murat Arslan said in his acceptance speech of the Vaclav Havel Human Rights Prize: "I am speaking to you from a jail in a country where the rule of law is suspended, that moves far away from democratic values, where dissidents are silenced, human rights defenders, journalists, people asking for peace, people who shout out that children should not die are labeled as terrorists and jailed. . . . The price that we are paying just raises our faith in the coming days where the rule of law and democracy will be internalized" (MEDEL 2019).

20.6 Conclusion

The whole world is watching the human rights violations taking place in Turkey with concern. As a signatory to the European Convention on Human Rights, Turkey has pledged to abide by the protection of fundamental rights and freedoms. However, after the July 15, 2016 coup, human rights violations have escalated.

Almost every day, the European Convention on Human Rights is violated in Turkey. The pressure on journalists falls under Article 10 (freedom of expression) of the European Convention on Human Rights. Arbitrary arrests and the absence of legal representation for imprisoned prisoners are evidently violations of the European Convention on Human Rights. Torture corresponds to Article 3 of the European Convention on Human Rights. As a result, the European Court of Human Rights has seen a significant uptick in the number of cases being heard that have originated from Turkey.

In the aftermath of the 15 July 2016 failed coup attempt, a state of emergency was declared that was renewed several times (Girdap 2020). As a result, human rights violations grew, a fact about which the European Union has taken due notice. Federica Mogherini, High Representative of the European Union for Foreign

Affairs, made a speech in Strasbourg on 6 February 2018. She said, "We care about Turkey, we care about the Turkish people, we care about Turkey's democracy, security, and stability, and we care about security and stability in the Turkish region because it is also our region" (European Union External Action 2018). She continued saying, "The negative trend of the human rights situation in the country has not been reversed. There have been some small steps in certain human rights cases, but violations have continued, affecting prominent civil society figures, users of social media, medical staff, and the list could continue. This is on top of the initial violations we have seen in recent years, which have not been resolved. The ongoing state of emergency also remains a key issue of concern. We all know that it was established in one of the most difficult moments in Turkish history, we remember those hours very well, in which we expressed our concern, our proximity with the people and the leadership of Turkey after the attempted coup d'état. Yet, one-and-a-half years later, the state of emergency has allowed measures that go well beyond those initially foreseen, and this has to be clearly stated." (European Union External Action 2018).

As tensions have risen, the European Union has taken measures. These have included withholding funding and freezing Turkey's accession to the Union. As a result, Turkey has turned to Russia. What will happen over time is unclear. One great hope is that the European Union and Turkey will continue their dialogue.

20.7 Chronology

1950: Turkey became a member of the Council of Europe (COE).

1952: Turkey became a NATO member.

July 31, 1959: Turkey applies for associate membership in the European Economic Community.

July 12, 1963: The Ankara Treaty was signed.

September 12, 1980: A coup occurred in Turkey, and relations were suspended with the European Economic Community.

1987: Turkey's application for membership of the European Economic Community.

1989: The European Economic Community rejected Turkey's application. Justification for the Greek and Cypriot economy.

1993: The Copenhagen criteria for candidate countries to meet are determined.

1996: Entry into force of the Customs Union between Turkey and the EU.

1999: Turkey's membership application was formally approved.

2001–2004: Reforms within the scope of the military's role and power was weakened in Turkey.

2002: AKP wins the general elections.

March 2003: Erdoğan becomes prime minister and has run the country ever since.

October 3, 2005: EU-Turkey negotiations began.

December 2006: After opening and closing 35 chapters, the EU froze 8 chapters due to the Cyprus issue.

2007–2010: 12 chapters were opened for negotiation.

November 2007: In its report, the European Commission stated that negotiations would last for at least 10–15 years.

November 2008: The European Commission is to decide what is an acceptable level of Turkey's economy.

May 2012: For the removal of blockage between the EU and Turkey, a "Positive Agenda" study was initiated.

July 1, 2012: Cyprus refuses to join the European Union took over the rotating presidency of the meeting of Turkey.

May 29, 2013: Anti-government Gezi protests began in Istanbul.

5 November 2013: Regional Policy chapter was opened.

2015: Erdoğan steps back from the Kurdish initiative.

March 18, 2016: Refugee agreement signed between the EU and Turkey. In the first year, the number of asylum seekers from Turkey to Greece declined by 90 percent.

June 2016: Finance and Budget chapter was opened for negotiation after France lifted its veto.

July 15, 2016: Coup attempt - 290 dead.

July 20, 2016: The state of emergency was declared and then renewed many times. Turkey Council of Europe European Convention on Human Rights reported that been violated.

March 2017: Many EU countries banned Erdoğan supporters.

March 12, 2017: The Netherlands forbids Turkish ministers from entering the country. Erdoğan accused the authorities of being "Nazis."

March 25, 2017: EU-Turkey Erdoğan said that he wants to make a referendum on the EU treaty threatens immigrants.

April 17, 2017: A constitutional referendum was held to extend the powers of the President. Conclusion: yes.

August 2017: Erdoğan calls on Turks living in Germany not to vote for Merkel.

March 2018: Turkish army enters Afrin

March 15, 2019: After 4 years in the Brussels meeting of the EU-Turkey association council was held. Mogherini raises concerns over human rights violations.

References

Alan, Gülsüm. 2019. The Council of the European Union is Concerned but Is in Favor of Continuing the Dialogue with Ankara. *Euronews*, March 15. https://tr.euronews.com/2019/03/15/mogherini-ab-turkiye-deki-insan-haklari-ihlallerinden-buyuk-kaygi-duyuyor.

Amnesty International. 2017. *Amnesty International Report 2016/17- The State of the World's Human Rights*. London, England. https://www.amnesty.org/download/Documents/POL1048002017ENGLISH.PDF.

Aydin, Hasan, and Koksal Avincan. 2020. Intellectual Crimes and Serious Violation of Human Rights in Turkey: A Narrative Inquiry. *The International Journal of Human Rights* 24 (8): 1127–1155. https://doi.org/10.1080/13642987.2020.1713108.

Bartunek, Robert. 2016. Turkey Government Seemed to Have List of Arrests Prepared: EU's Hahn. *Reuters*, July 18. https://www.reuters.com/article/us-turkey-security-eu-hahn-idUSKCN0ZY0EA.

Billion, Didier. 2008. Brève histoire des relations Turco-Européennes depuis 1963. *Le Monde Diplomatique*, June. https://www.monde-diplomatique.fr/2008/06/BILLION/16009.

Cavusoglu from visa liberalization statement. 2016. *Cumhuriyet*, June 7. http://www.cumhuriyet.com.tr/haber/turkiye/547011/Cavusoglu_ndan_vize_serbestisi_aciklamasi.html.

Chislett, William. 2015. *Turkey's 10 Years of EU Accession Negotiations: No End in Sight – Analysis*. Elcano Royal Institute, October 7. https://www.eurasiareview.com/07102015-turkeys-10-years-of-eu-accession-negotiations-no-end-in-sight-analysis/.

Collett, Elizabeth. 2016. *The Paradox of the EU-Turkey Refugee Deal*. Migration Policy Institute. https://www.migrationpolicy.org/news/paradox-eu-turkey-refugee-deal.

Council of Europe. 2006. *27th Plenary Meeting of GRECO*. Strasbourg, France. https://rm.coe.int/CoERMPublicCommonSearchServices/DisplayDCTMContent?documentId=09000016806c946e.

———. 2019. *European Anti-corruption Group Highlights Continuing Lack of Progress in Turkey*. Strasbourg, France. https://www.coe.int/en/web/greco/-/european-anti-corruption-group-highlights-continuing-lack-of-progress-in-turkey.

Council of the European Union. 1993. *Accession Criteria*. Brussels, Belgium. https://ec.europa.eu/neighbourhood-enlargement/policy/glossary/terms/accession-criteria_en.

———. 2005. *Brussels European Council, 16/17 December 2004, Presidency Conclusions*. https://www.consilium.europa.eu/ueDocs/cms_Data/docs/pressData/en/ec/83201.pdf.

Dunér, Bertil, and Edward Deverell. 2001. Country Cousin: Turkey, the European Union and Human Rights. *Turkish Studies* 2 (1): 1–24.

Emmott, Robin. 2017. In Warning to Ankara, EU Cuts Funds for Turkey's Membership bid. *Reuters*, November 30. https://www.reuters.com/article/us-eu-turkey/in-warning-to-ankara-eu-cuts-funds-for-turkeys-membership-bid-idUSKBN1DU2D4.

Erdoğan: If the Parliament Makes a Death Sentence, I Will Approve. 2016. *BBC*, July 19. https://www.bbc.com/turkce/haberler-turkiye-36831255.

European Commission. 2006. *Turkey 2006 Progress Report*. Brussels, Belgium. https://ec.europa.eu/neighbourhood-enlargement/sites/near/files/pdf/key_documents/2006/nov/tr_sec_1390_en.pdf.

———. 2008. *Turkey 2008 Progress Report*. Brussels, Belgium. https://ec.europa.eu/neighbourhood-enlargement/sites/near/files/pdf/press_corner/key-documents/reports_nov_2008/turkey_progress_report_en.pdf.

———. 2013. *2013 Progress Report*. Brussels, Belgium. https://www.ab.gov.tr/files/2013%20ilerleme%20raporu/tr_rapport_2013_en.pdf.

———. 2016. *Turkey 2016 Report*. https://ec.europa.eu/neighbourhood-enlargement/sites/near/files/pdf/key_documents/2016/20161109_report_turkey.pdf.

European Council. 2016. *EU and Turkey Agree European Response to Refugee Crisis*. Brussels, Belgium. https://europa.eu/rapid/press-release_AC-16-2132_en.html.

———. 2019. *Press Statement Following the 54th Meeting of the Association Council Between the European Union and Turkey, Brussels*, 15 March 2019. Brussels, Belgium. https://www.consilium.europa.eu/en/press/press-releases/2019/03/15/press-statement-following-the-54th-meeting-of-the-association-council-between-the-european-union-and-turkey-brussels-15-march-2019/.

European Court of Human Rights. 2019. *Overview ECHR 1959-2018*. https://www.echr.coe.int/Documents/Overview_19592018_ENG.pdf.

European Parliament. 2016. *Freeze EU Accession Talks with Turkey until it Halts Repression, Urge MEPs*. http://www.europarl.europa.eu/news/en/press-room/20161117IPR51549/freeze-eu-accession-talks-with-turkey-until-it-halts-repression-urge-meps.

———. 2019a. *Parliament Wants to Suspend EU Accession Negotiations with Turkey*. Strasbourg, France. http://www.europarl.europa.eu/news/en/press-room/20190307IPR30746/parliament-wants-to-suspend-eu-accession-negotiations-with-turkey.

———. 2019b. *2018 Commission Report on Turkey*. http://www.europarl.europa.eu/doceo/document/TA-8-2019-0200_EN.html.

European Union. 2019. *Remarks by HR/VP Federica Mogherini at the Joint Press Conference Following the 54th EU-Turkey Association Council*. https://eeas.europa.eu/headquarters/headquarters-homepage_gl/59719/Remarks%20by%20HR/VP%20Federica%20Mogherini%20at%20the%20joint%20press%20conference%20following%20the%2054th%20EU-Turkey%20Association%20Council.

European Union External Action. 2018. *Speech by High Representative/Vice-President Federica Mogherini at the European Parliament Plenary Session on the Human Rights Situation in Turkey and the Situation in Afrin, Syria*. https://eeas.europa.eu/topics/crisis-response/39509/speech-high-representativevice-president-federica-mogherini-european-parliament-plenary_en.

Ezikoglu, Caglar. 2014. Turkish Human Rights and EU Accession: The Gezi Park Protests. *Open Democracy*. https://www.opendemocracy.net/en/turkish-human-rights-and-eu-accession-gezi-park-protests/.

Flausch, Manon. 2017. Le Parlement veut couper le robinet des aides à la Turquie. *Euractiv*, October 24. https://www.euractiv.fr/section/l-europe-dans-le-monde/news/eu-parliament-wants-up-to-e80-million-cuts-to-turkeys-2018-pre-accession-funds/.

Gauthier, Ursula. 2016. Turquie: la vérité sur la "dictature fascisante" d'Erdoğan. *L'OBS*, November 7. https://www.nouvelobs.com/monde/20161107.OBS0847/turquie-la-verite-sur-la-dictature-fascisante-d-erdogan.html.

Girdap, Hafza. 2020. Human Rights, Conflicts, and Dislocation: The Case of Turkey in a Global Spectrum. *American Journal of Qualitative Research* 4 (1): 69–84. https://doi.org/10.29333/ajqr/8266.

Gogou, Kondylia. 2017. *The EU-Turkey Deal: Europe's year of Shame*. Amnesty International, March 20. https://www.amnesty.org/en/latest/news/2017/03/the-eu-turkey-deal-europes-year-of-shame/.

Gunes, Gokan. 2016. French FM Rankles Turkey with State of Emergency Comments. *Digital Journal*, October 24. http://www.digitaljournal.com/news/world/french-fm-rankles-turkey-with-state-of-emergency-comments/article/477997.

Gunter, Michael M. 2007. Turkey's Floundering EU Candidacy and Its Kurdish Problem. *Middle East Policy* 14 (1): 117–124.

Hale, William. 2003. Human Rights, the European Union and the Turkish Accession Process. *Turkish Studies* 4 (1): 107–126.

Keyman, E. Fuat, and Senem Aydin Düzgit. 2007. Europeanization, Democratization and Human Rights in Turkey. In *Turkey and the European Union*, 69–89. London: Palgrave Macmillan.

Konings, Jeroen. 2018. *Revising the Turkey-EU Narrative: A Historical Institutional Approach to Turkey's EU Accession (1963–2017)*. Unpublished Master's thesis. https://duckduckgo.com/l/?kh=-1&uddg=https%3A%2F%2Fdspace.library.uu.nl%2Fbitstream%2Fhandle%2F1874%2F371074%2FJ.%2520Konings%2520Thesis%2520Final%2520Version.pdf%3Fsequence%3D2%26isAllowed%3Dy.

Leicht, Justus, and Peter Schwarz. 2003. Turkish Parliament Votes Down U.S. War Plans. *World Socialist Website*, March 4. https://www.wsws.org/en/articles/2003/03/turk-m04.html.

Magnien, Isaure, and Marianne Lazarovici. 2019. Adhésion de la Turquie à l'Union Européenne: où en est-on?. *Toute l'Europe*, August 5. http://europe.vivianedebeaufort.fr/adhesion-de-la-turquie-a-lunion-europeenne-ou-en-est-on/.

MEDEL. 2019. Letters from the Turkish Judiciary – 23rd of May – alert day for the Independence of Justice in Europe. https://www.medelnet.eu/index.php/news/60-featured-news/528-letters-from-the-turkish-judiciary-23rd-of-may-alert-day-for-the-independence-of-justice-in-europe.

Michael, Peter. 2018. EU Council Issues Strong Message about Turkey's Obligations. Cyprus Mail, 26 June. https://cyprus-mail.com/2018/06/26/eu-council-issues-strong-message-about-turkeys-obligations/.

News about Turkey. 2019. EP calls on EU Leaders to Formally Suspend Turkey's Accession Talks. https://newsaboutturkey.com/2019/03/13/news-about-turkey-ep-calls-on-eu-leaders-to-formally-suspend-turkeys-accession-talks/f.

Piri, Kati. 2019. *Report on Turkey*. European Parliament. Strasbourg, France. http://www.europarl.europa.eu/doceo/document/A-8-2019-0091_EN. html.

Radosavljevic, Zoran. 2017. Pour Juncker, la Turquie "s'éloigne de l'Europe à pas de géants." *Euractiv*, August 30. https://www.euractiv.fr/section/elargissement/news/juncker-says-erdogans-turkey-taking-giant-steps-away-from-eu/.

Rankin, Jennifer. 2016a. EU Strikes Deal with Turkey to Send Back Refugees. *The Guardian*, March 18. https://www.theguardian.com/world/2016/mar/18/eu-strikes-deal-with-turkey-to-send-back-refugees-from-greece.

———. 2016b. Turkey Reacts Angrily to Symbolic EU Parliament Vote on Its Membership. *The Guardian*, November 24. https://www.theguardian.com/world/2016/nov/24/eu-parliament-votes-freeze-membership-talks-turkey.

Republic of Turkey Ministry of Commerce. 2018. *Turkey and the EU*. https://www.trade.gov.tr/turkey-and-eu/turkey-and-the-eu.

Sengul, Ebru. 2015. *The EU's Positive Agenda with Turkey*. Sabah. https://www.sabah.com.tr/gundem/2015/11/13/turkiye-ile-abnin-pozitif-ajandasi.

Situation des droits de l'Homme en Turquie. que fais l'Europe?. 2018. *BlogActiv*, June 25. https://eulogos.blogactiv.eu/2018/06/25/situation-des-droits-de-lhomme-en-turquie-que-fait-leurope/.

The Law Society. 2019. Persecution of Lawyers in Turkey Must Stop. https://www.lawsociety.org.uk/news/press-releases/persecution-of-lawyers-in-turkey-must-stop/.

Tidey, Alice. 2019. EU Sanctions Turkey for Drilling off the Coast of Cyprus. *Euronews*, June 16. https://www.euronews.com/2019/07/16/eu-sanctions-turkey-for-drilling-off-the-coast-of-cyprus.

Timeline: A history of Turkish coups. 2016. *Aljazeera*, 16 July. https://www.aljazeera.com/news/europe/2012/04/2012447281468 7973.html.

Turkey corruption inquiry: eight arrested. 2013. *The Guardian*, December 20. https://www.theguardian.com/world/2013/dec/20/eight-arrested-turkish-corruption-investigation-Erdoğan.

Turkish Minute. 2017. Council of Europe's CPT: Ankara Won't Allow Report on Turkish Prisons to be published. https://www.turkishminute.com/2017/04/22/council-of-europes-anti-torture-committee-ankara-doesnt-allow-report-on-turkish-prisons-to-be-published/.

———. 2019. Our Red Line on Turkey has Been Crossed: EP Rapporteur Kati Piri. https://www.turkishminute.com/2019/03/14/our-red-line-on-turkey-has-been-crossed-ep-rapporteur-kati-piri/.

Vermot-Mangold, Ruth Gaby. 1998. *Humanitarian Situation of the Kurdish Refugees and Displaced Persons in South-East Turkey and North Iraq*. Strasbourg: Council of Europe. https://assembly.coe.int/nw/xml/XRef/X2H-Xref-ViewHTML.asp?FileID=8570&lang=en.

Gülsüm Alan was born and raised in Brussels. She works in the journalism sector since 2000. She holds her BA in Political Science, International Relations from the University of Brussels (ULB) and she also holds a Communication and Journalism degree. During her exchange program at Laval University in Canada, she conducted research on feminists in Quebec area. She began her career as a news anchor at the Francophone Catholic Radio (RCF) in Brussels. She worked in different leading media outlets in Belgium and France. These include the Belgian State Television RTBF and the French Parliamentary Television 'Public Senate'. Since November 2009, she has been working for the Euronews Turkish team, the most-watched International News Channel in Europe. Gülsüm Alan has been the Brussels representative of Euronews Turkish Service since 2011. Her research expertise is EU-Turkey relationships, human rights, and Turkish diaspora in Europe. Currently, she works as EU Correspondent for Euronews in Brussels. She speaks English, German, Dutch, French, and Turkish. Time to time she speaks on panels or teach at universities.

The manufacturer's authorised representative in the EU is Springer Nature Customer Service Centre GmbH, Europaplatz 3, 69115 Heidelberg, Germany. If you have any concerns regarding our products, please contact ProductSafety@springernature.com

Printed and bound by CPI Group (UK) Ltd, Croydon, CR0 4YY
30/09/2026
02225498-0018